# INTERNATIONAL LAW AND …

The European Society of International Law (ESIL) is known for its particularly dynamic character. After 10 years of existence it has proved that it is one of the most cutting-edge scholarly associations in the field of public international law. At its 10th Anniversary Conference in September 2014, which was held in Vienna, participants assembled in order to discuss 'International law and …', the proceedings of which are published here. Going beyond the usual related disciplines of political science, international relations, economics and history, this conference ventured into less well-trodden paths, exploring the links between international law and cinema, philosophy, sports, the arts and other areas of human endeavour.

As the proceedings show, it is clear that international law has long been influenced by other fields of law and other disciplines. They also explore whether the boundaries of international law have been crossed and, if so, in what ways.

# International Law and …

## Select Proceedings of the European Society of International Law

### Fifth Volume

'International Law and …': Boundaries of International Law and
Bridges to Other Fields and Disciplines
Vienna, 4-6 September 2014

Edited by
August Reinisch, Mary E Footer
and Christina Binder

·HART·
PUBLISHING
OXFORD AND PORTLAND, OREGON
2016

**Hart Publishing**
An imprint of Bloomsbury Publishing Plc

Hart Publishing Ltd
Kemp House
Chawley Park
Cumnor Hill
Oxford OX2 9PH
UK

Bloomsbury Publishing Plc
50 Bedford Square
London
WC1B 3DP
UK

**www.hartpub.co.uk**
**www.bloomsbury.com**

Published in North America (US and Canada) by
Hart Publishing
c/o International Specialized Book Services
920 NE 58th Avenue, Suite 300
Portland, OR 97213-3786
USA

**www.isbs.com**



First published 2016



**British Library Cataloguing-in-Publication Data**
A catalogue record for this book is available from the British Library.

ISBN: PB: 978-1-50990-813-4
ePDF: 978-1-50990-815-8
ePub: 978-1-50990-814-1

Typeset by Compuscript Ltd, Shannon

# *Foreword*

LAURENCE BOISSON DE CHAZOURNES* AND ANDRÉ NOLLKAEMPER**

At the invitation of Professor August Reinisch, the European Society of International Law (ESIL) celebrated its tenth anniversary at the University of Vienna.

Ten years ago, ESIL organised its inaugural conference in Florence. Although ESIL has matured rapidly since then with the development of a wide array of activities, the Society is still in its formative stage. There is nonetheless a real sense that ESIL is beginning to realise its enormous potential for understanding and influencing international law in Europe and throughout the world.

As the Society continues to develop, it is important to remain mindful of the origins of ESIL. Looking back on what motivated the founders of ESIL, there is one theme that dominated: ESIL was established out of the perceived need to create a European forum for Europe-wide discussions, against a background of a rich European tradition of international legal issues of concern to Europe. ESIL has indeed become a European forum in the widest sense, and it is an important space for reflection and the exchange of ideas. The Vienna Conference amply demonstrated this feature.

This conference was a great success, bringing together a large number of participants, academics and practitioners from Europe and other regions of the world. This conference also allowed for the participation of specialists from other disciplines, such as psychology, philosophy or economics, who have brought insights on the rule of law and its effectiveness. This book is a selection of very stimulating papers that were presented at this conference. The discussions and exchanges were rich and the book reflects this.

We express our profound gratitude to Professor August Reinisch and his team for organising this tenth conference and for allowing the papers to be published in a book. Our thanks also go to Professors Christina Binder and Mary Footer who co-edited the book.

* President of the European Society of International Law, 2012–2014.
** President of the European Society of International Law, 2014–present.

# *Table of Contents*

PART VII: INTERNATIONAL LAW AND SPORT



PART VIII: INTERNATIONAL LAW AND THE ARTS AND HUMANITIES



PART IX: INTERNATIONAL LAW AND THE AESTHETIC

# *Introduction*

AUGUST REINISCH,* MARY E FOOTER** AND CHRISTINA BINDER***

THE EUROPEAN SOCIETY of International Law (ESIL) is known for its particularly dynamic character. After 10 years of existence it has proved that it is one of the most cutting-edge scholarly associations in the field of public international law. At its 10th Anniversary Conference in September 2014, which was held in Vienna, an unprecedented number of 400 participants assembled in order to discuss 'International law and ...'. Going beyond the usual related disciplines of political science, international relations, economics and history, this conference ventured into less well-trodden paths, exploring the links between international law and cinema, philosophy, sports, the arts and other areas of human endeavour.

The Conference thus acknowledged the fact that international law has long been influenced by other fields of law and other disciplines but it also explored whether the boundaries of international law had been crossed and if so, in what ways.

Themes, such as international law as a generator of national law, and national law as a generator of international law, paid tribute to the increased cross-fertilisation between the different levels of law, that is, the expansion of international law into the domestic sphere as well as the influence of national law on international law. Particular emphasis was laid on the role of domestic courts as interpreters and enforcers of international law. Judicial dialogue—which is often regarded as crucial to secure the coherence of international law—on both a horizontal level (between international courts) and a vertical level (between international and domestic courts)—was likewise explored.

Some of the papers discussing these themes can be found in 'Part I: International Law and Human Rights Adjudication' and 'Part II: International Law and National Law' of these proceedings. Thus, in Part I, Anja Seibert-Fohr discusses judicial engagement in human rights comparativism while Magnus Killander examines jurisprudential dialogue in supranational human rights litigation in Africa. Samantha Besson provides a view of human rights adjudication as transnational adjudication with the proposition that domestic courts play a peripheral role as international law

* Professor of International and European Law at the University of Vienna.

** Professor of International Economic Law and co-director of the Nottingham International Law and Security Centre (NILSC), University of Nottingham School of Law.

*** Professor of International Law at the University of Vienna.

adjudicators while Başak Çali questions whether we are moving towards a responsible domestic courts' doctrine in her review of the European Court of Human Rights and the variable standard of judicial review of domestic court judgments.

In Part II, Hege Elisabeth Kjos leads with her contribution on international law through the national prism, in analysing the role of domestic law and jurisprudence in shaping international investment law. This is followed by Cecilia Bailliet who looks at national case law as a generator of international refugee law, especially in rectifying the imbalance within the UNHCR Guidelines on International Protection. Using the case of norm export at the WTO, Gregory Messenger considers how national law can be an unpredictable generator of international law while Mavluda Sattorova looks at norm and institutional design in terms of internationalisation and domestic rule-making through the lens of international investment treaties and the promise of good governance.

Other Conference panels dealt with the interconnections between public and private international law by focusing particularly on cultural heritage & the arts and investment law, as distinct examples for fields at the crossroads between public and private. Another panel was dedicated to international and EU law, especially in view of the tendencies to emancipate and even isolate EU law from the wider body of international law and the unsettled relationship between both. Special emphasis was laid on a core issue at the junction between international and European law: the question of trade and investment.

Some of the papers that represent the crossroads between the public and private in investment and trade, include the papers in 'Part III: International Law and Trade and Investment' by Andrea K Bjorklund, Georgios Petrochilos, Stephan W Schill and Diane A Desierto from the joint panel on 'Investment Law at the Crossroads of Public and Private International Law'. Catherine Titi similarly explores what she describes as the forced co-existence of trade and investment provisions in preferential trade and investment agreements and the regulatory architecture of trade and investment law. Anastasios G Gourgourinis considers the shared responsibility of the EU for Member States' financial crisis measures as a defence in international investment claims.

Other panels discussed international law and other disciplines, sciences and arts and what they can learn and how they can benefit from each other. These included international law and philosophy together with possible legitimacy deficits of international law against the background of the increased broadening of its domains as well as international law and international relations with a special focus on stability and change as a particularly productive terrain especially in the case of international politics. In addition, more broadly, the need for international law and political science to learn from each other was examined. Another panel dealt with international law and the human sciences: anthropology and sociology. International law and psychology was discussed by focusing on the potential and the challenges of psychological approaches to international law. With 'law and economics' having become an established branch of interdisciplinary research, another panel investigated the possibilities to apply '(behavioural) law and economics' approaches more widely to core issues of international law such as treaty negotiation or compliance. In yet other panels, the challenges posed to international law by new information technologies and the interrelation between international law and sports were addressed. Likewise, a criticism/de-construction of international law from a feminist perspective was taken up with particular focus on the current stage of the debate. The contributions in 'Part IV: International Law and International Relations', by Georg Nolte on the work of the International Law Commission with respect to subsequent treaty practice and Jeffrey L Dunoff's piece on changing conceptions of regime interaction and interdisciplinarity both relate to differing aspects of international law and international relations in practice.

In 'Part V: International Law and New Technologies', Irène Couzigou deals with the challenge posed by cyber-attacks on the law of self-defence while Jamie Trinidad looks at international law and new technologies from a different angle with his contribution on culturomics and international law research.

'Part VI: International Law and the Social and Human Sciences' contains a contribution from Jessie Hohmann in which she uses opium as an object of international law to explore the age-old notions of sovereignty and intervention, while Emma Nyhan looks at the concept of indigenous peoples from the perspective of the Negev Bedouin to explore the notion of international law in transit. Finally, Gina Heathcote brings a critical perspective to bear on the topic of feminism with her chapter on fragmented feminisms in which she applies critical feminist thought to the post-Millennium era.

A trilogy of contributions on International Law and Sport can be found in Part VII. First, Lars Schönwald analyses the human rights obligations of international sports associations; second, Jernej Letnar Černič looks at emerging fair trial guarantees before the Court of Arbitration for Sport; and third, Carmen Pérez González considers the topical issue of international sports law and the fight against doping from an international human rights law perspective.

Other panels centered on international law and literature as well as on international law and philology/linguistics, which seemed of particular interest given their focus on written texts and methodological overlaps as regards interpretation and textual analysis; this even more so, since international law is a multilingual discipline. Questions such as how new research into the history of international law is changing our understanding of the past and the present were raised in a panel on international law and history. The similarities and differences concerning international law and religion and theology were addressed in yet another panel: International Law and Theology.

'Part VIII: International Law and the Arts and Humanities' contains a selection of contributions from Ekaterina Yahyaoui Krivenko on engaging international law and literature with Kafka, Deleuze and Guattari, while Mieke van der Linden uses the case law of the International Court of Justice and its interpretation of the inter-temporal rule to provide an interesting analysis of the inextricable connection between historical consciousness and international law. Similarly, two papers on the relationship between international law and theology can be found in Part VIII. One is from Aleš Weingerl who introduces the idea of international law and the international community in contemporary Catholic theology, while Dimitrios Kourtis situates his enquiry in the ideology of the early *ius gentium* to discuss its implications for the current debate about normative hierarchy and public policy in the international community.

International law and film, the power of pictures and how international law is portrayed in fiction as well as in documentary movies was addressed in yet another panel. The relationship between international law and various manifestations of art more broadly—ranging from visual arts such as painting, sculpture and video to performing arts such as music, dance and theatre—was explored in the panel 'international law and the aesthetic'.

'Part IX: International Law and the Aesthetic' brings together international law and cultural heritage with Janet Blake's chapter on an interdisciplinary approach to safeguarding intangible cultural heritage. Meanwhile, the relationship between international law and the performing and visual arts is discussed in the contribution by Eva Brems and Hilde van Gelder on engaged visual art as a tool for normative renewal in the field of international human rights, in which they use the work of Ariella Azoulay's *Potential History* to portray this relationship. In terms of international law and film, Part IX contains an analysis from Daniel Joyce and Gabrielle Simm of the film *Zero Dark Thirty* to discuss the link between international law, torture and representation while Olivier Corten does the same with respect to *The West Wing* (or *À la Maison Blanche*).

Overall, following a very competitive selection process through the call for papers, 15 agorae plus eight fora, with invited speakers, dealt with the various sub-themes of the Vienna conference. A poster-presentation was also organised in order to provide another avenue for disseminating the theme of 'International Law and …'. The 'Epilogue' to the Proceedings contains the Conference presentation given by Emeritus Professor Vera Gowlland-Debbas, in which she reflects critically on the theme and its various components as well as offers her own views on how international law has changed and developed over her life-time. Sadly, this was to be one of Vera's last public appearances. She died in September 2015 and we are publishing the written version of her presentation posthumously. As one of the founding members of ESIL and a former member of the ESIL Executive Board, she is remembered for her scholarship, her warmth of personality, and her spontaneity.

This volume of Proceedings combines the best written contributions arising from the Conference. As editors we are particularly pleased to present such a broad variety of cross-cutting investigations which were typical of this conference. We rearranged some of the presentations in order to fit them into meaningful chapters for the purpose of publication, as explained in the foregoing paragraphs.

We are particularly grateful to have had the assistance of Jane Alice Hofbauer, Bernhard Scherzer and Ralph Janik who were very helpful at the editing stage of the individual contributions and in coordinating with the individual authors.

Thanks are also due to the authors who have patiently complied with our editing requests and punctually submitted their final written versions.

We are likewise grateful for the language check performed by Mark Rogers and for the final formatting and copy-editing by Tom Adams of Hart Publishing.

We would like to thank the ESIL as well as the University of Vienna for supporting both the Conference and the publication of these Proceedings.

Vienna/Nottingham, December 2015

# PART I

# INTERNATIONAL LAW AND HUMAN RIGHTS ADJUDICATION

# 1

# *Judicial Engagement in International Human Rights Comparativism*

ANJA SEIBERT-FOHR*

## I. INTRODUCTION

FRAGMENTATION IN INTERNATIONAL law and jurisprudence has become a significant concern of academic discourse over the past decade.[1] It thus does not come as a surprise that the notion of judicial dialogue is attracting increasing attention as a potential means for enhancing coherence.[2] At the same time, the role of judges in the context of 'government networks' attracts academic interest.[3] The dialogue among international judges has become a subject of empirical research which considers different motivations for and channels of this interaction.[4] Less attention has been paid so far to the extent to which the notion of dialogue has

* The author is Vice-Chair of the UN Human Rights Committee and holds the Chair for International Law and Human Rights at Göttingen University. All views expressed in this contribution are those of the author individually and do not represent the views of the Committee. The author would like to thank Sahra Golghalyani and Torsten Stirner for their research assistance, and Katrin Bensler and Florina Neßmann for their editing assistance.

[1] Martti Koskenniemi and Päivi Leino, 'Fragmentation of International Law? Postmodern Anxieties' (2002) 15 *Leiden Journal of International Law* 553; Ole Kristian Fauchald and André Nollkaemper (eds), *The Practice of International and National Courts and the (De-)Fragmentation of International Law* (Hart Publishing, 2012); Isabelle Buffard and others (eds), *International Law between Universalism and Fragmentation: Festschrift in Honour of Gerhard Hafner* (Brill, 2008).

[2] Rosalyn Higgins, 'A Babel of Judicial Voices? Ruminations From the Bench' (2006) 55 *International & Comparative Law Quarterly* 791, 804; Ruti Teitel and Robert Howse, 'Cross-Judging: Tribunalization in a Fragmented but Interconnected Global Order' (2009) 41 *New York University Journal of International Law and Politics* 959; Nathan Miller, 'An International Jurisprudence? The Operation of "Precedent" across International Tribunals' (2002) 15 *Leiden Journal of International Law* 483.

[3] Anne-Marie Slaughter, *A New World Order* (Princeton University Press, 2004); Anne-Marie Slaughter, 'A Global Community of Courts' (2003) 44 *Harvard International Law Journal* 191.

[4] Erik Voeten, 'Borrowing and Nonborrowing among International Courts' (2010) 39 *Journal of Legal Studies* 547; Daniel Terris and others, *The International Judge: An Introduction to the Men and Women who Decide the World's Cases* (Brandeis, 2007); Laurent Scheeck, 'Inter-Judicial Dialogue: Institutional and Functional Legitimacy in Supranational Judiciary Space' (2008), available at citation.allacademic.com/meta/p_mla_apa_research_citation/2/5/1/2/2/pages251223/p251223-1.php; Cesare PR Romano, 'Deciphering the Grammar of the International Jurisprudential Dialogue' (2008–2009) 41 *New York University Journal of International Law and Politics* 755. See also Miller (n 2).

become manifest in international human rights jurisprudence and the normative basis on which it is grounded. Human rights law is particularly interesting for this debate because of its multiplicity of international and regional instruments. Arguably, the variety of judicial bodies entrusted with the interpretation of these instruments might foster fragmentation and jeopardise universal human rights protection. Therefore the question arises of whether and to what extent this risk can be overcome by the respective bodies' mutual engagement with each other's jurisprudence.

In an effort to answer this question, the following contribution takes the Human Rights Committee as an example and considers whether and to what extent the Committee is part of an international judicial dialogue. Based on an analysis of the Committee's views in the individual communication procedure, it describes the relevant partners and the Committee's jurisprudential practice of referring to international jurisprudence. It analyses the Committee's methodology and endeavours to identify the normative foundations of its international human rights comparativism. In order to recognise the Committee's impact on international human rights protection more generally, the contribution advocates a more inclusive approach to judicial interchange which goes beyond the customary notion of judicial dialogue.[5] It identifies modes of interaction which go beyond the formal confines of a dialogue. To capture them the author introduces the notion of judicial engagement, and distinguishes between different degrees of engagement depending on their respective rationales.

## II. THE OBJECT OF ENGAGEMENT

Before considering whether and to what extent the Human Rights Committee takes part in an international judicial dialogue, the question arises whether the Committee is capable of taking part in a 'judicial' dialogue in the first place. Its denomination as a committee, not a court, may point at a different direction. However, under the International Covenant on Civil and Political Rights (ICCPR) the Committee is entrusted with the competence of interpreting the ICCPR by its States parties.[6] Those who have ratified or acceded to the Optional Protocol recognise the Committee's competence to consider individual communications.[7] The 'views' which the Committee adopts at the end of this process reflect and conclude the Committee's examination of each individual communication. They are based on its interpretation

[5] For the term 'interchange', see Sabino Cassesee, 'Jurisdictional Redundancy and Interjudicial Interchanges' in Anja Seibert-Fohr and Mark E Villiger (eds), *Judgments of the European Court of Human Rights—Effects and Implementation* (Nomos/Ashgate, 2014).

[6] International Covenant on Civil and Political Rights (adopted 16 December 1966, entered into force 23 March 1976) 999 UNTS 171 (ICCPR) Arts 40–41.

[7] Optional Protocol to the International Covenant on Civil and Political Rights (adopted 16 December 1966, entered into force 23 March 1976) 999 UNTS 171 (ICCPR) Art 1.

of the Covenant as a legally binding instrument and result from the legal analysis of individual cases thereunder. For this reason the Committee in its General Comment No 33 on 'The Obligations of States Parties under the Optional Protocol to the International Covenant on Civil and Political Rights' explained its task as follows:

> While the function of the Human Rights Committee in considering individual communications is not, as such, that of a judicial body, the views issued by the Committee under the Optional Protocol exhibit some important characteristics of a judicial decision. They are arrived at in a judicial spirit, including the impartiality and independence of Committee members, the considered interpretation of the language of the Covenant, and the determinative character of the decisions.[8]

To put it concisely, it is not the nature of the institution, but the task, the nature of the decision-making process, and the procedural safeguards which render the individual communication procedure quasi-judicial.[9] Hence, to the extent that the Committee engages in this type of norm-interpretation, it is a potential partner for a judicial interchange with other jurisdictions.

## III. THE PARTNERS OF ENGAGEMENT

The Committee's norm-interpretative role and quasi-judicial nature is commonly recognised by international courts. The International Court of Justice (ICJ), for example, described the Committee in the *Diallo* case (*Republic of Guinea v Democratic Republic of the Congo*) as an 'independent body that was established *specifically* to supervise the application of that treaty [the ICCPR]'.[10] The Court interpreted Article 13 ICCPR as requiring that the expulsion of an alien lawfully in the territory of a State party must comply with domestic law. In support of its interpretation it pointed out that it was 'fully corroborated by the *jurisprudence* of the Human Rights Committee established by the Covenant to ensure compliance with that instrument by the States parties'.[11] The ICJ even went so far to describe the Committee's findings in response to individual communications and General Comments as 'interpretative case law'.[12]

[8] UN HRC 'General Comment 33: The Obligations of States Parties under the Optional Protocol to the International Covenant on Civil and Political Rights' (5 November 2008) UN Doc CCPR/C/GC/33, para 11.

[9] *Case Concerning Ahmadou Sadio Diallo (Republic of Guinea v Democratic Republic of the Congo)* (Judgment) [2010] ICJ Rep 640, 663–64, para 66; *Legal Consequences of the Construction of a Wall in Occupied Palestinian Territory* (Advisory Opinion) [2004] IJC Rep 136, 179–80, paras 109–10.

[10] *Case Concerning Ahmadou Sadio Diallo* (n 9) 663–64, para 66 (emphasis added).

[11] Ibid (emphasis added) with reference to *Maroufidou v Sweden*, UN HRC Communication No 58/1979 (1984) UN Doc CCPR/C/OP/1 65, para 9.3; UN HRC 'General Comment 15: The Position of Aliens under the Covenant' (11 April 1986) UN Doc HRI/GEN/1/Rev.1.

[12] *Case Concerning Ahmadou Sadio Diallo* (n 9) 663–64, para 66.

Though the Court did not consider itself bound by the Committee's interpretation, it acknowledged that, given the Committee's mandate and independence, the Court 'should ascribe great weight to the interpretation adopted by this independent body'.[13] It explained that the object of its consideration of this case law was 'to achieve the necessary clarity and the essential consistency of international law, as well as legal security'.[14]

The ICJ took a similar approach in its Advisory Opinion on the *Legal Consequences of the Construction of a Wall in the Occupied Palestinian Territory.*[15] When confronted with the question of whether the ICCPR applies extraterritorially, it recognised that States parties are bound by it when exercising jurisdiction outside their national territory. The Court explicitly pointed out that its interpretation was consistent with the Human Rights Committee's previous practice.[16]

Both cases demonstrate that the ICJ's engagement with the Human Rights Committee's interpretation is based on a recognition of the Committee's quasi-judicial task and composition. By referring to its interpretation the ICJ recognises the Committee as an appropriate partner for judicial interchange and aims at a coherent interpretation of the ICCPR as a treaty which is shared by both jurisdictions.

The ICJ is not the only international court which considers the Committee's human rights jurisprudence. While the European Court of Human Rights ECtHR is entrusted with the interpretation of the European Convention on Human Rights (ECHR), the regional counterpart to the ICCPR, it also keeps an eye on the Human

[13] Ibid.

[14] Ibid.

[15] *Legal Consequences of the Construction of a Wall in Occupied Palestinian Territory* (n 9). In her Separate Opinion Judge Higgins even asked whether it was appropriate to ask for an Advisory Opinion from the ICJ on the compliance by States parties of the two covenants with their obligations under the two covenants 'which are monitored, in much greater detail, by a treaty body established for that purpose', ibid Judge Higgins (Separate Opinion) 213, paras 26–27.

[16] *Legal Consequences of the Construction of a Wall in Occupied Palestinian Territory* (n 9) 179–80 paras 109 and 111 with reference to *López Burgos v Uruguay*, UN HRC Communication No 52/1979 (1981) UN Doc CCPR/C/13/D/52/1979; *Lilian Celiberti de Casariego v Uruguay*, UN HRC Communication No 56/1979 (1984) UN Doc CCPR/C/OP/1 para 92; *Montero v Uruguay*, UN HRC Communication No 106/81 (1983) UN Doc Supp No 40 (A/38/40) para 186; see also the reference to the Committee's Concluding Observations on Israel in *Legal Consequences of the Construction of a Wall in Occupied Palestinian Territory* (n 9) 179, para 110 and the reference in 192, para 136 to UN HRC, 'General Comment 27: Freedom of Movement (Art 12) (2 November 1999) UN Doc CCPR/C/21/Rev.1/Add.9 para 14; for a reference to the Committee's jurisprudence on 'continuing events', see Judge Higgins (Separate Opinion) in *Case Concerning Legality of Use of Force (Serbia and Montenegro Belgium)* (Order, Request for the Indication of Provisional Measures) [1999] ICJ Rep 124, 161–62, para 5 with reference to *Gueye and Others v France*, UN HRC Communication No 196/1985 (1989) UN Doc CCPR/C/35/D/196/1985 and *Simunek v The Czech Republic*, UN HRC Communication No 516/1992 (1995) UN Doc CCPR/C/54/D/516/1992; many other Separate Opinions also make reference to the Human Rights Committee's interpretation of the ICCPR, eg Judge Weeramantry (dissenting) in *Legality of the Threat or Use of Nuclear Weapons* (n 9) 507; Judge Kreca (dissenting) in *Application of the Convention on the Prevention and Punishment of the Crime of Genocide (Bosnia and Herzegovina v Serbia and Montenegro)* (Provisional Measures) [1993] ICJ Rep 631, 463; Judge Koroma (dissenting) in *Armed Activities on the Territory of the Congo (New Application: 2002) (Democratic Republic of the Congo v Rwanda)* (Judgement) [2006] ICJ Rep 911, 58–59, para 15.

Rights Committee's interpretation of the Covenant.[17] The Court's overview of relevant case law of foreign jurisdictions and international bodies and the section on relevant international law and practice as part of the Court's judgments include Human Rights Committee's cases.[18] The references indicate that the Court at some point in its analysis takes note of relevant Committee cases. At times the Court examines whether and to what extent its jurisprudence is in line with the Committee's cases. A recent example is *SAS v France*, where the Court held that the ban on full-face veils in public places was not in violation of the European Convention. Before arriving at this conclusion, the Grand Chamber distinguished the facts at issue in this case from the Committee's views in *Hudoyberganova v Uzbekistan*. In the latter case the Human Rights Committee had found a student's exclusion from university for wearing a headscarf to be in violation of the freedom of religion.[19] In the ECtHR's overview of the relevant international law and practice, it explicitly pointed out that the Human Rights Committee 'has not yet ruled on the question of a blanket ban on the wearing of the full-face veil in public places'.[20] As the case before it could be distinguished from earlier Committee cases the Court continued with its own legal analysis.

Citations of Committee views can also be found in the merits section of ECtHR judgments.[21] At times, the Court seeks information from the Committee with respect to the broader context or the evaluation of the particular situation in a State party.[22] In other instances the Court considers the Committee's practice in respect to procedural issues.[23] For example, when the Court determined the legal force of its interim measures in *Mamatkulov and Askarov v Turkey*, it pointed inter alia to the Committee's similar practice as part of the broader international legal context.[24]

In a few cases the Court has referred to the Committee in its interpretation of substantive rights.[25] The purpose is usually to confirm its own interpretation.

[17] *Babar Ahmad and Others v UK* App nos 24027/07, 11949/08, 36742/08, 66911/09 and 67354/09 (ECtHR, 10 April 2012) paras 118, 175; *El-Masri v The Former Yugoslav Republic of Macedonia* App no 39630/09 (ECtHR, 13 December 2012) para 109; *Othman (Abu Qatada) v UK* App no 8139/09 (ECtHR, 17 January 2012) para 151; *Janowiec and Others v Russia* App nos 55508/07 and 29520/09 (ECtHR, 16 April 2012) paras 80, 81, 152, 163; *Maskhadova and Others v Russia* App no 18071/05 (ECtHR, 6 June 2013) para 147; *Mamatkulov and Askarov v Turkey* App nos 46827/99 and 46951/99 (ECtHR, 4 February 2005) paras 111, 124; *Öcalan v Turkey* App no 46221/99 (ECtHR, 12 May 2005) paras 60, 166; *SAS v France* App no 43835/11 (ECtHR, 1 July 2014) paras 38, 39.

[18] See eg *Maskhadova and Others v Russia* (ECtHR) (n 17) para 147; *SAS v France* (ECtHR) (n 17) paras 38–39; in *SAS v France* the Grand Chamber also referred to the Committee's General Comments Nos 22, 27 and 28; see *SAS v France* (ECtHR) (n 17) para 38.

[19] *SAS v France* (ECtHR) (n 17) para 38; *Hudoyberganova v Uzbekistan*, UN HRC Communication No 931/2000 (2004) UN Doc CCPR/C/82/D/931/2000.

[20] Ibid; see also Judges Nussberger and Jäderblom (Separate Opinions), *SAS v France* (ECtHR) (n 17) para 19.

[21] For a statistical survey of citations by the ECtHR to other international courts, see Voeten (n 4) 565.

[22] *El-Masri v The Former Yugoslav Republic of Macedonia* (ECtHR) (n 17) para 109.

[23] See eg *Janowiec and Others v Russia* (ECtHR) (n 17) para 106.

[24] *Mamatkulov and Askarov v Turkey* (ECtHR) (n 17) para 111.

[25] *Janowiec and Others v Russia* (ECtHR) (n 17) paras 152, 163 with references to *Mariam Sankara and Others v Burkina Faso*, UN HRC Communication No 1159/2003 (2006) UN Doc CCPR/C/86/D/1159/2003; *Schedko v Belarus*, UN HRC Communication No 886/1999 (1999) UN Doc CCPR/C/77/D/886/1999; see also *Öcalan v Turkey* (ECtHR) (n 17) para 166.

Occasionally the Committee's views are cited to underscore that the Court's interpretation of a right protected under the European Convention is in accordance with that of the Committee's interpretation of the ICCPR, provided that the respective provisions are 'substantially similar in wording'.[26] In *Babar Ahmad et al v the UK* the ECtHR explicitly derived 'interpretative assistance' from the Human Rights Committee's interpretation of the prohibition on torture and ill-treatment.[27] It had to deal with the question of whether non-refoulement applied only to torture or also to other forms of ill-treatment. In the context of its legal analysis of Article 3 ECHR, the Court pointed out that Article 7 ICCPR according to the Committee's General Comment No 20 prevents refoulement, both when there is a real risk of torture and when there is a real risk of other forms of ill-treatment. The Court decided to share this interpretation in its legal analysis of Article 3 ECHR.

Another example is the ECtHR judgment in *Svinarenko and Slyadnev v Russia* of July 2014 which concerned degrading treatment during criminal trials. Here, again, the Grand Chamber referred to and agreed with the interpretation by the Human Rights Committee. Only a few months before the Chamber rendered its judgment, the Committee had found that the placement of a defendant in a metal cage with his hands handcuffed behind his back during his trial was degrading.[28] The Strasbourg Court followed this approach and applied it to the cases before it accordingly. The judgment shows once again that the ECtHR takes part in a jurisprudential interchange with the Human Rights Committee, not only with respect to procedural issues but also with respect to the interpretation of substantive rights.

Apart from the ECtHR, other regional human rights courts also cite Human Rights Committee's cases in their jurisprudence. The African Court of Human and Peoples' Rights and the Inter-American Court of Human Rights often refer to the interpretation given by the Committee to rights which are also protected under their respective treaties.[29] Taking these instances together with the above given example it is fair to conclude that international and regional courts consider the Human Right Committee's jurisprudence in their decision-making processes and respect the Human Rights Committee as a competent partner for judicial interchange.

[26] *Janowiec and Others v Russia* (ECtHR) (n 17) paras 106, 152, 163.

[27] *Babar Ahmad and Others v UK* (ECtHR) (n 17) para 175, it is interesting to observe that subsequently the Human Rights Committee in turn referred to this judgment of the ECtHR in a case involving non-refoulement in case of a life-sentence, see *Sholam Weiss v Austria*, UN HRC Communication No 1821/2008 (2012) UN Doc CCPR/C/106/D/1821/2008, para 9.3 (fn 13).

[28] *Svinarenko and Slyadnev v Russia* App nos 32541/08 and 43441/08 (ECtHR, 17 July 2014), para 132 with reference to *Pustovoit v Ukraine*, UN HRC Communication No 1405/2005 (2014) UN Doc CCPR/C/110/D/1405/2005, paras 9.3 and 10.

[29] See Magnus Killander, 'African Human Rights Law in Theory and Practice' in Sarah Joseph and Adam McBeth (eds), *Research Handbook on International Human Rights Law* (Edward Elgar Publishing, 2010) 388, 401, 402. For the Inter-American Court of Human Rights, see eg *Herrera-Ulloa Case*, IACtHR Series C No 107 (2004) paras 166–67 and 117; *Ricardo Canese Case*, IACtHR Series C No 111 (2004) paras 115–35; *Velásquez Rodríguez Case* (Compensatory Damages), IACtHR Series C No 7 (1989) para 28; *YATAMA Case*, IACtHR Series C No 127 (2005) para 208. See also Gerry L Neuman, 'Import, Export, and Regional Consent in the Inter-American Court of Human Rights' (2008) 19 *European Journal of International Law* 101, 110.

## IV. THE PRACTICE OF ENGAGEMENT

Turning now to the Committee's practice and the question of whether and to what extent it participates in a judicial dialogue with the aforementioned courts, it should be noted at the outset that the number of cases making explicit reference to international jurisprudence is limited.[30] One reason for this is the fact that the Committee's views, and particularly its legal reasoning, are much shorter than the judgments of the ICJ and regional human rights courts, a matter which will not be improved by the UN General Assembly's recent imposition of a 10,700 word limit in the context of the so-called 'strengthening process'.[31]

A case in which the Committee made reference to the ECtHR was *Atasoy and Arda Sarkut v Turkey*.[32] The reference, however, was not to inform its original interpretation but to reinforce an approach it had adopted prior to the Strasbourg Court. The case was about a conscientious objector and raised the question of whether the reference in Article 8 ICCPR precludes a right of conscientious objection under Article 18. The Committee referred to its earlier views in *Yoon and Choi v the Republic of Korea* that Article 8 neither recognises nor excludes this right.[33] In a footnote the Committee noted that 'the European Court of Human Rights subsequently reached a similar conclusion regarding comparable language in art. 4 of the European Convention on the Protection of Human Rights and Fundamental Freedoms, subsequent to the Committee's interpretation'.[34]

The Committee referred here to the judgment in *Bayatyan v Armenia* where the Strasbourg Court had followed the Human Rights Committee's approach by pointing to the 'important developments concerning recognition of the right to conscientious objection in various international fora. The most notable is the interpretation by the UNHRC of the provisions of the ICCPR (Articles 8 and 18), which are similar to those of the Convention (Articles 4 and 9).' The Court went on to describe the historical evolution of the Committee's interpretation:

> Initially the UNHRC adopted the same approach as the European Commission, excluding the right of conscientious objection from the scope of article 18 of the ICCPR. However, in 1993, in its General Comment No 22, it modified its initial approach and considered that a right to conscientious objection could be derived from article 18 of the ICCPR inasmuch as the obligation to use lethal force might seriously conflict with the freedom of conscience and the right to manifest one's religion or belief. In 2006 the UNHRC explicitly refused to apply article 8 of the ICCPR in two cases against South Korea concerning conscientious

30 For an earlier account of the Committee's practice, see LR Helfer and Anne-Marie Slaughter, 'Toward a Theory of Effective Supranational Adjudication' (1997) 107 *Yale Law Journal* 273, 358–61.

31 UNGA Res 68/268 Strengthening and Enhancing the Effective Functioning of the Human Rights Treaty Body System [without reference to a Main Committee (A/68/L.37)] (9 April 2014) para 15.

32 *Atasoy and Arda Sarkut v Turkey*, UN HRC Communication Nos 1853/2008 and 1854/2008 (2012) UN Doc CCPR/C/104/D/1853–54/2008, para 10.3.

33 See *Yoon and Choi v Republic of Korea*, UN HRC Communications Nos 1321/2004 and 1322/2004 (2006) UN Doc CCPR/C/88/D/1321–1322/2004, para 8.2.

34 *Atasoy and Arda Sarkut v Turkey*, UN HRC Communication (n 32) para 10.3 with reference to *Bayatyan v Armenia* App no 23459/03 (ECtHR, 7 July 2011) paras 62–64. See also *Erçep v Turkey* App no 43965/04 (ECtHR, 22 November 2011).

objectors and examined their complaints solely under article 18 of the ICCPR, finding a violation of that provision on account of the applicants' conviction for refusal to serve in the army for reasons of conscience.[35]

The mutual references by the Court and the Committee in these cases are not only a matter of courtesy but provide evidence for the cross-fertilisation in human rights jurisprudence where courts and treaty bodies make use of each other's jurisprudence in order to sustain their evolving case law. Their jurisprudence is mutually reinforcing and the references to each other seek to add further legitimacy to their jurisprudential advances.

There are additional cases which show that the Committee takes note of other judicial bodies when it has to deal with similar issues. In *Vos v The Netherlands*, for example, the Committee in its legal analysis noted that the ECJ had already decided a parallel case involving discrimination.[36] At issue was the difference in calculation of civil service pensions for married men and women and its compatibility with the non-discrimination provision of the Covenant. The ECJ had found this provision to be in violation of the then EEC Treaty provision on equal pay for men and women.[37] But due to a cut-off date established by the Court for the submission of such claims, the Committee was later confronted with a similar case to determine whether the difference amounted to a violation of Article 26 ICCPR. The Committee took note of the ECJ decision but it stressed that the issue of the communication was different as it concerned the compatibility of the Dutch legislation with Article 26 of the Covenant. It therefore proceeded with its own analysis thereunder.[38]

The Committee went a step further in *Paksas v Lithuania* and considered the jurisprudence of the ECtHR in an effort to inform its own approach to the exhaustion of local remedies rule. In its consideration on admissibility, the Committee referred to an earlier judgment by the ECtHR and explicitly shared its analysis, according to which a request to Lithuania's Constitutional Court for clarification of the meaning of a legal provision would not have led to an examination of the author's particular situation and therefore was not to be exhausted under the local remedies rule.[39]

Another case, in which the ECtHR's practice regarding procedural issues became relevant for the Committee's decision, was *Aleksei Pavlyuchenkov v Russian Federation*. The Committee in its decision on admissibility referred to *Ananyev and others v Russia*.[40] In this case, the Strasbourg Court had found that the Russian legal system did not provide for an effective remedy for inadequate conditions of detention.[41] This general appraisal of the judicial system in the State party supported the

[35] *Bayatyan v Armenia* (ECtHR) (n 34) para 105.

[36] *AP Johannes Vos v The Netherlands*, UN HRC Communication No 786/1997 (1999) UN Doc CCPR/C/66/D/786/1997, para 7.3.

[37] Case C-7/93 *Bestuur van het Algemeen Burgerlijk Pensioenfonds v GA Beune* [1994] ECR I-4502.

[38] *AP Johannes Vos v The Netherlands*, UN HRC Communication (n 36) para 7.6.

[39] *Paksas v Lithuanina*, UN HRC Communication No 2155/2012 (2014) UN Doc CCPR/C/110/D/2155/2012, para 7.9.

[40] *Aleksei Pavlyuchenkov v Russian Federation*, UN HRC Communication No 1628/2007 (2012) UN Doc CCPR/C/105/D/1628/2007, para 8.6 (fn 5).

[41] *Ananyev and Others v Russia* App nos 42525/07 and 60800/08 (ECtHR, 10 January 2012) para 119.

Committee's holding that no other remedies were available to the author while he was in detention so that his claim was held to be admissible.

Whereas the previous examples relate to questions of admissibility, there are also a few cases demonstrating that the Committee is very well aware of international and regional jurisprudence in regard to substantive human rights issues and considers it in its deliberations. One example is *Larrañaga v The Philippines*[42] where the Committee referred to the ECtHR's *Öcalan* judgment of 2005.[43] A citation in a footnote served as a reference for its finding that the imposition of the death sentence after an unfair trial amounted to inhuman treatment.[44] The reference, however, did not go unchallenged. Nisuke Ando, then a member of the Committee, stated in his individual opinion: 'I do not think it proper for the Committee to quote here a judgment of the European Court of Human Rights.'[45] His colleague on the Committee, Ruth Wedgwood, also took issue with this reference and criticised the Committee's holding as an 'importation from the European Court of Human Rights'.[46] Both individual opinions show that references are not necessarily unanimous. However, the opposition to comparativism in this case was not of a general nature. It was case-specific and related to the substantive question of whether Article 7 was implicated by violations of the right to a fair trial in capital punishment cases. We will come back to the reasons for the dissenters' opposition to this reference below when we discuss the prerequisites for judicial interaction.[47]

At any rate, as the previous examples show, the Human Rights Committee is not opposed to referring to international and regional human rights jurisprudence. This is also evidenced by numerous individual opinions of Committee members with citations of a broad array of international and regional courts and other bodies, including the ECtHR, the Inter-American Court and Commission of Human Rights, the African Commission, the Committee against Torture, the ICJ and Permanent Court of International Justice (PCIJ) and the ECJ.[48] Even Ruth Wedgwood, who objected

[42] *Francisco Juan Larrañaga v The Philippines*, UN HRC Communication No 1421/2005 (2006) UN Doc CCPR/C/87/D/1421/2005.

[43] *Öcalan v Turkey* (ECtHR) (n 17) paras 167–75.

[44] *Francisco Juan Larrañaga v The Philippines*, UN HRC Communication (n 42) para 7.11 (fn 59). The reference was renewed in *Munguwambuto Kabwe Peter Mwamba v Zambia*, UN HRC Communication No 1520/2006 (2010) UN Doc CCPR/C/98/D/1520/2006, para 6.8 (fn 13) where the Committee reiterated its jurisprudence and in the respective footnote referred not only to its views in *Francisco Juan Larrañaga v The Philippines* (n 42), but also to the ECtHR judgment in *Öcalan v Turkey* (n 17).

[45] Nisuke Ando in *Francisco Juan Larrañaga v The Philippines*, UN HRC Communication (n 42) 23, para 2.

[46] Ruth Wedgwood, ibid 26.

[47] See below under section VII.

[48] See eg Christine Chanet in *Randolph Barrett and Clyde Sutcliffe v Jamaica*, UN HRC Communication No 271/1988 (1992) UN Doc CCPR/C/44/D/271/1988, 71 with reference to the ECtHR; Bertil Wennergren in *Arvo O Karttunen v Finland*, UN HRC Communication No 387/1989 (1992) UN Doc CCPR/C/46/D/387/1989; Kurt Herndl (dissenting) in *Charles Chitat Ng v Canada*, UN HRC Communication No 469/1991 (1994) UN Doc CCPR/C/49/D/469/1991 with reference to the ECtHR; Kurt Herndl and Waleed Sadi (concurring) in *Cox v Canada*, UN HRC Communication No 539/1993 (1994) UN Doc CCPR/C/52/D/539/1993, with reference to the ICJ (with respect to the means of interpretation); Ivan Shearer (dissenting) in *Nabil Sayadi and Patricia Vinck v Belgium*, UN HRC Communication No 1472/2006 (2008) UN Doc CCPR/C/94/D/1472/2006 with reference to the ECJ; Sir Nigel Rodley

to the majority's reference to the 2005 *Öcalan* judgment in *Larrañaga v The Philippines*, made active use of Strasbourg human rights jurisprudence in several other individual opinions.[49]

Admittedly, the instances in which the Human Rights Committee cites international jurisprudence are rare. But this does not mean that it is irrelevant to its decision-making when it does not actively cite other jurisdictions.[50] A closer study of Committee views can help to reveal many parallels of its and other judicial and quasi-judicial bodies' reasoning.[51] This usually goes unnoticed because most research is limited to explicit references.[52] But in order to identify such parallels, which are not purely incidental, the legal reasoning and the arguments in support of a holding should be compared in more detail. Such an analysis can help to identify conceptual resemblance and even similar language which reveal unspoken interchanges.

Whereas it would be outside the scope of this article to give a full account of this phenomenon, I will refer to an example by the Human Rights Committee which is evidence of converging terminology. *Winata v Australia* was a case which involved an Australian minor and his stateless parents who had lived unlawfully in Australia for many years. They claimed that the parent's removal would violate their right to a family. Arguably the authors' son could have travelled with his parents to continue living with them abroad. However, the Committee refuted this counter-argument.

(concurring) in *Nabil Sayadi and Patricia Vinck v Belgium*, UN HRC Communication (this note) with reference to the ECtHR and the Court of First Instance of the European Communities; Yuji Iwasawa (concurring) in *Nabil Sayadi and Patricia Vinck v Belgium*, UN HRC Communication (this note) with reference to the ICJ (with respect to the interpretation of Arts 25, 103 UNC); Fabián Salvioli (partially dissenting) in *Weerawansa v Sri Lanka*, UN HRC Communication No 1406/2005 (2009) UN Doc CCPR/C/95/D/1406/2005 with reference to the PCIJ, ECtHR and the IACtHR; Rafael Rivas Posada and Krister Thelin (dissenting) in *Raihman v Latvia*, UN HRC Communication No 1621/2007 (2010) UN Doc CCPR/C/100/D/1621/2007 with reference to the ECtHR; Helen Keller, Iulia Antoanella Motoc, Gerald L Neuman, Michael O'Flaherty and Sir Nigel Rodley (concurring) in *Pillai v Canada*, UN HRC Communication (n 16), with reference to the Committee against Torture and the ECtHR; Yuji Iwasawa in *Pillai v Canada*, UN HRC Communication (n 16) with reference to the CAT and ECtHR; Fabián Salvioli (partly dissenting) in *Prutina v Bosnia-Hercegovina*, UN HRC Communications Nos 1917/2009, 1918/2009, 1925/2009 and 1953/2010 (2013) UN Doc CCPR/C/107/D/1917, 1918, 1925/2009 and 1953/2010 with reference to the IACtHR, the ECtHR, the Inter-American Commission on Human Rights, the African Commission on Human and Peoples' Rights, and the former European Commission of Human Rights. The practice to cite other jurisdictions more frequently in separate opinions is shared by the ECtHR and the ICJ. See Voeten (n 4) 566–68, 572.

[49] See eg Ruth Wedgwood (dissenting) in *Lederbauer v Austria*, UN HRC Communication No 1454/2006 (2007) UN Doc CCPR/C/90/D/1454/2006, para 3.2 with reference to *Pellegrin v France* App no 28541/95 (ECtHR, 08 December 1999); Ruth Wedgwood (concurring) in *Hudoyberganova v Uzbekistan*, UNHRC Communication No 931/2000 (2004) UN Doc CCPR/C/82/D/931/2000 with reference to *Leyla Şahin v Turkey* App no 44774/98 (ECtHR, 29 June 2004).

[50] See also Voeten who finds international courts to be hesitant in acknowledging external sources; according to him the number of citations is not representative of influence. Voeten (n 4) 550 and 572; see Higgins who points to the tremendous efforts that courts and tribunals make to be consistent *inter se* and to the striking similarity of approaches across the various courts and tribunals. Higgins, (n 2) 797.

[51] For example, according to Slaughter, the Human Rights Committee adopted styles of reasoning which are similar to the ECtHR, but without them acknowledging this, Anne-Marie Slaughter, 'A Typology of Transjudicial Communication' (1994) 29 *University of Richmond Law Review* 99, 106.

[52] See eg Voeten (n 4); Miller (n 2).

It used instead the notion of 'long-settled family life' in order to find a violation.[53] The Committee reasoned that the decision to deport the parents compelled the family to choose whether their 13-year-old son either remained alone in the State party or accompanied his parents and that this was an 'interference' with their family, at least in circumstances where 'substantial changes to long-settled family life would follow in either case'.[54] The reference to 'long-settled family life' was not found in the Article 17 ICCPR which merely refers to the right to a family. It moved this provision closer to Article 8 ECHR which provides for the right to respect for 'family life' and its interpretation by the ECtHR. While this step was not taken explicitly in reference to the European human rights jurisprudence, apparently the Committee's interpretation of the Covenant was informed thereby.[55] The case demonstrates that a careful analysis of the Committee's formulations and legal reasoning can reveal judicial interchanges which go unnoticed when the examination of the Committee's views is restricted to explicit citations.

## V. METHODOLOGY OF ENGAGEMENT

The above cited cases illustrate that the Human Rights Committee considers international and regional jurisprudence in the course of its interpretation of the ICCPR. However, whether this practice can be qualified as a dialogue is doubtful. As Vicki Jackson pointed out in her work on transnational constitutional comparison, dialogue usually involves the expectation of a response.[56] But considering the limited number of citations to/by other bodies, it is questionable whether the Human Rights Committee expects a response. Neither is there any indication in the Committee's practice which would indicate an attempt to influence other courts in their interpretation of their respective human rights treaties.[57] Furthermore, a great part of its practice of consulting the case law of other jurisdictions is unexpressed, whereas the term dialogue would suggest an utterance. Nevertheless, the Committee is quite aware of the jurisprudence of other jurisdictions and takes their interpretations into account in its legal analysis.[58]

In order to capture this approach, the term 'deliberative engagement' is more appropriate. It is borrowed from Vicki Jackson who uses it in the context of constitutional comparison, a field which is different but related to international human rights comparativism.[59] The term engagement indicates that the Committee does

[53] See *Winata v Australia*, UN HRC Communication No 930/2000 (2001) UN Doc CCPR/C/72/D/930/2000 para 7.2.

[54] Ibid.

[55] See Individual Opinions by Committee members Prafullachandra Natwarlal Bhagwati, Tawfik Khalil, David Kretzmer and Max Yalden (dissenting) in *Winata v Australia*, UN HRC Communication (n 53).

[56] Vicki Jackson, *Constitutional Engagement in a Transnational Era* (Oxford University Press, 2010).

[57] But see for this potential motivation more generally, Slaughter, *A New World Order* (n 3) 74–75.

[58] See the above cited cases; see also *Sholam Weiss v Austria*, UNHRC Communication (n 27) para 9.3.

[59] Jackson (n 56) 103–104.

not, strictly speaking, rely on the human rights interpretation of international and regional courts, but rather seeks inspiration and information from their case law when it interprets the Covenant. Engagement is without prejudice to the outcome of this exercise. Whether the interpretation of other bodies influences the Committee's interpretation evidently is not a matter of binding precedent but a matter of persuasion. After all, they work on the basis of different legal instruments with varying communities of States parties.

That the Committee is not always persuaded by other jurisdictions and reserves the right to take a different approach became evident, for example, in *Ranjit Singh v France*. In this case the Committee was aware that the author had not brought the case to the ECtHR because the Court's jurisprudence on freedom of religion was more deferential and thus would have been presumably less favourable to the author.[60] But this did not prevent the Committee from holding that the French requirement that an individual appear bareheaded in the identity photograph used for a residence permit violated the Sikh author's freedom of religion under Article 18 of the Covenant.[61]

The difference between the two jurisdictions in balancing the right to religion against public safety became apparent again in a later case. In *Mann Singh v France*, the same author successively brought similar claims to both jurisdictions.[62] After the ECtHR had found that the requirement of bareheaded individuals on photographs for driving licences was not in violation of the freedom of religion,[63] the same author submitted a communication to the Human Rights Committee challenging the regulation for passports. In this case the Committee found a violation of the freedom of religion with respect to passport photos.[64] Though the cases before the Court and the Committee can be distinguished in terms of the identity documents, the major difference arguably is a different application of the proportionality principle. Whereas the Strasbourg Court concedes to States parties a margin of appreciation in the application of the proportionality principle, the notion of discretion is not to be found in the Committee's jurisprudence.

Such differences indicate that the engagement with the case law of other human rights jurisdictions ultimately does not prevent the Committee from pursuing a different line of legal reasoning. The Committee maintains its autonomy in interpreting and applying the ICCPR. This also applies to its relations to other universal human rights treaty bodies as evidenced in *Alzery v Sweden*. In this case the parties in

[60] See *Ranjit Singh v France*, UN HRC Communication No 1876/2009 (2011) UN Doc CCPR/C/102/D/1876/2009, para 4.2; for a similar case decided by the ECtHR, see decision of the European Court of Human Rights, *Mann Singh v France* App no 24479/07 (ECtHR, 13 November 2008).

[61] See *Ranjit Singh v France*, UN HRC Communication (n 60) para 8.4.

[62] See *Mann Singh v France* (ECtHR) (n 60); cf also *Hudoyberganova v Uzbekistan*, UN HRC Communication No 931/2000 (2004) UN Doc CCPR/C/82/D931/2000 and *Leyla Sahin v Turkey* App no 44774/98 (ECtHR, 29 June 2004).

[63] See *Mann Singh v France* (ECtHR) (n 60).

[64] See *Mann Singh v France*, UN HRC Communication No 1928/2010 (2013) UN Doc CCPR/C/108/D/1928/2010, para 9.5.

their submission to the Human Rights Committee referred to the Committee against Torture's findings in a parallel case which had involved similar facts.[65] The Committee, however, stressed that it must '*independently* ascertain that in the circumstances of the case violations of the relevant provisions of the Covenant or the Optional Protocol had occurred' and proceeded with its own examination of the case without further reference to the Committee against Torture.[66]

Another example is the above-mentioned *Vos v The Netherlands* case. Though the Committee had noted that the ECJ had decided the same issue under the EEC Treaty, the Committee made clear that it had come to its conclusion independently and stressed that its analysis was based on Article 26 of the Covenant, not on the principle of equality between men and women with regard to pay and social security which the ECJ had decided.[67]

The need for the Committee to make autonomous findings was also stressed by Committee members Mr Lallah, Mr Bouzid and Mr Salvioli in an individual opinion. In *Panagiotis v Greece* they explained that 'it is the primary function of the Committee itself under the Covenant (and not simply that of other fora or jurisdictions) to interpret and apply the Covenant' and that:

> [It] would be odd if the Committee were to seek to delegate this primary responsibility elsewhere and wait for other jurisdictions to effect developments in the universality and effective protection of Covenant rights, when it is the Committee itself which has primary responsibility, at least for questions which are expressly mandated to it under the Covenant and the Optional Protocol.[68]

These cases show that the Committee engages with other jurisdictions largely from an internal perspective which uses the jurisprudence of other judicial bodies in order to develop the best understanding of the ICCPR and to improve its deliberation thereon. In other words, the jurisprudence of other human rights bodies informs the process of its own treaty interpretation.[69] Vicki Jackson qualifies such intrinsic approaches to comparative law as 'deliberative engagement'.[70] She distinguishes it from 'relational engagement' which is motivated by a relational understanding to other legal systems.[71] According to her definition, relational engagement is the result

[65] See *Mohammed Alzery v Sweden*, UN HRC Communication No 1416/2005 (2006) UN Doc CCPR/C/88/D/1416/2005, paras 4.3 and 9.1.

[66] See ibid para 11.2 (emphasis added).

[67] See *A P Johannes Vos v The Netherlands*, UN HRC Communication (n 36) para 7.6. with reference to the ECJ, Case C-7/93 *Bestuur van het Algemeen Burgerlijk Pensioenfonds v GA Beune* [1994] ECR I-4502.

[68] See Individual Opinion by Committee members Mr Lazhari Bouzid, Mr Rajsoomer Lallah and Mr Fabian Salvioli concerning merits (dissenting) in *Panagiotis v Greece*, UN HRC Communication No 1507/2006 (2011) UN Doc CCPR/C/100/D/1507/2006, para 14.

[69] Slaughter considers this as a matter of 'learning' which motivates international judges to refer to each other, see Slaughter, 'A Global Community of Courts' (n 3) 201.

[70] Jackson (n 56) 103.

[71] Ibid 117–18.

of a felt obligation to consider other systems, even if they are not legally binding as a matter of a moral obligation or the acknowledgment of interdependence.[72]

The Committee's current practice, especially its emphasis on the Covenant's autonomy tends to be more deliberative than relational. Otherwise one would expect more references to other jurisdictions. Furthermore, the large asymmetry and modest extent to which the Human Rights Committee and other international judicial bodies rely on each other's jurisprudence suggests that reciprocity considerations are not a predominant motivation for their engagement with other jurisdictions.[73] Nevertheless, the above examination of the Committee's practice under the individual communication procedure shows at least a few instances which indicate that the engagement can be a mutual undertaking.[74]

## VI. NORMATIVE REASONS FOR ENGAGEMENT

Turning now to the purposes of the Committee's deliberative engagement, a closer look at the cases outlined above, reveals a threefold objective. Its engagement with other human rights jurisdictions exhibits *rationalising*, *legitimising* and *coordinating* elements.

First and foremost the Committee's human rights comparativism serves a *rationalising function*. It engages with international and regional jurisprudence as part of its legal reasoning in which different possible interpretations are duly taken into account. Other bodies' case law informs the Committee's deliberation without, however, determining its outcome. As such, it becomes relevant for the Committee's textual and teleological interpretation of the ICCPR. To the extent that the latter is guided by the Covenant's object and purpose[75] which is the international protection of human rights, the interpretation of other judicial and quasi-judicial bodies becomes relevant.

Secondly, its human rights comparativism serves a *legitimising function*. References to other jurisdictions seek to strengthen the normative acceptability of the Committee's holding and thus the effectiveness of its views.[76] It is for this reason that references are likely to be made in those instances in which the Human Rights Committee goes beyond its prior jurisprudence.[77] It thus does not come as a surprise that most of the cases outlined above in which reference was made to other

[72] Ibid 118.

[73] For a similar result with respect to the ECtHR, see Voeten (n 4) 572.

[74] See eg *Atasoy and Arda Sarkut v Turkey*, UN HRC Communication (n 32) and *Bayatyan v Armenia* (ECtHR) (n 34).

[75] Vienna Convention on the Law of Treaties (adopted on 22 May 1969, entered into force 27 January 1980) 1155 UNTS 331 (VCLT) Art 31(1).

[76] For the relevance of judicial dialogue for the effectiveness of the Committee's adjudication see Helfer and Slaughter (n 30) 358–61.

[77] See eg *Atasoy and Arda Sarkut v Turkey*, UN HRC Communication (n 32); see also *Bayatyan v Armenia* (ECtHR) (n 34).

jurisdictions involved controversial issues, such as the death penalty,[78] deportation of family members,[79] non-refoulement[80] and conscientious objection.[81] In such contentious cases cross-references are particularly useful to be persuasive and mutually reinforcing.

The third rationale for the Committee's engagement with other human rights jurisdictions is *coordination*. By taking due account of other bodies' interpretations of similar rights contradictions can be avoided.[82] But this does not prevent the Committee from taking a different approach if it is persuaded to have better reasons for its own conclusions. Coordination does not mean uniformity. As we have seen in *Mann Singh v France*, there is room for different levels of protection without necessarily jeopardising the notion of universal human rights protection.[83]

## VII. SCOPE AND LIMITS OF ENGAGEMENT

All three objectives together inform the decision of whether and to what extent the Committee engages with other human rights jurisdictions. The decision depends on the particularities of each case. In some cases the need for coordination may be stronger than in other cases. The same holds true for the need to rationalise and the need to legitimise. For example, comparative engagement is less important in cases of detailed provisions whereas abstract formulations require more deliberation. Furthermore, in some instances the demand for being persuasive in terms of legitimacy may be less compelling than in other situations.

Rationality, legitimacy and coordination do not only inform the extent to which the Committee engages in human rights comparativism. These rationales also determine the limits of its engagement. This becomes apparent when we consider the prerequisites for the Committee's deliberative engagement. Evidently, in order to be relevant for the Committee's *rationale*, the interpretation by other human rights bodies must be based on substantially similar wording.[84] Furthermore, comparison

[78] See *Francisco Juan Larrañaga v Philippines*, UN HRC Communication (n 42).

[79] See *Winata v Australia*, UN HRC Communication (n 53).

[80] *Kindler v Canada*, UN HRC Communication No 470/1991 (1993) UN Doc CCPR/C/48/D/470/1991; *Sholam Weiss v Austria*, UN HRC Communication (n 27).

[81] See *Atasoy and Arda Sarkut v Turkey*, UN HRC Communication (n 32).

[82] For this rationale see also Neuman (n 29) 101, 112.

[83] Compare *Mann Singh v France*, UN HRC Communication (n 64) with *Mann Singh v France* (ECtHR) (n 60).

[84] For this concept see ECtHR, *Janowiec v Russia* App nos 55508/07 and 29520/09 (ECtHR, 21 October 2013) para 166 ('analogous'); HRC in *Mohammed Alzery v Sweden*, UN HRC Communication (n 65) para 11.2 ('substantially similar provisions'); HRC in *Lederbauer v Austria*, UN HRC Communication (n 49) para 7.3 where it points out the different scope of application of the right to a fair trial under the Covenant and the ECHR. A difference in wording between Art 17 ICCPR and Art 8 ECHR was also pointed out by the dissenters (Kretzmer and others) in *Winata v Australia*, UN HRC Communication (n 53) para 3.

with other cases requires similar facts.[85] And finally, the respective legal context is to be considered.[86] For example, if the Committee is confronted with a case in which different rights protected under the Covenant are in conflict, it is less likely to refer to jurisprudence by another treaty body which has only considered the issue under one of the rights. In other words, if competing rights are both protected under the Covenant but not under the legal instrument that served as a basis for another treaty body's interpretation, the Committee is likely to maintain its autonomy in interpreting and applying the ICCPR which allows a proper balancing of the competing rights.

Considerations of *legitimacy* and *coordination* inform the degree of engagement, too. For example, there may be cases in which reference to regional jurisprudence is more persuasive for countries which belong to the respective regional human rights system than for non-State parties. It is for this reason that a certain dynamic interpretation widely shared in one region of the world may not be equally persuasive in other parts of the world.[87] This is not to question the fundamental principle of universal human rights. However, it is a relevant aspect when we consider the pace and legitimacy of progressive interpretation. This is why Ruth Wedgwood objected to the 'importation' of the European Court's *Öcalan* interpretation with respect to the death penalty in *Larrañaga v Philippines*. She explained that the European Court's progressive interpretation in the *Öcalan* case was justified by the Court with a wide consensus in the Council of Europe, whereas the Second Optional Protocol to the ICCPR on the abolition of the death penalty had only been ratified by a minority of States parties.[88]

To my mind there are good reasons to defend the Committee's substantive legal position in *Larrañaga v Philippines*. But irrespective of the substantive legal issue, the case reveals that when answering the question of whether borrowing from other jurisdictions is legitimate, the context of the decision which is resorted to needs to be considered. This is especially true if a particular context has led to a regional consensus that justifies a dynamic interpretation of the respective regional human rights instrument. Considerations of legitimacy counsel a cautious context-oriented approach towards comparativism in such instances. This approach is not necessarily to the detriment of universal human rights protection. A regional consensus may spread to other regions to the effect that it provides a proper basis for similar jurisprudential developments there. Even if not, a higher regional standard does not put at risk the protection of essential human rights at the universal level. Though there

[85] It is for this matter that the Committee distinguished the facts in *Kindler v Canada*, UN HRC Communication (n 80) from the ones in *Soering v UK* App no 14038/88 (ECtHR, 7 July 1989) para 15.3:

[T]he Committee has had careful regard to the judgment given by the European Court of Human Rights in the *Soering v UK* case [European Court of Human Rights, judgment of 7 July 1989]. It notes that important facts leading to the judgment of the European Court are distinguishable on material points from the facts in the present case. In particular, the facts differ as to the age and mental state of the offender, and the conditions on death row in the respective prison systems.

[86] See also Higgins (n 2) 795 and 804.

[87] See also Neuman (n 29) 123.

[88] Ruth Wedgwood in *Francisco Juan Larrañaga v Philippines*, UN HRC Communication (n 42).

are good reasons to coordinate international and regional human rights protection in order to avoid contradictions, this does not require rigorous uniformity.

Evidently, the situation is different when two judicial bodies adjudicate cases on the same legal basis. In these instances the degree of their mutual engagement needs to be stronger. Concerns about fragmentation become more prevalent here because divergent interpretations of the same legal norms would jeopardise their validity and the legitimacy of their interpretation. This is why the ICJ, when applying the ICCPR in the *Diallo* case and in *Wall* Opinion, stressed that its interpretation was in accordance with the Human Rights Committee. It did so in an effort to preserve the 'essential consistency of international law, as well as legal security'.[89] But this rationale does not apply to the same extent to the interpretation of different human rights treaties with different States parties. To demand strict uniformity in these situations would ignore the difference of their substantive legal scope as well as the scope of their applicability.

## VIII. CONCLUSION

The answer to the question of how and to what extent international human rights courts engage with each other ultimately depends on their jurisprudential premises. Those courts which emphasise the common moral foundation of international human rights are likely to actively engage with other human rights jurisdictions from a relational perspective. From this perspective, international and regional human rights instruments form part of a unitary human rights system even though the respective courts operate under different treaty regimes with different States parties. The *corpus juris* concept of the Inter-American Court of Human Rights, with its multiple references to other jurisdictions, serves as an example.[90] On the other hand, courts which emphasise the consensual basis of human rights treaties and consider that their task is to adjudicate on the basis of their respective treaties are more likely to adopt an internal perspective which calls attention to the consensual foundation of these treaties.

The Human Rights Committee's approach features both aspects, however, in varying degrees. It engages with other jurisdictions primarily in a deliberative way. Its consent-based approach leads it to maintain its autonomy in the interpretation of the Covenant. But this does not prevent it from seeking interpretative input when it

[89] *Case Concerning Ahmadou Sadio Diallo* (n 9) 664, para 66.

[90] For the notion of *corpus juris*, see *Case of the 'Street Children'*, IACrtHR Series C No 63 (1999) para 194; *Case of the Ituango Massacres*, IACrtHR Series C No 148 (2006) para 157 (fn 177), see also *'Other Treaties' Subject to the Advisory Jurisdiction of the Court (Article 64 American Convention on Human Rights)*, Advisory Opinion OC-1/82, IACtHR Series A No 1 (1982) paras 40 and 41 where according to the IACtHR '[m]ankind's universality and the universality of the rights and freedoms which are entitled to protection form the core of all international protective systems' and '[a] certain tendency to integrate the regional and universal systems for the protection of human rights can be perceived in the Convention'. For a detailed and critical analysis of the IACtHR's approach to comparativism see Neuman (n 29).

considers the interpretation of similar provisions by other courts and judicial bodies persuasive. The Committee's engagement in international human rights comparativism is thus foremost a matter of rationalising its interpretation of the Covenant. At the same time it is informed by the desire to legitimise and to coordinate its jurisprudence with other bodies in an effort to address common legal issues. This coordinating function can help to prevent fragmentation and foster the notion of universal human rights protection. But it does not call for uniformity. After all, the advancement of human rights protection is a continuous process which can be driven by different dynamics.

# 2

# *Jurisprudential Dialogue in Supranational Human Rights Litigation in Africa*

MAGNUS KILLANDER[*]

## I. INTRODUCTION

HUMAN RIGHTS LAW is both national and international. Today almost all states have bills of rights in their constitutions and are at the same time bound by international treaties that they have ratified, and by customary international law. The extent to which human rights norms, national or international, can be brought before national courts varies from state to state. Where there is no remedy at the national level a case may be taken to an international court or quasi-judicial body with jurisdiction over the state in question.[1]

The content of a human rights norm is rarely self-evident. Norms need to be interpreted. The use of comparative legal materials from other jurisdictions, national and international, by national courts has been discussed extensively in the literature.[2] Though there is much literature on interpretation of human rights treaties, scholars have not extensively discussed why and how international courts and quasi-judicial bodies with a human rights mandate make use of comparative material.[3]

The focus of this article is on how African international courts and quasi-judicial bodies with a human rights docket use comparative jurisprudence.[4] The contribution

[*] Associate Professor, Centre for Human Rights, Faculty of Law, University of Pretoria.

[1] Before some international courts such as the ECOWAS Community Court of Justice there is not even a requirement to exhaust local remedies.

[2] See eg C Saunders, 'Use and misuse of comparative constitutional law' (2006) 13 *Indiana Journal of Global Legal Studies* 41.

[3] However, see C Romano, 'Deciphering the grammar of the international jurisprudential dialogue' (2008–2009) 41 *New York University Journal of International Law and Politics* 755; N Miller, 'An international jurisprudence? The operation of "precedent" across international tribunals' (2002) 15 *Leiden Journal of International Law* 483; E Voeten, 'Borrowing and nonborrowing among international courts' (2010) 39 *Journal of Legal Studies* 547; D Terris, C Romano and L Swigart, *The International Judge: An Introduction to the Men and Women who Decide the World's Cases* (Oxford University Press, 2007).

[4] On the definition of a human rights court, see ST Ebobrah, 'International human rights courts' in C Romano, K Alter and C Avegrou (eds), *The Oxford Handbook of International Adjudication* (Oxford University Press, 2013).

also briefly considers the extent to which national courts in Africa consider African supranational human rights jurisprudence and whether international courts outside Africa make use of African jurisprudence.

It should be noted that as is the case with international courts in general,[5] there is no international judicial hierarchy in Africa between the four institutions considered in this article: the African Commission on Human and Peoples' Rights (African Commission), the African Court on Human and Peoples' Rights (African Court), the Community Court of Justice of the Economic Community of West African States (ECOWAS Court) and the East African Court of Justice.[6]

## II. JUDICIAL DIALOGUE

In Africa, courts in common law countries make much more reference to case law than courts in civil law jurisdictions. The main comparative reference is the former colonial power. Thus courts in common law jurisdictions frequently cite English case law but also case law from other English-speaking jurisdictions such as the United States, Canada, India, Australia and New Zealand, while courts in Francophone Africa, when they do cite case law, cite cases from France, even ahead of national jurisprudence.[7] Inter-African judicial dialogue is minimal, apart from Southern African countries with a Roman-Dutch legal heritage where South African precedent dominates. There is no dispute that international courts may also cite comparative jurisprudence which, as will be discussed below, they extensively do.

One of the reasons for use of comparative case law is to achieve coherence. Coherent human rights law would not necessarily require citation as courts may have a thorough understanding of existing case law on a particular issue without citing it. Citation may also be used to enhance legitimacy which is as much a concern for international courts as national courts. What constitutes legitimacy is also similar: 'judgments that are well reasoned, appear constrained by the law, and require actions that the public views as acceptable'.[8]

While not strictly bound by precedent, international courts extensively cite their own judgments to provide legitimacy.[9] As at the national level, expansive interpretation supported by decisions of other courts (and other comparative material not

[5] Romano (n 3) 758.

[6] The exception is that the African Court can set aside a decision of the African Commission where the complainant by choice or necessity first has had to approach the Commission. On how individuals and NGOs can access the Court, see F Viljoen, *International Human Rights Law in Africa* (Oxford University Press, 2012). The African Committee on the Rights and Welfare of the Child which has decided one individual complaint is not discussed in this contribution.

[7] M Killander and H Adjolohoun, 'International law and domestic human rights litigation in Africa: An introduction' in M Killander (ed), *International Law and Domestic Human Rights Litigation in Africa* (Pretoria University Law Press, 2010).

[8] S Dothan, 'How international courts enhance their legitimacy' (2013) 14 *Theoretical Inquiries in Law* 455, 457.

[9] Ibid 471; Y Lupu and E Voeten, 'Precedent in international courts: A network analysis of case citations by the European Court of Human Rights' (2012) 42 *British Journal of Political Science* 413.

binding on the respondent state) may be controversial as states may feel that the court has moved away from the meaning of the treaty thereby threatening the legitimacy of the Court.[10]

Romano argues that international courts cite other international judgments 'sparingly, selectively, and reluctantly' because they may feel that 'relying too much on other courts' jurisprudence is tantamount to abdicating [their] own role'.[11] While it is clear that international jurisprudence is cited selectively, the empirical basis for Romano's finding that such citation is used sparingly and reluctantly is questionable. Indeed, Romano seems to contradict himself when he says that 'whenever given a chance, international courts will try to reinforce each other's jurisprudence by citing each other's decisions'.[12]

A judge of the European Court has noted that the judgments of the Court 'will have real effect only when national constitutional/supreme courts become genuinely attracted by the ECtHR's legal positions'.[13] The Court's impact at the national level is partly dependent on 'the transparency and the accountability of its rulings, that is, on the fact that they are published and supported by good reasons'.[14] The judicial style of the European Court is to divide the judgment into three sections: the facts, general principles, and the application of the principles to the facts. Under 'general principles' (or similar heading) the Court will summarise 'the existing case law and ... identify the precedents that control the outcome of the case'.[15] In *Demir and Baykara v Turkey* the European Court noted that it would consider not only other treaties ratified by the state but also other 'relevant instruments [which] denote a continuous evolution in the norms and principles applied in international law or in the domestic law of the majority of member states of the Council of Europe and show, in a precise area, that there is common ground in modern societies'.[16] Comparative jurisprudence (from national and international courts) has played an important role in the Court's determination of the 'common ground' in many cases.

The Inter-American Court has in a few cases made references to the national case law of the member states establishing a regional consensus similar to the approach of the European Court.[17] However, in general the approach is to illustrate the

[10] L Helfer, 'Nonconsensual international lawmaking' (2008) *University of Illinois Law Review* 71, 75; G Neuman, 'Import, export, and regional consent in the Inter-American Court of Human Rights' (2008) 19 *European Journal of International Law* 101.

[11] Romano (n 3) 758.

[12] Ibid 759.

[13] L Garlicki, 'Judicial deliberations: The Strasbourg perspective' in N Huls, M Adams and J Bomhoff (eds), *The Legitimacy of Highest Courts' Rulings: Judicial Deliberations and Beyond* (Asser Press, 2009) 391.

[14] MA Loth, 'Courts in quest for legitimacy: A comparative approach' in Huls, Adams and Bomhoff (n 13) 276. See also Garlicki (n 13) 394–95; H Keller and A Stone Sweet, *A Europe of Rights: The Impact of the ECHR on National Legal Systems* (Oxford University Press, 2008).

[15] Garlicki (n 13) 395.

[16] *Demir and Baykara v Turkey*, 34503/97 (ECtHR, 12 November 2008) para 86.

[17] See eg in relation to forced disappearances *Radilla Pachecho v Mexico*, Preliminary Objections, Merits, Reparations and Costs, IACtHR Series C No 209 (23 November 2009) para 140; *Gudiel Alvarez et al ('Diario Militar') v Guatemala*, Merits, Reparations and Costs, IACtHR Series C No 253 (20 November 2012) para 193.

universality of a particular interpretation, often with reference to the judgments and decisions of international courts and quasi-judicial bodies.[18] Already in its first advisory opinion the Inter-American Court held:

> It would be improper to make distinctions based on the regional or non-regional character of the international obligations assumed by States, and thus deny the existence of the common core of basic human rights standards.[19]

Reference by the Inter-American Court to national case law is rare, sometimes chosen to illustrate international consensus[20] and sometimes that no international consensus exists.[21]

## III. AFRICAN COMMISSION ON HUMAN AND PEOPLES' RIGHTS

The African Commission was established in 1987 following the entry into force of the African Charter on Human and Peoples' Rights in 1986. All African Union member states have ratified the African Charter and individuals and NGOs can submit petitions alleging violations of the rights set out in the Charter. The Commission has issued roughly 200 decisions on petitions since its establishment (including inadmissibility decisions and withdrawals) finding violations in 75 of these.[22]

In *Wetsh'okonda Kosa and Others v DRC*, the African Commission held that it has 'always deplored lack or inadequacy of motives for legal decisions as a violation of the right to fair trial'.[23] However, the early decisions of the Commission itself were a brief summary of facts with a finding without providing any reasoning. To the extent that case law was cited in the Commission's early jurisprudence it was generally references to its own case law. However, the Commission has on occasion deviated from its own previous case law[24] without providing reasons for its change of opinion and has, as Viljoen points out, a 'weak institutional memory'.[25]

[18] M Killander, 'Interpreting regional human rights treaties' (2010) 7 *SUR—International Journal on Human Rights* 145.

[19] Advisory Opinion OC-1/82, IACtHR Series A No 1 (24 September 1982) para 40.

[20] *Pueblo Saramaka v Suriname*, Preliminary Objections, Merits, Reparations and Costs, IACtHR Series C No 172 (28 November 2007) citing case law from Canada and South Africa; *Atala Riffo and children v Chile*, Merits, Reparations and Costs, IACtHR Series C No 239 (24 February 2012) para 109 citing national case law from Australia, Philippines and South Africa; *Hilaire, Constantine and Benjamin v Trinidad and Tobago*, Merits, Reparations and Costs, IACtHR Series C No 94 (21 June 2002) para 103 citing cases from India and South Africa in addition to cases of the UN Human Rights Committee, and paras 105, 167 citing cases from the US Supreme Court.

[21] *Artavia Murillo v Costa Rica*, Preliminary Objections, Merits, Reparations and Costs, IACtHR Series C No 257 (28 November 2012) para 185.

[22] Based on decisions published by the Commission as of August 2014 in its activity reports and on its website.

[23] *Wetsh'okonda Kosa and Others v DRC* (2008) AHRLR 93 (ACHPR 2008) para 89 citing the Human Rights Committee decision in *Pinkney v Canada* in relation to delay in providing the judgment, another problem that often arises with regard to the Commission's own decisions.

[24] Viljoen (n 6) 325.

[25] Ibid 289. In this it differs from the European Court, see Garlicki (n 13) 395.

The first Commission case to mention comparative case law is the 1995 case *Courson v Zimbabwe*,[26] which dealt with the criminalisation of homosexuality. The Commission noted that the complainant had attached the UN Human Rights Committee's decision in *Toonen v Australia*[27] to the complaint. The case was never decided as the communication was withdrawn.

Viljoen notes the 14th Annual Activity Report (2000–2001) as the turning point in relation to more 'reasoned and well-researched findings'.[28] It is also around this time that the Commission slowly started to cite comparative case law more consistently in addition to citation of comparative treaties, resolutions, general comments, legal doctrine and so on. As with other human rights bodies, the focus has remained on its own case law. The Commission also extensively relies on its other interpretive tools such as resolutions and guidelines which it has adopted as authoritative guidelines on the provisions of the Charter, similarly to the general comments of UN treaty monitoring bodies.

With regard to comparative case law, the Commission has highlighted the similarities with the Inter-American human rights system.[29] However, the Commission has also cited extensively from the case law of the European Court and the UN treaty monitoring bodies, in particular the Human Rights Committee and to a lesser extent the Committee against Torture. In addition, it has extensively relied on general comments of the Human Rights Committee. The Commission cites national case law less often than judgments of international courts and even more rarely national case law from African states. The Commission has only cited the sub-regional courts with a human rights mandate in one case. Viljoen notes 'the irony in the fact that in interpreting some of the distinctly "African" features of the Charter, as in the *Ogoniland* case,[30] the Commission only relied on non-African sources'.[31] However, it is noticeable that in this case the Commission only cites two comparative cases, the European Court case of *X and Y v Netherlands*[32] and the landmark Inter-American Court case *Velásquez Rodríguez v Honduras*,[33] as reinforcing the obligation of the state to prevent human rights violations by private actors as set out by the Commission in its earlier case law.[34]

The Commission has used comparative case law in relation to both issues of admissibility and of merits. The Commission in some cases includes lengthy summaries

[26] *Courson v Zimbabwe* (2000) AHRLR 335 (ACHPR 1995).

[27] *Toonen v Australia*, Communication No 488/1992, UN Doc CCPR/C/50/D/488/1992 (1994).

[28] Viljoen (n 6) 325. There have been some brief decisions without much reasoning also after 2001, see eg *Odjouriby v Benin* (2004) AHRLR 15 (ACHPR 2004).

[29] Communication 301/05, *Haregewoin Gabre-Selassie and IHRDA (on behalf of former Dergue Officials) v Ethiopia* (ACHPR 2012).

[30] *Social and Economic Rights Action Centre* (SERAC*) and Another v Nigeria* (2001) AHRLR 60 (ACHPR 2001).

[31] Viljoen (n 6) 326.

[32] *X and Y v Netherlands* 8978/80 (1985) 8 EHRR 235.

[33] *Velásquez Rodríguez v Honduras*, IACtHR Series C No 4 (1988).

[34] *Commission Nationale des Droits de l'Homme et des Libertés v Chad* (2000) AHRLR 66 (ACHPR 1995).

of the parties' submissions, including cases cited.[35] For example, in a case decided by the Commission in 2011 dealing with the fair trial rights of terrorism suspects and the prohibition against torture, the complainants cited case law from the European Court,[36] the International Criminal Tribunal for the former Yugoslavia (ICTY),[37] the Committee against Torture,[38] the Human Rights Committee,[39] the Inter-American Court,[40] and the Inter-American Commission[41] in their submissions on the merits which are 'summarised' in 53 paragraphs in the decision.[42] Only a few of these decisions are cited in the Commission's 'analysis on the merits'.[43]

The quality of the decisions of the Commission and how it engages with comparative case law vary significantly. The Commission in its 2000 decision on *Huri-Laws v Nigeria*,[44] quoted the European Court's judgment in *Ireland v UK*[45] with regard to the minimum threshold for treatment to be cruel, inhuman or degrading ('minimum level of severity').[46] Eight years later the Commission considered the same substantive issue as in *Huri-Laws* (conditions of detention) in *Institute for Human Rights and Development in Africa v Angola*. The Commission cited case law of the Human Rights Committee in relation to medical assistance to detainees,[47] case law which was decided several years before the decision in *Huri-Laws*.[48]

In *Doebbler v Sudan* the complaint argued that corporal punishment was a grossly disproportionate sentence in relation to the offence for which a group of students had been convicted.[49] The Commission went further than the complaint and investigated the compatibility of corporal punishment as such with the African Charter. The Commission's only reference to comparative material was citing *Ireland v UK* and a quote from the European Court's judgment in *Tyrer v UK*.[50] In contrast, the Inter-American Court judgment of *Caesar v Trinidad and Tobago* decided two years

[35] *Zimbabwean Human Rights NGO Forum v Zimbabwe* (2006) AHRLR 128 (ACHPR 2006) paras 90, 91, 96, 99, 100, 103, 104.

[36] *Egyptian Initiative for Personal Rights and Interights v Egypt I* (2011) AHRLR 42 (ACHPR 2011) paras 109, 117, 125, 132, 136.

[37] Ibid para 110.

[38] Ibid paras 116, 137.

[39] Ibid paras 119, 125.

[40] Ibid para 125.

[41] Ibid.

[42] See similarly the extensive citation of cases of the IACtHR and ECtHR by the complainant in *Zitha v Mozambique* (2011) AHRLR 138 (ACHPR 2011) where the Commission cited none of these cases in its analysis.

[43] See *Egyptian Initiative for Personal Rights and Interights v Egypt I* (n 36) paras 168, 185, 186, 214, 216.

[44] *Huri-Laws v Nigeria* (2000) AHRLR 273 (ACHPR 2000).

[45] *Ireland v UK*, (5310/71) [1978] ECHR 1 (18 January 1978).

[46] The Commission also cited the European Commission's decision in *Urrutikoetxea v France* App no 31113/96 (5 December 1996).

[47] *Institute for Human Rights and Development in Africa v Angola* (2008) AHRLR 43 (ACHPR 2008) para 52.

[48] *Kelly v Jamaica*, Communication No 537/1993 CCPR/C/57/D/537/1993 (17 July 1996); *Kalenga v Zambia* UN Doc CCPR/C/48/D/326/1988 (2 August 1993).

[49] *Doebbler v Sudan* (2003) AHRLR 153 (ACHPR 2003) para 6.

[50] *Tyrer v UK*, 5856/72 (ECtHR, 25 April 1978) para 38.

after *Doebbler*, cited, in addition to *Tyrer*, case law from the Human Rights Committee, the ICTY and national courts from across the world, including from Africa, to establish 'the growing trend towards recognition, at international and domestic levels, of the impermissible character of corporal punishment'.[51] To base the decision in *Doebbler* solely on *Tyrer*, in particular given the particular circumstances of that case, is inadequate.[52]

In *Tembani*, the Commission quoted the case of *Maksimov v Russia*[53] to the effect that 'the Convention guarantees the availability at the national level of a remedy to enforce the substance of the Convention rights'.[54] This was taken by the Commission to mean that access to justice is limited to national courts and could not apply to an international tribunal. The reasoning is very weak considering that *Maksimov* dealt with access to justice at the national level.

Since 2006 the Commission has cited comparative case law in almost all of its decisions on the merits. This is linked to the increased length of the decisions of the Commission in recent years.[55] In the *Endorois* decision, the Commission extensively relied on reports of the UN special rapporteur on indigenous peoples and general comments and other materials of UN treaty monitoring bodies but also placed heavy reliance on the judgments of the Inter-American Court in relation to the rights of indigenous peoples, and to a lesser extent the European Court, in relation to the definition of property and protection of minorities. It is noticeable that in its discussion on the merits, the Commission did not consider the extensive case law of the Inter-American Commission cited by the complainant but instead focused on the case law adopted by the Inter-American Court.[56]

The increased length of decisions has not necessarily led to a more thorough and accurate engagement with comparative case law. In a 2011 case dealing with gender-based violence in Egypt, the Commission quoted extensively from case law of the European Commission and Court dating from the 1960s to the early 1980s. The emphasis on deliberate treatment as expressed in the European Commission's case law of the 1960s and 1970s as cited by the Commission[57] has clearly been replaced by later case law of the Court.[58] The main point made by the quotations from the

[51] *Caesar v Trinidad and Tobago*, Merits, Reparations and Costs, IACtHR Series C No 123 (11 March 2005) paras 60–70.

[52] Cf Killander (n 18) 155–58.

[53] *Maksimov v Russia*, 43233/02 (ECtHR, 18 March 2010).

[54] Communication No 409/12, *Luke MunyanduTembani and Benjamin John Freeth (represented by Norman Tjombe) v Angola and Thirteen Others* (ACHPR 2013) para 140.

[55] The exception to the citation of comparative case law is *Mouvement Ivorien des Droits Humains (MIDH) v Côte d'Ivoire (I)* (2008) AHRLR 62 (ACHPR 2008) where the state did not dispute that its legislation violated the Charter. In *Zimbabwe Lawyers for Human Rights and Another v Zimbabwe* (2008) AHRLR 120 (ACHPR 2008) the Commission only cited the US Supreme Court decision in *Brown v Board of Education* of Topeka, 347 US 483 (1954) in its own analysis and no international case law despite the complainant citing case law from the Inter-American Commission and Court.

[56] *Saramaka People v Suriname*, IACtHR Series C No 172 (28 November 2007).

[57] *Egyptian Initiative for Personal Rights and Interights v Egypt II* (2011) AHRLR 90 (ACHPR 2011) para 195.

[58] See N Rodley, *The Treatment of Prisoners under International Law* (Oxford University Press, 2009) 127.

European Court's case law is that whether something is considered prohibited ill-treatment must be decided on a case-by-case basis. Judicial economy should mean that this point could be made in one paragraph of the decision rather than four. The section of the same case dealing with investigation cites the relevant European Court case law on this point in a much more concise manner.[59]

Engagement with comparative case law is, of course, not necessary in all cases. *Kazingachire v Zimbabwe*[60] is a clear example where UN soft law instruments provide clear direction in relation to use of force. Comparative case law cited by the complainants did not play an important role. In its only inter-state decision to date, dealing with violations by armed forces from Burundi, Rwanda and Uganda in the Democratic Republic of the Congo (DRC), the Commission cited the *Delalić* case[61] of the ICTY in relation to the prohibition of pillage.[62] Considering that the Commission cited extensively from international humanitarian law treaties, the additional benefit of this case law reference is doubtful.

The increased citation of comparative case law in recent years does not mean that such jurisprudence was not considered in earlier years. This can be seen from the fact that more recent cases cite both African Commission cases and comparative case law to the same effect. A clear and consistent format for the Commission's decisions would help in understanding its approach, which comes across as haphazard.

## IV. AFRICAN COURT ON HUMAN AND PEOPLES' RIGHTS

The judges of the African Court were elected in 2006. The Court has had a slow start, partly as a result of a lack of cases referred to it from the Commission and a low number of states having allowed direct access. The Court can find violations of not only human rights instruments adopted by the African Union, but any human rights instrument ratified by the respondent state.

In its first merits judgment in June 2013, *Mtikila v Tanzania*, the Court made extensive reference to the case law of the African Commission as well as the Inter-American and European courts in relation to exhaustion of local remedies.[63] With regard to the merits issue, the right of independent candidates to stand in elections, the Court cited *Castañeda Gutman v Mexico* where the Inter-American Court held that Mexico had shown 'compelling' social need for not allowing independent candidates.[64] The African Court cited the case law of the African Commission and

[59] *Egyptian Initiative for Personal Rights and Interights v Egypt II* (2011) (n 57) paras 228–29.

[60] Communication No 295/04, *Kazingachire and Others v Zimbabwe* (ACHPR 2012).

[61] *Prosecutor v Zejnil Delalić et al*, Case No IT-96-21-A.

[62] *DR C v Burundi, Rwanda and Uganda* (2004) AHRLR 19 (ACHPR 2003) para 85.

[63] *Tanganyika Law Society, the Legal and Human Rights Centre and Rev Christopher R Mtikila v Tanzania* App no 009, 011/2011 (ACtHPR, 14 June 2013) para 82.1.

[64] Para 103 quoting *Castañeda Gutman v Mexico*, IACtHR Series C No 184 (6 August 2008) paras 192–93.

the European and Inter-American Court in relation to limitations of rights.[65] The African Court found a violation of the right to political participation, trying to distinguish the case before it from *Castañeda Gutman v Mexico* in that a candidate in Mexico could be sponsored by a political party without being a member, while membership in the political party was required in Tanzania.[66] The Court further made reference to the position of the UN Human Rights Committee General Comment 25 'as an authoritative statement of interpretation of Article 25 of the ICCPR'.[67]

The recent judgment of the African Court in *Zongo v Burkina Faso*[68] is noticeable in its different approach to citation of comparative case law to *Mtikila*. The only citation to comparative case law is where the Court cites two European Court cases against France as indicating that 'cassation' must be exhausted as part of the requirement of exhaustion of local remedies.[69]

With regard to the merits, the Court held that Burkina Faso had 'failed to act with due diligence in seeking, trying and judging the assassins'.[70] The Court did not cite any comparative material in relation to what would constitute due diligence in this context. The same applies to the Court's finding of a violation of freedom of expression as set out in Article 9 of the African Charter read with Article 66(2)(c) of the revised ECOWAS Treaty (freedom of expression for journalists).

The lack of citation is clearly not because there is no comparative case law to discuss on the issue at hand (accountability for extrajudicial executions). It is mentioned in the judgment that the parties cited case law from the African Commission,[71] though the judgment does not mention which cases. However, it should also be noted that the relevant issues are covered extensively in UN soft law.[72] However, not even these instruments were cited in the judgment.

## V. ECOWAS COMMUNITY COURT OF JUSTICE

The ECOWAS Community Court of Justice was established in 1991 but it was only with the provision of a human rights mandate and individual access in 2005 that the Court became active. The Court does not require exhaustion of local remedies in order to be accessed. In human rights related cases the ECOWAS Court applies the ECOWAS Treaty, the African Charter, the Universal Declaration of Human Rights and UN human rights treaties ratified by the defendant state.

65 *Mtikila v Tanzania* (n 63) para 106.
66 Ibid para 107.3.
67 Ibid.
68 *Affaire ayant droit de feus Norbert Zongo, Abdoulaye Nikiema dit Ablasse, Ernest Zongo et Blaise Ilboudo & Le mouvment Burkinabé des droits de l'homme et des peuples c Burkina Faso*, requête No 013/2011 (ACtHR 28 March 2014).
69 *Zongo* case (n 68) para 70 indicating that France belongs to the same legal family as Burkina Faso.
70 Ibid para 156 (unofficial translation).
71 Ibid para 141.
72 Cf the Commission decision in *Kazingachire v Zimbabwe* (n 60) discussed above.

The Court has relied heavily on a textual interpretation of the relevant treaty provisions combined with reliance on its own case law. It is noticeable that there is less reliance on soft law by the ECOWAS Court than by the African Commission.[73]

In *Manneh v The Gambia* the Court noted:

> Although this Court is not bound by the precedents of other international courts, it can draw some useful lessons from their judgments, especially when the issues involved are similar; in other words, such decisions can be of persuasive value to this Court.[74]

It then cited two European Court judgments in relation to that Court awarding damages, before turning to the issue at hand, that is, whether to award punitive damages and finding that: 'Notwithstanding the fact that the European and the Inter-American Courts have been in existence for long, there is no record available to us that showed that any of them had awarded punitive damages.'[75] The Court then cited *Silver v UK*[76] as a case where punitive damages were called for by the complainant but rejected by the European Court without motivation. The Court further cited UK national case law to the effect that the aim of compensation is restoration.

In *Ocean King*, the fact that the ECOWAS Court does not require exhaustion of local remedies was challenged. The Court noted that the International Court of Justice (ICJ) had held that the general requirement of exhaustion could be waived through treaty.[77]

The most famous judgment of the ECOWAS Court is the so-called slavery judgment, *Koraou v Niger*. On the merits of the case the Court cited the judgment of the ICTY in *Kunarac* in relation to what constitutes enslavement[78] and the finding of the Nuremberg tribunal that slavery can occur without evidence of other ill-treatment.[79] Allain has criticised the Court for going beyond the definition in the Slavery Convention with regard to a case that clearly fell within the scope of the definition of the Convention.[80] He also criticises the misquoting of the ICJ judgment in *Barcelona Traction* in relation to *erga omnes* obligations.[81]

Allain concluded his discussion of the *Koraou* judgment as follows:

> [T]he judges of the Community Court of Justice appeared to be out of their depth in going beyond the ECOWAS acquis, to consider issues of international human rights law. Yet, the

[73] The assessment of the Court's case law is based on a sample of 22 judgments of the Court available to the author.

[74] *Manneh v The Gambia* (2008) AHRLR 171 (ECOWAS 2008) para 33.

[75] Ibid para 36.

[76] *Silver v UK* (1983) 5 EHRR 347.

[77] *Ocean King Nigeria Limited v Senegal* (2011) ECW/CCJ/APP/05/08 para 39. See also the reference in *Koraou v Niger* (2008) AHRLR 182 (ECOWAS 2008) para 39 to the European Court judgment in *De Wilde, Ooms and Versyp v Belgium*. For a critique of the use 'out of context' of this case see J Allain, '*Hadijatou Mani Koraou v Republic of Niger*, judgment No ECW/CCJ/JUD/06/08, Economic Community of West Africa States Community Court of Justice, October 27, 2008' (2009) 103 *American Journal of International Law* 311, 315–16.

[78] *Koraou v Niger* (n 77) para 77.

[79] Ibid para 79.

[80] Allain (n 77) 316.

[81] *Koraou v Niger* (n 77) para 81; Allain (n 77) 316.

> manner in which the judges played fast and loose with the judgments of both the International Court of Justice and European Court of Human Rights speaks to a more fundamental flaw in the makeup of the ECOWAS Court.[82]

In finding that there had not been a violation of the principle of equal pay for equal work, the Court in *Essien v The Gambia* cited the Court of Justice of the European Union and the French Court of Cassation.[83] In *Yovo et 31 autres v Societe Togo Telecom et Etat Togolais*, the Court cited the European Court case of *Burdov v Russia* as *Burlov* and *Hornsby v Greece* as *Honsbly*.[84] What is indicated as a quote from the judgment does not appear in either of the two judgments.

In *Ehivet and Gbagbo v Côte d'Ivoire* the Court deals extensively with the European Court's case law on derogation in a state of emergency, concluding that Côte d'Ivoire did not act in accordance with Article 4 of the International Covenant on Civil and Political Rights (ICCPR) and Article 48 of the Ivorian Constitution. It is noticeable that the Court did not consider the African Commission's case law on the non-derogability of the African Charter or the general comment of the UN Human Rights Committee in relation to derogation from the ICCPR.[85]

In *Ibrahim v Niger*,[86] the Court cited the Appeals Chamber of the Special Court for Sierra Leone and the Inter-American Court judgment in *Barrios Altos*[87] in relation to the prohibition of amnesties for gross violations of human rights.[88] The Court concluded that the violations in the case at hand were not massive without any discussion of what constitutes the threshold.[89]

The facts in *SERAP v Nigeria*[90] were similar to those informing the African Commission's 2001 decision in the *Ogoniland* case. However, the Commission decision was only cited as part of the complainant's submissions.[91] In interpreting Article 24 of the Charter, the Court cited an advisory opinion of the ICJ in relation to the relationship between a healthy environment and human health.[92]

In one of its most far-reaching judgments the Court ordered that the Nigerian government should cover a shortfall resulting from corruption in relation to funding for education. The order was made without any reference to comparative material and despite a finding that cases of embezzlement could not be treated as human rights violations.[93]

82 Allain (n 77) 317.
83 *Essien v The Republic of The Gambia and Another* (2007) AHRLR 131 (ECOWAS 2007).
84 *Yovo et 31 autres v Societe Togo Telecom et Etat Togolais* 34, ECW/CCJ/APP/08/11.
85 *Ehivet et Michel Gbagbo v Côte d'Ivoire* (2013) ECW/CCJ/JUD/03/13.
86 *Ibrahim v Niger*, ECW/CCJ/APP/12/09.
87 *Barrios Altos v Peru*, IACtHR Series C No 87 (2001).
88 *Ibrahim v Niger* (n 86) para 51.
89 Ibid para 52.
90 *SERAP v Nigeria*, ECW/CCJ/APP/08/0.
91 Ibid para 64.
92 Ibid para 100.
93 Ibid para 21.

Comparative jurisprudence citation by the ECOWAS Court is not widespread. As indicated above, this may not be a bad thing considering that comparative case law is quite often misquoted or is not applicable to the case.

## VI. EAST AFRICAN COURT OF JUSTICE

The East African Court of Justice was established in 2001. It is unique among international courts in that it did not need to build a set of its own precedents from scratch. Instead it has relied extensively on the case law of the Court of Appeal for Eastern Africa (EA) which operated from 1902 to 1977.[94] As with other courts, it also relies extensively on its own case law as precedent. The Court at present explicitly lacks a human rights mandate. However, this has not prevented the Court from interpreting principles set out in the EAC Treaty such as the rule of law in a broad manner, allowing it to consider some cases that would clearly fall under the banner of human rights case law.[95]

In *Katabazi* the Court cited the EA and the Court of Appeal of Tanzania in relation to preliminary objections.[96] In dealing with what constitutes the rule of law, the Court first quoted Wikipedia and Kanyeihamba's *Commentaries on Law, Politics and Governance* before asking the question 'how have the courts dealt with it?' and citing Kenyan and British case law.[97] In subsequent case law the Court has continued to rely on Wikipedia and other websites, dictionaries and various NGO and UN reports as well as doctrine to define the rule of law, governance and so on.[98]

In *Katabazi*, the Court noted that counsel for the applicant 'left no stone unturned to persuade us to find that what the soldiers did breached the rule of law'. The Court found that the African Commission's decision in *Constitutional Rights Project and Another v Nigeria*,[99] cited by the complainant, 'are on all fours with the present

[94] 'Overview of the East African Court of Justice by Justice Harold R Nsekela, President, East African Court of Justice', A paper for presentation during the sensitisation workshop on the role of the EACJ in the EAC integration, Imperial Royale Hotel, Kampala, Uganda 1–2 November 2011 (on file with author). On the history of the EAC see also LL Kato, 'The Court of Appeal for East Africa: From a colonial court to an international court' (1971) 7 *East African Law Journal* 1.

[95] A 2013 publication of the Open Society Justice Initiative sees 12 judgments in relation to eight cases as being of relevance to human rights. See Open Society Justice Initiative (June 2013) 'Human rights decisions of the East African Court of Justice', available at www.opensocietyfoundations.org/sites/default/files/east-african-court-digest-june-2013-20130726.pdf.

[96] *Katabazi and Others v Secretary-General of the EAC and Another* (2007) AHRLR 119 (EAC 2007) para 13.

[97] Ibid paras 43–45.

[98] See eg *Hon Sitenda Sebalu v Secretary General of The East African Community* Ref 1 of 2010 (22 December 2013) paras 34–35; *Mary Ariviza & Okotch Mondoh v Attorney General of the Republic of Kenya & Secretary General of the East African Community* No 3 of 2010 (EACJ, 29 November 2011) paras 21–22; *Samuel Mukira Mohochi v Attorney General of the Republic of Uganda* No 5 of 2011 (EACJ, 17 May 2013) para 17.

[99] *Constitutional Rights Project and Another v Nigeria* (2000) AHRLR 235 (ACHPR 1999).

reference and we find that the independence of the judiciary, a cornerstone of the principle of the rule of law, has been violated'.[100]

In *Plaxeda Rugumba*, dealing with illegal detention, the First Instance Division did not cite any comparative case law apart from quoting a section from *Katabazi* which includes references to two British cases.[101] The Appellate Division also did not cite any comparative material in finding:

> To hold a citizen in preventive detention without lawful authority and in breach of the laws of the State of Rwanda; to deprive him of his liberty for a period of about five (5) months; not to inform him or his family of the reason(s) for detention, obviously breach the principles set out in the EAC Treaty to which the Republic of Rwanda is a signatory.[102]

The Court only cited the *Interhandel* case of the ICJ (though incorrectly citing it as the *International* case) in relation to the customary international law nature of the requirement of exhaustion of local remedies.[103] While finding that there were no remedies to exhaust in the case at hand it contradicted its own case law in relation to there not being a requirement to exhaust local remedies for cases brought to the Court.

Comparative case law is cited more in cases dealing with procedure,[104] than in cases dealing with substantive issues, in particular human rights, and used more extensively by the Appellate Division than the First Instance Division. The most extensive use of comparative case law is in the judgment of the Appellate Division in the application for review of its judgment in *Independent Medico Legal Unit v Attorney General of Kenya*. In this case the Court cited the position of the courts of four member states, Uganda, Tanzania, Kenya and Rwanda in relation to the possibility of review of judgments and also comparative case law from South Africa, Zimbabwe, Australia and India before concluding that review is obviously allowed since the EAC Treaty provides for it. On page 20 of the judgment it then turns to the actual issue, whether the jurisdiction of review extends to the Appellate Division. It first sets out that the issue 'was put to rest, for regional courts' by two judgments of the Common Market for Eastern and Southern Africa (COMESA) Court of Justice.[105]

The Court has on occasion rejected the comparative case law put forward by a party as irrelevant. In *Awadh Omar*, the Appellate Division tried to distinguish itself

[100] *Katabazi* case (n 96) para 49.

[101] *Plaxeda Rugumba v Secretary General of the East African Community and Attorney General of the Republic of Rwanda* Ref No 8 of 201(EACJ, 1 December 2011).

[102] *Attorney General of the Republic of Rwanda v Plaxeda Rugumba* Appeal No 1 of 2012 (EACJ, 21 June 2012) para 29.

[103] *Plaxeda Rugumba* (n 101) para 35.

[104] See eg *Secretary General of The East African Community v Hon Sitenda Sebalu* No 9 of 2012 (EACJ, 14 February 2013).

[105] Cf eg *Independent Medical Legal Unit v Attorney General of the Republic of Kenya and Four Others* Ref 3 of 2010 (EACJ, 29 June 2011) citing its own case law and one Kenyan case, and the Appellate Division ruling in the same case, *Independent Medical Legal Unit* Appeal No 1 of 2011 (EACJ, 15 March 2012) citing EA, its own case law, the IACtHR and the European Court of Justice.

from a human rights court and explain the reason why the precedents cited by counsel were not applicable before the Court:

> The respondents laboured valiantly to avail to us all the abundant jurisprudence of the European Human Rights Court, the Inter-American Court, the African Commission and others that recognize the principle of 'continuing violations'. While this jurisprudence is perfect for its particular circumstances, it is all about human rights violations, governed by particular conventions on human rights.[106]

The Court's attempt to distinguish itself as a regional integration court is also evident in its many instances of citing the Court of Justice of the European Union[107] also in relation to human rights issues such as deportation.[108]

## VII. IMPACT OF SUPRANATIONAL HUMAN RIGHTS LITIGATION AT THE NATIONAL LEVEL

The extent to which reliance on the case law of the European Court has penetrated constitutional law and litigation in European states has not been replicated in other regions with established regional human rights systems.[109] In the case of Africa this may be because of the so far limited issues dealt with by regional jurisprudence. Clearly, training and access to material for lawyers and judges also play a role.[110]

References to the African Commission's case law in domestic African case law are quite rare. The South African Constitutional Court has made reference to the Commission's case law in one case[111] as has the Supreme Court of Appeal, the Supreme Court of Zambia,[112] the Supreme Court of Zimbabwe[113] and the High Court of

[106] *Omar Awadh* Appeal No 2 of 2012 (EACJ, 15 April 2013) para 55. In this case the Court cited ECJ and Ugandan and US national cases. See also *Samuel Mukira Mohochi v Attorney General of the Republic of Uganda*, Case No 5 of 2011 (17 May 2013); *Omar Awadh Omar and Six Others v Attorney General of the Republic of Kenya, Attorney General of the Republic of Uganda and Secretary General of the East African Community* No 4 of 2011 (EACJ, 1 December 2011).

[107] See eg *Anyang Nyongo'o*, Ref 1 of 2006 (EACJ, 6 February 2007) paras 107–108; Independent *Medical Legal* Appeal No 1 of 2011 (EACJ, 15 March 2012) para 16; *Mohochi* (n 106) para 55.

[108] *Mohochi* (n 106) paras 75, 116.

[109] Centre for Human Rights *The Impact of the African Charter and Women's Protocol in Selected African States* (Pretoria University Law Press, 2012); A Huneeus 'Rejecting the Inter-American Court: Judicialization, National Courts, and Regional Human Rights' available at papers.ssrn.com/sol3/papers.cfm?abstract_id=1911383; A Huneeus, 'Courts resisting courts: Lessons from the Inter-American Court's struggle to enforce human rights' (2011) 44 *Cornell International Law Journal* 493. On some examples of reliance on Inter-American jurisprudence by national courts in the Americas, see JM Pasqualucci, *The Practice and Procedure of the Inter-American Court of Human Rights* (Cambridge University Press, 2012) 77.

[110] Killander and Adjolohoun (n 7).

[111] *Koyabe and Others v Minister for Home Affairs and Others* (CCT 53/08) [2009] ZACC 23; 2009 (12) BCLR 1192 (CC); 2010 (4) SA 327 (CC) (25 August 2009) para 42.

[112] *Attorney General v Clarke* (96A/2004) [2008] ZMSC 4 (24 January 2008).

[113] *Capital Radio (Pvt) Limited v Broadcasting Authority of Zimbabwe and Others* (162/2001); *Kachingwe and Others v The Minister of Home Affairs and Others* (2005) AHRLR 228 (ZwSC 2005).

Kenya.[114] In contrast, the South African Constitutional Court has extensively cited the European and Inter-American human rights courts.[115] African national courts have in some instances referred to the resolutions of the Commission.[116] Sometimes the findings of the courts in relation to this case law are not correct.[117]

## VIII. AFRICA IN THE GLOBAL HUMAN RIGHTS DIALOGUE

The European Court does not only cite European national case law. For example, in *IB v Greece*, the Court sets out the 'Judgment of the South African Constitutional Court in the case of *Hoffman v South African Airways*' as a three-paragraph sub-heading under the main heading 'relevant European and international instruments'.[118] In addition to the Constitutional Court of South Africa, the European Court has also cited other African national courts such as the supreme courts of Mauritius and Namibia.[119] The African Commission's case law has only been referred to in one case by the Court in its exposition of 'international law and practice'.[120] The lack of references to the Commission's case law is not because it lacks

[114] *Satrose Ayuma and Eleven Others v Registered Trustees of the Kenya Railways Staff Retirement Benefits Scheme and Three Others*, Petition No 65 of 2010; *New Vision Kenya (NVK Mageuzi) and Three Others v Independent Electoral and Boundaries Commission and Eight Others* [2012] eKLR, Petition 331 of 2012; *Republic v Milton Kabulit and Six Others* [2012] eKLR, Criminal Case No 115 of 2008; *David Njoroge Macharia v Republic* [2011] eKLR, Criminal Appeal No 497 of 2007; *John Swaka v Director of Public Prosecutions, Attorney General and Two Others* [2013] eKLR, Constitutional Petition No 318 of 2011.

[115] Search terms 'European Court of Human Rights' and 'Inter-American Court' in SAFLII database. For example, *S v Makwanyane and Another* (CCT3/94) [1995] ZACC 3; 1995 (6) BCLR 665; 1995 (3) SA 391; [1996] 2 CHRLD 164; 1995 (2) SACR 1 (6 June 1995); *Ferreira v Levin NO and Others; Vryenhoek and Others v Powell NO and Others* (CCT5/95) [1995] ZACC 13; 1996 (1) SA 984 (CC); 1996 (1) BCLR 1 (6 December 1995); *Doctors for Life International v Speaker of the National Assembly and Others* (CCT12/05) [2006] ZACC 11; 2006 (12) BCLR 1399 (CC); 2006 (6) SA 416 (CC) (17 August 2006).

[116] *Charles Onyango Obbo and Another v Attorney General* (Constitutional Appeal No 2 of 2002); *Fakudze and Others v Director of Public Prosecutions and Another* (237/08) [2008] SZHC 161 (22 August 2008); *International Centre for Policy and Conflict v Attorney General and Another* [2012] eKLR, Petition 398 of 2012; *Famy Care Limited v Public Procurement Administrative Review Board and Another and Four Others* [2012] eKLR, Petition No 43 of 2012; *Kahindi Lekalhaile and Four Others v Inspector General National Police Service and Three Others* [2013] eKLR, Petition No 25 of 2013.

[117] *Civil Liberties Committee v The Minister of Justice and Registrar General* MSCA Civil Appeal No 12 of 1999 (Malawi Supreme Court of Appeal, 8 April 2004) stating that *action popularis* is not allowed under the African Charter.

[118] *Hoffmann v South African Airways* (CCT17/00) [2000] ZACC 17; 2001 (1) SA 1; 2000 (11) BCLR 1235; [2000] 12 BLLR 1365 (CC) (28 September 2000) paras 36–38.

[119] *Babar Ahmad and Others v UK*, 24027/07, 11949/08, 36742/08, 66911/09 and 67354/09 (ECtHR, 10 April 2012) paras 153, 154.

[120] *Sitaropoulos and Giakoumopoulos v Greece*, 42202/07 (ECtHR, 15 March 2012) para 31 citing the *Purohit* case. See also the lengthy quotation in *Margus v Croatia* 4455/10 (ECtHR, 27 May 2014) para 63 from the judgment of the Inter-American Court of Human Rights in *Gelman v Uruguay*, Merits and Reparations, IACtHR Series C No 221 (24 February 2011) which includes a reference to the Commission's case law on amnesty laws.

relevance as it has been referred to in a number of separate opinions[121] and submissions before the Court.[122] There is clearly no reason to neglect African perspectives in determining what constitutes 'common ground in modern societies'.

The Inter-American Court has cited the African Commission in relation to amnesty laws,[123] rights of indigenous peoples,[124] expulsion of foreign nationals,[125] judicial independence[126] and the importance of freedom of expression in a democratic society.[127] Most of the Commission cases cited have themselves cited earlier Inter-American Court judgments related to the same issue, illustrating how comparative case law is used to reinforce the position of the Court where it has already established a jurisprudence of its own.

## IX. CONCLUSION

Supranational case law is meant to set the standard to be followed at the national level. Ideally, repeat cases should be dealt with at the national level. However, regional courts which handle cases related to human rights are still a new phenomenon in Africa. Africa is thus still precedent weak at the regional level. Arguably, this should invite increased reliance on comparative case law.

The case law surveyed indicates that comparative case law is cited quite often, whether or not cited by counsel.[128] Authority is often given to support conclusions. It is rare that there is discussion about different approaches taken in different jurisdictions in relation to an issue leading to what is seen as the most persuasive authority.

[121] *Souza Ribeiro v France*, 22689/07 (ECtHR, 13 December 2012) concurring opinion of Judge Pinto de Albuquerque, joined by Judge Vucinic; *Konstantin Markin v Russia*, 30078/06 (ECtHR, 7 October 2010) partly concurring, partly dissenting opinion of Judge Pinto de Albuquerque; *Hirsi Jamaa and Others v Italy*, 27765/09 (ECtHR, 23 February 2012) concurring opinion of Judge Pinto de Albuquerque.

[122] *CLR on behalf of Campeanu v Romania*, 47848/08 (ECtHR, 17 July 2014) para 88; *Janowiec and Others v Russia* 55508/07 and 29520/09 (ECtHR, 21 October 2013) para 196; *El-Masri v The Former Yugoslav Republic of Macedonia*, 39630/09 (ECtHR, 13 December 2012) para 175.

[123] *Gelman v Uruguay* (n 120) paras 195, 212, 214; *Gomes Lund and Others v Brazil*, Preliminary Objections, Merits, Reparations and Costs, IACtHR Series C No 219 (24 November 2010) paras 146, 147, 160, 162.

[124] *Pueblo Indigena Kichwa de Sarayaku v Ecuador*, Merits and reparations, IACtHR Series C No 245 (27 June 2012) para 216; *Pueblo Saramaka v Suriname*, Preliminary Objections, Merits, Reparations, and Costs Series C No 172 (28 November 2007) para 120.

[125] *Nadege Dorzema and Others v Dominican Republic*, Merits, Reparations and Costs, IACtHR Series C No 251 (24 October 2012) para 162, 163, 175; *Velez Loor v Panama*, Preliminary Objections, Merits, Reparations and Costs, IACtHR Series C No 218 (23 November 2010) para 100.

[126] *Apitz Barbera et al ('first court of administrative disputes') v Venezuela*, Preliminary Objection, Merits, Reparations and Costs, IACtHR Series C No 182 (5 August 2008) para 84 (citing the Principles and Guidelines on the Right to Fair Trial and Legal Assistance in Africa).

[127] *Herrera Ulloa v Costa Rica*, Preliminary Objections, Merits, Reparations and Costs, IACtHR Series C No 107 (2 July 2004) para 114.

[128] See eg *African Network for Animal Welfare (ANAW) v Attorney General of Tanzania* Ref 9 of 2010 (EACJ, 20 June 2014) para 42: 'Mr Malata gave us no authority to support his arguments in that regard, neither have we found any such authority.'

Intra-institutional citation is still rare. The East African Court of Justice (EACJ) cited a relevant Commission case when dealing with the same issue, while the ECOWAS Court did not. The African Commission and African Court have cited each other.

All too often, authority is given that is taken out of context, or simply does not deal with the issue at hand, or is misquoted. Such an approach hardly enhances legitimacy. The remark by Justice Kriegler of the South African Constitutional Court in relation to comparative case law cited by counsel applies equally to citation by courts, whether at the national or international level: 'Far too often one sees citation by counsel of, for instance, an American judgment in support of a proposition relating to our Constitution, without any attempt to explain why it is said to be in point.'[129]

A court or quasi-judicial body can clearly be influenced without citing a judgment. However, the advantage of citation is that it makes it clear to those concerned that the decision is in line with developments elsewhere, in particular if a court is dealing with issues that have not come before it previously. There is not much indication that citation of comparative material would cause a decision to be viewed as more legitimate and thus influence compliance with the decision, or make the decision more prominent in legal discourse.

Reasons not to cite include reducing length of decisions as citation is often accompanied by lengthy, often unnecessary quotes, and the risk of not citing the best sources or citing them incorrectly, even if the outcome of the case is in line with the international jurisprudence in relation to the case at hand.

Romano sets out four hypotheses in relation to the use of international judges of comparative jurisprudence: 'jurisprudential harmony', 'jurisprudential teamwork' (creating international law through repeated multiple reference), acculturation, and lack of judicial hierarchy.[130] The African experience is consistent with these hypotheses. Though the reasoning of African regional courts and quasi-judicial bodies often appears haphazard, the outcome of the cases is in most instances in line with the view of international human rights law as a universal endeavour. That comparative case law is not cited more than it is, could arguably be explained by the fact that case law is only one of a multitude of possible material to cite without any hierarchy in relation to what is seen as the most authoritative except for the treaties applied and own case law. Thus there is not only a lack of judicial hierarchy but also case law is not viewed as superior (or inferior) to other authorities in line with the hypothesis of acculturation.

Africa could arguably play a more important role in the global judicial dialogue on human rights. In particular, the European Court could more frequently cite relevant jurisprudence of African courts. One weakness of African courts and quasi-judicial bodies is lack of visibility. The judgments of the ECOWAS Court are difficult

[129] *Bernstein and Others v Bester NO and Others* (CCT 23/95) [1996] ZACC 2; 1996 (4) BCLR 449; 1996 (2) SA 751 (27 March 1996) para 133.

[130] Romano (n 3).

to obtain; the African Court only puts its judgments in heavy scanned pdf files on the web and different language versions are not released at the same time; and the African Commission lags behind in publishing a number of its decisions and is often late in even letting the parties know about the outcome.

Judicial dialogue does not only take place in judgments but also through workshops and seminars where judges and members of quasi-judicial bodies meet and are exposed to each other's case law. Counsel also play an important role in putting relevant material before the courts.

Africa is quite a new entrant to the global dialogue on human rights. African regional courts and quasi-judicial bodies should reflect on how to ensure that their decisions are clear and well reasoned and accurately cite good authority to the benefit of all stakeholders including the parties to the dispute, other African states and other courts in Africa and elsewhere.

# 3

# *Human Rights Adjudication as Transnational Adjudication: A Peripheral Case of Domestic Courts as International Law Adjudicators*

SAMANTHA BESSON*

## I. INTRODUCTION

THE ROLE DOMESTIC courts should play in the adjudication of international law, not only in its enforcement, but also in the interpretation and hence the 'development' of international law is of increasing interest to international lawyers.[1]

This chapter contributes to this most recent and normative turn in the discussion of the role of domestic courts in international law. It does not aim to do so generally, however, but looks at the adjudication and hence interpretation of international human rights law by domestic courts. It argues that international and domestic human rights adjudication processes are best understood together as one single process: transnational human rights adjudication. After explaining the specificities of that process, the contribution argues that international human rights law and adjudication should not be taken too readily as a core case or example in the general discussion of domestic judicial law-making in international law, or at least not without serious qualifications.

* Professor of Public International Law and European Law, University of Fribourg, Switzerland. Many thanks to Yuval Shany for his invitation to contribute to the 2014 ESIL Conference in Vienna and for his comments, and to August Reinisch for his invitation to publish in the Proceedings. I would also like to thank Odile Ammann, my research assistant, for her help with the editing and formal layout of the piece.

[1] On the 'enforcement' and 'interpretation' or 'development' functions of international adjudication and their tensions, see Samantha Besson, 'International Judges' Function(s) between Dispute-Settlement and Law-Enforcement—From International Law without Courts to International Courts without Law' (2012) 34 *Loyola Law Review* 33; Samantha Besson, 'Legal Philosophical Issues of International Adjudication—Getting Over the *amour impossible* between International Law and Adjudication' in Karen Alter, Cesare Romano and Yuval Shany (eds), *Oxford Companion to International Adjudication* (Oxford University Press, 2014).

The proposed argument is four-pronged. Section II maps the discussion of international law adjudication by domestic courts and explains how it is becoming more normative. Against the background of those discussions, Section III identifies where the puzzle of international human rights adjudication lies. In Section IV, the argument explores the specificities of international human rights adjudication by international and domestic courts, before articulating, in Section V, a transnational interpretation of those unique features and functions.

Methodologically, the contribution approaches the question of international human rights adjudication from the perspective of human rights theory, and, more precisely, from the perspective of a legal theory of human rights. It aims to provide the best interpretation and justification of the existing practice of international human rights law, that is, one that puts the practice in its best light.[2] To that extent, the contribution does not merely aim to propose a moral theory of the legitimacy of domestic adjudication in the human rights context that could then be used to reform existing practice. Nor, however, is it about reconstructing the practice as a theory and hence merely about justifying it. There is a space between utopia and apology. The practice of international human rights law entails its own immanent justifications and critiques, and those are the justifications and critiques that need to be identified and interpreted in the proposed theory of human rights adjudication so as to best fit the practice while at the same time justifying and criticising it.[3]

For reasons of scope, the argument advanced focuses mostly on the Convention for the Protection of Human Rights and Fundamental Freedoms (European Convention on Human Rights (ECHR)). While this may be criticised for falling prey to a regionalist bias as well as to a judicial one, both critiques may be countered. As I will explain in the conclusion, much of what I will argue may be transposed *mutatis mutandis* to the universal level and to the future World Court of Human Rights if it ever comes into existence. The same may be said, albeit with some fine-tuning, about United Nations (UN) human rights treaty bodies that are non-judicial in their reasoning and interpretation of international human rights law.[4] One may argue, indeed, that they have jurisdiction to monitor and not to interpret international human rights law,[5] but that this provides for even more scope for interpretation by domestic courts in human rights adjudication in the end. In any case, it is actually quite common for human rights scholars to include all those judicial and non-judicial international bodies in the same discussion.[6]

[2] See eg Samantha Besson, *Human Rights as Law* (forthcoming, manuscript on file with author).

[3] Of course, this assumes that judges are moral reasoners (albeit of a special kind), and that their motivation is to develop the best interpretation of international human rights law in their democratic domestic context and, when necessary, to convince the ECtHR to change its consolidated European interpretation as well.

[4] See eg Birgit Schlütter, 'Aspects of Human Rights Interpretation by the UN Treaty Bodies' in Helen Keller and Geir Ulfstein (eds), *Human Rights Treaty Bodies: Law and Legitimacy* (Cambridge University Press, 2012).

[5] On this distinction in international adjudication in general, see Besson, 'Legal Philosophical Issues of International Adjudication' (n 1).

[6] See eg Schlütter (n 4).

## II. INTERNATIONAL LAW ADJUDICATION BY DOMESTIC COURTS

After a summary of the discussion of the role of domestic courts in the adjudication of international law to date, I will introduce what one may take as a recent normative turn in the debate.

### A. The Discussion to Date

To date, international legal scholars' discussions of the role of domestic courts in the adjudication of international law have been largely descriptive and of a sociological kind. Most authors have sought to assess the 'effects' of domestic courts on international law, and more generally, to explain the 'role' domestic courts' decisions have played in the interpretation and hence development of international law.[7] This has been done mostly in general terms, but also, recently, within specific regimes of international law where the role of domestic courts has been greater, such as international responsibility law or international immunities law.[8]

In a nutshell, those discussions may be said to have branched out in three directions. Authors have identified and discussed: the legal bases for domestic courts' engagement with international law and the various types of engagement therewith; the variables in the international law framework that affect that engagement in practice; and the various effects domestic courts' decisions have had in international law.

[7] See eg Antonios Tzanakopoulos, 'Domestic Judicial Law-Making' in Catherine Brölmann and Yannick Radi (eds), *Research Handbook on the Theory and Practice of International Law-Making* (Edward Elgar, 2016 forthcoming); Antonios Tzanakopoulos and Christian Tams, 'Introduction: Domestic Courts as Agents of Development of International Law' (2013) 26 *Leiden Journal of International Law* 531; Shaheed Fatima, *Using International Law in Domestic Courts*, 2nd edn (Hart Publishing, 2013); Antonios Tzanakopoulos, 'Domestic Courts as the "Natural Judge" of International Law: A Change in Physiognomy' in James Crawford and Sarah Nouwen (eds), *Select Proceedings of the European Society of International Law*, vol 3 (Hart Publishing, 2012); Study Group: Principles on the Engagement of Domestic Courts and with International Law, 'Principles on the Engagement of Domestic Courts with International Law' in International Law Association Preliminary Report (2012); Jean d'Aspremont, 'The Systemic Integration of International Law by Domestic Courts: Domestic Judges as Architects of the Consistency of the International Legal Order' in Ole Kristian Fauchald and André Nollkaemper (eds), *The Practice of International and National Courts and the (De-)Fragmentation of International Law* (Hart Publishing, 2011); André Nollkaemper, *National Courts and the International Rule of Law* (Oxford University Press, 2011); Anthea Roberts, 'Comparative International Law? The Role of National Courts in Creating and Enforcing International Law' (2011) 60 *International & Comparative Law Quarterly* 57; Yuval Shany, 'National Courts as International Actors: Jurisdictional Implications' (2009) 15 *Federalismi.it*, available at www.federalismi.it/nv14/articolo-documento.cfm?artid=13810; Eyal Benvenisti and George Downs, 'National Courts, Domestic Democracy and the Evolution of International Law' (2009) 20 *European Journal of International Law* 59; Yuval Shany, *Regulating Jurisdictional Relations between National and International Courts* (Oxford University Press, 2007); Karen Knop, 'Here and There: International Law in Domestic Courts' (2000) 32 *New York University Journal of International Law and Politics* 501, and before them: Hersch Lauterpacht, 'Decisions of Municipal Courts as a Source of International Law' (1929) 10 *British Yearbook of International Law* 65; Lassa Oppenheim, 'The Science of International Law: Its Task and Method' (1908) 2 *American Journal of International Law* 313; Robert Jennings, 'The Judiciary, International and National Law and the Development of International Law' (1996) 45 *International & Comparative Law Quarterly* 1.

[8] See eg the various contributions in the special issue of the (2013) 26 *Leiden Journal of International Law* edited by Antonios Tzanakopoulos and Christian Tams.

### *i. The Legal Bases for Domestic Courts' Engagement with International Law and the Types Thereof*

Some of the legal bases or grounds for the duty or, at least, for the right or power of domestic courts to apply, and hence to interpret international law in their decisions have been clarified in the literature.[9] The first distinction one has to draw in this regard is between international and domestic legal bases.

With respect to *international* legal bases, one should mention the following in particular. First of all, the principle of primacy of international law binding the state (and its courts as agents of the responsible state in case of violation of international law), and the principle of consistent interpretation of international law that derives from it (in monist and dualist orders alike). This duty of compliance extends to a duty of domestic courts to abide by the international framework of interpretation of international law (and in particular to comply with Articles 31 and 32 of the Vienna Convention on the Law of Treaties (VCLT)).[10,11] Second, one should mention the principle of exhaustion of local judicial remedies that applies in some cases in order for an international court to then acquire jurisdiction.[12] This principle implies a primary obligation for states to set up domestic judicial remedies in cases of violation of international law. This may be connected, thirdly, to the explicit duty of states under international human rights law to guarantee a judicial remedy for any violation of international law, including a domestic judicial remedy.[13] Fourth, the principle of 'substantive' subsidiarity[14] applies in some cases, mostly in the context of international human rights law,[15] and governs the ability of an international court to impose a new interpretation. As we will see, this principle requires that international courts observe a 'consensus' or 'common approach'[16] among states before identifying a new interpretation of international law on that basis, thus implying that

[9] See in particular, Tzanakopoulos, 'Domestic Judicial Law-Making' (n 7); Tzanakopoulos and Tams (n 7).

[10] Vienna Convention on the Law of Treaties (adopted 23 May 1969, entered into force 27 January 1980) 1155 UNTS 331 (VCLT).

[11] See d'Aspremont (n 7).

[12] See below section IV.B, in the international human rights context. See also Yuval Shany, 'Towards a General Margin of Appreciation Doctrine in International Law?' (2006) 16 *European Journal of International Law* 907 on subsidiarity in international law in general.

[13] See Council of Europe, High Level Conference on the Future of the European Court of Human Rights 'Interlaken Declaration' (19 February 2010), available at wcd.coe.int/com.instranet.InstraServlet?command=com.instranet.CmdBlobGet&InstranetImage=2045095&SecMode=1&DocId=1547616&Usage=2 and, more recently, Council of Europe, *Dialogue between Judges 2012: 'How Can We Ensure Greater Involvement of National Courts in the Convention System?'* (European Court of Human Rights Publications, 2012).

[14] See Samantha Besson, 'The "Erga Omnes" Effect of Judgments of the European Court of Human Rights—What's in a Name?' in Samantha Besson (ed), *La Cour européenne des droits de l'homme après le Protocole 14—Premier bilan et perspectives* (Schulthess, 2011) on the three forms of subsidiarity in international human rights law: procedural, substantive and remedial.

[15] See below sections IV.B and D.

[16] On the use of this other term, privileged recently by some judges, see *Christine Goodwin v the United Kingdom* ECHR 2002-VI, para 85.

domestic courts in particular are the actors responsible for changes in the interpretation of international law. Finally, one can allude to the requirement of domestic judicial enforcement in some cases. This makes domestic courts the main agents of the *restitutio in integrum* following a violation of international law and the condemnation by an international court.[17]

As to the *domestic* legal bases for domestic courts' engagement with international law, one should mention the following bases. First of all, the constitutional requirement of incorporation or transposition of international law into domestic law (for example, whether the domestic legal order is monist or dualist), and hence into the corpus of valid domestic law applicable by domestic courts and their material jurisdiction. Second, the principle of separation of powers, and that of judicial review of the executive and the legislature based on any valid law under the jurisdiction of the domestic court and that may include international law. Finally, constitutionalism, and the related principle of (internationalised) constitutional review of other domestic institutions and their decisions.

Three remarks are in order with respect to these various legal bases and in particular to the types of engagement with international law they justify or require. First of all, while some of these legal bases are legal grounds for *duties* of domestic courts to apply and interpret international law, others give rise to mere *rights* or powers for them to do so. Only a few of them ground both rights and duties. This is a factor that needs to be taken into account in the discussion of the legitimacy of domestic courts' engagement with international law and of the authority of their interpretations. Secondly, while some of those legal bases cover the right or duty to both enforce *and* interpret international law, not all of them do so. This should also be kept in mind later on when considering the legitimacy of domestic courts' decisions. Finally, some of these legal bases and the various duties/rights they foresee may enter into conflict, and this makes things complicated. There may in particular be tensions between the *domestic* and *international* legal duties and/or rights of domestic courts. One may, for instance, think of tensions between the courts' duty of constitutional fidelity, on the one hand, and the identification of a customary rule on state immunities, on the other.[18]

### *ii. The International Framework Variations in Domestic Courts' Engagement with International Law*

Various factors in the international law framework, which affect the engagement of domestic courts with international law in practice, have been uncovered in the literature.[19] One could mention the following in particular.

First of all, there are the sources of international law at stake. When the international law norms interpreted stem from customary international law or general

[17] For a discussion, see Besson (n 14).

[18] Of course, one could argue that those conflicts may also be internal to the international legal bases themselves.

[19] See in particular, Tzanakopoulos, 'Domestic Judicial Law-Making' (n 7); Tzanakopoulos and Tams (n 7).

principles, the effects of domestic courts' judicial interpretations on the interpreted norm are greater than they are in the case of treaties. This has to do with the validating role of the judiciary with respect to norms stemming from those sources of international law. This is as true for domestic courts as it is for international courts.[20] Secondly, there are the norms of international law at stake. When the norms of international law interpreted are indeterminate, there is more scope for their interpretation and contextualisation, and hence there is a greater role for any interpreter, including a domestic court. Thirdly, there are the duties of international law at stake. When norms of international law give rise to interstate duties, it is less likely that domestic courts will be called to enforce and hence interpret them. Even when they do, they are not usually alone in doing so. Things are different when the norms applied generate intra-state duties, as is the case with international immunities law or international human rights law, for instance. Fourthly, there may be an international court with jurisdiction. The existence of one or many international courts with (compulsory or non-compulsory) jurisdiction affects the leeway given to domestic courts in the interpretation of international law. This is clear from areas such as international humanitarian law and international environmental law, for instance, where there are few or no international courts exercising jurisdiction. Finally, there is the monist or dualist nature of the domestic legal order at stake. This feature of the relevant domestic legal order affects the scope of its domestic courts' jurisdiction and hence whether and how they interpret international law. This point has, however, become largely moot in practice, especially with respect to customary international law and general principles.[21]

### *iii. The Effects of Domestic Courts' Engagement with International Law*

With respect to the effects of domestic courts' engagement with international law, the primary distinction to draw is between their legal effects (that is, whether or not domestic decisions have some kind of legal authority for subjects of international law based on the existing sources of international law) and their non-legal effects (that is, whether or not domestic decisions trigger other kinds of reaction on the part of subjects of international law, international institutions and courts or other domestic institutions and courts).[22]

When assessing the legal effects of domestic courts' decisions pertaining to international law, it is important to distinguish between the role of domestic courts as enforcers of international law (*qua* organs of their respective states) and the corresponding (relative) decisional authority of their decisions, on the one hand, and their

[20] On this question, see Donald Regan, 'International Adjudication: A Response to Paulus—Courts, Custom, Treaties, Regimes, and the WTO' in Samantha Besson and John Tasioulas (eds), *The Philosophy of International Law* (Oxford University Press, 2010); Besson, 'Legal Philosophical Issues of International Adjudication' (n 1).

[21] See Giorgio Gaja, 'Dualism: A Review' in Janne Nijman and André Nollkaemper (eds), *New Perspectives on the Divide between National and International Law* (Oxford University Press, 2007).

[22] On those various 'formal' and 'informal' reactions, see Tzanakopoulos, 'Domestic Judicial Law-Making' (n 7).

role as interpreters and hence as judicial law-makers of international law and the corresponding (general) interpretative authority of their decisions, on the other.[23] This is a key distinction mentioned above by reference to the legal bases for domestic courts' engagement with international law, and hence to the different powers or duties of domestic courts with respect to either the enforcement or the interpretation of international law. Note that I am not considering the legal effects of domestic courts' interpretations of international law in domestic law *qua* (source of judicial) domestic law. Those effects are obvious, and are only of indirect interest within international law (for example, for the establishment of state nationality for the purpose of diplomatic protection).

If one focuses exclusively on the *legal authority* of domestic courts' *interpretations* of international law from the perspective of the *sources of international law*, different ways for these courts to exercise legal authority can be identified by reference to different sources of international law.

First of all, domestic courts' interpretations of international law may be considered as evidence of or even as the content of either one of the two constitutive elements of customary international law (either *opinio juris* or general practice[24]), but also of treaty law (Article 38(1)(a) and (b) of the Statute of the International Court of Justice (ICJ Statute)).[25] This might be evidence provided to an international court or another domestic court, or to any subject of international law. This has been confirmed by the practice of the ICJ in the context of intra-state duties in particular, for instance in decisions pertaining to the international law of immunities.[26] Such sources of legal authority are sometimes referred to as material sources of international law.

Secondly, domestic courts' interpretations of international law may also be considered as evidence or as content of the general principles of law recognised by civilised nations and, most of the time, by domestic courts in those civilised nations (Article 38(1)(c) ICJ Statute).[27] This might be evidence provided to an international court or another domestic court, or to any subject of international law. Again, such sources of legal authority are referred to as material sources of international law.

Thirdly, domestic courts' interpretations of international law may also be considered as a process of validation of another source of international law such as customary international law or general principles, or treaty law (Article 38(1)(d)

[23] On this distinction, see Besson (n 14).

[24] On these two elements, see ILC, 'First Report on Formation and Evidence of Customary International Law by Special Rapporteur Sir Michael Wood' (17 May 2013) UN Doc A/CN.4/663; and ILC, 'Second Report on Identification of Customary International Law by Special Rapporteur Sir Michael Wood' (22 May 2014) UN Doc A/CN.4/672.

[25] Statute of the International Court of Justice (adopted 26 June 1945, entered into force 24 October 1945) 33 UNTS 993 (ICJ Statute).

[26] See eg Peter Tomka, 'Custom and the International Court of Justice' in Council of Europe (ed), *The Judge and International Custom* (Council of Europe, 2013); *Jurisdictional Immunities of the State (Germany v Italy: Greece intervening)* (Judgment) [2012] ICJ Rep 99.

[27] See Samantha Besson, 'General Principles in International Law—Whose Principles?' in Samantha Besson and Pascal Pichonnaz (eds), *Les principes en droit européen—Principles in European Law* (Schulthess, 2011).

ICJ Statute).[28] Here, one refers to domestic courts' interpretations as an auxiliary or subsidiary formal source of international law. Indirectly, this acknowledges international judicial law-making as a process of international law-making.[29] It is rarer for domestic courts to be recognised as such than for international courts, however.[30] This would be even more controversial with respect to domestic courts.[31] And thus, fourthly, when domestic courts' interpretations of international law are considered as a process of validation of international law, they are usually taken to so operate only in a gradual and collective fashion: it requires many simultaneous domestic courts' interpretations for them to validate a norm stemming from a formal source of international law applicable to all of them.[32] This is due to the principle of 'self-interpretation' by states that prevails in international law. In this context, the interpretation by one of those self-interpreting state's domestic courts cannot claim any authority outside that state's legal order. If it does, then it is as one among many states' practices constitutive of the general 'subsequent practice' of states which establishes the agreement of those states according to Article 31(3)(b) VCLT, and hence as a constitutive element of some form of interpretative custom.[33] Of course, domestic courts' interpretation of international law may be trumped by that of an international court with the ultimate authority to interpret (provided there is such an ultimate international interpreter in the case at hand, which is rare).

Interestingly, in all four types of legal authority of domestic courts' interpretations of international law, but especially in the first two, interpretations of international law may be taken not only for what they are formally (that is, domestic courts' decisions) with the legal authority that goes with it, but also, more substantially, as epistemic emulations of what the international courts' interpretations of that same norm of international law could look like.[34] When this is the case, what is at stake is some form of theoretical or epistemic authority distinct from the practical legal authority discussed so far. Furthermore, the self-referential dimension of the judicial law-making process may be worth emphasising. While the self-referential nature of the reasoning of international courts which know that, when they interpret

[28] On this question, see Regan (n 20); Besson, 'Legal Philosophical Issues' (n 1).

[29] See Besson, ibid; Armin von Bogdandy and Ingo Venzke (eds), *International Judicial Lawmaking—On Public Authority and Democratic Legitimation in Global Governance* (Springer, 2012); Marc Jacob, 'Precedents: Lawmaking Through International Adjudication' (2011) 12 *German Law Journal* 1005; Alain Pellet, 'Article 38' in Andreas Zimmermann, Christian Tomuschat and Karin Oellers-Frahm (eds), *The Statute of the International Court of Justice: A Commentary* (Oxford University Press, 2006).

[30] See eg Pellet (n 29); Roberts (n 7).

[31] See Besson, 'Legal Philosophical Issues' (n 1).

[32] See Roberts (n 7).

[33] I am not deciding here between considering subsequent practices of domestic courts as customary law in itself, and considering them as mere interpretations of treaties and hence between a new interpretation of the same treaty norm and its modification, for the difference is largely moot and a new interpretation implies a new norm even when its source is a treaty. See also ILC, 'Second Report on Subsequent Agreements and Subsequent Practice in Relation to the Interpretation of Treaties by Special Rapporteur Georg Nolte' (26 March 2014) UN Doc A/CN.4/671, 51. See also *Al-Saadoon and Mufdhi v the United Kingdom* ECHR 2010, paras 119–20 for an interpretation of Art 3 ECHR that goes against the wording of Art 2 para 1 ECHR.

[34] See also ILC, 'First Report by Sir Michael Wood' (n 24).

international law, their interpretation will become part of the law they are interpreting is a well-known and inescapable difficulty, it is more problematic in the case of domestic courts. Indeed, the latter courts' impact on their object of interpretation is less immediate and the concurrent interpretation by other domestic courts largely indeterminate for them. This is particularly the case as, along the lines discussed above, their rights and duties to engage with international law under international and domestic law may enter into conflict.

### B. A Normative Turn

Most recently, the discussion about the role of domestic courts in international law seems to have been taking a normative turn, leaving previous sociological considerations aside, but also providing more than the usual passing reference to Scelle's *dédoublement fonctionnel*.[35] Authors have started to focus on the evaluation of the impact, but also of the justification of the authority of domestic courts' decisions in international law.[36]

In short, the questions one should be asking now are: How can the authority of the decisions by domestic courts be justified in international law? How should the decisions be issued or reasoned, that is, what are the applicable principles, standards or criteria? What priorities can be justified in cases where they conflict?

Various positions could be defended. Some authors have mentioned, for instance, a duty of 'systemic integration' based on a systemic argument about the international legal order.[37] Others have proposed an argument drawing from the international rule of law.[38] But there could be many others. Whatever they are, it is important that their discussion is conducted with sufficient precision and rigour.

At this stage, the main difficulty seems to be that adjudication as a source and function in international law is the least mature of all sources and functions. Without entering into too much detail, it is sufficient to remember that most of the time there is no single court of international law, but many of them. In fact, there is not always a court and, when there is one, its jurisdiction is not always compulsory. Moreover, judicial law-making still sits uneasily with the original sources of international law, and in particular with state-made international law and especially the self-interpretation of international law. It is no wonder that international law adjudication remains one of the most difficult questions from the perspective of international

[35] Georges Scelle, 'Le phénomène juridique du dédoublement fonctionnel' in Wolfgang Schätzel and Hans-Jürgen Schlochauer (eds), *Rechtsfragen der internationalen Organisation—Festschrift für Hans Wehberg zu seinem 70. Geburtstag* (Klostermann, 1956).

[36] See eg Massimo Iovane, 'Domestic Courts Should Embrace Sound Interpretative Strategies in the Development of Human Rights-Oriented International Law' in Antonio Cassese (ed), *Realizing Utopia—The Future of International Law* (Cambridge University Press, 2012); d'Aspremont (n 7); Nollkaemper (n 7).

[37] See eg d'Aspremont (n 7).

[38] See eg Shany, 'National Courts' (n 7).

legal philosophy today.[39] In turn, this uncertainty necessarily hampers the discussion of the legitimate authority of domestic courts' decisions in international law. Secondly, a connected legal theoretical difficulty is the distinction between domestic and international law, and the way one should best conceive of their relationship in one or many legal orders. Clarity on those issues is a pre-condition to any discussion of the relationship between domestic judicial law-making and international law.

Finally, whatever the duties of domestic courts and the standards applied, there are also important practical issues to consider. For instance, the problem of resources and the sheer difficulty for domestic courts to work with international law, hence the enhanced risk of selectivity in the choice of the international law applied or interpreted (for instance, many domestic courts focus on international courts' decisions only and not on primary sources of international law) or even some of the strategic biases present (for instance, there is a lot of cherry-picking of the international legal norms that best suit the domestic court's purpose or argument). This is especially problematic in the context of the interpretation of general international law (for example, of international law rules on sources, interpretation and responsibility). Of course, whether these practical difficulties, and especially the strategic risk, are greater for domestic courts than they are for international courts remains to be demonstrated.

This chapter contributes to this most recent and normative turn in the discussion of the role of domestic courts in international law. It does not aim to do so generally, however, but looks at the adjudication and hence interpretation of international human rights law by domestic courts.

## III. THE PUZZLE OF INTERNATIONAL HUMAN RIGHTS ADJUDICATION BY DOMESTIC COURTS

There is a very simple puzzle about the role of domestic courts in international human rights adjudication which anyone familiar with both international human rights law and international dispute settlement will recognise. It has to do with the sources of international human rights law, on the one hand, and with the international courts in place to monitor its application, on the other.

To start with, the sources of international human rights law are largely conventional. There are countless international and regional human rights treaties in place, and at least most of them are ratified very broadly. Thus, the sources of international human rights are not only or mainly customary international law. To that extent, they differ from other areas of international law where domestic courts have contributed effectively to the interpretation of international law in practice (including to the latter's identification as exemplified in the law of international responsibility or of international immunities).

[39] See Besson, 'Legal Philosophical Issues' (n 1); Samantha Besson, 'The Egalitarian Dimension of Human Rights' (2012) *Archiv für Sozial- und Rechtsphilosophie Beiheft* 19.

Moreover, international human rights law is one of the few international law regimes with international courts in place (though only regional so far) that exercise compulsory jurisdiction. In this respect again, it is unlike other areas of international law where the impact of domestic courts has been important in the absence of an ultimate international law interpreter (in lieu of self-interpretation). In areas such as the law of international responsibility or the international law on immunities, indeed, domestic courts have gradually contributed to the development of an interpretative custom in the absence of an international court's authoritative interpretation.

Still, and this is the puzzle, domestic courts' decisions do actually contribute to a high degree to the interpretation of international human rights law in practice. Furthermore, their interpretations of international human rights law are granted, at least by international human rights courts, a form of legal authority that goes further than any of the four types of legal authority of domestic courts' interpretations of international law mentioned before.

In response to this puzzle, this contribution makes two claims: one is substantive and the other is methodological.

First of all, international human rights law, and hence its adjudication, are special because human rights are special. Based on their special nature, I would like to argue that domestic courts should be understood as the primary adjudicators of human rights, and that this should in turn be reflected in the way international human rights adjudication works in relation to domestic courts. To reflect this, I defend the view that both levels of human rights adjudication are best referred to as forms of 'transnational' human rights adjudication.

Secondly, and as a result, international human rights law and adjudication should not be taken too hastily as a core example in the general discussion of the role of domestic courts in international law, or at least not without serious qualifications. It is confusing to take international human rights law as a central example, besides international investment law or trade law, and then to consider the specificities of international human rights law (in particular, as giving rise to inter-state and non-reciprocal duties) as generalisable and then transferrable into other areas of international law.[40]

## IV. THE SPECIFIC FEATURES OF INTERNATIONAL HUMAN RIGHTS LAW ADJUDICATION

The specific features of international human rights adjudication in practice, and especially the role of domestic courts, are best justified by reference to the democratic argument of mutual validation between domestic and international human rights law. More specifically, this argument fits and justifies three dimensions of our contemporary human rights practice: the kind of norms, sources and adjudication one encounters in international human rights law.

[40] See eg Tzanakopoulos and Tams (n 7); Tzanakopoulos, 'Domestic Judicial Law-Making' (n 7).

## A. The Mutual Validation of Domestic and International Human Rights Law

Given the mutual relationship between human rights *qua* equal rights and (basic moral) equality, and in turn between (basic moral) equality and political equality and hence democracy,[41] human rights ought to be mutually identified and their duties specified, allocated and fulfilled in a democratic community and through democratic processes.[42] In the current state of international relations, this means in the relevant state having jurisdiction over the individual in question. Of course, because human rights and democracy are in mutual tension and constitution, human rights should also constrain those democratic communities in return, and cannot merely be defined by democratic procedures. This mutuality between human rights and democracy is one of the many complexities of human rights.[43]

Interestingly for our purpose, the egalitarian and hence democratic dimension of human rights, but also the mutuality between them, is actually reflected in the way in which international human rights law developed: through the practice of democratic states, but in a way of transnational consolidation that has gradually constrained their practice in return. Historically, indeed, much of the content of international human rights treaties was drawn from domestic bills of rights existing in 1945, and many of the latter were then revised post 1945 to be in line with the former. So, international human rights law consolidated out of that practice and constrained that practice in return.

No wonder then that in the current human rights law system one can no longer figure out domestic or internal human rights without their international or external counterparts and, of course, vice versa. This virtuous circle has been perpetuated since then in the way in which domestic and international legal norms pertaining to human rights have been interpreted and developed together. This is what I have referred to elsewhere as the mutual validation and legitimation of domestic and international human rights law.[44]

## B. The Mutuality of Human Rights Norms, Sources and Adjudication

The argument about the mutual validation and legitimation between domestic and international human rights law helps account for at least three dimensions of

[41] On the egalitarian dimension of human rights, see Allen Buchanan, 'The Egalitarianism of Human Rights' (2010) 120 *Ethics* 679; Besson, 'The Egalitarian Dimension of Human Rights' (n 39).

[42] See for a confirmation in the European human rights practice, *Ždanoka v Latvia* ECHR 2006-IV, para 98.

[43] See Samantha Besson, 'Human Rights and Democracy in a Global Context—Decoupling and Recoupling' (2011) 4 *Ethics & Global Politics* 19; Samantha Besson, 'Human Rights and Constitutional Law: Mutual Validation and Legitimation' in Rowan Cruft, Matthew Liao and Massimo Renzo (eds), *Philosophical Foundations of Human Rights* (Oxford University Press, 2015); Samantha Besson, 'The Legitimate Authority of International Human Rights: On the Reciprocal Legitimation of Domestic and International Human Rights' in Andreas Føllesdal, Johan Karlsson Schaffer and Geir Ulfstein (eds), *The Legitimacy of International Human Rights Regimes* (Cambridge University Press, 2013); Besson (n 2).

[44] See Besson (n 2); Besson, 'Human Rights and Constitutional Law' (n 43) 288-9; Besson, 'The Legitimate Authority of International Human Rights' (n 43).

international human rights law and its practice: the type of norms, sources and, most importantly for us in this contribution, adjudication one encounters in international human rights law.[45]

First of all, the argument for the mutual validation and legitimation between domestic and international human rights law accounts for the special type of *norms* one encounters in international human rights law. To start with, in a very unusual fashion for international law norms, international human rights law gives rise to (inter-state and even *erga omnes*) duties to incur (intra-state) human rights duties vis-à-vis individuals under the given state's jurisdiction. Those duties to recognise human rights correspond, I have argued elsewhere, to the international right to have (domestic) human rights.[46] Thus, international human rights have to be matched by corresponding domestic human rights, which they then complement as minima both in content and with respect to their (personal and territorial) scope. Despite sharing the same content and structure (albeit minimally), international human rights are therefore not redundant alongside domestic human rights.[47] Nor, however, are they merely about filling the latter's gaps. On the contrary, they fulfil complementary functions that make them interdependent with domestic human rights, and necessarily arise and function together. Furthermore, international human rights norms are (abstract) rights, and, as such, their corresponding duties need to be specified every time anew. This can only be done in the relevant domestic and political context by domestic institutions. The corresponding international duties can only be abstracted therefrom *ex post* by international courts.

Secondly, the mutual validation between domestic and international human rights law also accounts for the special type of *sources* of international human rights law and their relation to domestic sources of human rights law. First of all, international human rights have long been guaranteed by treaties that developed out of domestic human rights guarantees. International human rights are also, however, concurrently of a customary nature[48]—and not only additionally so when there are gaps in the conventional protection of human rights.[49] Indeed, international human

[45] Much of the argument below has been developed elsewhere, and in particular in Besson, 'Human Rights and Constitutional Law' (n 43); Besson, 'The Legitimate Authority of International Human Rights' (n 43); Besson, 'Human Rights and Democracy in a Global Context' (n 43).

[46] See eg Besson, 'Human Rights and Constitutional Law' (n 43); Besson, 'Human Rights and Democracy in a Global Context' (n 43); Ronald Dworkin, *Justice for Hedgehogs* (Harvard University Press, 2011); Stephen Gardbaum, 'Human Rights as International Constitutional Rights' (2008) 19 *European Journal of International Law* 749; Gerald Neuman, 'Human Rights and Constitutional Rights: Harmony and Dissonance' (2003) 55 *Stanford Law Review* 1863.

[47] Unlike Tzanakopoulos, 'Domestic Judicial Law-Making' (n 7), I am not referring to the 'consubstantiality' of international human rights norms for the term is a theological one that is out of place in the human rights context, and more importantly, it glosses over the minimality of the content of international human rights law and its complementarity to domestic human rights law. On the latter, see Besson, 'Human Rights and Constitutional Law' (n 43).

[48] See Jean-François Flauss, 'La protection des droits de l'homme et les sources du droit international' in Société française pour le droit international (ed), *La protection des droits de l'homme et l'évolution du droit international* (Pedone, 1998); Besson (n 27).

[49] As claimed by Bruno Simma and Philip Alston, 'The Sources of Human Rights Law: Custom, *Jus Cogens*, and General Principles' (1988–1989) 12 *Australian Yearbook of International Law* 82.

rights law, even when primarily of a conventional nature, also actually includes the interpretation of international human rights treaties that is constitutive of an evolutive and subsequently consolidated practice and *opinio juris*, that is, of an international human rights custom. Such a custom may be assessed in the traditional way—involving both practice and *opinio juris* and not in a diluted fashion only (for example, based on *opinio juris* only).[50] As to objections to the existence of customary international law in the human rights context, they may all be met by reference to the type of state practice required (for example, intra-state and not only interstate practice, and including omissions, not only actions) and the kind of consistency it should display (for example, justifications of violations count towards consistency).[51] Last but not least, international human rights may also be regarded as general principles of international law, although here the intimate relationship between principles as norms and principles as sources in international law does not make for much clarity.[52]

All three sources work as bottom-up processes of international human rights law-making drawing from domestic practices of human rights and constraining them in return. This combination of sources in international human rights law explains why international human rights treaties themselves are often regarded as sources of general (non-party relative) and objective (non-consent-based) international law.[53] It also explains how international human rights treaties can relate directly to domestic human rights in practice. International human rights are, for instance, the only treaty norms that are immediately valid in domestic law independently of whether the domestic legal order endorses monism or dualism. Of course, one may wonder in those conditions why one should still hold onto human rights treaties as the main source of international human rights law. This may be explained by the need to set interpretative minima and constraints. The latter may evolve in practice, as demonstrated by the adoption of protocols to the ECHR, for instance.

Finally, and centrally for this contribution, the mutual validation between domestic and international human rights law also accounts for the specific kind of adjudication one encounters in international human rights law, both at the international and the domestic levels.

Internationally, human rights protection has long been monitored by *international* (although mostly regional so far) courts (or bodies) that guarantee the respect of the minima consolidated in international human rights law. Importantly, however, those courts may only proceed with their monitoring function once domestic judicial

[50] See also Besson (n 27); Simma and Alston (n 49); contra see John Tasioulas, '*Opinio Juris* and the Genesis of Custom: A Solution to the "Paradox"' (2007) 26 *Australian Yearbook of International Law* 199.

[51] See also Besson (n 27); Simma and Alston (n 49); and more generally on customary international law, ILC, 'Second Report by Sir Michael Wood' (n 24).

[52] See eg Besson (n 27).

[53] See more generally, Samantha Besson, 'The Sources of International Human Rights Law' in Samantha Besson and Jean d'Aspremont (eds), *Oxford Handbook on the Sources of International Law* (Oxford University Press, 2017 forthcoming).

remedies have been exhausted ('procedural subsidiarity').[54] In turn, their review[55] decisions are declaratory (albeit binding, of course), thus most of the time calling for some form of domestic remedial enforcement ('remedial subsidiarity').[56] Finally, and most importantly, those courts may and should only offer new interpretations of international human rights law in the course of their monitoring activity when those are based on an existing transnational human rights practice ('substantive subsidiarity').[57] They also have to adapt their past interpretations when those no longer correspond to the existing transnational human rights practice.

In short, therefore, international human rights courts do not work as ultimate interpreters or umpires. To that extent, they are really unlike other international law courts whose interpretative authority derogates from the principle of self-interpretation that prevails in international law (for example, the Court of Justice of the European Union (CJEU) for European Union law or the ICJ for international law). Instead, international human rights courts are facilitators of the self-interpretation of their human rights law by states: they help crystallise and consolidate states' interpretations and practices of human rights and the custom stemming from their subsequent practice of human rights treaties. Once identified and entrenched as international law, the minimal human rights interpretation can then be re-imposed on domestic authorities. This is often referred to as the interpretative authority or *erga omnes* effect of an international human rights interpretation or decision, an authority very different from an autonomous and ultimate supranational interpretative authority.[58] This mode of adjudication and its interpretative authority actually fit the customary nature of international human rights law itself: international human rights courts work as custom-identifiers and -validators.[59]

[54] See Besson (n 14).

[55] On the adequacy of the term 'review' in the context of the ECtHR's decisions, see Samantha Besson, 'European Human Rights, Supranational Judicial Review and Democracy—Thinking outside the judicial box' in Patricia Popelier, Catherine Van den Heyning and Piet Van Nuffel (eds), *Human Rights Protection in the European Legal Order: Interaction between European Courts and National Courts* (Cambridge University Press, 2011); Başak Çali, 'Towards a Responsible Domestic Courts Doctrine? The European Court of Human Rights and the Variable Standard of Judicial Review of Domestic Court Judgments' in Oddny Mjöll Arnadóttir and Antoine Buyse (eds), *Shifting Centres of Gravity in Human Rights Protection* (Routledge, 2016).

[56] See Besson (n 14).

[57] Ibid. There are fluctuations in the ECtHR's decisions and in the literature on the meaning of subsidiarity and on related concepts like states' margin of appreciation or European consensus, see eg Luzius Wildhaber, Arnaldur Hjartarson and Stephen Donnelly, 'No Consensus on Consensus? The Practice of the European Court on Human Rights' (2013) 33 *Human Rights Law Journal* 248; Dean Spielmann, 'Allowing the Right Margin: the European Court of Human Rights and the National Margin of Appreciation Doctrine: Waiver or Subsidiarity of European Review?' (2011–2012) 14 *Cambridge Yearbook of European Legal Studies* 381; George Letsas, 'Two Concepts of the Margin of Appreciation' (2006) 26 *Oxford Journal of Legal Studies* 705. The key is to distinguish between the justifications of individual restrictions by a given state and its margin of appreciation in that context, on the one hand, and the interpretation of ECHR rights for the future and states' margin of appreciation as a whole in that context, on the other.

[58] See Besson (n 14) on the specificities of that authority and the inapplicability of international and constitutional analogies.

[59] Ibid; Besson, 'Human Rights and Constitutional Law' (n 43).

All this in turn explains why the interpretation methods used by international human rights courts are often described as being specific by comparison to those that apply within other regimes of international law:[60] their interpretation should evolve with their subsequent transnational practice which the international human rights courts identify and validate (Article 31(3)(b) VLCT). This is how the European Court of Human Rights (ECtHR) approaches what it refers to as the 'European consensus',[61] that is, a form of interpretative custom among states parties.[62] It is based on states' general practice (based on an average ratio of 6 out of 10 states)[63] and their *opinio juris* verified by reference, for instance, to domestic and international courts' decisions and to other international human rights law norms.[64] The evolutive nature of this joint or transnational interpretative process by reference to consensus in practice is sometimes also referred to as the 'dynamic interpretation' of international human rights law. Interestingly, it is then used as a basis for either a systemic

[60] See eg Schlütter (n 4); Başak Çali, 'Specialised Rules of Treaty Interpretation: Human Rights' in Duncan B Hollis (ed), *The Oxford Guide to Treaties* (Oxford University Press, 2012); George Letsas, 'Strasbourg's Interpretive Ethic: Lessons for the International Lawyer' (2010) 21 *European Journal of International Law* 509; Laurence Burgorgue-Larsen, 'Les méthodes d'interprétation de la Cour interaméricaine des droits de l'homme—Justice in Context' (2014) 97 *Revue trimestrielle des droits de l'homme* 31; contra see Jonas Christoffersen, 'Impact on General Principles of Treaty Interpretation' in Menno Kamminga and Martin Scheinin (eds), *The Impact of Human Rights Law on General International Law* (Oxford University Press, 2009).

[61] On 'European consensus' in the case law of the ECtHR, see eg Samantha Besson and Anne-Laurence Graf-Brugère, 'Le droit de vote des expatriés, le consensus européen et la marge d'appréciation des Etats—Un commentaire de l'arrêt *Sitaropoulos et Giakoumopoulos c. Grèce*' (2014) 100 *Revue trimestrielle des droits de l'homme* 937; Wildhaber, Hjartarson and Donnelly (n 57); Spielmann (n 57); Andrew Legg, *The Margin of Appreciation in International Human Rights Law—Deference and Proportionality* (Oxford University Press, 2012); Besson (n 14); Hanneke Senden, *Interpretation of Fundamental Rights in a Multilevel Legal System—An Analysis of the European Court of Human Rights and the Court of Justice of the European Union* (Intersentia, 2011); Kanstantsin Dzehtsiarou, 'Does Consensus Matter? Legitimacy of European Consensus in the Case Law of the European Court of Human Rights' (2011) 3 *Public Law* 534; Catherine Van de Heyning, 'No Place Like Home: Discretionary Space for the Domestic Protection of Fundamental Rights' in Patricia Popelier, Catherine Van de Heyning and Piet Van Nuffel (eds), *Human Rights Protection in the European Legal Order: Interaction between European Courts and National Courts* (Intersentia, 2011); Laurence Helfer, 'Redesigning the European Court of Human Rights: Embeddedness as a Deep Structural Principle of the European Human Rights Regime' (2008) 19 *European Journal of International Law* 125; Yutaka Arai-Takahashi, *The Margin of Appreciation Doctrine and the Principle of Proportionality in the Jurisprudence of the ECHR* (Intersentia, 2002).

[62] See eg Ineta Ziemele, 'Customary International Law in the Case Law of the European Court of Human Rights' in *The Judge and International Custom* (Council of Europe, 2013); Paul Mahoney, 'The Comparative Method in Judgements of the European Court of Human Rights: Reference Back to National Law' in Guy Canivet, Mads Andenas and Duncan Fairgrieve (eds), *Comparative Law Before the Courts* (British Institute of International and Comparative Law, 2004).

[63] Wildhaber, Hjartarson and Donnelly (n 57) 258.

[64] See *Demir and Baykara v Turkey* ECHR 2008-V, paras 85–86; *Sitaropoulos and Giakoumopoulos v Greece* ECHR 2012-II, para 66. Note that this broadening of the assessment of the existence of a state practice and of *opinio juris* confirms the customary and hence general (and not regional only) reading of the reasoning of the ECtHR in its identification of a European consensus. See also Besson and Graf-Brugère (n 61); Ziemele (n 62) for a defence of this general international law approach to regional human rights law.

or a teleological interpretation; dynamic interpretation does not therefore amount to a distinct method of interpretation, but only to a tool in any of the latter.[65] European states' common approach or consensus constrains the Court's dynamic interpretation and guides it. According to the ECtHR, the reference to consensus and the evolution of state practice amounts to a duty, and not just a possibility.[66]

In turn, the special features of human rights adjudication by international human rights courts also imply an enhanced role for *domestic* courts. This is what all three types of subsidiarity require. It is also a consequence of the democratic contextualisation of international human rights law given the crucial role of the judiciary in post-1945 constitutional democracies and the entrenchment of conventional judicial review in international human rights law. As a matter of fact, international institutional and procedural standards for the implementation and monitoring of human rights have been developed internally in cooperation between democratic states, transnationalised and internationalised bottom-up, and then imposed top-down again as external constraints on domestic institutions and procedures.

This explains in turn why international courts work in priority with domestic courts in the interpretation and development of international human rights law, and only indirectly with domestic legislative or executive authorities.[67] It is rare, for instance, to find an international human rights court refer, in its assessment of a new consensus between states, to state practices outside of the decisions of domestic courts and their interpretations of international human rights law.[68] Their legal authority (for international human rights courts, in particular) is much greater than that of domestic courts' other interpretations of international law. It is with respect to the fourth kind of authority described previously, in particular, that their authority seems to be enhanced: domestic courts' custom-identifying and custom-validating role is largely recognised in international human rights law.

## V. DOMESTIC AND INTERNATIONAL HUMAN RIGHTS ADJUDICATION AS TRANSNATIONAL ADJUDICATION

The proposed argument and reading of international human rights law has various implications for international human rights adjudication in practice: some general, pertaining to its transnational nature, and others more specific, pertaining to the respective functions of international and domestic courts.

[65] See also Schlütter (n 4); contra see Julian Arato, 'Subsequent Practice and Evolutive Interpretation: Techniques of Treaty Interpretation over Time and Their Diverse Consequences' (2010) 9 *The Law and Practice of International Courts and Tribunals* 443. This is in line with ILC, 'Second Report by Special Rapporteur Georg Nolte' (n 33) 49ff.

[66] See *Sitaropoulos and Giakoumopoulos v Greece* ECHR 2012_II, para 66; Besson and Graf-Brugère (n 61).

[67] See eg *Von Hannover v Germany (No 2)* ECHR 2012-I, paras 105–107; Çali (n 55).

[68] See also Besson (n 27); Dworkin (n 46).

## A. Transnational Human Rights Adjudication

The mutual regime of international human rights law-making I have just argued for and its anchoring in state practice I have presented, are best referred together to as 'transnational',[69] and not merely as domestic and international respectively.[70] The transnational nature of human rights law has implications for the role of human rights adjudication in transnational human rights law-making and the relations between domestic and international human rights courts in that process.

First of all, adjudication plays a specific role in the transnational development of human rights law. Judicial interpretations are sufficiently flexible to evolve with the practice of states and the customary nature of international human rights law. Judicial distinction and overruling may always be possible either way.[71] Moreover, the 'judicial custom' that stems from international courts' decisions[72] can in turn be incorporated into the customary corpus of international human rights law. Finally, more substantive justifications for the role of adjudication in the development of human rights law may be put forward, including the kind of moral reasoning that characterises judicial reasoning when contrasted with other forms of legal reasoning.[73]

Secondly, transnational human rights adjudication implies its mutuality, and this in turn means that neither domestic nor international interpretations should take priority in case of conflict. Since international and domestic human rights law complement each other and are in productive tension, their interpreting institutions should be understood as situated in a joint albeit complementary interpretative endeavour over the same human rights[74] and not as mutually exclusive interpretative authorities.[75] There is no clear priority of either judicial body in case of conflicting

[69] The term 'transnational' is used here to refer to horizontal and accretive processes of law-making between domestic institutions from different states as opposed to international processes and sources that do not necessarily include domestic institutions in their domestic capacities. Transnational law and adjudication should be distinguished from the transnational or extra-territorial jurisdiction of domestic courts, on the one hand, and from hybrid law-making processes that integrate domestic public and private actors, on the other.

[70] See also for the term 'transnational' human rights law, Christopher McCrudden, 'A Common Law of Human Rights: Transnational Judicial Conversations on Human Rights' (2000) 20 *Oxford Journal of Legal Studies* 499, 530; Kristen Hessler, 'Resolving Interpretive Conflicts in International Human Rights Law' (2005) 13 *Journal of Political Philosophy* 29, 37; Jeremy Waldron, 'Rights and the Citation of Foreign Law' in Tom Campbell, Keith D Ewing and Adam Tomkins (eds), *The Legal Protection of Human Rights—Sceptical Essays* (Oxford University Press, 2011) 423.

[71] See also Van de Heyning (n 61) 91–94; Jonas Christoffersen, 'Individual and Constitutional Justice: Can the Power of Adjudication Balance be Reversed?' in Jonas Christoffersen and Mikael Rask Madsen (eds), *The European Court of Human Rights between Law and Politics* (Oxford University Press, 2011) 198–200.

[72] On judicial law as customary law, see Besson (n 27).

[73] See eg Jeremy Waldron, 'Judges as Moral Reasoners' (2009) 7 *International Journal of Constitutional Law* 2.

[74] This may be exemplified by *Hirst v the United Kingdom (No 2)* ECHR 2005-IX and *Scoppola v Italy (No 3)* ECHR 2012-I.

[75] See Hessler (n 70); Samantha Besson, 'Human Rights Pluralism in Europe' in Kaarlo Tuori and Miguel Maduro (eds), *Transnational Law—Rethinking Legal Thinking* (Cambridge University Press, 2014).

interpretations of the corresponding human rights duties, unlike in other regimes of international law. This differs from the way they would relate if they belonged to different political communities and corresponding legal orders.[76] This is because their respective claims to legitimate authority are not distinctly justified on different bases and in an exclusive fashion, but, on the contrary, share a mutually reinforcing democratic justification. Thus, it is the international human rights institutions' potential contribution to democratic processes or compensation for the lack thereof domestically that helps justify its legitimate authority in those cases in which they impose certain human rights interpretations on domestic authorities.[77] Just as international human rights contribute to protecting the right to democratic membership and the right to have human rights in a democratic polity, international human rights institutions protect domestic democratic institutions and guarantee their ability to respect human rights.

All this explains in turn how domestic courts are sometimes justified when diverging from international human rights courts' interpretations, while, on the other hand, having to comply with them in other cases. The transnationality of the system may lead to a significant amount of levelling-up, but it also allows for some levelling-down if most states change their practice together. On an individual state level too, saving clauses are usually in place in international human rights treaties to protect higher domestic protection (for example, Article 53 ECHR). One should also mention the possibility of a persistent objection to the transnational practice of states and their consensus, for instance in a sensitive moral context.[78] Conversely, if the state practice shows that a given interpretation and type of human rights duties are to be entrenched and should not be restricted for any reason, then the high degree of protection of those core duties should be regarded as ensuing from state practice and a prior consensus of states parties, and not as being imposed top-down by the international human rights court.

Note that the idea of 'pluralism' of human rights' interpretations is not an adequate model to capture the way in which complementary and distinct human rights' interpretations relate in case of conflict.[79] It is perceptive with regard to the immediate validity and lack of hierarchy among international or regional and domestic human rights norms, but misses the mutuality and reciprocal validation and legitimation process at stake. There is, in fact, much more than judicial politics and judicial dialogue at work here, if one is to explain the process of mutual interpretation and reasoning at play. There are reasons, in other words, behind international or European judges' and domestic judges' cooperation, reasons that go beyond judicial attitudes and strategies and their mutual respect for each other's beliefs.

[76] See eg Neuman (n 46) 1873–74.

[77] See also Hessler (n 70) 45ff.

[78] See eg in the context of abortion, *A, B and C v Ireland* ECHR 2010-VI, and despite the existence of a contrary European consensus.

[79] See Besson (n 75); Hessler (n 70); contra see Nico Krisch, 'The Open Architecture of European Human Rights Law' in *Beyond Constitutionalism: The Pluralist Structure of Postnational Law* (Oxford University Press, 2010).

## B. The Transnational Functions of Domestic and International Human Rights Courts

Specific normative implications of the proposed transnational reading of international human rights law ensue for the respective functions of domestic and international human rights courts.

With respect to *international* human rights adjudication, one should mention the following. International human rights courts should not behave as ultimate interpreters and authorities unlike other international courts interpreting international law (and, actually, unlike domestic constitutional courts in any constitutional system),[80] but merely help in identifying and validating a general subsequent state practice that has turned, or is turning, into a custom.

This is particularly important for the way international human rights courts approach the authority of their decisions, with respect to both their interpretative and their decisional authority.[81] More specifically, in terms of reasoning and method, international human rights courts should focus more openly on the customary nature of international human rights law and adjudication. This means a more consistent and systematic reference to state consensus (and related concepts such as subsidiarity, states' margin of appreciation, evolutive interpretation and so on),[82] and clarity about the ways to identify that consensus *qua* subsequent practice and agreement of states and interpretative custom.[83] Specifically, this may imply adopting a comparative human rights law method.[84] Of course, it would have to be adapted to international law for it to be sufficiently transnational and reciprocal.[85] It should not only be unilateral, therefore, and merely applied as a way to ascertain other sources of theoretical or epistemic authority as opposed to practical or legal authority. Nor should it exclude international law from its scope. More resources and more rigour with respect to the scope and depth of the comparative survey (for example, how many states, which practice in those states, and what degree of variation) are required to do so effectively in practice.

With respect to *domestic* human rights adjudication, the following implications of the transnational endeavour may be identified. Domestic courts should engage with international human rights law more strongly than they usually do with other

[80] Against the constitutional analogy, see Besson, 'Human Rights and Constitutional Law' (n 43); Besson (n 14); contra see Gardbaum (n 46).

[81] For this critique, see eg Besson (n 14).

[82] See eg Dean Spielmann, 'Allowing the Right Margin: the European Court of Human Rights and the National Margin of Appreciation Doctrine: Waiver or Subsidiarity of European Review?' (2011–2012) 14 *Cambridge Yearbook of European Legal Studies* 381; Jan Kratochvíl, 'The Inflation of the Margin of Appreciation by the European Court of Human Rights' (2011) 29 *Netherlands Quarterly of Human Rights* 324.

[83] See also Besson and Graf-Brugère (n 61); Wildhaber, Hjartarson and Donnelly (n 57); Ineta Ziemele, 'Other Rules of International Law and the European Court of Human Rights: A Question of a Simple Collateral Benefit?' in Dean Spielmann, Marialena Tsirli and Panayotis Voyatzis (eds), *La Convention européenne des droits de l'homme, un instrument vivant—Mélanges en l'honneur de Christos L Rozakis* (Bruylant, 2011).

[84] See eg Mahoney (n 62); Arai-Takahashi (n 61).

[85] See eg Roberts (n 7) on this kind of 'comparative international law'.

regimes of international law. They should make the most of the procedural, substantive and remedial subsidiarity that are protected by international human rights law. Specifically, this means engaging with international human rights courts' past decisions and reasoning, but also with other domestic courts'. Through constant distinguishing of and reasoning with those decisions, they can contribute to the development of their transnational human rights law.[86]

Of course, there is no duty of integrity or consistency with international courts' decisions or other domestic decisions, and no obligation to consider transnational human rights decisions as precedents: this would jeopardise the dynamic development of a democratic consensus on human rights. It is the role of international human rights courts to identify and validate that consensus but only once it has occurred, and not to trigger it. Otherwise, the democratic dimension of the contextualisation and allocation of human rights would not be respected, and the consensus would become a strategic one. Of course, once transnational decisions have become a general subsequent practice and a new consensus or transnational custom is validated by a given international human rights court, they bind domestic courts *qua* new international human rights custom. To that extent, domestic courts' duties when interpreting international human rights law differs from their duties in other fields of international law adjudication: there is no maximal international standard to be interpreted uniformly out there, but that standard is moulded and developed through concurrent domestic interpretations.

At the same time, however, engaging effectively with other international and domestic human rights courts means treating transnational precedents as at least persuasive.[87] Local circumstances may be comparable and domestic human rights interpretations could be consciously 'boiler-plated', to borrow Jeremy Waldron's terms,[88] in real time as it were and before being constrained by international interpretations based on their transnational consensus. Paying attention to those transnational decisions helps domestic courts contribute more quickly and more efficiently to the development of a consensus and state practice that will become binding for them in return. It also enables them to make an argument of change with respect to the transnational interpretative consensus of a given human right and to hope to trigger a judicial dialogue with international human rights courts and maybe bring about a new international interpretation of that right, as I have argued above. This interpretation actually fits and justifies the new advisory procedure under ECHR Protocol 16. That procedure provides domestic courts which request it with a non-binding interpretation of the state of the European consensus or, at least, the emerging consensus[89] on any human rights question, thus enabling the domestic court to decide by reference to that consensus.

[86] See eg Van de Heyning (n 61).

[87] See McCrudden (n 70) 513; Besson, 'Human Rights and Constitutional Law' (n 43).

[88] Waldron (n 70) 423.

[89] On the importance of those emerging trends in states' human rights practice and their identification by international human rights courts before identifying a consensus *stricto sensu*, see Ziemele (n 83).

Interestingly, an important argument against this kind of one-to-one practice of comparative human rights law is that using human rights' interpretations stemming from other domestic institutions than those of one's own country would be a clear violation of the democratic principle.[90] It follows from the argument in this chapter about the mutual validation and legitimation of domestic and international human rights law, however, that comparative constitutional law may not only provide the best way to grasp the interpretative content of the transnational human rights practice at stake.[91] It also means that transnational human rights may be vested with some indirect democratic legitimation through the respective democratic processes by which they have gradually been recognised.

## VI. CONCLUSIONS

There are three conclusions one may draw from the proposed argument.

First of all, international and domestic human rights adjudication are best understood together as one single process: transnational human rights adjudication. One cannot and should not work without the other, and this has implications for the way domestic and international human rights courts should respectively apply and interpret international human rights law. This first conclusion also applies outside the jurisdiction of the ECtHR and other regional human rights courts. It is the case for a future World Court of Human Rights, although the identification and consolidation of the subsequent state practice and agreement may be far more difficult to achieve on a global scale.[92] It also matters for non-judicial human rights treaty-bodies. Although they do not have the judicial authority to function directly as international custom-validators,[93] they can contribute to the clarification of a subsequent state practice and are part of the transnational adjudication process (for example, through general comments collating and systematising domestic case law).

Secondly, international human rights law and adjudication should not be taken too readily as a core example in the general discussion of domestic judicial law-making in international law, or at least not without serious nuancing. This would imply, for instance, bearing in mind the lack of ultimate authority of international human rights courts' interpretations, the international and domestic courts' duties to consider other domestic decisions and international decisions and law, and the joint custom-validating function of domestic courts' interpretations. The norms, sources and adjudication of international human rights law are very different from laws which prevail in other regimes of international law. No wonder then that the types

[90] On those critiques, see McCrudden (n 70) 501ff, 529ff; Waldron (n 70) 412ff.

[91] See Besson, 'Human Rights and Constitutional Law' (n 43).

[92] For a similar critique, see Philip Alston, 'Against a World Court of Human Rights' (2014) 28 *Ethics & International Affairs* 197.

[93] See also André Nollkaemper and Rosanne van Alebeek, 'The Legal Status of Decisions by Human Rights Treaty Bodies in National Law' in Helen Keller and Geir Ulfstein (eds), *Human Rights Treaty Bodies: Law and Legitimacy* (Cambridge University Press, 2012).

and grounds of domestic courts' powers and duties to engage with international law differ a lot between international human rights law and other regimes of international law. And so does their legal authority. This second conclusion should be a concern both for future scholarship on domestic courts and international law, and for future scholarship on human rights. Of course, one cannot exclude the possibility that more international law will develop on the model of international human rights law in the future and become transnational in this way, especially in the remaining constitutional areas that have not yet been covered by international law, where intra-state duties are at stake and where judicial reasoning is central. If this happened, then the same implications for the engagement of domestic courts with international law would probably ensue. But it is too early to say and there is too much to lose in the way we conceive of the rights and duties of domestic courts engaged in the interpretation of international law, on the one hand, and of domestic human rights adjudication, on the other, if we continue to merge the two discussions.

Last but not least, politically speaking, the proposed transnational reading of human rights adjudication has important implications for the way we deal with the growing resistance to international human rights courts and bodies in democratic and non-democratic states alike. The message that academics should convey is that those courts and bodies cannot be identified with other international courts, and cannot and should not claim ultimate interpretative authority over domestic courts. More importantly, provided they comply with the duties stemming from their complementary and mutual functions with domestic courts, those international human rights courts and bodies should not be disparaged from a democratic perspective. Quite the contrary: they contribute to the consolidation and development of our democratic values and principles. Nor should domestic judges fear to engage with international human rights law and courts for this is the only way international human rights law can develop and be interpreted transnationally and hence democratically. In this respect, and contrary to what many human rights scholars have been saying, recent restatements of the principle of subsidiarity and the margin of appreciation in major international human rights instruments, like the new ECHR Protocol 15, are a step in the right direction.

# 4

# *A New Doctrine on the Block? The European Court of Human Rights and the Responsible Courts Doctrine*

BAŞAK ÇALI*

## I. INTRODUCTION

THE RELATIONSHIP BETWEEN the highest domestic courts and the European Court of Human Rights (ECtHR) has been subject to much debate in the past decade.[1] A great deal of criticism of the ECtHR has relied on the assumption that it has attempted to micromanage domestic high courts that are perfectly capable of carrying out Strasbourg-proof rights interpretation themselves. This criticism has typically come from strong apex courts with a long-standing tradition of interpreting the human rights and fundamental freedoms enshrined in the European Convention on Human Rights (ECHR). Whilst the judges of the ECtHR have on occasion addressed in public speeches and articles such criticisms by their domestic counterparts,[2] the ECtHR has also taken up the challenge of this criticism doctrinally in its jurisprudence. This paper focuses on the doctrinal response.

* Başak Çalı, Koç University. This contribution was initially presented at the 'Shifting Centres of Gravity in European Human Rights Protection: Oscillating between the ECHR, the EU and national legal orders' Conference in Reykjavík, Iceland on 6–7 March 2014. I would like to thank the conference participants, and in particular Rory O'Connell and Philip Leach, for comments and Cem Tecimer for research assistance. The chapter builds on my earlier work on emerging standards of judicial review at the European Court of Human Rights, in particular, 'Domestic Courts and the European Court of Human Rights: Towards Developing Standards of Weak International Judicial Review?' (Opinio Juris, 11 January 2013), available at opiniojuris.org/2013/01/11/domestic-courts-and-the-european-court-of-human-rights-towards-developing-standards-of-weak-international-judicial-review/.

[1] Richard S Kay, 'The European Convention on Human Rights and the Control of Private Law' (2005) 5 *European Human Rights Law Review* 466; Jochen A Frowein, 'The transformation of constitutional law through the European Convention on Human Rights' (2008) 41 *Israel Law Review* 489; Laurence R Helfer, 'Redesigning the European Court of Human Rights: Embeddedness as the Deep Structural Principle of the European Human Rights Regime' (2008) 19 *European Journal of International Law* 125; Leonard Hoffmann, 'The Universality of Human Rights' (2009) 125 *Law Quarterly Review* 416; Brenda Hale, 'Common Law and Convention Law: The Limits to Interpretation' (2011) 16 *European Human Rights Law Review* 534.

[2] Cf European Court of Human Rights, Dialogue between Judges 2012: How can we ensure greater involvement of national courts in the Convention system? (European Court of Human Rights Publications, 2012), available at www.echr.coe.int/Documents/Dialogue_2012_ENG.pdf; see also Nicolas

Specifically, I argue that the ECtHR is developing a new standard of judicial review of domestic court judgments. I call this a nascent 'responsible courts doctrine',[3] allowing domestic courts a larger discretionary space with regard to making rights violation determinations, provided that domestic courts take ECtHR case law seriously. The responsible courts doctrine at its core signals that the ECtHR is willing to carry out a lenient form of judicial review of the decisions of those domestic courts that responsibly take into account the interpretation of the European Convention of Human Rights (ECHR) as developed through ECtHR case law. This stands in contrast to the stricter forms of judicial review it reserves for the judgments of domestic courts that fail to take Strasbourg case law into account or interpret it inadequately.

The responsible courts doctrine is nascent and contested. Its relationship to other forms of deference to domestic authorities under the umbrella of the margin of appreciation is also under-determined. A series of dissenting opinions from judges in cases where the doctrine has been hinted at or failed to be employed further points to deeper divisions on the ECtHR bench over whether the doctrine, if officially adopted, supports or hinders the effective application of the ECHR.[4] In this paper my aim is to assess whether this new standard of judicial review is a transient approach largely developed to improve relationships with well-established domestic courts that resent being supervised by the ECtHR, or a more principled doctrinal development indicating a constitutionalisation of the European Human Rights system.[5]

In what follows, I start with the characteristics of judicial review with respect to the ECtHR. In particular, I hold that the ECtHR has *sui generis* characteristics as a supranational human rights court and that this has been reflected in how it appropriates standards of judicial review from domestic contexts. The ECtHR is well known for placing a significant emphasis on 'case-by-case' and 'right-by-right' review, alongside the diverse uses of the margin of appreciation doctrine as its core approaches to judicial review.[6] Next, I review the development of the nascent responsible courts doctrine with reference to a number of paradigmatic cases

Bratza, 'The Relationship between the UK Courts and the Strasbourg Court' (2011) 5 *European Human Rights Law Review* 505.

[3] In characterising the doctrine in this way, I am inspired by the 'Responsible Governments Doctrine' espoused by the World Trade Organization Appellate Body, in particular in its decision WTO, EC Measures Concerning Meat and Meat Products (Hormones)—Complaint by Canada—Report of the Appellate Body (16 January 1998) WT/DS26/AB/R and WT/DS48/AB/R, available at docs.wto.org/dol2fe/Pages/FE_Search/FE_S_S005.aspx.

[4] See *Dissenting Opinions in Palomo Sanchez and Others v Spain* App nos 28955/06, 28957/06, 28959/06 and 28964/06 (12 September 2011); *Aksu v Turkey* App nos 4149/04 and 41029/04 (ECtHR, 15 March 2013).

[5] KS Ziegler and PM Huber (eds), *Current Problems in the Protection of Human Rights* (Hart Publishing, 2013).

[6] For a comprehensive analysis of how the margin shifts according to rights, see Howard C Yourow, *The Margin of Appreciation Doctrine in the Dynamics of European Human Rights Jurisprudence* (Martinus Nijhoff Publishers, 1996). For a view that argues that the ECtHR is precedent-bound, see Luzius Wildhaber, 'Precedent in the European Court of Human Rights' in Paul Mahoney (ed), *Protection des droits de l'homme: la perspective européenne, mélanges à la mémoire de Rolv Ryssdal* (Carl Heymanns, 2000) 1529–45.

representative of this doctrine. I then compare this doctrine to the existing margin of appreciation doctrine used by Strasbourg and argue that we potentially have a new doctrine that seeks to positively entrench Convention rights interpretation amongst domestic judiciaries. I conclude by discussing the desirability, feasibility and pitfalls of this doctrine.

## II. THE EUROPEAN COURT OF HUMAN RIGHTS AND THE STANDARDS OF JUDICIAL REVIEW: BETWEEN PURPOSIVE INTERPRETATION AND MARGIN OF APPRECIATION

The ECtHR can best be characterised as a supranational court that has variable review standards of domestic court decisions. There is no doubt that in a general sense the ECtHR carries out a Convention-based review (akin to Constitutional Courts) and does not seek a retrial of a case.[7] The Court has been vocal about rejecting the fourth instance type review.[8] The Court, however, has not approached all domestic courts in the same way due to the human rights standard-setting mission it has taken on over the years.

How the ECtHR sets human rights standards is deeply entrenched in the principles of effective and dynamic interpretation of the rights enshrined in the Convention.[9] Effective interpretation requires the Court to take due regard of the consequences of the interpretation of the rights for the real (not illusory) enjoyment of rights by the applicant who brings the case before the Court.[10] The dynamic interpretation of rights, on the other hand, requires the Court to be responsive to the constantly changing political, economic, social and moral developments in the *espace juridique* of the Council of Europe, and more recently beyond.[11]

These two aspects of effective and dynamic interpretation, taken together, have led the ECtHR to operate on a case-by-case basis without clearly formulating what type of deference it should owe to domestic courts.[12] This is not to suggest that the

[7] There have been exceptions to this, in particular in situations in which the Court (and the Commission) have carried out fact-finding missions and declared domestic courts unable to deliver a domestic remedy, cf *Kurt v Turkey* App no 24276/94 (ECtHR, 25 May 1998); *Timurtas v Turkey* App no 23531/94 (ECtHR, 13 June 2000); *Akdeniz and Others v Turkey* App no 23954/94 (ECtHR, 31 May 2001); *Ipek v Turkey* App no 25760/94 (ECtHR, 17 February 2004); see also Philip Leach, Costas Paraskeva and Gordana Uzelac, 'Human Rights Fact-finding: the European Court of Human Rights at a Crossroads' (2010) 28 *Netherlands Quarterly of Human Rights* 41.

[8] The rejection of the 'fourth instance doctrine' has been frequently discussed, in particular when the ECtHR reviews allegations of the violation of right to fair trial by domestic courts, cf *Rowe and Davis v United Kingdom* (2000) 30 EHRR 1.

[9] Başak Çali, 'Specialised Rules of Treaty Interpretation: Human Rights' in Duncan B Hollis (ed), *The Oxford Guide to Treaties* (Oxford University Press, 2012) 525–50.

[10] *Airey v Ireland* App no 6289/73 (9 October 1979).

[11] *Baykara v Turkey* App no 34503/97 (ECtHR, 12 November 2008); *Bayatyan v Armenia* App no 23459/03 (ECtHR, 7 July 2011).

[12] *Christine Goodwin v United Kingdom* App no 28957/95 (ECtHR, 11 July 2002).

ECtHR does not seek to build general principles or persuasive precedents.[13] The ECtHR, however, has insisted that the standards of review developed by it are meant to be transient, fluid and open to revision in the face of the facts of an individual case. In *Christine Goodwin v United Kingdom* the ECtHR sets out the relationship between predictability and effectiveness as follows:

> While the Court is not formally bound to follow its previous judgments, it is in the interests of legal certainty, foreseeability and equality before the law that it should not depart, without good reason, from precedents laid down in previous cases (see, for example, Chapman v. the United Kingdom [GC], no. 27238/95, ECHR 2001-I, § 70). However, since the Convention is first and foremost a system for the protection of human rights, the Court must have regard to the changing conditions within the respondent State and within Contracting States generally and respond, for example, to any evolving convergence as to the standards to be achieved (see, amongst other authorities, the Cossey [v.UK] judgment, p. 14, § 35, and Stafford v. the United Kingdom [GC], no. 46295/99, judgment of 28 May 2002, to be published in ECHR 2002, §§ 67-68). It is of crucial importance that the Convention is interpreted and applied in a manner which renders its rights practical and effective, not theoretical and illusory. A failure by the Court to maintain a dynamic and evolutive approach would indeed risk rendering it a bar to reform or improvement (see the above-cited Stafford v. the United Kingdom judgment, § 68).[14]

This historic and transformative mission of the ECtHR sets it apart from ordinary courts bound by legislation, and constitutional courts bound by their own social contract. In fact, the intrinsic relationship between identifying and assigning meaning to relevant facts and interpretation of the Convention has been openly acknowledged by the ECtHR jurisprudence.

This can be best seen in the early doctrinal formulation by the ECtHR of its relationship with domestic courts. The ECtHR has traditionally demanded that all domestic courts, to the best of their ability, formulate 'relevant' or 'sufficient' reasons when assessing whether they have made a genuine effort to decide whether a right was engaged or violated.[15] The 'relevant and sufficient reasons' doctrine is in fact a standard of review of domestic courts. But whether the reasons are indeed relevant or sufficient in the particular case is ultimately decided by the ECtHR.[16] The 'relevant and sufficient reasons' doctrine has been employed by the ECtHR as both a backward-looking and a forward-looking doctrine. In cases where the Court decides that its previous case law has established a clear guideline as to what these reasons are, the ECtHR is content to refer to this older case law.[17] When the Court decides that the particulars of the case warrant a fresh restatement of the Convention

[13] Michal Balcerzak, 'The Doctrine of Precedent in the International Court of Justice and the European Court of Human Rights' (2004–2005) 27 *Polish Yearbook of International Law* 131, 139 and Wildhaber (n 6).

[14] *Christine Goodwin v United Kingdom* (n 12) para 74.

[15] *Coster v United Kingdom* App no 24876/94 (ECtHR, 18 January 2001); *Nikula v Finland* App no 31611/96 (ECtHR, 21 June 2002); *Sidabras v Lithuania* App nos 55480/00 and 59330/00 (ECtHR, 27 October 2004).

[16] *Axel Springer AG v Germany* App no 39954/08 (7 February 2012).

[17] *Marper v United Kingdom* App nos 30562/04 and 30566/04 (ECtHR, 4 December 2008).

in the light of the principles of effective and dynamic interpretations, the ECtHR is in a position to more substantively assess whether it believes the reasons given, in the light of the facts of the case and the human rights questions surrounding it, are relevant or sufficient or both. The relevant and sufficient reasons, therefore, can lend themselves both to a strict review of the facts of the case in the light of a forward-looking interpretation of human rights and to a more constitutional standard-based review of the decision of the domestic court based on the previous case law of the ECtHR.

The standard of judicial review of the ECtHR is further complicated by the use of the margin of appreciation doctrine. When defined as a deference to the state authorities taking into account their proximity to the facts and other extra-legal phenomena, such as political circumstances and background historical, social and political conditions on a case-by-case basis,[18] the margin of appreciation doctrine directs the ECtHR not to carry out a strict review of a particular case, but to defer to the state authorities in assigning meaning to the facts and measures taken by a state to limit a right.

The margin of appreciation, however, is not a standard of judicial review in and of itself.[19] It merely indicates that the standard of judicial review may vary from case to case, if the ECtHR decides that a margin of appreciation of state authorities is in and of itself a relative criterion to apply a weaker or a more interventionist standard of judicial review.

This shifting character of standard review based on the effectiveness of the Convention, the living instrument doctrine and the formulation of a view regarding the relevance of the margin is reflected in one of the standard statements of the Court:

> Under Article 10 of the Convention, the Contracting States have a certain margin of appreciation in assessing whether an interference with the right to freedom of expression was 'necessary in a democratic society'. However, this margin goes hand in hand with a European supervision, embracing both the legislation and the decisions applying it, even those given by an independent court (see Tammer v. Estonia, no. 41205/98, § 60, ECHR 2001-I; Peck v. the United Kingdom, no. 44647/98, § 77, ECHR 2003-I; and Karhuvaara and Iltalehti v. Finland, no. 53678/00, § 38, ECHR 2004-X). The Court's task in exercising its supervision is not to take the place of the national authorities but rather to review, in the light of the case as a whole, the decisions that they have taken pursuant to their margin of appreciation (see Petrenco v. Moldova, no. 20928/05, § 54, 30 March 2010; Polanco Torres and Movilla Polanco v. Spain, no. 34147/06, § 41, 21 September 2010; and Petrov v. Bulgaria (dec.), no. 27103/04, 2 November 2010).[20]

This statement, with its emphasis on 'the case as a whole', the review function of the Court and the margins of state authorities, attests to multiple tensions and the

[18] *Şahin v Turkey* App no 44774/98 (10 November 2005).

[19] Başak Çali, 'Between Legal Cosmopolitanism and a Society of States: The Limits of International Justice at the European Court of Human Rights' in Marie-Benedicte Dembour and Tobias Kelly (eds), *Paths to International Justice: Social and Legal Perspectives* (Cambridge University Press, 2007) 111–33.

[20] *Aksu* (n 4) para 65; See *Petrenco v Moldova* App no 20928/05 (ECtHR, 4 October 2010); *Petrov v Bulgaria* App no 27103/04 (ECtHR, 23 November 2010).

difficulty of formulating a stable standard of review in the case law of the Court. The standard of judicial review that the Court uses is that of review of the compatibility of the case in hand with the ECHR.[21] This, however, may be disrupted by the case as a whole leading to outcomes that lead to strict review,[22] or a lenient review.[23]

## III. RESPONSIBLE COURTS DOCTRINE: A NEW STANDARD OF REVIEW IN THE MAKING?

The nascent responsible courts doctrine is a culmination of the Court's growing confidence in its interpretation of the ECHR standards, as well as the growing trust the Court has in domestic courts to responsibly apply these standards. The responsible courts doctrine has seen its clearest formulation in cases where the ECtHR recognises that more than one outcome may be possible and acceptable provided that a domestic court applies the standards developed by the ECtHR appropriately. This is sometimes referred to as a 'corridor of solutions', referring to the possibility of more than one right answer in rights adjudication.[24] It is, therefore, no wonder that cases that exhibit a tension between the enjoyment of more than one right have been the breeding ground for this doctrine. The *Von Hannover Case (2) v Germany* is the paradigmatic example of this.[25]

The *Von Hannover (2)* case was the second appearance of Princess Caroline of Monaco before the Strasbourg Court, arguing that the German press had violated her right to privacy. In the first *Von Hannover* case of 2004, Princess Caroline advanced the argument that given that she does not hold a public office or have any public functions, the continuous publication of pictures depicting her private life in the German press violated her right to privacy, and the German Courts had failed to protect her. In its first review of the case in 2004, the ECtHR held that, as a matter of principle, when the right to privacy and the right to freedom of expression are in competition, domestic courts had to show themselves to be considering the adequate protection of each right. The Strasbourg Court stated that the standard of human rights review developed by the German Constitutional Court in its judgment of 15 December 1999 was a test that a priori favoured freedom of expression and risked under-protecting the right to privacy. The standard afforded protection to a figure in contemporary society 'only if she was in a secluded place out of the public eye to which persons retire with the objectively recognisable aim of being alone and where, confident of being alone, they behave in a manner in which they would not

[21] *Schenk v Switzerland* App no 10862/84 (ECtHR, 12 July 1988) paras 45–49; *Bernard v France* App no 22885/93 (ECtHR, 23 April 1998) paras 37–41; *G v the United Kingdom* App No 37334/08 (ECtHR, 30 August 2011) paras 28–30.

[22] *DH and Others v Czech Republic* App no 57325/00 (13 November 2007).

[23] *Şahin* (n 18) and the dissenting opinion of Judge Tulkens.

[24] *Axel Springer* (n 16) para 62.

[25] For cases with similar reasoning structures see *Obst v Germany* App No 425/03 (ECtHR, 23 September 2010); *Siebenhaar v Germany* App no 18136/02 (ECtHR, 3 February 2011); *Schüth v Germany* App no 1620/03 (ECtHR, 23 December 2010).

behave in public'.[26] The Strasbourg Court held that 'the criterion of spatial isolation, although apposite in theory, is in reality too vague and difficult for the person concerned to determine in advance'[27] and that, therefore, the standard failed to offer real and practical protection of human rights, a central object and purpose of the whole Convention system. The Court consequently found a violation of the right to privacy based on the argument that the German Courts' conduct in reviewing the case was out of step with the European human rights law that demanded equal consideration of both rights in cases when rights compete.

In *Von Hannover (2)* the princess, in the aftermath of the printing of more pictures of her in the German press, returned to the Strasbourg Court alleging that new violations of her right to privacy had taken place. The applicant thought the German Courts had paid no heed to the Strasbourg Court's judgment. The Strasbourg Court disagreed with the applicant, deciding that the fact that the German press had been allowed to print pictures of her did not in itself point to a violation of the Convention. What concerned it was whether the German Courts had appropriately balanced the rights of privacy and expression in their reasoning for allowing the publication of further pictures and that they did not favour freedom of expression at the expense of the right to privacy in applying principles to the facts of the case. The Court went on to make one of the most explicit definitions so far of its role as an international court.

> In exercising its supervisory function, the Court's task is not to take the place of the national courts, but rather to review, in the light of the case as a whole, whether the decisions they have taken pursuant to their power of appreciation are compatible with the provisions of the Convention relied on.[28]

Where the balancing exercise has been undertaken by the national authorities in conformity with the criteria laid down in the Court's case law, the Court would require strong reasons to substitute its view for that of the domestic courts.[29]

These statements clearly indicate a departure from the 'relevant and sufficient' reasons doctrine of the ECtHR. Firstly, the ECtHR introduces a new concept, namely 'the power of appreciation' of domestic courts. In so doing, the Court distinguishes domestic courts from other domestic authorities, which, according to the ECtHR, have a 'margin of appreciation' rather than a power of appreciation. The ECtHR, therefore, accords the domestic courts higher status with regard to the appreciation of facts than other domestic institutions. Secondly, the power of appreciation of domestic courts is conditional. The ECtHR empowers domestic courts only when it decides that the domestic courts are interpreting the rights in a Convention-compatible way. Thirdly, the ECtHR explicitly imposes a judicial restraint on itself on carrying out a full review of the case, if the domestic court has acted in a responsible way.

[26] *Von Hannover v Germany* App no 59320/00 (24 September 2004) para 54.

[27] Ibid para 75.

[28] *Von Hannover v Germany (No 2)* App nos 40660/08 and 60641/08 (ECtHR, 7 February 2012) para 105.

[29] Ibid para 107.

As a formal structure, therefore, the responsible courts doctrine operates as follows:

1. The ECtHR declares that the domestic court has dealt convincingly and comprehensively with the Convention as interpreted by the ECtHR in its previous case law.
2. After declaring this finding, the Court asks whether there are 'strong reasons' to differ from the analysis of the facts as offered by the domestic court.
3. If the ECtHR answers the question it posed in Step 2 negatively, it defers to the domestic court with regard to whether or not there is a violation of the Convention rights.

## IV. RESPONSIBLE COURTS DOCTRINE: YET ANOTHER FORM OF MARGIN OF APPRECIATION?

The deference to responsible courts, as formulated above, differs from standards of review that build in a deference to domestic courts, legislative or judicial authorities under the traditional umbrella of the margin of appreciation. The significant mark of distinction here is that in the case of the responsible courts doctrine, deference to domestic courts is conditional upon taking and applying the Convention principles seriously. In contrast, the margin of appreciation doctrine, as originally developed, has operated according to an a priori declaration that the authorities enjoy a margin of appreciation by virtue of their qualities that is not dependent on their ability to interpret the Convention standards.[30] In this respect, the responsible courts doctrine is a qualified form of margin of appreciation. The domestic courts earn the margin by showing their loyalty to the Convention standards rather than by their other virtues *qua* domestic courts.

An illustrative example of the difference between responsible courts and the more traditional forms of margin is how the ECtHR constructs the margin of appreciation in relation to the interpretation of Article 6 of the ECHR in non-criminal proceedings. In a string of case law examples, starting with *Roche v United Kingdom*, the ECtHR has developed a doctrine of direct deference to domestic courts in non-criminal Article 6 cases as a standard of review.[31] In its recent 2012 Grand Chamber case of *Boulois v Luxembourg*, in particular, the ECtHR recognised that the starting point of the interpretation of Article 6 in the sphere of civil rights and obligations must be the provisions of the relevant domestic law and their interpretation by domestic courts.[32] In particular, the ECtHR requires that a 'right', at least on arguable grounds, be recognised under domestic law, irrespective of whether it is protected under the Convention. Alongside this, the dispute must be genuine and serious;

[30] Cf *Şahin* (n 18).
[31] *Roche v United Kingdom* App no 32555/96 (19 October 2005) paras 116–26.
[32] *Boulois v Luxembourg* App no 37575/04 (3 April 2012) para 91. Cf *Roche* (n 31) paras 119–20.

it may relate not only to the actual existence of a right but also to its scope and the manner of its exercise; and the result of the proceedings must be directly decisive for the right in question.[33] The ECtHR here, too, would need 'strong reasons to differ from the conclusions reached by the superior national courts by finding, contrary to their view, that there was arguably a right recognised by domestic law'.[34]

In this way, the ECtHR explicitly recognises the role of superior national courts in deciding the interpretation of the applicability of fair trial rights to non-criminal disputes. Furthermore, by basing its own interpretation on at least the 'arguable' existence of the right in domestic law and interpretation, the ECtHR defers to all domestic courts and not only to the responsible domestic courts in this instance.

In the light of the contrast between *Von Hannover* and *Boulois*, we may conclude that deference to domestic courts based on whether they internalised ECtHR case law or not shows important dissimilarities to other uses of the margin of appreciation. The leeway to apply the Convention standards to the facts of a case is only accorded to states that the ECtHR deems trustworthy and Convention-compliant in the first place.[35] In this regard, *Von Hannover* represents a more nuanced deference doctrine than the margin of appreciation doctrine.

## V. IS THE RESPONSIBLE COURTS DOCTRINE FEASIBLE AND DESIRABLE?

The doctrine, if it becomes a more regular feature of the Court's interpretive toolkit, however, is not without problems. As with other doctrines of the court, there is no clear consistency in the usage of the responsible courts doctrine. A survey of dissenting opinions on instances in which this nascent doctrine has been employed points to two different types of issues raised by ECtHR judges. On the one hand, supporters of the responsible courts doctrine are worried about its consistent use. On the other, sceptics of the doctrine are worried that a doctrine of principled deference to domestic courts faces the risk of undermining the effective interpretation of rights and giving undue credit to domestic courts for adequately interpreting Convention rights.

The *Axel Springer AG Germany* judgment of the Grand Chamber, and in particular the dissenting opinions of Judges Lopez Guerra, Jungwiert, Jaeger, Villiger and Poalelungi, is an important illustration of the first issue. Decided on the same day as the *Von Hannover* decision, the *Axel Springer AG* case also involved a tension between the Article 10 rights of a publisher and the Article 8 rights of a TV celebrity. Unlike the *Von Hannover* case, in this instance the publisher was the applicant arguing for his violation of freedom of expression. The Grand Chamber, in this case, reiterated that what matters in competing expression and privacy cases is that the

[33] *Boulois* (n 32) para 90.

[34] Ibid para 91.

[35] For a view that regards this doctrine as a mere variant of the margin of appreciation doctrine, see Dean Spielmann, 'Allowing the Right Margin: The European Court of Human Rights and The National Margin of Appreciation Doctrine: Waiver or Subsidiarity of European Review?' (2011–2012) 14 *Cambridge Yearbook of European Legal Studies* 381.

domestic courts have duly considered both rights, taking into account the published information's contribution to a debate of general interest, the previous behaviour and degree of notoriety of the person affected, the content and veracity of the information and the nature of the sanctions and penalties imposed. The Grand Chamber went on to decide that despite the 'margin of appreciation enjoyed by Contracting States', the 'grounds advanced by the respondent State although relevant, are not sufficient to establish that the interference was necessary in a democratic society'.[36]

In their dissenting opinion, five judges queried the standard of review that the ECtHR had employed in this case. In particular, they argued that the finding that the 'Convention rights were not duly considered' by the domestic courts was unfounded.[37]

The dissenting judges, following the logic of the responsible courts doctrine espoused in the *Von Hannover* case, further argued that:

> In order to exercise this Court's powers of review without becoming a fourth instance our task in guaranteeing respect for Convention rights in this type of case is essentially to verify whether domestic courts have *duly* balanced the conflicting rights and have taken into account the relevant criteria established in our case law without any manifest error or omission of any important factor.[38]

Dissenting judges placed more weight on the consideration of Convention standards by domestic courts than on the correct application of the standards to the facts of the case. As stated in the dissenting opinion, unless the application of standards to facts was 'arbitrary, careless, or manifestly unreasonable', the domestic court's decision should not be interfered with by the ECtHR.[39] On the contrary, the majority of judges have referred to the 'relevant, but not sufficient test' in this particular judgment, carrying out a stronger form of Conventionality review than that set out in the *Von Hannover* judgment.

At the other end of the spectrum, some judges are concerned that the responsible courts doctrine could lead to an undermining of human rights standard development. This was the concern of the dissenting judges in the *Palomo Sanchez v Spain* judgment of the Grand Chamber of the ECtHR.[40] The *Palomo Sanchez* case involved delivery workers who were dismissed from their jobs by an industrial bakery company in Barcelona. The applicants had earlier brought proceedings against that company before Spanish employment tribunals seeking recognition of their status as salaried workers (rather than self-employed or non-salaried delivery workers), in order to be covered by the corresponding social security regime. Representatives of a committee of non-salaried delivery workers within the same company had testified

[36] *Axel Springer* (n 16) para 110.

[37] Ibid Dissenting Opinion.

[38] Dissenting Opinion in *Axel Springer* (n 16) para 4 (emphasis added).

[39] See also Joint Partly Dissenting Opinion of Judge Jungwiert, Judge Vajic, Judge Gyulumyan, Judge Jaeger, Judge Myjer, Judge Berro-Lefevre and Judge Vucinic in *Orsus and Others v Croatia*.

[40] Joint Dissenting Opinion of Judge Tulkens, Judge David Thor Björgvinsson, Judge Jociene, Judge Popovic and Judge Vucinic in *Palomo* (n 4).

against the applicants in those proceedings. The applicants set up the trade union NAA (*Nueva alternativa asamblearia*) in 2001 to defend their interests and subsequently published a cartoon in the NAA newsletter showing the company manager and two workers who testified against them in an undignified position. They were dismissed from work as a result of this cartoon.

In this case, the Grand Chamber signalled that it would employ the responsible courts doctrine stating that 'if the reasoning of the domestic courts' decisions concerning the limits of freedom of expression in cases involving a person's reputation is sufficient and consistent with the criteria established by the Court's case law, the Court would require strong reasons to substitute its view for that of the domestic courts'.[41] The Grand Chamber went on to accept that the domestic Spanish Court paid due attention to the criteria of whether (a) harmfulness to others, and (b) the sanction of dismissal, was proportionate to the degree of seriousness of the impugned remarks. In particular, the Grand Chamber decided that the domestic courts duly recognised the importance of freedom of expression and considered these criteria and that the outcome of the reasoning of the domestic courts was not 'manifestly disproportionate'.[42]

Dissenting judges took issue with this qualification and charged the Grand Chamber with refusing to carry out a proper proportionality analysis between the aim of the limitation (to protect the reputation of others) and the means of the limitation (the dismissal of the applicants). According to the dissenting judges, the ECtHR failed to give full effect to the importance of freedom of expression in the field of labour relations and trade union activity. The fact that the ECtHR was interested in whether the situation was manifestly disproportionate meant that the Court approved 'in their entirety and almost word for word, the findings of the domestic courts, which, without taking Article 10 of the Convention into account, took the view that the cartoon and articles in question were offensive and impugned the respectability of the individuals and company concerned'.[43]

The dissenting opinions in *Axel Springer AG* and *Palomo Sanchez* show the difficulties the ECtHR judges have in deciding both the appropriate review standards and whether they should also scrutinise how review standards are applied to the facts of the cases by domestic courts. In *Palomo Sanchez* the dissenting judges thought the review standards were wrongly identified through a failure to take into account the importance of freedom of expression for trade unions. In so arguing, they take their cue from the effective interpretation of Convention rights so that they are not merely theoretical or illusory.[44] In *Axel Springer AG*, the dissenting judges believed that the Grand Chamber had failed in its promised effectiveness, whilst it exercised its new deferential standards to responsible courts.

[41] *Palomo* (n 4) para 57.
[42] Ibid para 77.
[43] Joint Dissenting Opinion in *Palomo* (n 40) para 10.
[44] Ibid.

## VI. CONCLUSION

At first sight, the responsible courts doctrine appears to be a promising doctrine for mediating the relationship between domestic courts that take the ECtHR case law seriously and the Strasbourg Court. Domestic courts that apply the ECtHR standards demand a lenient review of their judgments by Strasbourg. The ECtHR does not see itself as an appeal court, but it also does not want to share the ultimate interpretive responsibility of the Convention with domestic courts. The responsible courts doctrine is able to speak to all of these concerns by recognising the space for manoeuvre of domestic courts within a framework that identifies Strasbourg as the ultimate interpretive authority.

The nascent responsible courts doctrine also represents an advance from the margin of appreciation doctrine as it formulates a principled account of deference.

The frequent and inconsistent use of the doctrine, however, is not without problems. The core problem is the, perhaps unintended, consequences of the stabilisation effect that the doctrine has on the case law of the ECtHR. Unlike the case-by-case approach, the doctrine binds the ECtHR to its past case law and can hamper its dynamism. From a legal/policy perspective, there are also two risks with the doctrine. Firstly, the doctrine may encourage an internalisation of ECtHR standards as well as a mimicking of ECtHR standards by domestic courts. In the case of the latter, Courts may dress rights restrictions in the correct language in order to reap the benefits of being perceived to be a responsible court. Secondly, the ECtHR may provoke a new backlash from domestic courts that have not been classified as a responsible domestic court, on the grounds of double standards.

# PART II

# INTERNATIONAL LAW AND NATIONAL LAW

# 5

# *International Law through the National Prism: The Role of Domestic Law and Jurisprudence in Shaping International Investment Law*

HEGE ELISABETH KJOS*

## I. INTRODUCTION

DESPITE THEIR PROLIFERATION and the large amount of scholarship they continue to inspire, international courts and tribunals stand in the shadow of domestic courts when it comes to the number of cases rendered with a public international law dimension. This observation also applies to disputes between foreign investors and host states.

In my contribution, I discuss domestic law as a generator of international investment law, focusing on domestic court decisions. This area of law constitutes a particularly rich field of study for several reasons. First, the constellation of the disputants—a private party and a sovereign state—entails the applicability of both domestic and international law. Going back to the minimum standard of treatment of aliens, there are also several parallels to be found between international and domestic law. A further reason is the steep increase in the number of investment disputes being settled by arbitration and the corollary growth of jurisprudence.[1]

A separate motivation for this study stems from the larger role that the domestic judiciary of the host state may play in the settlement of investment disputes following calls for reform of the investment law and arbitration regime. Several states have

* Amsterdam Center for International Law, University of Amsterdam. Email address: H.E.Kjos@uva.nl.
This research forms part of the research project 'International Law through the Prism of National Law: the Impact of Judicial Dialogue' funded by the European Science Foundation (ESF) as a European Collaborative Research Project in the Social Sciences (ECRP). The presentation draws in part from a recent publication: HE Kjos, 'Domestic Courts under Scrutiny: The Rule of Law as a Standard (of Deference) in Investor-State Arbitration' in M Kanetake and A Nollkaemper (eds), *The Rule of Law at the National and International Levels: Contestations and Deference* (Hart Publishing, 2016).

[1] UNCTAD, *World Investment Report 2014* (2014) 125. ('By the end of 2013, the number of known [investor-state dispute settlement] cases reached 568.')

sought to bolster the role of their judiciary in cases involving foreign investors, inter alia by imposing the requirement that investors first seek a remedy before domestic courts; by narrowing the dispute settlement clause in international investment agreements (IIAs); excluding recourse to investor-state arbitration in IIAs; or withdrawing from IIAs.[2] This development is likely to increase the number of foreign investment disputes before domestic courts. Without recourse to international arbitration, what level of protection awaits foreign investors in the courts of the host state?

Drawing from domestic court decisions and arbitral jurisprudence, I intend to shed light on the core issue discussed in this agora: the possible swing-back effect from domestic courtrooms to the international legal order in the area of investment law. Besides the questions of whether and how international and domestic courts and tribunals can and do refer to (other) domestic court decisions in interpreting and applying international investment law, I also consider the normative dimension of whether and when it is appropriate to do so.

The chapter is divided into three parts: first, I show the substantive overlap between domestic and international sources in the area of foreign investment law, also referencing domestic case law. Second, I point to various legal bases for investor-state tribunals to refer to domestic law and jurisprudence. I then give some examples of how investor-state tribunals have engaged in this practice, while also considering more normative reasons and obstacles therefor. In brief, tribunals tend to refer explicitly only to the domestic law and jurisprudence of the host State. Such reference is to be recommended as it can enhance the legitimacy of the award for the disputants. The selectivity is also understandable in light of the difficulties entailed in comparative research.

## II. NORMATIVE OVERLAP BETWEEN DOMESTIC AND INTERNATIONAL FOREIGN INVESTMENT LAW

Both domestic and international law apply to the investor-state relationship[3] and in light of a normative overlap, relevant domestic judgments for investor-state tribunals may include pronouncements on domestic law as well as public international law. Indeed, practice shows that foreign investors invoke and domestic courts apply norms originating in both legal orders. These 'consubstantial' or 'multi-sourced equivalent norms'[4] include constitutional law, foreign investment codes, customary international law, general principles of international law, IIAs and human rights law. This normative convergence has led scholars to refer to international investment

[2] Cf ibid 127; UNCTAD, 'Reform of the IIA Regime: Four Paths of Action and a Way Forward' *IIA Issue Note* No 3 (July 2014) 7.

[3] JW Salacuse, *The Three Laws of International Investment: National, Contractual, and International Frameworks for Foreign Capital* (Oxford University Press, 2013); HE Kjos, *Applicable Law in Investor-State Arbitration: The Interplay Between National and International Law* (Oxford University Press, 2013).

[4] A Tzanakopoulos, 'Preliminary Report' International Law Association Study Group on Principles on the Engagement of Domestic Courts with International Law, para 29.

arbitration as an 'internationalized discipline of public law', and a 'form of global constitutional and administrative law'.[5]

Starting with the minimum standard for the treatment of aliens, foreign investment law has a comparatively long existence as a separate field of international law.[6] There are several examples of domestic courts applying customary international law and general principles of law in investor-state disputes. An illustration (which is also one of courts citing foreign courts) is the *Anglo-Iranian Oil Company* case from 1954.[7] The Civil Court of Rome was faced with a claim for ownership of oil acquired in Persia by the respondent company and then transported in vessels to Italy. The respondent had acquired this oil following nationalisation of the oil industry by Persia in 1951. The claimant argued that the nationalisation laws were not applicable in Italy because they were (i) contrary to the Persian Constitution; (ii) contrary to Italian public policy; (iii) contrary to the generally accepted provisions of international law referred to in the Italian Constitution; (iv) of a political, discriminatory and confiscatory nature; and (v) because they decreed expropriation without compensation.

The action failed as the Court found that the oil had been validly acquired in Persia by the respondent company. Also, the nationalisation laws were neither unconstitutional by Persian law, nor were they confiscatory in nature since they provided for the payment of at least some compensation. Since they did not offend against either Italian public policy or international public policy, the Court could not refuse to apply those laws or to recognise the validity of a purchase from a vendor who had derived title under them. The Court stated inter alia:

> The legality of the nationalization was explicitly confirmed … by the Court of Tokyo in its judgment of September 21, 1953 …. The principle of nationalization and the power of Governments to expropriate any real or personal right, and even the right of ownership, belonging to their own or foreign citizens, for reasons of public interest and against compensation which does not appear to be merely illusory, is, moreover, recognized by the case-law of every country. … The principle that Governments must, when dealing with foreign nationals, comply with the fundamental rules by which the more civilized Governments abide in relation to private individuals and which constitute the 'minimum standard' of the idea of justice of civilized countries—the international 'ethical minimum'—need not be invoked if there is the right of compensation, as has been confirmed, moreover, by, inter alia, the judgment of the Tribunal of Le Havre of July 22, 1939, in connection with the expropriation of oil concessions by the Mexican Government, prescribed by its Decree of March 18, 1938. The judgment of the Civil Court of Antwerp of February 21, 1939, relating to the same question, that of the Court of Appeal of Arnhem of June 12, 1939, and that of the District Court of New York (Southern District) of April 13, 1939, definitely deny that

[5] SW Schill, 'Enhancing International Investment Law's Legitimacy: Conceptual and Methodological Foundation of a New Public Law Approach' (2011) 52(1) *Virginia Journal of International Law* 57, 59; S Montt, *State Liability in Investment Treaty Arbitration: Global Constitutional and Administrative Law in the BIT Generation* (Hart Publishing, 2009) 4.

[6] H Dickerson, 'Minimum Standards' in R Wolfrum (ed), *The Max Planck Encyclopedia of Public International Law* (Oxford University Press, October 2010), available at mpepil.com.

[7] *Anglo-Iranian Oil Company v S.U.P.O.R.*, Civil Court of Rome, Italy [1954] 22 ILR 23.

> any foreign court is entitled to decide on the lawfulness of an expropriation carried out by a foreign Government; the same conclusion was reached by the Court of Tokyo in its judgment of September 21, 1953, relating to the Persian oil nationalization.[8]

Besides customary international law and general principles of law, there are now more than 2,900 bilateral investment treaties (BITs) and several hundred other IIAs.[9] These IIAs are designed to stimulate foreign investments, and for that purpose they impose—on a reciprocal basis—obligations on the host state vis-à-vis investors from (the) other contracting state(s), such as 'national', 'most-favoured-nation' and 'fair and equitable' treatment (FET); and 'full protection and security'; and they stipulate criteria for expropriation.[10]

Examples can be given of domestic courts applying IIAs or their 'predecessors': treaties of friendship, navigation and commerce. In *Kessl v Minister of Lands and Resettlement* (2008) the High Court of Namibia referred to the Germany–Namibia BIT to settle an expropriation dispute between three German nationals and Namibia.[11] The Germans asserted that the way in which the expropriation had been carried out violated the Namibian Constitution and the land reform law, as well as constituting discrimination prohibited by the BIT. While primarily relying on the Namibian Constitution, the decision in favour of the applicants was also based on the BIT:

> As German citizens, the three applicants are entitled to the same treatment as Namibian citizens in terms of the Encouragement and Reciprocal Protection of Investments Treaty ... which was entered into by the Republic of Namibia and the Government of the Federal Republic of Germany.[12]

[8] Ibid 42. See also *Anglo-Iranian Oil Company v Jaffrate (The Rose Mary)*, Supreme Court of Aden [1953] 20 ILR 316, 324–27 (citing French, Polish, German and Italian case law, as well as inter-state arbitral awards, on the question of compensation for expropriation); *Lauritzen v Chile*, Supreme Court of Chile [1955] 23 ILR 208, 716 (referring, on the right of angary, to German, US and Peruvian legislation); *Argentine Necessity Case*, German Constitutional Court, ILDC 952 (DE 2007) para 62 ('An inspection of national case law on the question of State necessity also fails for lack of agreement to suggest that the recognition of State necessity impacting on private-law relationships is established in customary law.'); *Yemen v Compagnie d'Enterprises CFE SA*, Supreme Court of Cyprus, ILDC 630 (CY 2002) (applying the principle of acquired rights to arbitration agreements in cases of successor states).

[9] UNCTAD (n 1) 114. By the end of 2013, the number of IIAs was 3,236 (2,902 BITs and 334 'other IIAs'.)

[10] C Brown (ed), *Commentaries on Selected Model Investment Treaties* (Oxford University Press, 2013).

[11] *Günther Kessl v Minister of Lands and Resettlement*, High Court of Namibia, Case No 27/2006 and 266/2006, 6 March 2008, appended to SL Harring and W Odendaal, '*Kessl*: A New Jurisprudence for Land Reform in Namibia' (April 2008), available at www.lac.org.na/projects/lead/Pdf/kessl.pdf. See also W Ben Hamida, 'Investment Treaties and Domestic Courts: A Transnational Mosaic Reviving Thomas Wälde's Legacy' in J Werner and AH Ali (eds), *A Liber Amicorum: Thomas Wälde Law Beyond Conventional Thought* (Cameron May International Law & Policy, 2009) 69, 74.

[12] Ibid para 106. See also *Case Concerning Kristensen*, Constitutional Court of Latvia, Case No 2009-113-0106, 6 October 2010, available at http://www.satv.tiesa.gov.lv/wp-content/uploads/2009/12/2009-113-0106_Spriedums_ENG.pdf (applying the Latvian Constitution, the Denmark-Latvia BIT and the European Convention on Human Rights to an expropriation claim). For other domestic court decisions on IIA provisions, see eg *Investment Treaty Arbitration*, available at italaw.com/treaty-interpretation. For domestic jurisprudence on friendship treaties, see eg *Town and Country Planning (United States Citizens in Germany) Case*, German Federal Supreme Court [1957] 24 ILR 8, 9 (applying the 1954 German-American Treaty of Friendship to an expropriation claim); *American International Group Inc v Iran*, US

Moreover, court decisions on domestic law may also be of relevance for investor-state tribunals. FET, for instance, has been interpreted to guarantee eg independent and impartial judges, due process and avoidance of undue delay, arbitrariness and discrimination.[13] These 'rule of law' criteria[14] as well as the protection of property[15] are reflected in the domestic laws of most, if not all, states.[16] Thus, in a case from 1931, the US Supreme Court applied the Fifth Amendment to the US Constitution when ruling against the United States in a case brought by a Russian corporation, whose contracts for the construction of two vessels had been requisitioned under a 1917 Act providing for war-time expropriation of ships.[17] The Court held that:

> The Fifth Amendment gives to each owner of property his individual right. The constitutional right of owner A to compensation when his property is taken is irrespective of what may be done somewhere else with the property of owner B. As alien friends are embraced within the terms of the Fifth Amendment, it cannot be said that their property is subject to confiscation here because the property of our citizens may be confiscated in the alien's country. The provision that private property shall not be taken for public use without just compensation establishes a standard for our government which the Constitution does not make dependent upon the standards of other governments ....
>
> Nor do we regard it as an admissible construction of the Act of June 15, 1917, to hold that the Congress intended that the right of an alien friend to recover just compensation should be defeated or postponed because of the lack of recognition by the government of the United States of the regime in his country. A fortiori, as the right to compensation for which the act provided sprang into existence at the time of the taking, there is no ground for saying that the statute was not to apply, if at a later date, and before compensation was actually made, there should be a revolution in the country of the owner and the ensuing regime should not be recognized. The question as presented here is not one of a claim advanced by or on behalf of a foreign government or regime, but is simply one of compensating an owner of property taken by the United States.

District Court, DC [1980] 63 ILR 452 (applying the 1955 US-Iran Treaty of Amity, Economic Relations and Consular Rights, and referring to 1962 UN General Assembly Resolution 1803 in an expropriation claim); *Parzinger e Nowak v Provincia autonoma di Bolzano and Comune di Renon*, Italian Court of Cassation, Decision No 4811, 28 July 1986, (1987) Rivista di diritto internazionale private e processuade 788 (applying the 1957 Germany-Italy Treaty of Friendship, Commerce and Navigation to an expropriation claim).

[13] C Liebscher, 'Monitoring of Domestic Courts in BIT Arbitrations: A Brief Inventory of Some Issues' in C Binder and others (eds), *International Investment Law for the 21st Century: Essays in Honour of Christoph Schreuer* (Oxford University Press, 2009) 105, 123; P Dumberry, 'The Prohibition against Arbitrary Conduct and the Fair and Equitable Treatment Standard under NAFTA Article 1105' (2014) 15(1–2) *Journal of World Investment & Trade* 117, 119.

[14] Cf Report of the Secretary-General Kofi Annan, 23 August 2004, UN Doc S/2004/616 (2004) para 6.

[15] The protection of property may also be seen as a 'rule of law' criterion. See The World Justice Project, 'What is the Rule of Law?', available at worldjusticeproject.org/what-rule-law.

[16] SW Schill, 'Fair and Equitable Treatment under Investment Treaties as an Embodiment of the Rule of Law' Institute for International Law and Justice Working Paper 2006/6, 9, available at www.iilj.org/publications/documents/2006-6-GAL-Schill-web.pdf ('The rule of law is a wide-spread positive legal concept that can be found with similar characteristics in most legal systems that adhere to liberal constitutionalism.' (references omitted)).

[17] *Russian Volunteer Fleet v US*. US Supreme Court, 282 US 481 (1931).

The same 'rule of law' criteria are reflected in human rights law, which domestic courts can also apply in investor–state disputes. One example here is *Blascaod Mór Teoranta v Commissioners of Public Works in Ireland* (1998), which related to a compulsory acquisition of property under the Blascaod Mór National Historic Park Act.[18] Among the many grounds of challenge to the Act, the plaintiffs argued that the 1989 Act was expropriatory in nature and also a discriminatory anti-American measure. Besides Irish law, they relied on the 1950 Treaty of Friendship, Commerce and Navigation between Ireland and the US as well as the European Convention on Human Rights (ECHR). With respect to the 1950 Treaty, the Court held that:

> The contents of the Treaty of Friendship, Commerce and Navigation between Ireland and the USA dated the 21st January, 1950 is not enforceable by individual citizens of the United States or of Ireland against either of the States; being a treaty, it does not take precedence over an Act of the Oireachtas. It is not part of our national law, and does not give rise to a cause of action by an individual.[19]

The plaintiffs were more successful with their human rights arguments. Finding the 1989 Act to be unconstitutional, the Court applied the Irish Constitution's provisions on fundamental rights, citing also jurisprudence of the European Court of Human Rights and the European Court of Justice.[20] Regarding the claim that the Act did not provide a constitutionally adequate or valid mechanism for assessing the quantum of compensation, the Court stated that while 'the issue is to be determined particularly by reference to the Irish Constitution and case law', it found helpful a 'quick survey of the position in kindred jurisdictions'.[21]

A more recent example is a case from 2013 brought by numerous parties from different countries, challenging the Dutch Government's seizure of the bank SNS REAAL's shares and subordinated loans after real estate losses brought the bank to the brink of collapse.[22] In assessing the lawfulness of the expropriation, the Dutch Council of State looked to the ECHR, as well as the Charter of Fundamental Rights of the European Union.[23]

Moreover, a number of states have adopted a special legal regime to attract investment in the form of domestic investment codes with language paralleling international investment law. One example here is a 2004 case brought by a Hong Kong company against the Bangladesh Export Processing Zones Authority.[24] The

[18] *Blascaod Mór Teoranta v Commissioners of Public Works in Ireland*, Irish High Court [1998] IEHC 38. See also Ben Hamida (n 11).

[19] Ibid para 127.

[20] Ibid paras 129, 136, 168–69. See also ibid paras 172, 247 (referring to ECHR Arts 14 and 6).

[21] Ibid paras 217–23. See also ibid paras 61–62, 72–73, 153–54, 173, 187–88, 198–207, 236, 266.

[22] *Vereniging VEB NCVB v Minister van Financiën*, Dutch Council of State, Case No 201301173/1, 25 February 2013.

[23] Ibid paras 7–8, 33. See also *Plexus Investments USA Inc and Northlight Oil AS v Ministry of the Environment*, Norwegian Supreme Court, ILDC 1327 (NO 2008) (applying to an expropriation claim the 1814 Constitution of Norway and the 1999 Act relating to the strengthening of the status of human rights in Norwegian law, and relying on European Court of Human Rights jurisprudence).

[24] *Northpole (BD) Ltd v Bangladesh Export Processing Zones Authority*, Bangladesh Supreme Court, ILDC 478 (BD 2004).

company argued that the decision to remove tents from the list of products it had previously been granted permission to manufacture was arbitrary and discriminatory. It invoked the 1980 Foreign Private Investment Act of Bangladesh, which in Sections 4 and 5 provides that:

> 4. Protection and equitable treatment—The government shall accord fair and equitable treatment to foreign private investment which shall enjoy full protection and security in Bangladesh.
>
> 5. Terms of sanction, etc: The terms of sanction, permission or licence granted by the government to an industrial undertaking having foreign private investment shall not be unilaterally changed so as to adversely alter the conditions under which the establishment of such undertaking was sanctioned; nor shall foreign private investment be accorded a less favourable treatment than what is accorded to similar private investment by the citizens of Bangladesh in the application of relevant rules and regulations.[25]

In holding in favour of the company, the Bangladesh Supreme Court stated:

> The petitioner having invested millions of dollars for setting up a tent manufacturing industry is not being allowed to utilise his investment for the export market due to deliberate withholding of decision from the respondent No. 1 for reasons not known to them and such inaction can at best be considered arbitrary and unreasonable.[26]

It further held:

> Government action must be passed as per law and the law itself must be reasonable and fair with reference to some legitimate object to be achieved. Democratic formal Government demands equality and absence of arbitrariness and discrimination. There must be fairness in Government dealings based on the principle of rationality, duty to act promptly and ensure fair play and economic due process.[27]

These are just a few examples of relevant domestic court decisions in the area of foreign investment law. In the following, we consider the legal bases for an arbitral tribunal to take into account such decisions when solving investor-state disputes.

## III. LEGAL BASES FOR REFERRING TO DOMESTIC LAW AND JURISPRUDENCE

Taking Article 38(1) of the Statute of the International Court of Justice (ICJ) as our starting point, it is uncontroversial that domestic sources can constitute elements in the formation and identification of international law. A first possibility for arbitrators to draw from domestic sources is when determining customary international law. The IIA provision invoked by the foreign investor may reflect custom, and custom can also constitute a separate cause of action depending on the dispute

[25] Ibid para 9.
[26] Ibid para 10.
[27] Ibid para 12.

settlement clause.[28] It is generally accepted that domestic legislation and jurisprudence can be consulted for evidence of state practice and *opinio juris*.[29]

Second, treaty provisions may find a parallel normative source in general principles of law. Fair and equitable treatment has been stated to constitute such a principle applicable to the investor-state relationship:

> The notions of FET form core elements of any legal system—of any legal 'family' or 'tradition' .... As most developed and developing countries recognize in their domestic laws that FET ought to be applied to foreign investments and investors, one has to conclude that FET is a general principle of law in the realm of foreign investment. This is the case, even though the term FET itself may not be applied as such, but the content of FET, namely the absence of arbitrary action of courts and governmental agencies, is found in national provisions.[30]

Since general principles of law derive from 'the consistent provisions of the various municipal legal systems',[31] arbitration tribunals can rely on domestic law and jurisprudence when interpreting IIA provisions.[32] In fact, it is likely that reliance by tribunals on domestic law and jurisprudence was envisaged by the drafters of some IIAs. For instance, the US Model BIT (2012) includes in the definition of FET 'the obligation not to deny justice in criminal, civil, or administrative adjudicatory proceedings in accordance with the principle of due process embodied in the principal legal systems of the world'.[33]

Third, Article 38(1)(d) ICJ Statute stipulates that judicial decisions may be considered as subsidiary means for the determination of rules of law. Hence, it could for instance be possible for a tribunal to refer to a decision by a domestic court applying an international norm on due process, or to a judgment in which the court interprets domestic legislation on the right to property in the light of international law.[34]

[28] Cf *Chevron Corporation and Texaco Petroleum Corporation v Ecuador*, Partial Award on Merits, 30 March 2010 (Böckstiegel, Brower, van den Berg arbs) IIC 421 (2010) para 209.

[29] T Treves, 'Customary International Law' in R Wolfrum (ed), *The Max Planck Encyclopedia of Public International Law* (Oxford University Press, November 2006) para 26, available at mpepil.com. But see PM Moremen, 'National Court Decisions as State Practice: A Transnational Judicial Dialogue?' (2006) 32(2) *North Carolina Journal of International Law & Commercial Regulation* 259, 308 ('[T]here are various difficulties in relying on national court decisions as evidence of custom.')

[30] A Diehl, *The Core Standard of International Investment Protection* (Kluwer, 2012) 173–74.

[31] H Thirlway, *The Law and Procedure of the International Court of Justice: Fifty Years of Jurisprudence*, vol I (Oxford University Press, 2013) 233. See also Restatement (Third) of the Foreign Relations Law of the United States s 102 (1987).

[32] JW Salacuse and NP Sullivan, 'Do BITs Really Work?: An Evaluation of Bilateral Investment Treaties and their Grand Bargain' in KP Sauvant and LE Sachs (eds) *The Effect of Treaties on Foreign Direct Investment: Bilateral Investment Treaties, Double Taxation Treaties, and Investment Flows* (Oxford University Press, 2009) 109, 159.

[33] US Model BIT (2012) Art 5(2)(a). Cf Liebscher (n 13) 122–23 (on the 2004 US Model BIT). See also France-Guatemala BIT Art 4(1); Dominican Republic-Central America-US Free Trade Agreement Art 10.5(2)(a); Columbia Model Investment Treaty Art III(4)(a). See also A Roberts, 'Clash of Paradigms: Actors and Analogies Shaping the Investment Treaty System (2013) 107 *The American Journal of International Law* 45, 82.

[34] Cf H Thirlway, *The Sources of International Law* (Oxford University Press, 2014) 124–26. But see A Pellet, 'Article 38' in A Zimmerman and others (eds), *The Statute of the International Court of Justice: A Commentary* (Oxford University Press, 2006) 731, 862 ('[T]hese decisions should better be treated as elements of State practice in the customary process or, maybe, as being at the crossroads between evidence of practice and *opinio juris*.' (references omitted)).

The Vienna Convention on the Law of Treaties (VCLT) provides other avenues for tribunals to consider domestic court decisions. First, they can be viewed as 'subsequent practice' providing evidence of how states parties understand their treaty obligations.[35] Yet this might be difficult, as the conduct must be 'concordant', that is, the treaty parties have done essentially the same thing expressly in pursuance of the treaty; and for unilateral conduct, it must reveal the agreement of the other party or parties.[36] A second and more promising avenue is Article 31(1)(3)(c) VCLT which provides that when interpreting a treaty, account shall be taken of 'any relevant rule of international law applicable in the relations between the parties'.[37] As noted by Simma and Kill, human rights law qualifies as 'relevant rules' within the meaning of this Article.[38] In light of the foregoing discussion of Article 38(1) ICJ Statute, it would seem that in interpreting 'relevant rules', investor-state tribunals could consider also domestic (human rights) law and jurisprudence.

Further, the IIA itself may provide reasons for relying on domestic law and jurisprudence. Many investments explicitly allow the foreign investor to invoke the norm—national or international—that offers the best protection.[39] For example, the Greece-Romania BIT stipulates:

> If the provisions of law of either Contracting Party or obligations under international law existing at present or established hereafter between the Contracting Parties in addition to this Agreement, contain a regulation, whether general or specific, entitling investments by investors of the other Contracting Party to a treatment more favourable than is provided for by this Agreement, such regulation shall to the extent that it is more favourable, prevail over this Agreement.[40]

In *Middle East Cement Shipping and Handling Company SA v Egypt* (2002), the Tribunal considered that an identical clause in the Egypt-Greece BIT 'requires the application of additional provisions ... if more favourable for the investor', and even when they are not more favourable, such provisions can be 'taken into account' in order to 'supplement' rules set out in the BIT.[41]

Last, but not least, IIAs often list domestic law as part of the applicable substantive law.[42] The UK-Argentina BIT, for example, provides that disputes between investors and host states shall be decided 'in accordance with the provisions of this Agreement, the laws of the Contracting Party involved in the dispute, including its

[35] 1969 Vienna Convention on the Law of Treaties (VCLT), 1155 UNTS 331, Art 31(3)(b); R Gardiner, *Treaty Interpretation* (Oxford University Press, 2008) 228–30. (Practice may consist of executive, legislative, and judicial acts.)

[36] Gardiner (n 35) 227.

[37] VCLT (n 35) Art 31(3)(c).

[38] B Simma and T Kill, 'Harmonizing Investment Protection and International Human Rights: First Steps Towards a Methodology' in C Binder and others (eds), *International Investment Law for the 21st Century: Essays in Honour of Christoph Schreuer* (Oxford University Press, 2009) 678, 695–70.

[39] Kjos (n 3) 300–301.

[40] Greece-Romania BIT, Art 10.

[41] *Middle East Cement Shipping and Handling Company SA v Egypt*, ICSID Case No ARB/99/6, Award, 12 April 2002 (Böckstiegel, Bernardini, Wallace Jr arbs) IIC 169 (2002).

[42] Kjos (n 3) 6–7.

rules on conflicts of laws, the terms of any specific agreement concluded in relation to such an investment and the applicable principles of international law'.[43] Domestic law can also be relied upon in cases where the IIA does not stipulate the applicable law, for example, by virtue of Article 42(1) of the International Centre for Settlement of Investment Disputes (ICSID) Convention which provides for the application of domestic law and international law in the absence of party agreement.[44] When the disputants invoke norms from both legal orders, the frequent reliance by arbitrators on consistency not only demonstrates the importance arbitrators place on reaching a mutually acceptable solution, but also instances the simultaneous applicability of both national and international law to the investor-state relationship.[45]

## IV. REFERENCE TO DOMESTIC LAW AND JURISPRUDENCE: EXAMPLES, REASONS AND OBSTACLES

Arbitrators may thus draw from and sometimes apply domestic law and jurisprudence in investor-state arbitration. As was just noted, many examples can be offered of tribunals emphasising normative convergence between national and international law; and arbitrators often refer to the national law of the host State in support of their findings on the substantive applicable law.[46]

One example is the *Loewen* case (2004), in which the Tribunal cited US jurisprudence when observing that:

> In the United States and in other jurisdictions, advocacy which tends to create an atmosphere of hostility to a party because it appeals to sectional or local prejudice, has been consistently condemned and is a ground for holding that there has been a mistrial, at least where the conduct amounts to an irreparable injustice.[47]

We can also refer to *Sempra v Argentina* (2007), where the Tribunal stated:

> [T]he obligations and commitments which the Argentine Republic owed in relation to the License were not observed. Whether the question is examined from the point of view of the Constitution, the Civil Code or Argentine administrative law, the conclusion is no different ... [T]hese conclusions are no different from those that could be reached under the Treaty and international law.[48]

[43] UK-Argentina BIT Art 8(4).

[44] 1965 Convention on the Settlement of Investment Disputes between States and Nationals of Other States (ICSID Convention), 575 UNTS 159, Art 42(1). See also UNCITRAL Arbitration Rules as revised in 2010, GA Res 65/22, UN GAOR, 65th Session, 57th plen mtg, UN Doc A/RES/65/22 (6 December 2010) Art 35(1).

[45] Kjos (n 3) 271ff, 301.

[46] Ibid 271–93.

[47] *Loewen v US*, ICSID Case No ARB(AF)98/3, Award, 26 June 2003 (Mason, Mustill, Mikva arbs) IIC 225 (2004) para 123 (citing *New York Central RR Company v Johnson* 279 US 310, 319 (1929); *Le Blanc v American Honda Motor Company Inc* 688 A 2d 556, 559; *Walt Disney World Company v Blalock* 640 So 2d 1156, 1158; *Whitehead v Food Max of Mississippi Inc* 163 F 3d 265, 276–78; *Norma v Gloria Farms Inc* 668 So 2d 1016, 1021, 1023; *Pappas v Middle Earth Condominium Association* 963 F 2d 534 539, 540; *Koufakis v Carvel* 425 F 2d 892, 900).

[48] *Sempra Energy International v Argentine Republic*, ICSID Case No ARB/0/16, Award, 18 September 2007 (Vicuña, Lalonde, Rico, arbs) IIC 304 (2007) para 268.

The case *Desert Line Projects v Republic of Yemen* (2008) is also illustrative.[49] Having found that the respondent had violated the BIT's FET provision by exerting pressure on the claimant to sign a settlement agreement subsequent to the rendering of an arbitral award in favour of the claimant, the Tribunal concluded that the award had to be implemented in its entirety. According to the Tribunal:

> This conclusion emerges from the combined effect of two basic rules having paramount place within the Yemeni legal order and shared by all other systems of law as well as by international law .... First, *pacta sunt servanda* .... Second, the mandatory implication of the fundamental general principle of law commonly known as the legal doctrine of estoppel, which originated over twelve centuries ago in the Islamic Jurisprudence ... the precise wording of which can be translated in English to read: 'whoever tries to undo what he previously undertook, such act on his part shall be turned against him.'[50]

Other tribunals, while not explicitly citing domestic law, have supported a comparative approach. In *Total v Argentina* (2010), it was stated:

> In determining the scope of a right or obligation, Tribunals have often looked as a benchmark to international or comparative standards. Indeed, as is often the case for general standards applicable in any legal system (such as 'due process'), a comparative analysis of what is considered generally fair or unfair conduct by domestic public authorities in respect of private firms and investors in domestic law may also be relevant to identify the legal standards under BITs. Such an approach is justified because, factually, the situations and conduct to be evaluated under a BIT occur within the legal system and social, economic and business environment of the host State. Moreover, legally, the fair and equitable treatment standard is derived from the requirement of good faith which is undoubtedly a general principle of law under Article 38(1) of the Statute of the International Court of Justice.[51]

A similar reference to domestic legal systems was made by the Tribunal in *Mobil Corporation v Venezuela* (2010):

> The Tribunal first observes that in all systems of law, whether domestic or international, there are concepts framed in order to avoid misuse of the law. Reference may be made in this respect to good faith ('bonne foi'), 'détournement de pouvoir' (misuse of power) or 'abus de droit' (abuse of right).[52]

And according to the Tribunal in *Toto v Lebanon* (2012): 'The fair and equitable treatment standard of international law does not depend on the perception of the frustrated investor, but should use public international law and comparative domestic public law as a benchmark.'[53]

[49] *Desert Line Projects (DLP) v Republic of Yemen*, ICSID Case No ARB/05/17, Award, 6 February 2008 (Tercier, Paulsson, El-Kosheri, arbs) 319 IIC (2008).

[50] Ibid paras 205–207.

[51] *Total SA v Argentina*, ICSID Case No ARB/04/1, Decision on Liability, 21 December 2010 (Sacerdoti, Álvarez, Marcano arbs) IIC 484 (2010) para 111.

[52] *Mobil Corporation Venezuela Holdings BV and Others v Venezuela*, ICSID Case No ARB/07/27, Decision on Jurisdiction, 10 June 2010 (Guillaume, Kaufmann-Kohler, El-Kosheri arbs) IIC 435 (2010) para 169.

[53] *Toto Costruzioni Generali SPA v Lebanon*, ICSID Case No ARB/07/12, Award, 30 May 2012 (van Houtte, Schwebel, Moghaizel arbs) IIC 545 (2012) para 166.

This approach has been encouraged by scholars as a means to give substance and meaning to IIA provisions, but also to help balance investment protection and non-investment concerns. To Schill, for instance: 'While the arbitral jurisprudence continuously develops a more precise meaning of fair and equitable treatment, it nevertheless meanders around without any clear conceptual vision of the principle's function.'[54] He therefore suggests that 'tribunals should draw—in a comparative approach—on the jurisprudence of domestic and international courts on rule of law standards in order to further concretize fair and equitable treatment'.[55]

Montt also favours a comparative study of domestic legal systems.[56] To him, the best perspective is '*BITs-as-developed-countries-constitutional-law-and-no-more*', referring in particular to jurisprudence from the US, France, Germany and the European Court of Human Rights.[57] According to Montt, this methodology can ensure that IIAs positively influence the domestic laws of developing countries and increase the rule of law not only for foreign investors, but more generally.[58]

Relatedly, reliance by tribunals on domestic law, including human rights law, can have the effect of progressive development as well as contributing to less fragmentation. Wälde explains:

> [T]erms and concepts used in investment law (eg fair and equitable treatment, indirect expropriation, denial of justice, due process) should reflect the progress of law in the specialized fields of international, but also national law. The concept of 'general principles of law recognized by civilized nations' of Article 38(1)(c) of the ICJ statute allows us to take into account not just significant progress in special areas of international law (eg the guarantees of a fair judicial procedure under Article 6 of the ECHR), but also, identified through a comparative public law approach, common approaches to due process and good governance, indirect expropriation, scope of anti-avoidance measures in tax law, or mine reclamation standards, to name but a few.[59]

An additional reason why tribunals might point to domestic law concerns the legitimacy of the award vis-à-vis the respondent state. Apart from the fact that references to both domestic and international law avoids or mitigates a potentially controversial finding on the applicable law, the award will also be more persuasive, especially

[54] Schill (n 16) 37.

[55] Ibid. Cf SW Schill, 'Comparative Public Law Methodology in International Investment Law' EJIL *Talk!*, 3 January 2014, available at www.ejiltalk.org/comparative-public-law-methodology-in-international-investment-law (listing purposes and effects of comparative public analysis, eg to help balance investment protection and non-investment concerns; to ensure consistency in the interpretation and application of IIAs; to ensure cross-regime consistency and mitigate the negative effects of fragmentation; to legitimise existing arbitral jurisprudence if solutions adopted are analogous to those of domestic courts or other international courts or tribunals; to suggest changes to arbitral practice in view of different, or more nuanced, solutions; to suggest changes to the current practice of investor-State arbitration; and to develop general principles of law in the sense of Art 38(1)(c) of the ICJ Statute).

[56] Montt (n 5) 165–67.

[57] Ibid 369 (emphasis in original); ibid 21–23, 75.

[58] Ibid 80–82.

[59] TW Wälde, 'Interpreting Investment Treaties: Experiences and Examples' in C Binder and others (eds), *International Investment Law for the 21st Century: Essays in Honour of Christoph Schreuer* (Oxford University Press, 2009) 724, 774 (references omitted).

for the party who is unsuccessful on the merits.[60] As noted by Paulsson, the value of referring to domestic law 'is that the outcome is shown not to be an international imposition on national law, but a vibrant affirmation of that same law'.[61]

The recent case *Lahoud v Democratic Republic of the Congo* (DRC) (2014) illustrates the interrelationship between domestic and international law pertaining to the investor-state relationship.[62] It is also instructive in that it offers a reason why tribunals do not look to domestic law when assessing court behaviour: lack of reliance on such law by the disputants.

The arbitration proceedings were initiated by a Lebanese couple following a dispute about rental premises and the couple's eviction and subsequent folding of their business. The DRC investment code provided for fair and equitable treatment 'in conformity with the principles of international law'.[63] It also included criteria for expropriation, without an explicit reference to international law.[64] The Tribunal observed that the parties had offered little argumentation on the question concerning the applicable law in the written and oral pleadings.[65] Thereafter, and at the request of the Tribunal, the claimants gave reasons for the application of international law and relied on international law sources;[66] while the respondent state pleaded the application of its domestic law.[67] In light of the lack of agreement, the Tribunal held that it would apply both the domestic law of the host state and international law, in accordance with Article 42(1) of the ICSID Convention.[68]

Still, the decision on the merits in favour of Lahoud was rendered solely by reference to international law. While it quoted from the Constitution's provision on

[60] Kjos (n 3) 273–74.

[61] J Paulsson, 'Unlawful Laws and the Authority of International Tribunals' (2008) 23(2) *ICSID Review* 215, 230. See also O Lando, 'The Law Applicable to the Merits of the Dispute' in JDM Lew and others (eds), *Contemporary Problems in International Arbitration* (Centre for Commercial Law Studies, 1986) 101, 107–108; *Sociedad Minera el Teniente SA v Norddeutsche Affinerie AG*, Provisional Court of Hamburg, Germany [1973] ILR 230, 239, 245 (referring in support to a 1964 decision of the Supreme Court of Chile); and by analogy Rome Statute of the International Court, 17 July 1998, UN Doc A/ CONF.183, Art 21(1)(c) ('The Court shall apply … general principles of law derived by the Court from national laws of legal systems of the world including, as appropriate, the national laws of States that would normally exercise jurisdiction over the crime …').

[62] *Antoine Abou Lahoud and Leila Bounafeh-Abou Lahoud v Democratic Republic of the Congo*, ICSID Case No ARB/10/4, Final Award, 7 February 2014 (Park, Hafez, Ngwe arbs) IIC 637 (2014) (in French).

[63] Ibid para 359 (referring to DRC Investment Code, Art 25: 'La République Démocratique du Congo s'engage à assurer un traitement juste et équitable, conformément aux principes du droit international, aux investisseurs et aux investissements effectués sur son territoire, et à faire en sorte que l'exercice du droit ainsi reconnu ne soit entravé ni en droit, ni en fait.')

[64] Ibid para 362 (referring to DRC Investment Code, Art 26. 'Les droits de propriété individuelle ou collective acquis par un investisseur sont garantis par la Constitution de la République Démocratique du Congo. Un investissement ne peut pas être, directement ou indirectement, dans sa totalité ou en partie, nationalisé ou exproprié par une nouvelle loi, et/ou d'une décision d'une autorité locale ayant le même effet, excepté: pour des motifs d'utilité publique et moyennant le payement d'une juste et équitable indemnité compensatoire.')

[65] Ibid para 305.

[66] Ibid paras 351–53.

[67] Ibid paras 354–55 (own translation).

[68] Ibid paras 358, 364.

expropriation,[69] the Tribunal justified the lack of reference to domestic law by noting on several occasions that apart from the copy of the Constitution, neither party had submitted any authority on Congolese law as concerned FET and expropriation.[70]

Although arbitrators certainly could conduct their own investigation of domestic law, the principle *jura novit curia* (the court knows the law) does not generally impose on tribunals a duty to go beyond requesting relevant material and to consider material submitted by the parties.[71] If the parties fail to do so, it is difficult to see how arbitrators should be required to draw on domestic law and jurisprudence to further concretise applicable norms; especially considering the additional time and costs involved.[72] Keeping in mind also the difficulties involved in comparative law research,[73] this observation applies with even greater force to the proposition that arbitrators should draw not just from the law of the respondent state but from a multitude of jurisdictions.

The award in *Saar Papier Vertriebs GmbH v Poland* (1995) stands out in this respect, as the arbitrators looked to domestic law without much assistance from the parties.[74] It is also noteworthy in that it illustrates the consubstantial nature of foreign investment law. The case concerned a claim by a German company that the prohibition on importation of raw material for its production of tissue rolls and toilet paper constituted indirect expropriation in violation of the Germany-Poland BIT. While the facts were not disputed, the parties disagreed on the law.[75] According

[69] Ibid para 492 (quoting from the Transitional Constitution, Art 37: 'L'expropriation pour cause d'intérêt général ou d'utilité publique ne peut intervenir qu'en vertu d'une loi prévoyant le versement préalable d'une indemnité équitable. Nul ne peut être saisi en ses biens qu'en vertu d'une décision prise par une autorité judiciaire compétente').

[70] Ibid paras 365, 437, 476, 491. Cf *Biloune and Marine Drive Complex Ltd v Ghana Investments Centre and the Government of Ghana*, Award on Jurisdiction and Liability, 27 October 1989 (Schwebel, Wallace, Lee arbs) 95 ILR 183, Section VI ('neither Party brought to the attention of the Tribunal any interpretation of ... the prohibition of expropriation, peculiar to the law of Ghana').

[71] HE Kjos, 'Knowing the Law: A Power or a Duty? The Role of Arbitrators and Counsel in Ascertaining the Applicable Law in Investor-State Arbitration' paper presented at the ESIL Research Forum (Amsterdam, May 2013) 40–42.

[72] Cf JE Alvarez, 'Beware: Boundary Crossings (draft 19 March 2013) (forthcoming as a chapter in Tsvi Kahana and Anat Schnicov (eds), *Boundaries of Rights, Boundaries of State*) 28, available at https://www.law.yale.edu/sites/default/files/documents/pdf/sela/Bewareboundarycrossings_nofootnotes_(2).pdf ('BIT parties and investors originally turned to investor-state arbitration, in all likelihood, at least in part because it is supposed to be a party-driven adversarial process focused on solving the particular dispute and not on the making systemic precedents. The appeal of arbitration, after all, is that these characteristics make it presumptively less expensive and more expeditious than domestic courts.'); WW Park, 'Arbitrators and Accuracy' (2010) 1 *Journal of International Dispute Settlement* 25, 28 ('On a small street in downtown Boston stands a shoe repair shop with a proactive approach to customer complaints. In the window, an equilateral triangle links three options: fast service, low price, high quality. "Pick any two", patrons are advised.').

[73] VS Vadi, *Critical Comparisons: The Role of Comparative Law in Investment Treaty Arbitration* (2010–2011) 39(1) *Denver Journal of International Law and Policy* 67; Schill, EJIL *Talk!* (n 55) (recognising the need for 'rigorous methodology'); Alvarez (n 72) 40-42 (warning of unintended consequences of the comparative public law approach).

[74] *Saar Papier Vertriebs GmbH v Poland*, Final Award, 16 October 1995 (Karrer, Szurski, Ahrens arbs). See also J Hepburn, 'Comparative Public Law at the Dawn of Investment Treaty Arbitration: *Saar Papier Vertriebs GmbH v Republic of Poland*' (2014) 15(3–4) *Journal of World Investment & Trade* 705.

[75] Ibid paras 23–24.

to the Tribunal, 'administrative law practice in Germany and Poland would be helpful',[76] and it had asked the parties to be prepared to discuss at the hearing '"the law of expropriation matérielle" and "Vertrauensschutz im Verwaltungsrecht [legitimate expectations in administrative law]", under the laws of Poland and Germany, and in comparative law, including the [ICSID] Convention and ICSID awards'.[77] Despite repeated requests, the Tribunal received little help from the parties on German and Polish administrative law.[78] For this reason, it relied on its own understanding of general administrative law and the principle of good faith when interpreting the BIT.[79]

Before concluding that Poland was liable for indirect expropriation, the arbitrators considered two approaches in administrative law practice that 'converge to deal with this type of problem'. The first originated in the constitutional guarantee of the right to property.[80] Here, they relied on German administrative law, and particularly the *Sonderopfer*-theory on special sacrifice.[81] The second approach started from the proposition that there is an obligation of good faith in public law which applies to all branches of government.[82] Here, the Tribunal quoted from the Swiss Supreme Court setting out various circumstances in which originally wrong information by a state authority entails a right to compensation.[83]

## V. CONCLUSION

In conclusion, we recall the substantive overlap between domestic and international sources on foreign investment law. A few examples were given of the many domestic court decisions to which investor-state tribunals could refer, and we considered legal bases for engaging in such practice.

More normative reasons that have been offered for referring to domestic jurisprudence include the need to concretise and/or limit the scope of open-ended IIA provisions, which also helps balance investment protection and non-investment concerns. However, it appears that while several tribunals have supported a comparative law approach, they generally only expressly refer to the domestic law and jurisprudence of the respondent state. This is not surprising considering that this law also governs the investor-state relationship; and even when not directly applicable in the arbitration proceedings, taking it into account may enhance the legitimacy of the award for the disputants.

When tribunals follow Paulsson's recommendation to resort to domestic law, they might even be seen to engage in a converse form of *dédoublement fonctionelle* in

[76] Ibid para 79.
[77] Ibid para 15.
[78] Ibid para 79. See also ibid para16.
[79] Ibid para 79.
[80] Ibid paras 79–80.
[81] Ibid paras 80–91.
[82] Ibid para 92.
[83] Ibid paras 92–94.

the sense suggested by Scelle.[84] To Paulsson, 'when a government has overreached, when it has cowed legislators or judges, when it has followed a practice of weakening the judiciary, even citizens of the country whose law is in question may come to see the international tribunal as a defender of enduring national values'.[85] As we thereby can compare the role of investor-state arbitration tribunals to that of agents of the domestic legal order of the respondent State, this approach demonstrates how arbitrators can play an important contribution 'in advancing the rule of law at the international and national levels'.[86]

From the perspective of the larger theme of the 2014 European Society of International Law (ESIL) Conference agora on 'National Law as a Generator of International Law', such practice also illustrates a 'pendulum effect' with respect to the national and international dimensions of foreign investment law: international investment law may originate in domestic law and when applying international law, tribunals may inform its interpretation by reference to domestic law. However, this possibility does not only lie in the hands of the arbitrators. Legal counsel play a crucial role in presenting to tribunals relevant domestic material. Scholars can certainly help in that respect; first, in pointing to and demonstrating the possibilities that lie in the interplay between national and international law, and second, in unearthing and shedding light on relevant domestic law and jurisprudence.

[84] Paulsson (n 61) 232; G Scelle, 'La phénomène juridique de dédoublement fonctionnel' in W Schätzel and HJ Schlochauer (eds), *Rechtsfragen der Internationalen Organisation: Festschrift für Hans Wehberg zu seinem 70. Geburtstag* (Klosterman, 1956) 324; H Lauterpacht, *International Law: Being the Collected Papers of Hersch Lauterpacht* Vol 2 (Cambridge University Press, 1970) 567 (domestic courts may 'regard themselves, in addition to their normal function, as administering a law of a unit greater than the State').

[85] Paulsson (n 61) 232.

[86] Declaration of the High-level Meeting of the General Assembly on the Rule of Law at the National and International Levels ('GA Declaration'), A/RES/67/1 (30 November 2012) para 32.

# 6

# *National Case Law as a Generator of International Refugee Law: Rectifying an Imbalance within the UNHCR Guidelines on International Protection*

CECILIA M BAILLIET*

## I. INTRODUCTION

THE EVOLUTION OF international refugee law is marked by the fact that it lacks an international refugee court to provide authoritative statements on the interpretation of the 1951 Convention on the Status of Refugees. Instead, it relies on soft law guidelines produced by the United Nations High Commissioner for Refugees (UNHCR); and case law issued at the national level by refugee tribunals, administrative agencies, and other courts; as well as decisions from international courts for other regimes, such as human rights or international criminal law. There are initiatives to promote transnational judicial dialogues, such as the International Association of Refugee Law Judges, but these have been criticised as having 'no real impact' at the European level.[1]

In 2000, the UNHCR convened Global Consultations on International Protection with academic experts, governments, the International Association of Refugee Law Judges, legal practitioners and NGOs in order to pursue 'greater clarity and coherence of interpretation' of the 1951 Convention on the Status of Refugees.[2] The papers commissioned for the Global Consultations served as background notes for the elaboration of soft law guidelines. Volker Türk, the Director of International Protection at UNHCR headquarters, noted that: 'Their purpose was to take stock of the state of law and practice in these areas, to consolidate the various positions taken and to develop concrete recommendations on the way forward to achieve

* Professor, Department of Public & International Law/PluriCourts University of Oslo, Norway.
I warmly thank Laura Letourneau-Tremblay for her helpful research assistance.

[1] See Guy S Goodwin-Gill and Helene Lambert, *The Limits of Transnational Law: Refugee Law, Policy Harmonization and Judicial Dialogue in the European Union* (Cambridge University Press, 2010) 9.

[2] Erika Feller, Volker Türk and Frances Nicholson, *Refugee Protection in International Law: UNHCR's Global Consultations on International Protection* (Cambridge University Press, 2003) xv.

more consistent understandings of these various interpretative issues.'[3] The Background Papers led to the publication of *Guidelines on International Protection*, which are characterised as issued pursuant to the UNHCR's supervisory role under its Statute and the 1951 Convention.[4] To date, the UNHCR has produced ten official *Guidelines on International Protection* addressing: gender-related persecution, 'membership of a particular social group', cessation of refugee status, internal flight alternative, exclusion clauses (for persons who have committed crimes against peace, war crimes, crimes against humanity, or serious non-political crimes), religion-based claims, victims of trafficking, child asylum claims, claims based on sexual orientation and/or gender identity, and claims related to military service.[5] These issues present challenging interpretation dilemmas according to the 1951 Convention on the Status of Refugees, and the guidelines are intended to provide 'UNHCR's authoritative legal position on the various interpretive issues that arise and to provide legal guidance for governments, legal practitioners, decision-makers and the judiciary'.[6]

Türk explains that the UNHCR is a type of treaty-monitoring body of the 1951 Convention and that the 'issuance of the Guidelines has been preceded by an analysis of State practice (including jurisprudence) and an examination of the applicable international legal framework'.[7] According to the UNHCR, they are intended to have an authoritative status because of the process behind the drafting of the guidelines, consisting of the production of a Background Note, a Consultation and an Expert Roundtable. The Roundtables include representatives from governments, NGOs, academia, the judiciary and the legal profession, producing Summary Conclusions which reflect the discussions held.[8] The *Guidelines on International Protection* are linked to the 1979 *UNHCR Handbook on Procedures and Criteria for Determining Refugee Status* (hereinafter *Handbook*) which was intended to provide states with guidance on the meaning and interpretation of the 1951 Convention. However, the *Handbook* itself has been subject to debate as to whether it is to be viewed as persuasive, discretionary, or mandatory.[9] Indeed, North and Chia note that with regard to the *Handbook* 'It remains true, at least in Australian courts, that where there is a conflict of opinion, greater weight is generally accorded to decisions

[3] Volker Türk, Introductory Note to UNHCR, *Guidelines on International Protection* (2003) 15(2) *International Journal of Refugee Law* 303.

[4] Feller et al (n 2) 9 citing the Stature of the Office of the United Nations High Commissioner for Refugees, A/RES/428 (V), 14 December 1950, Art 35 of the 1951 Convention, and Art II of the 1967 Protocol.

[5] The UNHCR *Guidelines on International Protection* are available at www.unhcr.org/cgi-bin/texis/vtx/search/?page=&comid=4a2789926&cid=49aea93ae2&keywords=GIP.

[6] Türk (n 3) 304. The UNHCR Statute sets forth in para 8 that the High Commissioner shall promote the conclusion and ratification of international conventions for the protection of refugees, supervise their application and propose amendments thereto.

[7] Ibid 304.

[8] Feller et al (n 2) 8.

[9] Satvinder Singh Juss, 'The UNHCR Handbook and the Interface between "Soft Law" and "Hard Law" in International Refugee Law' in Satvinder Singh Juss and Colin Harvey (eds), *Contemporary Issues in Refugee Law* (Edward Elgar, 2013) 38.

of other common law courts and learned commentators.'[10] Regarding the *Guidelines on International Protection*, they conclude that they have had some impact in common law jurisdictions, including Australia, the US and Canada, but have been endorsed most enthusiastically so far by the UK.[11] They call for a global character interpretation of the 1951 Convention that will promote consistency. Hence it is necessary to review the *Guidelines on International Protection* to examine whether or not they can be characterised as reflecting a global character.[12]

Goodwin-Gill confirms that the supervisory role of the UNHCR has been interpreted:

> to mean that UNHCR does not have binding authority to interpret the 1951 Convention and, even though states have asked UNHCR to provide 'guidance', they and national courts have emphasised, perhaps all too often, that such views are not binding ... If guidelines are to be treated as authoritative—and courts know full well that they are not 'bound' by what UNHCR may say—then the methodology needs very careful consideration. First, this means identifying novel protection needs with some precision—the area or issue should be one in which guidance is evidently necessary, and where clarification or development of the refugee definition or other provisions of the Convention is feasible. Second, guidelines must be soundly based in basic principles of international law, particularly those related to the interpretation of treaties and the development of customary international law. Third, UNHCR need to recognize, and closely analyse and understand, even if they do not adopt, the reasoning and approaches of national and international courts, as well as the views and practices of other stakeholders in refugee protection.[13]

This contribution will seek to discuss discrepancies in the citation of national case law in the evolution of refugee law within UNHCR *Guidelines on International Protection*. Section II will assess the UNHCR's limited references to national case law in its guidelines. It is suggested that there is a dominance of common law/English-language national decisions which renders UNHCR output subject to legitimacy challenges as it seeks to provide objective guidance on interpretation of the 1951 Convention on the Status of Refugees. It will also discuss the nature of reference to case law from international human rights and criminal tribunals within UNHCR guidelines. Section III will present an alternative view of the importance of transnational judicial dialogues within Refugee Law. Section IV will assess whether the

[10] Anthony M North and Joyce Chia, 'Towards convergence in the interpretation of the Refugee Convention: A Proposal for the Establishment of an International Judicial Commission for Refugees' in James C Simeon, *The UNHCR and the Supervision of International Refugee Law* (Cambridge University Press, 2013) 226.

[11] Ibid 226–27.

[12] North and Chia also advocate the creation of an International Judicial Commission for Refugees, ibid 235–55. Indeed, Jane McAdam confirms that Australian courts make little reference to EU law, more often refer to jurisprudence from the UK, New Zealand and Canada (with exception of cases influenced by the Canadian Charter of Rights and Freedoms which has no parallel in Australia) to explore treaty interpretation. Jane McAdam, 'Migrating Laws? The "plagiaristic dialogue" between Europe and Australia' in Helene Lambert, Jane McAdam and Maryellen Fullerton (eds), *The Global Reach of European Refugee Law* (Cambridge University Press, 2013) 25.

[13] Guy S Goodwin-Gill, 'The Dynamic of International Refugee Law' (2014) 25(4) *International Journal of Refugee Law* 655.

Background Papers demonstrate parallel citation biases. Section V will offer a conclusion calling for greater pluralism in the reference to national case law by the UNHCR in its soft law guidelines and policy documents in order to improve the legitimacy of international refugee law.

As a caveat, it should be noted that there are procedural variances in the production of the *Guidelines on International Protection*, for example, the consultation on sexual orientation and gender occurred *after* the *Guidelines* were issued. The guideline on victims of trafficking was issued without an expert meeting or a background paper. The UNHCR also produces additional *guidance notes* on particular topics (such as on organised criminal gangs, blood feuds, female genital mutilation and so on) but they are considered to be less authoritative than the *Guidelines on International Protection* due to the fact that a simpler process is pursued. Nevertheless, because of the special status of the *Guidelines*, the representativeness of their case citations is of particular interest.

## II. REFERENCE TO NATIONAL AND INTERNATIONAL CASE LAW WITHIN UNHCR GUIDELINES

A review of the *Guidelines* found a clear bias in favour of citation of common law jurisdictions over civil law jurisdictions, and no citations from the developing world whatsoever. In terms of the use of reference to the jurisprudence of international tribunals, UNHCR *Guidelines on International Protection* has turned to these institutions for progressive analysis of the risk or form of persecution, recognition of gender-related persecution, articulation of the state duty to protect against persecution by non-state actors, the need to limit the application of the internal flight alternative, and the scope of the non-refoulement principle.

### A. Guideline on Membership of a Particular Social Group

The Guideline on 'membership of a particular social group' cites only one national case from the High Court of Australia addressing whether the fear of persecution by forcible sterilisation pursuant to China's 'One Child Policy' was legitimate in order to define the particular social group.[14] Nevertheless, Volker Türk states that the *Guidelines* sought to reconcile two approaches arising from common law jurisdictions, protected characteristics and social perception, so the absence of the case references is surprising.[15] The paper did not refer to any cases from international courts, tribunals or committees.

[14] *Applicant A v Minister for Immigration and Ethnic Affairs* (1997) 190 CLR 225, 264, 142 ALR 331 (Australia).

[15] Türk (n 3) 304.

### B. Guideline on Child Asylum Claims

The Guideline on child asylum claims contains citations of Canadian case law (11), US case law (8), Australian case law (7), UK case law (4), New Zealand case law (3), French case law (3) and Belgian case law (1). There is a clear dominance of cases from common law jurisdictions.

However, when we turn to the international level, there is a majority of citations of the Inter-American Court of Human Rights as opposed to the European Court of Human Rights (ECtHR). The *Guidelines* cite the jurisprudence of the Inter-American Court of Human Rights in order to underscore the risk or form of persecution such as that facing street children who may be subjected to violence or murder as part of 'social cleansing'.[16] The relevant *Guideline* additionally relies on the Inter-American Court of Human Rights to ground the perspective that persecution may be established where children with disabilities or stateless children lack access to birth registration and are excluded from education, health care and other services.[17] Further, it refers to an Advisory Opinion by the Inter-American Court to support the call for assessment as to whether or not the State or its agents are unable or unwilling to protect children against persecution by non-State actors (such as gangs, parents, etc.).[18] The Guideline also refers to both the Inter-American Court of Human Rights and the ECtHR's contentious case articulation of an obligation of states to conduct effective investigation and punishment of non-state persecutors.[19] The Guideline also cites case law of the ECtHR to explain how children may have a well-founded fear of persecution if they have witnessed violence or experienced the disappearance or killing of a parent or other person on whom the child depends.[20] It turns to the ECtHR to underscore limits against the application of internal flight alternatives to children, as this may result in inhuman treatment.[21]

[16] *Case of the 'Street Children' (Villagrán-Morales et al) v Guatemala*, Inter-American Court of Human Rights, 19 November 1999, paras 190–91. 'The Court found that there was a prevailing pattern of violence against street children in Guatemala. The Court noted that the State had violated their physical, mental, and moral integrity as well as their right to life and also failed to take any measures to prevent them from living in misery, thereby denying them of the minimum conditions for a dignified life.'

[17] See *Case of the Yean and Bosico Children v The Dominican Republic*, Inter-American Court of Human Rights, 8 September 2005. Two girls of Haitian origin were denied the right to nationality and education because, among other matters, they did not have a birth certificate; *Case of the 'Juvenile Reeducation Institute' v Paraguay*, Inter-American Court of Human Rights, 2 September 2004. The Court found that failure to provide severely marginalised groups with access to basic health-care services constitutes a violation of the right to life.

[18] *Advisory Opinion on Juridical Condition and Human Rights of the Child*, No OC-17/02, Inter-American Court of Human Rights, 28 August 2002.

[19] *Velásquez Rodríguez Case*, Series C, No 4, Inter-American Court of Human Rights, 29 July 1988, para 174; *MC v Bulgaria*, App no 39272/98 (ECtHR, 3 December 2003).

[20] *Cicek v Turkey*, App no 67124/01 (ECtHR, 18 January 2005) paras 173–74; *Bazorkina v Russia*, App no 69481/01 (ECtHR, 27 July 2006) paras 140–41.

[21] *Mubilanzila Mayeka and Kaniki Mitunga v Belgium*, App no 13178/03 (ECtHR, 12 October 2006) which concerned the return (not internal relocation) of an unaccompanied five-year-old girl. The Court was 'struck by the failure to provide adequate preparation, supervision and safeguards for her deportation', noting further that such 'conditions were bound to cause her extreme anxiety and demonstrated such

Finally, the Guideline refers to the Special Court for Sierra Leone which has concluded that the recruitment of children under the age of 15 years into the armed forces constitutes a crime under general international law.[22] Hence, international citations demonstrate a reverse dominance of the South because of the specialised jurisprudence applicable to child protection.

## C. Guideline on Sexual Orientation and/or Gender Identity

The Guideline on sexual orientation and/or gender identity contains more citations of common law: US case law (20 including UNHCR amicus briefs filed in cases), UK case law (10 including UNHCR amicus briefs filed in cases), Canadian case law (9), Australian case law (9), New Zealand case law (3), French case law (3), Belgian case law (3), German case law (1) and Finnish case law (1).

In terms of citation of international cases, the *Guidelines* turn to the UN Human Rights Committee to confirm that the proscribed grounds of 'sex' and 'other status' contained in the non-discrimination clauses of the main international human rights instruments have been accepted as encompassing sexual orientation and gender identity.[23] The *Guidelines* refer to the ECtHR to establish the risk of harm to transgender persons.[24] It refers to the International Criminal Courts to ground the view that rape may constitute persecution, noting that: 'International criminal tribunals in their jurisprudence have broadened the scope of crimes of sexual violence that can be prosecuted as rape to include oral sex and vaginal or anal penetration through the use of objects or any part of the perpetrator's body.'[25] It also sets forth

a total lack of humanity towards someone of her age and in her situation as an unaccompanied minor as to amount to inhuman treatment [violation of Article 3 of the European Convention on Human Rights]' paras 66, 69.

[22] *Prosecutor v Sam Hinga Norman*, Case No SCSL-2004-14-AR72(E), Decision on Preliminary Motion Based on Lack of Jurisdiction (Child Recruitment) 31 May 2004, paras 52–53.

[23] The UN Human Rights Committee held in 1994 in the landmark decision *Toonen v Australia* that the International Covenant on Civil and Political Rights (adopted by the UN General Assembly on 16 December 1966, (ICCPR)) prohibits discrimination on the grounds of sexual orientation, see CCPR/C/50/D/488/1992, 4 April 1994.

[24] The European Court of Human Rights has established that authorities must legally recognise the altered gender. See, *Goodwin v United Kingdom*, App no 28957/95 (ECtHR, 11 July 2002), finding a violation of the applicant's right to privacy, noting that 'the stress and alienation arising from a discordance between the position in society assumed by a post-operative transsexual and the status imposed by law which refuses to recognise the change of gender cannot, in the Court's view, be regarded as a minor inconvenience arising from a formality', para 77, and that 'Under Article 8 of the Convention in particular, the notion of personal autonomy is an important principle underlying the interpretation of its guarantees, protection is given to the personal sphere of each individual, including the right to establish details of their identity as individual human beings' para 90.

[25] See, for instance, *Prosecutor v Anto Furundžija (Trial Judgment)* IT-95-17/1-T, International Criminal Tribunal for the former Yugoslavia (ICTY), 10 December 1998, 185; *Prosecutor v Dragoljub Kunarac, Radomir Kovač and Zoran Vuković* (Appeal Judgment), IT-96-23 and IT-96-23/1-A, ICTY, 12 June 2002, para 128.

that rape may constitute torture, citing case law of the ECtHR.[26] It cites the International Criminal Tribunal for Rwanda (ICTR) to state that rape is also characterised as a violation of dignity.[27]

The *Guidelines* refer to UN Committee on the Elimination of Discrimination Against Women (CEDAW) to discuss corrective surgery as persecution.[28] Moreover, they cite the UN Working Group on Detention to support the view that detention, including in psychological or medical institutions, on the sole basis of sexual orientation and/or gender identity is considered to be in breach of the international prohibition against arbitrary deprivation of liberty and would normally constitute persecution.[29]

Finally, the *Guideline* notes that the UN Human Rights Committee and the Inter-American Commission on Human Rights have concluded that the inaction of States vis-à-vis death threats constitutes a violation of the right to life. It further remarks the discriminatory nature of criminal penalties against same-sex consensual relations.[30] This *Guideline* also refers to secondary sources containing jurisprudence.[31] The Guideline appears to refer to both common law and international jurisprudence to pursue an expansive approach to LGBT protection.

## D. Guideline on Claims related to Military Service

The Guideline on claims related to military service cites only two UK cases. It excludes review of other national jurisprudence, albeit indirect reference is made via the international cases which address other countries, such as Armenia, Finland, France, the Netherlands, Korea and Turkey. At the international level, there are citations from the the UN Human Rights Committee (11), the ECtHR (5), Inter-American Court of Human Rights (2), the Special Court for Sierra Leone (2), the International Criminal Court (ICC) (1), the ICJ (1), and the UN Working Group on Arbitrary Detention (1).

26 *Aydin v Turkey*, 57/1996/676/866, Council of Europe, European Court of Human Rights, 25 September 1997, para 83.

27 *The Prosecutor v Jean-Paul Akayesu* (Trial Judgment), ICTR-96-4-T, International Criminal Tribunal for Rwanda, 2 September 1998, para 687.

28 The assessment needs to focus on whether the surgery or treatment was voluntary and took place with the informed consent of the individual, citing UN Committee on the Elimination of Discrimination against Women (CEDAW), Communication No 4/2004, 29 August 2006, CEDAW/C/36/D/4/2004, which considered non-consensual sterilisation as a violation of women's rights to informed consent and dignity, para 11.3.

29 UN Working Group on Arbitrary Detention, Opinions No 22/2006 on Cameroon and No 42/2008 on Egypt; A/HRC/16/47, annex, para 8(e).

30 Noting *Toonen v Australia* the sodomy law of the territory concerned violated the rights to privacy and equality before the law.

31 International Commission of Jurists, *Sexual Orientation and Gender Identity in Human Rights Law, References to Jurisprudence and Doctrine of the United Nations Human Rights System*, 2010, fourth updated edition, ICJ, *Sexual Orientation and Gender Identity in Human Rights Law, Jurisprudential, Legislative and Doctrinal References from the Council of Europe and the European Union*, October 2007, ICJ, *Sexual Orientation and Gender Identity in Human Rights Law: References to Jurisprudence and Doctrine of the Inter-American System*, July 2007.

These guidelines were eviscerated by Guy Goodwin-Gill who noted that the UNHCR needed to 'closely analyse and understand, even if they do not adopt, the reasoning and approaches of national and international courts ... combining "best law" with progressive development.'[32] He criticised the guidelines for failing to cite an appeals decision by the House of Lords and accepting the views of the UN Human Rights Committee over the jurisprudence of the ECtHR.[33]

The *Guidelines* point out that the UN Human Rights Committee's case law has shifted from characterising the right as derived from the right 'to manifest' one's religion or belief and thus subject to certain restrictions in Article 18(3) to viewing it as one that 'inheres in the right' to freedom of thought, conscience and religion in Article 18(1) itself.[34] The Guideline states: 'The shift suggests that the right to conscientious objection is absolute, and that states may not impose restrictions on the right to freedom of thought, conscience and religion by way of compulsory military service.'

Essentially, the problem is that by framing the right to conscientious objection as absolute, the UNHCR guidelines may then be interpreted as supporting crystallisation of the right of conscientious objection under international customary law. It should be noted that Goodwin-Gill's concern for the lack of citation of the UK House of Lords decision may be given less weight as the legitimacy issue is not resolved just by adding additional common law cases. Instead, I suggest that more attention should be paid to tracing the transnational judicial dialogues addressing particular protection issues and normative interpretive questions within refugee law, as is discussed in the next section.

## III. TRANSNATIONAL JUDICIAL DIALOGUES

There is significant diversity in the interpretation of the 1951 Convention by national tribunals, ranging from variances in the interpretation of 'membership in a particular social group', assessment of cases originating from civil wars, recognition of persecution by non-state agents or gender-related persecution, application of exclusion and cessation clauses, and diverse conceptions of 'effective protection by the state', as well as criteria for return due to an internal flight alternative in the country of

[32] Guy Goodwin-Gill, 'The Dynamic of International Refugee Law' (2014) 25(4) *International Journal of Refugee Law* 651, 657–61.

[33] *Sepet and Bulbul v Secretary of State for the Home Department* (2003) UKHL 15 (2003) 1 WLR 856. See UN Human Rights Committee, *Atasoy and Sarkut v Turkey* Communications Nos 1853/2008 and 1854/2008, Views adopted 12–30 March 2002 UN doc CCPR/C/104/D/1853-1854/2008 19 June 2012. See also *Bayatyan v Armenia* App No 23459/03 (ECtHR Grand Chamber, 7 July 2011); *Savda v Turkey* App No 42730/05 (ECtHR Second Session Judgment, 12 June 2012).

[34] *Atasoy and Sarkut v Turkey* CCPR/C/104/D/1853-1854/2008, UN Human Rights Committee (HRC), 19 June 2012, available at www.refworld.org/docid/4ff5b14c2.html. Note the separate opinions: Individual opinion of Committee member Mr Gerald L Neuman, jointly with members Mr Yuji Iwasawa, Mr Michael O'Flaherty and Mr Walter Kaelin (concurring). See also *Min-Kyu Jeong et al v The Republic of Korea*, CCPR/C/101/D/1642-1741/2007, UN Human Rights Committee (HRC), 27 April 2011, available at www.refworld.org/docid/4ff59b332.html.

origin. North and Chia observe 'Even within the "harmonized" European Union, recognition rates for Iraqi refugees in 2007 ranged from 0 per cent in Greece and Slovakia to 97 per cent in Hungary.'[35] This underscores the importance of guidance by the UNHCR in terms of articulating universal protection standards.

Nevertheless, I suggest that more attention needs to paid to the evolution of the transnational judicial dialogue within refugee law. Specifically, there should be increased reference to national cases within UNHCR *Guidelines* in order to illuminate developments within jurisprudence and its impact on refugee law theory. As an example, one may consider the assessment of deserters who escape conscription into an army and seek asylum abroad, and the issue of whether the desertion itself may be considered to ground a finding of a risk of persecution on account of imputed political opinion. The UNHCR *Guidelines on Military Service* address this issue in Paragraph 52 without reference to national case law:

> Depending on the facts, an objection to military service ... may be viewed through the prism of actual or imputed political opinion. In relation to the latter, the authorities may interpret the individual's opposition to participating in a conflict or in act(s) as a manifestation of political disagreement with its policies. The act of desertion or evasion may in itself be, or be perceived to be, an expression of political views.

In 2011, the Norwegian Immigration Appeals Board granted asylum to 40 Eritreans based on the finding that they would risk persecution upon return due to the fact that the Eritrean state authorities would *impute a political opinion* to them on account of their desertion.[36] This perspective was reflective of a decision issued the same year by the Australian Refugee Review Tribunal (RRTA) which held that 'there is a real chance that the applicant will face persecution in Eritrea because an adverse political opinion will be attributed to him by the authorities and the government ... because of ... his decision not to return to Eritrea to comply with his military service'.[37] France and Switzerland also upheld desertion as imputed political opinion within their case law.[38] In contrast, the Israeli Population, Immigration and Border Authority articulated that they granted only two Eritrean deserters asylum because of their additional political engagement, thereby not relying on the desertion as imputing political opinion by itself.[39] Hence, there is disagreement among

[35] North and Chia (n 10) 224.

[36] Immigration Appeals Board of Norway (*Utlendingsnemda*), Practice Report Eritrea (2011).

[37] 1103210 (2011) RRTA 382 (24 May 2011).

[38] See French cases: Cour National du droit d'asile (CNDA National Asylum Court), 23 November 2011 case no MA: no 11018030C+, Recuiel 2011, 55. Recognising an Eritrean deserter as a refugee due to a threat of persecution on account of his imputed political opinion, see also Cour National du droit d'asile CNDA (National Asylum Court) 28 February 2012, case no M et Mme M no S II015298, Recuiel 2012, 43–44. The Eritrean deserter and his wife were granted asylum on account of imputed political opinion. Swiss Asylum Appeal Commission, excerpts from the judgment of the ARK of 20 December 2005, iSLH, Eritrea, involving an Eritrean deserter in which it was noted that 'In Eritrea, military service is used as a mean for nation-building. Evasion or desertion, is therefore understood not only as damaging the effectiveness of the troops, but as questioning the legitimacy of the political leadership and the state as such.' It also cited a British case: UKIAT from 22 March 2005, para 15.

[39] See Ilan Lior, 'Two Eritreans granted refugee status in rare decision' Haaretz, 27 January 2014.

jurisdictions on this point, and it is suggested that the *Guidelines* would have benefited from illuminating this.

It is interesting to note that the UNHCR actually produced specific Eligibility Guidelines for Assessing the International Protection Needs of Asylum Seekers from Eritrea (UNHCR April 2009). They advocate the position that 'even where a claim is not based on actual political opinion, or not perceived by the draft evader or deserter as being an expression of political opinion, refusal to perform military service may nevertheless amount to imputed political opinion'.[40] The UNHCR further argues that:

> Military service has become politicized in Eritrea and actual or perceived evasion or desertion from military service is regarded by the Eritrean authorities as an expression of political opposition to the regime. Persons who evade or desert military service are regarded as disloyal and treasonous towards the Government and are punished for their perceived disloyalty. Hence, persons of, or approaching, military service age, who are medically fit, are at risk of persecution on return to Eritrea as actual or perceived draft evaders or deserters on the ground of imputed political opinion.

This section actually cites case law from Australia, New Zealand and Canada.[41] It is suggested that reference to these cases would have been positive for the UNHCR *Guidelines on Military Service*, and it is curious that they were omitted. As a point of clarification, it should be noted that the UNHCR Refworld database contains a significant collection of jurisprudence that goes beyond the case citations in the guidelines and this is fully accessible to asylum adjudicators, including UNHCR staff.[42] The next section addresses whether UNHCR Background Papers contain a common law bias similar to the UNHCR *Guidelines*.

## IV. UNHCR BACKGROUND NOTES/PAPERS

Six UNHCR guidelines do not include *any* references to national case law: gender-related persecution, cessation of refugee status, internal flight alternative, exclusion clauses, religion-based claims, and victims of trafficking. Hence, it is necessary to review the background papers produced for the guidelines. Background papers are commissioned from individual refugee law experts and therefore present the position of that consultant. It is noted that:

> Sometimes a paper advocates one particular interpretation rather than a range of approaches which may exist. The papers do not therefore purport to be a definitive position, but rather

[40] It cites Guy S Goodman-Gill and Jane McAdam, *The Refugee in International Law*, 3rd edn (Oxford University Press, 2007) 111.

[41] Refugee Appeal No 75378, 19 October 2005 (New Zealand Refugee Status Appeals Authority) para 116; Refugee Appeal No 76183, 13 May 2008 (New Zealand: Refugee Status Appeals Authority) paras 50–51; *Erduran v Minister for Immigration & Multicultural Affairs* [2002] FCA 814, 27 June 2002 (Federal Court of Australia); and *Zolfagharkhani v Canada* (Minister of Employment and Immigration) [1993] 3 FC 540, 15 June 1993 (Federal Court of Canada).

[42] The UNHCR Refworld database of case law is available at www.refworld.org/type,CASELAW,,,,,0.html.

are part of a process of taking the debate forward on key issues of interpretation on which opinion and jurisprudence continue to differ.[43]

The background paper on cessation of refugee protection does not refer to *any* case law, relying instead on a rich collection of interviews, UNHCR and UN policy materials, and national administrative and legislative sources.[44]

The background paper on claims for protection of religion or belief states clearly that reference to jurisprudence is limited to the US, Canada, New Zealand, and the UK.[45] The citations are a thorough collection of common law cases: New Zealand (37), Canada (33), US (28) and UK (22). However, this is problematic particularly given the special nature of the topic which behooves a more universal perspective, including civil law cases and international jurisprudence.

Similarly, the background paper on Gender-related persecution contains citations of common law cases from the UK (9), New Zealand (6), Australia (5) and US (3).[46] With regard to the international level, it refers to cases from the International Criminal Tribunal for Rwanda (ICTR) (1) and International Criminal Tribunal for the former Yugoslavia (ICTY) (1). The paper cites the ICTR, *Prosecutor v Jean-Paul Akayesu*, which defines rape in international law and holds that rape can constitute genocide, and the ICTY, *Prosecutor v Kunarac, Kovac and Vukovic* cases.[47] Further, the paper contains one footnote which recommends secondary literature by Walter Kälin for 'discussion of the French, German and Swiss law' regarding the interpretation of a 'well-founded' fear of persecution.[48]

The background paper on membership of a particular social group indeed contains references to cases from both common law and civil law jurisdictions: France (18), the US (17), Australia (5), Germany (5), the UK (3), New Zealand (3), the Netherlands (1) and Canada (1.)[49]

The background paper on internal flight alternative reveals a further improvement, as there is more inclusion of civil law cases, although common law cases remain in the majority: Canada (25), the UK (19), Australia (19), the US (11), Germany (10), New Zealand (9), the Netherlands (7), Switzerland (2), Austria (1) and France (1).[50] In terms of cases from international jurisdictions, the paper cites

43 Feller et al (n 2) 8.

44 Joan Fitzpatrick and Rafael Bonoan, 'Cessation of Refugee Protection' in Feller et al (n 2) 491.

45 Karen Musalo, Claims for Protection Based on Religion or Belief: Analysis and Proposed Conclusions (UNHCR Department of International Protection PPLA/2002/01, December 2002) 9, fn 43.

46 Roger Haines QC, 'Gender-related persecution' in Feller et al (n 2) 319.

47 Ibid at 336, fn 80, citing *The Prosecutor v Jean-Paul Akayesu* (Trial Judgment), ICTR-96-4-T, International Criminal Tribunal for Rwanda (ICTR), 2 September 1998, www.refworld.org/docid/40278fbb4.html and *Prosecutor v Dragoljub Kunarac, Radomir Kovac and Zoran Vukovic* (Trial Judgment), IT-96-23-T and IT-96-23/1-T, International Criminal Tribunal for the former Yugoslavia (ICTY), 22 February 2001, available at www.refworld.org/docid/3ae6b7560.html.

48 Ibid at 338, fn 84 citing W Kälin, 'Well-founded Fear of Persecution: A European Perspective' in J Bhabha and G Coll (eds), *Asylum Law and Practice in Europe and North America: A Comparative Analysis*, 1st edn (Federal Publications, 1992).

49 T Alexander Aleinikoff, 'Protected Characteristics and Social Perceptions: An Analysis of the Meaning of "Membership of a Particular Social Group"' in Feller et al (n 2) 263.

50 James C Hathaway and Michelle Foster, 'Internal protection/relocation/flight alternative as an aspect of refugee status determination' in Feller et al (n 2) 357.

the ECtHR (2), the Permanent Court of International Justice (1) and the Convention against Torture CAT (1). The paper cites the ECtHR, *Chahal v UK* establishing that an internal flight alternative is not possible where the State (police) is the persecutor; also confirmed in *Hilal v UK*,[51] and by the CAT in *Alan v Switzerland*.[52]

In contrast, the background paper on exclusion contains a majority citation of civil law decisions, in spite of the fact that the author has a common law background himself: Switzerland (10), Canada (3), the UK (3), France (3), the US (2) and Belgium (2). Furthermore, reference to jurisprudence from the international level includes citations of the judgment of the ICTY (5), the ECtHR (2), the ICJ (2), the International Military Tribunal at Nuremberg (1) and the UN Human Rights Committee (1).[53] The judgment at Nuremberg and ICTY jurisprudence is cited for definition of international crimes.[54] It cites the ECtHR to establish the non-refoulement standard and fair trial standards.[55] On torture, it also cites the ECtHR and the CAT.[56] It turns to the ICTY to address the exclusion of underage persons at ICC.[57]

The consultants who produced the background notes for these guidelines tend to come from common law backgrounds and hence this may in part explain the focus on common law cases, although there was one exception. Another worrisome trend, similar to the *Guidelines*, is the complete absence of references to cases from developing countries. This is particularly surprising given the fact that most refugees seek asylum in developing countries.[58] At present, through selective citation of national case law, both the soft law UNHCR *Guidelines* and Background Papers appear to lack the universal characteristic they are intended to have and this requires rectification in order to preserve the legitimacy of international law-making.

## V. CONCLUSION

This chapter sought to deconstruct the UNHCR *Guidelines on International Protection* and Background Papers in order to demonstrate the importance of increased

[51] *Hilal v The United Kingdom*, 45276/99, Council of Europe: European Court of Human Rights, 6 June 2001.

[52] *Ismail Alan v Switzerland*, Communication No. 21/1995, U.N. Doc. CAT/C/16/D/21/1995 (1996).

[53] Geoff Gilbert, 'Current Issues in the Application of the Exclusion Clauses' in Feller et al (n 2) 425.

[54] *Duško Tadić*, Decision on the Defence Motion for Interlocutory Appeal on Jurisdiction before the Appeals Chamber of the ICTY, Case No IT-94-1-AR72, 2 October 1995, para 134. *The Prosecutor v Kupreškić*, Case No IT-95-16-T, 14 January 2000, crimes against humanity, *Prosecutor v Jean-Paul Akayesu*, Case No ICTR-96-4-T, 2 September 1998, *Prosecutor v Furundzija*, Case No IT-95-17/1-T 10, 10 December 1998.

[55] *Chahal v United Kingdom* (70/1995/576/662), 15 November 1996 (1997), and *Jabari v Turkey*, Appeal No 40035/98 11 July 2000 ECtHR on non-refoulement according to Article 3. See *Maoaouia v France* App no 39652/98 (ECtHR, 5 October 2000) for the fair trial standard.

[56] *Selmouni v France*, App no 25803/94 (ECtHR, 28 July 1999); *Labita v Italy* App no 26772/95 (ECtHR, 6 April 2000); *Mutombo v Switzerland*, Communication No 13/1993, CAT/C/12D/13/1993, 27 April 1994, *Khan v Canada*, Communication No 15/1994, CAT/C/13/D/15/1994, 18 November 1994, para 12.2.

[57] *Prosecutor v Drazen Erdemović*, ICTY, Appeals Chamber judgment, Case No IT-96-22-A, 7 October 1997.

[58] UNHCR, 'World Refugee Day: UNHCR Report finds 80 per cent of the world's refugees in developing countries' (20 June 2011), available at www.unhcr.org/4dfb66ef9.html.

pluralistic references to national case law. Change is required in order to ensure that comprehensive citation of national law is pursued, as well as to correct a bias towards common law judgments and omission of cases from the developing world, thereby avoiding the appearance of selectivity in case law. The UNHCR's Department of International Protection needs to be expanded in order to enable it to legitimately fulfill its mandate of providing a truly global assessment of protection standards as they evolve within refugee law tribunals around the world. It is recommended that the UNHCR *Guidelines on International Protection* be revised in order to achieve this purpose. Furthermore, since there appears to be no political will to amend the 1951 Convention to recognise and address new forms of forced migration, it is likely that creation of international soft law in the form of guidelines will continue to be a primary means by which to evolve refugee law.

The UNHCR should be given appropriate funding to strengthen the Department of International Protection in terms of competent staffing and related support (at present it has only seven to eight lawyers), and consultancy should ensure representativeness of both civil law and common law traditions, as well as developing country jurisdictions.[59] There is a need for greater transparency of the role of the international civil servants, experts, NGOs, judges, and government officials in soft law evolution, for example all Background Papers should be published. Although it may be argued that the UNHCR's primary focus is field assistance, addressing immediate protection needs such as providing shelter, water and so on, it is essential to reinvigorate its normative mandate as well, in order to respond to the changing dynamics of forced migration and the need for legal guidance in asylum determination. This requires reform and buttressing of the process behind the drafting of the *Guidelines* and Background Papers.

[59] In comparison the International Labour Organization has over 100 lawyers on staff to develop international labour standards.

# 7

# *National Law as an Unpredictable Generator of International Law: The Case of Norm Export at the World Trade Organization*

GREGORY MESSENGER*

## I. INTRODUCTION

ONE OF THE most identifiable instances of national law generating international law is through the use of domestic legislation as the model for a treaty provision. This contribution seeks to identify some consequences of using domestic legislation in this way by examining the World Trade Organization (WTO) where numerous obligations are modelled on national law. It argues that, far from straightforward, such a process is a particularly unpredictable form of law-making, the results of which are intelligible only as part of a complex process of 'norm export'.

In international trade, as in many areas of international relations, law plays a defining role. While economic globalisation has encouraged a broad consensus on the merits of liberalisation and the role of the market, there still exist a wide range of varied approaches to this paradigm.[1] Different States structure their relationship between market and government differently, using different legal arrangements to regulate this relationship.[2]

The legal framework that regulates the appropriate role of government and market results from internal debates over where States (and their communities) identify

* Lecturer in Law, University of Liverpool. This contribution is adapted from sections in G Messenger, *The Development of World Trade Organization Law: Examining Change in International Law* (Oxford University Press, 2016). I am grateful to a number of people who have offered comments on the ideas presented in one form or another, but in particular Dan Sarooshi, Mary Footer and Dapo Akande. All errors and omissions are my own.

[1] It is notable that in spite of the global financial crisis beginning in 2007/2008 there has been no substantial shift toward rejecting the fundamentals of a market economy by policy-makers.

[2] For the purposes of this contribution, 'government' refers to the aggregate of public authority within the State. This is broader than its traditional usage that would, for example, exclude judicial bodies that are included here. See C Molyneux, *Domestic Structures and International Trade* (Hart Publishing, 2001) 7.

the 'correct' balance.[3] International organisations such as the WTO offer States (and members of their constituent communities) the opportunity to project their conception of the correct relationship between the market and government onto the international plane. By embedding norms within the WTO system ('norm export'), they thus influence the ways in which participants in other States are free to determine the appropriate role of the market or government.[4]

The WTO provides a particularly attractive target for norm export as WTO legal obligations cover nearly all world trade, binding 162 Members (and with a further 22 countries in accession talks). One might expect, therefore, that inserting a treaty provision into WTO law, which incorporates a State's own national law, would ensure that their perception of the correct balance between market and government filters down through to the membership via the covered agreements, enforced by a (comparatively) effective dispute settlement system.[5]

However, the outcomes of incorporating domestic legal texts into the covered agreements have been wildly inconsistent. While 23 of the original 26 articles in the General Agreement on Tariffs and Trade (GATT) 1947[6] were largely based on US proposals[7] and numerous provisions of the covered agreements were modelled on US law,[8] the Appellate Body's interpretation of these articles has often diverged from that taken under US trade law. Indeed, in the case of trade remedies especially, this has caused particular consternation in the US where the Appellate Body has been accused of judicial activism.[9]

This chapter proceeds in three parts: first, it outlines the motivation for norm export, and identifies one method, embedding domestic legislation in an international legal system; second, it identifies an example from international trade remedies law modelled on US provisions, and the subsequent unexpected interpretation

[3] These debates may take any number of forms from discussions in legislative assemblies to informal social discourse. Overlaps can be found with J Habermas, *Between Facts and Norms: Contributions to a Discourse Theory of Law and Democracy* (Polity Press, 1996).

[4] The WTO 'system' as defined here includes both its normative and institutional aspects. On the distinction, see M Footer, *An Institutional and Normative Analysis of the World Trade Organization* (Martinus Nijhoff, 2006) 6–8.

[5] Considered 'on any view, the most successful inter-state system of dispute settlement ever', J Crawford, 'Continuity and Discontinuity in International Dispute Settlement: An Inaugural Lecture' (2010) 1 *Journal of International Dispute Settlement* 4, 4.

[6] General Agreement on Tariffs and Trade (30 October 1947) 55 UNTS 194 (GATT 1947).

[7] D Sarooshi, 'Sovereignty, Economic Autonomy, the United States, and the International Trading System' (2004) 15(4) *European Journal of International Law* 651 fn 74.

[8] Compare Article 2.1, Agreement on Safeguards, Multilateral Agreements on Trade in Goods, Annex 1A of the Agreement Establishing the World Trade Organization, 1869 UNTS 154, entered into force 1 January 1995 (the 'Safeguards Agreement') and s 201 Trade Act 1974 (Pub L 93–618, 88 Stat 1978).

[9] For example, statements in Congress such as: 'Who would have ever thought that Antigua and Barbados would have more control over what goes on in Utah than the people of Utah themselves do?' in response to the *US—Gambling* dispute proceedings (Congressional Record H1739, 5 April 2005), or, in a statement Resolution of the US House of Representatives, 'the WTO dispute settlement process is not working and has been guided by politics rather than by legal principles' (H Res 441, 17 November 2003) in response to the *US—Steel* dispute. For an overview of the typical concerns, see I Fergusson and L Sek, 'World Trade Organization: Issues in the Debate on US Participation' CRS Report for Congress, Order Code RL32918 (9 June 2005).

by the Appellate Body; third and finally, it analyses the seeming failure of the US to establish uniform provisions consistent with its own law in this area, reframing critiques of the Appellate Body's treatment of these US-originated WTO provisions. It does this by acknowledging the multiple exercises of norm export by actors, not only in these specific agreements but also in others, most notably in this case, the constituent document of the WTO's dispute settlement system, the Dispute Settlement Understanding. Further, it stresses the complexities involved in norm export and the inherent unpredictability of such an exercise.

The chapter concludes by stressing the need to examine the consequences of norm export not only on a specific legal provision but also on the constitutive texts of the institutions entrusted with its oversight. In doing so, it encourages an appreciation of the limitations of using national law as a model for international law, and an awareness that institutions interpreting these provisions, such as the Appellate Body, are both subject to, and the result of, a process of norm export themselves.

## II. INTRODUCING THE PROCESS OF NORM EXPORT

Norm export is (in its most general sense) a key element of many accounts of international law, especially process-based accounts.[10] Such depictions involve transnational actors (including States)[11] attempting to determine the rules that apply to the relevant communities of actors by structuring normative frameworks in their favour. Rather than viewing international organisations as sites of cooperation,[12] many accounts view them instead as battlegrounds for pursing the objectives of interest groups.[13] The process of norm export, however, is more profound and more complex than many accounts often indicate: it results not only from the pursuit of interests but also involves continual contestations over the appropriate scope of (in our subject of analysis) international trade regulation and, consequently, the nature and role of the State.

The argument in this section is as follows: the constitutive influence of law encourages transnational actors to project their trade-related value preferences onto others by a process of norm export, as the interests of these actors in pursuing norm export is not determined only by their material circumstances but are instead constituted by the normative (including legal) frameworks in which they exist. One notable method

[10] H Koh, 'Transnational Legal Process' (1996) 75 *Nebraska Law Review* 181, Symposium in *Yale Journal of International Law* (2007), R Higgins *Problems and Process: International Law and How We Use It* (Clarendon Press, 1996). See also Cass Sunstein's work on norm entrepreneurs, C Sunstein, 'Social Norms and Social Roles' (1996) 96 *Columbia Law Review* 903.

[11] Any actor which engages across jurisdictional boundaries is considered a transnational actor for the purposes of this contribution. It thus includes, inter alia, States, international organisations, civil service organisations, and multinational corporations.

[12] For example, K Abbott and D Snidal, 'Why States Act through Formal Organizations' (1998) 42(1) *Journal of Conflict Resolution* 3; S Krasner, *International Regimes* (Cornell University Press, 1983).

[13] Thus extending the insights of international liberalism, A Moravcsik, 'Taking Preferences Seriously: A Liberal Theory of International Politics' (1997) 51(4) *International Organization* 513, 518.

of norm export is through the crystallisation of norms in treaty texts using national law as a model.

## A. Norm Export and the Constitutive Role of Law

A core element in understanding the current trading system is the relationship between market and government, and one of the principal tools in structuring the relationship between the market and government is law; there is an implicit connection between the values that underpin the relationship between government and market, and the legal structures put into place to regulate this relationship.

A consequence of the syllogistic relationship between law and values is that international organisations such as the WTO offer transnational actors the opportunity to project their values by exporting norms. By providing a space for Members to negotiate, create rules and resolve disputes at the international level, the WTO offers a target for actors who want to ensure that their own value preferences are established as the international standard through encouraging the acceptance of certain norms.

Norms, in this context, are defined as a 'prescription for action in situations of choice'.[14] They 'give rise to feelings of obligation and when violated engender regret or a feeling that the deviation or violation requires justification'.[15] Norms encourage actors to understand and interpret their obligations in a determined way, taking into account the underlying values within a legal agreement. 'Norm export'[16] is the process whereby actors export norms with the aim that their preferences for certain types of behaviour in instances of choice take preference over others.

For example, one can take 'fairness' as a starting point, a socially determined value that has multiple facets. One actor may view fairness in terms that prioritise intergenerational equity: this is to say that current generations ought to consider the consequences to future generations in their decision-making processes.[17] The subsequent norm within the context of the WTO system, which focuses on the role of development as a tool for peace and prosperity,[18] might be that States should not use the overarching aims of the covered agreements to ignore their environmental

[14] A Chayes and AH Chayes, *The New Sovereignty: Compliance with New Regulatory Agreements* (Harvard University Press, 1995) 113.

[15] A Cortell and J Davis, 'When Norms Clash: International Norms, Domestic Practices, and Japan's Internalisation of the GATT/WTO' (2005) 31 *Review of International Studies* 3, 4.

[16] The term itself is not new, though its use here is different from prior uses: cf A Björkdahl, 'Norm-maker and Norm-taker: Exploring the normative influence of the EU in Macedonia' (2005) 10 *European Foreign Affairs Review* 257.

[17] See Rio Declaration on Environment and Development (3–14 June 1992) A/Conf.151/26 (Vol I), Principles 3 and 21.

[18] Preamble to the GATT 1947, second paragraph: 'Recognizing that their relations in the field of trade and economic endeavour should be conducted with a view to raising standards of living, ensuring full employment and a large and steadily growing volume of real income and effective demand, developing the full use of the resources of the world and expanding the production and exchange of goods.'

obligations to future generations. One formulation of the specific resultant rule can be found within the exceptions of Article XX GATT, specifically Article XX(b)[19] and Article XX(g).[20] Thus a value suggests a norm that, in turn, crystallises into a specific legal obligation under the GATT. This is not to say that this is the only interpretation, but rather that within systems such as the WTO, terms are continually contested and respond to the behaviour of actors.[21] Even foundational terms such as 'free trade' alter over the years as a consequence of cognitive changes.[22]

Norm export by transnational actors may take place at the point of creating new obligations (for example, negotiations of new agreements or ministerial conferences) or during the judicial processes of interpretation, or during quasi-administrative processes at the committees of the WTO and elsewhere. In each instance, transnational actors compete to project their conception of the correct balance between market and government with the expectation that the 'correct' interpretation filters down through the WTO membership via their obligations under the covered agreements.

For many, projection requires embedding such values where possible.[23] Having captured certain institutions, there is an interest in ensuring that the values of the actors are entrenched as far as possible. By prescribing certain forms of behaviour within these institutions, actors protect their own value preferences.[24] This applies within the State but also, importantly, for our purposes, within institutions that claim authority over the State such as the WTO. Actors need to be able to engage internationally to protect their preferences from threats both within the State and without.

Thus, instead of coercing or co-opting other States, a State might instead attempt to influence the structure and activity of the WTO.[25] The logic is clear:

> If a country can shape international rules that are consistent with its interests and values, its actions will more likely appear legitimate in the eyes of others. If it uses institutions and follows rules that encourage countries to channel or limit their activities in ways it prefers, it will not need as many costly carrots and sticks.[26]

[19] Relating to the protection of human, animal or plant life or health.

[20] Relating to the conservation of exhaustible natural resources. On its relationship to intergenerational fairness, through the principle of sustainable development: Panel Reports, *China—Measures Related to the Exportation of Rare Earths, Tungsten, and Molybdenum*, WT/DS431/R / WT/DS432/R / WT/DS433/R / and Add 1, adopted 29 August 2014, para 7.277.

[21] For a vivid account, see J Ruggie, 'International Regimes, Transactions, and Change: Embedded Liberalism and the Postwar Economic Order' (1982) 36 *International Organization* 379.

[22] A Lang, 'Reflecting on "Linkage": Cognitive and Institutional Change in The International Trading System' (2007) 70 *Modern Law Review* 523, 525–30.

[23] Embedding values can be understood as encouraging a form of structural bias, the influence of which is well documented, J Goldstein, 'Ideas, Institutions, and American Trade Policy' in GJ Ikenberry, D Lake and M Mastanduno (eds), *The State and American Foreign Economic Policy* (Cornell University Press, 1988); M Koskenniemi, 'The Politics of International Law—20 Years Later' (2009) 20 *European Journal of International Law* 1.

[24] In support, J Nye, *Soft Power: The Means to Success in World Politics* (Public Affairs, 2004) 10.

[25] Ibid 10.

[26] Ibid 10–11.

At the WTO there are numerous cases of such behaviour,[27] indeed, policy-makers openly use the potential success of norm export through international legal structures to justify their positions. For example, President Clinton did so writing on China's accession to the WTO. While he made the traditional arguments about the benefits to US traders and farmers from the reduction of tariffs and inclusion of China into the WTO's dispute settlement system, the president also placed considerable focus on the importance of projecting US values through the trading system, stating:

> This deal [China's accession to the WTO] not only expands trade, it also projects our values and enhances our security. To understand why, we need to see China clearly—its progress and problems, its policies and perceptions of us, of itself, and the world …
>
> The agreement obligates China to deepen its market reforms, empowering leaders who want their country to move further and faster toward economic freedom …
>
> In the past, the Chinese state was employer, landlord, shopkeeper, and news provider all rolled into one. This agreement will accelerate a process that is removing the government from vast areas of China's economic life. China's people will have greater scope to live their lives as they see fit. And as they become more mobile, more prosperous, more aware of alternative ways of life, they will seek greater say in the decisions that affect their lives.[28]

The expectation was that China would bring its national law into conformity with its WTO obligations but also that the WTO would provide a framework in which compliance procedures (both formal and informal) would be available.

The following section examines one such method of achieving this aim: the transplant of national legal provisions into an international agreement, in our case, at the WTO. It is not the only method of norm export though it is the most easily identifiable. It also provides a number of interesting insights regarding the consequences of using national law as a model for creating international law.

### B. Textual Transplant: Norms Export through Crystallisation

Determining what is to be regulated by international agreement at the WTO, and how the related rights and obligations under the covered agreements are defined and developed is key to ensuring that a transnational actor's objectives are met. This both sets the agenda and the rules of the game.

As actors seek to export their normative preferences, one obvious target is the creation of new international obligations in treaties such as the covered agreements, often using domestic legislation as a model. This contribution argues that while crystallising norms as treaty obligations is an obvious choice for actors, it is limited in effect due to numerous influences that constrain their pursuit of this goal. These

[27] See D Sarooshi, 'Sovereignty, Economic Autonomy, the United States, and the International Trading System' (2004) 15 *European Journal of International Law* 651, 664–669 for an account of the US–UK steel dispute in light of a debate over competing values.

[28] President Clinton, 'Expanding Trade, Projecting Values' *The New Democrat* (1 January 2000).

can include material factors (the need for power asymmetries), temporal factors (the timing must be right to gain agreement for a new treaty or amendment) and unintended consequences as embedded norms may interact with other norms producing unexpected results.

One of the most obvious ways of ensuring that the normative preferences of an actor are embedded within the WTO system is to introduce a provision in the foundational legal texts of the WTO: the covered agreements.[29] The history of international affairs is replete with examples of disagreements over what should be included in a treaty and how each article and paragraph should be worded. It is the legally binding nature of these international obligations that encourages such focus from the negotiating parties. As the Members of the WTO are bound by the obligations within the covered agreements as a matter of international law (and, depending on their domestic systems, as a matter of national law), one might expect that inserting a treaty provision that incorporates an actor's preferences would be a logical objective for those actors engaged in a process of norm export.

While norm crystallisation within treaty obligations may be the objective of actors engaged in norm export, they are also constrained by three limitations: material, temporal, and behavioural. The material limitation results from the need for consent by all relevant parties to incorporate a desired treaty obligation wholesale; considerable power asymmetries are thus needed to achieve this aim. While this has occurred previously (the aforementioned examples of US involvement in the GATT), the wholesale dictation of a treaty by one party in multilateral negotiations is rare. In spite of US dominance, its relative decline in the international trading system, accompanied by the increased influence of the EU as a (largely) single voice and the increasing economic strength of large emerging countries, has led to a reduction in the concentration of power than was the case in the 1940s. With a larger group of powerful trading States or regional bodies involved in the negotiations on new treaties or agreements, the scope for forcing one provision on the WTO's membership is diminished.

This is particularly the case with new multilateral agreements, which require unanimity.[30] More likely, Members could act through the Ministerial Conference or General Council and attempt to adopt an authoritative interpretation under Article IX(2) WTO Agreement, a waiver under Article IX(3) WTO Agreement, Decision under Article IX(1) WTO Agreement or amendment by the Ministerial Conference under Article X WTO Agreement. However, these bodies require (inter alia) consensus or majority in the case of Decisions, three-fourths majority for an authoritative interpretation or waiver and a two-thirds majority for amendments (though

[29] Those agreements listed under Appendix 1 Understanding on Rules and Procedures Governing the Settlement of Disputes, (DSU) Annex 2 of the Agreement Establishing the World Trade Organization, 1869 UNTS 401, entered into force 1 January 1995.

[30] So as not to breach Article 34 Vienna Convention on the Law of Treaties (VCLT) (23 May 1969) 1155 UNTS 331; 8 ILM 679 (1969).

the consequences of amendments vary depending on the circumstances).[31] These are not easy hurdles to overcome: with the exception of waivers which have proved less 'exceptional' than the terms of Article IX(3) WTO Agreement would indicate,[32] there has only been one amendment[33] and no authoritative interpretations.[34] The adoption of new plurilateral agreements also requires consensus under Article X(9) WTO Agreement, while their scope is commonly between more powerful Members where power asymmetries are less.[35]

The second limitation is the temporal limitation: the need for the timing to be right to arrive at an agreement. Timing plays a role in whether or not consensus can be reached over new agreements or amendments to the existing ones.[36] Not only do the negotiations at the multilateral level need to be favourable but all the parties involved have to be capable of consenting to a new agreement: this is a frequent issue for the US executive which requires a Congressional delegation of authority in order to conclude a trade agreement.[37] With the completion of the Uruguay Round, there have been few agreements at the multilateral level,[38] most notably the four protocols[39] to the General Agreement in Trade in Services (GATS),[40] Ministerial Declarations such as the Information Technology Agreement[41] or documents passed by a specific working group such as the Telecommunications Services Reference Paper.[42]

[31] In practice, Members do not vote in the majority of these instances and consensus is maintained as the underlying rule: M Footer, 'The WTO as a 'Living Instrument' in T Cottier and M Elsig (eds), *Governing the World Trade Organization: Past, Present and Beyond Doha* (Cambridge University Press, 2011) 223.

[32] However, most waivers have been granted to individual Members thus not having the broader systemic impact that an amendment has. Council for Trade-Related Aspects of Intellectual Property Rights—Paragraph 6 of the Doha Declaration on the TRIPS Agreement and Public Health: Note by the Secretariat (24 October 2002) IP/C/W/387 Annex 1.

[33] Decision of the General Council, Amendment of the TRIPS Agreement (6 December 2005) WT/L/641.

[34] There have only been two requests: Communication from the European Communities, 'Request for an Authoritative Interpretation Pursuant to Article IX:2 of the Marrakesh Agreement Establishing the World Trade Organization' (25 January 1999) WT/GC/W/133 and Communication from the European Communities, 'Request for an Authoritative Interpretation Pursuant to Article IX:2 of the Marrakesh Agreement Establishing the World Trade Organization' (5 February 1999) WT/GC/W/143.

[35] For example, Agreement on Government Procurement, Plurilateral Trade Agreements, Annex 4(b) of the Agreement Establishing the World Trade Organization, 1869 UNTS 508 (text available at 1915 UNTS 103), entered into force 1 January 1995.

[36] Article X Agreement Establishing the World Trade Organization (WTO Agreement) (15 April 1994) 1867 UNTS 154; (1994) 33 ILM 1144, entered into force 1 January 1995.

[37] Under the 'Fast-Track' or Trade Promotion Authority system.

[38] This is in stark contrast to the exponential growth of regional and preferential trade agreements.

[39] Second Protocol to the General Agreement on Trade in Services (24 July 1995) S/L/11, Third Protocol to the General Agreement on Trade in Services (24 July 1995) S/L/12, Fourth Protocol to the General Agreement on Trade in Services (30 April 1996) S/L/20 and Fifth Protocol to the General Agreement on Trade in Services (3 December 1997) S/L/45.

[40] General Agreement on Trade in Services, Annex 1B of the Agreement Establishing the World Trade Organization, 1869 UNTS 183, entered into force 1 January 1995 (GATS).

[41] Ministerial Declaration on Trade in Information Technology Products (13 December 1996) WT/MIN(96)/16.

[42] Negotiating Group on Basic Telecommunications, 'Telecommunications Services: Reference Paper' (24 April 1996).

Where treaties have come into question it has been to terminate them, as was the case with the Agreement on Textiles and Clothing.[43]

The textual transplant of national law to treaty obligations has a final disadvantage: the often unintended consequence of embedding norms within an institutional structure in a different area of regulation which nonetheless impact on the subject-matter at hand.

Take the prior example of an intergenerational conception of fairness as a societal value. When expressed in environmental matters, the resulting norm-proscribing acts prejudicial to the interests of future generations for short-term development crystallises as a treaty obligation. In the context of the GATT, this relates specifically to Article XX (b) and Article XX (g), providing for exceptions to the GATT obligations where in pursuance of the protection of exhaustible natural resources or protection of human, animal or plant life. While an actor may be encouraged by the inclusion of these provisions, this says nothing of the method of interpretation used by the panel in the particular dispute, nor the institutional procedures for the adoption of the report, nor the method of compliance should a Member be found in violation.[44] At each stage, it is not only the specific rights and obligations under the GATT that matter but rather also the relevant provisions under the Dispute Settlement Understanding (DSU), WTO Agreement and others. It is not only the narrow treaty obligation that matters but also the environment in which it exists, an environment which constrains and enables actors as a result of successful norm exports by that same Member or others.

The following section identifies one such process of norm crystallisation through textual transplant and its unexpected consequences for the principal norm exporter in question, the US.[45]

## III. SAFEGUARD MEASURES

Safeguard measures allow Members of the WTO to protect their domestic industries from unexpected import surges. This reprieve from the rigours of competition is designed (in theory) to permit the industries of the protecting Member to adapt to new conditions.[46] Unsurprisingly, such a measure is open to abuse and thus the WTO and domestic legal systems of the Members limit their use; Article XIX

[43] Terminated on 1 January 2005.

[44] Note the novel interpretation of the Appellate Body in *United States—Import Prohibition of Certain Shrimp and Shrimp Products*, WT/DS58/AB/R, adopted 6 November 1998, DSR 1998:VII, 2755.

[45] Elements of the following analysis borrows from G Messenger, 'The Development of International Law and the Role of Causal Language' (2015) *Oxford Journal of Legal Studies* 1.

[46] The success of safeguard measures to achieve such an aim is questionable: the more common outcome is for industry to direct further investment toward lobbying for continued protection rather than restructuring. See CP Bown and R McCulloch, 'Trade Adjustment in the WTO System: Are More Safeguards the Answer?' (2007) 23(3) *Oxford Review of Economic Policy* 415 at 416.

GATT[47] and the subsequent Safeguards Agreement require Members to conduct an investigation and determine whether or not the conditions for the introduction of a safeguard measure have been met.[48] Both Article XIX GATT and Article 2.1 Safeguards Agreement are based on US models.

Article XIX GATT was modelled on the escape clause introduced in the US—Mexico Reciprocal Trade Agreement 1942[49] and incorporated into national law requiring the inclusion of such escape clauses in all future agreements and implement a procedure at the domestic level for industry to petition for relief in the form of safeguard measures.[50]

The formulation of the safeguards clause displayed key elements that are still present: temporary in application, the requirement that domestic producers suffer injury (or are threatened by injury) and the 'emergency' nature of safeguards requiring a connection to 'unforeseen developments'. This final requirement and its development is the subject of the analysis which follows.

## A. The 'Unforeseen Developments' Clause under Article XIX GATT

Article XIX:1(a) of the GATT reads:

> If, *as a result of unforeseen developments and of the effect of the obligations incurred* by a contracting party under this Agreement, including tariff concessions, any product is being imported into the territory of that contracting party in such increased quantities and under such conditions as to cause or threaten serious injury to domestic producers in that territory of like or directly competitive products, the contracting party shall be free, in respect of such product, and to the extent and for such time as may be necessary to prevent or remedy such injury, to suspend the obligation in whole or in part or to withdraw or modify the concession.[51]

In spite of its inclusion, the application of the 'unforeseen developments' clause has been contentious as domestic legal systems excluded this requirement.[52]

In 1951 the US Trade Agreements Extension Act replaced Executive Order 9832 as the obligation to include an escape clause, placing the requirement on a legislative

[47] General Agreement on Tariffs and Trade (1994); Multilateral Agreements on Trade in Goods; Annex 1A of the Agreement Establishing the World Trade Organization (15 April 1994) 1867 UNTS 187, entered into force 1 January 1995 (GATT 1994).

[48] Article 3(1) Safeguards Agreement: 'A Member may apply a safeguard measure only following an investigation by the competent authorities of that Member pursuant to procedures previously established ...'

[49] Negotiated as part of a warming of US–Mexico relations. In essence, to reward Mexican entry into World War II earlier in the year, the US eased its restrictions on the exportation of Mexican oil to the US: L Zorrilla, *Historia de las Relaciones enre Mexico y los Estados Unidos de América 1800–1958* (Porrua, 1965) 495.

[50] Executive Order No 9832, signed 25 February 1947. Later this obligation was placed on a legislative footing: US Trade Agreements Extension Act 1951 [Ch 141 sec 10, 65 Stat 75].

[51] Emphasis added.

[52] P Mavroidis, *Trade in Goods* (Oxford University Press, 2007) 366 fn 101.

footing. In doing so it also removed the 'unforeseen developments' requirement from US law in response to the perception that it was too difficult to obtain an affirmative determination by the Tariff Commission on safeguard relief by domestic industries.[53] Trading partners followed suit, excluding the 'unforeseen developments' clause from their safeguard investigations.[54] By 1994, of the major global economies, only Japan maintained an 'unforeseen developments' requirement within its legislation.[55]

1951 was a significant year not only for initiating domestic alterations in safeguards practice but also for marking the year of a key GATT dispute, which, in the eyes of many, confirmed the inoperability of the 'unforeseen developments' clause as a matter of international law.

The *Hatters' Fur Case*[56] is the only dispute arising from the GATT system over the meaning and scope of the 'unforeseen developments' clause. In *Hatters' Fur* the US granted concessions on certain types of women's fur felt hats. Following a change in the fashion, imports into the US from Czechoslovakia increased to such an extent that the US, invoking Article XIX, withdrew its concessions. The Working Group[57] took the position[58] that:

> the term 'unforeseen development' should be interpreted to mean developments occurring after the negotiation of the relevant tariff concession which it would not be reasonable to expect that the negotiators of the country making the concession could and should have foreseen at the time when the concession was negotiated.[59]

The Working Group continued, noting the peculiarities of the fashion industry and its propensity to change.[60] It concluded that changing fashions in and of themselves could not constitute 'unforeseen developments', the implicit reasoning being that it would be reasonable for a negotiator to expect that there would be a change in the circumstances of the industry in the foreseeable future. The issue was therefore, '*the degree to which* the change in fashion affected the competitive situation, could not reasonably be expected to have been foreseen by the United States authorities'.[61]

The traditional account of *Hatters' Fur* was that it was responsible for 'reading out' of the GATT the 'unforeseen developments' clause by virtue of its lax

[53] T Stewart, *The GATT Uruguay Round: A Negotiating History Vol II* (Kluwer Law International, 1993) 1731. This would appear to be at variance with the position that the further from the 1947 tariff bindings one got, the easier it became to comply with the 'unforeseen developments' criterion; A Sykes, 'The Safeguards Mess: A Critique of WTO Jurisprudence' (2003) 2 *World Trade Review* 261, 265.

[54] For example, neither Council Regulation (EC) No 260/2009 nor its antecedents: *Council Regulation (EEC) No 288/82 of 5 February 1982 on common rules for imports* [1982] OJ L35/1 (repealed), Council Regulation (EC) No 3285/94 of 22 December 1994 on the common rules for imports and repealing Regulation (EC) No 518/94 [1994] OJ L349/53 (repealed).

[55] Article 9*bis*, Law No 68 of March 1963.

[56] *Hatters' Fur Case*, Report on the Withdrawal by the United States of a Tariff Concession under Article XIX of the General Agreement on Tariffs and Trade (27 March 1951) CP/106).

[57] The form of dispute settlement used under the GATT (1947–1995) was, particularly in the early years, largely consensual in nature, hence the use of Working Groups rather than panels.

[58] The US representative dissented.

[59] *Hatters' Fur Case*, para 9.

[60] '[C]hange is the law of fashion', ibid para 10.

[61] Ibid para 12 (emphasis added).

interpretation.[62] This account had been widely followed and expanded by commentators arguing, for example, that the *Hatters' Fur* report is indicative of 'the fact that this particular clause [that is, the 'unforeseen developments' requirement] is too ambiguous and equivocal to create objective legal criteria'.[63]

Within the US, the law on safeguards continued to develop: the influence from groups that desired a greater willingness on the part of the State to protect their industry (or the industry of their constituents) led to a relaxation of the legal requirements for an affirmative petition, thus channelling their aims through legislative amendment. However, the Tariff Commission (the quasi-judicial body empowered to make determinations on petitions) applied the domestic legislation so strictly that the possibility of negative GATT determinations was of secondary concern. Further, the president could negotiate his own Voluntary Export Restraints (VERs) with trading partners, limiting imports and thus offering protection to concerned domestic industries. This resulted in the use of VERs as a 'second-best' solution.[64]

The traditional view was thus that *Hatters' Fur* read the 'unforeseen developments' clause out of Article XIX, and the lack of an equivalent provision in national law confirmed this. This view was influential and when the new Safeguards Agreement came into force the consensus view was that the 'unforeseen developments' clause was not legally operative.

### B. The 'Unforeseen Developments' Clause in the WTO Era

In the years that followed the inclusion of the GATT, the US had witnessed many changes to its own safeguards legislation, reflecting the changing circumstances the US found itself in. In the seventies, confronted with international economic disorder and progressive competition, partly from the EC but more importantly from Japan,[65] Congress pushed for a safeguard system that would provide protection for domestic industries in the light of this new competition and curtail the president's powers to override determinations of the US International Trade Commission (USITC), the Tariff Commission's replacement.

The current petitioning procedure is found in sections 201 to 204 of the Trade Act 1974. A domestic industry[66] may petition the USITC to conduct an investigation into whether 'an article is being imported into the United States in such increased

[62] J Jackson, *The World Trading System*, 2nd edn (MIT Press, 1997) 187.

[63] YS Lee, 'Destabilization of the Discipline on Safeguards' (2001) 35 *Journal of World Trade* 6, 1241.

[64] Between 1943 and 1951, only one petition was found to merit safeguard relief by the Tariff Commission (T Stewart, *Vol II*, 1731), from 1951 to 1958 10 industries out of 87 petitions received protection (T Stewart, *Vol II*, 1732), three out of 28 petitions were successful under the 1962 Trade Expansion Act (T Stewart, *Vol II*, 1736), 19 industries received some sort of relief out of 62 petitions under the Trade Act of 1974 (T Stewart, *Vol II*, 1737), with the 1988 Omnibus Trade and Competitiveness Act still setting the requirements for successful petitions particularly high (T Stewart, *Vol II*, 1738).

[65] S Strange, *The Retreat of the State* (Cambridge University Press, 1996) 21–22.

[66] By means of an 'entity, including a trade association, firm, certified or recognized union, or group of workers, which is representative of an industry.' 19 USC s 2252(a)(1).

quantities as to be a substantial cause of serious injury, or the threat thereof, to the domestic industry producing an article like or directly competitive with the imported article'.[67] Despite the relaxation of certain requirements, a determination by the USITC requesting relief is still a difficult goal to achieve. Since the 1988 Omnibus Trade and Competitiveness Act domestic industries must now also show how they intend to adapt if relief is to be granted. This includes whether or not they will focus their resources on improving competitiveness or instead focus on a separate area of business.

Once a petition has been lodged, the USITC conducts detailed investigation and produces a report. Where three or more of the six Commissioners vote in favour of a determination of serious injury (or threat thereof), they pass their recommendations on to the president. The president then has a wide range of considerations to factor in (from national security to trade diversion)[68], and an even wider range of actions available to him from the list found in the Act, including the broad catchall 'any other action ... which the President considers appropriate and feasible'.[69]

The Safeguards Agreement follows the tradition of Article XIX and once again uses a US legal instrument as its model. During the Uruguay Round the US representative at the Working Group preparing the Safeguards Agreement stated somewhat coyly:

> The purpose of this paper is not to advocate that the specific procedures of the United States be incorporated into a safeguards agreement or that the United States experience readily lends itself to use by other contracting parties. This paper is presented more for the purpose of demonstrating how one country has defined injury in its national trade law and developed a transparent process for making injury determinations consistent with Article XIX.[70]

The resulting Safeguards Agreement, however, does incorporate the US position. With the exception of certain procedural requirements (which are more detailed under US law), the WTO Safeguards Agreement is overtly modelled on the US system under section 201 Trade Act of 1974,[71] including a lack of the 'unforeseen developments' clause.

The Safeguards Agreement marked one of the great successes of the Uruguay Round, and led to an increase in the use of safeguard measures by Members and a rekindling in the interest of their application and the legal disciplines to be applied.

The difference between the wording of Article XIX and Article 2(1) Safeguards Agreement arose during two separate disputes raised by the EU against Korea and Argentina. Amongst the claims of the EU, was that the appropriate trade bodies in Korea and Argentina had not fulfilled their obligations under Article XIX by showing that the increase in imports was a result of 'unforeseen developments'. The importing Members' claims can be divided into three separate threads.

[67] 19 USC s 2251(a).
[68] 19 USC s 2253(a)(2).
[69] 19 USC s 2253(a)(3)(i).
[70] Communication from the United States (3 March 1988) GATT Doc MTN.GNG/NG9/W/13, 1.
[71] URAA Statement of Administrative Action, H.Doc 103–316 (I), 4298.

First, it was argued that the Safeguards Agreement contained the full set of disciplines relating to the use of such measures and compliance with it satisfied the legal requirements.[72] Second, that where a conflict exists between the GATT and the Safeguards Agreement, it is to be resolved in favour of the Agreement, as per the Interpretative Note to the WTO Agreement.[73] Third, engaging with the possibility of the validity of the 'unforeseen developments' clause, that the rise in imports could not have been foreseen.[74] The EU, for its part, submitted that the obligations under the covered agreements were part of a 'single undertaking' and as such were cumulative in nature. The entirety of both Article XIX and the Agreement has to be applied.[75] In the context of the Argentinean case, the EU also pointed out that as Argentina had pursued a conscious policy of liberalisation over the period of 1989/1990, an increase in imports could not be 'unforeseen' for the purposes of Article XIX.[76]

The *Korea—Dairy* panel in this case took an approach in line with academic opinion at the time; it interpreted the text so as to avoid conflict (citing the principle of *l'effet utile*)[77] and proceeded to examine the text of Article XIX:1 'based on the ordinary meaning of the terms' in it.[78] The conclusion was that the 'unforeseen developments' clause did not create any specific obligation but was instead explanatory.[79] The panel elucidated the *raison d'être* of Article XIX in light of the historic commitments made in 1947 and in doing so, cited both the *Hatters' Fur* dispute as well as (via Article XVI:1 of the WTO Agreement) 48 years of State practice.[80] It concluded that Article XIX contained no obligation with reference to the 'unforeseen developments' clause.[81]

The *Argentina—Footwear* panel's reasoning was somewhat distinct, citing Article 11.1(a) of the Safeguards Agreement which stipulates the requirement to enact safeguard measures in compliance with Article XIX 'applied in accordance with Agreement [on Safeguards]'.[82] The panel then concluded, both that, due to this provisio, Article XIX and the Safeguards Agreement were 'intrinsically linked' and that Article XIX was to be read in light of the 'subsequently negotiated and much more specific provisions of the Agreement on Safeguards'.[83] The 'unforeseen developments' clause is then read in light of the object and purpose of the Safeguards Agreement. The Agreement is intended (as per its Preamble) to 'clarify and reinforce' the disciplines found in Article XIX.[84]

[72] *Korea—Definitive Safeguard Measure on Imports of Certain Dairy Products, Panel Report (21 June 1999) WT/DS98/R (Korea—Dairy Panel)* para 7.33.
[73] WTO Agreement Annex 1a.
[74] *Argentina—Safeguard Measures on Imports of Footwear*, Panel Report (25 June 1999) WT/DS121/R (*Argentina- Footwear Panel*) para 848.
[75] *Korea—Dairy Panel* (n 72) para 7.36.
[76] *Argentina—Footwear Panel* (n 74) para 847.
[77] *Korea—Dairy Panel* (n 72) para 7.37.
[78] Ibid para 7.39.
[79] Ibid para 7.45.
[80] Ibid para 7.46.
[81] Ibid para 7.48 '[W]e consider that Article XIX of GATT does not contain such a requirement.'
[82] Article 11.1(a) Safeguards Agreement.
[83] *Argentina—Footwear Panel* (n 74) para 8.56.
[84] Ibid para 8.62.

The 'unforeseen developments' clause fits into the panel's analysis by virtue of two conceptual exercises. First, it posits that the omission of the 'unforeseen developments' clause in the Safeguards Agreement was an intentional, express omission. There is no detailed examination of negotiating histories but this is instead based upon speculation of the mindset of negotiators at the time.[85] Second, a division is made between the provisions in the Safeguards Agreement in light of its aim to reassert control over the multilateral system of safeguards; on the one hand the tightening of disciplines (for example, elimination and restriction of VERs) and on the other hand, the relaxing of disciplines (for example, flexibility over compensation actions).[86] By making the omission of the 'unforeseen developments' clause an intentional alteration the panel is free to include it in the latter category. In this manner, the panel can view the omission of the unforeseen developments clause as part of the new provisions in the Safeguards Agreement that are designed to make it easier to apply safeguard measures, echoing the motivations in 1951 for the omission of the unforeseen developments requirement under US law. While paying lip-service to the limits on adding to or diminishing rights or obligations under the covered agreements[87] it still concludes that 'conformity with the explicit requirements and conditions embodied in the Agreement on Safeguards must be sufficient for the application of safeguard measures within the meaning of Article XIX of GATT'.[88]

### C. Norm Export and the Dispute Settlement Understanding

The two panel reports in *Korea—Dairy* and *Argentina—Footwear* were consistent in general terms with the prevailing views of the time, however, they did not engage with the institutional shift that had taken place following 1994 with the introduction of the DSU and creation of the Appellate Body.

The Appellate Body's status as 'World Trade Court' in all but name[89] was by no means inevitable,[90] and has had a profound influence on the way that the Appellate Body examines cases before it.

[85] Ibid para 8.65.
[86] Ibid para 8.63.
[87] Article 3.2 DSU.
[88] *Argentina—Footwear Panel* (n 74) para 8.67.
[89] C-D Ehlermann, 'Six Years on the Bench of the "World Trade Court": Some Personal Experiences as Member of the Appellate Body of the WTO' (2002) 36 *Journal of World Trade* 605. An alternative name previously suggested is the 'International Court of Economic Justice'; JHH Weiler, 'The Rule of Lawyers and the Ethos of Diplomats: Reflections on the Internal and External Legitimacy of WTO Dispute Settlement' Harvard Jean Monnet Working Paper 9/00 (2000) IV:1.
[90] P Van Den Bossche, 'The Making of the "World Trade Court": The Origins and Development of the Appellate Body of the World Trade Organization' in R Yerxa and B Wilson, *Key Issues in WTO Dispute Settlement: The First Ten Years* (Cambridge University Press, 2005) 63–64. Also, P Van Den Bossche, 'From Afterthought to Centerpiece: The WTO Appellate Body and its Rise to Prominence in the World Trading System', Maastricht Faculty of Law Working Paper 2005/1.

It was not clear at the founding of the WTO, that the Appellate Body would take the form that it has since taken.[91] Indeed, the negotiating history clearly indicates that the then Contracting Parties considered dispute settlement under the WTO to be an entirely different creature to that found in other areas of international relations,[92] not concerned with the development of a clear jurisprudence[93] but rather to settle specific disputes between the parties to it.[94] The proposal of appellate review raised concerns not of potential institution building (at that point in time) but rather that it would add delays to the settlement of disputes with all Members lodging appeals.[95] Such a concern speaks to the expectation that there would be no necessary connection between instituting a more rule-based approach with the subsequent judicialisation of the dispute settlement system.

Article 17 DSU sets out the competences of the Appellate Body and is cautious in its terminology. There is no mention of a 'court', 'tribunal' or 'judges' and the number of permanent members is considerably lower than comparable international tribunals.[96] Though permanent, members of the Appellate Body are not contracted on a full-time basis but rather maintained on a monthly retainer with daily fees factored in.[97] They do not sit together but in divisions of three,[98] potentially minimising their ability to lay down particularly authoritative decisions of the full Appellate Body as is customary in other legal systems.[99] Finally, the negative consensus rule[100] in theory constitutes a serious limitation on the autonomy of the Appellate Body, at the very least creating opportunities for public criticism of Appellate Body decisions by the Membership.[101]

[91] R Steinberg, 'Judicial Lawmaking at the WTO: Discursive, Constitutional, and Political Constraints' (2004) 98 *American Journal of International Law* 247, 250.

[92] 'The GATT dispute settlement machinery is original and specific; there is no equivalent in other areas of international relations.' Communication from EEC (24 September 1987) GATT Doc MTN.GNG/NG13/W/12, para 1.

[93] Ibid. 'The machinery cannot and must not be used to create, through a process of deductive interpretation, new obligations for contracting parties, or to replace the negotiating process. One of the objectives of the Uruguay Round is to eliminate certain ambiguities and diverging interpretations of the General Agreement and Codes, and this will make a fundamental contribution to dispute settlement.'

[94] 'The dispute settlement procedures should be used essentially as a conciliation mechanism whose final stage, if conciliation fails, should not be of a judicial nature.' Communication from Brazil (7 March 1988) GATT Doc MTN.GNG/NG13/W/24.

[95] See Note by the Secretariat (13 November 1989) GATT Doc MTN.GNG/NG13/16, para 21; Note by the Secretariat (15 December 1989) GATT Doc MTN.GNG/NG13/17, para 9; Note by the Secretariat (28 May 1990) GATT Doc MTN.GNG/NG13/19, para 8.

[96] Van Den Bossche, 'The Making of the "World Trade Court": The Origins and Development of the Appellate Body of the World Trade Organization' (n90) 65–66 citing the numbers of other permanent judges on international tribunals: 15 on the International Court of Justice, 18 on the International Criminal Court and 21 on the International Tribunal for the Law of the Sea.

[97] Establishment of the Appellate Body: Recommendations by the Preparatory Committee for the WTO approved by the Dispute Settlement Body on 10 February 1995 (19 June 1995) WT/DSB/1, paras 10–12.

[98] Article 17.1 DSU.

[99] The practice of sitting *en banc* to enhance the authority of decisions of a court and thus provide greater certainty is principally found in courts within common law systems.

[100] Article 17.14 DSU.

[101] For an account of the WTO General Council Meeting following the reception of *amicus curiae* briefs by the Appellate Body in the Shrimp-Turtle dispute: P Mavroidis, 'Amicus Curiae Briefs Before the WTO: Much Ado About Nothing' Jean Monnet Working Paper 2/01, 8.

The role of judicial actors in creating novel institutions is not new; Stein identified the process in the European context in 1981.[102] The WTO has been little different with the Appellate Body acting to consolidate its position and maintain its own legitimacy.[103] In spite of limited, though central, guidance from the DSU[104] and a weak mandate from its accompanying negotiating history, the Appellate Body members constituted their identity through their decisions (some considered of particular 'constitutional' importance)[105] and own Working Procedures[106] that served to 'cure' some of the obstacles to the Appellate Body's legitimacy; Van den Bossche identifies Rule 4 of the Working Procedures, which sets out a mechanism for the 'exchange of views' between all members before finalising a report, as a key way to resolve the dangers of inconsistency and reduced authority that the three member divisions might otherwise have caused.[107] More generally, the Working Procedures have served to ensure the judicial character of the procedures at the Appellate Body as opposed to the more informal pre-WTO dispute settlement practices.[108]

One consequence of the judicialisation of the Appellate Body system has been its need to ensure its own legitimacy in face of claims of activism, and it has done so in response to the guidance given in the DSU, in particular through Article 3.2, ensuring that its reports (once adopted by the Dispute Settlement Body) 'cannot add to or diminish the rights and obligations provided in the covered agreements'. Such a provision is unusual in the extreme, embodying a deep concern for judicial 'activism' or overreaching.

## D. The *Korea—Dairy* and *Argentina—Footwear* Appellate Body Reports and the Subsequent Fallout

The Appellate Body's response to the *Korea—Dairy* and *Argentina—Footwear* panel reports was released almost simultaneously and the relevant passages were essentially the same. In particular, it took issue with the panels' approach by stressing the

102 E Stein, 'Lawyers, Judges, and the Making of a Transnational Constitution' (1981) 75(1) *American Journal of International Law* 1.

103 Van Den Bossche 'The Making of the "World Trade Court": The Origins and Development of the Appellate Body of the World Trade Organization' (n90) 69: 'most, if not all, members appointed in November 1995 shared a nearly missionary belief in the importance of the task entrusted to them'.

104 The limited guidance offered by the DSU to the members of the Appellate Body may well further explain their fixation with what little guidance exists: ie Article 3.2 DSU and thus the textual methodology on which their legitimacy rests.

105 J Jackson, 'The Varied Policies of International Juridical Bodies—Reflections on Theory and Practice' (2004) 25 *Michigan Journal of International Law* 869, D Cass, 'The "Constitutionalization" of International Trade Law: Judicial Norm Generation as the Engine of Constitutional Development in International Trade' (2001) 12 *European Journal of International Law* 39.

106 Currently, *Working Procedures for Appellate Review* (4 January 2005) WT/AB/WP/5.

107 Van Den Bossche, 'The Making of the "World Trade Court": the Origins and Development of the Appellate Body of the World Trade Organization' (n90) 69–71.

108 R Hudec, 'The New Dispute Settlement System of the WTO: An Overview of the First Three Years' (1999) 8 *Minnesota Journal of Global Trade* 1.

need to give meaning and effect to all provisions in the text[109] and reversed the panels' findings that the 'unforeseen developments' clause created no legal obligation.[110]

The Appellate Body also took the opportunity to clarify the aim of this interpretation; that is, in line with the object and purpose of the Safeguards Agreement, to reassert control over the multilateral disciplines on safeguards.[111] This is useful in clarifying the position of the 'unforeseen developments' clause during the intervening years. By stressing the need to reassert control over the safeguard system the clear implication is not that the 'unforeseen developments' clause had been legally inoperative but instead that there was lacking a suitable enforcement method or cases raised.

The fallout of the Appellate Body response was felt later as, in case after case, the US had its safeguard measures identified as WTO-incompliant.[112] The 'unforeseen developments' clause was one key issue, though a similar process has been reflected by the refusal of the Appellate Body to flesh out the requirements for causation tests under the Safeguards Agreement, even in spite of a pre-existing US methodology.[113] The exasperation from the US is palpable, stating '[it would] be important for us in terms of understanding what our obligations are under the *Agreement [on Safeguards]* and what we have to do to comply with them'.[114]

The result of the domestic (predominately US) influence on a strictly limited scope of action for the WTO dispute settlement system and its textual focus has led to an inability to discount the 'unforeseen developments' clause. Criticisms of the Appellate Body's position in these cases, arguing that too rigorous an application of Article XIX and the Safeguards Agreement undermines the 'safety valve' purpose of the provisions,[115] miss the broader imperatives that drive the Appellate Body. This is its concern with prioritising its own legitimacy in the face of criticism, resulting in a focus on 'hermeneutic prudence' to defend itself.[116]

This is not to argue that neither the Appellate Body nor the panels have extended the text of the Agreements but, instead, stresses their need to justify clearly such an

[109] *Korea—Definitive Safeguard Measure on Imports of Certain Dairy Products*, Report of the Appellate Body (14 December 1999) WT/DS98/AB /R (*Korea—Dairy Appellate Body*) para 82.

[110] Ibid.

[111] Ibid para 88.

[112] For example, *United States—Definitive Safeguard Measures on Imports of Wheat Gluten from the EC*, Report of the Appellate Body (22 December 2000) WT/DS166/AB/R, *United States—Safeguard Measures on Imports of Fresh, Chilled or Frozen Lamb Meat From New Zealand and Australia*, Report of the Appellate Body (1 May 2001) WT/DS177-178/AB/R, *United States—Definitive Safeguard Measures on Imports of Certain Steel Products*, Report of the Appellate Body (10 November 2003) WT/DS248-259/AB/R.

[113] '[A] series of wooden, largely useless and often logically incoherent decisions that simply underscore the deficiencies of the treaty text without clarifying them in the least.' A Sykes, 'The Fundamental Deficiencies of the Agreement on Safeguards: A Reply to Professor Lee' (2006) 40(5) *Journal of World Trade* 979, 993.

[114] US statement in *US—Steel* (n 112) para 484.

[115] A Sykes, 'The "Safeguards Mess" Revisited—A Reply to Professor Jones' (2004) 3 *World Trade Review* 93, 95–96.

[116] JHH Weiler, 'The Rule of Lawyers and the Ethos of Diplomats: Reflections on the Internal and External Legitimacy of WTO Dispute Settlement' *Harvard Jean Monnet Working Paper* 9/00 (2000).

act. For example, the position taken by the Appellate Body that safeguard measures ought to be extraordinary has been described as 'an exercise in policy-making' rather than 'even-handed interpretation'.[117] This position is justified by the Appellate Body, grounding its stance in the text of Article 11.1(a) of the Safeguards Agreement and the title of Article XIX GATT that safeguard measures are to be emergency actions. 'Thus, Article XIX is clearly, and in every way, an extraordinary remedy.'[118] Indeed, 'policy-making' as a criticism is routed in the view that there is a clear identifiable rule that can be applied apolitically: it is an understanding of law as a mechanistic system of rules rather than a complex process subject and responsive to the behaviour of actors. The case here, however, is one where both the text and the institution have been influenced by a process of norm export. The expectation that by using national law as a model for international law, similar approaches will be taken by adjudicative bodies fails not as a result of differing legal cultures, but instead for failing to take into account corresponding processes of norm export that have taken place in other areas such as the creation of a dispute settlement system.[119]

## IV. CONCLUSION

Contrasting expectations from the use of national law to create new provisions of international law and the results, draws our attention to the utility and effectiveness of such activities. It also, and more importantly, tells us about how law functions, as part of a complex process involving numerous actors, institutional and otherwise, pursuing and responding to competing interests and values. At the WTO, expectations seem to have been confounded: the use of domestic legislation as a model, carrying not only its specific meaning but also an accompanying tradition of application, to embed norms internationally has had limited success in the area of safeguard measures. And this example is not unique at the WTO: the debates regarding standard of review under the Anti-Dumping Agreement, definitions of key terms such as 'public body' under the Agreement on Subsidies and Countervailing Measures (SCM Agreement) or approaches to provisional measures under the Agreement on the Application of Sanitary and Phytosanitary Measures (SPS Agreement), all paint a larger picture of the limited ability of national law to produce predictable outcomes internationally.

The example taken from safeguards has identified the equally important role that norm export has when not only using specific provisions of national law as a model, but also domestic concepts: the concern of the US with judicial activism and the desire to restrict the interpretative freedom of panels and the Appellate Body

[117] K Greenwald, 'WTO Dispute Settlement: An Exercise in Trade Legislation?' (2003) *Journal of International Economic Law* 113.

[118] *Argentina—Footwear Appellate Body* (n 74) paras 93–94.

[119] This speaks to a broader cultural context for the existence, understanding and interpretation of the legal rule: P Legrand, 'What "Legal Transplants?"' in D Nelken and J Feest (eds), *Adapting Legal Culture* (Hart Publishing, 2001) 55, 61.

through Article 3.2 DSU speaks strongly to an internal debate over the appropriate scope of authority between legislative and judicial branches within the federal government. Superficially concerned with sovereignty, Congressional debates that informed US positions at the Uruguay Round were nonetheless steeped in the constitutional traditions of the US.[120] This example has been strongly focused on the US, an influence which is not representative of all instances of norm export: nonetheless, as an extreme case it allows us to identify certain key features of this process.

National law thus influences international law, though not always in the way we expect. To understand *how* it actually does this, we are required to reframe our view of the law away from mechanistic approaches to 'appropriate' application of rules and to appreciate the complex and complicated, and far messier, realities of a multiplicity of systems and actors all engaged in a web of competing interests, ideas and objectives.

[120] For an account, see J Jackson, 'The Great 1994 Sovereignty Debate: United States Acceptance and Implementation of the Uruguay Round Results' in J Charney et al (eds), *Politics, Values and Functions: International Law in the 21st Century—Essays in Honor of Professor Louis Henkin* (Martinus Nijhoff, 1998).

# 8

# *International Investment Agreements and Good Governance: Norm and Institutional Design, Internalisation and Domestic Rule-making*

MAVLUDA SATTOROVA*

## I. INTRODUCTION

THIS CONTRIBUTION FORMS part of the author's ongoing project which examines the role of international investment law in fostering good governance and rule of law at a national level. What role does international investment law play in generating national law? Can investment treaty remedies induce governments into compliance with the rule of law and good governance standards? To what extent and how do investment treaty norms influence government decision-making in host states? To answer these questions, the project examines the evolving objectives of international investment law and undertakes socio-legal and interdisciplinary analysis of the impact, both *ex ante* and *ex post*, of international investment law on governmental conduct. The aim of this contribution is to introduce the key strands of the argument developed in the project and to discuss some of the preliminary findings stemming from the empirical case studies and interviews conducted to date.

While much has already been written on why states sign international investment agreements (IIAs), there is a dearth of studies on the connection between such agreements and state actions in both the domestic and international arenas. What effect do international investment law and its dispute settlement mechanism have on state behaviour? With the exception of some recent scholarly contributions, the existing literature makes little effort to engage with causal assumptions about how the investment treaty regime influences host state behaviour. One such assumption is readily discernible in the arguments which justify both the existence of the regime and its increasingly expanding reach. The proliferation of voices criticising IIAs and investment arbitration coincided with a rapid uptake of the good governance narrative

* Senior Lecturer, University of Liverpool School of Law and Social Justice.

among the regime's supporters as though it was felt that international investment law 'must fulfill *some* useful societal function'.[1] International investment law and investor-state arbitration, it has been claimed, are necessary and desirable not just to ensure effective protection of foreign investors but also to promote host state compliance with the rule of law and good governance precepts. Thus, one of the investment treaty regime's broader objectives, as well as one of its projected collective benefits, is the transformation of governance institutions and practices in host states. It has been argued that 'investment treaties aim at binding States into a legal framework that gives them an incentive and a yardstick for transforming their legal systems into ones that are conducive to market-based investment activities and provide the institutions necessary for the functioning of such markets'.[2] 'Indirect collective benefits' of international investment law for host societies comprise not only the ability of host states to attract investment but also the potential for change in 'the political dynamic of reform of domestic dispute resolution and policy making institutions'.[3]

The increasing frequency of such claims in legal discourse compels one to question their conceptual and juridical underpinnings. 'Good governance has a very powerful and apparently universal appeal: all peoples and societies would surely seek good governance—in much the same way that all peoples and societies were seen as desiring development.'[4] Just as is the case with economic development, which has long been regarded as one of the primary objectives of IIAs, it is barely questioned by either proponents or critics of the investment treaty regime that fostering good governance (and the rule of law) is a desirable end. However, what remains underexplored is the capacity of international investment rules to bring about change in domestic governance institutions and practices. This contribution questions the good governance narratives in the investment treaty context from conceptual, doctrinal and empirical angles. First, it will critically examine the regime's internal capacity to influence host state behaviour by analysing its existing make-up through the eyes of political science scholarship on state compliance with international law. Does international investment law possess the necessary tools to influence domestic governance? Is it inherently compliant with rule-of-law and good governance precepts to be able to export them successfully into national legal environments? The focus will then shift to findings emerging from empirical investigations, including the small-scale interviews and case studies conducted by the author in two developing countries. Finally, the contribution will draw attention to the variety of forms in which investment treaty law can influence government behaviour, highlighting the

[1] Thomas Schultz and Cédric Dupont, 'Investment Arbitration: Promoting the Rule of Law or Over-Empowering Investors? A Quantitative Empirical Study' available at ssrn.com/abstract=2399179, 2.

[2] Stephan Schill, *The Multilateralization of International Investment Law* (Cambridge, Cambridge University Press, 2009) 377.

[3] David Gaukrodger and Kathryn Gordon, 'Investor-state dispute settlement: A scoping paper for the investment policy community' (OECD Working Papers on International Investment, No 2012/3, OECD Investment Division), available at www.oecd.org/daf/investment/workingpapers,13.

[4] Antony Anghie, 'Civilisation and Commerce: The Concept of Governance in Historical Perspective' (2000) 45 *Villanova Law Review* 887, 893.

importance of peering behind the state and identifying domestic actors and factors that shape the ways in which host states respond to investment treaty disciplines.

## II. INVESTMENT TREATY LAW AND ITS CAPACITY TO FOSTER GOOD GOVERNANCE IN HOST STATES

### A. Norm-embedding and Compliance with Good Governance Standards

At the heart of the good governance narrative in investment law scholarship lies the claim that, although legally enforceable only by foreign investors, strict investment protection standards create a 'spillover' effect that benefits national citizens and residents as the host country gradually develops better administrative practices to comply with international investment best practices.[5] The need to comply effectively with the rule of law and principles of due process imposed by investment treaties may arguably entail legal reforms and foster more legalistic and rule-oriented governance practices.[6] An inquiry into the capacity of international investment law to bring about a positive change in domestic governance may provide new and useful insights into the currently largely unexplored question of compliance in the investment treaty context. One can distinguish three layers of compliance: pre-dispute compliance with good governance standards, post-dispute compliance with concrete arbitral prescriptions, and post-dispute adjustment of domestic governance norms and practices. The rate of compliance with the concrete arbitral prescriptions stage may well be high, which is not surprising given the strength of the enforcement mechanism undergirding the investment treaty regime. In an effort to enforce arbitral awards, investors can go as far as resorting to judicial proceedings and discovery subpoenas seeking information about the respondent host state's banking assets and transactions.[7] Compliance with arbitral awards may be involuntary and is frequently carried out against the respondent state's will. Moreover, arbitral awards rarely if ever prescribe concrete changes in governance practices. What is more interesting for the purposes of this project, however, is *ex ante* and *ex post* compliance by host states with investment treaty obligations which explicitly or implicitly compel states to maintain good governance standards in daily practices of domestic bureaucratic and legal institutions. Can international investment law, with its strategy of substituting domestic governance mechanisms by international structures, effectively induce states into compliance with the rule of law and good governance standards at a national level?[8]

[5] Roberto Echandi, 'What Do Developing Countries Expect from the International Investment Regime?' in Jose E Alvarez et al, *The Evolving International Investment Regime: Expectations, Realities, Options* (Oxford, Oxford University Press, 2011) 13.

[6] Ibid 14.

[7] See *Republic of Argentina v NML Capital* 134 SCt 2250 (2014).

[8] Of note is the study conducted by Tom Ginsburg, 'International substitutes for domestic institutions: Bilateral investment treaties and governance' (2005) 25 *International Review of Law and Economics* 107.

What appears to be problematic in the investment treaty context is that the institution of investor-state arbitration, with its predominantly externalised, decentralised and frequently ad hoc nature does not provide the necessary bedrock of support to facilitate effective and consistent embedding of good governance and rule of law values in the legal and bureaucratic practices of host states. When compared with other international regimes, the investment treaty regime appears to lack some of the vital characteristics necessary for the fulfilment of its promise to transform domestic governance in host states. One considerable impediment to the effective embedding of good governance standards in the legal and bureaucratic practices of host states is the lack of national judicial involvement, precipitated by the waiver of the local remedies exhaustion—a unique feature and cornerstone of the investment treaty regime. Political science scholarship has long stressed the role of embeddedness in promoting compliance with international rules. As observed by proponents of liberal institutionalist theory, when international legal commitments are embedded in domestic legal systems it is no longer necessary for governments, and in particular national executives, to take positive action to ensure enforcement of international judgments.[9] 'Instead, enforcement occurs through domestic courts and executive agents who are responsive to judicial decisions.'[10] Thus, 'other things being equal, the more firmly embedded an international commitment is in domestic law, the more likely is compliance with judgments to enforce it'.[11]

Other theories of compliance, among them notably the theory of transnational legal process, have also stressed the importance of embedding and norm internalisation as a precondition of compliance. Koh has argued, for example, that 'self-enforcing patterns of compliance' are generated through internalisation of international norms in domestic structures through executive, legislative and judicial action. It is through repeated participation in the transnational legal process—the interaction between transnational legal actors and national epistemic communities—that states comply with international law. In Koh's view: 'True compliance is not so much the result of externally imposed sanctions ... as internally felt norms.'[12]

Social science theories of governance also point in the direction of iterative interaction between external and internal actors; after all, governance is defined as 'the creation of a structure or an order which *cannot be externally imposed* but is the result of the interaction of a multiplicity of governing and each other influencing actors'.[13] Since international investment law is largely premised on the transfer of adjudicatory powers from national courts to international tribunals, the former are removed

[9] Robert O Keohane, Andrew Moravcsik and Anne-Marie Slaughter, 'Legalized dispute resolution: interstate and transnational' (2000) 54(3) *International Organization* 457, 476.

[10] Ibid 476.

[11] Ibid 478.

[12] Harold Koh, 'How Is International Human Rights Law Enforced?' (1998) 74 *Indiana Law Journal* 1397, 1407; see also Oona A Hathaway, 'Do Human Rights Treaties Make a Difference? (2002) 111 *Yale Law Journal* 1935, 1961.

[13] Gerry Stoker, 'Governance as theory: five propositions' (1993) 50(155) *International Social Science Journal* 17.

from 'the transnational iterative process'. Lack of vertical interaction between international tribunals and national courts prevents the latter from exercising a key role in embedding good governance standards in domestic legal orders.[14] Three notable dimensions of this problem are: (1) the absence of mandatory recourse to domestic remedies prevents national judicial involvement in embedding rule of law norms and practices; (2) the fact that lack of domestic remedies in the national legal order in itself can constitute a breach and form a basis of a host state's liability; and (3) as evidenced by recent arbitral practice, judicial attempts to enforce good governance standards and thus to provide effective remedies also can lead to host state liability.

To provide an example of how the lack of consistent interaction between the external agency and domestic actors currently impedes the fulfilment of the good governance agenda of investment treaty law, one could take a look at recent arbitral practice. A number of investment protection instruments, including certain US IIAs and Article 10 of the Energy Charter Treaty, expressly require that states provide investors with 'effective means of asserting claims and enforcing rights'.[15] This 'effective means' provision has been invoked in a number of investment disputes, including *AMTO v Ukraine*, where the claimants went as far as contending that the host state should be held to monetary responsibility for failing to create and maintain effective bankruptcy legislation.[16] The desirability and fairness of sanctioning developing states for their lack of legal and institutional capacity provides yet another ground for contesting the investment treaty regime's promise of good governance for host communities. To echo Harlow's criticism of global administrative law, there is 'a measure of hypocrisy in seeking to impose external standards on the poor and under-privileged, which the self-styled "good countries" are unwilling and sometimes unable to meet'.[17] That is, however, a separate question which falls outside the scope of this contribution. What is more troubling and relevant for the discussion at hand is the fact that attempts by national courts to restore the rule of law in domestic settings and to rectify wrongs committed by administrative bodies may lead to a host state's liability under the relevant IIA.

The case of *Arif v Moldova* provides a curious example of the internally contradictory set of obligations imposed by international investment law on host states, thus highlighting problems with the feasibility of the good governance promise (and mandate) of investment treaty law. The dispute arose after Moldovan courts had found illegality in actions of Moldovan airport authorities. The Moldovan judiciary held that the airport authorities failed to follow the competitive tender process

[14] See Diane A Desierto, 'ASEAN's Constitutionalization of International Law: Challenges to Evolution under the New ASEAN Charter' (2011) 49 *Columbia Journal of Transnational Law* 268, 316 highlighting the importance of norm embedding in the context of ASEAN.

[15] See eg Art II(7) of the Treaty Between the United States of America and the Republic of Ecuador Concerning the Encouragement and Reciprocal Protection of Investment (adopted 27 August 1993, entered into force 11 May 1997); also Art 10(12) of the Energy Charter Treaty (signed 17 December 1994, entered into force 16 April 1998) 2080 UNTS 100.

[16] *AMTO LLC v Ukraine*, Final Award, SCC Case No 080/2005 (26 March 2008) paras 75, 85.

[17] Carol Harlow, 'Global Administrative Law: The Quest for Principles and Values' (2006) 17 *European Journal of International Law* 187, 211.

required by the law, thereby preventing the foreign investor's competitors from participating in a tender for the right to operate duty-free shops at the Chisinau Airport. Disgruntled by this judicial ruling, the investor initiated investor-state arbitration. The investment tribunal acknowledged that the courts of Moldova had acted in what was an exemplary manner by transition economy standards. Yet the courts' effort to restore the rule of law by pronouncing on the illegality of the administrative action was found to be in violation of Moldova's IIA commitments, simply because the court rulings discouraged Arif's investment, while the executive branch encouraged the same.[18] This inconsistent treatment of the investor by the two branches of the Moldovan government was found to constitute a breach of the fair and equitable treatment standard. The executive branch committed a further treaty breach when it enforced the national court's orders against the investor, so as to restore legality and compliance with national laws.[19] The case of Arif is unsettling because it shows that, on the one hand, the lack of domestic remedies could itself lead to state liability, including under the effective means standard. On the other hand, the availability of such remedies and their utilisation by national courts could also be a problem, as attempts to restore legality in domestic law by national courts could be regarded as a breach of investment treaty law. This leaves host states in a situation when any attempt to rectify the original wrongfulness in executive conduct by judicial organs may be seen not only as superfluous but also in violation of IIAs. Can suppressing domestic judicial oversight of domestic executive action promote the rule of law? How can IIA prescriptions of good governance be embedded and implemented in domestic legal orders if restoring the rule of law by judicial bodies can itself be condemned and sanctioned as an investment treaty breach? 'If States cannot simultaneously respect arbitral norms and facilitate the integrity of institutions that support development, one of the key justifications for IIAs—their contribution to economic development—can be brought into question.'[20] If states cannot simultaneously respect the rule of law prescriptions of IIAs and maintain legality and integrity in the functioning of national institutions, the contribution of IIAs to the creation of rule-orientated governance practices is just as questionable.

## B. Does the Investment Treaty Regime Comply with Good Governance Standards?

When analysing state compliance with good governance standards through the lens of liberal institutionalist theory, one is pushed to question what role the existing design of international investment arbitration institutions plays in determining the regime's capacity to affect state behaviour. 'Institutions ... need to be consistent with the basic normative commitments of their members, so that having a reputation for

[18] *Mr Franck Charles Arif v Republic of Moldova*, Award, 8 April 2013 (ICSID Case No ARB/11/23) para 547.

[19] Todd Tucker, 'Investment Agreements versus the Rule of Law?' available at papers.ssrn.com/sol3/papers.cfm?abstract_id=2379283 1.

[20] Ibid 3.

supporting the institution has intrinsic, as well as instrumental, value.'[21] Does the investment treaty regime possess the necessary institutional consistency that would enable it to have a transformative impact on domestic governance? To be able to foster good governance and compliance with the rule of law in host states, international investment law must be guided by the same governance precepts, including transparency, predictability, consistency and accountability. There is a considerable body of scholarly contributions that have criticised both the institutional framework and the procedural mechanisms of investment treaty law for falling short of these benchmarks.[22] In this contribution, mention should be made of another shortcoming of the existing investment treaty regime, which detracts from its capacity to foster *ex ante* compliance and can discourage rather than encourage positive change in host states: its lop-sided nature and the resulting ambiguity of normative values that it stands for and is able to export into domestic regimes. Of particular interest here is the much-criticized failure of international investment law to balance investment rights with investment responsibilities, particularly in the context of corruption. Well-evidenced and much-discussed cases of misconduct by foreign investors and their complicity in illegal acts committed by governmental agencies in host states is an illustration of how investments can affect local communities not by eliminating inadequate governance practices but rather by entrenching them. Cases such as *World Duty Free v Kenya*, *Inceysa v Ecuador* and *Fraport v Philippines* have divided academics and practitioners as to how international investment law (IIL) should tackle the incidence of corruption.[23] At one end of the spectrum are those who advocate a zero-tolerance approach to investor participation in corruption, and in particular bribery. Others argue that 'a zero-tolerance approach undermines the general welfare of non-parties to the arbitration, who may be, as described by the *World Duty Free* tribunal with reference to the peoples in Kenya, "the mass of tax-payers and other citizens making up one of the poorest countries in the world."'[24] Furthermore, commentators have even suggested that 'upholding corrupt investors' claims in appropriate circumstances, such as where the state has condoned or demanded bribes from investors, is a more effective method of combating corruption and *enhancing the rule of law*'.[25] The claim that the rule of law could be strengthened through condoning investors' complicity in bribery and corruption appears to be dubious at best. It is true that countries which suffer from endemic government corruption usually lack a *culture*

[21] Robert O Keohane, 'International Relations and International Law: Two Optics' (1997) 38 *Harvard International Law Journal* 487, 502.

[22] See eg Gus Van Harten, 'Investment Treaty Arbitration, Procedural Fairness, and the Rule of Law' in Stephan W Schill (ed), *International Investment Law and Comparative Public Law* (Oxford, Oxford University Press, 2010) 627.

[23] *World Duty Free Company Limited v Kenya*, Award 4 October 2006 (ICSID CASE NO. ARB/00/7); *Inceysa Vallisoletana S.L. v. El Salvador*, Award 2 August 2006 (ICSID Case No. ARB/03/26); *Fraport AG Frankfurt Airport Services Worldwide v. The Republic of the Philippines*, Award 16 August 2007 (ICSID Case No. ARB/03/25).

[24] Kevin Lim, 'Upholding Corrupt Investors' Claims Against Complicit or Compliant Host States—Where Angels Should *Not* Fear to Tread' in Karl P Sauvant (ed), *Yearbook on International Investment Law & Policy* 2011–2012 (Oxford, Oxford University Press, 2013) 601, 620.

[25] Ibid 622.

of legitimate and transparent business practices and the political will to encourage such practices by enforcing anti-corruption laws.[26] Should tribunals grant investors compensation even despite their claims being tainted by corruption, the host communities would not benefit from such awards but would rather be taxed twice: once through the perpetuation of corrupt practices by foreign companies, and then by having to shoulder the financial burden of the monetary award rendered against the host state. If IIL continues to allow corrupt investors to recover their losses despite their participation in corrupt practices, the function of IIAs as instruments of good governance can be legitimately doubted.

A troubling illustration of the impact of foreign investment—and of international rules on foreign investment protection—can also be found in the much-publicised instances of environmental neglect by foreign companies. Hirsch observes that 'existing literature consistently emphasises the importance of foreign investment as a channel for the diffusion of knowledge, technology and management practices'.[27] What role do foreign investments *and* investment protection rules play in entrenching, rather than eliminating, weaknesses in governance practices in host states, in particular environmental governance? One cannot but agree with Miles's observation that 'sourced from a purely instrumentalist conceptualisation of the environment, [international investment law] is indifferent to the effects of investor activity on the local communities and environments of host states'.[28] The negative impact of international investment law on domestic governance, and in particular environmental governance, is considered as one of the legacies of imperialism which lies at the roots of the modern IIL. It finds its reflection in the historical 'commodification of the environment of host state for the use of the foreign investor'[29] and the entrenchment of such commodification in host states' neglect of the environment. Just as with corporate complicity in corruption, both integrity and feasibility of the good governance promise of the investment treaty regime hinges on the stance investment treaties and arbitration take on environmental misconduct of foreign investors.

## III. SOME INSIGHTS INTO EMERGING EMPIRICAL EVIDENCE ON THE PATTERNS OF INTERNALISATION OF INVESTMENT TREATY PRESCRIPTIONS IN HOST GOVERNMENTS

At the heart of the argument that posits a transformative impact of investment treaty law on governance in host states is an assumption that investment treaty rules act as 'a deterrent mechanism against short-term policy reversals and assist developing

[26] Ibid.

[27] Moshe Hirsch, 'The Sociology of International Investment Law' in Zachary Douglas, Joost Pauwelyn and Jorge E Viñuales (eds), *The Foundations of International Investment Law: Bringing Theory into Practice* (Oxford, Oxford University Press, 2014) 4–5, available at papers.ssrn.com/sol3/papers.cfm?abstract_id=2322328.

[28] Kate Miles, *The Origins of International Investment Law: Empire, Environment and the Safeguarding of Capital* (Cambridge, Cambridge University Press, 2013) 139–40.

[29] Ibid 134.

countries in promoting greater effectiveness of the rule of law at the domestic level'.[30] 'While tribunals cannot quash domestic acts or compel States to bring their domestic legal order into line with investment treaty obligations, the monetary sanctions they can impose exert considerable pressure on states to bring their domestic legal orders into conformity with their investment treaty obligations.'[31] However, just as with many areas of international law and policy, the claims regarding effectiveness of international investment law, including in the context of fostering good governance and the rule of law in host states, remain by and large empirically and theoretically untested.[32]

The project intends to fill this gap and examine the interplay between investment treaty disciplines and governmental conduct by focusing on the so-called incentive effects of investment treaty rules on bureaucratic behaviour. If host states are expected to respond to investment treaty norms by adjusting their legal orders and ensuring *ex ante* compliance with the prescribed standards of governmental conduct, government officials ought to understand the scope and meaning of investment protection guarantees under existing bilateral and multilateral agreements. To what extent are government officials actually aware of and influenced by investment treaty disciplines in making their decisions? In empirically evaluating the interplay between investment treaty rules and host state behaviour it is important to disentangle two distinct but interrelated issues: (1) the extent of awareness of investment treaty law; and (2) the ways in which investment treaty law is internalised leading to changes in government behaviour.

Recent empirical studies provide useful insights into the extent to which government officials are aware of investment treaty prescriptions. For instance, Poulsen and Aisbett's survey of government officials in 13 developing countries has shown that 'all officials, including stakeholders, noted that they had been unaware of the far-reaching scope and implications of bilateral investment treaties (BITs) during the 1990s, when the treaties proliferated'.[33] Although the primary focus of their survey was on the making of BITs rather than the impact of BITs on host state behaviour, it nevertheless elucidates the extent to which government officials, including those who were directly involved in signing BITs, were and are aware of investment treaty law.

[30] Echandi (n 5) 13.

[31] Stephan W Schill, 'System Building in Investment Treaty Arbitration and Lawmaking' (2001) 12 *German Law Journal* 1083, 1085.

[32] Except for a burgeoning body of research, including recent studies authored by Jonathan Bonnitcha, Emma Aisbett, Lauge Poulsen, Jason Yackee and Susan Franck. Although Bonnitcha has examined the impact of investment treaty law on government decision-making, the focus and methodology of his research are different from this project. See respectively, Jonathan Bonnitcha and Emma Aisbett, 'An Economic Analysis of the Substantive Protections Provided by Investment Treaties' in Sauvant et al (eds), *Yearbook on International Investment Law & Policy 2011–2012* (New York, Oxford University Press, 2013) 681–704; Lauge N Skovgaard Poulson and Emma Aisbett, 'When the Claims Hit: Bilateral Investment Treaties and Bounded Rational Learning' (2013) 65 *World Politics* 273–313; Jason Webb Yackee, 'Do Bilateral Investment Treaties Promote Foreign Direct Investment? Some Hints from Alternative Evidence' (2010–2011) 51 *Virginia Journal of International Law* 397; Susan D Franck, 'Development and Outcomes of Investment Treaty Arbitration' (2009) 50 *Harvard Journal of International Law* 435.

[33] Poulsen and Aisbett (n 32) 281–82.

Of course, the question can be raised as to whether the historically low levels of awareness have changed after the number of investment treaties and investment arbitrations proliferated. Poulsen and Aisbett's study also reveals that: 'In twelve out of 13 countries where officials were interviewed, respondents thus noted that it was not until the first claim was filed against their country that stakeholders realized that BITs exposed them to serious liabilities.'[34] This finding resonates with those made by this author in the course of case studies conducted in two developing states. The case studies comprised interviews with government officials and analysis of national legislative material relating to investment policy-making and dispute settlement, as well as rules on the enforcement of judgments against government agencies and officials in two developing countries which (1) have a number of investment treaties; and (2) have been exposed to investment arbitration on a number of occasions. The interviews (21 respondents in total) were conducted among government officials working in ministries and agencies that have had involvement in investment treaty making and dispute settlement, as well as government officers who interact with foreign investors outside the context of investment treaty law and dispute settlement, that is, in making, implementing and otherwise applying national laws in domestic, not international, settings. The interviews showed that the first exposure to investment arbitration claims entailed a spike in the level of awareness of investment treaty law among government officials who were directly involved in regulating and implementing foreign investment projects (for example, ministries of energy, economic development, justice and foreign affairs).

What is perhaps even more interesting for the purposes of this project is that the case studies show a remarkable lack of awareness of investment treaty law among officials in lower tiers of government. Even before the emergence of empirical scholarship on international investment law and policy-making, it was argued that decision-makers—particularly those in administrative agencies of developing states—who do not have direct or regular dealings with foreign investors are unlikely to be aware of international investment agreements and their prescriptions.[35] As a consequence, such decision-makers are unlikely 'to internalise the constraints of investment treaty protections'[36] not only when evaluating the adoption of new governmental measures but also in exercising their day-to-day decision-making powers vis-à-vis foreign investors. The case studies suggest that, even after the respective governments became exposed to a number of investment treaty arbitrations, government officials in the executive and judicial organs have remained unaware of both the very existence of investment treaty law and of the fact that their acts or omissions affecting foreign investors may lead to investment arbitration claims. This preliminary finding is noteworthy, not least because recent statistical analyses of the International

[34] Ibid 282.

[35] J Coe and N Rubins, 'Regulatory Expropriation and the *Tecmed* Case: Context and Contributions' in T Weiler (ed), *International Investment Law and Arbitration: Leading Cases from the ICSID, NAFTA, Bilateral Treaties and Customary International Law* (London, Cameron May, 2005) 599.

[36] Jonathan Bonnitcha, *Substantive Protection under Investment Treaties: A Legal and Economic Analysis* (Oxford, Oxford University Press, 2014) 122.

Centre for the Settlement of Investment Disputes (ICSID) case load show that the majority of government decisions that lead to investor-state arbitrations are associated with actions taken by the executive branch and that, beyond ministries, it was the conduct of subnational actors such as provincial, state and municipal authorities and agencies that eventually led to investment disputes.[37] If government officials involved in making executive and judicial decisions vis-à-vis investors are unaware of investment treaty law and its prescriptions, even after the country has had to defend itself in a number of investment arbitration cases, it becomes very difficult to agree with the argument that such arbitration would lead to changes in governmental practices and culture within these agencies.

Another noteworthy aspect that emerges from the case studies is that investment treaty law can be internalised by government officials but not necessarily in the way predicted by the proponents of the good governance narrative. Although anecdotal, evidence from the interviews reveals that, in some cases, despite the previous exposure of the host state to investment treaty arbitration claims, government officials chose to ignore the risk of a new claim which their action could entail. One interviewee, for instance, referred to an incident where a high-ranking official disregarded legal advice about the potential risk of investment arbitration on the ground that the governmental action at issue was economically significant and thus more important. It appears that even though, as some scholars have suggested, the country may scale back its IIA policy after experiencing their bite,[38] the existence of IIAs may not necessarily influence government decision-making vis-à-vis a concrete foreign investment project even after the country had been exposed to investment arbitration. This suggests that, due to various factors, the awareness of IIAs and of their implications does not necessarily lead to internalisation in the sense of engendering more risk-averse and IIA-compliant patterns of behaviour on the part of government officials.

Governments' failure to learn from their previous experience may also be reflected in their failure to adjust both their investment treaty policies and domestic legal frameworks. Since many cases of compliance or non-compliance with international law are ultimately made by individuals,[39] it can be questioned whether holding a host government to monetary liability would have a subsequent deterrent effect and promote *ex ante* compliance with investment treaty rules, thus arguably leading to improved governance at a national level. In theory, the imposition of monetary liability on the state should compel a governmental agency to assume responsibility for detecting, identifying and controlling risk-increasing activities in which its departments and employees engage.[40] Governments are expected to put in place

[37] Jeremy Caddel and Nathan M Jensen, 'Which host country government actors are most involved in disputes with foreign investors?' Columbia FDI Perspectives No 120 April 28, 2014, available at ccsi.columbia.edu/files/2013/10/No-120-Caddel-and-Jensen-FINAL-WEBSITE-version.pdf.

[38] Aisbett and Poulsen (n 32) 282.

[39] Tomer Broude, 'Behavioral International Law' *Hebrew University of Jerusalem International Law Forum Research Paper No 12–13* (2013) available at papers.ssrn.com/sol3/papers.cfm?abstract_id=2320375, 52–53.

[40] David Cohen, 'Regulating Regulators: The Legal Environment of the State' (1990) 40 *University of Toronto Law Journal* 245.

risk management measures to identify potential exposure to, and reduce the probability and magnitude of, monetary liability.[41] Such measures may include employee training programmes and remuneration policies that link the cost of governmental responsibility to salaries and promotions. The capacity of an external governance regime to induce government officials to act in a certain manner and to refrain from certain types of behaviour will hinge on the targeted government's 'monitoring ability'.[42] A lack of proper incentive to avoid harm arises where neither the government nor its employees bear the costs of the harms that they cause.[43] Thus, in order for investment treaty law to have an incentivising and transformative effect on national governance practices in a host state, an internal loss-allocation regime should be in place to ensure that monetary losses incurred as a result of damages awards are shifted to a governmental agency which has managerial, supervisory and budgetary authority, and political power over bureaucrats whose activities lead to state liability.[44]

However, in practice, imposing liability on host governments does not necessarily lead to risk-averse bureaucratic behaviour. This preliminary conclusion draws on interviews as well as sample case studies of national legal rules governing the payment of damages in connection with claims against state organs and government officials. It transpires that governments often fail to respond to liability rules in the expected manner, that is, they fail to take measures aimed at identifying the causes of investment disputes and preventing officials from engaging in the forms of conduct that may lead to a dispute and host state liability. It has emerged from one case study, for example, that the only monitoring mechanism the government introduced after its exposure to investment arbitration was a new agency tasked with dealing with investment claims. No attempt was made to identify the potential causes of investment disputes and to put in place measures to change governance practices that fell short of investment treaty prescriptions.

'Individuals' behaviour and normative choices are significantly affected by the social context and socio-cultural factors.'[45] The very ability of the host government to act sensitively and thus respond to the harmful consequences of international liability by changing relevant practices can be severely circumscribed by the very weaknesses in the domestic legal and bureaucratic culture which international investment law allegedly aims to improve. Such shortcomings interfere with government ability to put in place and maintain an effective internal monitoring and loss-prevention mechanism. Governments in democratic states with high levels of institutional capacity are more likely to show sensitivity to the imposition of international liability than

[41] Ibid 246.

[42] Eric A Posner and Alan O Sykes, *Economic Foundations of International Law* (Cambridge, Mass, Harvard University Press, 2013) 115.

[43] Ibid 115.

[44] Cohen (n 40) 213.

[45] Moshe Hirsch, 'The Sociology of International Investment Law' in Zachary Douglas, Joost Pauwelyn and Jorge E Viñuales, *The Foundations of International Investment Law: Bringing Theory into Practice* (Oxford, Oxford University Press, 2014).

those with a long and pervasive record of corruption and cronyism.[46] Liberal institutionalist theorists have long argued that 'the domestic regime type is essential to understanding international law compliance'.[47]

> Governments based on the rule of law and, especially, the independence of the judicial branch are, in this view, much more likely to comply with international obligations than those that are not. Liberal democracies are likely to commit to rules that reflect their ideological biases and to comply with them.[48]

Although this proposition 'has not been put to a rigorous test',[49] host state compliance with international investment law may provide an interesting empirical case to support this theory, by illustrating how different countries vary in their response to the pressure of investment treaty law, that is, reform-orientated response in developed states and withdrawal and backlash in less developed states.

More to the point, the specificity of the host state regime needs to be taken into account in designing or recalibrating deterrence and incentive devices through which international investment law is to transform national governance cultures. Scholarship on law and development has made considerable advance in analysing rule of law initiatives and their impact on governance in host states. For instance, Trebilcock and Daniels highlight the role of socio-cultural values as a critical success factor in rule of law reform.[50] The use of top-down, one-size-fits-all reform blueprints and the ensuing insensitivity to the needs and contexts of target states have caused many a reform initiative to founder.[51] Furthermore, scholars sound a note of caution that: 'Governments unequivocally opposed to rule of law reform will rarely be sensitive to state-level pressure mechanisms.'[52] These observations expose the fallacy of assumptions which lie at the heart of the good governance narratives: those who advocate that investment treaty law and its monetary sanctions can act as a catalyst of governance reforms in developing states disregard the complexity of factors which shape governance practices and the diversity of incentives through which such practices could be changed.

[46] A somewhat similar conclusion has been made by Aisbett and Poulsen, who suggest that developing country governments may be 'more prone to biased processing of information about the implications of BITs than developed country counterparts with higher levels of administrative capacity'. See Aisbett and Poulsen (n 32) 302.

[47] Anne-Marie Slaughter, 'International Law in a World of Liberal States' (1995) 6 *European Journal of International Law* 503.

[48] Beth A Simmons, 'International Law and State Behavior: Commitment and Compliance in International Monetary Affairs' (2000) 94(4) *American Political Science Review* 819, Oona Hathaway, 'Between Power and Principle: An Integrated Theory of International Law' (2005) 72 *The University of Chicago Law Review* 469, 524: 'Perhaps the most robust finding in the empirical literature to date is that democratic nations behave differently with regard to international law than do non-democratic nations'; Andrew Moravcsik, The Origins of Human Rights Regimes: Democratic Delegation in Postwar Europe (2000) *International Organization* 217, 220: international treaties offer states a means of consolidating democratic achievements.

[49] Simmons (n 48) 819.

[50] Michael J Trebilcock and Ronald J Daniels, *Rule of Law Reform and Development: Charting the Fragile Path of Progress* (Cheltenham, Edward Elgar, 2008) 336.

[51] Ibid 336.

[52] Ibid 354.

## IV. THE VARYING IMPACT OF INVESTMENT TREATY REMEDIES: ON FORMS OF IMPACT AND THE ROLE OF DOMESTIC ACTORS IN SHAPING IT

If investment treaty law is capable of producing a transformative effect on government behaviour, there is a likelihood that such an effect will not always be positive (that is, it will stimulate compliance with good governance standards) but in some cases negative (that is, it will inhibit governments from otherwise desirable action and lead to the so-called regulatory chill). The existence of a chilling effect of investment treaty law on national regulatory activity is a matter of an ongoing scholarly debate, particularly in the context of a clash between investment protection and states' regulatory freedom to pursue environment protection, health and safety, and other public policy measures. Some scholars have argued that investment treaties '*should* not lead to a chill on environmental regulation nor obstruct measures that are introduced in an attempt to mitigate climate change'.[53] This proposition, however, does not engage with empirical and theoretical studies on the effect of international rules on government conduct. Other contributions to the debate indicate that international investment treaties are likely to, and in some cases do, have a chilling effect on regulatory conduct.[54] The aim of this project is not to record the fact that investment treaties restrict regulatory powers but rather to test this claim from various angles. In particular, attention will be drawn to the interface between good governance and regulatory chill. One aspect of this interface is the variety of ways in which international investment law can influence host state behaviour—known examples include regulatory chill, withdrawal (treaty chill), and arguably domestic governance reforms. This variety in turn gives rise to the question about the factors that determine the way in which host states respond to investment treaty disciplines.

First, we suggest that regulatory chill should be examined as a form of excessive risk-reduction strategy triggered by the imposition of monetary liability on the host state. Host states where internal risk-reduction mechanisms are in place are likely to be more susceptible to the chilling effect of investment treaty norms. This preliminary conclusion not only draws support from the liberal institutionalist and managerial theories of compliance but is also supported by a recent study on bounded rationality, which suggests that decision-making in the investment treaty context varies with the extent of expertise in the relevant government agencies, whereby developed countries with higher levels of administrative capacity may display different patterns of learning from their investment treaty experience.[55]

[53] Stephan W Schill, 'Do Investment Treaties Chill Unilateral State Regulation to Mitigate Climate Change?' (2007) 5 *Journal of International Arbitration* 469.

[54] See eg Emily Barrett Lydgate, 'Biofuels, Sustainability, and Trade-related Regulatory Chill' (2012) 15 *Journal of International Economic Law* 157; Kyla Tienhaara, 'Regulatory Chill and the Threat of Arbitration: A View From Political Science' in Chester Brown and Kate Miles (eds), *Evolution in Investment Treaty Law and Arbitration* (Cambridge, Cambridge University Press, 2011) 606–28.

[55] Aisbett and Poulsen (n 32) 302.

Secondly, in examining the impact of investment treaty law on national governance it is important to consider the role of domestic actors in shaping a host state's response to investment treaty disciplines. Just like many of the existing theories of compliance with international law, investment law scholarship leaves unaddressed the question of how international legal rules advance the interests of different constituencies within the target state and how those constituencies shape the way host states respond to and internalise investment treaty prescriptions.[56] This is particularly pertinent in the context of discussing a potentially negative impact of investment treaty law on national governance whereby the imposition or threat of sanctions produces regulatory chill. To what extent, and how, is this causal relationship between investment treaty sanctions and government decision-making influenced by various domestic constituencies? As Trachtman has observed:

> A theory of formation and compliance with international law that focuses on the role of domestic political coalitions achieves important theoretical advances. ... It allows for the possibility of greater explanatory and predictive power than 'unitary state' theories of compliance. Second, it encompasses the role of individuals in domestic politics, and therefore moves toward a more liberal and cosmopolitan understanding of the role and dynamics of international law. A domestic coalition-based theory of international law transcends the state and examines individual preferences, but takes the state as the partial mediator of individual preferences.[57]

It seems that, with its focus on individuals and its departure from state-centric approaches, such theory would provide a suitable analytic frame for examining *ex ante* compliance with good governance prescriptions of IIAs. 'State behaviour is the result of complex interactions between political players at the domestic level, and cannot be explained as simply resulting from power-maximizing behaviour or strategic calculation by a unitary actor.'[58] Why despite sharing similar socio-economic and political characteristics, do states—both developed and developing—differ in the way they respond to investment treaty law? For instance, some developed states have amended their investment treaty models whilst others continue to use the traditional drafting patterns. What lies beneath this variation in the ways developed states have approached investment treaty reform? There are some instances where host states have moved towards a more participatory investment treaty policy[59] (that is, United States, South Africa and more recently the European Union). The exposure to investment treaty claims has generated different responses among developing states too; some have reacted by withdrawing from the investment arbitration

[56] Joel P Trachtman, 'International Law and Domestic Political Coalitions: The Grand Theory of Compliance with International Law' (2010) 11 *Chicago Journal of International Law* 128, 129.

[57] Ibid 133.

[58] Hathaway (n 48) 484.

[59] David Schneiderman, 'Power and Production in Global Legal Pluralism: An international political economy approach' in Amanda Perry-Kessaris, *Socio-legal Approaches to International Economic Law: Text, Context, Subtext* (Routledge, 2013) 116.

regime, others moved to adjust their treaties, yet others continued their participation in the regime by leaving investment treaty texts intact. In order to better understand the interplay between investment treaty law and governance in host states, we need to '[p]eer inside the state, looking for the individuals and groups that influence governments through political institutions and social practices'.[60]

Closely linked to the place of domestic actors in the shaping of host state responses to IIAs is the position of stakeholders other than investors and host states within the emerging architecture of the global investment regime. In their recent political science perspective on government behaviour in signing IIAs, Aisbett and Poulsen question 'whether more participants in the policy-making process reduce the aggregate impact of individual biases'.[61] For example, the role of civil society groups in international investment law has received some attention in recent legal discourse, but what remains little explored is whether and how such actors shape the impact of investment treaty law on domestic governance. It has been pointed out that 'host state grassroots activism remains a source of pressure to reform the unbalanced nature of international investment law, to give voice to those affected by the activities of foreign investors, and to reflect the role of resistance in shaping the regulatory network of investment protection'.[62] Could the emerging variation in the drafting of treaty models and different patterns of response to treaty disciplines be explained by a more inclusive process in some countries and a relatively limited involvement of stakeholders other than the business community and its lobby in the treaty-making process of other countries?

## V. CONCLUSION

Can international investment law foster good governance in host states? This contribution has discussed some of the questions that arise when the good governance narratives in the investment treaty law context are subjected to critical scrutiny. Leaving aside the question of whether fostering good governance at a domestic level is, or ought to be, the function of investment treaty law, the chapter has instead focused on the capacity of investment treaties and the investment arbitration mechanism to bring about change in the legal and bureaucratic culture and practices of states.

In an effort to make a novel contribution to the emerging debate about the impact of investment protection instruments on host state behaviour, the chapter adopted an interdisciplinary and a socio-legal perspective. In particular, it drew on political science scholarship concerning state compliance in international law as well as on empirical case studies aimed at identifying the ways in which international investment law is perceived and internalised by national institutions and actors.

[60] Hathaway (n 48) 485.
[61] Poulsen and Aisbett (n 32) 273, 303.
[62] Miles (n 28) 105.

The chapter also proposed examining the impact of investment treaty law by retreating from a unitary notion of state and acknowledging the diversity of domestic epistemic communities that shape the ways in which host states respond to investment treaty disciplines. As the aim of the contribution has been to introduce some of the key arguments and empirical insights emerging from the case studies so far, the relevant findings are not conclusive and require further methodological and conceptual refinement. Rather than offering a comprehensive and detailed critique of good governance narratives in investment law scholarship, it highlights the novel doctrinal and conceptual questions that arise when examining the interplay between investment treaty law and national governance.

# PART III

# INTERNATIONAL LAW AND TRADE AND INVESTMENT

# 9

# *Investment Law at the Crossroads of Public and Private International Law*

ANDREA K BJORKLUND, GEORGIOS PETROCHILOS,
STEPHAN W SCHILL AND DIANE A DESIERTO

## I. INTRODUCTION

UNDER THE CHAIRMANSHIP of Christoph Schreuer, the Forum panelists discussed the myriad intersections between public and private international law found in the realm of investment arbitration. The mix of ideas, raised by the four panelists in their individual papers, and developed during the course of lively exchanges between them, characterised the session.

The contributions to these proceedings, which arise out of the Forum panel, grapple with such challenging issues as identifying the multiple facets of the 'public' interest raised in and by investment law; identifying the appropriate guardians of the public interest, given their multi-faceted nature and the ever-increasing number of persons and entities with claims to represent some aspect of the public interest; offering innovative theories about the possibility of viewing those competing actors as having shared responsibility for guarding the public interest; and turning a critical eye to dismantling the overly simplistic view of investment law as a battle between the binaries of private contract or public governance, and again urging a public-private partnership.

Taken together, the following contributions suggest the gradual emergence of a complex but functional conceptualisation of an important and controversial governance mechanism to serve public interests without jeopardising private rights.

## II. THE PUBLIC INTEREST IN INTERNATIONAL INVESTMENT LAW

ANDREA K BJORKLUND*

We tend to talk blithely about the 'public interest' in international investment law—and certainly today the public *is* interested in international investment law, particularly in Europe but also in Australia, Canada, the United States (US) and Uruguay, to name just a few countries. This interest is partly the result of such high-profile disputes as *Vattenfall v Germany*[1] (which involves a Swedish investor's challenge to Germany's decision to phase out nuclear power) and *Philip Morris v Uruguay*[2] and *Philip Morris v Australia*[3] (both involving challenges to the countries' respective 'plain-packaging' laws for cigarettes). Negotiations for the Trans-Atlantic Trade and Investment Partnership (TTIP) between the European Union (EU) and the US and the Trans-Pacific Partnership (TPP) may be scuttled because of public concern about investor-state dispute settlement, and even the concluded Comprehensive Economic and Trade Agreement (CETA) between Canada and the EU may yet fail to be ratified.

Public interest, in the popular sense, can be evanescent. In 1999 and 2000 several cases brought under the investment Chapter (Chapter XI) of the North American Free Trade Agreement (NAFTA) provoked alarm in Congressional circles. Then-Senator John Kerry said that senators had not understood what was in NAFTA. According to Senator Kerry: 'When we debated NAFTA, not a single word was uttered in discussing Chapter 11. Why? Because we didn't know how this provision would play out. No one really knew just how high the stakes would get.'[4]

In 2002 Senator Kerry sponsored an amendment to Trade Promotion Authority (aka 'fast-track') legislation that would have directed the president to limit, though not eliminate, investor-state dispute settlement in future US investment agreements.[5] This amendment was not added to the bill, although a watered-down version gave the president directions 'to reduce or eliminate artificial or trade-distorting barriers to foreign investment, while ensuring that foreign investors in the United States are not accorded greater substantive rights with respect to investment protections than United States investors in the United States'.[6]

* Full Professor and L Yves Fortier Chair in International Arbitration and International Commercial Law, McGill University Faculty of Law. I thank my fellow panelists and our chairman for a thought-provoking and lively session, and the ESIL for including our panel in the conference programme.

[1] *Vattenfall AB et al v Germany*, ICSID Case No ARB/12/12, Notice of Arbitration (31 May 2012).

[2] *Philip Morris Brands SARL et al v Uruguay*, ICSID Case No ARB/10/07, Request for Arbitration (19 February 2010).

[3] *Philip Morris v Australia*, UNCITRAL, PCA Case No 2012-12, Notice of Arbitration (21 November 2011).

[4] See Adam Liptak, 'Review of US Rulings by Nafta Tribunals Stirs Worries' *New York Times* 18 April 2004, 20.

[5] Proposed Kerry Amendment to HR 3009, SA 3430, 107th Cong, 148 *Congressional Record* S4504 (2002). The Kerry Amendment would have introduced a government screening mechanism for claims under the investment chapters of free trade agreements.

[6] Trade Act of 2002, Pub L No 107-210, s 2102(b)(3), 116 Stat 933, 995 (2002).

Notwithstanding these directives, subsequent to 2002 the US negotiated and ratified some dozen free trade agreements and bilateral investment treaties (BITs) that contain investor-state dispute settlement procedures, which were very similar to those found in NAFTA,[7] though the US made some attempts to limit investor redress by according only the minimum standard of treatment (rather than free-standing fair and equitable treatment) and restricting recovery for interference with property pursuant to a state's police powers.[8] But at least to date the US has not abandoned its commitment to ensuring that investor-state dispute settlement will be in its future agreements, including the TTIP and the TPP.

Ordinarily when we talk about the 'public interest' in investment law we use the term in a different sense—that many investments themselves, and disputes arising from them, have potentially broad societal implications, whether or not the general public evinces interest in them at any given time. Talking about '*the* public interest' in this narrower sense can be misleading because in fact there are multiple facets of public interest implicated by international investment law and by investor-state dispute settlement in particular.

The baseline trigger for public interest is simply the fact that the government is involved, because these are disputes about governmental measures and challenges to them. Thus, in a broad sense any dispute involving the government triggers the public interest—this is true whether the claim at issue involves negligence in the driving of postal vehicles by government employees, or whether it involves claims of violation of constitutional law.

[7] These include the US—Chile Free Trade Agreement (adopted 6 June 2003, entered into force 1 January 2004) TIAS; the US—Morocco Free Trade Agreement (adopted 15 June 2004, entered into force 1 January 2006) TIAS; the US—Singapore Free Trade Agreement (adopted 6 May 2003, entered into force 1 January 2004) TIAS; the US—Colombia Free Trade Agreement (adopted 22 November 2006, entered into force 15 May 2012); the Dominican Republic/Central American Free Trade Agreement (adopted 5 August 2004, entered into force 1 March 2006); the US—Peru Trade Promotion Agreement (adopted 12 April 2006, entered into force 1 February 2009) TIAS; the Agreement between the Government of the United States of America and the Government of the Sultanate of Oman on the Establishment of a Free Trade Area (adopted 19 January 2006, entered into force 1 January 2009) TIAS; the Free Trade Agreement between the United States of America and the Republic of Korea (adopted 30 June 2007, entered into force 15 March 2012) TIAS; the US—Panama Trade Promotion Agreement (adopted 28 June 2007, entered into force 31 October 2012) TIAS; the Treaty Between the Government of the United States of America and the Government of the Hashemite Kingdom of Jordan Concerning the Encouragement And Reciprocal Protection of Investment (adopted 2 July 1997, entered into force 12 June 2003) TIAS; the Treaty Between the United States of America and the Oriental Republic of Uruguay Concerning the Encouragement And Reciprocal Protection of Investment (adopted 4 November 2005, entered into force 1 November 2006) TIAS; and the Treaty Between the United States of America and the Republic of Rwanda Concerning the Encouragement And Reciprocal Protection of Investment (adopted 19 February 2008, entered into force 1 January 2012).

[8] Examples of these provisions can be found in the US Model BIT of 2004, and were carried through to the US Model BIT of 2012. Article 5(2) of the 2004 Model BIT states: 'For greater certainty, paragraph 1 prescribes the customary international law minimum standard of treatment of aliens as the minimum standard of treatment to be afforded to covered investments. The concepts of 'fair and equitable treatment' and 'full protection and security' do not require treatment in addition to or beyond that which is required by that standard, and do not create additional substantive rights.'

There is further elaboration in Article 5 as well as in Annex A. As for expropriation, Annex B Article 4(b) provides that 'Except in rare circumstances, non-discriminatory regulatory actions by a Party that are designed and applied to protect legitimate public welfare objectives, such as public health, safety, and the environment, do not constitute indirect expropriations.' available at www.state.gov/documents/organization/117601.pdf.

More specifically, the type of public interest that sparks concerns about investor-state dispute settlement is the nature of the claims, almost all of which are public law matters: discrimination, violations of due process or abuses of governmental authority, and the taking of property for governmental purposes. These are public law claims that pit individual interests against sovereign authority. These cases are often viewed as zero-sum games, because if the individual wins the government (and by extension the public) loses, at least insofar as monetary payment is concerned. Many treaties permit investors to submit claims against host states but do not permit counterclaims, which means an investor can prevail against a host state, but a host state can only defeat an investor's claim without affirmative recovery.[9] In addition, absent investment arbitration the state might well have the ability to move against the investor without the investor having any real redress.

Yet this is only one side of the story. Note the assumption that the government is representing the public, rather than the individual. In domestic constitutional law cases the reverse is often true. The core idea of government according to the rule of law is that governmental exercises of authority should be scrutinised, questioned and even constrained. Insofar as one person challenges the government and prevails, that person is sometimes lauded as a standard-bearer for others who will share in the victory should the government be brought to heel.

Some cases involve breaches of contract. Those claims tend to attract less attention insofar as the substance of the claim is concerned, although whether that should be the case is doubtful—governments which fail to honour their contractual obligations should be called to account just as are those which do not honour their public law obligations. Moreover, those contracts involve public interests as well in that they concern the expenditure of public monies and often the allocation of public resources. Contract law is quintessential private law, yet state contracts do involve the public interest and it is illogical to suggest that they ought not, at least sometimes, to cause at least equal concern about government activity and accountability.

The second public interest of note is that of the subject matter of the dispute. Certain issues—environmental protection, access to public drinking water, hazardous waste disposal and the ability to respond to economic crises—are the best known and most closely watched cases.[10] They have captured the interest especially of the NGO community, whose representatives have frequently sought to participate as amici curiae or as fully fledged interveners in investment law cases.[11] These issues

[9] On counterclaims, see Andrea K Bjorklund, 'The Role of Counterclaims in Rebalancing Investment Law' (2013) 17 *Lewis & Clark Law Review* 461.

[10] See eg some of the more iconic cases, such as *Methanex v United States*, UNCITRAL, Final Award of the Tribunal on Jurisdiction and Merits (3 August 2005); *SD Myers v Canada*, UNCITRAL, Partial Award (13 November 2000); *Metalclad v Mexico*, ICSID Case No ARB(AF)/97/1, Award (30 August 2000); *Tecmed v Mexico*, ICSID Case No ARB(AF)/00/2, Award (29 May 2003); *Aguas del Tunari v Boliva*, ICSID Case No ARB/02/3, Decision on Respondent's Objections to Jurisdiction (21 October 2005) (withdrawn); *Biwater Gauff v Tanzania*, ICSID Case No ARB/05/22, Award (24 July 2008). The Argentine cases are described in multiple places, one of which is José E Alvarez and Tegan Brink, 'Revisiting the Necessity Defense' (2011) *2010–2011 Yearbook on International Investment Law and Policy* 315.

[11] See Andrea K Bjorklund, 'The Emerging Civilization of Investment Arbitration' (2009) 113 *Pennsylvania State Law Review* 1269, 1290.

are important because of their broader societal implications—their potential to have an impact on others besides the parties to the dispute.

More garden-variety subject matter is often seen as less interesting—the garbage cases that do not involve hazardous waste, the government contracts and permit cases, the road-building cases—and is less likely to spark widespread concern, yet such cases also involve core governmental functions regarding the allocation of public resources. In fact, these cases should trigger more scrutiny than some of the cases that do excite the public interest given their potential to affect broad swathes of the population. Investment law could be said to have its own version of the charismatic megafauna phenomenon whereby public attention is captured by certain types of subjects and certain types of claims but not by others that might be equally deserving of attention.

The third public interest is the process by which disputes involving the government are settled—and this is true for investor-state dispute settlement as well as for domestic dispute resolution. The actions of government respondents are of particular interest to their constituents and should be open to scrutiny. One might say that the government is itself representing the public interest, and the arguments it makes on behalf of the people can be criticised or praised, or very likely both of those things. And, of course, to the extent that arbitral decisions contribute to the development of international investment law, those decisions themselves should be, and generally are, examined and commented upon for their contribution to the development of international law.

Thus, the decisions of arbitral tribunals should be public, and hearings should be accessible. Ideally, all of the materials in a case should be publicly available, too. Arbitrators will also be more constrained in what they can do, and their performance can be more fairly assessed if measured against the arguments made to them. The new United Nations Commission on International Trade Law (UNCITRAL) Rules on Transparency embrace this degree of openness, albeit somewhat late in the game.[12] Since 2001, the NAFTA parties have made publicly available all materials in cases brought against them under NAFTA and under other investment agreements,[13] and the CETA has provisions that go beyond those found in the UNCITRAL Rules.[14]

When these three public interests are involved at once—a constitutional-law-like challenge to a government measure regarding a social issue that will be settled in international arbitration—there is a veritable trifecta and the interest of the public as well as the public interest are at their zenith. Yet each case offers the opportunity to serve the public interest by encouraging examination of governmental activity, even

[12] UNCITRAL Rules on Transparency in Treaty-based Investor-State Arbitration (January 2014) UNGA Res 68/109 (16 December 2013) UN Doc A/RES/68/109.

[13] Canada Department of Foreign Affairs and International Trade, available at www.international.gc.ca/trade-agreements-accords-commerciaux/topics-domaines/disp-diff/gov.aspx?lang=eng; Mexico Secretaría de Economía, available at www.gob.mx/se/acciones-y-programas/comercio-exterior-solucion-de-controversias?state=published; US Department of State, International Claims and Investment Disputes, available at www.state.gov/s/l/c3433.htm.

[14] Consolidated CETA Text, ch 10, Art X.33 (26 September 2014), available at trade.ec.europa.eu/doclib/docs/2014/september/tradoc_152806.pdf.

if the case involves a one-off measure with little apparent societal impact. This is the rule-of-law aspect of international investment law, which deserves greater prominence than it has been given in the past.

## III. WHO ARE THE APPROPRIATE GUARDIANS OF THE PUBLIC INTEREST (STATES, INTERNATIONAL ORGANISATIONS OR NGOS)?

GEORGIOS PETROCHILOS*

Those familiar with the workings of Whitehall will know of the time-honoured tradition of the postcard: Ministers may insist that advice from the civil service, on any topic, be expressed in a length of words that can fit on the back of a postcard. Each of us on this panel has the equivalent of a postcard's worth of time. Here are six propositions I would include in my postcard.

The first proposition is that on the face of it, all investment treaties are designed to serve the public interest. Their predicate, which is invariably reflected in their preambles, is that: (a) foreign investment is good for the host state; (b) limitations and scrutiny—substantive and procedural—on the host state's sovereign powers will encourage investment; and (c) such limitations are not only good instrumentally, that is, to attract foreign investment, but are also worthy in and of themselves, from the perspective of good governance.

In the 1990s states entering into so-called 'Europe Agreements', which paved the way for their accession to the EU, were encouraged by those Agreements to enter into investment treaties with other EU Member States. It was all part of a good-governance agenda. Whether that was right or wrong policy is one point, and one can explore it; but it is beyond debate that, as a matter of fact, achievement of good governance is the predicate of investment-protection treaties.

The point can be pressed further, in saying that (opposition in some quarters notwithstanding) the 3,000 or so investment treaties extant are evidence of a core set of protections that have customary international law status, and—taking a leaf from European Court of Human Rights jurisprudence—these core rules reflect the public policy of the community of states.[15]

The second proposition follows from the first. Investment treaties curb sovereign powers that a state would otherwise be unfettered to exercise in regulating investments in its territory, and therefore they are a form of public law.[16] It would, I think,

* Three Crowns, Paris.

[15] Cf *Austria v Italy (Pfunders Case)* App no 788/60 (EComHR, 11 January 1961) 138; *Chrysostomos, Papachrysostomou and Loizidou v Turkey* App nos 15299/89, 15300/89, 15318/89 (EComHR, 4 March 1991) paras 20–22; and *Cyprus v Turkey* App no 25781/94 (ECtHR, 10 May 2001) paras 37, 44.

[16] On investment law as a species of public law, see W Burke-White and A von Staden, 'The need for public law standards of review in investor-state arbitrations' in SW Schill (ed), *International Investment Law and Comparative Public Law* (Oxford University Press, 2010) 689, 691–95; and B Kingsbury and SW Schill, Investor-State Arbitration as Governance: Fair and Equitable Treatment, Proportionality

be perfectly cogent to say that, given that investment treaties *are* binding law, the public interest from a rule-of-law perspective is served precisely by ensuring compliance with them. That is to say, there is a public interest in ensuring that states do not overstep the limitations on their powers under the treaties, and also that investors do not seek to curb sovereign powers any more than the treaties require.

Who are the guardians of ensuring proper compliance on both sides? Evidently, they are the arbitral tribunals who resolve disputes about compliance, either in an investor-state context or, more rarely (and rather more controversially), in an inter-state context.

The third proposition is that investors are not guardians of the public interest. They are, rather, the enforcers of their own interests. Whichever way one comes down on the debate over whether or not investment treaties confer individual investor rights,[17] it is not open to doubt as a matter of treaty practice that there have been several examples of protections granted to investors in the past which were to be enforced, in case of dispute, at the inter-state level only.[18] Thus, conferring on investors a direct right of action before an international tribunal is the procedural mechanism permitting such a tribunal to determine the proper limits of the contracting states' sovereign powers under the applicable treaty.

The fourth proposition is that states are not the guardians of duties under an investment treaty. They are doubtless the creators of these duties: they can seek to define them however they wish when they conclude the treaty; they can vary the treaty in the course of its life in various ways; and they can terminate the treaty if they wish. But there are important limitations on what the contracting states can do—even when they act in concert—in respect of investor rights or claims that have already arisen. Just as one example, in the *Pope & Talbot* case[19] it was held that the interpretative statement of the NAFTA states regarding the scope of the duty to accord fair and equitable treatment (FET)[20] was an amendment to, rather than an interpretation of, NAFTA; and as a result it could not affect state liability for conduct that predated the statement.[21]

Or suppose that the two contracting states under a BIT issue a statement that a particular investor's claim, pending before a tribunal, has no merit, jurisdictionally or substantively. Then a number of questions arise. Does this statement in and of itself terminate the proceedings? I should think not. Does it legally bind the tribunal

and the Emerging Global Administrative Law' in Albert J van den Berg (ed), *50 Years of the New York Convention: ICCA International Arbitration Conference* (ICCA Congress Series No 14, Kluwer Law International, 2009) 5, 68.

[17] M Paparinskis, 'Investment Treaty Arbitration and the (New) Law of State Responsibility' (2013) 24 *European Journal of International Law* 617, 621–27; and Z Douglas, *The International Law of Investment Claims* (Cambridge University Press, 2009) para 276.

[18] The historical example is the Pakistan and Federal Republic of Germany Treaty for the Promotion and Protection of Investments (adopted 25 November 1959, entered into force 28 April 1962) 457 UNTS 24, Art 11. Previous FCN treaties proceeded on the same footing.

[19] *Pope & Talbot Inc v Canada*, UNCITRAL, Award in Respect of Damages (31 May 2002).

[20] Free Trade Commission, *Notes of Interpretation of Certain Chapter Eleven Provisions*, 31 July 2001.

[21] *Pope & Talbot Inc v Canada* (n 19) para 47.

to follow it and dispose of the case? I submit it would be difficult to imagine on what basis a tribunal could conclude that it did. After all, by submitting to arbitration an investor foregoes diplomatic protection. Can the two states agree to bar, that is terminate, access to arbitration by that investor? Again, it is difficult to see how they could. So once more, the guardian of treaty duties and rights is a third party, that is, the tribunal.

For all that, and this is the fifth proposition, one must recognise that it is unsatisfactory today to just stay with the classical legal analysis outlined above. There are factors at play which qualify—certainly in practice, and arguably also in theory—the primary role of states in defining the content of investment law and the primary role of arbitral tribunals in resolving investment claims.

There are two salient qualifications. First, there is an emerging corpus of standards of conduct for enterprises which emanates from international organisations. The UN Guiding Principles on Business and Human Rights (UNGP)[22] is a prime example here of course.[23] One can acknowledge and attest from personal experience, and from materials in the public domain, that not only corporations but also states and the EU take these Guiding Principles extremely seriously.[24] The Guiding Principles seek to be part of a corporation's 'social licence to operate'[25] and they have serious traction. It is not straightforward to fit such emerging norms into the classical list of considerations that can be taken into account in treaty interpretation. Yet the day will surely come—and it is probably nigh—that an investment tribunal will be confronted with this question.

The second qualification stems from the procedural ability of NGOs to intervene in investment-related arbitration proceedings as amici curiae. There are two strands of thought here. The principal one is that amici curiae interventions may be apt in cases which involve directly and materially a domestic community at large. The

[22] 'Guiding Principles on Business and Human Rights' UN HRC Res 17/4 (2011) UN Doc HRC/RES/17/4.

[23] See also eg the revised OECD 'Guidelines for Multinational Enterprises' (2011) available at www.oecd.org/daf/inv/mne/48004323.pdf.

[24] See eg European Commission 'A Renewed EU Strategy 2011–14 for Corporate Social Responsibility' (Communication) COM (2011) 681 final, 14; Statement of the European Union at the second UN Business and Human Rights Forum, 3 December 2013; The Secretary of State for Foreign and Commonwealth Affairs, 'Good Business—Implementing the UN Guiding Principles on Business and Human Rights' (September 2013), available at www.gov.uk/government/uploads/system/uploads/attachment_data/file/236901/BHR_Action_Plan_-_final_online_version_1_.pdf; Dutch Ministry of Foreign Affairs, 'National Action Plan on Business and Human Rights' (April 2014) available at business-humanrights.org/sites/default/files/documents/netherlands-national-action-plan.pdf; Italian Government, 'The Foundations of the Italian Action Plan on the United Nations "Guiding Principles on Business and Human Rights"' (March 2014) available at business-humanrights.org/sites/default/files/media/documents/foundations-ungps-nap-italy.pdf; Danish Government, 'Danish National Action Plan—implementation of the UN Guiding Principles on Business and Human Rights' (March 2014) available at www.ohchr.org/Documents/Issues/Business/NationalPlans/Denmark_NationalPlanBHR.pdf; and The Special Representative of the United Nations Secretary-General for Business and Human Rights, 'Applications of the UN "Protect, Respect and Remedy" Framework' (30 June 2011) available at business-humanrights.org/sites/default/files/media/documents/applications-of-framework-jun-2011.pdf.

[25] UN HRC, 'Report of the Special Representative of the Secretary-General on the issue of human rights and transnational corporations and other business enterprises' (2009) UN Doc A/HRC/11/13, para 46.

*Suez v Argentina* cases illustrate this perfectly. The tribunal was at pains to explain that while all investment-treaty cases can be seen as involving the public interest, a case concerning water distribution and sewage services for a large urban area involved a specific public interest of a particular constituency. (However, the tribunal also accepted—and I think this is significant, though often overlooked—that there was a separate, international public interest involved, in that the decision in these cases could affect similar privatisations of water and sewage services in other countries.)[26] The second strand, endorsed by the *Biwater v Tanzania* tribunal, is that there is a public interest in ensuring transparency through the participation of amici curiae in arbitration proceedings.[27] The recent addition of a 'transparency chapter' in the UNCITRAL Arbitration Rules,[28] and the text of a Transparency Convention that has also been endorsed by UNCITRAL,[29] reflect this line of thought.

What do these two qualifications mean? In my view, they certainly show that international organisations and NGOs are to an extent and for certain purposes stakeholders in investment law. They have legitimate viewpoints and can, in varying measures, shape decisions by tribunals. They can also help in forming standards of conduct by states and investors, but also standards for the procedural conduct of tribunals in respect of added transparency in the dispute-resolution process. What I think is less clear is whether this means that we are moving towards a new definition of public interest in investment law; or whether international organisations and NGOs are recognised as more legitimate or authentic representatives of the public interest than states are.

This brings me to my sixth and last proposition. It is perfectly possible to say—and I think with some force—that the developments I have just outlined enhance, rather than diminish, the role of arbitral tribunals as guardians of the public interest. The task of arbitral tribunals is becoming increasingly more demanding than merely resolving a dispute between two parties based on a legal instrument and the record before them. They may have to take into consideration various viewpoints other than those of the litigants in the proceedings; they may have regard, in addition to the applicable treaty, to customary international law and emerging norms of conduct; and in so doing they ultimately have to satisfy the international community that arbitration remains a fair and cogent means for safeguarding the integrity of investment law.

26 *Suez, Sociedad General de Aguas de Barcelona, SA and Vivendi Universal, SA v The Argentine Republic*, ICSID Case No ARB/03/19, Order in Response to a Petition for Transparency and Participation as *Amicus Curiae* (19 May 2005) para 19; *Suez, Sociedad General de Aguas de Barcelona, SA and Vivendi Universal, SA v The Argentine Republic*, ICSID Case No ARB/03/19, Order in Response to a Petition by Five Non-Governmental Organizations for Permission to Make an Amicus Curiae Submission (12 February 2007) paras 17–18; and *Suez, Sociedad General de Aguas de Barcelona SA, and InterAguas Servicios Integrales del Agua SA v The Argentine Republic*, ICSID Case No ARB/03/17, Order in Response to a Petition for Participation as *Amicus Curiae* (17 March 2006) para 18. See generally, F Grisel and J Vinuales, 'L'amicus curiae dans l'arbitrage d'investissement' (2007) 22 *ICSID Review* 380, 419–20.

27 *Biwater Gauff (Tanzania) Ltd v United Republic of Tanzania*, ICSID Case No ARB/05/22, Procedural Order No 5 (2 February 2007) paras 53–55.

28 UNCITRAL Arbitration Rules 2013, UNGA Res 68/109 (16 December 2013) UN Doc A/RES/68/109, Art 1, para 4.

29 United Nations Convention on Transparency in Treaty-Based Investor-State Arbitration (adopted 10 December 2014, open for signature 17 March 2015).

## IV. 'SHARED RESPONSIBILITY': STOPPING THE IRRESPONSIBILITY CAROUSEL FOR THE PROTECTION OF PUBLIC INTERESTS IN INTERNATIONAL INVESTMENT LAW

STEPHAN W SCHILL*

### A. Introduction

The interaction between private and public in international investment law and investor-state arbitration also raises the question of who should be responsible for deciding the boundaries between both, about where to draw the line between investor rights and public interests. Depending on the perspective, this involves either the question of who should ultimately determine the scope of protection of private rights against illegitimate public interference, or who should ensure that legitimate public interests are protected and not hampered due to an over-expansive protection of investor rights. The latter perspective has given rise to the large majority of concerns in the current debates about the 'legitimacy crisis' in international investment law[30] and the future of the investment regime.[31] For this reason, it constitutes the focus of the following remarks. Moreover, this perspective is also the more interesting one. While it is clear that investment treaties and investment treaty tribunals are given responsibility to protect foreign investors, potentially together with the investor's home state exercising diplomatic protection, it is less clear who is responsible for protecting competing public interests under the existing investment regime and who should be responsible under the future rules that are being considered in the various reform initiatives in the field.[32]

* Stephan W Schill, Dr iur (Frankfurt am Main, 2008); LLM (New York University, 2006); LLM (Augsburg, 2002) is Professor of International and Economic Law and Governance at the University of Amsterdam and Principal Investigator in the ERC-project 'Transnational Private-Public Arbitration as Global Regulatory Governance: Charting and Codifying the Lex Mercatoria Publica' (LexMercPub, Grant agreement no 313355). He is admitted to the Bar as a German Rechtsanwalt and as Attorney-at-Law (New York) and is a Member of the List of Conciliators of the International Centre for Settlement of Investment Disputes.

[30] See Charles N Brower and Stephan W Schill, 'Is Arbitration a Threat or a Boon to the Legitimacy of International Investment Law?' (2009) 9 *Chicago Journal of International Law* 471, 473 (with further references).

[31] See, inter alia, Roberto Echandi and Pierre Sauvé (eds), *Prospects in International Investment Law and Policy: World Trade Forum* (Cambridge University Press, 2013); Armand de Mestral and Céline Lévesque (eds), *Improving International Investment Agreements* (Routledge Chapman & Hall, 2012); José E Alvarez, Kamil Gerard Ahmed, Karl Sauvant and Gabriela del P Vizcaino (eds), *The Evolving International Investment Regime: Expectations, Realities, Options* (Oxford University Press, 2011); Jean E Kalicki and Anna Joubin-Bret (eds), *Reshaping the Investor-State Dispute Settlement System: Journeys for the 21st Century* (Brill, 2015); Karl P Sauvant and Federico Ortino, *Improving the International Investment Law and Policy Regime: Options for the Future* (Ministry for Foreign Affairs of Finland, 2013).

[32] See eg the work done by the United Nations Conference on Trade and Development (UNCTAD). UNCTAD, *World Investment Report 2012—Towards a New Generation of Investment Policies* (United Nations Publication, 2012) 97ff; UNCTAD, *World Investment Report 2013—Global Value Chains: Investment and Trade for Development* (United Nations Publication, 2013) 110ff; UNCTAD, *World Investment Report 2014—Towards a New Generation of Investment Policies* (United Nations

Potential candidates for the responsibility to protect public interests are arbitral tribunals, home states, host states, or international organisations active in the field of foreign investment. Yet when considering who is responsible—both *de lege lata* as well as *de lege ferenda*—we face a significant collective action problem that arises out of the decentralised structure of international investment law and investor-state arbitration, in which every class of actors is able to pass on the responsibility for protecting public interests to another class of actors. To address this collective action problem, I suggest having recourse to the idea of 'shared responsibility' of all actors involved in protecting public interests. This concept is not used in the technical sense of the law on state responsibility or the responsibility of international organisations as referring to the secondary norms governing the consequences of a breach of international law, but rather to indicate that we need to develop conceptual approaches that allow us to consider primary obligations for the protection of public interests that no class of actors in the international investment regime can escape.[33]

In the following remarks, I will not deal in detail with how the idea of shared responsibility should be operationalised in international investment law. I will only present its contours and the *problématique* to which it reacts. For this purpose, I will first turn to the characteristics of the structure of the investment regime: while it is decentralised and heterarchical, it nevertheless has significant governance effects that are able to impact public interests and, therefore, are in need of protection. Second, I will turn to the difficulties the decentralised structure poses in attributing responsibility for the protection of public interests from a practical point of view: it can result in what I call an 'irresponsibility carousel' that makes it difficult, if not impossible, to hold a specific class of actors, or in fact any actor, accountable for protecting the public interest. Finally, I will introduce the idea of 'shared responsibility' as a solution to conceptualise the duty of all actors involved to protect public interests.

## B. The Governance Structure of International Investment Law and Its Impact on Public Interests

Analysing who should decide about the protection of public interests is closely connected, and has to respond, to the structure of international investment law and investor-state dispute settlement. This structure is decentralised and heterarchical.[34]

Publication, 2014) 126ff. Similarly, the Organisation for Economic Co-operation and Development (OECD) is engaged in reform activities. See eg David Gaukrodger and Kathryn Gordon, 'Investor-State Dispute Settlement: A Scoping Paper for the Investment Policy Community' (2012) OECD Working Papers on International Investment 2012/3 available at dx.doi.org/10.1787/5k46b1r85j6f-en. For further information on the OECD's activities in international investment law, see www.oecd.org/daf/inv/investment-policy/oecdworkoninternationalinvestmentlaw.htm.

[33] My use of the notion thus differs from the same notion used by André Nollkaemper and Dov Jacobs, 'Shared Responsibility in International Law: A Conceptual Framework' (2013) 34 *Michigan Journal of International Law* 359, even though I share a similar motivation, namely to address collective action problems.

[34] See Stephan W Schill, *The Multilateralization of International Investment Law* (Cambridge University Press, 2009) 281–93.

The governing law is based largely on bilateral treaties, not a single multilateral framework; it is implemented not by a centralised dispute settlement body but by one-off arbitral tribunals, which are constituted under a variety of institutional rules and apply different rules of procedure;[35] and finally, there is formal review of arbitral decision-making in set-aside or annulment proceedings as well as the enforcement of awards, depending on the applicable institutional rules, which is in the hands of ad hoc annulment committees and/or domestic courts.[36] In international investment law, we therefore face a multi-actor structure, or network, without hierarchical order among the actors and without a clearly discernible centre.

Notwithstanding this decentralised structure, international investment law as a whole, and investor-state arbitration in particular, have governance effects.[37] These effects are due to the fact that decisions and awards by investment treaty tribunals become public, and thereby are able to, and actually do, function as precedents in other investment arbitrations somewhat independently of which investment treaty concretely applies.[38] In addition, the relatively close-knit community of investment arbitrators, which has developed its own epistemic, or interpretive culture, and comprises a core of particularly influential 'elite arbitrators',[39] exercises a pull towards

[35] Most investment treaty arbitrations take place under the Convention on the Settlement of Investment Disputes Between States and Nationals of Other States (adopted 18 March 1965, entered into force 14 October 1966) 575 UNTS 159 (ICSID Convention). Other procedural rules that regularly apply, depending on the agreement of the parties and/or the consent in an investment treaty, are the Rules Governing the Additional Facility for the Administration of Proceedings by the Secretariat of the International Centre for Investment Disputes (ICSID Additional Facility Rules) (latest version effective as of 10 April 2006) reprinted in 'ICSID Additional Facility Rules' Document ICSID/11 (April 2006) available at icsid.worldbank.org/apps/ICSIDWEB/icsiddocs/Documents/AFR_English-final.pdf, the United Nations Conference on International Trade Law (UNCITRAL) Arbitration Rules (the original 1976 version, the revised version of 2010, and the latest version of 2013 incorporating the UNCITRAL Rules on Transparency for Treaty-Based Investor-State Arbitration) available at www.uncitral.org/uncitral/en/uncitral_texts/arbitration/2010Arbitration_rules.html; the Rules of Arbitration of the Arbitration Institute of the Stockholm Chamber of Commerce (SCC Arbitration Rules) (the latest version adopted 1 January 2010 and previous versions) available at www.sccinstitute.com/dispute-resolution/rules/; the Rules of Arbitration of the International Chamber of Commerce (ICC Arbitration Rules) (the latest version in force as of 1 January 2012) available at www.iccwbo.org/Data/Documents/Buisness-Services/Dispute-Resolution-Services/Mediation/Rules/2012-Arbitration-Rules-and-2014-Mediation-Rules-ENGLISH-version/, or ad hoc arbitration. Cf Rudolf Dolzer and Christoph Schreuer, *Principles of International Investment Law*, 2nd edn (Oxford University Press, 2012) 238–39.

[36] In arbitrations under the ICSID Convention the only remedy against an arbitral award is an application for annulment pursuant to Art 52 ICSID Convention. ICSID awards have to be recognised and enforced in all member states of the Convention; see Art 54 ICSID Convention. In non-ICSID arbitration, the remedies against arbitral awards depend on the law applicable at the place of arbitration. Recognition and enforcement is usually governed by the United Nations Convention on the Recognition and Enforcement of Foreign Arbitral Awards (adopted 10 June 1958, entered into force 7 June 1959) 330 UNTS 38 (New York Convention). In this context, domestic courts play a more prominent, but still limited role, as compared to ICSID arbitrations.

[37] See further, Benedict Kingsbury and Stephan W Schill, 'Investor-State Arbitration as Governance: Fair and Equitable Treatment, Proportionality, and the Emerging Global Administrative Law' in Albert Jan van den Berg (ed), *50 Years of the New York Convention* (ICCA Congress Series No 14, Kluwer Law International, 2009).

[38] On the use and function of precedent in investment treaty arbitration see Schill (n 34) 321–57.

[39] The classic analysis of the sociological composition of international arbitration has been presented by Yves Dezalay and Bryant G Garth, *Dealing in Virtue—International Commercial Arbitration and the Construction of a Transnational Legal Order* (University of Chicago Press, 1996). How the arbitration

convergence, rather than divergence. These factors not only contribute to international investment law constituting a relatively uniform regime for the governance of investor-state relations despite its decentralised structure; they also enable arbitrators as a group to nudge investment treaty jurisprudence in a certain direction.[40] This is all the more important considering that the investment regime exercises pressure on all branches of government at the domestic level to comply with the state's investment treaty obligation by granting monetary compensation and damages in cases of breach.

The governance structure of international investment law raises a number of concerns for the protection of public interests. First, problems for the protection of public interests can arise because of the lack of sufficiently hierarchical and centralised governance structures. After all, the fragmentation of investment law into a myriad number of treaties and their application by one-off dispute settlement bodies actually creates, or at least risks creating, inconsistencies and a lack of predictability in the governing law.[41] This can be harmful for the protection of public interests because governments may refrain from regulating in the light of unforeseeable liability risks.[42]

Second, problems for the protection of public interests stem from the asymmetric nature of investment treaties that protect foreign investments against government interference without, in most cases, mentioning host state rights or competing non-economic concerns, and from only giving foreign investors, not host states, nor affected third parties, the right to bring claims for breach of treaty in investment treaty arbitration.[43]

Third, the mechanism of party-appointment of arbitrators leads to different dispute-resolvers than those who would otherwise be appointed in a state-only system.

community's *esprit de corps* translates into legal culture is discussed in Joshua Karton, *The Culture of International Arbitration and the Evolution of Contract Law* (Oxford University Press, 2013). On the structure of the network of arbitrators and the importance of a relatively small number of individuals in this network, see Sergio Puig, 'Social Capital in the Arbitration Market' (2014) 25 *European Journal of International Law* 387.

[40] On law-making by arbitrators through precedent see Schill (n 34) 332–38.

[41] Examples of such inconsistencies can be found in Schill (n 34) 282–87, 339–55.

[42] On this notion in the context of investment law, see Kyla Tienhaara, 'Regulatory Chill and the Threat of Arbitration: A View from Political Science' in Chester Brown and Kate Miles (eds), *Evolution in Investment Treaty Law and Arbitration* (Cambridge University Press, 2011) 607; Christian Tietje and Freya Baetens, 'The Impact of Investor-State-Dispute Settlement (ISDS) in the Transatlantic Trade and Investment Partnership' (Study prepared for Minister for Foreign Trade and Development Cooperation [and] Ministry of Foreign Affairs, the Netherlands, Reference: MINBUZA-2014.78850, 2014) paras 66–86, available at www.rijksoverheid.nl/bestanden/documenten-en-publicaties/rapporten/2014/06/24/the-impact-of-investor-state-dispute-settlement-isds-in-the-ttip/the-impact-of-investor-state-dispute-settlement-isds-in-the-ttip.pdf. Notably, regulatory chill is not necessarily connected to inconsistent decision-making but may result more generally from a lack of clarity in the applicable law, but cases of inconsistent decision-making decrease predictability and therefore increase the potential for governments to refrain from taking action to protect public interests.

[43] On the asymmetric nature of investment treaties, see Jochen von Bernstorff, 'Reflections on the Asymmetric Rule of Law in International Relations' (2010) 3 *Select Proceedings of the European Society of International Law* 381, 382–83; Benedict Kingsbury, 'International Courts: Uneven Judicialization in Global Order' in James Crawford and Martti Koskenniemi (eds), *The Cambridge Companion to International Law* (Cambridge University Press, 2012) 203, 211–12.

It is certainly difficult to argue that the appointment mechanism, as some claim,[44] generally leads to a pro-investor bias in investment treaty arbitration, given that both the state's nominee as well as the chair or president of the tribunal will usually have been appointed with the consent of the respondent.[45] This notwithstanding, the dynamic of a tribunal's decision-making, in particular in deliberations and reasoning, and hence the outcome of a decision, will certainly be influenced by the investor's nominee who may, but need not, be chosen for his preference for private, rather than public interests.

Finally, the sociological composition of the group of investment treaty arbitrators, in particular the background of many of them in international commercial arbitration, may be a ground to fear that their decision-making is less public interest-minded than that of tenured judges in national or international courts.[46]

## C. The Irresponsibility Carousel in International Investment Law

All of the above illustrate that public interests may be significantly affected in international investment law and arbitration. Yet, when considering which actors have a responsibility to protect public interests in international investment relations, the decentralised structure of the regime causes considerable headache. After all, the structure makes it difficult, if not impossible, to pinpoint a specific actor, or a class of actors, that can be effectively held accountable for protecting the public interest. Instead, the decentralised structure of international investment law risks leading to an irresponsibility carousel, where everybody who is asked to assume responsibility for protecting the public interest points to somebody else as being in charge. This is a textbook-like collective action problem.[47]

In fact, we can witness the irresponsibility carousel going round in the current practice of international investment law and arbitration. Some arbitrators and arbitral tribunals, when confronted with the charge of giving too little weight to public interests, point out that they are only applying the governing law, suggesting that if there is insufficient protection of public interests it is of the contracting states' making. After all, states are responsible for making treaties that only explicitly

[44] For this claim, see Gus Van Harten, *Investment Treaty Arbitration and Public Law* (Oxford University Press, 2007) 167–75; Gus Van Harten, 'Investment Treaty Arbitration, Procedural Fairness, and the Rule of Law' in Stephan W Schill (ed), *International Investment Law and Comparative Public Law* (Oxford University Press, 2007) 627, 628, 648; Pia Eberhardt and Cecilia Olivert, *Profiting from Injustice: How Law Firms, Arbitrators and Financiers Are Fuelling an Investment Arbitration Boom* (Corporate Europe Observatory and the Transnational Institute, 2012) available at www.tni.org/files/download/profitingfrominjustice.pdf.

[45] Susan Franck's work suggests that the claimed bias cannot be sustained when empirically analysing the outcome of investment treaty arbitrations, see Susan D Franck, 'Empirically Evaluating Claims About Investment Treaty Arbitration' (2007) 86 *North Carolina Law Review* 1; Susan D Franck, 'Development and Outcomes of Investment Treaty Arbitration' (2009) 50 *Harvard International Law Review* 436.

[46] For the impact of professional socialisation on decision-making in investment arbitration, see Stephan W Schill, 'W(h)ither Fragmentation? On the Literature and Sociology of International Investment Law' (2001) 22 *European Journal of International Law* 875.

[47] See Nollkaemper and Jacobs (n 33) 391–92.

mention the protection of foreign investment, but hardly refer to competing rights and public interests. Some tribunals even appear to deny responsibility for the entire system of international law and instead emphasise that they are only serving the disputing parties in settling an individual dispute without regard to the overall system.[48] Systemic considerations for the protection of public interests are thus shunned.

Host states whose measures protecting public interests are scrutinised as to their conformity with investment treaty disciplines equally pass on their responsibility for protecting public interests by pointing to the circumstances they are in. Not only do many of them not have well-working domestic institutions that could protect public interests effectively, such as the protection of consumers, the environment, or labour standards; they also point to the structural constraints they suffer due to the decentralised structure of investment law. One such argument emphasises host states' competition in attracting foreign investment with other capital-importing countries. This competition, in turn, is said to lead to a race to the bottom and requires capital-importers to lower the protection of the public interest and restrict taxation.[49] This puts them, they claim, in a weak bargaining position in relation to capital-exporting states and to investors.[50] In this view, it would be home states, through domestic regulation of outward investment, or the international community as a whole, through concluding a multilateral treaty, that are responsible for protecting public interests effectively.

Home states, however, equally do not necessarily feel responsible for taking principal responsibility for protecting public interests. Instead, they may point to host states as the main bearers of responsibility. After all, what constitutes a public

[48] See eg *GEA Group Aktiengesellschaft v Ukraine*, ICSID Case No ARB/08/16, Award (31 March 2011) para 90: 'The Tribunal has carefully reviewed the pleadings, evidence and legal authorities submitted by the Parties and has relied exclusively on those in the analysis below. This applies in particular to legal authorities, as the Tribunal adheres to the principle that it should remain within the confines of the debate between the Parties. Thus, this Award is a decision in the dispute as pleaded between the Parties, and the Tribunal will not address arguments that have not been raised by them.' *RosInvestCo UK Ltd v Russian Federation*, SCC Case No V 079/2005, Award on Jurisdiction (October 2007) para 137 stressing that 'it is the primary function of this Tribunal to decide the case before it rather than developing further the general discussion on the applicability of MFN clauses to dispute-settlement-provisions.'

Other tribunals, by contrast, stress the importance of embedding their decision-making and reason-giving in a broader framework that aims at creating convergence in investment treaty jurisprudence. See eg *Saipem SpA v People's Republic of Bangladesh*, ICSID Case No ARB/05/07, Decision on Jurisdiction and Provisional Measures (21 March 2007) para 67: 'The Tribunal considers that it is not bound by previous decisions. At the same time, it is of the opinion that it must pay due consideration to earlier decisions of international tribunals. It believes that, subject to compelling contrary grounds, it has a duty to adopt solutions established in a series of consistent cases. It also believes that, subject to the specifics of a given treaty and of the circumstances of the actual case, it has a duty to seek to contribute to the harmonious development of investment law and thereby to meet the legitimate expectations of the community of States and investors towards certainty of the rule of law.'

[49] For this argument, see Andrew T Guzman, 'Why LDCs Sign Treaties that Hurt Them: Explaining the Popularity of Bilateral Investment Treaties' (1998) 38 *Virgina Journal of International Law* 639. On competition as the driving factor for the spread of BITs see further Zachary Elkins, Andrew T Guzman and Beth Simmons, 'Competing for Capital' (2006) 60 *International Organization* 811.

[50] For an understanding of investment treaties as expressions of hegemonic behaviour of capital-exporting States, see Eyal Benvenisti and George W Downs, 'The Empire's New Clothes: Political Economy and the Fragmentation of International Law' (2007) 60 *Stanford Law Review* 595, 611–12.

interest is normally an internal matter that is for the host state to decide and to implement. Furthermore, unilateral regulation in home states is not necessarily effective in protecting public interests in investor-state relations because investors could escape unilateral home state regulation by moving the home base of problematic investment activities to another home jurisdiction without comparably strict regulation of outward foreign investment.

Similarly, international organisations active in the field of foreign investment by themselves cannot necessarily act effectively to protect public interests without the necessary competences and support of their respective Member States, as these are themselves home and host states of foreign investment activities. They may not only have opposing interests, but may make each other responsible for closing the gaps in the protection of public interests.

This irresponsibility carousel must be stopped in order to effectively protect public interests. The question is how.

## D. Shared Responsibility to Protect Public Interests

One way to stop the irresponsibility carousel would be to destroy the decentralised system as it exists altogether and to replace it with more centralised structures, both in substance and procedure. A multilateral treaty combined with a permanent international investment court would achieve that aim. While a multilateral regime would indeed be attractive in providing uniform rules for investor-state relations worldwide, the prospects that such an ambitious project will see the light of day any time soon are dim. The creation of a multilateral investment treaty has failed repeatedly in the not-too-distant past, first in the Multilateral Agreement on Investment negotiated under the auspices of the Organisation for Economic Co-operation and Development (OECD) in the late 1990s, and later on as part of the Singapore Issues in the World Trade Organization (WTO).[51] The closest we are currently likely going to get to multilateralism is through a consolidation of BITs into mega-regionals, such as the Trans-Pacific Partnership (TPP) or the Transatlantic Trade and Investment Partnership (TTIP), currently under negotiation.[52] This does not mean that multilateral approaches on some aspects of investment law are not possible. The Convention on Transparency in Treaty-based Investor-State Arbitration, adopted by the United Nations General Assembly on 10 December 2014, which will introduce broad transparency rules into investment treaty-based arbitrations, independently of the applicable institutional rules, is an example.[53] However, more general multilateral reform projects are likely to require many more years to ripen.

Another way, and one that is more immediately effective, is to develop conceptual approaches that are able to ensure accountability and responsibility for the protection of public interests already in the existing structure and to explore whether and how such approaches can be brought to bear as part of the law that already exists

[51] See Schill (n 34) 49–60.
[52] See ibid 49–60.
[53] UNGA Res 69/116 (10 December 2014) UN Doc A/RES/69/116.

and in the context of existing investment treaty negotiations. A concept that, in my view, could address responsibility and accountability successfully in a decentralised system and provide a remedy against the irresponsibility carousel is the concept of 'shared responsibility'.

Instead of asking who among several actors and institutions is responsible for protecting public interests, this concept posits that in principle all actors and institutions bear responsibility for achieving policy goals that are in the common interests of all actors, such as the protection of public interests, be it the environment, human rights, labour standards, public health and morals, or international peace and security. The idea of shared responsibility prevents individual actors, or classes of actors, from denying responsibility for protecting public interests by pointing to alternative addressees who should be in charge. Instead, the concept of shared responsibility requires them to work jointly in achieving a common goal or public policy, which is the protection of public interests through mutual support and mutual control.

Certainly, the idea of 'shared responsibility' is not yet mainstreamed in international law and global governance theory. This notwithstanding, it is actively being developed in the light of the need to prevent harm to affected rights and interests in the context of coordination and joint action of international actors to meet certain common policy goals. André Nollkaemper's project on Shared Responsibility in International Law (SHARES), for example, spearheads efforts to adapt the law of international responsibility, of states as well as of international organisations, so as to deal more effectively and fairly with injury caused to third parties by joint activities of international actors through the concept of 'shared responsibility'.[54]

Yet the idea of 'shared responsibility' does not only resonate in connection with the law of international torts. It also falls on fruitful ground as a concept to address the interrelationship of independent public actors that operate under a common governance regime, which aims at achieving certain policy goals but does not have hierarchical structures among those actors. An example of such a situation can be found in the context of the EU, where both EU organs and Member States act jointly in order to achieve common European policy goals without the existence of a strictly hierarchical order among Member States and in relation to the EU.

Rather, EU organs and Member States in many contexts interact in what many scholars of EU constitutional law, in particular in Germany, conceptualise as a 'composite structure' (*Verbund*).[55] This concept highlights the autonomy of the actors at different levels (EU and national) and transcends ideas of supra- and subordination, while stressing their mutual dependence and the need to cooperate in order to be able to achieve common goals.[56] The need to cooperate, in turn, corresponds to a duty

[54] See Nollkaemper and Jacobs (n 33); André Nollkaemper and Ilias Plakokefalos (eds), *Principles of Shared Responsibility in International Law: An Appraisal of the State of the Art* (Cambridge University Press, 2014).

[55] See Christoph Schönberger, 'Die Europäische Union als Bund' (2004) 129 *Archiv des öffentlichen Rechts* 81 (with further references). For similar views outside Germany, see Leonard FM Besselink, *A Composite European Constitution* (Europa Law Publishing, 2007); Luis I Gordillo, *Interlocking Constitutions—Towards an Interordinal Theory of National, European and UN Law* (Hart Publishing, 2012).

[56] Eberhard Schmidt-Aßmann, 'Einleitung: Der Europäische Verwaltungsverbund und die Rolle des Europäischen Verwaltungsrechts' in Eberhard Schmidt-Aßmann and Bettina Schöndorf-Haubold (eds),

of both the EU and its organs, on the one hand, as well as Member States, on the other, to exercise what Piet Eeckhout calls 'limited and shared jurisdiction' in the context of an integrated legal system.[57] While every actor in that system continues to exercise jurisdiction according to its own rules and mandates, this jurisdiction is limited to the extent that the norms at stake are shared with other systems and actors in order to avoid conflicts and incoherence across actors. Limited and shared jurisdiction, therefore, comprise the idea of a duty to further and to protect what is in the common/public interest.

Similar considerations as those developed in the context of developing structures of responsibility and accountability in multi-actor action under international law and in situations of multi-level governance are also informative when asking which actors in international investment law should protect public interests. The idea of shared responsibility suggests that all actors—tribunals, host states, home states, international organisations, and the international community as a whole—bear responsibility for protecting public interests.

The form that action of each class of actors can take, of course, differs. Host and home states can recalibrate investment treaties in order to meet their responsibilities towards clarifying the fact that investment protection cannot unduly restrict governments' policy space to protect public interests.[58] Similarly, they can agree on joint interpretations of existing investment treaties to that effect, in particular where investment tribunals do not sufficiently take account of public interests in their decision-making practice.[59]

Arbitral tribunals, in turn, can make use of interpretative techniques that integrate the protection of public interests into their decision-making,[60] such as proportionality analysis,[61] and exercise appropriate degrees of deference vis-à-vis government action that is taken to pursue non-investment public interests.[62] Finally, international

*Der Europäische Verwaltungsverbund* (Mohr Siebeck, 2005) 1, 6ff; Andreas Voßkuhle, 'Multilevel Cooperation of the European Constitutional Courts: Der Europäische Verfassungsgerichtsverbund' (2010) 6 *European Constitutional Law Review* 175, 183–84.

[57] Piet Eeckhout, 'Human Rights and the Autonomy of EU Law: Pluralism or Integration?' (2013) 66 *Current Legal Problems* 169.

[58] On this recalibration, see José E Alvarez, 'Why Are We "Re-calibrating" Our Investment Treaties?' (2010) 4 *World Arbitration and Mediation Review* 143.

[59] On the dual role of states as parties to disputes and makers of the applicable law, see Anthea Roberts, 'Power and Persuasion in Investment Treaty Interpretation: The Dual Role of States' (2010) 104 *American Journal of International Law* 179.

[60] For public interests protected under international law, the principle of systemic integration contained in Art 31(3)(c) of the Vienna Convention on the Law of Treaties (adopted 23 May 1969, entered into force 27 January 1980) 1155 UNTS 331 is of particular importance in this context, see Campbell McLachlan, 'The Principle of Systemic Integration and Article 31(3)(c) of the Vienna Convention' (2005) 54 *International and Comparative Law Quaterly* 279.

[61] See Benedict Kingsbury and Stephan W Schill, 'Public Law Concepts to Balance Investors' Rights with State Regulatory Actions in the Public Interest—The Concept of Proportionality' in Schill (n 44) 75; Alec Stone Sweet, 'Investor-State Arbitration: Proportionality's New Frontier' (2010) 4 *Law and Ethics of Human Rights* 47; Erlend Leonhardsen, 'Looking for Legitimacy: Exploring Proportionality Analysis in Investment Treaty Arbitration' (2012) 3 *Journal of International Dispute Settlement* 95; Caroline Henckels, 'Indirect Expropriation and the Right to Regulate: Revisiting Proportionality Analysis and the Standard of Review in Investor-State Arbitration' (2012) 15 *Journal of International Economic Law* 223.

[62] See further, Stephan W Schill, 'Deference in Investment Treaty Arbitration: Re-conceptualizing the Standard of Review' (2012) 3 *Journal of International Dispute Settlement* 577.

organisations, to the extent covered by their mandate, could assist states and tribunals in taking action to protect public interests, for example, through assistance in concluding public-interest-friendly investment treaties,[63] or in developing soft law instruments that can help to conduct investor-state arbitrations in a public-interest-friendly manner or to interpret and apply investment treaties in such a way.[64]

### E. Conclusion

To conclude, what all actors in the international investment regime need to appreciate fully is that they do not only deal with interests that are specific to individual disputes or to specific bilateral treaty relationships. Instead, every investment treaty concluded, and every investment treaty dispute settled, not only serves the immediate interests of those involved, but has effect on a global level as part of a global governance structure for investor-state relations. This structure does not serve the protection of private investors for their own sake, but ultimately aims at enhancing prosperity and well-being in all countries that participate in the global investment regime because an appropriate level of investment protection is necessary for global markets to work and create growth and welfare effects.

Accordingly, the goal of the investment regime to protect private investment, while ensuring that the pursuance of non-investment public interests is not hampered, is not a private aim for private gain but is of itself in the public interest. In order to live up to the expectations and exigencies of this system, all actors in international investment law, that is, arbitral tribunals and home and host states, as well as international institutions, should be seen as subject to the shared responsibility of protecting both investment and non-investment public interests.

## V. CONTRACT, GOVERNANCE, OR A 'PUBLIC-PRIVATE PARTNERSHIP' LENS? METHODOLOGICAL CONSEQUENCES IN INTERNATIONAL INVESTMENT LAW

DIANE A DESIERTO[*]

When one recalls that a foreign investment dispute is, at its core, 'one between an investor from one country and a government that is not its own but that relates to

[63] One example is UNCTAD's Investment Policy Framework for Sustainable Development. See UNCTAD, *World Investment Report 2012—Towards a New Generation of Investment Policies* (United Nations Publication, 2012) 97; see further the dynamic version of the framework on UNCTAD's website at investmentpolicyhub.unctad.org/ipfsd.

[64] On the potential of soft law in international investment law, see Marc Jacob and Stephan W Schill, 'Going Soft: Towards a New Age of Soft Law in International Investment Law?' (2014) 8 *World Arbitration and Mediation Review* 1.

[*] JSD, LLM, Yale; JD *cum laude*, BSc Economics *summa cum laude*, University of the Philippines, Michael J Marks Distinguished Professor and tenured Associate Professor of International Law,

an investment in the host country',[65] the vivid image of a private actor (the investor), disputing with the public agent (the government of the host state) might appear to translate easily into a strict clash of 'private claims' versus 'public interests'.[66] This characterisation, however, yields a false binary,[67] since the host state's 'public interests'[68] all tend to span a complex spectrum of constituencies and stakeholders in economic development.[69] (After all, it is also difficult to delineate, with complete objective precision, the state's 'public' interests *acta jure imperii*, from its 'private' commercial interests *acta jure gestionis*.)[70]

The government of a host state owes multiple simultaneous duties to numerous constituencies, all of which demand constant calibration and assessment in the host state's investment decision-making. These include, for example, the host state's competing normative obligations to ensure conditions for long-term economic growth while reducing income inequality; to expand employment while maintaining labour protections and decent conditions of work; to encourage technology transfers/spillovers while preserving cultural heritage and protecting intellectual property; and to

International Economic Law, International Investment and Commercial Arbitration Law, and ASEAN Law at the University of Hawai'i William S Richardson School of Law; Co-Director of ASEAN Law & Integration Center; 2016–2017 CASBS Fellow, Stanford University; Law Partner at Desierto Law (Manila, Phils); and Legal Expert for the USAID and the ASEAN Coordinating Committee on Investment. With thanks to my co-panelists for the thoughtful exchanges.

[65] R Doak Bishop, James Crawford and W Michael Reisman, *Foreign Investment Disputes: Cases, Materials and Commentary* (Kluwer Law International, 2005) 9.

[66] Much of the ongoing reform critiques have zeroed in on investor-state dispute settlement (ISDSs); see among others, United Nations Conference on Trade and Development (UNCTAD), 'Reform of Investor-State Dispute Settlement: In Search of a Roadmap' (2013) IIA Issues Note No 2 available at unctad.org/en/publicationslibrary/webdiaepcb2013d4_en.pdf; Manuel Perez-Rocha, 'When Corporations Sue Governments' *New York Times*, 3 December, 2014, available at www.nytimes.com/2014/12/04/opinion/when-corporations-sue-governments.html?_r=0; Pia Eberhardt and Cecilia Olivet, *Profiting From Injustice: How law firms, arbitrators, and financiers are fuelling an investment arbitration boom* (Corporate Europe Observatory and Transnational Institute 2012) available at www.tni.org/sites/www.tni.org/files/download/profitingfrominjustice.pdf.

[67] 'A false dichotomy (sometimes called a false binary) inaccurately divides possible views on a subject into two opposing camps, forcing a choice between black and white, when some shade of gray may be fairer and more accurate.' David Rosenwasser and Jill Stephen, *Writing Analytically*, 5th edn (Thomson Wadsworth, 2009) 83; see Anthea Roberts, 'Clash of Paradigms: Actors and Analogies Shaping the Investment System' (2013) 107 *American Journal of International Law* 1, 45; Julie A Maupin, 'Public and Private in International Investment Law: An Integrated Systems Approach' (2014) 54 *Virginia Journal of International Law* 2; Andreas Kulick, *Global Public Interest in International Investment Law* (Cambridge University Press, 2014) 269–306.

[68] See Alexander J Bělohlávek, 'Public Policy and Public Interest in International Law and EU Law' (2012) 3 *Czech Yearbook of International Law* 117, 126–27: 'Public interest is an interest vested in a loosely defined, but basically identifiable circle of persons that allows the label "public" ... Interest becomes public if and when a broader group of (potential) individuals draws benefit from it ... The problem here is how to define the "good", which opens a can of worms in practical terms.'

[69] UNCTAD spearheads recent global reform efforts, see James Zahn and Diana Rosert, 'UNCTAD Multi-Stakeholder Meeting Seeks Reform of Investment Treaties and Investment Dispute 'Settlement', *Investment Treaty News*, 19 November 2014 available at www.iisd.org/itn/2014/11/19/unctad-multi-stakeholder-meeting-seeks-reform-of-investment-treaties-and-investment-dispute-settlement/.

[70] Sir Ian Sinclair, 'The Law of Sovereign Immunity: Recent Developments' (1980) 167 *Recueil De Cours/Collected Courses of the Hague Academy of International Law* 210–13.

optimise property use while internalising environmental sustainability.[71] Long-term reform efforts for the international investment system make it imperative to engage the paradigms of justification behind 'balancing'[72] techniques, while also recognising the shifting landscape of interests and players involved in the host state's investment decision-making process.[73]

Investor-state arbitral jurisprudence illustrates the kinds of analytical lens that international decision-makers (specifically, investor-state arbitral tribunals) adopt, when examining international investment protection as part of the spectrum of the host state's numerous 'public' interests.[74] These decisions are suggestive, but not at all definitive, of how a subset of the global corpus of international investment decision-makers treats international investment obligations, and they are particularly telling on arbitral dispositions in regard to the relationship dynamic between the host state, the investor, and any other investment stakeholders. By nature, investor-state disputes are highly political, and are usually lodged in the aftermath of host state regulatory breakdowns that adversely impact guaranteed investment protections and expected investment returns.[75]

Since investor-state disputes are often lodged as a result of host state regulatory breakdowns impacting upon guaranteed investment protections, I find that arbitral tribunals oscillate between treating investment more as a *contract* in some legal issues, and characterising investment more as a matter of *governance*, in others,[76] based on decision trends in five recurring legal issues in investor-state disputes. These are: (1) the consent of parties to the offer of arbitration; (2) the definition of property or covered investment; (3) the standard of treatment applied; (4) the

[71] See Markus Gehring and Andrew Newcombe, 'An Introduction to Sustainable Development in World Investment Law' in Marie-Claire Cordonier Segger, Markus W Gehring and Andrew Newcombe (eds), *Sustainable Investment in World Investment Law* (Kluwer Law International, 2011) 3–12.

[72] For some of the rich literature seeking 'balance' between human rights concerns and investment protection objectives, see among others, Todd Weiler, 'Balancing Human Rights and Investor Protection: A New Approach for a Different Legal Order' (2004) 27 *Boston College International and Comparative Law Review* 429; Pedro Nikken, 'Balancing of Human Rights and Investment Law in the Inter-American System of Human Rights' in Pierre-Marie Dupuy, Ernst-Ulrich Petersmann and Francesco Francioni (eds), *Human Rights in International Investment Law and Arbitration* (Oxford University Press, 2009) ch 12.

[73] See José E Alvarez, 'The Public International Law Regime Governing Foreign Investment' (2011) 344 *Recueil de Cours/Collected Courses of the Hague Academy of International Law* 193, 434–41, 470–79.

[74] Investor-state arbitral jurisprudence does not describe the entire process of international investment decision-making, since analysing investor-state dispute settlement is a matter of scrutiny *ex post*, rather than *ex ante* in the investment planning stages, see Diane A Desierto, *Public Policy in International Economic Law: The ICESCR in Trade, Finance, and Investment* (Oxford University Press, 2015) 308–79.

[75] See Zoe Williams, 'Domestic Demands and International Agreements: What Causes Investor State Disputes?' in Shaheeza Lalani and Rodrigo Polanco Lazo (eds), *The Role of the State in Investor-State Arbitration* (Martinus Nijhoff Publishers, 2014) 187–210; Jeswald W Salacuse, 'Is There A Better Way? Alternative Methods of Treaty-Based, Investor-State Dispute Resolution' (2007) 31 *Fordham International Law Journal* 138, 140–48.

[76] Note that other scholars have long argued the potential applicability of contract theory or constitutionalist/public law governance theory in international investment laws, see Anne van Aaken, 'International Investment Law between Commitment and Flexibility: A Contract Theory' (2009) 12 *Journal of International Economic Law* 507; Stephan W Schill, 'International Investment Law and Comparative Public Law—an Introduction' in Stephan W Schill (ed), *International Investment Law and Comparative Public Law* (Oxford University Press, 2010).

scope of participation and fact-finding permitted; and (5) the valuation approach taken in the liability phase. As I show below, it is interesting to see that neither the 'contract' nor the 'governance' methodology proves completely outcome-determinative for all issues. This may perhaps suggest that a 'public-private partnership'[77] cooperative methodology—fully accepting the hybrid public and private dimensions of investment—might be more suitable than the strict application of dichotomies between 'public' and 'private' in international investment law.[78]

### A. Consent of Parties to the Arbitration

The host state's offer of arbitration arises either from, or due to, some combination of three sources: the international investment agreement (IIA), the host state's domestic legislation, or the foreign investment contract itself.[79] The *private contract lens* would view this offer of, and consent to, arbitration as a matter governed by some degree of 'legal privity' existing between the disputants. This privity could be created as a result of the arbitral clause explicitly contained in the foreign investment contract; a separate arbitral agreement (*compromis*); or after the investor accepts the host state's standing offer of arbitration, as contained in either an applicable IIA or the host state's domestic legislation.[80] The host state's offer of arbitration in an IIA, in particular, is presumed to be a valid sovereign act, representing the will of the state's constituents. As such, the host state cannot invoke its internal law as a justification for the failure to perform this treaty obligation,[81] unless the host state can show that the violation of its internal law affects its competence to conclude the

[77] The metaphor draws from the 'cooperative', rather than conflicting, nature of public–private partnerships; see Graeme A Hodge, Carsten Greve and Anthony E Boardman, 'Introduction: the PPP phenomenon and its evaluation' in Graeme A Hodge, Carsten Greve and Anthony E Boardman (eds), *International Handbook on Public-Private Partnership* (Edward Elgar Publishing, 2010) 4: 'PPPs are a classic public policy issue. They are simultaneously a form of governance, a public policy delivery tool, and a language-game involving multiple grammars. So they are a political tool, a technical device, and a rhetorical framing device for governments ... PPPs are loosely defined as cooperative institutional arrangements between public and private sector actors ... an organizational and financial arrangement.'

[78] See Alex Mills, 'Antinomies of Public and Private at the Foundations of International Investment Law and Arbitration' (2011) 14 *Journal of International Economic Law* 469, noting the technical issues in investor-state arbitration as a product of the deeper theoretical uncertainty between 'public' and 'private' in international investment law.

[79] See Jeswald W Salacuse, *The Three Laws of International Investment: National, Contractual, and International Frameworks for Foreign Capital* (Oxford University Press, 2013) 35–50.

[80] See Guiguo Wang, 'Consent in Investor-State Arbitration: A Critical Analysis' (2014) 13 *Chinese Journal of International Law* 335; Michael Nolan and Frederic Sourgens, 'Limits of Consent—Arbitration without privity and beyond' in Miguel Angel Fernandez-Ballesteros and David Arias (eds), *Liber Amicorum Bernardo Cremades* (Kluwer Law International, 2010). On methods of accepting the government's offer to arbitrate, such as filing of a request for arbitration or communication to the host State, see Christopher F Dugan, Don Wallace Jr, Noah D Rubins and Borzu Sabahi, *Investor-State Arbitration* (Oxford University Press, 2008) 221–22.

[81] Vienna Convention on the Law of Treaties (adopted 23 May 1969, entered into force 27 January 1980) 1155 UNTS 331 (VCLT), Art 27.

IIA in a manner that is objectively manifest, and also involves a violation of a rule of the host state's internal law that is of fundamental importance.[82]

Investor-state arbitral tribunals tend to reject a restrictive interpretation of the host state's consent to arbitration in an arbitral clause, as well as any conditional qualifications embedded in the host state's standing offer to arbitrate under an IIA or its domestic legislation.[83] There is at least some evidence of a presumption of effective interpretation to favour affirming jurisdiction over disputes involving IIA-covered investments.[84] The operational influence of this presumption appears tacitly demonstrable in a recent case. In *Churchill Mining PLC v Indonesia*, the arbitral tribunal rejected Indonesia's interpretation of Article 7 of the UK–Indonesia BIT (stating that Indonesia '*shall assent* to any request on the part of such national or company to submit, for conciliation or arbitration') as one that articulated Indonesia's desire to 'balance the policy of encouraging investment ... with other policies or considerations ... [such as] to preserve the ability to avoid ICSID arbitration of disputes relating to investments outside the protection of the BIT in question'.[85]

Notwithstanding evidence presented by Indonesia that Aron Broches, the architect of the ICSID Convention, and Christoph Schreuer, the leading commentator on the ICSID Convention, along with many other scholars, all found that the ordinary meaning of a 'shall assent' clause does not result in a standing offer of the host state to arbitrate, the *Churchill Mining* arbitral tribunal held that the ordinary meaning of the phrase 'shall assent' was at best 'inconclusive'.[86] It also found that treaty context 'rather supports Churchill's interpretation, without however delivering a fatal blow to Indonesia's interpretation'.[87]

The tribunal then went on to state that the object and purpose of the BIT was 'neutral' for the purposes of interpretation because the preamble of the UK–Indonesia BIT 'refers to both the private interests of the investor as well as the public interests of the State'.[88] Discarding the relevance of the text, context, object and purpose of the UK–Indonesia BIT, the *Churchill Mining* tribunal, instead, invoked supplementary means of interpretation, under Article 32 of the Vienna Convention on the Law of Treaties (VCLT), to examine doctrinal writings, case law, the treaty practice of Indonesia and the UK with third states, and preparatory materials regarding the negotiation of the UK–Indonesia BIT. It thus reached its strained hindsight conclusion that 'the treaty drafters considered the "shall assent" language as functionally equivalent to "hereby consents" or similar wording ... [that] Indonesia has given its advance consent to arbitrate the dispute presently before it'.[89]

[82] Ibid Art 46.

[83] See Andrea M Steingruber, *Consent in International Arbitration* (Oxford University Press, 2012) paras 12.48–12.57.

[84] Ibid paras 12.56 and 12.57.

[85] *Churchill Mining PLC v Indonesia*, ICSID Case No ARB/12/14 Decision on Jurisdiction (24 February 2014) para 177.

[86] Ibid para 171.

[87] Ibid para 179.

[88] Ibid para 178.

[89] Ibid para 230.

The *Churchill Mining* award provides thin reasoning on the supposed obscurity of the 'shall assent' clause, and is equally sparse in showing that the integrated method of interpretation of VCLT Article 31 produces an absurd result,[90] which are the two critical requirements before any treaty interpreter can resort to the supplementary means of interpretation in VCLT Article 32. The arbitral tribunal's unusual exclusive reliance on its interpretation of supplementary materials qua VCLT Article 32, at the very least, call to mind Mahnoush Arsanjani and Michael Reisman's reminder regarding the interpreter's duty of good faith. They are of the view that:

> [I]t would be bad faith to pretend a text is ambiguous or obscure so as to open the door to *travaux* and then to rummage about for something to support a litigating position, when the application of the canons of Article 31 would produce an unambiguous interpretation that is neither absurd nor unreasonable.[91]

Shortly after the *Churchill Mining* award, Indonesia announced its decision to terminate its BIT programme altogether.[92]

The *Churchill Mining* case demonstrates how strict adherence to a *private contract lens* ensures that the investor does not assume the burden of any potential political agency breakdown between the host state and its constituents, much less any ensuing ambiguity in IIA language. On the one hand, there is no room, under the *private contract lens*, for determining whether the host state adequately represented the interests of all its constituents at the time that it made its standing offer to arbitrate under an IIA or national law. On the other hand, tribunals that have leant more towards a *public governance lens* may also lend more scrutiny to the political agency between the central or federal government of the host state that made the standing offer to arbitrate, and the local organs tasked with direct regulation of the investment transaction. Generally, political agency problems between central or federal governments with local or state governments of the host state do not pose a material jurisdictional bar, although the consequences for host state liability may well differ. Cases such as *Metalclad Corporation v Mexico*[93] and *Tecmed v Mexico*,[94] among others, show how lack of federal coordination and oversight with local state governments can cause injury to guaranteed investor protection under IIAs; while cases such as *Glamis Gold Ltd v United States*[95] and *Methanex Corporation v United States*[96] depict how well-devised, transparent and nondiscriminatory

[90] Ibid paras 156–71.

[91] Mahnoush H Arsanjani and W Michael Reisman, 'Interpreting Treaties for the Benefit of Third Parties: The "Salvors" Doctrine and the Use of Legislative History in Investment Treaties' (2010) 104 *American Journal of International Law* 597, 601.

[92] Ben Bland and Shawn Donnan, 'Indonesia to terminate more than 60 bilateral investment treaties' *Financial Times*, 26 March 2014, available at www.ft.com/cms/s/0/3755c1b2-b4e2-11e3-af92-00144feabdc0.html#axzz3ROj41NrU.

[93] *Metalclad Corporation v Mexico*, ICSID Case No ARB(AF)/97/1, Award (25 August 2000).

[94] *Tecnicas Medioambientales Tecmed SA v Mexico*, ICSID Case No ARB(AF)/00/2, Award (29 May 2003).

[95] *Glamis Gold Ltd v United States*, UNCITRAL, Award (14 May 2009).

[96] *Methanex Corporation v United States*, UNCITRAL, Final Award on Jurisdiction and Merits (3 August 2005).

regulatory environments by local state governments would not give rise to liability to investors for supposed IIA breaches.

However, when such political agency matters are themselves material to determining the legality of the investment for the purposes of admission and establishment of the investment under an IIA (for example, compliance with local state regulations as part of 'investment in accordance with host State law' clauses in an IIA)[97] they can certainly attain jurisdictional significance. The arbitral tribunals in *Plama v Bulgaria*,[98] *Anderson v Costa Rica*,[99] *Fraport v Philippines*,[100] *Hamester v Ghana*[101] and *Inceysa Vallisoletana v El Salvador*,[102] affirm readings of the host state's consent, or standing offer to arbitrate, that preclude treaty coverage for investments made through acts that are either illegal, fraudulent, or contrary to good faith and public policy. Host states that insist arbitral tribunals adopt a *public governance lens* will very likely argue more bases for termination of their consent or offer to arbitrate, seek to denounce their IIAs, and insist on constitutional challenges and exceptions to IIA coverage.[103]

Both the *private contract lens* and the *public governance lens* contain their respective paradigms of justification. Neither lens fully apprehends the political agency breakdown. On the one hand, it is unreasonable to expect that the competence of the arbitral tribunal extends to resolving the patent breakdown of political agency (either between the central/federal government of a host state and its local/state governments, or between the host state itself and citizens that insist on restrictions to the standing offer to arbitrate) at the back end when the dispute has already arisen. Doing so risks undermining established principles of state sovereignty and *pacta sunt servanda* duties in assuming treaty obligations.

At the same time, if the actual parties negotiating the IIA (or other arbitral consent instrument) seek to anticipate these political agency breakdowns, then the host state's domestic procedures should provide, at the outset, for better consultations and participation by its constituencies. Locally-affected communities rarely, if at all, have a meaningful voice in, or significant influence over, how language is framed under an IIA between the host state and home state of the investor, the host state's domestic investment statute and regulations, or the host state's foreign investment contract with a foreign investor, joint venture or consortium partner. Where the concerns of locally-affected communities (for example, environmental, labour, social or cultural) are articulated and internalised early on in the foreign investment due diligence process, investors would be able to properly anticipate and

[97] See Christina Knahr, 'Investments "in accordance with host State law"' (2007) 5 *Transnational Dispute Management* 44; Rahim Maloo and Alex Kachaturian, 'The Compliance with the Law Requirement in International Investment Law' (2011) 34 *Fordham International Law Journal* 1473.

[98] *Plama Consortium Ltd v Bulgaria, ICSID*, Award (27 August 2008).

[99] *Alasdair Ross Anderson v Costa Rica*, ICSID Case No ARB(AF)/07/3, Award (10 May 2010).

[100] *Fraport AG v Philippines*, ICSID Case No ARB/03/25, Award (16 August 2007).

[101] *Gustav F W Hamester GmbH v Ghana*, ICSID Case No ARB/07/24, Award (10 June 2010).

[102] *Inceysa aVallisoletana SL v El Salvador*, ICSID Case No ARB/03/26, Award (2 August 2006).

[103] See UNCTAD, 'Denunciation of the ICSID Convention and BITs: Impact on Investor-State Claims' (2010) IIA Issues Note No 2, available at http://unctad.org/en/Docs/webdiaeia20106_en.pdf.

design their risk calculus with consideration for the increased costs of obtaining and monitoring such information bearing on the future of their investment operations in the host state.

### B. Property or Covered Investment

Both the *private contract lens* and the *public governance lens* also affect the interpretation of the property or subject matter that could properly be covered in an investor-state arbitration. Briefly, investor-state arbitral tribunals that demonstrate a *private contract lens* tend to construe the 'object' of the dispute (for example, covered investment) in a broad manner, one that most accommodates the various forms and permutations of property interests to the extent permissibly contemplated in the IIA design[104]—from standard real property, plant and equipment in foreign direct investments (FDIs), to shareholdings in corporate vehicles, goodwill, intellectual property rights, debt instruments and derivatives, among other things. The *Abaclat*[105] and *Ambiente Ufficio*[106] tribunals affirmed that IIA coverage extended to investor interests in sovereign bonds traded in secondary and tertiary markets, in the process of rejecting the argument that the investment's contribution to the host state's development should be regarded as a mandatory criterion for qualifying asserted property interests as IIA-covered investments, that, in turn, would be entitled to access investor-state dispute settlement mechanisms.[107] While arbitral tribunals have been repeatedly urged to take on a *public governance lens* in restricting the kinds of investments (and investors) that are permitted gateway access to treaty-based investor-state arbitration,[108] absent treaty reform and the actual linguistic elasticity in the IIA texts themselves,[109] one cannot expect investor-state arbitral tribunals to perform interpretive calisthenics on behalf of host states' interests to exclude specific interests, given the fluid range of property types that could likely be accommodated within many IIA definitions of investment.[110]

Tribunals would be better positioned to adopt a *public-private partnership lens* when construing the scope of covered investments to include all stakeholders'

[104] See UNCTAD, *Scope and Definition* (United Nations, 2011) 21–71.

[105] *Abaclat and Others v Argentina*, ICSID Case No ARB/07/5, Decision on Jurisdiction and Admissibility (4 August 2011).

[106] *Ambiente Ufficio SpA and Others v Argentina*, ICSID Case No ARB/08/9, Decision on Jurisdiction and Admissibility (8 February 2013).

[107] See Diane A Desierto, 'Development as an International Right: Investment in the New Trade-Based IIAs' (2011) 3 *Trade Law and Development* 296.

[108] See among others, Andreas Kulick, *Global Public Interest in International Investment Law* (Cambridge University Press, 2012) 168–71.

[109] See Annamaria Viterbo, 'Sovereign Debt Restructuring and Investment Protection' in Tullio Treves, Francesco Seatzu and Seline Trevisanut (eds), *Foreign Investment, International Law and Common Concerns* (Routledge, 2014) 346; UNCTAD, *Investor-State Dispute Settlement* (United Nations, 2014) 37–54.

[110] See Amnon Lehavi, *The Construction of Property: Norms, Institutions, Challenges* (Cambridge University Press, 2013) 274–316.

interests, when the IIA itself purposely enables such wholesale scrutiny. In this respect, the International Institute for Sustainable Development (IISD) Model International Investment Agreement for Sustainable Development, for example, puts forward qualifying criteria to enable tribunals to conduct an 'overall examination' of public and private interests (for example, investment's effects on third persons and local communities, environment and global commons and so on) when it comes to the application of the national treatment standard.[111] Perhaps this could be usefully analogised into future IIA language on the scope of covered investments. IIA language could also be reformed towards shaping the extent of arbitral discretion (or restraint, as recently argued)[112] to be applied when an investor-state tribunal scrutinises the scope of investment.

## C. Treatment Standards

The most visceral debates today arise from how investor-state tribunals, ultimately, take on either a *private contract lens* or a *public governance lens* when it comes to assessing breaches of IIA standards of investor treatment (for example, national treatment standard,[113] most favoured nation (MFN) treatment standard,[114] the prohibition against direct and indirect expropriations,[115] and the controversial and the interpretively-amorphous fair and equitable treatment (FET) standard)[116], alleged to have arisen from a host state's assertion of 'policy space' through its regulatory measures.[117] Tribunals which appear to frame their analysis through the *private contract lens* tend to interpret investment protection standards in a certain way. Thus, they often focus on the envisaged economic equilibrium under the foreign investment contract—whether in conducting *ex post* armchair reconstruction of the

[111] International Institute for Sustainable Development (IISD) Model International Investment Agreement for Sustainable Development, available at www.iisd.org/pdf/2005/investment_model_int_agreement.pdf.

[112] Gus Van Harten, *Sovereign Choices and Sovereign Constraints: Judicial Restraint in Investment Treaty Arbitration* (Oxford University Press, 2013) 80–115.

[113] Kate Miles, 'Sustainable Development, National Treatment and Like Circumstances in Investment Law' in Segger, Gehring and Newcombe (n 71).

[114] UNCTAD, *Most Favoured-Nation Treatment* (United Nations, 2010) 102–18.

[115] Caroline Henckels, 'Indirect Expropriation and the Right to Regulate: Revisiting Proportionality Analysis and the Standard of Review in Investor-State Arbitration' (2012) 15 *Journal of International Economic Law* 223.

[116] Jonathan Bonnitcha, *Substantive Protection under Investment Treaties: A Legal and Economic Analysis* (Cambridge University Press, 2014) 143–228.

[117] Suzanne Spears, 'The Quest for Policy Space in a New Generation of International Investment Agreements' (2010) 13 *Journal of International Economic Law* 1037; Mark S McNeill, 'Investor-State Arbitration: Striking a Balance Between Investor Protections and States' Regulatory Imperatives' in Arthur W Rovine (ed), *Contemporary Issues in International Arbitration and Mediation: The Fordham Papers 2013* (Martinus Nijhoff Publishers, 2014); Thomas Schultz, 'Against Consistency in Investment Arbitration' in Zachary Douglas, Joost Pauwelyn and Jorge E Viñuales (eds), *The Foundations of International Investment Law: Bringing Theory Into Practice* (Oxford University Press, 2014).

'legitimate expectations of the investor' to determine breach of the FET clause;[118] ensure, through application of the MFN clause, investor access to third-party benefits (substantive or procedural) conferred by the host state in other IIAs;[119] treat a broad spectrum of governmental acts as constituting 'creeping' or indirect expropriatory measures that violate investor expectations;[120] or frame discriminatory treatment of the host state's governmental or regulatory measure, by means of a mainly factual comparison of disparate economic gains obtained by local firms, which are held to be 'in like circumstances' with the foreign investor.[121]

On the other hand, certain tribunals that appear to favour a *public governance lens* would endorse, to a certain extent, the notion that a host state inherently retains the ability to override such contractually promised protections at any time during the life of an investment, such as through a broad (if not highly contested) reading of 'exceptions clauses' or 'necessity clauses' in an IIA.[122] While many scholars advocate and dispute various terms of calibration and proportionality analysis for investor-state tribunals' application of these contested standards,[123] the lines of an analytical

[118] See Christopher Campbell, 'House of Cards: The Relevance of Legitimate Expectations under Fair and Equitable Treatment Provisions in Investment Treaty Law' (2013) 30 *Journal of International Arbitration* 361; *Suez and Others v Argentina,* ICSID Case No ARB/03/17, Decision on Liability (30 July 2010) para 203:

> In an effort to develop an operational method for determining the existence or nonexistence of fair and equitable treatment, arbitral tribunals have increasingly taken into account the legitimate expectations that a host country has created in the investor and the extent to which conduct by the host government subsequent to the investment has frustrated those expectations. When an investor undertakes an investment, a host government through its laws, regulations, declared policies, and statements creates in the investor certain expectations about the nature of the treatment that it may anticipate from the host State. The resulting reasonable and legitimate expectations are important factors that influence initial investment decisions and afterwards the manner in which the investment is to be managed. *The theoretical basis of this approach no doubt is found in the work of the eminent scholar Max Weber, who advanced the idea that one of the main contributions of law to any social system is to make economic life more calculable* and also argued that capitalism arose in Europe because European law demonstrated a high degree of "calculability." An investor's expectations, created by law of a host country, are in effect *calculations about the future.*' (emphasis added)

[119] See Tony Cole, 'The Boundaries of Most Favoured Nation Treatment in International Investment Law' (2012) 33 *Michigan Journal of International Law* 537.

[120] W Michael Reisman and Robert D Sloane, 'Indirect Expropriation and its Valuation in the BIT Generation' (2003) 74 *British Yearbook of International Law* 115. See *LG&E Energy Corporation and Others v Argentina*, ICSID Case No ARB/02/1, Decision on Liability (3 October 2006) paras 190–93.

[121] See *Feldman v Mexico,* ICSID Case No ARB(AF)/99/1, Award and Dissenting Opinion (16 December 2002)) paras 165–80; *Corn Products International Incorporated v Mexico,* ICSID Case No ARB(AF)/04/1, Decision on Responsibility (15 January 2008) paras 95, 119, 138–43.

[122] See discussion in Diane A Desierto, *Necessity and National Emergency Clauses: Sovereignty in Modern Treaty Interpretation* (Martinus Nijhoff Publishers, 2012) 145; Diane A Desierto, 'Necessity and Supplementary Means of Interpretation for Non-Precluded Measures in Bilateral Investment Treaties' (2010) 31 *University of Pennsylvania Journal of International Law* 827.

[123] See among many others, William W Burke-White and Andreas von Staden, 'Private Litigation in a Public Law Sphere: The Standard of Review in Investor-State Arbitrations' (2010) 35 *Yale Journal of International Law* 283, 333–43, arguing for a margin of appreciation by investor-state arbitral tribunals; Benedict Kingsbury and Stephan W Schill, 'Investor-State arbitration as governance: Fair and equitable treatment, proportionality, and the emerging global administrative law' in Benedict Kingsbury (ed), *El Nuevo Derecho Administrativo global en America Latina* (Buenos Aires, 2009); Stephan W Schill, 'Deference in Investment Treaty Arbitration: Reconceptualizing the Standard of Review' (2012) 3 *Journal of International Dispute Settlement* 577; Alec Stone Sweet, 'Investor-State Arbitration: Proportionality's New Frontier' (2010) 4 *Law and Ethics of Human Rights* 47.

paradigm for a more cooperative *public-private partnership* methodology have yet to surface in investor-state arbitral practice to date.

### D. Participation and Scope of Fact-Finding in Investor-State Arbitral Proceedings

Tribunals that adopt a *private contract lens* cannot be expected to warm to the idea of exercising mere arbitral discretion *proprio motu*, in order to open access for non-disputing parties to the investor-state arbitral proceedings.[124] Tribunals of this analytical persuasion appear more comfortable when permitting the transfer or assignment of investor interests to third parties because of the contractual fiction extended to the subrogee or assignee acquiring the investor's right to sue a host state.[125] Arbitral discretion has generally not been exercised to scrutinise or to investigate third-party funders that finance investor claims against host states,[126] although it has been argued that compelling disclosure of funding agreements falls well within such discretion.[127]

Taken in this light, ICSID's initiative to design some access to, and participation by, non-disputing parties in investor-state arbitrations demonstrates remarkable foresight and responsiveness to using a *public governance lens* in investor-state arbitration.[128] Without this reform of ICSID procedures, non-disputing parties (such as NGOs and public interest groups) could not seek recourse through any formal mechanism for intervention, such as that contained in Article 62 of the Statute of the International Court of Justice. Permission to submit amici curiae briefs would have depended on arbitral fiat alone, where arbitrators and disputing parties alike would have had to weigh the cost implications (for example, document production, among others) of such expanded participation in investor-state arbitral proceedings.

A *public governance lens* could be useful to the tribunal when seeking to obtain facts and information on the investment project, process, regulatory environment and investor conduct, from the widest possible range of sources. These sources could include, for example, the community impacts of the investment project, the degree and record of economic, social and cultural rights compliance of the host state towards its citizens, and other reports by UN specialised agencies in regard to the

[124] See the remarkable exception in *Suez and Others v Argentina*, ICSID Case No ARB/03/19, Order in Response to a Petition by Five Non-Governmental Organizations for Permission to make an Amicus Curiae Submission (12 February 2007).

[125] See Borzu Sabahi and Diora Ziyaeva, 'Unauthorized transfer or assignment of interests or shares in investor-state arbitration' (Oxford University Press's Investment Claims blog, 20 May 2014) available at blog.oup.com/2014/05/unauthorized-transfer-assignment-interests-shares-investor-state-arbitration/.

[126] Although see the first landmark order requiring claimants to disclose the name/s and identity/ies of any third-party funders and the terms of such funding in *Muhammet Çap & Sehil Inşaat Endustri ve Ticaret Ltd. Sti. v Turkmenistan,* ICSID Case No ARB/12/6, Procedural Order No 3, 12 June 2015, available at http://www.italaw.com/sites/default/files/case-documents/italaw4350.pdf.

[127] Eric De Brabandere and Julia Lepeltak, 'Third Party Funding in International Investment Arbitration' (2012) Grotius Centre Working Paper Series No 2012/1, available at papers.ssrn.com/sol3/papers.cfm?abstract_id=2078358.

[128] Eloise Obadia, 'Extension of Proceedings beyond the Original Parties: Non-Disputing Party Participation in Investment Arbitration' (2007) 22 *ICSID Review* 349.

host state and the investment at issue. Collectively, they could help generate a more well-rounded scientific discussion of the nature of the host state's regulatory measure and the investor's assessment and estimation of political and project risks.[129] At the very least, expanding the fact-finding process could help allay the perceived imbalance between tribunals permitting new entrants to the investor-state arbitration (for example, subrogees or assignees of the investor, as well as undisclosed third-party funders), while otherwise being reticent in regard to the participation of affected communities and other investment stakeholders.

## E. Valuation in the Liability Phase

Valuation of compensation as a form of reparation in investor-state arbitration is, indeed, both an art and a science—both a question of law and a question of fact.[130] While expropriation generally requires payment of the 'prompt, adequate, and effective compensation' (the Hull formula) favoured by 'the majority of capital-exporting 'states',[131] tribunals tend to award compensation for a host state's non-expropriation breaches of IIAs under valuation levels closely tracking (if not already at) the fair market value of the investment.[132] As a mode of reparation under international law, compensation for non-expropriation breaches of an IIA should indeed 'cover any financially assessable damage including loss of profits insofar as established'.[133] Such financially assessable damage is supposed to 'exclude compensation for what is sometimes referred to as "moral damage" to a state, that is, the affront or injury caused by a violation of rights not associated with actual damage to property or persons'.[134]

This kind of compensation 'is not concerned to punish the responsible State, nor does compensation have an expressive or exemplary character ... [m]onetary compensation is intended to offset, as far as may be, the damage suffered by the injured State as a result of the breach.'[135] While the International Law Commission (ILC) generally characterised valuation for losses suffered for infringement of property rights as capable of being broken down into heads of damage such as: '(i) compensation for capital value; (ii) compensation for loss of profits; and (iii) incidental

[129] Bruno Simma and Diane Desierto, 'Bridging the Public Interest Divide: Committee Assistance for investor-host State Compliance with the ICESCR' (2013) 10 *Transnational Dispute Management*, available at www.transnational-dispute-management.com/article.asp?key=1931.

[130] See Mark Kantor, *Valuation for Arbitration: Compensation Standards, Valuation Methods and Expert Evidence* (Kluwer Law International, 2008) 2.

[131] Muthucumaraswamy Sornarajah, *The International Law of Foreign Investment* (Cambridge University Press, 2010) 414.

[132] See Diane A Desierto, 'ICESCR Minimum Core Obligations and Investment: Recasting the Non-Expropriation Compensation Model During Financial Crises' (2012) 44 *George Washington International Law Review* 473.

[133] Draft Articles on the Responsibility of States for Internationally Wrongful Acts with commentaries' (2001) II *Yearbook of the International Law Commission* 1, Art 36(2).

[134] Ibid 99, para 1.

[135] Ibid 99, para 4.

"expenses"',[136] the ILC was also careful to point out first that there has been 'considerable' variability'[137] in over two centuries of reported cases on property claims of nationals arising out of internationally wrongful acts. Moreover, even in assessing compensation, as a mode of reparation, it will be necessary to take into account the investor's wilful or negligent action, or omissions, as the injured party, insofar as they contribute to the injury.[138]

The difficulty with valuing compensation in investor-state arbitrations lies precisely in the lack of disclosed reasoning in arbitral awards on how breaches of non-expropriation IIA standards (specifically the frequently invoked FET standard)—when taken alongside breaches of the expropriation standard—somehow still result in the same method of assessing compensable material injury.[139] Often the FET breach is linked directly to the deprivation or decimation of the investor's expectations of returns to justify applying compensation for material injury, usually pegged at the fair market valuation of the investment itself when the arbitral tribunal exercises its discretion to analogise cumulative FET breaches with property deprivation arising from indirect expropriation.[140]

Yet, this seeming trend in the reasoning and exercise of discretion in selection (and interpretation) of compensation standards appears to demonstrate the arbitral tribunal's reliance on a *private contract lens*, which is intended to affirm the investor's expectations of returns from the investment contract. But the method is not at all scientific or precise, since arbitral tribunals often demonstrate considerable subjectivity when reconstructing, in hindsight, their perceived appropriate level of compensation for breaches of non-expropriation standards in an IIA. In determining compensation for a state's alleged breach of FET, for example, do arbitral tribunals fully discuss and disclose reasoning on the interaction between the legal issue of *causation*, with the *nature* of the injury caused and their metric for evaluating the appropriate *quantum* of compensation? Is it consistent with the reparative, but also

[136] Ibid 102, para 21.

[137] Ibid 102, para 20.

[138] Ibid Art 39.

[139] See Horia Curtin, 'The Compensation Standard for FET Breaches: The Far Limits of Legal Analogy' (Kluwer Arbitration Blog, 30 January 2015), available at kluwerarbitrationblog.com/blog/2015/01/30/the-compensation-standard-for-fet-breaches-the-far-limits-of-legal-analogy/: 'when taking into consideration the high number of cases alleging non-expropriatory breaches of international law, it still proves difficult to conceptualize the type of compensation owed by the states in such situations, as *no precise standards have been put forth*. Although there has been recent debate in the academia following a set of decisions—part of the Argentinian 'lot'—addressing this question, no definitive answer was delivered by scholars.

The main difficulties in using a unitary and common standard for the compensation of FET breaches arise from the broad spectrum of possible acts that could qualify as such. For example, it would prove nearly impossible to equate a "denial of justice" claim with one of "frustration of legitimate expectations" in respect to damages. *However, as a majority of the FET breaches invoked prove to have dire consequences for the investor, most cases re-argued—partially or totally—the former customary law approaches toward compensation for expropriatory acts.*' (emphasis added.)

[140] See *Enron Creditors Recovery Corporation and Ponderosa Assets LP v Argentine Republic*, ICSID Case No ARB/01/3, Award (22 May 2007) para 363; *Sempra Energy International v Argentine Republic*, ICSID Case No ARB/02/16, Award (28 September 2007) para 403; *CMS Gas Transmission Company v The Argentine Republic*, ICSID Case No ARB/01/8, Award (12 May 2005) para 409.

purposely equitable, nature of compensation under Article 31 of the Articles of State Responsibility, that compensation for an FET breach be automatically equated with the fair market value of the investment, as with expropriation breaches, based on the arbitral tribunal's subjective reconstruction of the alleged 'legitimate expectations' of the investor at the time the investment was established?

In its Judgment on compensation in the *Case Concerning Ahmadou Sadio Diallo*, the International Court of Justice emphasised that '[q]uantification of compensation for non-material injury necessarily rests on equitable considerations'.[141] Equity has been considered, albeit sparingly affirmed, in the process of determining the quantum of compensation, only in a small subset of investor-state arbitration cases to date.[142] Certainly, arbitral tribunals have not appeared at all to consider using any *public governance lens* when examining current valuation methodologies for non-expropriation breaches of IIAs. In a previous work, I have suggested an alternative for arbitral tribunals to consider the relative situations of the 'injured' and 'injuring' parties in international investment transactions.[143] More work is certainly needed on this front, to aid investor-state arbitral tribunals to clarify their valuation methodologies in an attempt to develop a more cooperative *public-private partnership lens*.

## VI. CONCLUSION

The foregoing brief survey of issues in investor-state arbitration is by no means exhaustive, but intended only to illustrate some of the methodological consequences of treating international investment as more a matter of contract or an object of governance. Neither lens fully captures the complexity of institutional, informative, and interpretive coordination critical to recognising investment as a kind of cooperation analogous to a public-private partnership. The oscillating legal, institutional, and teleological hybridity of international investment, only makes it all the more imperative for international lawyers to dissect, as well as connect, the premises and processes behind investment decision-making.

[141] *Case Concerning Ahmadou Sadio Diallo* (Compensation, Judgment) [2012] ICJ Reports 24, 334, para 24.

[142] Irmgard Marboe, *Calculation of Compensation and Damages in International Investment Law* (Oxford University Press, 2009) paras 3.307–3.338; Borzu Sabahi, *Compensation and Restitution in Investor-State Arbitration: Principles and Practice* (Oxford University Press, 2011) 186–88.

[143] Diane A Desierto and Desiree A Desierto, 'Investment Pricing and Social Protection: A Proposal for an ICESCR-Adjusted Capital Asset Pricing Model' (2013) 28 *ICSID Review* 405.

# 10

# *The Forced Co-Existence of Trade and Investment Provisions in Preferential Trade and Investment Agreements and the Regulatory Architecture of the Systems of Trade and Investment Law*

CATHARINE TITI*

## I. INTRODUCTION

IN RECENT YEARS the discussions on the structural geometry of the international investment law universe have focused on the sharply increasing number of bilateral investment treaties (BITs) concluded by states wishing to promote investment inflows and protect their investors in their ventures abroad. It is only very recently that the rhetoric of the burgeoning BIT universe has started to subside, as although still rising, the number of these treaties has abandoned its impressive upward trajectory,[1] and the focus has turned instead to increased regionalism in international investment relations and the conclusion of comprehensive trade or economic cooperation agreements with fully fledged investment chapters.[2] The latter are also known as 'other international investment agreements' ('other IIAs')[3] or sometimes preferential trade and investment agreements (PTIAs).[4] Although states have been concluding these comprehensive treaties for some time—and indeed on occasion trade and investment rules had co-existed in the same treaty even before the

* Research Scientist at the French National Centre for Scientific Research (*CNRS*) and Member of the CREDIMI (*Centre de recherche sur le droit des marchés et des investissements internationaux*) of the University of Burgundy.

[1] According to UNCTAD, in 2012 only 20 BITs were concluded, the lowest number in a quarter of a century. See UNCTAD *World Investment Report 2013* (United Nations) 101.

[2] Ibid 101 *et seq*.

[3] Ibid 101 *et seq*. UNCTAD has now abandoned this term in favour of 'treaties with investment provisions' (TIPs).

[4] Notably, PTIAs were the focus of the 2012 Frankfurt Investment Law Workshop 2012 organised at Goethe-Universität Frankfurt am Main, Germany.

advent of PTIAs[5]—more recently a trend appears to have been set. In North America, in parallel with traditional BITs, the United States (US), Canada and Mexico have been negotiating free trade agreements (FTAs) with investment chapters.[6] The North American Free Trade Agreement (NAFTA) constitutes an early and probably the most prominent example of such a treaty in North America.[7] The three NAFTA parties are also currently participating in negotiations on the Trans-Pacific Partnership Agreement (TPPA), a regional FTA that aims to incorporate an investment chapter.[8] Parallel negotiations involving the Association of Southeast Asian Nations (ASEAN) and some of the TPPA countries have been launched on a Regional Comprehensive Economic Partnership (RCEP) Agreement.[9] Australia, party to both sets of negotiations, has also been strong on the PTIA front.[10] According to the United Nations Conference on Trade and Development (UNCTAD), eight out of ten other IIAs concluded in 2012 were regional agreements and, by 2013, at least 110 states were participating in 22 negotiations.[11] In contrast to BIT negotiations, those of PTIAs appear to go hand-in-hand with increased regionalism.

Remarkably, the negotiation of comprehensive agreements with investment chapters has taken a definitive turn in Europe.[12] In the wake of the entry into force of the Treaty of Lisbon and the transfer of competence over foreign direct investment from the Member States to the Union, the latter has likewise been focusing on the negotiation of comprehensive economic agreements with investment chapters. The first EU-wide investment treaties with, inter alia, Canada, Singapore[13] and the US,

[5] For example, this was the case with Friendship, Commerce and Navigation (FCN) treaties (see M Sornarajah, *The International Law on Foreign Investment*, 3rd edn (Cambridge University Press, 2011) 180 *et seq*) or, in the WTO context, the Agreement on Trade-Related Investment Measures (TRIMs), the unsuccessful Havana Charter of 1948 and recent efforts in the Doha Round to cover investment measures; available at www.wto.org/english/tratop_e/invest_e/invest_info_e.htm. See also F Baetens, 'Preferential Trade and Investment Agreements and the Trade/Investment Divide: Is the Whole More than the Sum of Its Parts?' (2012) available at papers.ssrn.com/sol3/papers.cfm?abstract_id=2212247, 13.

[6] For example, US-Morocco FTA (2006), US-Central America-Dominican Republic FTA (2004), US-Colombia Trade Promotion Agreement (TPA) (2006), US-Panama TPA (2012), Canada-Colombia FTA (2008), Canada-Peru FTA (2008), Canada-Costa Rica FTA (2001), Mexico-Nicaragua FTA (1997), Mexico-Central America FTA (2011), (which replaced the Mexico-Nicaragua FTA), Mexico-Chile FTA (1998), Mexico-Uruguay FTA (2003) and Mexico-Peru FTA (2011), details of which can be found in the UNCTAD database at http://investmentpolicyhub.unctad.org/IIA.

[7] North American Free Trade Agreement, signed in San Antonio, 17 December 1992, entered into force 1 January 1994, 32 ILM 289 (1993).

[8] See www.ustr.gov/tpp.

[9] See www.dfat.gov.au/fta/rcep/.

[10] For example, Australia-Thailand FTA (2004), Australia-Chile FTA (2008), Australia-Singapore FTA (2003), Australia-US FTA (AUSFTA) (2004). See further investmentpolicyhub.unctad.org/IIA/Country OtherIias/11#iiaInnerMenu.

[11] UNCTAD, *World Investment Report 2013* (United Nations) 103.

[12] C Titi, 'International Investment Law and the European Union: Towards a New Generation of International Investment Agreements' 26(3) *European Journal of International Law* (2015).

[13] A preliminary consolidated version of the EU-Canada Comprehensive Economic and Trade Agreement (CETA) of September 2014 is available at trade.ec.europa.eu/doclib/html/152806.htm and the Draft EU-Singapore FTA of October 2014 is available at trade.ec.europa.eu/doclib/docs/2014/october/tradoc_152844.pdf.

point in the direction of treaties that cluster together trade and investment provisions;[14] exceptions to this are few and far between, notably the prospective treaties with China and Myanmar.[15] Although bilateral in nature, the PTIAs in question are no less regional, in that they engage all EU Member States.

The new proliferation of 'regional' comprehensive FTAs may have significant ramifications for the regulatory architecture of the international investment and international trade law systems. Although the evolution of each system is influenced by a confluence of factors whose respective weight is difficult to determine, this contribution will consider three seminal aspects of the interaction between trade and investment rules brought together under the umbrella of the same treaty, with a focus on investment law. Concretely, the chapter will consider three spheres of influence of this cohabitation of rules and the new state of play: first, its impact on the drafting of treaty provisions and, notably, the new generation of investment agreements; secondly, the question of whether it is possible to import interpretative principles and jurisprudential solutions from trade law into investment law; and, finally, the structure of governance of the two systems. The discussion will take place in light of the EU's new competence over the conclusion of treaties covering foreign direct investment and actual EU negotiations that are set to have a definitive impact on future PTIAs.

## II. PREFERENTIAL TRADE AND INVESTMENT AGREEMENTS AND THE NEW GENERATION OF INTERNATIONAL INVESTMENT TREATIES

The growing popularity of PTIAs coincides with a move in investment treaty-making towards so-called new generation investment agreements.[16] The latter are associated with the adoption of 'state-friendly' rules and are broadly deemed to be balanced instruments that safeguard a modicum of the host state's regulatory flexibility.[17] Another feature of these new agreements is that they tend to extend their protections to the pre-establishment stage: this is equally true of North American investment treaties and EU comprehensive FTAs.[18] The ensuing paragraphs will consider the

[14] At the time of writing, negotiations have been concluded for the first two of these agreements. On the status of the TTIP negotiations, see ec.europa.eu/trade/policy/in-focus/ttip/. On these and other IIA negotiations involving the EU, see M Bungenberg and C Titi, 'Developments in International Investment Law' in C Herrmann, M Krajewski and J P Terchechte (eds), *European Yearbook of International Economic Law 2014* (Springer, 2014) 428 *et seq.*

[15] M Bungenberg and C Titi, The Evolution of EU Investment Law and the Future of EU-China Investment Relations in W Shan and Jn Su (eds), *China and International Investment Law: Twenty Years of ICSID Membership*, Silk Road Studies in International Economic Law (Brill, 2014); European Commission, Press Release: EU and Myanmar/Burma to negotiate an investment protection agreement, IP/14/285, Brussels, 20 March 2014.

[16] C Titi, 'The Arbitrator as a Lawmaker: Jurisgenerative Processes in Investment Arbitration' (2013) 14(5) *Journal of World Investment & Trade* 829, 843 *et seq.*

[17] C Titi, *The Right to Regulate in International Investment Law* (Nomos and Hart Publishing, 2014) *passim.*

[18] For example, see Articles X.4–X.7 of the consolidated CETA Chapter on Investment of September 2014.

linkages between such developments and the co-existence of investment and trade rules, taking as an example the negotiation of EU FTAs with investment chapters.

New generation IIAs were born with the North American investment policy shift in the mid 2000s and the promulgation of the US's and Canada's model BITs of 2004.[19] In particular, the experience of the US as respondent under NAFTA arbitration in the 1990s revealed a series of obligations undertaken under the US BIT programme, which had been understood by the US Administration in a way different than in the claims brought against it in investment arbitration.[20] The US, which had until that moment probably paid little attention to the arbitration clause in its investment treaties due to a confidence in the coherence and integrity of its internal legal system,[21] was led to reconsider the formulation of the protection standards in its IIAs. As is well known, these early cases against the US,[22] although finding in favour of the state,[23] resulted in the 2004 revision of its Model BIT, in an endeavour to cut back on arbitral discretion and increase the state's policy space.[24] If this new generation of investment agreements took concrete shape in North America about ten years ago, the EU Member States continued to conclude old generation BITs and it is only now with the EU negotiations on the first EU-wide FTAs, with investment chapters, that the wind of change is at last reaching Europe.[25] Prior to the entry into force of the Treaty of Lisbon, the EU had an exclusive competence over the conclusion of treaties that covered the pre-establishment phase (that is, market access),[26] while the competence of the Member States was limited to the post-establishment phase—in other words, to the protection of investments already established in the host state.[27]

In accordance with this apportioning of competences in the pre-Lisbon era, while the Member States 'focused on the promotion and protection of all forms of investment, the Commission elaborated a liberalisation agenda focused on market access for direct investment'.[28] This 'liberalisation agenda' has been expressed in the Union's FTAs, which in recent years have been modelled on the 'EU Minimum Platform on

[19] Titi (n 16) 843 *et seq*.

[20] Titi (n 17) 68; KJ Vandevelde, 'A Comparison of the 2004 and 1994 US Model BITs: Rebalancing Investor and Host Country Interests' in KP Sauvant (ed), *Yearbook on International Investment Law & Policy 2008–2009* (Oxford University Press, 2009) 290–92.

[21] Titi (n 17) 68; Vandevelde (n 20) 285.

[22] For example, *Loewen Group Inc and Raymond L Loewen v United States*, ICSID Case No ARB(AF)/98/3, also *Methanex Corporation v United States*, UNCITRAL, *Mondev International Ltd v United States*, ICSID Case No ARB(AF)/99/2, *ADF Group Inc v United States*, ICSID Case No ARB(AF)/00/1.

[23] For example, see JE Alvarez, *The Public International Law Regime Governing International Investment* (Hague Academy of International Law, 2011) 87, 259; also see www.nafta-sec-alena.org/Home/Dispute-Settlement/Decisions-and-Reports.

[24] Titi (n 17) 68 (with further citations); Vandevelde (n 20) 287 *et seq*, 298 *et seq*.

[25] See in general, Titi (n 12).

[26] Bungenberg and Titi (n 14).

[27] M Bungenberg and S Hobe, 'The Relationship of International Investment Law and European Union Law' in M Bungenberg, J Griebel, S Hobe and A Reinisch (eds), *International Investment Law: A Handbook* (Beck/Hart/Nomos, 2015); Bungenberg and Titi (n 14).

[28] European Commission Communication 'Towards a comprehensive European international investment policy' COM (2010) 343 final, Brussels, 7 July 2010, 11.

Investment'.[29] This negotiating template for EU FTAs—the equivalent of a Model BIT for trade negotiations without an investment chapter—is qualitatively different from EU Member State BITs, in that it appears to be cognisant of the parties' right to regulate in a similar manner to post-2004 North American investment treaties.[30]

An early version of the Platform[31] indicates that the final document would contain general exceptions modelled on Article XX of the GATT 1994,[32] but also provisions encompassing non-directly enforceable positive language on regulatory concerns, such as articles targeting the avoidance of a lowering of environmental and social standards, or laws concerning the protection and promotion of cultural diversity.[33] The 2008 EU-CARIFORUM Economic Partnership Agreement (EPA)[34] and the 2010 EU-South Korea FTA[35] are among the treaties negotiated on the basis of the Platform. They incorporate provisions on the non-relaxing of environmental, safety and labour standards,[36] references to the fight against corruption, and state commitments under the International Labour Organization (ILO),[37] security exceptions[38] and general exceptions modelled on Article XX of the GATT.[39] The EU-South Korea Free Trade Agreement seems to be the first EU document to expressly refer to the states' right to regulate.[40] When EU negotiations on the first investment chapters were afoot, the European Commission expressed the opinion that the principles that have guided EU FTA negotiations should inspire the Union's new investment policy. Notably, it suggested that the state's right to regulate should be safeguarded through EU investment treaties in the way that it is protected through the Union's FTAs.[41] This insistence on the part of the EU on the right to regulate as a guiding

[29] The leaked text of a preliminary draft on which the minimum platform on investment was based is available at www.iisd.org/pdf/2006/itn_ecom.pdf. See on the minimum platform, eg N Maydell, 'The European Community's Minimum Platform on Investment or the Trojan Horse of Investment Competence' in A Reinisch and C Knahr (eds), *International Investment Law in Context* (Eleven International Publishing, 2007) 73 *et seq*; for the revisited version of the Minimum Platform on Investment, see Council Document 7242/09, Limited, of 6 March 2009. See also European Commission, 'Note for the attention of the 133 Committee, Minimum platform on investment for EU FTAs—Provisions on establishment in template for a Title on "Establishment, trade in services and e-commerce"' D (2006) 9219, Brussels 28 July 2006, available at www.iisd.org/pdf/2006/itn_ecom.pdf.

[30] On the right to regulate, see Titi (n 16).

[31] See European Commission, 'Note for the attention of the 133 Committee' (n 29).

[32] Ibid 7–8. General Agreement on Tariffs and Trade 1994, signed in Marrakesh, 15 April 1994, entered into force 1 January 1995, Marrakesh Agreement Establishing the World Trade Organization, Annex 1A (GATT).

[33] Ibid 11; and 'Explanatory Memorandum', ibid 3.

[34] CM Brown, The European Union and Regional Trade Agreements: A Case Study of the EU-Korea FTA, in C Herrmann and J P Terchechte, *European Yearbook of International Economic Law 2011* (Springer, 2011) 302.

[35] See Bungenberg and Hobe (n 27).

[36] Article 73 EU-CARIFORUM EPA; see also Article 1.1 EU-South Korea FTA.

[37] Article 72 EU-CARIFORUM EPA; Article 13.4(3) EU-South Korea FTA.

[38] For example, Article 225 EU-CARIFORUM EPA; Article 15.9 EU-South Korea FTA, Article 2(7) of Annex 9 EU-South Korea FTA.

[39] For example, Article 224 EU-CARIFORUM EPA; Articles 2.15, 7.50, 8.3 EU-South Korea FTA.

[40] Article 7.1(4) EU-South Korea FTA; see also the Preamble and Articles 13.3, 13.4.3, 13.5.2 and 13.7 of the same treaty.

[41] C Titi, 'EU investment agreements and the search for a new balance: A paradigm shift from laissez-faire liberalism toward embedded liberalism?' *Columbia FDI Perspectives* No 86, 3 January 2013.

principle for investment negotiations is hardly surprising. The very first investment agreements concluded by the Union, and most of those for which negotiations are currently ongoing, are in fact PTIAs, in other words FTAs with investment chapters. And although the possibility could be envisaged whereby an investment chapter would stand as 'separate' within the overall agreement, there is no overwhelming reason to expect the EU to abandon its established negotiating canons simply because an investment chapter has been added to its FTA.[42]

In any case, the principles that guide the rest of the treaty would constitute part of the context of the investment chapter which, in light of the principle of systemic integration, would need to be taken into account when interpreting the investment provisions.[43] Intentions aside, for pragmatic reasons negotiation of the investment chapter would probably be influenced by the general principles that govern the rest of the FTA. At the same time, the new EU treaties are generally intended to offer market access along with post-establishment investment protections.[44] In this respect, their effect is more far-reaching than that of traditional Member States' BITs, since the latter made no commitments regarding investment liberalisation. For this reason, the Union's new PTIAs would in any case be likely to wish to safeguard more policy space than their post-establishment only 'predecessors'.[45]

The example of EU PTIA negotiations demonstrates the potential for interaction and influence between, on the one hand, FTA provisions and negotiating principles, and on the other, the negotiation of investment agreements. Apart from the close proximity of trade and investment rules, which may encourage emulation and a certain degree of 'convergence' between them, other considerations that may have been previously uncalled for, such as greater regulatory flexibility for host states in light of market access commitments, have become a reality and may shape new PTIA provisions.

## III. INTERPRETATION OF SIMILAR TRADE AND INVESTMENT PROVISIONS

The emulation of trade law provisions in IIAs renders imperative tackling the dilemma of whether interpretive principles and jurisprudential solutions drawn from World Trade Organization (WTO) law may be transposed to investment law. Even before the co-existence of trade and investment provisions within the same PTIA,

[42] Titi (n 12).

[43] Article 31 Vienna Convention on the Law of Treaties (1969). On the principle of systemic integration, see further C McLachlan, 'The Principle of Systemic Integration and Article 31(3)(c) of the Vienna Convention' (2005) 54 *International & Comparative Law Quarterly*; C McLachlan, L Shore and M Weiniger, *International Investment Arbitration: Substantive Principles* (Oxford University Press, 2007) paras 7.69–7.70; TW Wälde, 'Interpreting Investment Treaties: Experiences and Examples' in C Binder, U Kriebaum, A Reinisch and S Wittich (eds), *International Investment Law for the 21st Century—Essays in Honour of Cristoph Schreuer* (Oxford University Press, 2009) 769–77.

[44] For example, see Articles X.4 *et seq.* CETA Chapter on Investment.

[45] Titi (n 12).

investment law has often borrowed the phrasing of the former. The *problèmatique* of their interpretive interaction is pertinent, whether such trade rules are incorporated in a PTIA or in a standalone BIT. But the question is even more relevant when the provisions co-exist in different chapters in the same treaty, relating both to trade and to investment.

Interpretive questions may arise due to the co-existence of provisions, but also for pragmatic reasons, such as the increasing blurring of the line between trade and investment rules as well as trade and investment lawyers.[46] One such question, for instance, may be asked regarding the relevance of WTO jurisprudence to general exceptions clauses modelled on Article XX GATT 1994, or Article XIV GATS, or such rules that have been incorporated *mutatis mutandis* into an investment agreement.[47] It is naturally possible to invoke WTO jurisprudence in investment arbitration, and vice versa, but it must also be recognised that no rule obliges an arbitrator to accept the solutions found in the other system.[48] This is particularly evident in the light of divergent investment jurisprudence that on a number of issues has reached contradictory solutions, not allowing for the development of a *jurisprudence constante* in their respect.[49]

The topic of the relationship between WTO jurisprudence and investment provisions has already been taken up in arbitral awards. Arbitrators adjudicating the Argentine crisis disputes when uncertain about the interpretation of the 'necessary for' requirement in the US-Argentina BIT's essential security interests exception, turned to customary law for guidance, noting that 'necessity and the conditions for its operation' are determined under customary law.[50] Their approach, flawed in the author's opinion for a number of reasons which have been discussed elsewhere,[51] points to another potential oversight in ignoring the fact that the 'necessary for' requirement has also been interpreted in GATT/WTO law.[52] In another arbitration involving the Argentine crisis, the *Continental Casualty* tribunal directly considered this issue. Although in the presence of an exception modelled on Article XXI GATT 1994, rather than one modelled on Article XX GATT 1994, the tribunal considered that since the provision under interpretation echoed GATT language, it would be

> appropriate to refer to the GATT and WTO case law which has extensively dealt with the concept and requirements of necessity in the context of economic measures derogating to

[46] Comment put forward during the 2012 Frankfurt Investment Law Workshop 2012 organised at Goethe-Universität Frankfurt am Main, Germany.

[47] See eg Article X.02 CETA Chapter on Exceptions.

[48] Titi (n 17) 179.

[49] Marc Bungenberg and Catharine Titi, 'Precedents in International Investment Law' in M Bungenberg, J Griebel, S Hobe and A Reinisch (eds), *International Investment Law: A Handbook* (Beck/Hart/Nomos, 2015) *passim*.

[50] *Sempra Energy International v Argentina*, ICSID Case No ARB/02/16, Award, 28 September 2007, para 376. See also *Enron Creditors Recovery Corporation (formerly Enron Corporation) and Ponderosa Assets LP v Argentina* ICSID Case No ARB/01/3, Award, 22 May 2007, paras 333–34.

[51] Titi (n 17) *passim*.

[52] Ibid 178.

> [*sic*] the obligations contained in GATT, rather than to refer to the requirement of necessity under customary international law.[53]

WTO jurisprudence, although not generally pertinent to investment law disputes, may offer a better understanding of themes and issues that on occasion may not be so different, whether they are addressed in the investment or in the trade law context.[54] Nevertheless, any parallels between the two systems must be drawn with caution, since, despite their commonalities, they continue to be two different universes, which in principle regulate disparate relationships.[55] This does not in itself prevent, for instance, a party to an investment dispute from invoking GATT or WTO jurisprudence but tribunals are under no obligation to draw on WTO law any more than they are under an obligation to draw on any other system of international law, such as human rights law.[56] This freedom to follow or not to follow trade law jurisprudence was affirmed by the arbitrators in the *Methanex* case:

> [T]he Tribunal may derive guidance from the way in which a similar phrase in the GATT has been interpreted in the past. Whilst such interpretations cannot be treated by this Tribunal as binding precedents, the Tribunal may remain open to persuasion based on legal reasoning developed in GATT and WTO jurisprudence, if relevant.[57]

In other words, much will depend on the persuasiveness of counsel's argumentation.[58]

## IV. THE PERSPECTIVE OF CONVERGENCE BETWEEN TRADE AND INVESTMENT GOVERNANCE

The final question to consider is whether the proliferation of PTIAs may encourage a degree of convergence between the respective structures of governance of trade and investment law. Such convergence is possible to the extent that the two systems differ from each other.

One first important structural difference is that trade law has embraced multilateralism, namely within the WTO, while repeated attempts to conclude a multilateral

[53] *Continental Casualty Company v Argentina*, ICSID Case No ARB/03/9, Award, 5 September 2008, para 192. Contra: Alvarez (n 23) 301 *et seq.* and JE Alvarez and T Brink, 'Revisiting the Necessity Defense: Continental Casualty v. Argentina' in KP Sauvant (ed), *Yearbook on International Investment Law & Policy 2010–2011* (Oxford University Press, 2012) 335–52.

[54] UNCTAD, The Protection of National Security in IIAs, *UNCTAD Series on International Investment Policies for Development*, UNCTAD/DIAE/IA/2008/5 (UN 2009) 51.

[55] N DiMascio and J Pauwelyn, 'Nondiscrimination in Trade and Investment Treaties: Worlds Apart or Two Sides of the Same Coin?' (2008) 102 *American Journal of International Law* 1, 53–58; B Legum and I Petculescu, 'GATT Article XX and International Investment Law' in R Echandi and P Sauvé (eds), *Prospects in International Investment Law and Policy: World Trade Forum* (Cambridge University Press, 2013); see also JE Alvarez, 'Implications for the Future of International Investment Law' in KP Sauvant and M Chiswick-Patterson (eds), *Appeals Mechanism in International Investment Disputes* (Oxford University Press, 2008) 31. Cf Alvarez and Brink (n 53) 335–52.

[56] Titi (n 17) 178–79.

[57] *Methanex Corporation v United States*, UNCITRAL, Final Award on Jurisdiction and Merits, 3 August 2005, Part II—Chapter B, para 6.

[58] Titi (n 17) 179.

*investment* agreement have failed lamentably.[59] As already mentioned, the conclusion of PTIAs coincides with increased regional tendencies in new negotiations. Of course, trade rules in FTAs are bilateral or plurilateral but not multilateral. Yet it is possible that the cohabitation of trade and investment provisions will bring back to the table the discussion on multilateralism in investment negotiations. In this manner, regionalism in PTIA negotiations may, in the long run, open the door to multilateral solutions.[60] This potential is obvious, for example, when considering recent positions of the European Commission including on the creation of a permanent investment court.[61]

One other potential point of convergence relates to the two systems' respective dispute settlement mechanisms. The latter are at this stage distinct from each other for more than one reason. Trade law has focused on the state as both claimant and beneficiary of protected rights, while international investment law has made the investor, generally a private entity or an individual, its principal subject of protection.[62] Investment arbitration was developed in an express attempt to de-politicise disputes, giving the investor standing before an arbitral tribunal and bypassing the various hurdles involved in any attempt to invoke diplomatic protection.[63] The differences (and complementarities?) between the two dispute settlement systems have sometimes encouraged disputing parties to indirectly pursue the resolution of a dispute in both *fora*, such as in the context of the *Philip Morris* and *Repsol* cases, leading to a certain degree of 'convergence' between trade and investment disputes.[64]

Investor-state arbitration has proved to be a popular dispute resolution mechanism for investors but a little less so for host states that have found themselves in the constant role of respondent.[65] Criticism has recently been levelled at the

[59] For example, see P Juillard, 'MAI: A European View' (1998) 31 *Cornell International Law Journal*) 477; PT Muchlinski, 'The Rise and Fall of the Multilateral Agreement on Investment: Where Now?' (2000) 34 *International Lawyer*; TR Braun, 'Investment Protection under WTO Law—New Developments in the Aftermath of Cancún' (2004) 28 *Beiträge zum Transnationalen Wirtschaftsrecht*.

[60] M Bungenberg, 'Preferential Trade and Investment Agreements and Regionalism' in Rainer Hofmann, S Schill and CJ Tams (eds), *Preferential Trade and Investment Agreements: From Recalibration to Reintegration* (Nomos, 2013) *passim*.

[61] European Commission, 'Concept Paper: Investment in TTIP and beyond—the path for reform' (2015).

[62] See also Baetens (n 5) 18–19.

[63] IFI Shihata, 'Towards a Greater Depoliticization of Investment Disputes: The Role of ICSID and MIGA' (1986) 1 *ICSID Review—Foreign Investment Law Journal*, *passim*; IFI Shihata, 'Introduction by the Secretary General', *ICSID 1984 Annual Report* 5 (1984); S Puig, 'Emergence & Dynamism in International Organizations: ICSID, Investor-State Arbitration & International Investment Law' (2013) 44 *Georgetown Journal of International Law* 531, *passim*; Catharine Titi, 'Are Investment Tribunals Adjudicating Political Disputes? Some reflections on the repoliticization of investment disputes and (new) forms of diplomatic protection' (2015) 32(3) *Journal of International Arbitration* 261 *et seq*.

[64] *Philip Morris Asia Ltd v Australia, UNCITRAL*, PCA Case No. 2012-12; *Repsol, S.A. and Repsol Butano, S.A. v. Argentina*, ICSID Case No. ARB/12/38. See RP Alford, 'The Convergence of International Trade and Investment Arbitration' (2013) *Santa Clara Journal of International Law* 12(1); C Titi, 'Investment Arbitration in Latin America: The Uncertain Veracity of Preconceived Ideas' (2014) 30(2) *Arbitration International* 374; Titi (n 63).

[65] Patrick Juillard, 'The Law of International Investment: Can the Imbalance Be Redressed?' in KP Sauvant (ed), *Yearbook on International Investment Law & Policy 2008–2009* (Oxford University Press, 2009) 274, 280.

system followed by calls for reform,[66] sometimes so vocal that states have started to rethink the necessity of including investor-state dispute settlement provisions in their investment agreements. This is notably the case of a previous Australian Government,[67] and some Latin American states[68] and it has more recently been evidenced in Germany's reluctance to 'embrace' investor-state dispute settlement in the EU-led negotiations.[69] Despite these particularities and critiques, investment dispute settlement is here to stay, at least for the foreseeable future. And the question may be raised whether international arbitration may also gain in popularity in trade disputes.[70] Besides, although under the WTO's dispute settlement system access to arbitration is possible, the latter is hardly ever used in that context.[71] At the same time, the design of the WTO dispute settlement system may likewise influence investment arbitration. In contrast with investment tribunals, the WTO provides a permanent forum for the resolution of trade disputes, with an appellate mechanism.[72] Relevant suggestions have been put forward in the investment context, such as the creation of a permanent investment arbitral tribunal and the establishment of an appeals mechanism,[73] and more recently the creation of a permanent investment court.[74] It is also worth looking into whether a common, that is, investment-trade, system of dispute resolution may not be feasible.[75]

A further issue concerning the governance of the two systems is how to manage eventual overlaps between similar provisions of BITs and 'other IIAs'.[76] A considerable number of BIT clauses overlap with post-establishment protections afforded in PTIAs. This is not a feature unique to the relationship between stand-alone investment instruments and comprehensive agreements but here there is an increased likelihood of *inadvertent* overlaps. Difficulties could arise, for example, with respect

[66] See eg SD Franck, 'The Legitimacy Crisis in Investment Treaty Arbitration: Privatizing Public International Law through Inconsistent Decisions' (2005) 73 *Fordham Law Review*; Alvarez (n 23) 75–93, 257–63, 352–406; WW Burke-White, 'The Argentine Financial Crisis: State Liability under BITs and the Legitimacy of the ICSID System' (2008) 3 *Asian Journal of WTO & International Health Law & Policy* 1; G van Harten, 'Perceived Bias in Investment Treaty Arbitration' in M Waibel, A Kaushal, K-H Chung and C Balchin (eds), *The Backlash against Investment Arbitration* (Kluwer Law International, 2010).

[67] Australian Government, *Gillard Government Trade Policy Statement: Trading our way to more jobs and prosperity*, April 2011, available at blogs.usyd.edu.au/japaneselaw/2011_Gillard%20Govt%20Trade%20Policy%20Statement.pdf 14.

[68] Titi (n 64).

[69] See Titi (n 12).

[70] Baetens (n 5) 37 *et seq*.

[71] Ibid 37.

[72] P-T Stoll and F Schorkopf, *WTO—World Economic Order, World Trade Law* (Martinus Nijhoff, 2003) 69 *et seq*.

[73] European Commission Fact Sheet, 'Investment Protection and Investor-to-State Dispute Settlement in EU agreements' (November 2013) 9.

[74] Such a proposal has been put forward at the EU level, see European Commission, 'Concept Paper: Investment in TTIP and beyond—the path for reform' (2015). Analogous proposals, sometimes referring to a permanent court sometimes to a permanent tribunal, have also been put forward by some EU Member States, eg by Germany, see Project No 83/15 of the Federal Ministry for Economic Affairs and Energy, prepared by Markus Krajwski. An English version of the model with commentary is available at www.rph1.rw.fau.de/files/2016/02/150429-muster-bit-fr-industriestaaten-krajewski-englische-bersetzung.pdf.

[75] Cf Baetens (n 5) 37 *et seq*.

[76] Ibid 9–10.

to the application of the most-favoured-nation treatment or with how claims are brought to adjudication, given that an investment chapter would typically provide for investor-state arbitration, while claims relating to other PTIA chapters may need to be brought by the state.[77]

A final consideration in this respect is whether the conclusion of PTIAs may encourage states to undertake liberalisation commitments,[78] when concluding either their PTIAs or their BITs. This may be asked for instance in respect of the EU's investment treaty with China, a bilateral investment agreement that will probably aim to offer market access.[79]

In short, the co-existence of trade and investment rules may bring about—or at least encourage—a certain degree of convergence in the governance of the trade and international investment law systems. This is especially true in the areas where the two are most dissimilar, such as with respect to the bilateral-multilateral nature of the system or the settlement of disputes.

## V. CONCLUSION

International economic law is a field in constant, dynamic evolution and the new popularity of PTIAs, comprehensive treaties that combine liberalisation commitments with investment protection, is witness to and an outcome of this evolution. The co-existence of trade and investment rules under the umbrella of the same treaty inevitably influences negotiations, and ultimately treaty-making, in incremental but also radical ways, such as by encouraging market access commitments and state-friendly provisions in investment treaties. This interaction between rules and the emulation of trade provisions in investment treaties or investment chapters raises the question of the extent to which the interpretation of trade rules and trade jurisprudence may guide the understanding of investment provisions. Although the former are by no means binding on an investment tribunal, they may create interpretive presumptions in their favour. Finally, the close cohabitation of trade and investment rules may result in a certain convergence in the respective structure of governance of the two systems, and in particular it may provide a source of inspiration that works both ways in the persistent attempt to improve international trade and investment law.

[77] See also ibid *passim*.
[78] See further ibid *passim*.
[79] See Bungenberg and Titi (n 14).

# 11

# *The Shared Responsibility of the EU for Member States' Financial Crisis Measures as a Defence in International Investment Claims*

ANASTASIOS G GOURGOURINIS*

## I. INTRODUCTION

MUCH HAS BEEN said regarding the role and influence of European Union (EU) institutions, such as the European Commission and the European Central Bank (ECB), over measures taken by Member States in the context of the Eurozone's financial crisis.[1] In parallel, the enactment of such measures may have substantial repercussions at the investment treaty arbitration level, potentially leading to investment claims against the individual EU Member States concerned. The question that then arises is what happens when a measure, otherwise part and parcel of and prerequisite for an EU-backed financial assistance programme, is nevertheless challenged as inconsistent with an EU Member State's international obligations under a bilateral investment treaty (BIT)?

The European Commission's view regarding ownership of measures taken in the context of financial assistance programmes appears unequivocal:

> The ownership of the design of the programme belongs to the authorities of the Member State concerned, and the main measures are included in the authorities' Letter of Intent (LoI) to the IMF and the EU. In the preparatory phase of the programme and the subsequent MoU there are intense interactions between the national authorities and the Troika, but given that the MoU is signed by the national authorities, who are also responsible for its implementation, the ultimate responsibility rests with them.[2]

* Lecturer in International Law, National and Kapodistrian University of Athens, Faculty of Law; Research Fellow, Academy of Athens. The author is grateful to Anna Ventouratou for her excellence research assistance.

[1] See eg the analysis through the lens of fundamental and human rights in Andreas Fischer-Lescano, *Human Rights in Times of Austerity Policy: The EU Institutions and the Conclusion of Memoranda of Understanding* (Nomos, 2014).

[2] European Commission, Answer to the questionnaire supporting the own initiative report evaluating the structure, the role and operations of the 'troika' (Commission, ECB and the IMF) actions in euro area programme countries, Ref Ares (2013) 3736254—16 December 2013, available at www.europarl.europa.eu/document/activities/cont/201401/20140114ATT77315/20140114ATT77315EN.pdf.

Hence, if the Commission's view is accepted, then Member States concerned would ad infinitum bear any potential burden alone and potentially be obligated to compensate foreign investors (even those originating from other EU Member States), notwithstanding the EU institutions' role in the adoption of the challenged measure, which is often opposed by the concerned EU Member State itself. It is in this context that the present study argues that the EU's shared responsibility for specific measures taken by Member States under structural adjustment programmes can in fact operate as a 'shield', in terms of admissibility and/or the merits of investment claims against the EU Member States.

## II. SPECIFIC EU MEMBER STATES' FINANCIAL CRISIS MEASURES AS A CASE STUDY

As a necessary prelude, one must be able prima facie to identify EU-mandated measures undertaken by Member States to tackle the financial crisis in the Euro Area, currently, or likely to be, challenged in investment arbitral proceedings. For the purposes of this study, the recent structural adjustment programmes of Greece and Cyprus provide suitable case studies.

Greece initially requested financial assistance on 23 April 2010. In March 2012, a Second Economic Adjustment Programme was approved for the period 2012 to 2014, after the success of the private sector involvement (PSI) leading to the restructuring of Greece's sovereign debt, following the adoption of the Bondholder Act (Law 4050/2012)[3] which introduced collective action clauses (CACs) in the sovereign bond contracts governed by Greek law. After the activation of the CACs, the sum of amended domestic law sovereign bonds, and tendered guaranteed and foreign law bonds rose above 95 per cent. *Poštová banka*, a Slovak bank which had reportedly purchased Greek government bonds in 2010, was among the hold-out bondholders. On 20 May 2013 *Poštová banka* and its Cypriot shareholder *Istrokapital SE* filed an ICSID claim against the Hellenic Republic, alleging the violation of the protective guarantees contained in the BITs in force between Greece and Slovakia, as well as Greece and Cyprus, due to the losses suffered by virtue of the March 2012 Greek debt restructuring.[4] On 9 April 2015 the *Poštová banka* Tribunal eventually dismissed the claims for lack of jurisdiction *ratione materiae*, and the merits of the case were not examined,[5] hence not excluding the future possibility of foreign bondholders instituting investment arbitration proceedings under other Hellenic BITs in force (equipped with different definitions of covered investments and

[3] Law 4050/2012, 'Rules on the amendment of titles issued or guaranteed by the Hellenic Republic with the bondholders' agreement', Hellenic Government Gazette A 36 23 February 2012.

[4] Investment Arbitration Reporter on 'Bondholders' claim against Greece is registered at ICSID, as mandatory wait-period expires on another threatened arbitration', available at www.iareporter.com/articles/20130530_2; Karen Halverson Cross, 'Sovereign Arbitration' in Rosa Lastra and Lee Buchheit (eds), *Sovereign Debt Management* (Oxford University Press, 2014) 162–64.

[5] *Poštová banka, a.s. and ISTROKAPITAL SE v Hellenic Republic*, Final Award of 9 April 2015, ICSID Case No ARB/13/8 (hereinafter *Poštová banka case*). An ICSID ad-hoc annulment committee is currently reviewing the award.

investors).[6] Amongst the various merits issues raised here, one could single out the allegations of creditor discrimination, based on the fact that Greek sovereign bonds, governed by Greek law, and held by the ECB (as Greece's single largest bondholder) were de facto excluded from the Greek PSI bond exchange. For, just a few days before the enactment of Law 4050/2012 and the publication of the bond exchange offer, Greece consented to the exchange of ECB-held sovereign bonds with new ones, identical to the old ones in all respects, except their issue date and International Securities Identification Number (ISIN), that is, *the new bonds were issued in 2012*. At the same time, the March 2012 PSI Greek debt exchange covered only sovereign bonds issued *on 31 December 2011, or earlier*. Accordingly, the ECB-held sovereign debt under the Securities Market Programme would be serviced in full, in contrast to other Greek government bond creditors affected by the imposition of CACs under Law 4050/2012, such as the ones held by *Poštová banka* or *Cyprus Popular Bank*.[7]

In the case of Cyprus, actual or threatened investment claims relate to the infamous March 2013 bank 'bail-in'.[8] Cyprus initially requested financial assistance from the EU in June 2012 but on 19 March 2013 had rejected an initial draft programme which included bail-in of insured depositors in Cypriot banks. Amidst the political and financial turmoil that developed, Cyprus found no alternative to the conditional EU adjustment programme and agreed a few days later to the bail-in of uninsured depositors in the two largest Cypriot banks.

Both the examples of Greece and Cyprus demonstrate that specific measures taken by Member States, albeit in the context of EU-backed financial assistance programmes, are not 'immune' and may, indeed, be challenged in the investment arbitration arena. Moreover, even theoretically (assuming that jurisdictional and admissibility objections are overruled)[9], the possibility of a violation finding regarding the international obligations under the BITs of the Member State concerned,

[6] Sotiris Nikas, 'Cyprus seeks PSI damages for Laiki Bank', *Kathimerini*, 1 October 2015, available at http://www.ekathimerini.com/202112/article/ekathimerini/business/cyprus-seeks-psi-damages-for-laiki-bank. Although more information is not available, this seemingly indicates that the now defunct *Cyprus Popular Bank*, which reportedly held Greek sovereign debt, also challenges the Greek PSI, in addition to the refusal of Greece's Central Bank to grant emergency liquidity assistance to its Greek branch: *Cyprus Popular Bank Public Co. Ltd. v. Hellenic Republic*, ICSID Case No. ARB/14/16.

[7] Antonis Bredimas, Anastasios Gourgourinis and George Pavlidis, 'The Legal Contours of Sovereign Debt Restructuring under the UNCTAD Principles: Antagonism and Convergence between Standards of Domestic Insolvency Law and International Investment Protection Law' in Carlos Espósito, Yuefen Li and Juan Pablo Bohoslavsky (eds), *Sovereign Financing and International Law: The UNCTAD Principles on Responsible Sovereign Lending and Borrowing* (Oxford University Press, 2013) 135, 158–59; Jeromin Zettelmeyer, Christoph Trebesch and Mitu Gulati, 'Managing Holdouts: The Case of the 2012 Greek Exchange' in Rosa Lastra and Lee Buchheit (eds), *Sovereign Debt Management* (Oxford University Press, 2014) 27.

[8] See *Theodoros Adamakopoulos and others v. Republic of Cyprus*, ICSID Case No. ARB/15/49. Also, see Kyriaki Karadelis, 'Cyprus threatened with bailout claim' *Global Arbitration Review*, 14 July 2014, available at globalarbitrationreview.com/news/article/32810/cyprus-threatened-bailout-claim/.

[9] For instance, despite the most recent *Poštová banka* case and the restrictive approach of the Tribunal in the determination of its jurisdiction, tribunals have asserted jurisdiction in the sovereign debt-related investment claims against Argentina: see *Abaclat and Others v Argentina*, Decision on Jurisdiction and Admissibility of 4 August 2011, ICSID Case No ARB/07/5; *Ambiente Ufficio SpA and Others (Case formerly known as Giordano Alpi and Others) v Argentina*, Decision on Jurisdiction and Admissibility of 8 February 2013, ICSID Case No ARB/08/9. Note that after a change in government in Argentina in November 2015, most holders of Argentinian sovereign bonds have reached a settlement with the state.

may well be said to exist.[10] Assuming *arguendo*, without further ado, and only for the purposes of this study, that the measures of Greece and Cyprus could potentially violate their obligations under BITs, the question that then arises concerns the effect of the relevant role of EU institutions in their enactment, an issue which is addressed in the next section.

## III. THE INVOLVEMENT OF EU INSTITUTIONS IN SPECIFIC MEMBER STATES' FINANCIAL CRISIS MEASURES

It must be emphasised from the outset that the involvement of EU institutions in EU-backed financial assistance programmes constitutes a fact-intensive and complex exercise. Perhaps the most authoritative information regarding the role of EU institutions can be found on materials pertaining to the European Parliament's probe that led to the adoption of the resolution of 13 March 2014 on the enquiry into the relevant role and operations of the so-called 'Troika',[11] and on the basis of which the present study will proceed.

In the context of the probe, the Economic and Monetary Affairs Committee first sent a questionnaire to Member States concerned and the EU institutions involved. In response to the, admittedly sophisticatedly worded, question regarding the 'leeway', concerned Member States having 'to decide upon the design of the necessary measures (consolidation or structural reforms)', Greece's Ministry of Finance canvassed the inherent imbalances regarding negotiating leverage:

> Given the inability of Greece to access capital markets, its bargaining power was *de facto* weak. Against this background, the Government tried, within what was deemed feasible, to consent to measures with the lowest possible negative social impact.[12]

The reply by Cyprus's Ministry of Finance to the very same question displays an upfront and careful negation of the 'ownership' of the measures in relation to the March 2013 bank bail-in from the Cypriot side:

> The most controversial aspect of the final negotiation was the application of the bail-in instrument on bank deposits. The Cyprus government was forced to accept this measure under duress.[13]

[10] See eg Maurice Mendelson and Martins Paparinskis, 'Bail-ins and the international investment law of expropriation: in and beyond Cyprus' (2013) *Butterworths Journal of International Banking and Financial Law* 475.

[11] European Parliament resolution of 13 March 2014 on the enquiry on the role and operations of the Troika (ECB, Commission and IMF) with regard to the euro area programme countries (2013/2277(INI), (hereinafter European Parliament resolution of 13 March 2014). The 'Troika' consists of the European Commission acting as an agent of the Eurogroup, the European Central Bank (ECB) and the International Monetary Fund (IMF). The Eurogroup finds formal recognition in Article 137 of the Treaty on the Functioning of the European Union (TFEU), while certain formalities regarding its meetings have been introduced in Protocol No 14, attached to the Treaties).

[12] Ministry of Finance of Greece, Answer to the questionnaire supporting the own initiative report evaluating the structure, the role and operations of the 'troika' (Commission, ECB and the IMF) actions in euro area programme countries, (5 January 2014), available at www.europarl.europa.eu/document/activities/cont/201401/20140114ATT77323/20140114ATT77323EN.pdf, 3.

[13] Ministry of Finance of Cyprus, Answer to the questionnaire supporting the own initiative report evaluating the structure, the role and operations of the 'troika' (Commission, ECB and the IMF) actions in euro area programme countries, available at www.europarl.europa.eu/document/activities/cont/201401/20140114ATT77319/20140114ATT77319EN.pdf, 3.

The Ministry of Finance of Cyprus, when asked to describe 'the quality of the cooperation' with the Troika, again took the opportunity to emphasise that the bail-in measures were a result of a Eurogroup decision, rather than its own:

> After the Eurogroup decision to apply the bail-in on deposits which was contested by the Cypriot side, a close and continuous cooperation between the Troika and the authorities of the Republic of Cyprus, has been established.[14]

At this point it is also worth referring to the statements by the recently elected Greek government regarding the negotiations on the latest EU-backed bailout programme. Alexis Tsipras, the Prime Minister of Greece since late January 2015, announced on 27 June 2015 (following several months of negotiation in Brussels) a referendum calling for the Greek people to decide whether Greece 'should accept the extortionate ultimatum that calls for strict and humiliating austerity'.[15] Yanis Varoufakis, the then Finance Minister of Greece, further claimed that '[c]ommon ground was sacrificed in favour of imposing upon our government a humiliating retreat'.[16] In the days following the referendum's announcement, and the Eurogroup's decision not to grant an extension of the previous financial programme until the vote, the government's statements became gradually harsher, with the Prime Minister stating that 'the objective of the Eurogroup's and ECB's decisions is to attempt to blackmail the will of the Greek people and to hinder democratic processes, namely holding the referendum'.[17] The peak of these statements was reached after the final agreement between the Greek government and the EU institutions in the 12 July EU Summit. The government did not miss any opportunity presented to stipulate that the final agreement did not reflect its own will or policy, the Prime Minister stating that:

> We were faced with a difficult compromise, having exhausted all of our negotiating efforts. The Greek economy and the banking system were stretched to their limits. Europe's limits were also exposed: its limits and tolerance of democracy and the democratic choice of its people … The conservative forces—without a doubt—achieved a Pyrrhic victory against the Greek Government, against the Greek people, against Greece.[18]

Meanwhile, the Euro Summit statement of 12 July 2015, describing the legislative measures that the Greek Parliament should adopt without delay, referred once more to the 'ownership by the Greek authorities' as 'key' for the agreement's successful implementation.[19] Although it is too early to see whether and how any potential

[14] Ibid 4.

[15] Prime Minister Alexis Tsipras' address concerning the referendum of 5 July, available at www.primeminister.gov.gr/english/2015/06/27/prime-minister-alexis-tsipras-address-concerning-the-referendum-to-be-held-on-the-5th-of-july/.

[16] Yanis Varoufakis' intervention during the 27 June 2015 Eurogroup Meeting, available at yanisvaroufakis.eu/2015/06/28/as-it-happened-yanis-varoufakis-intervention-during-the-27th-june-2015-eurogroup-meeting/.

[17] Prime Minister Alexis Tsipras' statement on the latest developments, 28 June 2015, available at www.primeminister.gov.gr/english/2015/06/28/prime-minister-alexis-tsipras-statement-concerning-on-the-latest-developments/.

[18] Excerpts from Prime Minister Alexis Tsipras' speech in the Greek Parliament, 23 July 2015, available at www.primeminister.gov.gr/english/2015/07/23/extracts-from-prime-minister-alexis-tsipras-speech-in-the-greek-parliament/.

[19] Euro Summit Statement Brussels, 12 July 2015, SN 4070/15, available at www.consilium.europa.eu/en/press/press-releases/2015/07/12-euro-summit-statement-greece/.

investment claims would arise out of Greece's latest agreement with the EU institutions, the crux of the matter remains—at least according to its government—that Greece was put under undue pressure to take on a number of measures, on the basis of a reported ultimatum by the EU institutions, so as to secure EU financial support and avoid a total collapse of its economy and its banking system. The trend *#ThisIsACoup* that was extensively used in the international press and social media during Greece's negotiations at the Euro Summit of 12 July 2015,[20] is also characteristic of this unprecedented pressure.

So, keeping the above in mind, the crucial question of whether and how, under both EU law and general international law, the conduct of EU institutions participating in the Troika is to be attributed to the EU as an international organisation, must now be addressed.

## IV. ATTRIBUTING THE CONDUCT OF EU INSTITUTIONS REGARDING SPECIFIC MEMBER STATES' FINANCIAL CRISIS MEASURES TO THE EU AS AN INTERNATIONAL ORGANISATION

The European Parliament resolution of 13 March 2013, adopted following the enquiry into the relevant role and operations of the Troika, constitutes a suitable point of departure regarding the above last issue. The resolution regrets 'the fact that the Cypriot Government was reportedly obliged to accept the bail-in instrument on bank deposits'.[21] Moreover, it points to conflicts of interest due to the European Commission's dual role in the Troika 'as both an agent of Member States and an EU institution'.[22] A similar potential conflict of interest was also pointed out between the positions of the ECB as 'technical advisor' and its position as creditor of the four Member States,[23] with the note that

> throughout the crisis the ECB has had crucial information on the health of the banking sector and financial stability in general, and that with this in mind it has subsequently exerted policy leverage on decision-makers, at least in the cases of the Greek debt restructuring, where the ECB insisted that CACs were to be removed from government bonds it held, the Cypriot ELA operations, and the Irish non-inclusion of senior-bondholders in the bail-in.[24]

Still, no reference is made in the resolution to the legal responsibility of EU institutions involved (even informal ones, such as the Eurogroup).[25]

[20] See eg '#ThisIsACoup: Germany faces backlash over tough Greece bailout demands', *The Guardian*, 13 July 2015, available at www.theguardian.com/business/2015/jul/13/thisisacoup-germany-faces-backlash-over-tough-greece-bailout-demands.

[21] European Parliament resolution of 13 March 2014 (n 10) recital 22.

[22] Ibid recital 53.

[23] Ibid recital 54.

[24] Ibid.

[25] Despite the informal nature of its meetings, the Eurogroup de facto plays a central political role in Eurozone monetary matters. See eg Jean Pisani-Ferry, 'Only One Bed for Two Dreams: A Critical Retrospective on the Debate over the Economic Governance of the Euro Area' (2006) 44 *Journal of Common Market Studies* 840; Francis Snyder, 'EMU—Integration and differentiation: Metaphor for European Union' in Paul Craig and Gráinne de Búrca (eds), *The Evolution of EU Law*, 2nd edn (Oxford University Press, 2011) 704–705; Claus Zimmermann, *A Contemporary Concept of Monetary Sovereignty* (Oxford University Press, 2014) 150.

While the applicable principles for attribution of internationally wrongful conduct to the EU itself are to be found in the International Law Commission's (ILC) Draft Articles on the Responsibility of International Organisations (hereinafter: DARIO),[26] and more specifically Articles 6 to 8 DARIO, one could observe that these are specifically designed for the attribution of unlawful acts, rather than general rules of attribution under which both wrongful and non-wrongful acts can be attributed to an international organisation. In a more technical sense, the DARIO principles on attribution, similar to their counterparts in the ILC's Articles on the Responsibility of States for Internationally Wrongful Acts (hereinafter: ASR),[27] are designed to apply solely with respect to the attribution of internationally unlawful acts, rather than establishing general rules of attribution of lawful conduct to international organisations, that is to determine when and via which organs and agents an international organisation may act in general. Still, and as has often been the case in investment treaty arbitration regarding contract claims and the question of whether the host-state contracted directly with the foreign investor,[28] one could plausibly argue that the rules on attribution in the DARIO, if not reflecting general rules of attribution, at least merit *mutatis mutandis* application.

Hence, Article 6 DARIO ('Conduct of organs or agents of an international organisation') provides:

> (1) The conduct of an organ or agent of an international organisation in the performance of functions of that organ or agent shall be considered an act of that organisation under international law, whatever position the organ or agent holds in respect of the organisation.
> (2) The rules of the organisation shall apply in the determination of the functions of its organs and agents.

The relevant commentary of the ILC clarifies, first, that the conduct of organs and agents of an international organisation[29] is attributable to it, 'when the organ or agent exercises functions that have been given to that organ or agent, and at any event is not attributable when the organ or agent acts in a private capacity'.[30] Second, it makes clear that the rules of the organisation are not strictly considered as the

[26] Report of the International Law Commission on the work of its sixty-third session (Draft articles on the responsibility of international organizations, with commentaries) UN Doc A/66/10 (2011) [hereinafter: DARIO with commentaries], General commentary, para 9.

[27] Report of the International Law Commission on the work of its fifty-third session (Draft Articles on the Responsibility of States for Internationally Wrongful Acts, with commentaries), UN Doc A/56/10 (2001) [hereinafter: ASR with commentaries], Commentary on Chapter II ('Attribution of Conduct to a State') para 5: 'the rules concerning attribution set out in this chapter are formulated for this particular purpose, and not for other purposes for which it may be necessary to define the State or its Government'.

[28] See eg Michael Feit, 'Attribution and the Umbrella Clause—Is there a Way out of the Deadlock?' (2012) 21 *Minnesota Journal of International Law* 28–32, and further citations therein.

[29] See Article 2 DARIO: For the purposes of the present draft articles, .... (c) "organ of an international organization" means any person or entity which has that status in accordance with the rules of the organization; (d) "agent of an international organization" means an official or other person or entity, other than an organ, who is charged by the organization with carrying out, or helping to carry out, one of its functions, and thus through whom the organization acts'.

[30] See DARIO with commentaries (n 26) commentary on Article 6, para 7.

sole criterion for attribution via the determination of which functions are entrusted to each organ or agent, so that

> the wording of paragraph 2 [of Article 6 DARIO] is intended to leave the possibility open that, in exceptional circumstances, functions may be considered as given to an organ or agent even if this could not be said to be based on the rules of the organisation.[31]

With the above in mind, it appears feasible to support the view that the Troika-related conduct of the European Commission, the ECB,[32] or even the Eurogroup (acting through the Commission as its agent), are attributable to the EU as an international organisation. According to the Treaty of Lisbon, they form part of the EU institutional framework and, thus, it can be argued that they all meet the requirements of Article 6 DARIO.

To elaborate, the European Parliament resolution repeatedly notes that in the context of the Troika, 'political responsibility' at the European level lies with the Eurogroup, EU finance ministers and their governments, and '[c]alls on the Eurogroup, the Council and the European Council to assume full responsibility' for the operations of the Troika.[33] The resolution also takes as its starting point the observation that the role of the Troika has been defined in Regulation (EU) No 472/2013[34] and mentioned in the Treaty on the European Stability Mechanism (ESM).[35] Moreover, it takes note of the *Pringle* judgment,[36] where the Court of Justice of the European Union (CJEU) found that the duties allocated to the European Commission and to the ECB in the European Stability Mechanism (ESM) Treaty do not alter the essential character of the powers conferred on those institutions by the founding treaties. This is because, even in their involvement in the ESM (that is, notwithstanding its intergovernmental character), the Commission carries out Union functions, since it 'promotes the general interest of the Union' and ensures that 'the memoranda of understanding concluded by the ESM are consistent with European Union law'. Similarly the ECB 'supports the general economic policies in the Union, in accordance with Article 282(2) TFEU'.[37]

So even though, according to recent rulings of the CJEU, the Eurogroup's decision regarding Cyprus was issued only for the purposes of informing the public of the

[31] Ibid commentary on Article 6, para 9.

[32] Despite its distinct international legal personality, the ECB still remains a formal institution of the EU, according to Article 13 of the EU Treaty: see further analysis in Robert Schütze, *European Constitutional Law* (Cambridge University Press, 2012) 139–45.

[33] European Parliament resolution of 13 March 2014 (n 14) recital 61.

[34] Regulation (EU) No 472/2013 of the European Parliament and of the Council of 21 May 2013 on the strengthening of economic and budgetary surveillance of Member States in the euro area experiencing or threatened with serious difficulties with respect to their financial stability, OJ L140, 1.

[35] Treaty Establishing the European Stability Mechanism, 2 February 2012, 2011 OJ L91, 1 (ESM Treaty).

[36] Case C-370/12, *Thomas Pringle v Governement of Ireland, Ireland and The Attorney General* [2012] ECR I-756. For further analysis, see eg Pieter-Augustijn Van Malleghem, 'Pringle: A Paradigm Shift in the European Union's Monetary Constitution' (2013) 14 *German Law Journal* 141–68; Etienne de Lhoneux and Christos A Vassilopoulos, *The European Stability Mechanism Before the Court of Justice of the European Union: Comments on the Pringle Case* (Springer, 2014).

[37] Ibid paras 155–69. Cf though that 'the activities pursued by those two institutions within the ESM Treaty solely commit the ESM' (ibid para 161).

political agreements reached, never gave rise (nor was it meant to give rise) to legal consequences for third parties, and did not dictate the bail-in measure,[38] this does not change the fact that attribution of the conduct of the EU institutions participating in the Troika, remains a matter of public international law. Thus, the responsibility of the EU, or any of its institutions, is to be determined under Article 6 DARIO regarding organs of international organisations.

Nor is this conclusion undermined by the European Parliament resolutions deploring the democratic deficit and the lack of accountability surrounding the Troika's operations;[39] rather, this further serves to verify that the urgent need for support of Member States experiencing financial distress and the negative prospects of disorderly sovereign default, contagion and meltdown of the Eurozone necessitates immediate and ad hoc action. Hence, the deployment of the Troika, whose operations took place in such exceptional circumstances, could in any event fall under the 'exceptional circumstances' envisaged in the ILC's commentary on Article 6 paragraph 2 DARIO, so that the EU institutions participating in the Troika would again be considered as entrusted with functions by the EU as an international organisation.

Thus, and on the basis of the working hypothesis that the Troika-mandated measures of Greece and Cyprus can be found to violate the two Member States' international obligations under their respective BITs, the next section will examine whether and how the EU's shared responsibility may be implemented in connection with Member States' measures linked with EU-backed structural adjustment programmes, under the secondary rules on responsibility of international organisations reflected in the DARIO.

## V. SCENARIOS OF THE EU'S SHARED RESPONSIBILITY IN CONNECTION WITH SPECIFIC MEASURES TAKEN BY GREECE AND CYPRUS UNDER THEIR STRUCTURAL ADJUSTMENT PROGRAMMES

The term 'shared responsibility' is loosely used herein and refers to situations 'where a multiplicity of actors contributes to a single harmful outcome, and legal responsibility for this harmful outcome is distributed among more than one of the contributing actors'.[40] Assuming that the exclusion of the ECB-held Greek sovereign bonds from the 2012 PSI and the bank bail-in in Cyprus are found not to be in conformity with the two Member States' obligations under the BITs they have concluded, one may then distinguish the following three potential scenarios of shared responsibility for the internationally wrongful acts in question, which are provided by

[38] See eg Case T-330/13, *Lella Chatziioannou v European Commission and European Central Bank (ECB)*, Order of the General Court (First Chamber) of 16 October 2014 (not yet reported) paras 48–62.

[39] European Parliament resolution of 13 March 2014 (n 10) recitals 48–63.

[40] See André Nollkaemper, 'Introduction' in André Nollkaemper and Ilias Plakokefalos (eds), *Principles of Shared Responsibility in International Law: An Appraisal of the State of the Art* (Cambridge University Press, 2014) 6–7 and generally on this issue, André Nollkaemper and Dov Jacobs, 'Shared Responsibility in International Law: A Conceptual Framework' (2013) 34(2) *Michigan Journal of International Law* 359.

Articles 14 to 16 DARIO,[41] by virtue of the conduct of EU institutions participating in the Troika. The first scenario, under Article 14 DARIO,[42] is that Greece and Cyprus were aided and assisted by the EU in the commission of the alleged internationally wrongful acts. The second scenario, under Article 15 DARIO,[43] is that Greece and Cyprus were directed and controlled by the EU over the commission of the alleged internationally wrongful acts. Or finally, the third scenario, under Article 16 DARIO,[44] is that Greece and Cyprus were coerced by the EU to commit the alleged internationally wrongful acts.

To start with, there exist a number of similarities between the above scenarios which should be mentioned from the outset. First, both Articles 14 and 15 DARIO require the commission of an internationally unlawful act by the aided or assisted, or directed and controlled actor, in order for the aiding or assisting, or directing and controlling actor to incur responsibility.[45] This prerequisite is considered met in the cases of Greece and Cyprus, as this has been the working hypothesis in this study, that is the de facto exclusion of the Greek sovereign bonds held by ECB from the 2012 PSI, as well as the bank bail-in in Cyprus, could allegedly be in violation of BITs concluded by the two countries. The case of Article 16 DARIO is different since it is exactly the phrase 'but for the coercion' which is crucial and verifies that only one internationally wrongful act (that of the coercing actor) exists in this specific instance of shared responsibility.[46]

Second, both Articles 14 and 15 DARIO require that the EU would commit a wrongful act if it acted itself, that is, that the EU's indirect responsibility would have

[41] However, for the theoretical and practical difficulties regarding the responsibility of an international organization in connection with the act of a State or another international organization, cf August Reinisch, 'Aid or Assistance and Direction and Control between states and International Organizations in the Commission of Internationally Wrongful Acts' (2010) 7 *International Organizations Law Review* 65.

[42] Article 14 DARIO ('Aid or assistance in the commission of an internationally wrongful act'): 'An international organization which aids or assists a State or another international organization in the commission of an internationally wrongful act by the State or the latter organization is internationally responsible for doing so if: (a) the organization does so with knowledge of the circumstances of the internationally wrongful act; and (b) the act would be internationally wrongful if committed by that organization.'

[43] Article 15 DARIO ('Direction and control exercised over the commission of an internationally wrongful act'): 'An international organization which directs and controls a State or another international organization in the commission of an internationally wrongful act by the State or the latter organization is internationally responsible for that act if: (a) the former organization does so with knowledge of the circumstances of the internationally wrongful act; and (b) the act would be internationally wrongful if committed by that organization.'

[44] Article 16 DARIO ('Coercion of a State or another international organization'): 'An international organization which coerces a State or another international organization to commit an act is internationally responsible for that act if: (a) the act would, but for the coercion, be an internationally wrongful act of the coerced State or international organization; and (b) the coercing international organization does so with knowledge of the circumstances of the act.'

[45] Hence, the successful invocation of a circumstance precluding wrongfulness by the acting state, excludes, albeit indirectly, the wrongfulness of the conduct of the other actor. Christine Chinkin, 'The Continuing Occupation? Issues of Joint and Several Liability and Effective Control' in Phil Shiner and Andrew Williams (eds), *The Iraq War and International Law* (Hart Publishing, 2008) 178, fn 101.

[46] See ASR with commentaries (n 27) commentary on Article 18, para 1: 'Responsibility for the coercion itself is that of the coercing State vis-à-vis the coerced State, whereas responsibility under article 18 is the responsibility of the coercing State vis- à-vis a victim of the coerced act, in particular a third State which is injured as a result'.

to be linked to the breach of an obligation binding on it, when it contributed to the breach.[47] Mindful of the EU's competence, albeit not always exclusive, over foreign investment after the entry into force of the Lisbon Treaty,[48] Member States' measures aided or assisted, or directed and controlled, by the EU, could also be internationally wrongful if committed by the EU itself, so that the relevant requirement in Articles 14 and 15 DARIO would also be met.

To elaborate on this point, the CJEU has long held that the EU must respect international law in the exercise of its powers,[49] that is when acting in areas where it enjoys competences conferred on it by the Member States. This is in line with the oft-cited passage from the advisory opinion of the International Court of Justice (ICJ) on the interpretation of the agreement between the World Health Organization (WHO) and Egypt, according to which international organisations 'are bound by any obligations incumbent upon them under general rules of international law, under their constitutions or under international agreements to which they are parties'.[50] Accordingly, and in view of the EU's competence over foreign investment, it can also be maintained that the EU is bound by the customary international law rules of foreign investment protection law, such as the requirements for the legal expropriation of alien property or the international minimum standard of treatment of aliens, which are often reflected in the provisions of the myriads of BITs.[51]

Thus, insofar as the measures of Greece and Cyprus are allegedly found to be in violation of the expropriation clause in their BITs (most likely reflecting the relevant customary international law requirements), then it could indeed be feasibly supported that these measures, aided or assisted, or directed and controlled, by the EU, could also be internationally wrongful if committed by the EU itself, albeit not under a BIT, but rather under general international law.[52] This is especially so insofar as James Crawford has succinctly observed that Article 16 ASR 'merely requires that the conduct in question would have been internationally wrongful if committed by [the aiding or assisting actor] and says nothing about the identity of norms or

[47] DARIO with commentaries (n 26) commentary on Article 14, para 5 and commentary on Article 15, para 6.

[48] Following the entry into force of the Treaty of Lisbon, foreign direct investment matters fall under the common commercial policy, where, in accordance with Article 3(1)(e) TFEU, the EU has exclusive competence. For an overview of the more intimate facets of the relevant dialectic, see, among many, Angelos Dimopoulos, *EU Foreign Investment Law* (Oxford University Press, 2011) 122.

[49] See eg Case C-286/90, *Poulsen and Diva Navigation* [1992] ECR I-6019, para 9; Case C–162/96, *Racke v Hauptzollant Mainz* [1998] ECR I-3655, para 45

[50] *Interpretation of the Agreement of 25 March 1951 between the WHO and Egypt*, Advisory Opinion, ICJ Reports (1980), para 37. See also Moshe Hirsch, *The Responsibility of International Organizations Toward Third Parties: Some Basic Principles* (Martinus Nijhoff, 1995) 37.

[51] See eg Rudolf Dolzer and Christoph Schreuer, *Principles of International Investment Law* 2nd edn (Oxford University Press, 2012) 98–104, 134–39; Martins Paparinskis, *The International Minimum Standard and Fair and Equitable Treatment* (Oxford University Press, 2013) 64–98.

[52] While not also excluding also a potential violation of right to property under the Charter of Fundamental Rights of the European Union, itself being primary EU law. In this respect, Cypriot depositors have instituted proceedings against the Commission and the ECB regarding the bail-in for violations of EU law, albeit unsuccessfully so far: see eg Case T-290/13, *CMBG Ltd v European Commission and European Central Bank (ECB)*, Order of the General Court (First Chamber) of 10 November 2014 (not yet reported).

sources',[53] a proposition which is also applicable, by implication, in the context of the identical requirement of Article 17 ASR, as well as Articles 14 and 15 DARIO.

Third, what would transcend all three scenarios of the EU's shared responsibility under Articles 14 to 16 DARIO is the requirement of 'knowledge of the circumstances' of the aided or assisted, or directed and controlled or coerced act.[54] Even though the wording of the 'knowledge' requirement in Article 16 DARIO is slightly different ('knowledge of the circumstances of the act', instead of 'knowledge of the circumstances of the internationally wrongful act' as in Articles 14 and 15 DARIO),[55] its basic contours remain the same: the ASR and DARIO commentaries clarify that the assisting or aiding, or directing and controlling, or coercing actor must be aware of the circumstances in which its aid or assistance is intended to be used, or the circumstances making the conduct of the dependent (directed or controlled) state wrongful.[56] Referring to the commentary on Article 18 ASR,[57] James Crawford clarifies that the term 'circumstances' denotes factual, rather than legal knowledge, so that what is necessary is that the coercing (as well as the assisting or aiding, or directing and controlling) actor be aware of the relevant 'factual matrix' rather than the ultimate unlawfulness of the act.[58] Furthermore, this requirement of factual knowledge is not undermined by the fact that the ILC commentary on Article 16 ASR appears to provide for an *ab extra* subjective criterion of intent (arguably also applicable in the cases of direction and control and coercion under the ASR and the DARIO):

> A State is not responsible for aid or assistance under article 16 unless the relevant State organ intended, by the aid or assistance given, to facilitate the occurrence of the wrongful conduct and the internationally wrongful conduct is actually committed by the aided or assisted State.[59]

For, in effect, there can be circumstances where 'a lack of intent can be offset by sufficient knowledge'.[60]

With the above considerations in mind it would appear that the involvement of the EU institutions participating in the Troika does meet the threshold of 'knowledge'

[53] James Crawford, *State Responsibility: the General Part* (Cambridge University Press, 2013) 410.

[54] See also James Fry, 'Attribution of Responsibility' in André Nollkaemper and Ilias Plakokefalos (eds), *Principles of Shared Responsibility in International Law: An Appraisal of the State of the Art* (Cambridge University Press, 2014) 121–23.

[55] And with good reason, since it is exactly the phrase 'but for the coercion' in Article 16(b) DARIO which verifies that, in most cases, only the coercing actor would be internationally responsible for its act of coercion.

[56] ASR with commentaries (n 27) commentary on Article 18, para 1; DARIO with commentaries (n 26) commentary on Article 16, para 3.

[57] ASR with commentaries (n 27) commentary on Article 18, para 5: 'while ignorance of the law is no excuse, ignorance of the facts is material in determining the responsibility of the coercing State'.

[58] Crawford (n 53) 421.

[59] ASR with commentaries (n 27), commentary on Article 16, para 5. Cf *Case concerning Application of the Convention on the Prevention and Punishment of the Crime of Genocide (Bosnia and Herzegovina v Serbia and Montenegro)*, Judgment, ICJ Reports (2007), para 421, where the Court recognized the customary status of Article 16 ASR and used it by way of analogy in interpreting and applying the complicity rule in Article III (e) of the Genocide Convention.

[60] Georg Nolte and Helmut Philipp Aust, 'Equivocal Helpers: Complicit States, Mixed Messages and International Law' (2009) 58 *International and Comparative Law Quarterly* 15.

for the triggering of Articles 14 to 16 DARIO with regard to the shared responsibility of the EU for specific measures by Greece and Cyprus. To start with, it would seem feasible to argue that the Troika-participating EU institutions in fact orchestrated the enactment of said measures: in the case of ECB-held Greek sovereign bonds, the pros and cons of the exclusion from the haircut were weighed during the 'final decision by the ECB's Governing Council and the Eurogroup', even though a legal basis to accord 'preferred creditor status' to the ECB was admittedly lacking.[61] In the case of Cyprus, it would similarly appear that the enactment of the bail-in measure as such was dictated by the Troika.

Moreover, the, perhaps otherwise broadly accepted, principle that an international organisation, such as the EU, is not *ab initio* required to keep the obligations of all of its members in mind when acting through its organs or agents (*in casu*, the obligations under the Greek and Cypriot BITs) is substantially weakened in a field where the international organisation enjoys and exercises competences.[62] Thus, in the case of the measures of exclusion of ECB-held bonds from the Greek PSI and the bank bail-in in Cyprus, potentially giving rise to international adjudication over issues pertaining to foreign investment protection[63] (over which the EU has and exercises competence), one could easily point, for instance, to Article 2 of Regulation (EU) No 1219/2012, under which Member States were obliged to notify the Commission of all BITs with third countries signed before the entry into force of the Treaty of Lisbon.[64] One could also point to the series of third-party interventions by the European Commission in investment arbitral proceedings against Member States. Put differently, any alleged lack of factual knowledge on behalf of the EU, regarding the obligations of Greece and Cyprus under their BITs (and the possibility of their breach by the measures *in casu*), would be logically contradicted by the very reality of the existence and exercise of EU competences in the field of foreign investment protection.[65] Thus, once again, the relevant 'knowledge' requirement in Articles 14 to 16 DARIO appears, in principle, to have been met.

Finally, determining the existence of the objective requirements in the cases of aid or assistance, direction and control, and coercion, that is the involvement of the

[61] Antonio Sáinz de Vicuña, 'Restructuring in a Monetary Union: Legal Aspects', in: Rosa Lastra and Lee Buchheit (eds), *Sovereign Debt Management* (Oxford University Press, 2014) 184–87.

[62] See Nataša Nedeski and André Nollkaemper, 'Responsibility of International Organisations' in Connection with Acts of States' (2012) 9 *International Organizations Law Review* 38.

[63] For an early identification of the possibility of investment treaty arbitration proceedings under BITs due to the (then forthcoming) Greek debt restructuring, see eg Lee Buchheit and Mitu Gulati, 'How to Restructure Greek Debt' (7 May 2010), available at ssrn.com/abstract=1603304 or dx.doi.org/10.2139/ssrn.1603304 13; Kevin P Gallagher, 'The New Vulture Culture: Sovereign Debt Restructuring and Trade and Investment Treaties', IDEAs Working Paper Series, Paper No 02/2011, available at ase.tufts.edu/gdae/publications/GallagherSovereignDebt.pdf 17–18.

[64] Regulation (EU) No 1219/2012 of the European Parliament and of the Council of 12 December 2012 establishing transitional arrangements for bilateral investment agreements between Member States and third countries, OJ L351, 20.12.2012, 40.

[65] Perhaps the recent (and surprising) episode in the saga of EU competence over foreign investment has been the Commission's injunction to prevent a Member State (Romania) from complying with a US$250 million award rendered under the Sweden-Romania BIT: see Sebastian Perry, 'EU blocks ICSID payout', Global Arbitration Review (8.8.2014), available at globalarbitrationreview.com/news/article/32881/eu-blocks-icsid-payout/.

international organisation in the action under examination is a fact-intensive exercise, and the available information in the specific cases of Greece and Cyprus is sporadic and fragmented. Still, based on the previously mentioned European Parliament resolution's findings regarding the role of the Troika, there exists prima facie room to argue that, insofar as the other requirements under Articles 14 to 16 DARIO are met, the EU may indeed incur shared responsibility over the specific measures of exclusion of ECB-held bonds from the Greek PSI and the bail-in of uninsured depositors in Cyprus.

It must be observed that the first scenario of aid and assistance, corresponding to the concept of complicity in international law,[66] differs strikingly from the second and third scenarios (direction and control, and coercion) in terms of the objective element, that is the nature and degree of involvement of the EU as the directing and controlling or coercing actor: for,

> whereas the role of the complicit state is relatively minor insofar as it is only supporting the main actor, Articles 17 & 18 ASR [the ASR counterparts of Articles 15 & 16 DARIO] address the relationship between what is called the 'puppet master' and the 'puppet'.[67]

Or, to use the benchmark set in the ILC commentaries to Articles 18 ASR (and 16 DARIO):

> Coercion for the purpose of article 18 has the same essential character as *force majeure* under article 23. Nothing less than conduct which forces the will of the coerced State will suffice, giving it no effective choice but to comply with the wishes of the coercing State. It is not sufficient that compliance with the obligation is made more difficult or onerous, or that the acting State is assisted or directed in its conduct: such questions are covered by the preceding articles.[68]

Accordingly, under a *maiore ad minus* argumentation and in the context of responsibility of international organisations in connection with the act of a state, this study will now focus on whether the conduct of EU institutions participating in the Troika was such as to qualify as coercion (which need not be unlawful per se)[69] giving rise to force majeure,[70] where the coerced Member States (Greece

[66] For a delimitation of the concept of complicity in international law, see eg Miles Jackson, *Complicity in International Law* (Oxford University Press, 2015) 10–55.

[67] Helmut Philipp Aust, *Complicity and the Law of State Responsibility* (Cambridge University Press, 2011) 222.

[68] ASR with commentaries (n 27) commentary on Article 18, para 2; DARIO with commentaries (n 26) commentary on Article 16, para 4. Still note that the inclusion of coercion in the ASR which has met criticism in the literature: see James Fry, 'Coercion, Causation and the Fictional Elements of Indirect State Responsibility' (2007) 40 *Vanderbilt Journal of Transnational Law* 611–42.

[69] DARIO with commentaries (n 26) commentary on Article 16, para 3. Cf. earlier analysis regarding the legality of economic coercion, see eg Richard Lillich, 'Economic Coercion and the International Legal Order' (1975) 51 *International Affairs* 358; ibid 'Economic Coercion and the "New International Economic Order": A Second Look at Some First Impressions', (1976) 16 *Virginia Journal of International Law* 107–18; Stephen C Neff, 'The Law of Economic Coercion: Lessons from the Past and Indications of the Future' (1981) 20 *Columbia Journal of Transnational Law* 411.

[70] See Christian Dominicé, 'Attribution of Conduct to Multiple States and the Implication of a State in the Act of Another State', in: James Crawford, Alain Pellet and Simon Olleson (eds), *The Law of International Responsibility* (Oxford University Press, 2010) 289: 'This is justified by the rigorous conception of coercion which underlies article 18, and also by the consideration that if this were not so the injured

and Cyprus, *in casu*) lacked any effective 'sovereign capacity of decision' and had no choice but to submit to the coercing actor (the EU, via its institutions).[71] For, if an arguable case can be made that the higher threshold of coercion is met due to the EU institutions' involvement in specific Member States' financial crisis measures, then, all the more so, the threshold of involvement required by Articles 14 and 15 DARIO is also met.

At this point, it must be examined what the element of 'coercion' in Article 16 DARIO includes so as to determine whether the actions undertaken by the EU institutions could qualify as such. The term 'coercion' has been traditionally linked to the law of treaties,[72] as well as to prohibited interventions in the internal affairs of a state. Ergo, one could readily recall the 1970 Friendly Relations Declaration[73] or the *Nicaragua* case,[74] where the recognition of the right of every state to choose its political, economic, social and cultural systems, without interference, essentially denotes that, at least certain forms of economic coercion are prohibited under public international law. Be that as it may, in the context of Articles 18 ASR and 16 DARIO coercion is actually not limited to unlawful coercion for international responsibility to arise for a coercing international organisation;[75] moreover, it also covers cases of

State could find itself unable to invoke the coerced State's responsibility, which benefits from a circumstance precluding wrongfulness, and also unable to invoke the coercing State's responsibility, since it is not bound by the obligation breached.'

[71] Further on the relationship between coercion and force majeure, see Federica Paddeu, 'A Genealogy of Force Majeure in International Law' (2011) 82 *British Yearbook of International Law* 397–98.

[72] See eg Mark Villiger, *Commentary on the 1969 Vienna Convention on the Law of Treaties* (Martinus Nijhoff, 2009) 633, noting that in the context of Article 51 of the Vienna Convention on the law of treaties ('Coercion of a representative of a State') '[p]ersuasion, influence, argument, or advice do not constitute coercion unless carried out to such an extreme as to amount to undue pressure', albeit observing that within the meaning of Article 52 (Coercion of a State by the threat or use of force) coercion "does not comprise economic or political coercion"; Thilo Rensmann, 'Article 51' in Oliver Dörr and Kirsten Schmalenbach (eds), *Vienna Convention on the Law of Treaties: A Commentary* (Springer, 2012) 863: 'Any forms of pressure other than *vis compulsiva* ..., which do not involve the inducement of fear ..., such as argument, entreaty, advice and persuasion, do not qualify as coercion;' Georges Tenekides, 'Les effets de la contrainte sur les traités à la lumière de la Convention de Vienne du 23 mai 1969' (1974) 20 *Annuaire français de droit international* 92–93, referring to coercion as a case where a state is '*pratiquement subordonné*'; *Dubai-Sharjah Border Arbitration* (1981) 91 ILR 543, 571: 'Mere influences and pressures cannot be equated with the concept of coercion as it is known in international law.' Note also that the United Nations Conference on the Law of Treaties adopted the Declaration on the Prohibition of Military, Political or Economic Coercion in the Conclusion of Treaties as part of the Final Act of the Conference, condemning 'the threat or use of pressure in any form, whether military, political, or economic, by any State in order to coerce another State to perform any act relating to the conclusion of a treaty in violation of the principles of the sovereign equality of States and freedom of consent' (see UN Doc A/CONF.39/26).

[73] Declaration on Principles of International Law concerning Friendly Relations and Cooperation among States, UNGA Res 2625 (XXV) (24 October 1970). Similarly, see eg Declaration on the Inadmissibility of Intervention in the Domestic Affairs of States and the Protection of their Independence and Sovereignty, UNGA Res. 2131 (XX) (21 December 1965); Charter of Economic Rights and Duties of States, UNGA Res. 3281 (XXIX) (12 December 1974), Article 32; 'Non-interference in the Internal Affairs of States', UNGA Res. 31/91 (14 December 1976).

[74] *Military and Paramilitary Activities in and against Nicaragua* (Nicaragua v United States of America, Merits, ICJ Rep 1986, paras 205 and 241.

[75] ASR with commentaries (n 27) commentary on Article 18, para 3; DARIO with commentaries (n 26), commentary on Article 16, para 3.

economic coercion: for instance, the ILC commentary on Article 18 ASR explicitly states that

> coercion could possibly take other forms, eg serious economic pressure, provided that it is such as to deprive the coerced State of any possibility of conforming with the obligation breached.[76]

Moreover, in his Third report on the responsibility of international organisations, Rapporteur Giorgio Gaja explicitly referred to the hypothetical example of coercion 'of an international financial organisation imposing strict conditions for an essential loan and thereby coercing the recipient State to infringe obligations towards another State or certain individuals'.[77] The International Monetary Fund (IMF) considered the above example as 'inapposite', commenting, inter alia, that 'a member State always has an effective choice between following the conditions of IMF financing, having recourse to other sources of external financing, or not accepting any external financing'.[78] Arguably, when it comes to economic coercion in the context of Articles 18 ASR and 16 DARIO, it would all boil down to the existence of 'effective choices', if in fact any, of the coerced actor.

Thus, one would be tempted to pose the following (rhetorical) question: what if any other reasonable options were available to Greece and Cyprus, instead of conceding to the exclusion of the ECB-held bonds from the Greek debt restructuring and the bank bail-in in Cyprus, respectively? If one indeed attempts to answer this question, the answer must be the discontinuance of banks' liquidity, disorderly default of external debt and collapse of the countries' banking systems, with all the social and political unrest which that entails, which would emerge as the only possible remaining alternative to accepting the bail-out programmes as put forward, on the reported as 'take-it-or-leave-it' basis, by the Troika.[79] Indeed, 'sovereign capacity of decision' entails the existence of choices available to the sovereign; and sovereigns always make choices, often hard ones. But in the case of coercion, it is exactly the existence of 'do or die' dilemmas, externally posed, that absolve the coerced actor from its responsibility of making a choice, which was dictated as an alternative to

[76] ASR with commentaries (n 27) commentary on Article 18, para 3 *in fine*.

[77] International Law Commission, *Third report on responsibility of international organizations, by Mr Giorgio Gaja, Special Rapporteur*, A/CN.4/553, 13–14, para 28.

[78] International Law Commission, *Responsibility of international organizations: Comments and observations received from international organizations*, A/CN.4/582, Comments by the International Monetary Fund on Draft article 14 ('Coercion of a State or another international organization') 12.

[79] See, for instance, regarding the case of Cyprus the Address to the Nation by the President of the Republic, Mr Nicos Anastasiades (17 March 2013), available at www.presidency.gov.cy/Presidency/Presidency.nsf/All/0866D78CCB8AE38FC2257B3300233289?OpenDocument, stating (before the enactment of the first proposed bail-in measure) that 'Cyprus is in a state of emergency' and that the 'real options that were put before us in the European Council' included 'disorderly bankruptcy as a result of the decision of the European Central Bank to immediately discontinue the provision of emergency assistance to preserve the liquidity of the two large banks' on the one hand, and accepting the (first) bail-in measure, on the other. It was within the next few days that the Cypriot Parliament would reject the first bail-in measure (affecting insured depositors as well), to then finally accept the second bail-in measure (affecting uninsured depositors) under financial turmoil due to the threat of discontinuance of liquidity assistance by the ECB.

financial collapse, especially under the threat of the banks' liquidity cut-off by the ECB.

And this is how one may also read the previously mentioned reply by the Ministry of Finance of Cyprus that the Cyprus government 'was forced to accept' the bail-in 'under duress', denoting that the Troika went beyond the 'admissible threshold of coercion', to use Alain Pellet's words.[80] An agreement between Greece and Cyprus and the Troika was struck, and it is really about keeping to it, for better or for worse, that is, when measures dictated and imposed are later found to be inconsistent with the Member States' international obligations. Again, as mentioned above, a very characteristic example to this end is also the most recent financial deal reached between Greece and the EU institutions, where the agreement was not only presented as a 'take it or leave it' deal but was also allegedly accompanied by the threat of a Euro-exit.

Hence, a good case could be made for the applicability of Article 16 DARIO (or, at least and alternatively, Articles 14 and 15 DARIO) regarding the situations involving Greece and Cyprus analysed in this study.[81] But having said that, the fact remains that the said measures were applied and that both countries ran the risks associated with investment arbitral proceedings by aggrieved foreign investors (potentially even originating from other EU Member States (as is now evident in the context of the pending investment claims for crisis measures against Greece and Cyprus on the basis of the 1992 Greece-Cyprus BIT). It is thus necessary to see how the potential shared responsibility of the EU could be invoked in investment arbitration proceedings against Greece and Cyprus, challenging the exact measures that were adopted solely due to the Troika's pressures.

## VI. THE EU'S SHARED RESPONSIBILITY INVOKED AS A DEFENCE: NAVIGATING BETWEEN THE ADMISSIBILITY AND MERITS OF INVESTMENT CLAIMS

The discussion now turns to the ambit and scope of investment tribunals' jurisdictional powers, and their capacity to address the EU's shared responsibility scenarios, which have so far been examined. A Member State's objection pointing to the EU's shared responsibility over any alleged breach of investment protection guarantees

[80] Alain Pellet, 'The Normative Dilemma—Will and Consent in International Law' (1992) 12 *Australian Yearbook of International Law* (1992) 44.

[81] Similarly perhaps one could also mention that under Regulation No 912/2014 regarding investor-state disputes under agreements to which the EU and Member States are parties (such as the Energy Charter Treaty), includes cases where the EU will also bear exclusive or joint financial responsibility. See Regulation (EU) No 912/2014 of the European Parliament and of the Council of 23 July 2014 establishing a framework for managing financial responsibility linked to investor-to-state dispute settlement tribunals established by international agreements to which the European Union is party, Article 3 ('Apportionment criteria'). For further analysis on this issue, see Freya Baetens, Gerard Kreijen and Andrea Varga, 'Determining International Responsibility Under the New Extra-EU Investment Agreements: What Foreign Investors in the EU Should Know' (2014) 47 *Vanderbilt Journal of Transnational Law* 1233–45.

would first aim at challenging the admissibility of the investment claims presented because the EU would be an essential (absent) third party, under the *Monetary Gold* principle, articulated by the ICJ in the early 1950s, according to which no international judicial organ may exercise jurisdiction over a third party to the dispute without its consent.[82] More recently, the ICJ *sub silentio* verified the principle's applicability when it made it clear that international organisations are allegedly indispensable third parties to international disputes.[83]

The UNCITRAL Tribunal in *Chevron v Ecuador*, in its Third Interim Award on Jurisdiction and Admissibility, was the first investment arbitration tribunal to address a Monetary Gold-type objection. Ecuador had argued that the tribunal lacked jurisdiction over Chevron's claim since that would require the determination of the legal rights of the Lago Agrio plaintiffs against Chevron before Ecuadorian courts, as third parties to the investment dispute.[84] Essentially, Ecuador's argument went as follows: 'If Claimants' requested relief were granted, the rights of the third parties to relief in the Lago Agrio litigation [would] arguably be resolved and terminated',[85] since 'it is impossible for the Tribunal to adjudicate Claimants' rights without determining the rights of a party in absentia.'[86] To this end, Ecuador invoked the 'well-established principles of international law', distilled in the *Monetary Gold* principle, which dictated that the Chevron Tribunal was barred from exercising jurisdiction over the Lago Agrio plaintiffs as third parties without their consent, insofar as this would require an assessment of the legal rights of a non-party to the proceeding.[87]

While the Tribunal found it unnecessary to opine whether the *Monetary Gold* principle was in principle applicable in investor-state (mixed) arbitral proceedings, it still did not rule out its applicability, even in the case of individuals as third parties.[88] In any case, it would seem that insofar as 'not only is the consent of the litigants essential to the arbitrator's competence, but so is the consent of any third party whose rights may be in issue',[89] then investment tribunals enjoy the

[82] *Case of the Monetary Gold Removed from Rome in 1943 (Preliminary Question)*, Judgment, ICJ Reports (1954) at 32. For further analysis and case law, see Alexander Orakhelashvili, 'The Competence of the International Court of Justice and the Doctrine of the Indispensable Party: from Monetary Gold to East Timor and Beyond' (2011) 2 *Journal of International Dispute Settlement* 373–92; Martins Paparinskis, 'Procedural Aspects of Shared Responsibility in the International Court of Justice' (2013) 4 *Journal for International Dispute Settlement* 295.

[83] *Application of the Interim Accord of 13 September 1995 (the former Yugoslav Republic of Macedonia v Greece)*, Judgment of 5 December 2011, ICJ Reports 2011, paras 43–44, where the Court rejected, albeit summarily, the objection that NATO and its member States were indispensable third parties to the dispute.

[84] *Chevron Corporation and Texaco Petroleum Company v Ecuador*, PCA Case No 2009-23, Memorial on Jurisdictional Objections of the Republic of Ecuador of 26 July 2010, paras 168–81.

[85] Ibid para 168 *in fine*.

[86] Ibid para 171 *in fine*.

[87] Ibid para 177.

[88] *Chevron Corporation and Texaco Petroleum Company v Ecuador*, Third Interim Award on jurisdiction and admissibility of 27 February 2012, PCA Case No 2009-23, para 4.60.

[89] John Merrills, *International Dispute Settlement*, 5th edn (Cambridge University Press, 2011) 93.

*competenz-competenz* to hear and entertain well-founded *Monetary Gold* admissibility objections.[90]

It is therefore interesting to note that the ILC commentary on Article 16 ASR (also pertinent for Articles 17 and 18 ASR, as well as Articles 14 to 16 DARIO) notes that the *Monetary Gold* principle

> may well apply to cases under article 16, since it is of the essence of the responsibility of the aiding or assisting State that the aided or assisted State itself committed an internationally wrongful act. The wrongfulness of the aid or assistance given by the former is dependent, inter alia, on the wrongfulness of the conduct of the latter.[91]

Accordingly, if a case for the EU's shared responsibility over the exclusion of ECB-held bonds from the Greek PSI and the bank bail-in in Cyprus is made, then a *Monetary Gold* admissibility defence could be conceivable, to the extent that any finding of a breach of the obligations of Greece and Cyprus under their BITs would render a determination of the parallel responsibility of the EU unavoidable as well. As a result, the investment claims would be inadmissible and the tribunal would not address their merits.

Nevertheless, even if the investment arbitration tribunals deciding on possible investment claims against Greece and Cyprus were to eventually decline to entertain a *Monetary Gold*-type admissibility objection based on the shared responsibility of the EU, relevant evidence and/or argumentation could also be pertinent at the merits stage of the claims, that is, in terms of the analysis of the extraordinary preclusion of the coerced Member State's responsibility via *force majeure* as a circumstance precluding wrongfulness.[92]

In this respect, it should be noted that, on the one hand, the *Chevron* Tribunal did accept that the indispensable third party principle, as a corollary of the 'consent' principle, dictates that jurisdiction cannot be exercised when it entails deciding a question of the rights of an absent third party;[93] but, on the other hand, the Tribunal also hinted that, even when jurisdiction is exercised and the merits of a claim are examined, considerations flowing from the *Monetary Gold* principle may still be pertinent:

> [I]f there were a decision by the Tribunal in this arbitration that the 1995 Settlement Agreement releases Chevron from all liability, that might be said to decide the legal rights of the Lago Agrio plaintiffs. But that is something that depends upon the form and content of the

[90] See eg, indirectly affirming this proposition, *Niko Resources (Bangladesh) Ltd. v People's Republic of Bangladesh, Bangladesh Petroleum Exploration and Production Company Limited ('Bapex'), Bangladesh Oil Gas and Mineral Corporation ('Petrobangla')*, Decision on Jurisdiction of 19 August 2013, ICSID Case No ARB/10/11 and ICSID Case No ARB/10/18, paras 516–24. Also see Freya Baetens, 'Procedural Issues Relating to Shared Responsibility in Arbitral Proceedings' (2013) 4 *Journal of International Dispute Settlement* 336–40.

[91] ASR with commentaries (n 27) commentary on Article 16, para 11.

[92] See Crawford (n 53) 421: 'Paragraph (a) [of Article 18 ASR] thus reinforces the overlap between force majeure as provided for in [Article 23 ASR], and a successful act of coercion—if coercion is force majeure, then the coerced state will be excused from responsibility that would otherwise have accrued. Responsibility for the act is transferred to the coercing state, identifying it as the party against which an injured state might obtain satisfaction'.

[93] *Chevron* Third Interim Award (n 88) para 4.62.

> decision of this Tribunal: it is not an inevitable consequence of the Tribunal exercising its jurisdiction. The question of form and content of the decision is a matter to be addressed during the merits phase of this case.[94]

Essentially, the *Chevron* Tribunal's findings are interesting in that, while recognising that the indispensable third-party principle primarily relates to the question of the admissibility of claims, it also envisages its potential lasting authority during the merits phase of a dispute, as capable of influencing the eventual 'form and content of the decision'.

Importantly, and returning to possible investment claims against Greece and Cyprus, this may also mean that a successful invocation of coercion by the EU, leading to *force majeure*, may not only be presented as an admissibility objection but could also be scrutinised as a merits defence (along with other defences available under the BIT or customary international law, such as state of necessity and so on). It is perhaps with this approach in mind that the *Micula v Romania* Tribunal opined that the involvement of the EU, in the form of EU law, could potentially provide grounds for the invocation of circumstances precluding wrongfulness in investment treaty arbitrations against EU Member States, in the following passage:

> The Tribunal also sees merit in the Claimants' suggestion that, in theory, EU law could also possibly come into play as a circumstance precluding wrongfulness under ILC Articles 23, 24 or 25. However, as noted above, the Respondent has not put forth a case of force majeure, duress or necessity. Accordingly, the Tribunal does not address the relevance of EU law in this context.[95]

Thus, arbitral tribunals may address EU's shared responsibility as a matter belonging to the merits, rather than the jurisdiction/admissibility of investment claims, should they appear ready to adjust the 'form and content' of their decision, *qua* the *Chevron v Ecuador* tribunal. And, should such a defence of the merits indeed be entertained, this would perhaps be the sole 'win-win' scenario for the EU and the Member State(s) concerned.

## VII. CONCLUSION

This study has addressed specific facets of the multifarious overlap between investment law, European law and the law on the responsibility of international organisations in investment arbitration proceedings, stemming from anti-crisis measures in the Euro Area. While the relevant policy and normative repercussions are such that they warrant, or even lead to, a reconfiguration of the relationship between international and European law in general, it has been explained how and why the EU's shared responsibility for specific measures taken by Member States, which relate to

[94] Ibid para 4.66.

[95] Similarly, see *Ioan Micula, Viorel Micula, SC European Food SA, SC Starmill SRL and SC Multipack SRL v Romania*, Final Award of 11 December 2013, ICSID Case No ARB/05/20, para 329.

financial assistance programmes, may operate as a defence in terms of the admissibility and/or the merits of investment claims against the Member States concerned.

Even if the determination of the shared responsibility of the EU is considered to be an exceptional and extraordinary scenario (especially if coercion is made out), then this would still appear to fit neatly into the otherwise troublesome legal terrain of the Eurozone's efforts for recovery and return to growth. So, even though factual evidence (other than political statements) is otherwise scarce, a recognition of the EU's shared responsibility, if determined in investment arbitration proceedings, could verify that the outcome of negotiations imposed by international organisations on individual Member States in distress retains its collective and solidary character, even in the hazardous arena of international investment arbitration.

# PART IV

# INTERNATIONAL LAW AND INTERNATIONAL RELATIONS

# 12

# *Subsequent Treaty Practice: The Work of the International Law Commission*

GEORG NOLTE*

## I. INTRODUCTION

IT IS A characteristic of any legal system how it formulates the conditions under which it admits, and then deals with, subsequent developments and assertions of change, outside the available formal amendment procedures. This mostly takes place in the realm of interpretation, and much depends on the rules, institutions and practices of interpretation.

The most obvious question in this context is whether, and, if so, how far, there may be some kind of evolutive, or evolutionary interpretation.[1] The question of how far evolutive interpretation may go is unanswerable in the abstract. General definitions of the possible range of evolutive interpretation, at least, are not particularly helpful when it comes to deciding specific cases. Judicial reasoning and pronouncements by States regarding the possibility of evolutive interpretation are nevertheless useful and important since such reasoning provides signposts and a general sense of direction of the shared understanding in a particular legal community, at a particular point in time, concerning the proper practice of interpretation.[2]

## II. EVOLUTIVE INTERPRETATION AND THE INTERNATIONAL LAW COMMISSION PROJECT ON SUBSEQUENT PRACTICE

These considerations are true for every legal system, not only for international law. It is, however, a characteristic of international law that it offers an additional avenue for openly taking into account in the identification of the law, circumstances which

* Professor of Law, Humboldt University Berlin; Member of the International Law Commission.

[1] See most recently, Eirik Bjorge, *The Evolutionary Interpretation of Treaties* (Oxford University Press, 2014).

[2] International Law Commission, 'Report of the International Law Commission on the Work of its 65th Session' (6 May–7 June, and 8 July–9 August 2013) UN Doc A/68/10, 12 Draft Conclusion 3 on 'Subsequent agreements and subsequent practice in relation to the interpretation of treaties': 'Subsequent agreements and subsequent practice under Articles 31 and 32 may assist in determining whether or not the presumed intention of the parties upon the conclusion of the treaty was to give a term used a meaning which is capable of evolving over time'.

have arisen after the entry into force of a given legal rule. This is the role of subsequent practice.[3] Practice plays not only an acknowledged role in the formation of customary international law[4] but also in treaty law. Article 31(3) of the Vienna Convention on the Law of Treaties provides that subsequent agreements and the subsequent practice of the parties which establish their agreement regarding the interpretation of a treaty shall be taken into account, together with the other means of interpretation which are mentioned in this provision. Article 32 implies the possibility of taking subsequent practice into account which does not establish the agreement of the parties.[5] These provisions designate a point where international law self-reflexively opens itself to later developments and factors them in.

It is, of course, a matter of debate as to whether Articles 31 and 32 provide any meaningful orientation, and thus whether the role of subsequent practice can be specified in a way that gives a sense of direction to interpreters. There are, however, good reasons to think that these provisions do provide orientation, and it is useful, at least for less experienced treaty interpreters, to be aware of the ways in which subsequent practice is and should be taken into account. Thus, in 2012 the International Law Commission (ILC) started to work on the topic of 'Subsequent agreements and subsequent practice in relation to the interpretation of treaties'[6] and it has yielded results since 2013.[7] During its sixty-sixth session, in 2014, the Commission provisionally adopted a number of specific Draft Conclusions with Commentaries which are addressed here. The first five Draft Conclusions, which were provisionally adopted in 2013, are general in nature.

## III. THE DRAFT CONCLUSIONS 2014

The following points regarding the Draft Conclusions which the Commission provisionally adopted in 2014 may merit highlighting.

### A. The Purpose of the ILC Project

The first general point concerns the purpose of the ILC project. This purpose is modest. It is not to provide a new theory of interpretation, or to prescribe hard and fast rules concerning the role of subsequent practice in treaty interpretation. The purpose is rather to take stock of how subsequent agreements and subsequent practice, as means of interpretation, have developed and been applied, in the practice

[3] Georg Nolte (ed), *Treaties and Subsequent Practice* (Oxford University Press, 2013).

[4] ILC, 'Second Report on identification of customary international law by Special Rapporteur Sir Michael Wood' (22 May 2014) UN Doc A/CN.4/672, 7–14, paras 21–31.

[5] ILC, 'Report of the International Law Commission on the Work of its 65th Session' (n 2) Draft Conclusions 1(4) and 4(3).

[6] ILC, 'Report of the International Law Commission on the Work of its 64th Session' (7 May–1 June, and 2 July–3 August 2012) UN Doc A/67/10, 133.

[7] ILC, 'Report of the International Law Commission on the Work of its 65th Session' (n 2) ch IV; ILC, 'Report of the International Law Commission on the Work of its 66th Session' (5 May–6 June, and 7 July–8 August 2014) UN Doc A/69/10, ch VII.

of States and of judicial organs. This should sensitise, and provide some orientation for practitioners in particular domestic courts, who are less familiar with the usages and understandings in international law. By simultaneously looking at the interpretative practice in different treaty regimes, the project may also contribute to identifying the degree to which the process of treaty interpretation is uniform across such regimes. By identifying patterns of interpretation, the product of the Commission should give some orientation without becoming a straightjacket. This means that the Commentaries on the Draft Conclusions are almost as important as the Draft Conclusions themselves since they give life and illustration to the Draft Conclusions.

## B. The Approach of the Commission

The second general point concerns the approach of the Commission. The Commission operates on the basis of consensus and by way of a very elaborate, even cumbersome, procedure. This means that virtually every word and every comma is debated, on and off the record, and that every word needs to be agreed upon, including every word of the Commentaries. Under these circumstances, and given the composition of the Commission and the rather general nature of the topic, the approach of the Commission cannot be expected to be particularly innovative. It is, indeed, the consensus among the members of the Commission that the purpose of the exercise is to elaborate on the pertinent rule, or rules, of the Vienna Convention, and not to change them. For example, Draft Conclusion 7, by referring to the narrowing or widening of the possible range of interpretations, clearly only articulates in more detail what is already contained in Article 31.

## C. Interpretation or Modification?

Perhaps the most delicate issue is addressed in Draft Conclusion 7(3). This paragraph is based on observations of State practice and the case law of international courts concerning the question of whether a certain agreed treaty-related practice can still be considered an 'interpretation' of that treaty, or whether it goes beyond. The International Court of Justice (ICJ) has articulated the problem in the 2009 *Dispute Regarding Navigational and Related Rights case* (*Costa Rica v Nicaragua*) where it held, in an *obiter dictum*, that 'subsequent practice of the parties, within the meaning of article 31(3)(b) of the Vienna Convention, can result in a departure from the original intent on the basis of a tacit agreement.'[8] It is not entirely clear whether the Court thereby wanted to recognise that subsequent practice under Article 31(3)(b) may also have the effect of amending or modifying a treaty, or whether it was merely making a point relating to the interpretation of treaties.[9]

[8] *Dispute regarding Navigational and Related Rights (Costa Rica v Nicaragua)* (Merits) [2009] ICJ Rep 213, 242, para 64.

[9] ILC, 'Report of the International Law Commission on the Work of its 66th Session' (n 7) Commentary on Draft Conclusion 7(3), 188, para 24.

The question of how far agreed subsequent practice can be said to have an effect on the interpretation of a treaty, or whether it can have the effect of modifying it, has been debated since the elaboration of the Vienna Convention. It is well known that the Commission originally proposed that the Vienna Convention should recognise that agreed subsequent practice can have the effect of modifying the treaty and that the Vienna Conference then rejected this proposal.[10] Courts, State practice and writers have thereafter continued to grapple with this issue. Whereas most writers seem to recognise the possibility of a modification or amendment of a treaty by agreed practice, courts and States generally avoided a clear statement and instead recognised a wide scope for the interpretation of a treaty by the means of subsequent practice.[11] Although the ICJ has on several occasions left room for the possibility of a modification of a treaty by agreed subsequent practice, the Court and most other international courts and tribunals have typically shied away from actually recognising that this abstract possibility had taken place in a concrete case. They have instead preferred to give a particular treaty an interpretation which strains the 'ordinary meaning of the terms' of the treaty, rather than to openly recognise the possibility of an informal modification of the treaty by the subsequent practice of the parties. Cases in which the ICJ and other courts or tribunals have gone further than that, can be distinguished. The most notable exception is the European Court of Human Rights.[12]

Bearing in mind the dictum of the ICJ in the case *Land and Maritime Boundary between Cameroon and Nigeria* according to which the possibility of a modification of a treaty by subsequent practice 'cannot be wholly excluded as a possibility in law',[13] Draft Conclusion 7(3) does not propose more than a presumption that the parties to a treaty, by common subsequent practice, do not intend to modify a treaty, but to interpret it. The additional statement according to which 'the possibility of modifying a treaty by subsequent practice of the parties has not been generally recognized' strengthens the presumption in favour of interpretation, but only by somewhat ambiguously referring to a factual situation.

By formulating Draft Conclusion 7(3) in the way presented, the Commission attempts to walk a fine line between, on the one hand, the obvious reluctance to recognise and to apply the possibility of the parties modifying a treaty by informal practices, and on the other hand, the experience from many cases that the common practice of the parties should and needs to be accommodated as a preferred form of the application of treaties. The solution which the Commission proposes to this difficult problem of treaty law is that interpreters are encouraged to attempt, as far as possible, to regard subsequent agreements and agreed subsequent practice as efforts by the parties to interpret a treaty rather than as efforts to modify, or break out of a treaty.

[10] Ibid 187–88, paras 22 and 23.

[11] Ibid 191–92, paras 32–35.

[12] *Al-Saadoon and Mufdhi v the United Kingdom* App no 61498/08 (ECtHR, 2 March 2010) para 119.

[13] *Land and Maritime Boundary between Cameroon and Nigeria (Cameroon v Nigeria: Equatorial Guinea intervening)* (Merits) [2002] ICJ Rep 303, 353, para 68.

## D. Does Subsequent Practice need to be 'common, concordant and consistent'?

Draft Conclusion 8 does not refer to the formula that subsequent practice needs to be 'common, concordant and consistent'. The Commission found that this formula, which has been used by the Appellate Body of the World Trade Organization and which has some pedigree, is not sufficiently well established and that it risks being misconceived as 'overly prescriptive'.[14] Instead, Draft Conclusion 8 attempts to circumscribe some factors which typically give more or less interpretative weight to the subsequent practice of the parties.

## E. Must an 'agreement' under Article 31(3) Necessarily be Binding?

According to Draft Conclusion 9 an agreement under Article 31(3) requires a common understanding of the parties which, however, does not need to be legally binding. Here, the Commission has clarified that the term 'agreement' in Article 31(3) does not necessarily mean a legally binding agreement. Indeed, the original Draft Articles on the Law of Treaties from 1966 used the term 'understanding' which was changed by the Vienna Conference to 'agreement', but for no conceivable substantive reason.[15] Since the chapeau of Article 31(3) merely requires that an agreement be 'taken into account', among other means of interpretation, the Vienna Convention would have had to attribute to them a stronger legal force should they necessarily have to be binding.

It is true, however, that not all members of the Commission are in full agreement with this proposition. The Commentaries therefore contain a paragraph which articulates the alternative view according to which the term 'agreement' has the same meaning wherever it is used in the Vienna Convention.[16] This alternative position seems to be based on a misunderstanding: of course, the interpreter is 'bound', under the chapeau of Article 31(3), to 'take into account' any subsequent agreement or subsequent practice referred to in (a) and (b). This obligation, however, does not derive from a necessarily binding nature of such subsequent conduct, as such, but rather from the Vienna Convention itself which attributes a nuanced legal effect to such conduct, which is that it 'shall be taken into account'. Indeed, the Tribunal in the *Railway Land Arbitration* between Malaysia and Singapore seems to have confirmed this position when it held that '[t]he agreement referred to [in Article 31 (3)] is consensus, not a formal agreement that itself has the status of a treaty.'[17]

[14] ILC, 'Report of the International Law Commission on the Work of its 66th Session' (n 7) 195–96, para 11.

[15] *International Law Commission Yearbook 1966* Vol II (United Nations, 1966) 222, para 15.

[16] ILC, 'Report of the International Law Commission on the Work of its 66th Session' (n 7) 201, para 12.

[17] *In the matter of the Railway Land Arbitration (Malaysia v Singapore)* (Award of 30 October 2014) PCA Case No 2012-01, para 167, available at www.pca-cpa.org/showpage.asp?pag_id=1598.

## F. Decisions of Conferences of States Parties

Draft Conclusion 10 addresses decisions which are adopted within the framework of Conferences of States Parties. A Conference of States Parties is not a term which is contained in the Vienna Convention, or in any other treaty of a general nature. Paragraph 1 of Draft Conclusion 10 offers a definition for the purpose of the proposed Draft Conclusions which takes the diversity of such Conferences into account.

Whenever and wherever all the parties to a treaty assemble or communicate with each other, there is a possibility, in principle, that they will reach an agreement regarding the interpretation of this treaty. Since there is no requirement of a particular form for such an agreement, there is no reason why it should not be possible for the parties to reach such an agreement within the framework of a Conference of States Parties. And since the applicable treaty and the rules of procedure are not always clear or exhaustive regarding the possible effects of agreements on the interpretation of the treaty, the question of the possible legal effect of decisions which were adopted within the framework of Conferences of States Parties has arisen in some cases. The Commentaries describe some of those cases and the Draft Conclusion formulates that, 'depending on the circumstances, such a decision may embody, explicitly or implicitly, a subsequent agreement under article 31 (3) (a), or give rise to a subsequent practice under article 31, paragraph 3 (b), or to subsequent practice under article 32.'[18]

Paragraph 3 of Draft Conclusion 10 is an attempt to clarify a situation which has occasionally given rise to misunderstandings. While it is clear that a unanimous decision of a Conference of States Parties can embody an agreement regarding the interpretation of a treaty, it is less clear whether a decision which was adopted by consensus may have such an effect. Paragraph 3 directs the interpreter to make a necessary distinction. This is the distinction between the substance of the decision, which may or may not be 'regarding the interpretation of a treaty', and its form, consensus or otherwise, which may or may not reflect an agreement in substance. The adoption of a decision by consensus alone is not sufficient to establish an agreement in substance. In fact, consensus may conceal a disagreement regarding the substance, or the content, of a particular decision by the Conference of States Parties.[19] Finally, since interpreters should not be directed, by the Draft Conclusion, to single-mindedly look for agreement regarding interpretation, the Draft Conclusion mentions that the Conference of States Parties' decision may be limited to providing 'a non-exclusive range of practical options'. This does not exclude, however, the possibility that a provision of options implies the interpretation of the underlying treaty that these options are *permissible* under the treaty.[20]

[18] ILC, 'Report of the International Law Commission on the Work of its 66th Session' (n 7) 170.
[19] Ibid 214–16, paras 30–35.
[20] Ibid 213, para 25.

## IV. CONCLUSION

The topic certainly raises a host of other practical and theoretical aspects. But the purpose of this contribution is limited to drawing attention to a few pertinent aspects of the Draft Conclusions themselves and the context from which they originate. The work of the Commission on the topic continues according to the original work plan.[21]

[21] ILC, Report of the International Law Commission on the Work of its 64th Session (7 May–1 June, and 2 July–3 August 2012) UN Doc A/67/10, ch X (121); Report of the of the International Law Commission on the Work of its 60th Session (5 May–6 June, and 7 July–8 August 2008) UN Doc A/63/10, Annex A (365–89).

# 13

# *A Gap, a Map, and an Intellectual Trap: Changing Conceptions of Regime Interaction and of Interdisciplinarity*

JEFFREY L DUNOFF*

## I. INTRODUCTION

IT IS ENTIRELY appropriate that the European Society of International Law's 10th Anniversary conference was devoted to the theme of 'International Law and …'. During the Society's first decade, interdisciplinary studies and approaches made deep inroads into international legal scholarship. These developments, in turn, prompted fierce debates about the propriety and usefulness of interdisciplinary approaches to international law. Thus, this volume represents a welcome opportunity to take stock of international law's turn to other disciplines, to identify both the strengths and weaknesses of interdisciplinary approaches to international law, and to chart paths for future research.

This chapter, originally prepared for the forum on 'International Law and International Relations: Stability and Change', suggests that we can approach the theme of 'stability and change' from a variety of perspectives. I will highlight an international practice that promotes *doctrinal and legal change*, namely law-making through interactions among international organisations (IOs). But scholars interested in interdisciplinarity should examine other types of change as well. One area of interest should be the *conceptual change* that occurs when ideas and concepts migrate from one discipline to another, in particular as ideas from other disciplines are used by law. Finally, given the conference theme, we might also inquire into *changing notions of interdisciplinarity*. What prompts the turn to interdisciplinarity in the first place?[1] Why do certain 'law and …' approaches seem so promising at certain times, and so threatening at others? To be sure, these are large and complex questions, and they

* Laura H Carnell Professor of Law, Temple University Beasley School of Law, Philadelphia, PA, USA.
This is a slightly revised version of a paper presented at the ESIL 10th Anniversary Conference and retains the informality of the presentation. I am grateful to Duncan Hollis, Nikolas Rajkovic and Richard Stewart for thoughtful comments on earlier versions, to Jutta Brunnée and Anne van Aaken for the opportunity to participate in the conference, and to conference participants for their feedback.

[1] This question is examined by Vera Gowlland-Debbas in her provocative keynote presentation 'International Law and … Variations on a Theme'; see further the Epilogue to these Proceedings, at Chapter 30.

cannot be fully addressed in the space of this short essay. Therefore, my more modest goal is to explore three related issues.

First, I will briefly summarise the leading approaches to inter-institutional interactions in the literature, and highlight a practice that existing research overlooks. Second, I will provide a typology of the ways that actors from different international bodies engage each other. Finally, I will use these interactions to show why I think a common critique of international law/international relations (IL/IR) research is mistaken. Rather more succinctly, this paper will explore a gap, a map, and an intellectual trap.

## II. REGIME INTERACTION IN INTERNATIONAL LAW AND INTERNATIONAL RELATIONS SCHOLARSHIP

In recent years, international lawyers have devoted substantial attention to issues of regime overlap and conflict. One early cluster of writings focused on 'trade and ...' issues, such as 'trade and environment' or 'trade and human rights', and explored real or perceived collisions between liberal trade norms embedded in World Trade Organization (WTO) treaties and rules from other international law regimes.[2] Thereafter, writings on the proliferation of international tribunals and later, the 'fragmentation' of international law, explored concerns that international law's decentralised processes of law-making, institution-building and dispute resolution risked inconsistent judgments, conflicting jurisprudence and lack of legal certainty.[3]

IR scholarship focuses on 'regime complexes' formed when different international legal regimes intersect and overlap in a non-hierarchical manner. The term has been applied to policy domains ranging from intellectual property to climate change.[4] This work helpfully describes the institutionally dense environment IOs inhabit, variation in levels of regime integration, and the dynamics that lead to regime complexes.[5]

A more recent literature focuses on 'regime interactions'.[6] While this literature purports to examine a broad range of ways that regimes can overlap and interact, in fact many of these writings foreground regime collisions.[7] For example, in a

[2] See Jeffrey L Dunoff, 'The Death of the Trade Regime' (1999) 10 *European Journal of International Law* 733; Robert Howse, 'From Politics to Technocracy—and Back Again: The Fate of the Multilateral Trading Regime' (2002) 96 *American Journal of International Law* 94.

[3] International Law Commission, 'Report of the Study Group of the International Law Commission finalized by Martti Koskenniemi, "Fragmentation of International Law: Difficulties Arising from the Diversification and Expansion of International Law"' (1 May–9 June, and 3 July–11 August 2006) UN Doc A/CN.4/L.682 as corrected UN Doc A/CN.4/L.682/Corr.1.

[4] Laurence R Helfer, 'Regime Shifting: The TRIPs Agreement and New Dynamics of International Intellectual Property Lawmaking' (2004) 29 *Yale Journal of International Law* 1; Robert O Keohane and David Victor, 'The Regime Complex for Climate Change' (2011) 9 *Perspectives on Politics* 7.

[5] Kal Raustiala, 'Institutional Proliferation and the International Legal Order' in Jeffrey L Dunoff and Mark A Pollack (eds), *Interdisciplinary Perspective on International Law and International Relations: The State of the Art* (Cambridge, Cambridge University Press, 2013).

[6] Margaret A Young (ed), *Regime Interaction in International Law: Facing Fragmentation* (Cambridge, Cambridge University Press, 2012).

[7] There are exceptions that adopt broader perspectives on regime interaction similar to that urged in this paper. See Sebastian Oberthür and Thomas Gehring (eds), *Institutional Interaction in Global*

contribution to a leading volume on regime interactions, Gunther Teubner and Peter Korth explore the 'collision of transnational regimes in the double fragmentation of world society',[8] and James Crawford and Penelope Nevill highlight the various techniques courts use when asked to resolve conflicts generated by regime collisions.[9]

Despite many differences in research design and methodology, across all of these different bodies of literature, regime interactions are conceptualised as consisting of real or potential regime collisions. Moreover, in each of these literatures, they share a number of common structural elements. For example, they are typically understood to be bilateral in nature, pitting one state against another, even though many more actors are typically affected. Since the literature focuses on high-profile conflicts, regime interactions are frequently understood in court-centric terms. The interaction is typically understood as arising out of a discrete event or series of events. The disputes that arise out of these interactions are invariably retrospective or backward-looking. And the lawyer's task is to sort out the relationships among conflicting rules. In short, the literature treats regime interactions as international law's version of a car crash—a sudden, isolated event that can be localised in space and time. These discrete transactions are understood to provide the occasion for regimes to overlap, intersect or conflict.

However, most regime interactions—and the most important ones—are not discrete transactions. Instead they occur in ongoing relationships. Thus, most regime interactions are forward-looking, and take place outside of international courthouses. So the dominant approach in the legal literature—which focuses on normative conflict, rather than institutional interaction—is partial and misleading. It virtually ignores the more common and more important forms of regime interaction. Thus, it has not developed an analytic typology to classify the various types of interactions that take place. As a result, we know little about these actions and their role in contemporary global governance.

This scholarly gap is increasingly problematic. Given the ubiquity and importance of the regime interactions described below, the failure to attend to these interactions compromises dominant approaches to conceptualising regime interactions. Moreover, these activities raise challenging conceptual, doctrinal and normative issues. As an analytic matter, what are the drivers, mechanisms and pathways that determine the frequency and intensity of regime interactions? How should we characterise, measure and evaluate the outputs and impacts of regulatory interactions? As a doctrinal matter, what rules govern the production of legal norms through interactions among actors from different international bodies? Are these activities subject to judicial review, or other institutional checks and balances? And, as a normative matter,

*Environmental Governance: Synergy and Conflict among International and EU Policies* (Cambridge, MIT Press, 2006); Margaret A Young, *Trading Fish, Saving Fish: The Interaction between Regimes in International Law* (Cambridge, Cambridge University Press, 2011); and Claire R Kelly, 'Institutional Alliances and Derivative Legitimacy' (2008) 29 *Michigan Journal of International Law* 605.

[8] Gunther Teubner and Peter Korth, 'Two Kinds of Legal Pluralism: Collision of Transnational Regimes in the Double Fragmentation of World Society' in Young (n 6) 23.

[9] James Crawford and Penelope Nevill, 'Relations Between International Courts and Tribunals: The "Regime Problem"' in Young (n 6) 235.

in what sense are norms produced by international bureaucrats legitimate? To whom are actors in different IOs accountable? What role do power and inequality play in determining whether and how international regulatory cooperation takes place?

Finally, the activities described below will only increase. As the long-stalled trade and climate negotiations suggest, traditional forms of cooperation—prominently including efforts to create general rules via multilateral treaty—are increasingly perceived to be cumbersome and ineffective. The rapid rise of new powers has rendered multilateral negotiations more difficult. Many claim that we have entered an age of gridlock, perhaps even a crisis of multilateralism.[10] As a result, the non-traditional forms of law-making described below will only increase in importance.

## III. TOWARD A NEW UNDERSTANDING OF REGIME INTERACTIONS

In recent work, I have sought to address this gap in our understanding. To do so, I have attempted to map a largely hidden world of regime interaction.[11] For expository purposes, we can categorise these interactions along two different axes. One axis highlights the *form* or *function* of the interaction; and one highlights its *nature*.

### A. Forms of International Regime Interactions

Starting with the form of regime interactions, we can identify regulatory, operational and conceptual interactions. *Regulatory interactions* arise when two or more international bodies jointly produce legal norms.

Consider efforts to protect the ozone layer. The Montreal Protocol was highly successful.[12] Its innovative trade provisions helped produce a dramatic reduction in the use of ozone-depleting substances. For the treaty to work, customs officials must be able to accurately track legal trade, and deter illegal trade. But an unanticipated problem arose when the treaty entered into force. Many states could not keep accurate statistics on trade in ozone-depleting substances because they used a global tariff code that did not distinguish between different chemicals treated differently by the ozone treaties. For example, under the Montreal Protocol, different hydrochlorofluorocarbons (HCFCs) are treated quite differently, as they have very different ozone-depleting potentials.[13] But under the World Customs Organization's (WCO's) harmonised tariff schedule, all HCFCs were classified under the same

[10] See Thomas Hale, David Held and Kevin Young, *Gridlock: Why Global Cooperation is Failing When We Need it Most* (Cambridge, UK/Malden, MA, Polity Press, 2013).

[11] See Jeffrey L Dunoff, 'Mapping a Hidden World of International Regulatory Cooperation' (2015) 75 *Law and Contemporary Problems* 267.

[12] Montreal Protocol on Substances that Deplete the Ozone Layer (adopted 16 September 1987, entered into force 1 January 1989) 1522 UNTS 3 (Montreal Protocol).

[13] UNEP, 'Handbook for the Montreal Protocol on Substances that Deplete the Ozone Layer', 9th edn (UNEP, 2012) 25–27, available at www.ozone.unep.org/Publications/MP_Handbook/MP-Handbook-2012.pdf.

tariff heading.[14] Once this problem came to light, the Executive Director of United Nations Environmental Programme (UNEP) formally requested the WCO to modify its tariff codes. In response, the WCO revised its classification system, greatly facilitating implementation of the ozone treaties.

Variations on this dynamic are quite common. Nine different IOs created the Inter-Organization Programme for the Sound Management of Chemicals (IOMC).[15] Among other activities, the IOMC developed a Globally Harmonized System for the Labelling of Chemicals.[16] This system is used today by at least 67 states, including the US and the EU. Similarly, the International Civil Aviation Organization (ICAO), which sets standards for aircraft safety, and the International Telecommunications Union (ITU), which allocates radio spectrums, collaborate to develop numerous rules on aircraft navigation and communication. Staff from the Convention on International Trade in Endangered Species (CITES) and the Food and Agriculture Organization (FAO) interact on an ongoing basis over listings of endangered marine species. The International Labour Organization (ILO) and the International Maritime Organization (IMO) have jointly produced a series of guidelines on safety at sea. The Stockholm Convention and the World Health Organization (WHO) have an ongoing dialogue about permitted uses of DDT. In short, actors from different international bodies regularly and consistently collaborate on regulatory efforts across a wide range of issues.

Of course, IOs do more than produce norms. Many engage in *operational activities*. For example, the Organization for the Prohibition of Chemical Weapons (OPCW) is overseeing the destruction of chemical weapons in Syria.[17] Less well publicised is the wide mix of international bodies partnering to provide humanitarian assistance in Syria, including the International Organization for Migration (IOM), United Nations Development Programme (UNDP), UNESCO, the United Nations High Commissioner for Refugees (UNHCR), UNICEF, the World Food Organization and the WHO. The example is telling; when scholars consider the operational activities of IOs, they usually focus on a single body. But the model of international bodies undertaking operational activities on their own is increasingly obsolete.

The Joint United Nations Programme on HIV/AIDS (UNAIDS) is one high-profile example. By the early 1990s, a number of IOs had launched AIDS programmes.

[14] See the discussion in Stephen O Andersen and K Madhava Sarma, *Protecting the Ozone Layer: The United Nations History* (UNEP, 2002) 277.

[15] FAO-ILO-OECD-UNEP-UNIDO-WHO: Memorandum of Understanding Concerning Establishment of the Inter-Organization Programme for the Sound Management of Chemicals (13 March 1995) 34 ILM 1311. Currently, participating organisations include the FAO, ILO, UNDP, UNEP, UNIDO, UNITAR, WHO, World Bank and OECD, with the WHO as the administering organisation. See Inter-Organization Programme for the Sound Management of Chemicals (IOMC) available at www.who.int/iomc/en.

[16] United Nations, 'Globally Harmonized System of Classification and Labelling of Chemicals' (GHS), 5th edn (2013) available at www.unece.org/fileadmin/DAM/trans/danger/publi/ghs/ghs_rev05/English/ST-SG-AC10-30-Rev5e.pdf. See also IOMC, Coordinating Group for the Harmonization of Chemical Classification Systems, Revised Terms of Reference and Work Program, Doc IOMC/HCW/95, 14 January 1996.

[17] Convention on the Prohibition of the Development, Production, Stockpiling and Use of Chemical Weapons and on their Destruction (adopted 3 September 1992, entered into force 29 April 1997) 1974 UNTS 45 (Chemical Weapons Convention) Art 8.

However, concerns soon arose over a lack of coordination, and efforts to rationalise these activities led to the creation of UNAIDS.[18] The original co-sponsors were UNICEF, the UNDP, the United Nations Population Fund (UNFPA), UNESCO, the WHO and the World Bank, soon joined by the United Nations Drug Control Programme (UNDCP), the ILO, the United Nations Office on Drugs and Crime (UNODC), the World Food Programme (WFP) and the United Nations Entity for Gender Equality and the Empowerment of Women. This unique partnership oversees and implements a wide variety of joint and co-sponsored programmes, coordinated by the UNAIDS Secretariat in Geneva. Working together, the co-sponsors advance HIV prevention, treatment, and care and support at the country level, promote global advocacy, and guide technical support.

Similar examples of operational interactions can be found across a wide range of issue areas. For example, the Collaborative Partnership on Forests (CPF) consists of 14 international bodies that work on forest issues.[19] The Global Environment Facility provides funds in support of activities related to biodiversity, climate change, international waters, land degradation and chemicals. Originally a partnership among the UNDP, United Nations Environment Programme and the World Bank, it now operates through seven additional implementing agencies.

Notably, these operational interactions frequently generate complex cooperation problems that, in turn, result in the generation of new norms. For example, each of the UNAIDS partner agencies had rules on corruption and procurement. But these rules varied, sometimes considerably. Once UNAIDS was formed, the ten partner organisations had to work out common approaches to procurement, integrity in use of funds, record-keeping, reporting requirements and so on. Thus, operational interactions are an important source of norms and best practices that govern much day-to-day business in the international realm.

Finally, IOs increasingly engage in what I call *conceptual interactions*. IOs do not simply produce rules and standards, they also produce knowledge. They do so by, for example, 'defin[ing] shared international tasks (like "development"), creat[ing] and defin[ing] new categories of actors (like "refugee"), creat[ing] new interests for actors (like "promoting human rights"), and transfer[ing] models of organization around the world (like markets and democracy)'.[20] Again, scholarship

[18] See Lindsay Knight, 'UNAIDS: The First Ten Years: 1996–2007' (May 2008) 20, available at data.unaids.org/pub/report/2008/jc1579_first_10_years_en.pdf.

[19] The participating organisations include the Center for International Forestry Research, the Convention on Biological Diversity Secretariat, FAO, Global Environmental Facility (GEF) Secretariat, International Tropical Timber Organization (ITTO), International Union for Conservation of Nature (IUCN), International Union of Forest Research Organizations, Convention to Combat Desertification Secretariat, UNDP, UNEP, UN Forum on Forests, United Nations Framework on Convention on Climate Change (UNFCCC) Secretariat, World Agroforestry Centre, and the World Bank. See CPF, 'About the Collaborative Partnership on Forests', available at www.cpfweb.org/73947/en/. See also UN Economic and Social Council (ECOSOC), 'Report on the Fourth Session on the Intergovernmental Forum on Forests' (18 October 2000) E/RES/2000/35 (inviting the heads of relevant UN, international and regional bodies to form a collaborative partnership on forests).

[20] Michael N Barnett and Martha Finnemore, 'The Politics, Power and Pathologies of International Organizations' (1999) 53 *International Organization* 699. See also Michael N Barnett and Martha Finnemore, *Rules for the World: International Organizations in Global Politics* (Ithaca, Cornell University Press, 2004).

exploring these issues has tended to focus on specific legal regimes,[21] but increasingly knowledge production results from interactions *among*, as opposed to *within*, international legal regimes.

One current example of a conceptual interaction with potentially far-reaching consequences is a joint WTO-OECD initiative that seeks to reconfigure how we measure, if not understand, international trade.[22] Trade statistics currently attribute the full commercial value of a product to the country of export. Thus, as widely reported, when a United States (US) buyer imports an iPod from China at a cost of $150, current statistical methods would increase the value of US imports from China by $150—even though much of the iPod's value is licensed from US firms, and the value-added operations in China total less than $10. Thus, current measurement practices can distort debates over trade imbalances, and resulting trade policies. In response, the OECD and WTO are jointly developing new ways to measure trade flows. Notably, this initiative is not intended to produce new rules or regulations. Rather, it is intended to assist policy-makers, academics and the broader public to better understand contemporary trade flows, in the belief that 'better statistics today will contribute to better policies tomorrow'.[23]

Another set of conceptual interactions addresses the evolving relationship between climate change and human rights. For over two decades, the debate over climate change has focused on the nature, causes and consequences of climate change. However, in recent years actors from the human rights regime have initiated a series of conceptual interactions designed to change the terms of climate discourse.

These interactions started with a presentation by the UN Deputy High Commissioner for Human Rights to the Bali Climate Conference in 2007, which urged the use of a human rights perspective when discussing environmental issues.[24] At roughly the same time, a diverse range of international actors, including the UNDP and the Organization of American States (OAS), began to explore the interface between climate change and human rights. In 2008, the Human Rights Council asked the Office of the High Commissioner for Human Rights (OHCHR) to prepare a 'detailed analytical study of the relationship between climate change and human rights'. In undertaking the study, the OHCHR opened up a dialogue with a variety of other UN bodies, IOs, national human rights institutes and NGOs. The study, released in January 2009, concludes that climate change interferes with a wide range of human rights and that states have an obligation under international human rights

[21] William Drake and Kalypso Nicolaides, 'Ideas, Interests and Institutionalization: "Trade in Services" and the Uruguay Round' (1992) 46 *International Organization* 37; Andrew TF Lang, 'Legal Regimes and Professional Knowledges: the Internal Politics of Regime Definition' in Young (n 6); David Kennedy, *The Dark Side of Virtue: Reassessing International Humanitarianism* (Princeton, Princeton University Press, 2005).

[22] See OECD, 'Measuring Trade in Value Added: An OECD-WTO joint initiative', available at www.oecd.org/sti/ind/measuringtradeinvalue-addedanoecd-wtojointinitiative.htm.

[23] DG Pascal Lamy, 'New Steps in Measuring Trade in Value Added' (16 January 2013) available at www.wto.org/english/news_e/sppl_e/sppl261_e.htm.

[24] Kyung-wha Kang, Deputy High Commissioner for Human Rights, UNHCR, 'Address to Conference of the Parties to the United Nations Framework Convention on Climate Change and its Kyoto Protocol: Climate Change and Human Rights' (3–14 December 2007) available at www.ohchr.org/EN/NewsEvents/Pages/DisplayNews.aspx?NewsID=200&LangID=E.

law to protect those rights from the adverse effects of climate change, including in particular, through international cooperation.[25]

The study triggered an extended dialogue on the relationships between the two regimes. For example, in 2009 alone, the Special Rapporteur on adequate housing issued a report on the impact of climate change on the right to adequate housing;[26] the Representative of the Secretary General on the human rights of internally displaced persons issued a report on the nexus between climate change and internal displacement;[27] and 20 Special Procedures mandate-holders issued a joint statement to encourage the inclusion of human rights in the Copenhagen Climate Change Conference.[28] Thereafter, the UNHCR appointed an Independent Expert on Human Rights and the Environment.[29]

As one advocate explains, the goal of these efforts is to transform 'how climate change is perceived'.[30] To date, climate change 'has been viewed as a scientific projection—a kind of line graph stretching into the future with abstract measurements based on parts per million, degrees centigrade or centimeters'.[31] But the introduction of 'human rights thinking' is intended to change this conceptualisation by 'supplying a set of internationally agreed values around which policy responses can be negotiated and motivated' and hence 'contribute, qualitatively, to the construction of better policy responses at both the national and international level'.[32] In short, actors in the human rights community are provoking an ongoing set of conceptual interactions intended to change how we come to understand climate change, the problems it poses, and the range of appropriate responses.

## B. Nature of International Regime Interactions

We can also distinguish among regime interactions along another axis, by considering the *nature* of the interaction. From this perspective, regime interactions fall along a continuum that includes rationalisation of existing activities, expansion of jurisdiction, and conflict.

[25] UNCHR, 'Report of the Office of the High Commissioner for Human Rights on the Relationship Between Climate Change and Human Rights' (15 January 2009) UN Doc A/HRC/10/61.

[26] 'Report of the Special Rapporteur on adequate housing to the 64th session of the General Assembly on the impact of climate change on the fulfilment of the right to adequate housing' (6 August 2009) UN Doc A/64/255.

[27] 'Report of the Representative of the Secretary-General on the human rights of internally displaced persons' (3 August 2009) UN Doc A/64/214.

[28] See UNCHR, 'Joint Statement of the Special Procedure Mandate Holders of the Human Rights Council on the UN Climate Change Conference (Copenhagen, 7–18 December 2009)' (7 December 2009) available at www.ohchr.org/EN/NewsEvents/Pages/DisplayNews.aspx?NewsID=9667&LangID=E.

[29] UNCHR 'Report of the Human Rights Council on its Nineteenth Session' (19 April 2012) UN Doc A/HRC/RES/19/10.

[30] Marc Limon, 'Human Rights and Climate Change: Constructing a Case for Political Action' (2009) 33 *Harvard Environmental Law Review* 439, 451.

[31] Maumoon Abdul Gayoom, President of the Maldives, Statement at the Annual Meeting 2008 of the Global Humanitarian Forum (24 June 2008) quoted in Limon (n 30) at 451.

[32] Limon (n 30) at 452.

Many operational interactions arise because multiple international bodies often exercise concurrent jurisdiction over the same set of individuals or activities, and are designed to rationalise these efforts. UNAIDS is a representative example. As noted above, a number of IOs had developed AIDs programmes by the early 1990s. Donors soon complained about the 'inefficiency of coordination between different UN agencies', and that 'duplication of effort and territorial rivalries threaten to weaken the global response to AIDS'.[33] Thus, the original motivation behind UNAIDS was the desire to streamline disparate yet overlapping efforts and address policy gaps. One of UNAIDS's notable accomplishments has been the development of a detailed 'division of labour' among its partner agencies.

Similar rationalisation dynamics can be seen in the area of humanitarian aid. Due to the ad hoc and unpredictable nature of emergencies, international responses were traditionally highly disorganised. In 2005, the UN Emergency Response Coordinator introduced an Agenda for Reform, which eventually led to the formation of groups of organisations organised by 'cluster'. The WFP,[34] the world's largest humanitarian agency, is designated lead agency of the 'logistics cluster'.[35] As a result, the WFP is responsible for coordination, information management and, where necessary, logistics service provision to ensure effective and efficient operational logistics. In this role, the WFP facilitated cargo operations on behalf of 32 different IOs in the Philippines in the aftermath of Typhoon Haiyan,[36] and coordinated with 17 partners to respond to the Ebola outbreak in Liberia, Sierra Leone and Guinea.[37]

At other times, interactions provide opportunities for international bodies to expand their reach. Consider, for example, ongoing interactions between the United Nations Relief and Works Agency (UNRWA) and the UNHCR. The UNRWA was created to provide humanitarian relief to refugees and displaced persons forced to flee the British Mandated Palestine as a result of the 1948 Arab-Israeli war.[38] When founded, the UNRWA's geographic ambit was limited to Jordan, Lebanon, Syria, the Gaza Strip and the West Bank.[39] The UNHCR's geographic ambit is worldwide; however, its statute provides that its competence shall not extend to anyone '[w]ho continues to receive from other organs or agencies of the United Nations protection or assistance'.[40] These provisions raise questions as to whether and when Palestinian refugees fall within the UNHCR's mandate.[41]

[33] Joint United Nations Programme on HIV/AIDS, 'UNAIDS: The First Ten Years: 1996–2007' (May 2008) UNAIDS/07.20E, 20.

[34] UNGA Res 1714 (XVI) (19 December 1961).

[35] World Food Programme, Our Work, available at www.wfp.org/logistics.

[36] See World Food Programme, 'Multi-Cluster Needs Assessment (Final report): Philippines Typhoon Haiyan' (2013) available at documents.wfp.org/stellent/groups/public/documents/ena/wfp261996.pdf.

[37] See World Food Programme, 'Ebola Response from Crisis to Recovery' (2015) available at documents.wfp.org/stellent/groups/public/documents/communications/wfp276313.pdf.

[38] UNGA Res 302 (IV) (8 December 1949).

[39] UNRWA and UNHCR, 'The United Nations and Palestinian Refugees' (2007) available at www.unrwa.org/userfiles/2010011791015.pdf.

[40] Statute of the Office of the United Nations High Commissioner for Refugees, UNGA Res 428 (V) Annex (14 December 1950) UN Doc A/RES/U28 (V) ch II, para 7(c).

[41] UNHCR, 'Revised Note on the Applicability of Article 1D of the 1951 Convention relating to the Status of Refugees to Palestinian Refugees' (October 2009) available at www.refworld.org/docid/4add77d42.html.

Despite apparent textual limitations, over time the UNRWA and UNHCR have increasingly collaborated in operations that seem to push the boundaries of their respective mandates. Examples include joint activities after Libya expelled Palestinians in 1995[42] and, more recently, in the aftermath of attacks on Palestinians in Iraq, when the UNRWA and UNHCR coordinated on the provision of assistance.[43] Moreover, in recent years, the UNRWA and UNHCR have acted in coordination to provide assistance to Palestinian refugees in Jordan and Syria.[44] Through these joint activities, the UNRWA has acted in areas arguably outside its geographic mandate, and the UNHCR has been active on behalf of individuals who arguably fall outside of its mandate. While the various operational interactions between the UNRWA and the UNHCR have historically had a strongly ad hoc nature, in 2010 the two bodies established a joint expert working group to address issues related to the overlapping legal regimes in this area.[45]

Of course, interactions among actors from different international regimes are not always cooperative. One recent example involves efforts to address shipbreaking. This practice is heavily regulated in developed states, but regulation is substantially less stringent in many developing states.[46] A number of international legal instruments—all adopted within months of each other—address this activity, including IMO Guidelines on Ship Recycling,[47] ILO Guidelines on Safety and Health in Shipbreaking,[48] and Technical Guidelines for the Environmentally Sound Management of the Full and Partial Dismantling of Ships,[49] adopted by the Conference of Parties to the Basel Convention. This highly fragmented approach quickly raised concerns over regulatory gaps, overlaps and potential inconsistencies, and the IMO, ILO and Basel Secretariats formed a Joint Working Group to study the relationship among the various instruments.[50] The three bodies agreed to collaborate on the drafting of a new treaty to be concluded under IMO auspices.

[42] Press Release, 'UN Agencies Issue Joint Statement on Expulsion of Palestinians from Libya' (29 September 1995) available at unispal.un.org/DPA/DPR/unispal.nsf/eed216406b50bf6485256ce1007 2f637/53f734fb0da3bd99852562520064c3b1?OpenDocument.

[43] Noura Erakat, 'Palestinian Refugees and the Syrian Uprising: Filling the Protection Gap during Secondary Forced Displacement' (2014) 26 *International Journal of Refugee Law* 581.

[44] UNRWA and UNHCR (n 39).

[45] Erakat (n 43) at 595.

[46] Tony George Puthucherril, *From Shipbreaking to Sustainable Ship Recycling, Evolution of a Legal Regime* (Leiden, Martinus Nijhoff/Brill Publishers, 2010).

[47] IMO, Assembly Res A.962(23), A 23/Res.962 (4 March 2004) (amended by IMO, Assembly Res A.980(24), A 24/Res.980 (3 February 2006)).

[48] ILO Committee on Sectoral and Technical Meetings and Related Issues, 'Report of the Interregional Tripartite Meeting of Experts on Safety and Health in Shipbreaking for Selected Asian Countries and Turkey' (7–14 October 2003) GB.289/STM/5; ILO, Governing Body, 289th Session (March 2004) available at www.ilo.org/public/english/standards/relm/gb/docs/gb289/pdf/stm-5.pdf.

[49] Basel Convention Secretariat, 'Technical Guidelines for the Environmentally Sound Management of the Full and Partial Dismantling of Ships' Basel Convention series/SBC No 2003/2, available at archive.basel.int/meetings/sbc/workdoc/techgships-e.pdf.

[50] See Joint ILO–IMO–BC Working Group on Ship Scrapping, 1st Session (15–17 February 2005) 'Report of the First Session of the Joint Working Group on Ship Scrapping' para 3.8, Doc ILO/IMO/BC WG 1/8 (18 February 2005) (acknowledging the conflict between the IMO Guidelines and the Basel Convention guidelines).

Thereafter, the three organisations—along with other key actors, including major shipping states like Norway—became deeply involved in drafting what eventually became the Hong Kong International Convention for the Safe and Environmentally Sound Recycling of Ships.[51] The Hong Kong Convention, adopted in 2009, clearly shows the results of inter-agency cooperation; it expressly incorporates principles set forth in instruments prepared by the three institutions, and its Annex creates a process of continuing interactions among the three agencies in the promulgation of regulations under the treaty.[52]

However, the Convention has also given rise to controversy. In particular, critics claim that the Hong Kong Convention is weaker than the Basel Convention in several respects.[53] Against this backdrop, the Basel Convention parties formally examined whether the Hong Kong Convention provides 'an equivalent level of control and enforcement as that established under the Basel Convention'.[54] An Open-ended Working Group provided an assessment to the Conference of the Parties,[55] which debated the issue at an October 2011 meeting. The discussion revealed a sharp split among the Basel parties and, despite extensive dialogue, consensus could not be reached. The Conference of the Parties adopted a decision explicitly noting this ongoing disagreement. The decision also encourages states to ratify the Hong Kong Convention (suggesting equivalence) but at the same time acknowledges that the Basel Convention Secretariat should continue to assist countries to apply the Basel Convention as it relates to ships (suggesting a lack of equivalence).[56] The debate over whether the Hong Kong treaty supports or undermines the Basel Convention remains unresolved.

* * *

Having identified a typology of different types of regime interaction, we can juxtapose the two axes to create a three-by-three matrix (see Table 1, below). The matrix provides a synoptic overview of different modes of international regulatory cooperation between and among IOs. At the same time, it highlights the multi-dimensional nature of contemporary international regulatory cooperation.

[51] Hong Kong International Convention for the Safe and Environmentally Sound Recycling of Ships (opened for signature 1 September 2009) IMO Doc SR/CONF/45 (19 May 2009) (not in force).

[52] See ibid Annex.

[53] Critics note that the Basel Convention covers a broader range of ships and recycling facilities, and that the Basel Convention's technical guidelines rejects 'beaching' as a dismantling method, while the question is open under the Hong Kong Convention (at least until the IMO adopts guidelines). For an analysis of these, and other differences, see European Commission, COM (2010) 88 final.

[54] UNEP, 'Report of the Conference of the Parties to the Basel Convention on the Control of Transboundary Movements of Hazardous Wastes and their Disposal on its ninth meeting' (23–27 June 2008) UN Doc UNEP/CHW.9/39, Decision IX/30 on Dismantling of Ships.

[55] See UNEP, 'Report of the Open-ended Working Group of the Basel Convention on the Control of Transboundary Movements of Hazardous Wastes and Their Disposal on the Work of its Eighth Meeting' (31 October 2012) UN Doc UNEP/CHW/OEWG-VII/12.

[56] UNEP, 'Report of the Conference of the Parties to the Basel Convention on the Control of Transboundary Movements of Hazardous Wastes and Their Disposal on its Tenth Meeting' (1 November 2011) UN Doc UNEP/CHW.10/28/BC-10/17. The decision also underscored the importance of continued cooperation between the ILO, IMO and the Basel Convention on the issue of ship recycling.

Table 1: Synoptic Overview of Different Modes of International Regulatory Cooperation

| | Regulatory | Operational | Conceptual |
|---|---|---|---|
| Rationalisation | IMO/ILO<br><br>ICAO/ITU<br><br>FAO/CITES | UNAIDS<br><br>'Logistics Cluster' in humanitarian assistance<br><br>Collaborative Partnership on Forests | WTO/UNEP report |
| Expansion | ILO/IMO guidelines on liability and compensation (fills legal void)<br><br>CITES/WCO<br><br>Convention on Persistent Organic Pollutants/WHO | CITES/WCO<br><br>International Consortium on Combatting Wildlife Crime<br><br>UNRWA/UNHCR | OHCHR/UNFCCC<br><br>WTO/World Intellectual Property Organization/WHO |
| Conflictual | ILO/IMO/Basel (Hong Kong Convention)<br><br>WTO/CITES/UN Convention on the Law of the Sea/ FAO talks on fisheries subsidies<br><br>Montreal Protocol/ WCO (sometimes) | UNAIDS (early years)<br><br>UN/IMO—Flag State Implementation | Climate and human rights (sometimes) |

## IV. TOWARD AN INTERDISCIPLINARY RESEARCH AGENDA ON REGIME INTERACTIONS

Having sketched the outlines of a largely unexplored world of regime interaction, let us now shift our attention from the world of international affairs to the world of international law scholarship. Perhaps on the basis of the analysis above some readers are now intrigued by the ubiquity and importance of regime interactions. Perhaps some have become convinced—as I have—that regime interactions constitute a distinctive and important mode of governance. And suppose those scholars decide to undertake research in this area. What might that research look like?

The interactions highlighted above are under-studied and under-theorised. In these circumstances, scholars are often tempted to look outside their own disciplines, and draw on cognate fields. One obvious candidate would be IR. Would a turn to IR be useful? Well, for one thing, rationalist IR approaches can be used to identify circumstances where we might expect regime interactions to take different forms, or where we might expect to land in one or another square of the matrix, as set out in Table 1. Let me mention just a few possible hypotheses along these lines that could be tested:

*Actors*: Scholars could explore the variation in relationships between the relevant actors. For example, does it matter whether the relevant actors are from 'nested regimes', such as the WTO and a regional trade body; from 'parallel regimes', like two of the international financial institutions; or from 'unrelated regimes', such as actors from a trade and a labour body?

*Problem structure*: International regime interactions address coordination, cooperation, distribution and enforcement problems. Prior research reveals that problem structure helps explain the design and functioning of individual international organisations.[57] Does problem structure likewise shed light on interactions among actors from different international regimes? For example, do distributional problems more frequently lead to conflictual regime interactions than enforcement problems? Do coordination problems lend themselves more easily to operational interactions, as parties have little reason to defect?

*Issue area*: The international system is marked by uneven legalisation and institutionalisation across issue areas. Are regime interactions more common, and more successful, in some issue areas than others? Knowing these patterns would enhance our understanding of the possibilities and limits of regulatory interactions.

*Sequencing*: Regime interactions are often fluid and dynamic. Thus, the interactions among the ILO, IMO and Basel Secretariat concerning the Ship Recycling Convention shifted over time from cooperative to conflictual; the interactions among the international bodies that created UNAIDS changed from cooperative to conflictual to cooperative; and the regulatory interactions between UNEP and WCO in the ozone context have vacillated between cooperative and conflictual. This variation invites inquiry into why some interactions are relatively stable while others are not, and into the features that push interactions towards or away from cooperative outcomes.

To be sure, I join those who caution that this type of enquiry runs a risk of being a one-sided form of interdisciplinarity. In work with Mark Pollack, I have criticised scholarship that applies IR theory and method to IL as a subject, but ignores IL theory.[58] Others, including prominent members of this Society, have gone substantially further, and suggested that international lawyers actively resist IL/IR work. They argue that interdisciplinarity is 'a path to academic takeover'[59] and that interdisciplinarity involving IR 'is not really about disciplinary cooperation but conquest'.[60]

[57] Barbara Koremenos, Charles Lipson and Duncan Snidal, 'The Rational Design of International Institutions' (2001) 55 *International Organization* 701.

[58] Jeffrey L Dunoff and Mark A Pollack (eds), *Interdisciplinary Perspectives on International Law and International Relations: The State of the Art* (Cambridge, Cambridge University Press, 2013).

[59] Martti Koskenniemi, 'The Politics of International Law—20 Years Later' (2009) 20 *European Journal of International Law* 7, 16.

[60] Martti Koskenniemi, 'Miserable Comforters: International Relations as New Natural Law' (2009) 15 *European Journal of International Relations* 395, 410.

Interdisciplinary work does raise tricky methodological and epistemological challenges; nevertheless, I believe that fears of disciplinary conquest are substantially overblown, for at least two reasons.[61] The first reason is grounded in certain features of law as a discipline, in particular, law's epistemology. In contrast to other academic disciplines, law does not have a method that cumulates knowledge. Rather, legal knowledge is very much a professional knowledge, a set of rhetorical and argumentative practices. Law is, as the critics properly remind us, largely an interpretative practice. This means that legal arguments and legal truths are deeply contextual; the strength and success of an argument is, in part, a function of the setting in which it is offered.

What implications does this insight hold for interdisciplinary research? Consider the practical reality that practicing and academic lawyers use information, ideas and concepts from other disciplines all the time. Indeed, this reality motivates—and provides the theme for—this volume. Significantly, however, when lawyers use knowledge from other disciplines, the identification of the problem, the basic assumptions used, and the questions posed tend to be characteristically legal.

As a result, interdisciplinary work points us towards a different type of change than the doctrinal and legal change we have been discussing. It highlights change in the meaning of ideas—and more importantly the change in the uses to which ideas are put—as they migrate across disciplinary borders. For example, IR and IL scholars both study international law's compliance and effectiveness. So IL might learn from IR studies that identify features of treaties thought to increase compliance. But in doing so, lawyers need not endorse the IR assumption that compliance is simply the correspondence of state behaviour with rules. International lawyers can complicate this view by noting the relative indeterminacy of rules, that non-compliance is identified not simply by acts but also by the intentionality and acceptability attributed to those acts by other actors, and that law has many effects in addition to influencing state behaviour.

To generalise the point, conceptual terms and distinctions do not have meanings independent of particular contexts. When terms or concepts migrate from one discipline to another—say, from IR to IL—they will be received and used in ways that reflect the preoccupations and commitments of law, not IR. As a result, law will use, modify, alter, revise, adapt, extend and transform these ideas because law will use them for its own purposes. This does not strike me as conquest. Instead, in the process of interdisciplinary exchange, law is less a passive consumer than an active user. Interdisciplinarity permits, perhaps necessarily entails a type of change—*conceptual change*—to which we have paid insufficient attention.

Claims of disciplinary conquest seem to be based on a related fear as well. This is the fear that normative values and claims will be undermined if we allow ourselves to focus on and measure observable phenomena. But this concern, as well, seems exaggerated. I would suggest that the pursuit of moral values and normative

[61] I explore these issues in more detail in Jeffrey L Dunoff, 'From Interdisciplinarity to Counterdisciplinarity: Is There Madness in Martti's Method?' (2013) 27 *Temple International and Comparative Law Journal* 309.

goals associated with international law—like, say, reducing inter-state violence or enhancing respect for human rights—is more likely to succeed if based on rich empirical understandings of the obstacles that hinder and factors that promote progress toward these goals. To be sure, there is a risk that when measurement becomes important, one could mistakenly think that only what is measureable is important. But this is hardly inevitable, and for reasons just identified I think the potential gains greatly outweigh this risk. We should see empirically-informed IL/IR work as a tool for deepening our grasp of why international processes unfold as they do. We seek this information not for its own sake, but to better prescribe future policy. Thus, IL/IR work is a means for advancing normativity, and not a substitute for it.

## V. CONCLUSIONS

Let me close by returning to where we started, with the notion of change. I have described changes in specific rules. I have also outlined a change in the law-making process. What I have described is not treaty or custom or another traditional process. And I have detailed a change in the relevant international actors. In many regime interactions, individuals from different international regimes operate as rather autonomous actors, and not simply agents of states. But we should note a crucial analytical move behind these conclusions. It is implicit, and so we should bring it to the foreground. The issue is that whether something counts as change or as continuity is not straightforward. It is deeply perspectival. It is a function of the systemic and time perspectives that we adopt. And it depends on the unit of analysis. When FAO and CITES worked out a procedure for listing endangered species, it was a substantial change for both bodies. But it was hardly a major change to the post-War liberal legal order. We lack an objective or agreed baseline against which to determine whether an act constitutes change or continuity. Any conclusions along these lines are determined by the interests and perspectives of observers, the scales of time and space that they use, and whether they seek evolutionary or breakpoint change. Thus, whether the processes I've described constitute change is at least as much a function of one's underlying theory of change and continuity than the underlying phenomena. This suggests that change is a useful analytical category after we identify the relevant metrics by which we want to measure change. So perhaps the more difficult—and the more relevant—inquiry is how we decide which metrics to choose and which perspective to adopt. With these metrics in mind, then the framework of continuity and change can be useful.

# PART V

# INTERNATIONAL LAW AND NEW TECHNOLOGIES

# 14

# *The Challenges Posed by Cyber-Attacks to the Law on Self-Defence*

IRÈNE COUZIGOU*

## I. INTRODUCTION

STATES HAVE BECOME increasingly dependent on computers and the networks that connect them. The development of cyber-space enables states and non-state actors to increase their offensive capabilities significantly.[1] Cyber-technology is now likely to become an essential offensive tool, in particular for terrorist organisations. It is even more the case that cyber-attacks can be carried out more easily and with a lower risk of detection than attacks with conventional weapons: it is enough to have a computer and a connection to the internet. The concern that transnational terrorist or other non-state organisations may turn to cyber-operations as a means of attacking states is well-founded. For instance, al-Qaeda computers containing hacker tools have been seized and the membership of such a group has increasing computer expertise.[2] In his State of the Union Address of 2014, the President of the United States (US) referred to the need to 'combat new threats like cyberattacks'.[3]

A cyber-attack can be defined as a deliberate action 'taken through the use of computer networks to disrupt, deceive, degrade, manipulate, or destroy information resident in the target information system or computer networks, or the systems/networks themselves'.[4] Cyber-attacks may produce effects that are not only internal to a computer or network but also those effects that are external, by causing harm

* Lecturer in Law at the University of Aberdeen Law School (United Kingdom). Email address: irene.couzigou@abdn.ac.uk.

[1] The term 'non-state actor' refers to terrorist groups, rebel groups, other organised groups, and individuals.

[2] Michael N Schmitt, 'Cyber Operations and the *Jus Ad Bellum* Revisited' (2011–2012) 56 *Villanova Law Review* 600.

[3] President Barack Obama's State of the Union Address, The White House Office of the Press Secretary, 28 January 2014, available at www.whitehouse.gov/the-press-office/2014/01/28/president-barack-obamas-state-union-address.

[4] James E Cartwright, 'Memorandum for Chiefs of the Military Services Commanders of the Combatant Commands Directors of the Joint Staff Directorates, Washington, DC, November 2010' 5, available at www.nsci-va.org/CyberReferenceLib/2010-11-joint%20Terminology%20for%20Cyberspace%20Operations.pdf.

to connected facilities which could in turn lead to serious physical harm to property or individuals. Such would be the case, for example, when a computer network attack disables an air traffic control system and, thereby, causes an airliner to crash, resulting in material and physical destruction. In other words, a cyber-operation may treat the target computer or computer network as the conduit for an attack on a physical target.

To what extent does international law on self-defence allow a state to react to cyber-attacks? To implement the rules on the right to self-defence may entail certain difficulties in view of the specific characteristics of cyber-technology. In particular, given the fast and anonymous character of a cyber-attack, it may be difficult to attribute it to the author of that attack. Section II of this paper will outline the international criteria for the attribution of a cyber-operation to a state. Section III will argue that only cyber-attacks reaching the level of an armed attack give the right to the victim state to use self-defence. Section IV will explain that the law on self-defence does not offer an effective response to cyber-attacks because, as international law stands, only cyber-attacks attributed to states trigger the right to self-defence. Section V concludes that current international law on self-defence needs to be adapted to meet the challenges posed by cyber-attacks.

## II. THE DIFFICULT ATTRIBUTION OF A CYBER-ATTACK

A crucial issue in any response in self-defence to a cyber-attack is first to identify the author of the attack against whom action can be taken. Attribution is necessary for the effectiveness as well as for the lawfulness of the counter-action. International law does not know any specific standards of evidence with regard to issues involving the use of armed force in self-defence. There is, however, a general agreement that the more grave the charge the more confidence there must be in the evidence.[5] Therefore, a state should determine with a high degree of confidence the identity of the author of a cyber-attack before exercising its right to self-defence against it.

The author of a cyber-attack may claim responsibility for it. For instance, a group that commits a cyber-attack may claim credit for it in a message posted online or on a videotape given to the media. The style of a cyber-attack may also help to identify the organisation responsible for it.[6] Otherwise, attribution of a cyber-attack is a complicated exercise, because of the nature of the cyber-domain. Not only must the attack be traced back to its source, that is, to a computer, but the person who operated the computer must also be identified or his affiliation determined. Unlike the case of an attacker in the physical world, a cyber-attacker has the ability to launch an attack anonymously. In particular, in order to hide the real origin of an attack, cyber-attackers may route an attack through a number of servers based around the

[5] Separate Opinion of Judge Higgins in *Case Concerning Oil Platforms (Islamic Republic of Iran v United States of America)* [2003] ICJ Rep, paras 30–39.

[6] Susan W Brenner, 'At Light Speed: Attribution and Response to Cybercrime/Terrorism/Warfare' (2007) 97 *Journal of Criminal Law and Criminology* 379, 408.

globe prior to hitting the target system.[7] To trace back an attack through those computers will require assistance from government and civilian entities in the states in which the computers were used. It can take months before assistance from the relevant states is obtained and the attack tracked back to its true point of origin.[8] A further issue in identifying the perpetrator of a cyber-attack is caused by the volatility of electronic data, which may be altered, moved or deleted in seconds. Lastly, once the origin and the author of a damaging international cyber-operation are known, it may be difficult to assess its real purpose. The cyber-operation might not be hostile but attributable only to faulty software or to an accidental computer error or malfunction.[9]

In April and May 2007, Estonia's digital infrastructure was the victim of several computer network attacks. Distributed 'denial of service' attacks targeted Estonia's web services and brought Estonian web traffic to a halt. Since Estonia relied heavily on internet services, the impact of the cyber-assaults was very inconvenient. Most of the attacks emanated from abroad, principally Russia. It could not, however, be firmly demonstrated that the Russian government either conducted or orchestrated them. The origin of the attacks was also traced to at least 177 other states.[10] This example of cyber-attacks from at least 178 countries shows how challenging it could be to attribute a cyber-operation to its author. In order to be able to respond effectively to cyber-attacks, states should continue their technically based effort to enhance the capacity to trace their source in real-time.

It is expected that most electronic attacks will be performed by non-state actors.[11] They may also be committed by or on behalf of a state, as suspected of Russia. In that case, one would expect a state that commits a cyber-attack to attempt to make it look like that of a hacker. Under international law, a cyber-operation can be attributed to a state especially in the following four circumstances. The first is where a cyber-act is performed by an organ of a state, for example, a member of its armed forces. This conclusion does not change if the hacker is a civilian, non-military, organ of the state. In accordance with Article 4 of the 2001 Draft Articles of the International Law Commission, which mostly codifies customary international law on the responsibility of states, '[t]he conduct of any State organ shall be considered an act of that State under international law, whether the organ exercises legislative, executive, judicial or any other functions'.[12]

The second circumstance of attribution of a cyber-act to a state is when the act is performed by a person or entity empowered by the state to exercise governmental authority.[13] For instance, if a state charges a private defence company with elements

[7] Ibid 409.

[8] Ibid 420.

[9] Ibid 434–35.

[10] Schmitt (n 2) 569–70.

[11] Jason Barkham, 'Information Warfare and International Law on the Use of Force' (2001–2002) 34 *New York University Journal of International Law & Politics* 57, 58–59.

[12] *Official Records of the General Assembly, Fifty-sixth session, Supplement No 10* (A/56/10), ch IVE.1.

[13] Article 5 of the Draft Articles on the Responsibility of States, ibid.

of authority normally associated with the government, and asks it to conduct cyber-operations, these operations will be imputed to the state.

The third scenario in which a cyber-operation may be attributed to a state is where the acting entity operated under the instructions, direction or control of a state. Such would be the case if a state hires an individual or an organisation to commit a cyber-attack. Article 8 of the Draft Articles on the Responsibility of States reads:

> The conduct of a person or group of persons shall be considered an act of a State under international law if the person or group of persons is in fact acting on the instructions of, or under the direction or control of, that State in carrying out the conduct.[14]

The degree of direction or control must be high, which means that the state should have effectively directed or controlled the specific cyber-operation. The reality of the control exercised on the ground should be determined on a case-by-case basis.[15] It has been argued that the technical difficulty of attributing cyber-attacks could only be responded to effectively by using a lower threshold for attribution,[16] namely the criterion of 'overall control' that covers the case where a state coordinates or helps in the general planning of the relevant operation.[17] Such an approach would, however, extend the use of the right to self-defence in response to cyber-attacks in a dangerous manner and should be rejected.

Finally, in accordance with Article 11 of the Draft Articles on the Responsibility of States: '[c]onduct ... shall ... be considered an act of that State under international law if and to the extent that the State acknowledges and adopts the conduct in question as its own.'[18] However, in order to avoid counter-measures taken by the victim state, it is unlikely that a state will publicly acknowledge a cyber-attack.

## III. THE QUALIFICATION OF A CYBER-ATTACK AS AN ARMED ATTACK

### A. The Prohibition of Inter-State Armed Force

Article 2(4) of the UN Charter states: 'All Members shall refrain in their international relations from the threat or use of force against the territorial integrity or political independence of any State, or in any other manner inconsistent with the Purposes of the United Nations.' The mainstream view among states and international lawyers is that the 'other manner' language extends to any use of force not authorised by the Charter, even if it does not threaten the territorial integrity or the political independence of a state.[19] Since the expression 'force' in Article 2(4) is not preceded by

[14] Ibid.

[15] *Military and Paramilitary Activities in and against Nicaragua (Nicaragua v United States)* [1986] ICJ Rep 14, para 115.

[16] Scott J Shackelford, 'From Nuclear War to Net War: Analogizing Cyber Attacks in International Law' (2009) 27 *Berkeley Journal of International Law* 192, 235.

[17] *Prosecutor v Duško Tadić* (15 July 1994) ICTY, Appeals Chamber Judgment, IT-94-1-A, para 131.

[18] *Official Records of the General Assembly* (n 12).

[19] Albrecht Randelzhofer and Oliver Dörr, 'Article 2(4)' in Bruno Simma (ed), *The Charter of the United Nations*, 3rd edn, vol I (Oxford, Oxford University Press, 2012) 215–16.

the adjective 'armed', the scope of the 'force' to which Article 2(4) adverts remains unclear and, in particular, whether it extends to economic or political force.

The expression 'armed force' appears elsewhere in the UN Charter (in paragraph 7 of the Preamble to the Charter as well as in Articles 41 and 46). Furthermore, the first and principal purpose of the UN is, according to Article 1(1) of the Charter, to maintain international peace. Therefore, the interpretation of Article 2(4) in the context of the UN Charter is that it forbids the use of inter-state armed force by state parties. The preparatory work of the UN Charter confirms the fact that the prohibition contained in Article 2(4) is concerned only with military force.[20] This conclusion is corroborated by resolutions of the UN General Assembly that deal with issues of peace and security and which received the consent of a high majority of the members of the Assembly.[21] International state practice also confirms the narrow scope of Article 2(4).[22]

In conclusion, the prohibition of the use of inter-state force in the UN Charter, as well as in general public international law, covers only armed force and not economic, political and other types of coercion, unless coupled with the use, or at least the threat, of armed force.

## B. Is a Cyber-Attack Armed Force?

Is a cyber-act equivalent to armed force prohibited by Article 2(4) of the UN Charter? This can be the case only if the act is committed by a state against another state. A cyber-act of an individual or an entity that is not acting on behalf of a state is tried as criminal action even when the attacker acts from abroad and claims to be waging war against the victim state. Furthermore, in order to be covered by the prohibition of inter-state use of force, a cyber-act must be similar to armed force.

Neither the UN Charter nor the International Court of Justice (ICJ) provides a definition of 'armed force'. 'Armed' can be defined as '[e]quipped with a weapon' or '[i]nvolving the use of a weapon'.[23] A weapon is '[a]n instrument used or designed to be used to injure or kill someone'.[24] Or a weapon is 'a thing designed or used for inflicting bodily harm or physical damage'.[25] In its Advisory Opinion on the *Legality of the Use of Nuclear Weapons*, the ICJ stated that Article 2(4) of the UN Charter does 'not refer to specific weapons'. It applies 'to any use of force, regardless of the weapons employed'.[26] Therefore, should cyber-technology be used to injure or kill, it should be regarded as a 'weapon'.

[20] *Documents of the United Nations Conference on International Organization*, published in cooperation with the Library of Congress, New York, vol VI (New York, United Nations Information Organisation, 1945) 559 and 720.

[21] See in particular, 'Declaration on Principles of International Law Concerning Friendly Relations and Co-operation Among States in Accordance with the Charter of the United Nations', GA Res 2625 (24 October 1970) UN Doc A/Res/2625, Annex, para 1.

[22] Randelzhofer and Dörr (n 19) 209.

[23] Bryan A Garner (ed), *Black's Law Dictionary*, 8th edn (St Paul, Minn, Thomson West, 2009) 115.

[24] Ibid 1730.

[25] *Oxford Dictionary of English*, 2nd edn (Oxford, Oxford University Press, 2008) 1994.

[26] *Legality of the Threat or Use of Nuclear Weapons* (Advisory Opinion) [1996] ICJ Rep 226, para 39.

Two main approaches can be adopted to determine whether a cyber-attack constitutes 'armed force'. The first approach is an 'instrument-based' one. Using this model, an assessment is made as to whether a cyber-operation may intrinsically involve physical force in the same way as a conventional weapon. Physical force is traditionally understood as involving 'any explosive effect with shock waves and heat'.[27] Cyber-operations do not intrinsically imply such physical force and therefore the 'instrument-based' model does not fit them.

The second approach is the 'consequence-based approach'. Here an assessment is made as to whether the overall effects of a computer network attack are equivalent to those of an attack using a traditional weapon. The 'consequence-based approach' regards as armed force the use of any new means that leads to serious destructive effects. It is more flexible than the 'instrument-based' approach and can adapt to the technical evolution of warfare. It allows the inclusion of certain cyber-attacks in the notion of 'armed force' even if the drafters of the UN Charter did not think of this possibility in 1945 simply because it was then not technically possible.

The 'instrument-based' approach has already been applied by Brownlie to biological and chemical devices. For him, when these agents are used to destroy physical property and life, they are weapons involving the use of armed force.[28] Similarly, under the 'consequence-based approach' cyber-operations may cause damage to tangible property, injury (including illness), or death. There are many examples of computer network attacks that should be considered as armed force: a cyber-attack on the controlling system of air or train traffic, causing the crash of a plane or a train;[29] a cyber-operation creating a hammering phenomenon in oil pipelines causing them to burst; a cyber-attack that shuts down power to a hospital with no back-up generators, or disrupts emergency response communications systems; a cyber-attack that incapacitates the computers that control oil refineries, leading to the release of deadly effluents; a cyber-operation shutting down computers controlling waterworks and dams, generating flooding of inhabited regions; a cyber-attack disabling the systems that control the reactor of a nuclear power plant, leading to the release of radioactive materials. In these different situations, the severity of the overall consequences of the cyber-operation—material destruction, injuries and/or deaths—rises to a level equal to that of an attack with kinetic weapons.

In contrast, a cyber-attack that interferes with the computers through which financial transactions are recorded and settled, and that disrupts a state's financial system, would not constitute armed force because there is no destruction of objects or human injury.[30] In the opinion of this author, qualifying such a cyber-operation as a use of force would depart too much from the traditional definition of force and therefore

[27] Ian Brownlie, *International Law and the Use of Force by States* (Oxford, Clarendon Press, 1963) 362.

[28] Ibid.

[29] The Malaysia Airlines crash of 8 March 2014 may have been due to a cyber-attack on air traffic control systems.

[30] Daniel B Silver, 'Computer Network Attack as a Use of Force Under Article 2(4) of the United Nations Charter' in Michael N Schmitt and Brian T O'Donnell (eds), *Computer Network Attack and International Law* (Naval War College Newport, International Law Studies, 2002) 91–92.

also of an armed attack—an armed attack being a severe use of force[31]—and would thus expand too much the use of the right to self-defence in response to an armed attack. Like this author, the majority of commentators uses the 'consequence-based' model and concludes that cyber-operations committed with the intention to cause material destruction, injuries and/or deaths analogous to those produced by kinetic weapons are to be considered as armed force.[32]

The appropriateness of the 'consequence-based' model is today confirmed by state views where several states regard cyber-technology as a new form of warfare. By 2012, the 15 states with the biggest military budgets were all investing in offensive cyber-capabilities.[33] The US, China, Iran, Israel and Russia have already introduced cyber-technology into their military strategies and have established military units with specific cyber-expertise.[34] For instance, in 2010, the US created the United States Cyber Command (USCYBERCOM), a subdivision of the United States Strategic Command, whose role is, among others, to command military cyber-space operations.[35] In response to a UN General Assembly invitation to inform the UN Security Council on the states' position regarding information security, the United Kingdom (UK),[36] Australia,[37] the US,[38] and Iran[39] expressly stated that international law on the use of force applies.

States have not yet categorised empirical cases of cyber-attacks as constituting a use of force. In particular, since they did not lead to material damage or injury, the massive distributed 'denial of service' attacks that targeted Estonia's web servers in 2007, or similar attacks that targeted Georgia's websites when Russian forces invaded South Ossetia in 2008, were not qualified by states as uses of force.[40] More surprisingly, no state considered as a use of force the attack caused by the Stuxnet virus that damaged Iran's centrifuges for uranium enrichment at Natanz in 2010.[41]

[31] See below section III C.

[32] See in particular, rule 11 and the comments on it by the Group of Experts invited by the NATO Cooperative Cyber Defence Centre of Excellence in Michael N Schmitt (ed), *Tallinn Manual on the International Law Applicable to Cyber Warfare* (Cambridge, Cambridge University Press, 2013) 45 and 47. See also: Barkham (n 11) 79–80; Heather Harrison Dinniss, *Cyber Warfare and the Laws of War* (Cambridge, Cambridge University Press, 2013) 74; Oona A Hathaway et al, 'The Law of Cyber-Attack' (2012) 100 *California Law Review* 817, 848; Herbert S Lin, 'Offensive Cyber Operations and the Use of Force' (2010) 4 *Journal of National Security Law & Policy* 63, 73; Todd A Morth, 'Considering our Position: Viewing Information Warfare as a Use of Force Prohibited by Article 2(4) of the UN Charter' (1999) 30 *Case Western Reserve Journal of International Law* 567, 590–92; Michael N Schmitt, 'Computer Network Attack and the Use of Force in International Law: Thoughts on a Normative Framework' (1998–1999) 37 *Columbia Journal of Transnational Law* 885, 913; Silver (n 30).

[33] 'A new kind of warfare', *New York Times*, 9 September 2012.

[34] Marco Roscini, 'World Wide Warfare—*Jus ad bellum* and the Use of Cyber Force' (2010) 14 *Max Planck Yearbook of United Nations Law* 85, 107.

[35] See the US Cyber Command's website at www.arcyber.army.mil.

[36] 'Developments in the field of information and telecommunication in the context of international security' (20 July 2010) UN Doc A/65/154, 15.

[37] Ibid 6.

[38] Ibid 18–19.

[39] Ibid 12.

[40] Hathaway et al (n 32) 837.

[41] Even Iran, which did not reveal what amount of material damage the Stuxet attack caused, did not invoke the use of force. Russell Buchan, 'Cyber Attacks: Unlawful Uses of Force or Prohibited Interventions?' (2012) 17 *Journal of Conflict & Security Law* 211, 219–20.

The reason may be that this attack was unprecedented—the first computer operation that successfully targeted an industry and caused material destruction beyond the computer system itself. In any case, states increasingly acknowledge the possibility of a categorisation of severe cyber-attacks as a use of force, and may react differently if a cyber-attack with consequences as severe as, or more severe than those of the Stuxnet attack occurs in the future.

Some commentators have advanced another and third approach for categorising when a cyber-attack is to be considered as a use of force, namely the target-based or strict liability approach.[42] This approach treats any cyber-attack against a critical national infrastructure as a use of force because of the possible severe effects should such an infrastructure be disabled. There are several issues with such an approach.

First, there is no fixed international definition of the term of 'critical infrastructure'. States generally agree that critical infrastructures constitute services such as water distribution, health, energy, transportation, banking and finance.[43] However, as long as this term is not precisely defined by treaty law, states can transform and extend this enumerative list as they wish. Secondly, and most importantly, the target-based approach is dangerously over-broad. Indeed, it assumes that any critical infrastructure network penetration reveals hostile intent and justifies the use of the right to self-defence, including anticipatory self-defence, whatever the level of damage caused.[44] Third, this approach is not strongly supported by the views of states. For all these reasons, the target-based/strict liability approach should be rejected.[45]

## C. Is a Cyber-Attack a Grave Form of Armed Force?

In accordance with Article 51 of the UN Charter, '[n]othing in the present Charter shall impair the inherent right of individual or collective self-defence if an armed attack occurs against a Member of the United Nations'. This provision is also a part of customary international law.[46] The bedrock principle of self-defence is that it may be invoked in response to an armed attack. The question is then whether a cyber-attack can constitute an armed attack, triggering the victim state's right to respond through self-defence. In its *Nicaragua* Judgment, the ICJ referred to Article 3(g) of the 'Definition of Aggression' appended to a resolution of the UN General Assembly

[42] Sean M Condron, 'Getting It Right: Protecting American Critical Infrastructure in Cyberspace' (2007) 20 *Harvard Journal of Law & Technology* 403, 415–16; Eric T Jensen, 'Computer Attacks on Critical National Infrastructure: A Use of Force Involving the Right of Self-Defense' (2002) 38 *Stanford Journal of International Law* 207, 229–31.

[43] Condron (n 42) 416.

[44] Reese Nguyen, 'Navigating Jus Ad Bellum in the Age of Cyber Warfare' (2013) 101 *California Law Review* 1079, 1120. For the requirements for the use of the right to self-defence in reaction to a cyber-attack, see below section III C.

[45] For a more nuanced position, see Marco Roscini, *Cyber Operations and the Use of Force in International Law* (Oxford, Oxford University Press, 2014) 55–63. In particular at 62 'it is only cyber attacks that go beyond mere inconvenience and *significantly* disrupt the functioning of *critical* infrastructure that can potentially fall under the scope of Article 2(4)'.

[46] *Military and Paramilitary Activities in and against Nicaragua* (n 15) para 176.

as concerning an 'armed attack'.[47] The Court reaffirmed this approach in its *Armed Activities* judgment.[48] The Definition of Aggression can thus be used to define the concept of armed attack.

Article 2 of this definition states that aggression is 'the use of armed force by a State against the sovereignty, territorial integrity or political independence of another State, or in any other manner inconsistent with the Charter of the United Nations'.[49] Its Article 3 provides examples of aggression that are widely accepted by the international community. The list, however, deals only with conventional armed attacks involving the use of kinetic force. Article 2 of the Definition of Aggression also specifies that an act of aggression must be of 'sufficient gravity'. Similarly, the ICJ has stated that the 'most grave forms of the use of force' constitute armed attacks, not 'less grave forms'.[50] Therefore, not every use of armed force is necessarily deemed an armed attack. The scope, duration and intensity of the armed force must be assessed to determine whether an armed attack has occurred. The restriction of the implementation of self-defence to the use of serious armed force expresses the UN Charter's intent to limit inter-state force.

Furthermore, for the ICJ, an armed attack must be carried out 'with the specific intention of harming'.[51] If these statements are applied to cyber-operations, it appears that an intentional disruption of digitised communications that causes only a minor destruction of physical property will reach the level of armed force but not that of an armed attack. By contrast, when a cyber-operation is perpetrated with the intention of seriously destroying physical property and/or injuring or killing persons, that operation will qualify as an armed attack.[52] For instance, if a computer attack causes a wagon of a goods train to crash, this may be considered as an illegal use of armed force but is unlikely to be regarded as an armed attack. However, a computer attack that leads to the crash of several passenger trains would very likely be considered an armed attack.

The fact that a cyber-attack may reach the threshold of an armed attack, triggering the right to self-defence, has been accepted by the heads of state and government participating in the meeting of the North Atlantic Council in September 2014.[53] It remains up to state practice to determine what level of damage is required to allow the legal use of self-defence. In this author's opinion, only a limited number of cyber-attacks, those causing severe material destruction, injury or death, should be considered as armed attacks. Without any doubt the examples involving oil pipelines and refineries, dams, nuclear power plants and so on, which were cited above as uses of armed force, should also be regarded as armed attacks.

[47] Ibid para 195.

[48] *Armed Activities on the Territory of the Congo (Democratic Republic of the Congo v Uganda)* [2005] ICJ Rep 14, para 146.

[49] Definition of Aggression, GA Res 3314 (14 December 1974) UN Doc A/RES/3314.

[50] *Military and Paramilitary Activities in and against Nicaragua* (n 15) para 191.

[51] *Case Concerning Oil Platforms* (n 5) para 64.

[52] Yoram Dinstein, 'Computer Network Attacks and Self-Defense' in Schmitt and O'Donnell (n 30) 105.

[53] Wales Summit Declaration of the North Atlantic Council of 5 September 2014, para 72, available at www.nato.int/cps/en/natohq/official_texts_112964.htm.

It should be noted that state practice seems to be evolving towards the recognition of the 'accumulation of effects' doctrine, according to which the accumulation of several attacks from the same originator, which do not on their own achieve the threshold of an armed attack, constitute an armed attack in combination.[54] The US and Israel in particular approve the 'accumulation of effects' theory.[55] The ICJ has not expressly pronounced on the matter, but equally seems to have implicitly endorsed it.[56] Such accumulation theory may, however, be abused in order to justify the recourse to force. It is argued that cyber-attacks that do not reach the level of an armed attack individually can constitute an armed attack when aggregated only if they are related and only if they occur within a relatively short period of time.

## IV. THE INAPPROPRIATE LAW ON SELF-DEFENCE IN RESPONSE TO CYBER-ATTACKS

### A. Absence of a Right to Self-Defence Against Non-State Cyber-Attackers

Article 51 of the UN Charter does not expressly require that an armed attack be committed by a state in order to trigger the right to self-defence.[57] If the UN Charter and other regional defensive treaties do not envisage military defence against attacks committed by non-states actors, they nevertheless do not exclude them.[58] Could the state victim of a cyber-attack exercise its right to self-defence against a non-state actor author of the attack?

The ICJ has clearly stated that the Charter only 'recognizes the existence of an inherent right of self-defence in the case of armed attack by one State against another State'.[59] In another case, it declined to elaborate on whether actions by non-state actors would constitute an armed attack that would trigger an armed defensive response.[60] States, and in particular the US and Israel, have sometimes used force against non-state actors. After the defeat of the Taliban regime in November 2001, action in self-defence of the US and its allies was no longer directed against the State

[54] Christian J Tams, 'The Use of Force against Terrorists' (2009) 20 *European Journal of International Law* 359, 388.

[55] The US links the attack on the World Trade Centre in 1994, the attacks on American embassies in Kenya and Tanzania in 1998, the attack on the destroyer USS Cole in 2000, and the attacks on the World Trade Center and the Pentagon in 2001, attributing all of them to the al-Qaeda organisation.

[56] *Military and Paramilitary Activities in and against Nicaragua* (n 15) para 231; *Case Concerning Oil Platforms* (n 5) para 64; *Armed Activities on the Territory of the Congo* (n 48) para 146.

[57] Separate Opinion of Judge Kooijmans in ICJ, *Armed Activities on the Territory of the Congo* (n 48) para 28; Declaration of Judge Buergenthal and Separate Opinion of Judge Higgins in ICJ, *Legal Consequences of the Construction of a Wall in the Occupied Palestinian Territory* (Advisory Opinion) [2004] ICJ Rep, para 6 and para 33 respectively.

[58] Raphael Van Steenberghe, 'Self-defense in Response to Attacks by Non-State Actors in the Light of Recent State Practice: A Step Forward?' (2010) 23 *Leiden Journal of International Law* 183, 198.

[59] *Legal Consequences of the Construction of a Wall in the Occupied Palestinian Territory* (n 57) para 139.

[60] ICJ, *Armed Activities on the Territory of the Congo* (n 48) para 147. In his separate opinion, Judge Simma criticised the fact that the Court missed an opportunity to clarify whether there is a right to self-defence against non-state actors, at para 8.

of Afghanistan, but solely against the al-Qaeda terrorist organisation and Taliban forces. The legality of this action was not, at least at the beginning, contested.[61] In 2006 Israel took action in self-defence against Hezbollah in Lebanon, declaring that it was acting not against the state of Lebanon—to which it was not able to attribute Hezbollah's conduct—but against Hezbollah itself.[62] Although many states criticised the disproportionate way in which Israel exercised its right to self-defence, they accepted that Israel enjoyed such a right in reaction to the attacks of Hezbollah.[63]

When, in other precedents, states invoked the right to self-defence against non-state actors, in particular terrorist organisations, without showing any involvement of the state where they were based, third states were, however, reluctant to recognise the legality of the forcible action.[64] In recent state practice, there is no general and clear approval of the legality of the right to self-defence against non-state actors. Therefore, it can be concluded that customary international law has not broadened, at least not yet, the right to self-defence to encompass action against non-state actors, irrespective of whether they are the authors of a cyber-attack. Indeed, to recognise a right to self-defence against a non-state actor would be an infringement of the fundamental international principle of the territorial integrity of the state where the non-state actor is based. Furthermore, this could lead to a risk of abuse. States might engage in military operations against non-state actors although law enforcement through international organs would be the more normatively appropriate reaction.

## B. Absence of a Right to Self-Defence Against States Actively Supporting Non-State Cyber-Attackers

The right to self-defence can be carried out against a state that commits a cyber-operation, similar to an armed attack. Does the right to self-defence also exist against a state that supports an offensive cyber-act perpetrated by a non-state actor whose severity is equivalent to that of an armed attack and directed against another state? In accordance with Article 3(g) of the Definition of Aggression, what qualifies as an act of aggression is the substantial involvement of a state in one of the acts of aggression referred to by paragraphs (b) to (f) of Article 3 of the Definition of Aggression.[65] This definition can be used to define the notion of armed attack.[66] If a state provides financial, technical or other material support (below the level of direction and control) to an organisation, and if this support significantly helps the commission by that organisation of a cyber-attack whose level is equivalent to that of an armed attack and which is directed against another state, is the support of that

[61] Christine Gray, *International Law and the Use of Force*, 3rd edn (Cambridge, Cambridge University Press, 2008) 204.

[62] Identical letters from the Permanent Representative of Israel to the UN addressed to the Secretary-General and the President of the Security Council (12 July 2006) UN Doc S/2006/515.

[63] Van Steenberghe (n 58) 193.

[64] Tams (n 54) 379–81.

[65] Definition of Aggression (n 49).

[66] See above section III C.

state in the commission of the armed attack a 'substantial involvement' that corresponds to an armed attack?

The ICJ has advocated a strict interpretation of 'substantial involvement' and held that 'assistance to rebels in the form of provision of weapons or logistical or other support' does not fall into the category of armed attack.[67] This legal position does not appear to have changed since.[68] In current state practice, the supply of money, arms and logistical help has rarely been regarded as an armed attack.[69] However, even if it does not constitute an armed attack, such a supply is illegal and engages the responsibility of the state under international law. Indeed a state is bound by an obligation not to actively support damaging conduct of non-state actors directed against another state.[70] Concerning, for instance, activities of terrorist non-state actors, the Security Council has stressed that 'every Member State has the duty to refrain from organizing, instigating, assisting or participating in terrorist acts in another State or acquiescing in organized activities within its territory directed toward the commission of such acts'.[71]

In the opinion of this author, the law on self-defence should evolve in order to offer a more efficient response to internationally offensive cyber-operations. The concept of 'substantial involvement' should be reinterpreted and include a lesser degree of state involvement than the one that seems to be required by the ICJ. When a state provides practical assistance to an organisation for the purpose of assisting it with the commission of a computer network attack against another state—similar to an armed attack—and when this assistance substantially contributes to the commission of the attack, state practice should change in such a way that the state is regarded as having committed an armed attack itself.[72] In such a situation, the victim state should have the right to self-defence against the relevant state.

### C. Absence of a Right to Self-Defence Against States Passively Supporting Non-State Cyber-Attackers

Another question is whether a state that simply tolerates computer network attacks which are as severe as armed attacks and are mounted from within its territory or an area under its exclusive control against another state can be regarded as perpetrating an armed attack itself? This question was asked most famously in relation to

[67] *Military and Paramilitary Activities in and against Nicaragua* (n 15) para 195.
[68] The case law of the *Nicaragua* case was confirmed in *Armed Activities on the Territory of the Congo* (n 48) paras 106–47.
[69] Gray (n 61) 132.
[70] *Military and Paramilitary Activities in and against Nicaragua* (n 15) para 205.
[71] UNSC Res 1189 (1998) preamble, UN Doc S/RES/1189.
[72] In his dissenting opinion to the *Nicaragua* case, Judge Schwebel found that the concept of 'substantial involvement' could also include financial and logistical support. *Military and Paramilitary Activities in and against Nicaragua* (n 15) paras 170–71. Also in his dissenting opinion to this case, Judge Jennings thought that the provision of arms could constitute a very important element in what amounts to an armed attack, when coupled with other kinds of involvement. Ibid 533. For a similar academic opinion see: Tom Ruys and Sten Verhoeven, 'Attacks by Private Actors and the Right of Self-Defence' (2005) 10 *Journal of Conflict & Security Law* 289, 315–16.

non-cyber-activities, those of 11 September 2001 against the US, mounted by the al-Qaeda terrorist organisation from within Taliban-led Afghanistan. Afghanistan had harboured al-Qaeda, and had not complied with Security Council resolutions asking it to stop doing so. It did not, however, control the 11 September attacks.[73] These attacks were clearly similar in scale and effect to an armed attack.

The US (supported by allies, in particular the UK) began military action against the al-Qaeda organisation and also against the state of Afghanistan from 7 October 2001. Both the US and the UK reported to the Security Council that the military intervention was taken in accordance with their right to individual self-defence and to collective self-defence respectively.[74] The Security Council recognised the existence of such a right to self-defence.[75] The North Atlantic Treaty Organisation (NATO) and the Organization of American States (OAS) also invoked the right to self-defence to assist the US in its response to the attacks. Overall, the military action in self-defence against Afghanistan received massive support from the international community.[76]

Considering the international approval of the military intervention in Afghanistan, can one conclude that self-defence can be invoked against a state tolerating non-state actors' activities that amount to an armed attack? The problem is that it is impossible to adduce conclusive state practice and *opinio juris*—both of which are necessary for the emergence of a customary international rule in support of this argument—other than that shown in the Afghanistan case of 2001.[77] Therefore, it is not enshrined in current customary international law that self-defence can be implemented against a state tolerating the organisation of non-state actors' attacks, cyber or not, against another state from within its territory or an area under its exclusive control.

The tolerance by a state of the organisation of international attacks from within its territory is, however, illegal as will be shown in the following analysis. In accordance with the ICJ in the *Corfu Channel* case of 1949, every state is under an obligation 'not to allow knowingly its territory to be used for acts contrary to the rights of other States'.[78] More specifically, the 1970 Declaration on Friendly Relations adopted by consensus by the UN General Assembly urges states to 'refrain from … acquiescing [in] organized activities within [their] territory directed towards the commission of [civil strife or terrorism in another State]'.[79] Concerning cyber-attacks, the 2001 Resolution on combating the criminal misuse of information technologies calls upon states to prevent their territories from being used as a safe haven from which to

[73] Gray (n 61) 200–201.

[74] Letters of the Permanent Representatives of the US and of the UK to the UN, UN Docs S/2001/946 and S/2001/947 respectively.

[75] UNSC Res 1368 (2001) preamble 3rd sentence, UN Doc S/RES/1368 and UNSC Res 1373 (2001) preamble 4th sentence, UN Doc S/RES/1373.

[76] Gray (n 61) 193–94.

[77] Ibid 136–40 and 230–31; Olivier Corten, *The Law Against War* (Oxford and Portland, Oregon, Hart Publishing, 2012) 183–86.

[78] *The Corfu Channel Case (United Kingdom v Albania)* [1949] ICJ Rep 4, 22.

[79] Declaration on Principles of International Law Concerning Friendly Relations and Co-operation Among States in Accordance with the Charter of the United Nations (n 21) Annex, para 1, 10.

launch cyber-attacks, and to cooperate in the investigation and prosecution of such attacks.[80]

It is now widely recognised that a state has a positive customary obligation of due diligence to prevent the commission of unlawful activities from within its territory or any area under its exclusive control against another state. In particular, a state should take necessary and reasonable measures to prevent non-state actors using its internet gateways to perpetrate computer network attacks against another state. A state must not knowingly permit its territory, or any other space under its exclusive control, to be used as a sanctuary for cyber-actors bent on attacking targets in another country.[81] When a state is unable to meet its obligation to prevent such action, either because it lacks the territorial control necessary to do so, or because it does not have the human or logistical resources available, it is under an obligation to seek assistance in preventing cyber-attacks.

If a state fails to seek such assistance, this should be interpreted as an unwillingness to meet its obligation to prevent cyber-attacks against other states from its territory.[82] The unwillingness of a state to perform its obligation to counter international offensive cyber-operations does not trigger the right to self-defence of the victim state, but nevertheless does engage the international responsibility of the relevant state.[83] For instance, if states were unable to attribute to Russia the cyber-attacks against Estonia in 2007, but this state is nevertheless suspected of tolerating the private groups, authors of the cyber-attacks, that engages its international responsibility.[84]

In the author's view, the law on self-defence should change. When a state infringes its obligation to prevent unlawful acts against another state committed on its territory or in an area under its exclusive control, and knowingly harbours a group preparing and perpetrating cyber-attacks equivalent to armed attacks, the present author argues that the state forfeits its right to territorial integrity. In this scenario, state practice should evolve so as to entitle the victim state of a cyber-attack to use force in self-defence against the author of the cyber-attack. The host state should, however, be given the opportunity to comply with its obligation to prevent international cyber-offensives before there is a resort to action in self-defence.

Where international cyber-attacks, whose level is similar to that of armed attacks, are prepared and committed from the territory of a failed state, then in this situation too, the victim state should have the right to self-defence against the cyber-attackers. Indeed, if a state persists in not attempting to prevent cyber-attacks equivalent to

[80] Resolution on Combating the criminal misuse of information technologies GA Res 55/63 (22 January 2001) UN Doc A/RES/55/63, para 1.

[81] Jeffrey Carr, *Inside Cyber Warfare: Mapping the Cyber Underworld*, 2nd edn (Sebastopol, CA, O'Reilly Publishing, 2013) 62–67; David E Graham, 'Cyber Threats and the Law of War' (2010) 4 *Journal of National Security Law & Policy* 87, 93–94.

[82] Kimberley N Trapp, 'Back to Basics: Necessity, Proportionality, and the Right of Self-Defence against Non-State Terrorist Actors' (2007) 56 *International and Comparative Law Quarterly* 147.

[83] Ruys and Verhoeven (n 72) 306. For the extensive scope of the responsibility of a state knowingly harbouring terrorists committing terrorist armed attacks against another state, see Tal Becker, *Terrorism and the State* (Oxford and Portland, Hart Publishing, 2006) 322–36.

[84] Roscini (n 34) 102; Matthew C Waxman, 'Cyber-Attacks and the Use of Force: Back to the Future of Article 2(4)' (2011) 36 *Yale Journal of International Law* 421, 447.

armed attacks mounted from within its territory or any other area it controls, or if cyber-attacks similar to armed attacks are perpetrated from the territory of a failed state, the victim state has no other means available to defend itself against the non-state actor, author of the cyber-attacks, than to resort to force against it. The requirement of the necessity of the use of the right to self-defence is thus fulfilled.[85]

In order to be more effective in response to severe international cyber-attacks, a broader consensus in the international community needs to emerge towards the legality of the use of force in self-defence against cyber-attackers, who commit cyber-attacks equivalent to armed attacks and who are located in another state that fails to prevent such attacks. The rationale behind this proposal is that the victim state should be entitled to engage in measures of prevention and suppression of cyber-attacks which the host state should have performed itself. Therefore, the victim state should only target the cyber-attackers and should not be allowed to react in self-defence against institutions of the host state.[86] Furthermore, in the opinion of this author, the provision by a state of a safe haven to a cyber-attacker is not serious enough to constitute an armed attack, even if the safe haven is necessary to, for example, the planning and organising of a cyber-attack amounting to an armed attack. To argue otherwise would unduly increase the possibility for resort to the use of force in self-defence.[87]

The obligation of a state to prevent the perpetration by territorial actors of cyber-attacks against other states, especially if they reach the level of armed attacks, is to be implemented with due diligence. It does not require the prevention of every international offensive cyber-action but the adoption of reasonable measures in the light of the circumstances in order to generally prevent international cyber-attacks. To assess whether a state respects its obligation of due diligence in the prevention of international cyber-attacks, it should be checked: whether there has been a continuous pattern of cyber-attacks from the relevant state; whether the state criminalises the commission of cyber-attacks; whether the state conducts detailed investigations into cyber-attacks; whether the state prosecutes cyber-attackers; and whether the state cooperates with the victim states' investigations and prosecutions of the cyber-attackers, especially when it lacks the capacity itself to investigate and prosecute those who have committed the cyber-attacks.[88] A careful assessment of all these facts is needed in order not to over stretch the limits of self-defence. Resort to self-defence should here be the last means for reacting to cyber-attacks.

[85] Ashley S Deeks, '"Unwilling or Unable": Toward a Normative Framework for Extraterritorial Self-Defense' (2012) 52 *Virginia Journal of International Law* 483, 494; Trapp (n 82) 142.

[86] Yoram Dinstein, *War, Aggression and Self-Defence*, 4th edn (Cambridge, Cambridge University Press, 2005) 245.

[87] Sonja Cenic, 'State Responsibility and Self-Defence in International Law Post 9/11: Has the Scope of Article 51 of the United Nations Charter Been Widened as a Result of the US Response to 9/11?' (2007) 14 *Australian International Law Journal* 201, 214–15.

[88] Graham (n 81) 94. Parties to the Convention on Cybercrime of 2001 have already agreed, in Article 23, to 'co-operate with each other … to the widest extent possible for the purposes of investigations or proceedings concerning criminal offences related to computer systems and date' available at www.coe.int/en/web/conventions/full-list/-/conventions/treaty/185.

## V. CONCLUSION

The victim state of an international cyber-attack could react within its right to self-defence if the cyber-attack were attributable to a state and if the cyber-attack had consequences similar to those of a traditional armed attack, namely severe material damage, human injury or human loss. Given the strict criteria governing the attribution of conduct to a state, most electronic attacks will not be attributable to a state. The current international right to self-defence does not, however, provide the state, which is the victim of a serious international computer network attack by a non-state actor, with the legal possibility of reacting with force against that actor. Furthermore, it does not allow a reaction against a state that actively supports cyber-attackers and provides financial, logistical or other support to them so that they are able to commit a cyber-attack equivalent to an armed attack against another state. Finally, the current right to self-defence cannot be implemented against a state that harbours individuals or groups committing international cyber-attacks from within its territory even if they amount to armed attacks. Therefore, the current international right to self-defence offers an incomplete and inappropriate response to serious international cyber-attacks.

In the author's view, the law on self-defence should be amended and adapted to meet the distinctive challenges posed by severe international cyber-attacks that are likely to be committed mostly by non-state actors. First, when a state provides practical assistance to a non-state organisation for the purpose of assisting it with the commission of a computer network attack against another state, similar to an armed attack, and when this assistance substantially contributes to the commission of the attack, state practice should change in such a way that the state is regarded as having committed an armed attack itself. In such a situation, the victim state should have the right to self-defence against the relevant state. Second, and this scenario may occur more frequently than the first, when a state knowingly harbours a non-state group preparing and perpetrating cyber-attacks equivalent to armed attacks, it is here argued that it forfeits its right to territorial integrity. In this case, state practice should evolve so as to entitle the victim state of the cyber-attacks to act in self-defence against the group—and only against it. In the exceptional situation when a cyber-attack equivalent to an armed attack is committed against a state by a non-state actor, based in the territory of a failed state, the victim state should also be allowed to implement its right to self-defence against the non-state actor.

In all these circumstances, the action in self-defence could be traditional and take a military form, or it could be a cyber one, and thus have effects similar to those of a forcible action in self-defence. The proposed changes in the implementation of the law of self-defence could occur through treaty law. However, it is unlikely that a majority of states would agree on a text governing reaction with force to cyber-attacks in the near future, as there are fundamental differences between states about the interpretation of the international law of self-defence. It is therefore hoped that the proposed changes will emerge in customary international law through state practice.

# 15

# 'Culturomics' and International Law Research

JAMIE TRINIDAD*

## 1. INTRODUCTION

SCHOLARS IN THE social sciences and humanities are increasingly turning to quantitative research methods in order to gain a better qualitative understanding of the social world. International law scholars are no exception. In April 2014, Joseph Weiler, the Editor-in-Chief of the *European Journal of International Law*, noted that there had been a recent surge in the number of articles submitted to the journal 'making use of quantitative research methods and analysis', and he described this quantitative turn as a 'distinct trend'.[1]

The key drivers of this trend are the new information technologies that make it possible to harness and manipulate vast amounts of data. As datasets rapidly become larger, more accessible and more malleable, new and exciting avenues of research are opening up for the international law scholar. One such avenue involves the quantitative analysis of large volumes of digitised text with the aim of revealing information about words.

In a light-hearted EJIL:*Talk!* post concerning the strange insistence of the International Criminal Tribunal for the former Yugoslavia (ICTY) on calling its decisions 'judgements' (with an 'e') rather than 'judgments', Marko Milanović referred to a keyword search he had undertaken of English court decisions catalogued on the British and Irish Legal Information Institute (BAILII) database. His search revealed that: 'judgment' gets 47345 hits while 'judgement' gets 4030. That's a ratio of about 12:1 ... in a country where 'judgement' is otherwise more prevalent.[2]

The type of analysis undertaken by Milanović can be situated within a fast-developing methodological trend, the potential of which extends far beyond

* Fellow of Wolfson College, University of Cambridge, and of the Lauterpacht Centre for International Law. I am grateful to Michael Engel for introducing me to the Google ngram viewer.

[1] JHH Weiler, 'Quantitative Empirical International Legal Scholarship' EJIL:*Talk!*, 1 April 2014. www.ejiltalk.org/quantitative-empirical-international-legal-scholarship/

[2] M Milanović, 'Judgment or Judgement: What Has the ICTY Wrought?' EJIL:*Talk!*, 29 October 2013. www.ejiltalk.org/judgment-or-judgement-what-has-the-icty-wrought/

trivial matters of spelling. Information concerning word usage can yield fascinating insights into the cultural phenomena that the words encode, including—I wish to suggest in this chapter—the kind of cultural phenomena that international lawyers are interested in.

As more texts are digitised, more sophisticated tools are being developed for exploring databases of digitised texts. This new technological landscape has spawned the burgeoning field of 'culturomics', which emerged in association with the Google Books project and in conjunction with the development of an ingenious and freely available research tool—the Google ngram viewer.

This chapter will firstly explain what culturomics involves and how the ngram viewer works. It will then illustrate how this methodology and interface can be put to use by international law researchers. A cautionary note follows regarding some of the problems and pitfalls that accompany culturomic analysis. The chapter concludes with some reflections on how culturomics might be of use in interrogating the very concept and discipline of international law.

## II. 'CULTUROMICS' AND THE GOOGLE NGRAM VIEWER

The neologism 'culturomics' refers to a quantitative approach to the study of culture through the analysis of millions of digitised texts. The approach was developed by Harvard's Jean-Baptiste Michel and his colleagues, and is described by them in a 2011 article in the journal *Science*.[3] Their methodology is associated with the Google Books project, which has digitised some 30 million books of the 130 million ever published. The word count goes into the hundreds of billions, mostly in English (361 billion as of 2011), but also in French (45 billion), Spanish (45 billion), German (37 billion), Chinese (13 billion), Russian (35 billion) and Hebrew (2 billion). The corpus of digitised books stretches back to the 1500s. The authors of the *Science* paper note that the number of words in the corpus has increased markedly since that time: 60 million words by 1800, 1.4 billion by 1900 and 8 billion by 2000.[4] According to Michel et al 'computational analysis of this corpus enables us to observe cultural trends and subject them to quantitative investigation. "Culturomics" extends the boundaries of scientific inquiry to a wide array of new phenomena'.[5]

The computational analysis they refer to is conducted using the Google ngram viewer, a research tool that is freely available online at ngrams.googlelabs.com. This tool generates graphs depicting the frequency with which a string of characters uninterrupted by a space (a '1-gram'), or a sequence of 1-grams (an 'ngram') appears in the corpus, relative to the total number of words in a given year. This enables users to search for, and compare, the frequency with which words and phrases appear over time within, and across, the various digitised corpora.

[3] Jean-Baptiste Michel et al, 'Quantitative analysis of culture using millions of digitized books' (2011) 331(6014) *Science* 176–82.
[4] Ibid 177.
[5] Ibid 176.

Michel at al use the word 'slavery' to illustrate their methodology:

> [I]n 1861, the 1-gram 'slavery' appeared in the corpus 21,460 times, on 11,687 pages of 1,208 books. The corpus contains 386,434,758 words from 1861; thus the frequency is $5.5 \times 10^{-5}$. 'slavery' peaked during the civil war (early 1860s) and then again during the civil rights movement (1955–1968).[6]

When one inputs the term 'slavery' into the ngram viewer, the resulting graph tells the story in compelling visual form.

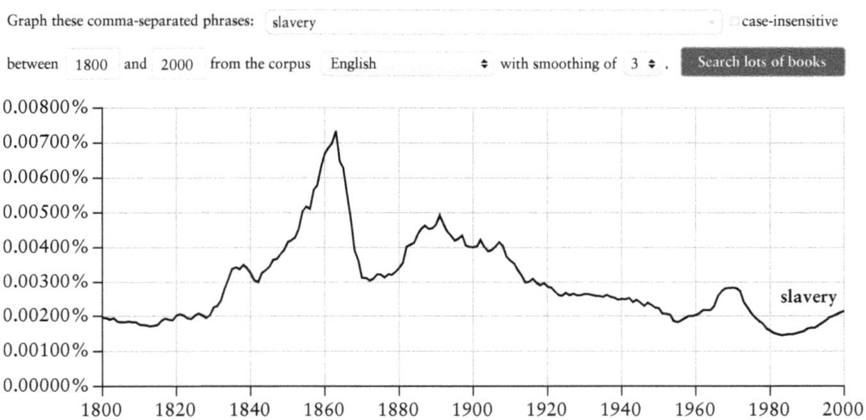


**Figure 1: Graph depicting frequency of usage of the word 'slavery' in the English corpus, from 1800 to 2000 (source: Google ngram viewer).**

One of Michel's collaborators, Erez Lieberman Aiden, told the *New York Times* that the aim of the Harvard project was ultimately 'to give an 8-year-old the ability to browse cultural trends throughout history, as recorded in books'.[7] Other culturomic interfaces exist, some of them as relatively simple as the keyword search function on the BAILII database deployed by Marko Milanović. However, the Google ngram viewer is currently by far the most impressive interface in terms of its sophistication, accessibility and the size of its target database.

## III. USING CULTUROMICS AND THE NGRAM VIEWER IN INTERNATIONAL LAW RESEARCH

The ngram viewer opens up remarkable possibilities for international law scholars. In the paragraphs that follow I seek to illustrate the potential of this tool, and to stimulate ideas for future research.

[6] Ibid 177.

[7] Patricia Cohen, 'In 500 Billion Words, New Window on Culture' *New York Times*, 16 December 2010.

## A. Spelling and Usage of Words

Returning to the 'judgment/judgement' dichotomy, a comparison of the phrases 'judgment of the ICTY' and 'judgement of the ICTY' suggests that while commentary on the ICTY's decisions has proliferated since the establishment of the Tribunal, commentators totally eschew the eccentric spelling favoured by the ICTY (to the point that 'judgement of the ICTY' does not even appear in the search results).

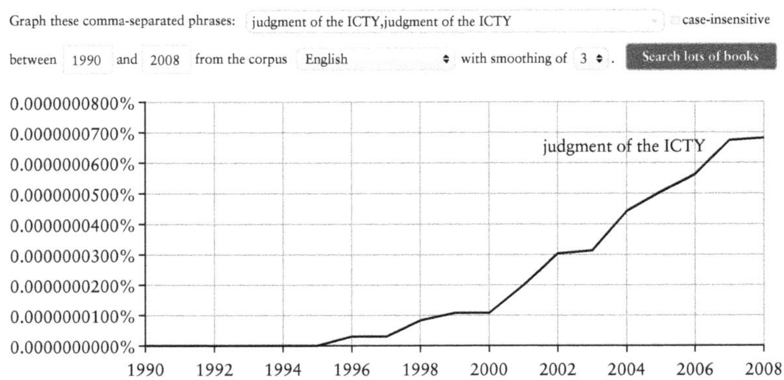


**Figure 2: Graph depicting frequency of usage of the phrases 'judgment of the ICTY' and 'judgement of the ICTY', from 1990 to 2008 (source: Google ngram viewer).**

## B. The Evolution of Concepts

Beyond matters of spelling, the graphs at Figure 3 and Figure 4 below show that a search for phrases like 'human rights/droits de l'homme' or 'fair and equitable treatment' can reveal interesting things about the concepts themselves.

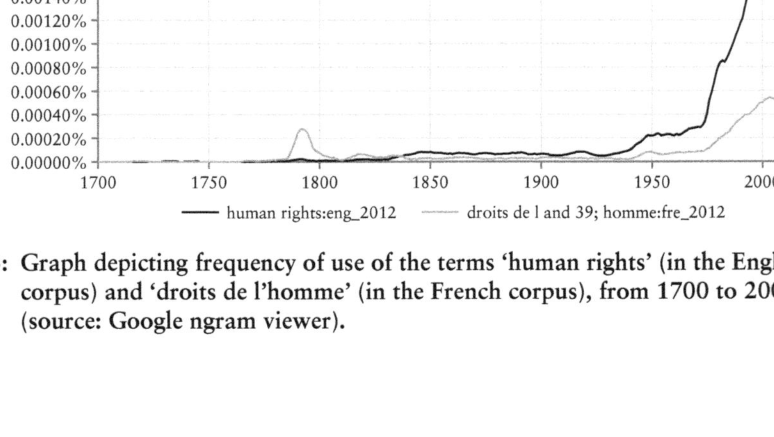


**Figure 3: Graph depicting frequency of use of the terms 'human rights' (in the English corpus) and 'droits de l'homme' (in the French corpus), from 1700 to 2008 (source: Google ngram viewer).**

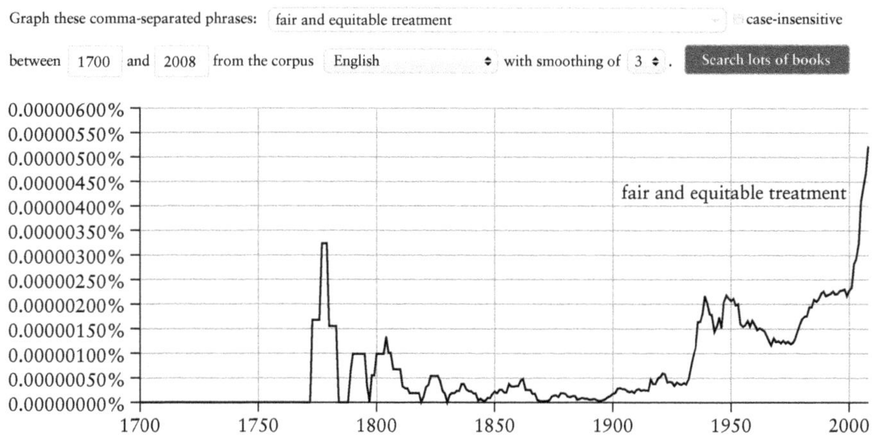


**Figure 4: Graph depicting frequency of usage of the phrase 'fair and equitable treatment' in the English corpus, from 1700 to 2008 (source: Google ngram viewer).**

As one might expect to find, the frequency of these terms has increased sharply in recent times. It is also interesting to observe that the phrase 'droits de l'homme' peaks abruptly in the French corpus in the early 1790s. A researcher curious to understand what may have precipitated the sudden interest in 'droits de l'homme' at the time might be inclined, upon viewing the graph, to examine the French literature of that period.

## C. Literature Searches

Literature searches are facilitated by another feature of the Google ngram viewer. Links beneath the search results direct the researcher to digitised books in which the relevant phrases appear. Clicking through to the book in question reveals its various metadata 'tags' (for example, title, name of author, publisher, year of publication and so on). However, it is not possible to read many of the texts directly from the Google Books database because Google has restricted access for copyright reasons. It is occasionally possible to read snippets. Copyright restrictions look set to continue, and physical access to a good library is likely to remain useful for some time to come.[8]

These restrictions notwithstanding, the benefits of being directed towards the relevant literature in this manner are significant. They can be illustrated with a simple example. In the case of 'fair and equitable treatment' the researcher is directed towards unexpected sources that have the potential to yield interesting insights into how the phrase found its way into political, and eventually legal, discourse. As the

[8] After an initial lawsuit in the US by the Authors Guild and Association of American Publishers of America in 2005 (which is still ongoing), other claims against Google for copyright infringement have followed in Germany, France and China. The Wikipedia entry on Google Books contains a useful summary of the claims and of Google's attempts to defend or settle them, en.wikipedia.org/wiki/Google_Books#Copyright_infringement.2C_fair_use_and_related_issues.

graph at Figure 4 shows, early use of the phrase in the English corpus first peaks in the 1770s.[9] The links below the ngram graph direct the researcher to, inter alia, the use of the phrase by Edmund Burke in a speech at the Bristol Guildhall, published in 1780.[10] Burke argues that, given Britain's interest in engaging on a friendly basis with certain Catholic allies, it should also offer 'fair and equitable treatment' to British Catholics, rather than 'furnish them with causes of eternal enmity'.[11] As can be seen from the graph, it would take many years from the time of Burke's speech for the term 'fair and equitable treatment' to be catapulted to prominence in the twentieth and twenty-first centuries. The upward surge in the first decade of the twenty-first century is nothing short of spectacular. Links to the more recent relevant literature confirm that international investment lawyers are responsible for this trend.[12]

## D. The Comparison of Concepts

The comparison of two or more phrases can be put to more sophisticated use than it was in the earlier 'judgement of the ICTY/judgment of the ICTY' example. For instance, a search comparing use of the phrases 'law of war' and 'law of peace' from 1600 to 2000 reveals that the former phrase eclipses the latter over time, with the exception of an intriguing little window in the 1930s.

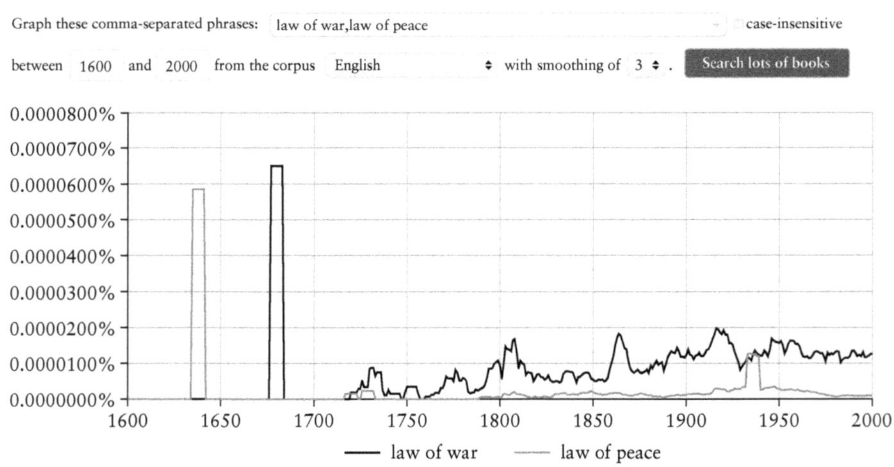


**Figure 5: Graph depicting frequency of usage of the terms 'law of war' and 'law of peace' in the English corpus, from 1600 to 2000 (source: Google ngram viewer).**

[9] The phrase appears at least a century earlier in Latin, in a treaty of Peace and Commerce between Britain and Denmark, 11 CTS 347, Art 24, cited by Martins Paparinskis at the beginning of his monograph *The International Minimum Standard and Fair and Equitable Treatment* (Oxford, Oxford University Press, 2013) 1.

[10] 'A Speech of Edmund Burke Esq at the Guildhall in Bristol' (J Dodsley, 1780) (digitised as a Google e-book).

[11] Ibid 40–41.

[12] The first three works on the list that appears when one clicks through to the relevant literature for the period 2005–2008 are: Ioana Tudor, *The Fair and Equitable Treatment Standard in the International law of Foreign Investment* (Oxford, Oxford University Press, 2008); Federico Ortino et al (eds),

When one follows the link provided to the literature containing the phrase 'law of peace' for the period 1909 to 1942, the second edition of JL Brierly's 'The Law of Nations: An Introduction to the Law of Peace' appears near the top of the list.[13] Brierly, then the Chichele Professor at the University of Oxford, was a major figure on the international law scene at the time and the work in question had been very well received.[14] It could be interesting to consider the nature and extent of Brierly's influence during this tumultuous historical period, in the debates surrounding the role of international law in the regulation of warfare. In such ways, culturomic analysis can spark hitherto unforeseen lines of investigation.

## E. Current Affairs and Futurology

Culturomic analysis can yield insights into current affairs, by placing them in historical context. Take, for example, the debate surrounding Scottish independence, which many international lawyers have taken an interest in. The graph at Figure 6 below can help a researcher to form an impression of how this debate has developed in recent decades, and how it compares to debates surrounding Irish independence, Welsh independence and English independence.

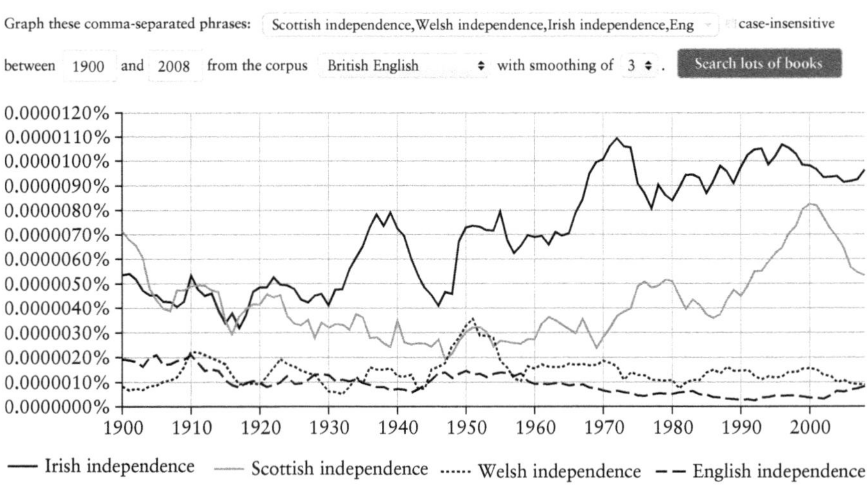


**Figure 6: Graph depicting frequency of usage of the terms 'Irish independence', 'Scottish independence', 'Welsh independence' and 'English independence' in the British English corpus, from 1900 to 2008 (source: Google ngram viewer).**

*Investment Law: Current Issues, Vol II* (London, British Institute of International and Comparative Law, 2007); and J Crawford, K Lee and E Lauterpacht, *ICSID Reports Vol 13* (Cambridge, Cambridge University Press, 2008).

[13] JL Brierly, *The Law of Nations: an Introduction to the International Law of Peace*, 2nd edn (Oxford, Oxford University Press, 1938).

[14] See eg the glowing review by Quincy Wright of the first print of Brierly's 2nd edn of *The Law of Nations* in (1936) 30(3) *American Journal of International Law* 558–60.

It is interesting to observe that in 1951, the year of a British general election in which the Welsh nationalist party Plaid Cymru succeeded for the first time in gaining a significant share of the vote, there are more references in the British English corpus to 'Welsh independence' than to 'Scottish independence'. However, after this point, the lines diverge and references to 'Scottish independence' increase steadily until the devolution settlement of 1998. The dip at the turn of the millennium appears significant, and it is a shame that no reliable data is available in Google Books after 2008, as this could potentially be used to gauge the tone of public discourse in the immediate run-up to the 2014 independence referendum.

As more recent reliable data become available, from a wider variety of sources (including news outlets), culturomic analysis may provide researchers with better insights into current international events and may even have predictive value. For example, one study claims that computational analysis of the text content of large-scale Twitter feeds can been used to measure 'collective mood states' and predict the behaviour of the stock market.[15] In another paper entitled 'Culturomics 2.0: Forecasting large-scale human behavior using global news media tone in time and space', Kalev Leetaru claims that 'global news tone', based on an analysis of a 30-year worldwide news archive, forecasted—inter alia—the revolutions in Tunisia, Egypt and Libya.[16] He rightly acknowledges that governments and corporations have long been using 'sentiment mining' techniques, processing data through a 'pre-compiled dictionary of "positive" and "negative" words', to predict large-scale behaviour (for instance, the British and American monitoring of the tone of Japanese radio broadcasts during World War II to determine attitudes towards the US).[17] Modern culturomic techniques represent a quantum leap in terms of the scale, sophistication and accessibility of this type of analysis. It is possible to imagine how such techniques might be employed by international law scholars for the purpose of speculating more intelligently on the future development of a particular dispute, protracted treaty negotiation, or normative concept.

## F. Gauging the Impact of Eminent Scholars

The ngram viewer can be a useful tool for researchers who are interested in tracking and comparing references to eminent international legal scholars. The graphs at Figure 7, Figure 8 and Figure 9 below depict occurrences of the proper names 'Hersch Lauterpacht', 'Louis Henkin', 'Ian Brownlie' and 'Martti Koskenniemi' in the British English, American English and German corpora respectively, from 1930 to 2008.

[15] Johan Bollen, Huina Mao, Xiao-Jun Zeng, 'Twitter mood predicts the stock market' (2011) 2(1) *Journal of Computational Science* 1.

[16] Kalev Leetaru, 'Culturomics 2.0: Forecasting large-scale human behavior using global news media tone in time and space', (2011) 16(9) *First Monday*, available at firstmonday.org/article/view/3663/3040.

[17] Ibid.

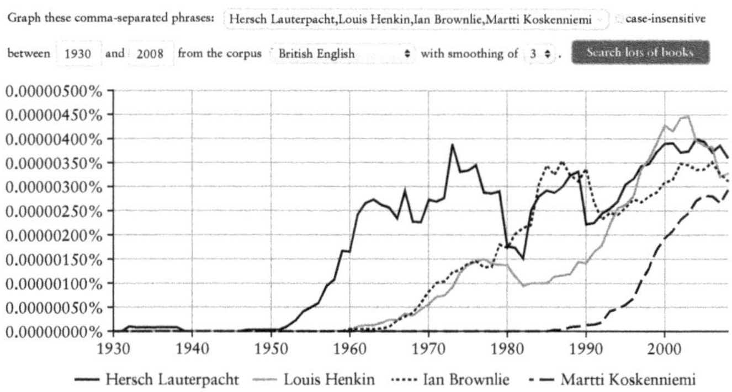


**Figure 7: Graph depicting frequency of usage of the names 'Hersch Lauterpacht', 'Louis Henkin', 'Ian Brownlie' and 'Martti Koskenniemi' in the British English corpus, from 1930 to 2008 (source: Google ngram viewer).**

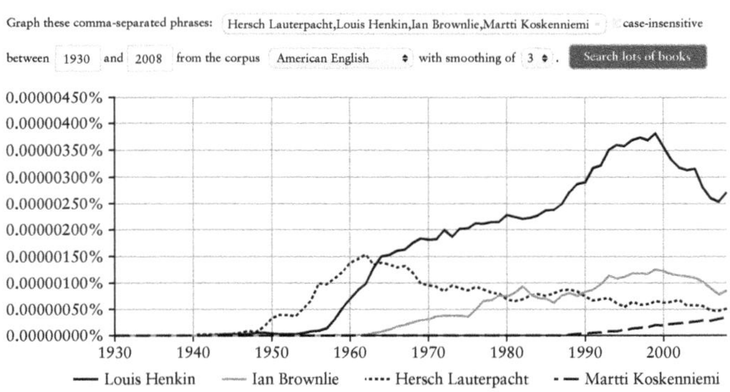


**Figure 8: Graph depicting frequency of usage of the names 'Hersch Lauterpacht', 'Louis Henkin', 'Ian Brownlie' and 'Martti Koskenniemi' in the American English corpus, from 1930 to 2008 (source: Google ngram viewer).**

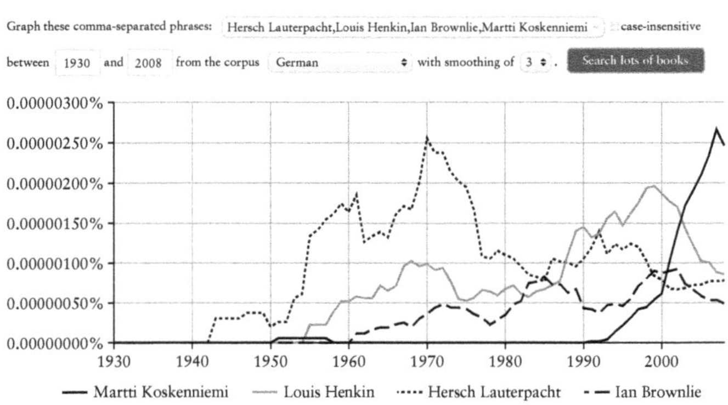


**Figure 9: Graph depicting frequency of usage of the names 'Hersch Lauterpacht', 'Louis Henkin', 'Ian Brownlie' and 'Martti Koskenniemi' in the German corpus, from 1930 to 2008 (source: Google ngram viewer).**

The above graphs are interesting in a number of ways. One might note, for instance, the relative dominance of Louis Henkin in the American English corpus, or the recent meteoric rise to prominence of Martti Koskenniemi in the German corpus. A more subtle observation is that, from the time of Hersch Lauterpacht's death in 1960, references to his name in the American English corpus have declined steadily, whereas in the British English corpus a definite (albeit somewhat inconsistent) posthumous upward trend can be observed.

When undertaking this type of research, one needs to be conscious of the problem of synonymy as a basic source of error. While late twentieth-century instances of the 2-gram 'Hersch Lauterpacht'—as depicted in Figures 7, 8 and 9—are almost certainly references to the celebrated international jurist, instances of the 2-gram 'Robert Jennings' could refer to any number of people who share that relatively common name. If one is interested in tracking the famous professor and former President of the International Court of Justice, it is possible to tweak the search so that it yields more reliable results. One way of improving reliability would be to search for the more specific 3-grams 'Robert Yewdall Jennings' or 'Robert Y Jennings'. The problem of synonymy is a fairly obvious potential source of error. The following section will deal more generally with some of the problems and pitfalls that accompany culturomic analysis.

## IV. PROBLEMS AND PITFALLS

As with all forms of data analysis, the potential for error and bias in culturomics is ever-present. Some of the sources of error and bias are of the merely technical variety. Some are more fundamental.

Technical sources of error include deficiencies in the system of optical character recognition (OCR) that Google uses to digitise books. It is not uncommon for words to be 'misread' by Google's digitising computers. A classic example of this, which Michel and his colleagues pick up on, is the OCR error of mistaking an old-fashioned long 's' for an 'f' in pre-nineteenth-century books.[18] A researcher of eighteenth-century Anglo-American relations engaged in culturomic analysis might never alight on Burke's impassioned comments regarding the 'fufferings and diftreffes of the people of America'.[19]

Technical problems with the data also arise when books are assigned the wrong date. In a year where the occurrence of a particular ngram is common this will not skew the data significantly. However, in a year where the occurrence of a particular ngram is rare (perhaps an early year when relatively few books have been published) the error can generate a spurious peak.[20] We know that the peak in the usage of

[18] Website of the Cultural Observatory, operated by Erez Lieberman Aiden, Jean-Baptiste Michel and others, available at www.culturomics.org/Resources/faq#datainterpretation, Part V: Data Interpretation, para 1.

[19] Burke speech at the Bristol Guildhall (n 10) 42.

[20] Website of the Cultural Observatory (n 18) Part V: Data Interpretation, para 1(ii).

'droits de l'homme' in the early 1790s is not a spurious peak, but this cannot be inferred from a face-value reading of the graph at Figure 3; we must go to the texts and try to figure out what was going on in France at the time. Interpretation is key. While culturomic analysis may serve as a valuable starting point by opening up new pathways towards qualitative insights, it is important to tread down these pathways with care.

The composition of the dataset presents more fundamental problems. For instance, the Google Books database is—as its name suggests—limited to books. Plans to extend the ngram viewer's scope to periodicals and other media have yet to materialise. Michel et al have stated that they 'hope to create similar resources based on magazines, journals, newspapers, patents, and many other aspects of recorded history in the future'.[21]

On a related point, it is important not to lose sight of the fact that the sum of 'culture'—whatever that may be—vastly exceeds what is included in the written record. Indeed, one scholar of Victorian literature, Matthew Bevis, notes that fewer references to a subject may not necessarily mean that it is disappearing from culture, but may instead mean 'that it has become such a part of the fabric of life that it no longer arouses discussion' (he quotes Emily Dickinson: 'Is it oblivion or absorption when things slip from our mind?').[22]

Another fundamental problem is that books in the English language are disproportionately represented in the Google Books database to a huge degree, and many widely spoken and written languages (for example, Arabic, Greek, Hindi and Portuguese, to name but a few) are not represented at all. The large size of the English corpus is a good thing if one is interested in English sources. However, it is important to realise that the Google Books database is very far from being a repository of *global* culture as recorded in books.

The final fundamental problem I will refer to here is what Michel et al call 'library acquisition bias'.[23] The books that Google digitises come from libraries that agree to cooperate with Google. An upward or downward trend in the data may therefore reflect the fact that participating libraries were more or less interested in acquiring books on a given topic. Such a trend does not necessarily reflect the fact that people generally were more or less interested in a given topic at a given time.

## V. CONCLUSION

The theme of this conference—'International law and …'—is explicitly outward-looking, encouraging us to draw connections with other fields and disciplines. I will nevertheless conclude by using culturomics to reflect inwards, and engage in the kind of navel-gazing that international lawyers are typically so fond of.

A relatively new 'wildcard' function in the ngram viewer, where an asterisk is used as a 'placeholder' in a search, allows for an interesting finding (depicted at

[21] Ibid, Part III: Data Contents, para 6.
[22] Matthew Bevis, 'Analyzing Literature by Words and Numbers' *New York Times*, 3 December 2010.
[23] Website of the Cultural Observatory (n 18) Part V: Data Interpretation, para 1(iii).

Figure 10 and Figure 11 below). In the English corpus, the word 'international' is followed much more frequently by the word 'law' than by any other word. In the French corpus, the word 'international' is most frequently preceded by the word 'droit' (although it nearly intersects with the word 'Comité' in the 1940s).

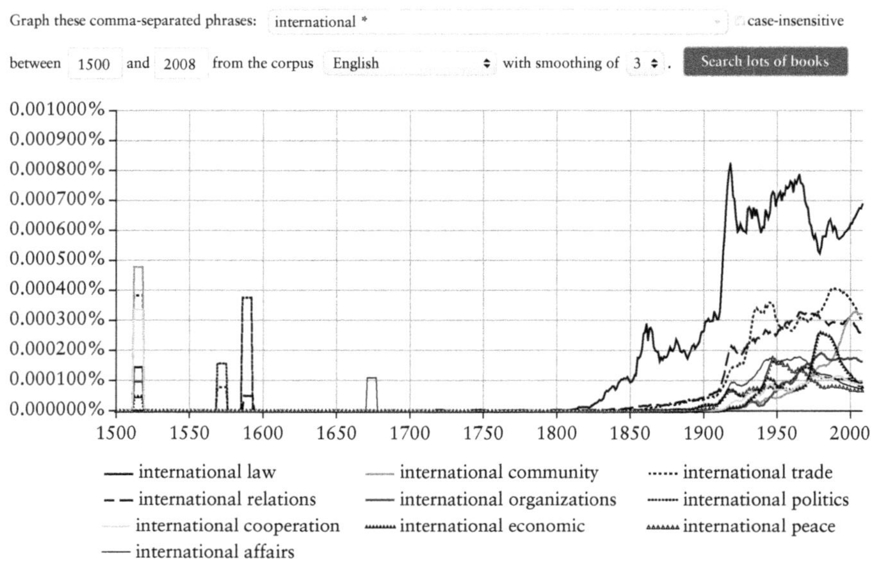


**Figure 10: Graph depicting results of wildcard search for 'international *' in the English corpus, from 1500 to 2008 (source: Google ngram viewer).**

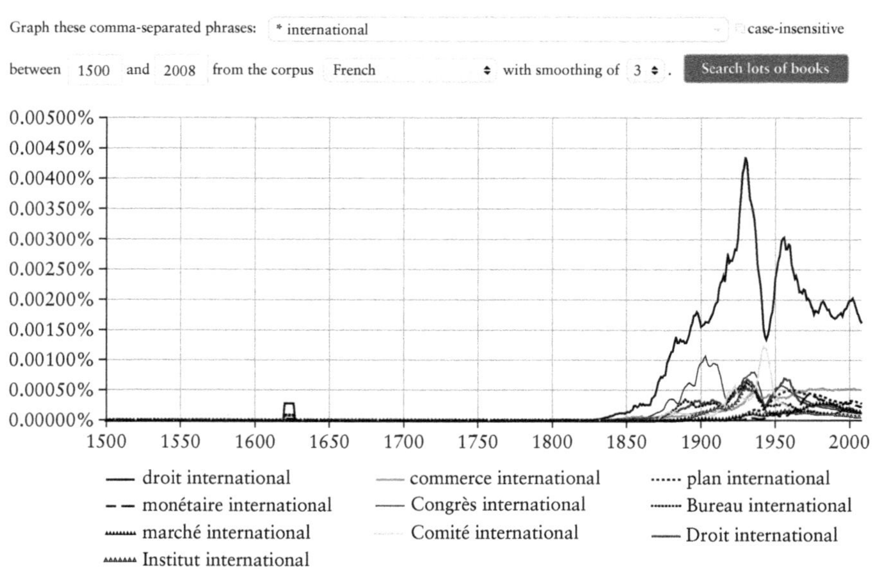


**Figure 11: Graph depicting results of wildcard search for '* international' in the French corpus, from 1500 to 2008 (source: Google ngram viewer).**

Of course, such graphs tell us nothing whatsoever about attitudes towards the concept of international law or about the health of the discipline. A different search can give us a better insight into the types of things people are saying about international law. For example, the graph below depicts the relative frequency of usage of the following phrases from 1800 to 2000: 'the limits of international law', 'the failure of international law', 'the value of international law', and 'the potential of international law'. It suggests, for instance, that the proliferation of writing in English about international law at the end of the First World War may have been, on balance, more cautious than celebratory in tone.

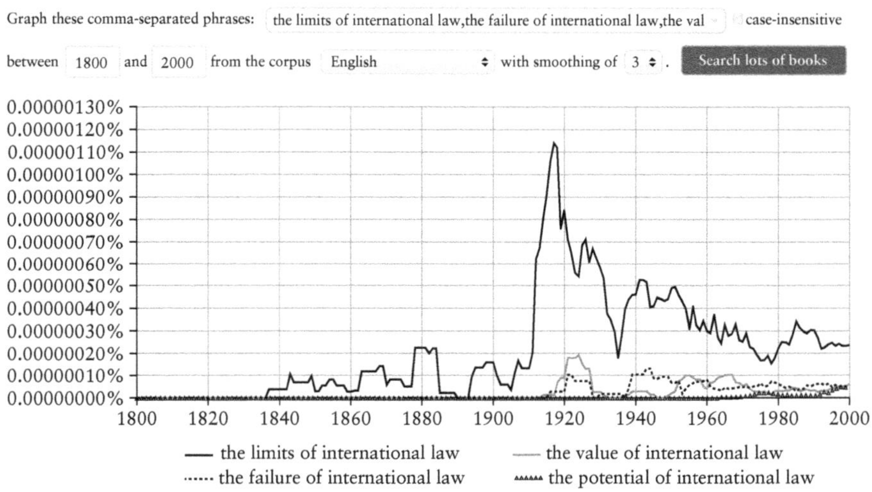


**Figure 12: Graph depicting frequency of usage of the phrases 'the limits of international law', 'the value of international law', 'the failure of international law' and 'the potential of international law' in the English corpus, from 1800 to 2000 (source: Google ngram viewer).**

Obviously, if we wish to acquire a valuable qualitative insight into what people were saying about international law after the First World War, we must read what they wrote. Culturomic analysis is no substitute for the close reading of texts. It may be valuable in and of itself for settling disputes over spelling usage of the 'judgment/judgement' variety, but for the most part it will serve the researcher as a mere point of departure.

While the insights to be gained from a face-value consideration of the graphs at Figure 10 and Figure 11 may be limited, the sheer frequency of usage of the terms 'international law' and 'droit international' suggests that authors in the English and French languages who are interested in international law are publishing rather than perishing. It seems likely that in years to come, the profusion of writing on the subject of international law will be enriched increasingly by insights derived from ever more sophisticated forms of culturomic analysis.

# PART VI

# INTERNATIONAL LAW AND THE SOCIAL AND HUMAN SCIENCES

# 16

# *Opium as an Object of International Law: Doctrines of Sovereignty and Intervention*

JESSIE HOHMANN*

## I. INTRODUCTION

THE STUDY OF international law is highly text-based. Whether as practice, scholarship or pedagogy, the discipline both relies on and produces a wealth of written material. Cases, treaties and volumes of academic writing are the legal sources through which most of us working in international law relate to the subject, and at times we might feel such texts are our major project and output.

Yet international law has a rich existence in the world. International law is often developed, conveyed and authorised through objects or images. From the symbolic (the regalia of the head of state), to the mundane (a can of dolphin-safe tuna certified as complying with international trade standards), international legal authority can be found in the objects around us. Similarly, the practice of international law often relies on material objects or images, both as evidence (satellite images, bones of the victims of mass atrocities) and to establish authority (for instance, maps and charts).

Drawing on these insights, this paper seeks to investigate two questions. First, what might studying international law through objects reveal? What might objects, rather than texts, tell us about the way international law constructs notions of sovereignty, the way it authorises practices of intervention, or the way it justifies participation in the international community through rights to trade?

Second, what might this scholarly undertaking reveal about the objects—as *aims* or *projects*—of international law? How do objects reveal, or perhaps mask, these aims, and what does this tell us about the reasons some (physical or material) objects are foregrounded, and others hidden or ignored?

In this chapter, I will investigate these questions through one specific material object: opium. Opium, the drug produced from the seed pods of the opium poppy

* PhD, Lecturer in Law, Queen Mary, University of London. This paper has emerged from an ongoing research project, 'International Law's Objects' which I am undertaking with Dr Daniel Joyce of the University of New South Wales. I am grateful to Professor Guglielmo Verdirame for his suggestion of opium as an object of study for this project during one of our (too infrequent but) always thought-provoking conversations.

(*papaver somniferum*), has long been traded between states and peoples.[1] Thus it has long been a subject of states' international relations. However, I will frame my argument around specific 'moments' when opium has surfaced as an object of international law in the last three centuries: first, in the Opium Wars fought between Britain and China in the 1800s, second, the United States (US)-led 'War on Drugs', and finally, the 'War on Terror'. Other moments might have been selected, and these might have illustrated quite different facets of international law, but they remain to be analysed on a future occasion.[2]

Each of these moments in which opium has emerged as an object of international law has revealed tensions between the legal doctrine of sovereignty under international law, and the commitments of the international system to particular forms of trade, and to certain moral norms. In this way, international law's relationship with opium's production, trade and even the morality of its use reveal particular fissures and discontinuities in international law, which remain hidden in text-centred accounts.

## II. OPIUM AS OBJECT

The opium poppy was traditionally cultivated across central Asia, and its products used for medicinal, spiritual and recreational purposes.[3] Historically, India, Afghanistan and Burma have figured prominently as producing states. But in recent times, the poppy has also been cultivated in Mexico and Columbia, among other regions.[4]

After the Second World War, scientific advances led to the development of a wide range of opiates derived from the poppy, which include heroin, codeine and morphine.[5] These drugs have had important—even revolutionary—medical applications.[6] But opiates have also been used recreationally by broad swathes of the public. As well as the smoking of opium, opiates have also been consumed in popular drinks and tonics, as well as taken through intravenous injection.[7]

Until 1961, opiates were regulated bilaterally,[8] and even in the 1960s, some states saw no reason at all to regulate their trade or use under international law.[9] Certainly,

[1] Ethan Nadelmann, 'Global Prohibition Regimes: The Evolution of Norms in International Society' (1990) 44(4) *International Organization* 479, 502–503.

[2] For interesting studies of other such moments, see Hans Derks, *History of the Opium Problem: Assault on the East ca 1600–1950* (Leiden, Brill, 2012).

[3] Jay Sinha, *The History and Development of the Leading International Drug Control Conventions, Prepared for the Senate Special Committee on Illegal Drugs* (Library of Parliament, Parliament of Canada, 2001) 1; Nadelmann (n 1) 502–503.

[4] Martin Jelsma, *The Development of International Drug Control: Lessons Learned and Strategic Challenges* (2010) 10 *Transnational Institute Series on Legislative Reform of Drug Policies* 4.

[5] Nadelmann (n 1) 504.

[6] Ibid 505.

[7] Ibid 504–505.

[8] Sinha (n 3) 8.

[9] Ibid 20.

the production, trade and consumption of opiates were not viewed as criminal and thus were not subject to international prohibition as they are now.

The current international law regime which controls opium responds to all facets of the drug's production, from cultivation to harvest, refinement and trade, with strict prohibition. The manufacture, use and sale of the drugs produced from the opium poppy are currently stringently regulated by international law through a variety of International Conventions, the most relevant being the 1961 Single Convention on Narcotic Drugs, and its 1972 Amending Protocol (hereinafter the 'Single Convention').[10] Thus, the vast majority of those involved in the cultivation, production or trade of opium and opiates are immediately plunged into a world of criminality. From the peasant farmer to the internationally-connected money launderer, every individual involved in the illicit opium trade steps outside the law.

Through its regulation by the Single Convention, opium is clearly and straightforwardly an object of international law. This conclusion is not particularly illuminating. However, beginning with opium as an object—a physical substance grown, harvested, refined, traded and consumed—allows us to consider how we have arrived at the point where *all* these aspects of opium's existence in the world are governed by a framework of prohibition and criminalisation.[11] Reflecting on this trend powerfully illuminates particular paradoxes in the logic of international law. Specifically, in this contribution I consider the paradoxes raised by interventions in sovereign territory; interventions through trade; and moral interventions.

## A. Opium, Sovereignty and Territorial Interventions

In order to enjoy sovereignty, a state must achieve two things. First, it must 'spatialise' territory: that is, it must establish control, authority and power over the geographical area of its territory.[12] Second, it must establish a framework of power—that is, sovereignty—over a geographical area, turning space *into* territory.[13] Both are necessary, and as such, make control over territory crucial to the existence of sovereignty.[14] Sovereignty attaches to a state, once recognised as a state, regardless of its internal political conditions or relative power position vis-à-vis other states.[15]

[10] Single Convention on Narcotic Drugs, 1961, New York, 30 March 1961, as amended by the 1972 Protocol Amending the 1961 Convention, Geneva, 25 March 1972 entered into force 8 August 1975, 976 UNTS, 105.

[11] Sinha (n 3) ii.

[12] Rachel Kallus and Hubert Law-Yone, 'National Home/Personal Home: Public Housing and the Shaping of National Space in Israel' (2002) 10 *European Planning Studies* 765, 767.

[13] *Nationality Decrees in Tunis and Morocco*, PCIJ Rep Series B No 4 (1923) (France, Pleadings) Series C No 2, 106, 108.

[14] Montevideo Convention on the Rights and Duties of States, Montevideo, 26 December 1933, entered into force, 26 December 1934, 19 LNTS (1933), Article 1.

[15] See Emer de Vattel, *The Law of Nations, Or, the Principles of Natural Law Applied to the Conduct and to the Affairs of Nations and of Sovereigns* (1758), with Three Early Essays on the Origin and Nature of Natural Law and on Luxury, edited and with an Introduction by Béla Kapossy and Richard Whitmore (Indianapolis, Liberty Fund 2008) Book I, Preliminaries s 18. See also Badinter Commission, Opinion No 1 (1991) 92 ILR 165.

And, at least post-UN Charter, 'sovereignty once achieved is entrenched'.[16] Once recognised as sovereign, a state's grip on territory is cemented in law, with little regard to the facts on the ground. The uninvited physical intrusion of one state into another's territory thus presents an affront to the most fundamental tenet of the international legal system, based as it is around the cardinal organisational principle of sovereign statehood. This is reflected, and protected, in Articles 2(4) and 2(7) of the UN Charter.

Yet a study of opium as an object of international law must consider how struggles to control opium's trade and production have led to or justified very real incursions into sovereign territory. This can be seen in all three of our examples: the Opium Wars, the 'War on Drugs', and the 'War on Terror'.

The Opium Wars were military conflicts, waged against China primarily by Britain. The purpose of the campaigns was to protect China as a lucrative market for Western opium exports from India.[17] The war for the Chinese populace as a market for opium had been hard fought and was seen as critical, as it gave Western states, and Britain in particular, the financial power to buy Chinese tea, porcelain and silk, for which the British had an insatiable appetite.[18] After China lost the First Opium War in 1842, it was forced by coercive 'unequal' treaties (most notably the treaty of Nanking)[19] to accept British merchant ships in its harbours, and traders in its ports. In addition to opening its territory to traders and government officials, it was also forced to surrender territory: the Island of Hong Kong was ceded to Britain in perpetuity.[20]

These incursions into China's sovereign territory were justified within the framework of international legal argument, rather than treated as a breach. The justification for the imposition of the unequal terms of the treaties was that China could not be seen as fully civilised, a test met only by a 'government capable of controlling white men [and] under which white civilisation can exist'[21] and was thus not fully sovereign. As such, it was not owed the territorial integrity which attached to fully sovereign states. Crucially, international law was used as a tool to force intervention, explicitly wielded against China, due to its refusal to accept the opium trade. If opium was the end, international law was the means to control and possess it.

[16] James Crawford, 'Sovereignty as a Legal Value' in James Crawford and Martti Koskenniemi (eds), *Cambridge Companion to International Law* (Cambridge, Cambridge University Press, 2012) 120.

[17] Studies of the Opium Wars, the details of which are beyond the scope of this paper, can be found in PW Fay, *The Opium War 1840–42* (Chapel Hill, University of North Carolina Press, 1975); Brian Inglis, *The Opium War* (London, Hodder & Stoughton, 1976).

[18] Alain Peyrefitte, *The Immobile Empire—The first great collision of East and West—the astonishing history of Britain's grand, ill-fated expedition to open China to Western Trade, 1792–94* (New York, Alfred A Knopf, 1992) 520.

[19] Treaty of Nanking (Treaty of Peace, Friendship and Commerce between Her Majesty the Queen of Great Britain and Ireland and the Emperor of China) Nanking, 29 August 1842 entered into force 26 June 1843, 93 Consolidated Treaty Series 465.

[20] Ibid Article 3.

[21] Lassa Oppenheim (ed), *The Collected Papers of John Westlake on International Law* (Cambridge, Cambridge University Press, 2014) 145 and see 143–44. See also Ellery C Stowell, *International Law: A Restatement of Principles in Conformity with Actual Practice* (New York, Henry Holt and Company, 1931) 367–68.

China was not a lone victim of such unequal treatment. Before the UN Charter, sovereignty had not attained its entrenched status, and states appeared and disappeared as the result of war and diplomacy. Force and power played more obvious roles in international relations. The Opium Wars, however, are of particular interest because these incidents illustrate how international law structures opportunities for intervention through its own doctrines, obscuring power's play behind the use of clear and objective rules. We return to other aspects of this point later in the chapter.[22] But for now, we will consider territorial interventions in the 'War on Drugs' and 'War on Terror'.

If sovereignty is now an entrenched fact, the 'War on Drugs' and the 'War on Terror' raise even more complex issues of intervention. Both are post-UN Charter phenomena, yet both have resulted in incursions into state territory justified by the role some states have played in the global production of opium and opiates.

One might be surprised to think of the US-led 'War on Drugs' as a moment when opium became an object of international law, given the fact that opium's international legal status as an illicit narcotic was cemented in 1961 with the Single Convention.[23] However, the US 'War on Drugs' had a clear international dimension from the very beginning. Making a war on drugs a foreign policy objective, the US tied its national drug policy to its strategic foreign policy goals and interests, and thus, inexorably perhaps, to future military interventions.[24]

Moreover, the enemy in this war on drugs, at least as portrayed in popular culture, was almost universally referred to as emanating from South America, and to be not opium but cocaine, refined from the coca plant.[25] Opium was, to a large extent, off the radar of the 'War on Drugs'. Yet this very silence should speak volumes to us about the relationship between opium and international law. The fact that opium did not figure strongly in this popular picture of the 'War on Drugs' has, partly, to do with fluctuating markets for coca-based products vis-à-vis opiates,[26] but much to do with the US's strategic interests in opium-producing countries, notably Afghanistan, as will emerge below.

The US 'certifies' drug producing states, in line with the requirements of the Single Convention.[27] Certification is given to states which can show falling production of illicit drug crops.[28] The certification system gives the appearance of a technical, dispassionate standard applied with scientific rigour. Yet certification is also based on a state's willingness to cooperate with the US in drug eradication *and* on the US's own foreign policy interests.[29] The low profile of opium-producing countries during

[22] See further sections II B and II C.

[23] Single Convention (n 10).

[24] Curtis Marez, *Drug Wars: The Political Economy of Narcotics* (Minneapolis, University of Minnesota Press, 2004) 4.

[25] Ibid 3.

[26] Julia Buxton, *The Political Economy of Narcotics: Production, Consumption and Global Markets* (Canada, Fernwood Publishing, 2006) ch 6.

[27] Single Convention (n 10) Article 21 (especially Article 21(4)) and Article 21 *bis*.

[28] Ibid Articles 20–25.

[29] Pierre-Arnaud Chouvy, *Opium: Uncovering the Politics of the Poppy* (Cambridge, Harvard University Press, 2010) 105–106.

the phases of highest rhetoric of the 'War on Drugs', when Colombia, for example, was seen as an outcast and regularly the arena of military intervention,[30] is thus a reflection of the US's cold war politics, not its stance on opium production *per se*.

This strategic approach to the producers of illicit opium has continued through the 'War on Terror'. Afghanistan has been certified by the US since the fall of the Taliban despite increased poppy cultivation within the state.[31] This again illustrates the role of strategic interests and foreign policy, which has carried on through the 'War on Terror', despite the rhetorical links made between illicit drug production, corruption and instability in Afghanistan.[32]

If we contrast Afghanistan's treatment with that meted out to Burma, we see that strategic foreign policy is an overriding concern. As Chouvy notes: 'Afghanistan is part of the democratization, state-building agenda and counter-terrorism efforts of the US administration, while Burma—a military dictatorship with a long record of human rights violations, and an ally of China—remains a pariah state.'[33] The intervention or non-intervention in a drug-producing state is, thus, not a decision based on a scientific formula dictated by international legal prohibition. Rather, power interests that are decidedly extra-legal are at play.

### B. Rights to Trade: Creating Licit and Illicit Markets in Opium

Military intervention in sovereign territory may be the most striking of interventions in a state. Yet the physical entry of forces into a state is by no means the only intrusion facilitated by international law that opium illuminates.

Regimes of trade, carried on the back of international law, have also constituted interventions in states where opium is produced or where it finds a market. These interventions may be subtle, as is the case where increased prohibition of opium's production and trade creates new markets or changes existing markets, resulting in shifts in livelihoods, criminal markets and patterns of official corruption.[34] Or, they may be striking. The British–Chinese Opium Wars are an example of trade-driven intervention in the extreme.

The international trade regime is founded on liberalisation as 'normalcy'. Freedom to trade rests at the heart of the system, and is seen as desirable.[35] Certainly, there are exceptions to freedom of trade, and some of these are significant: as Chantal Thomas puts it, trade liberalisation as normalcy is 'emphatically conceptual, rather than empirical'.[36] Nevertheless, the conceptual or ideological commitment to free trade is clear. The regime governing the trade of opium conflicts with efforts

[30] Ibid 113.
[31] Ibid 106.
[32] Ibid.
[33] Ibid 107.
[34] See Jonathan Goodhand, 'Corrupting or Consolidating the Peace? The Drugs Economy and Post-conflict Peacebuilding in Afghanistan' (2008) 15(3) *International Peacekeeping* 405.
[35] Chantal Thomas 'Disciplining Globalization: International Law, Illegal Trade, and the Case of Narcotics' (2003) 24 *Michigan Journal of International Law* 549, 558–59 and 563–64.
[36] Ibid 563.

to decrease trade regulation. Over the past 100 years, while regulation has been stripped away elsewhere, it has been laid in an increasingly tight net over the opium trade, both justifying further physical interventions in territory, and also resulting in more subtle interventions: those wrought by changed market conditions themselves.

Prior to the twentieth century, the opium trade was backed by the powerful British Empire, for which the trade in opium from its Indian colony to China was a highly significant source of revenue. It was so significant, in fact, that Britain was willing to protect this trade, against the wishes of the Chinese government, with military force in the Opium Wars.

It would not be fully accurate to describe this trade as *free*, of course: China was not a willing participant, and the British trade travelled through monopolies.[37] It is the case, however, that the trade was not the subject of criminalisation or prohibition through international law. Yet international law played a striking role in the Opium Wars, a point we return to below in our discussion of morality in international law.

It was not until the 1960s that an international legal framework for the prohibition and regulation of opium coalesced, slowly gelling from a miscellany of bilateral treaties, into the 1961 Single Convention.[38] The contemporary regime is based around strong criminal prohibitions. Opiates, along with other narcotic drugs, appear from this regime as strictly *illegal*. Yet legal trade interests have played a significant role in the way international law regulates opium.

First, it is important to note that only *illicit* markets are prohibited: the opium poppy remains the ultimate source of many important medical drugs, and the *licit* market in these drugs is preserved.[39] Afghanistan, Mexico and Burma are pariah states not because they produce the opium poppy, but because they do so for the illicit market. No such stigma attaches to Australia, France, Hungary or Turkey, for example, all of which are among the major licit producers for the world pharmaceutical market.[40]

The system of state-controlled and licenced production provided for by the Single Convention thus echoes the monopoly on trade exercised by Britain in the nineteenth century, when select states controlled the trade in opium and opiates, and others bore the brunt of their trade policies. More recently, states unable or unwilling to control the illicit market have also become pariahs, subject to sanction and censure. We see this clearly in both the 'War on Drugs', and the 'War on Terror'.

Although the 'War on Terror' had no necessary connection to the production of opium, and it was not initially a focus of the intervention in Afghanistan,[41]

[37] See further, Mark S Gaylord, 'Hong Kong' in Jurg Gerber and Eric L Jensen (eds), *Drug War American Style: The Internationalization of Failed Policy and its Alternatives* (London and New York, Routledge, 2001) 61–62. Gaylord notes that the Chinese condemned the taking of opium as a destructive vice and notes that the trade became a monopoly in 1844.

[38] Single Convention (n 10).

[39] Ibid Article 19. It is also noteworthy that the 1971 Convention on Psychotropic Substances (Convention on Psychotropic Substances, Vienna, 21 February 1971, entered into force 16 August 1976, 1019 UNTS, 175), which regulates synthetic drugs, is significantly weaker due to pressures from the states with strong pharmaceutical industries producing and trading in those substances. See eg Article 2 'Scope of Control of Substances'. See further Jelsma (n 4) 3.

[40] See Jelsma, ibid at 4.

[41] Goodhand (n 34) 405 and 409.

cultivation of the poppy was seen as increasingly linked to funding for terrorism, political corruption and instability,[42] and thus to the state's overall failed or outlaw status.[43] Ironically, perhaps, once opium became an illicit substance in Afghanistan, where it had previously been treated as a licit crop,[44] the nature of the market changed substantially with increases in prices reflecting the 'risk premium' borne by those involved in it.[45] Thus the imposition of the international legal framework changed, and even created, a new type of market for opium.

The 'War on Drugs', too, has created new markets. The US spends in excess of $35 billion each year in waging it.[46] As Curtis Marez notes:

> The aerospace industry (which supplies drug enforcement planes, helicopters, and other technology), chemical companies (which produce the poisons that are dropped on drug fields), and the prison industry directly benefit from the drug war and hence actively lobby for its continued expansion.[47]

And then there is the contribution of drug money, which accounts for US $400 billion per year (or 2 per cent of the global economy), to international investment and capital flows through money laundering.[48] Even government departments, notably the US's Drug Enforcement Administration (DEA), are beneficiaries of drug prohibition, with ever-increasing budgets and staffing as illicit opium production grows.[49]

The anomalous position of opium production as an ever-more regulated and criminalised market in an overall system of trade liberalisation also reflects the fact that a small handful of states constitute the potential producers, while other states can only be markets for the product. Those states which do not benefit from the production of opiates, and suffer only the social consequences of their misuse, have little market incentive to encourage a lucrative trade for others. Ethan Nadelmann writes:

> The fact that alcohol and tobacco have ended up with the official approval of international society while opium, coca and cannabis were in effect decertified did not, it should be stressed, reflect any objective calculation of their potential harm, since in many respects the former present greater health and societal risks than do the latter substances. Rather, alcohol was legitimized in good part by the fact that it could be produced and consumed in the great majority of societies.[50]

One factor, therefore, of opium's prohibited status is the trade interests of powerful states in regulating a product which they cannot produce. The irony lies in the fact

[42] World Bank, 'Afghanistan—State Building, Sustaining Growth and Reducing Poverty' (World Bank Country Study, Washington, DC, 2005). The assumption that failed or weak states provide good environments for organised criminal activity can, however, be challenged. See eg Diego Gambetta, *The Sicilian Mafia: The Business of Private Protection* (Cambridge, Harvard University Press, 1993). See also Goodhand (n 34) 416 and 419.

[43] Goodhand (n 34) 413.

[44] Ibid 409.

[45] Ibid.

[46] Moisés Naím, 'The Five Wars of Globalization' (2003) 134 *Foreign Policy* 28.

[47] Marez (n 24) 5.

[48] Ibid.

[49] Chouvy (n 29) 'As illicit opium production increased from 1,066 tonnes in 1971 to 6,610 tonnes in 2006, so the DEA grew from 1,470 special agents in 1973 to 5,320 in 2006 and its budget increased from US $65 million to US $2.4 billion' 105 [references omitted].

[50] Nadelmann (n 1) 511.

that such prohibition may create in the first place the very lucrative market which would not exist absent prohibition.

Yet another anomaly is illustrated if we focus on the subsistence farmers who grow the poppy in those pariah states in which opium is produced. For many of the often impoverished farmers who grow it, the opium poppy is an important cash crop, providing a source of income and livelihood. But growing the opium poppy is also an entry point as players, however small, in the global capitalist economy. The prohibition of these farmers' capitalist activities illustrates that participation in capitalism is not a matter of free enterprise, but is contingent on the parameters set by powerful players. That these contingencies involve moral judgements is the subject of the following section.

## C. Morality: The Indulgences of International Law

The increasing regulation of opium through international law over the last century powerfully illuminates the role of morality in international law. First, it shows the way moral norms influence the creation of international law, and second, the way in which international law can be used to impose a certain moral vision of behaviour on states and other actors.[51]

The campaign to criminalise and prohibit the production, use and trade in opium at the international level was undeniably a moral one. Moving from a situation in the nineteenth century where 'no global patterns were discernible in the norms and legal sanctions governing the trade and use of [opium]' we now find ourselves in a world where the vast majority of states support the global prohibition regime underpinned by the 1961 Single Convention.[52]

The role of moral norms in the creation of this regime is striking. Nadelmann notes that:

> The processes by which this regime has evolved must be understood as a confluence of the perceptions, interests, and moral notions among dominant sectors of the more powerful states along with the exceptional influence of American protagonists in shaping the regime according to their preferred norms.[53]

Among the important 'moral entrepreneurs' were religious movements such as the Quakers, and missionaries returned to the West from the Far East.[54] These actors—including key individuals[55]—were instrumental. The US, over all other states, was

[51] It goes without saying that opium also shows that international law can be used in highly immoral ways and to effect highly immoral outcomes.

[52] Nadelmann (n 1) 503.

[53] Ibid.

[54] Ibid 504.

[55] Sinha (n 3) 4 notes that 'Certain individuals stand out in the history of international drug control. While in positions of power, at opportune moments, their beliefs, morals, ambitions and single-minded determination enabled them to exert exceptional influence over the shape of the international drug regime.' He notes particularly Charles Henry Brent and Dr Hamilton Wright, both of whom were particularly important in setting the US agenda towards a global prohibition regime (at 7); and later, Harry J Anslinger, who was the head of the US Federal Bureau of Narcotics for 30 years (at 14).

the key driver behind the extant regime.[56] And behind the US's position was a particular moral stance on *vice*. Indulgence of any form (including not only the consumption of narcotics, but also alcohol, prostitution and tobacco) was viewed as abhorrent and sinful.[57] Rather than an innocent preoccupation with clean living, fears of immigrants and the poor, and concerns over the labour productivity of the worker, fuelled the prohibitionist climate.[58] Even now, as Marez argues, 'the "drug war" ultimately impacts intimate details of subjectivity and social relations, serving as formative, structuring content for ideas and practices concerning race, gender, class, sexuality and nation'.[59]

The Opium Wars, which occurred before the prohibition regime now governing opium in international law, illuminate the second aspect of morality and international law. Here, international law was used as an instrument through which certain moral standards could be demanded. China was forced to sign 'unequal treaties' which limited and regulated its sovereignty.[60] The justification for these treaties was that China could not be seen as fully civilised, a test met only by a 'government capable of controlling white men [and] under which white civilisation can exist'.[61] Even if these treaties were considered legal,[62] China's 'delinquency'[63] in meeting these standards was used to justify the imposition of highly unequal practices. Even where the treaties granted equal rights on paper, little equality ensued. As Jack Donnelly puts it: 'China's profound lack of interest in obtaining such rights was conveniently overlooked.'[64]

Such moves on the part of Britain and other members of the 'civilised' states were justified according to the theory of positivism. Positivism purported to give international law an objectivity, garnered from the facts as they were, thus giving it access to 'a higher and decisive truth'.[65] Yet the standard for admittance to the club of civilisation rested undeniably on a subjective assessment of what, ultimately, amounted to control over and existence of white civilisation. Such a standard carries with it a presumption that what civilisation entails is both unchallenged and unproblematic.

Far from a historical state of affairs, the morality of indulgence continues to fuel the ever-tighter net of regulation laid over opium, at the same time as it demands that particular moral standards are met. Hamid Karzai, president of Afghanistan between 2001 and 2014, has invoked a rhetoric of 'religious sin and collective shame' to combat the normalcy of opium production in Afghanistan.[66] Afghanistan's perceived

[56] See Nadelmann (n 1) 511. See further Sinha (n 3).
[57] Nadelmann (n 1) 506.
[58] Ibid.
[59] Marez (n 24) 4.
[60] This treaty formed the 'cornerstone' of the system of unequal treaties. See Jack Donnelly, 'Human Rights: A New Standard of Civilization?' (1998) 74(1) *International Affairs* 1, 7.
[61] Oppenheim (n 21) 145; see also 143–44.
[62] See Antony Anghie, *Imperialism, Sovereignty, and the making of International Law* (Cambridge, Cambridge University Press, 2007) 72.
[63] Stowell (n 21) 367–68.
[64] Donnelly (n 60) 7.
[65] Anghie (n 62) 66. See further, Monica Garcia-Salmones, *The Project of Positivism in International Law* (Oxford, Oxford University Press, 2013).
[66] Goodhand (n 34) 417.

failure to reach the standards of a modern state, with an accountable and democratically-elected central administration, equal rights for women, and other modern features of government, illustrates that international law has worked to construct modernity as a moral, not only factual, state of affairs. Reaching modern standards of morality accordingly carries with it certain privileges, conveyed through international legal norms, such as the right to be free from interventions in one's sovereign territory, and the benefits of membership in the international trade regime.

## III. CONCLUSION

As this contribution illuminates, the international regime governing the cultivation of the opium poppy, and the manufacture and trade of opium and opiates, powerfully illuminates the various interventions enabled by international legal prohibition and criminalisation. Control of opium through international law has facilitated obvious interventions into sovereign territory such as the forced opening of China's territories and the cession of Hong Kong under the Treaty of Nanking. International law's response to illicit opium production also reinforces and creates opportunities to intervene, as illustrated by the 'War on Drugs' and the 'War on Terror', even if these opportunities are exercised selectively as the US's different attitudes to Afghanistan and Burma illustrates.

But international law's relationship with opium also enables more subtle, if no less significant, interventions.The international legal regime of prohibition of opium also creates and structures markets, influencing the position of everyone involved in opium production. From the subsistence farmer hoping to gain a foothold on the first rung of the ladder of world capitalism, to the budgets of domestic government drug agencies, to the profits of global pharmaceutical companies, international law creates markets, and simultaneously controls their legitimacy or illegitimacy.

Opium as an object also reveals how powerfully moral norms structure international law. A positivist approach to international law, so long dominant in the Westphalian system, is couched in objective neutrality, yet attitudes to sin, indulgence and even what it means to be 'modern' infuse the regulation of opium's production, cultivation and trade, and have a direct influence on how states are governed under it.

Considering opium as an object of international law reveals the centrality of international law to the lives of those from the Afghan farmer to the head of a Swiss Bank, and shines a light on the way international law penetrates and intervenes in multiple aspects of each state's sovereignty. In sum, considering opium as an object is a way of interrogating the relationship between the doctrine of sovereignty and international law's commitment to moral norms and free trade, as well as the limits of these commitments.

# 17

# *International Law in Transit: The Concept of 'Indigenous Peoples' and its Transitions in International, National and Local Realms—the Example of the Bedouin in the Negev*

EMMA NYHAN*

## I. INTRODUCTION

THE QUESTION OF how global legal norms transit between international and national realms preoccupies scholars across disciplinary divides.[1] The objective of this contribution is to shed light on how the Bedouin in southern Israel have *gradually* become indigenous, and to illuminate the ways in which international legal concepts and categories become active and effective in the national

* Emma Nyhan is a PhD researcher at the European University Institute (Italy), and holds a LMM degree from Universität Konstanz (Germany) and Barrister-at-Law qualification from King's Inns (Ireland).

[1] Since the 1970s, anthropology and law have been actively, and in recent times collaboratively, engaged in questions on indigenous peoples. In law, for instance, Benedict Kingsbury's work on the concept of indigenous peoples and its application in South-East Asia offers a unique insight into law's production internationally and reproduction locally. In anthropology, and legal anthropology in particular, we witness how anthropologists are attempting to map law's movement in and outside different legal systems. Here, Sally Engle Merry's recent work on women's rights, focusing on gender violence, is fitting. Somewhat similar to Engle Merry but directing her focus on indigenous peoples, Karen Engle traces the development of global rights of indigenous peoples and their transplantation in the Caribbean context, looking at the case of the African-Colombians. See Benedict Kingsbury, *Indigenous Groups and the Politics of Recognition in Asia: Cases from Japan, Taiwan, West Papua, Bali, the People's Republic of China and Gilgit* (Brill, 2004); Benedict Kingsbury, 'The Applicability of the International Concept of "Indigenous Peoples" in Asia' in Joanne R Bauer and Daniel A Bell (eds), *The East Asian Challenge for Human Rights* (Cambridge University Press, 1999); Benedict Kingsbury, '"Indigenous Peoples" in International Law: A Constructivist Approach to the Asian Controversy' 92 *The American Journal of International Law* (1998) 414; Sally Engle Merry, *Human Rights and Gender Violence: Translating International Law into Local Justice* (University of Chicago Press, 2009); Karen Engle, *The Elusive Promise of Indigenous Development: Rights, Culture, Strategy* (Duke University Press Books, 2010).

realm. In particular, this chapter attempts to elucidate the mobilisation of the concept of 'indigenous peoples'[2] from the international to the national by the Bedouin in Negev,[3] who are increasingly employing the concept of indigenous peoples, and engaging in the indigenous peoples' movement, transnational networks and programmatic activities. Therefore, this intervention draws attention to the role of international law in the conceptualisation and legalisation of indigenous peoples and the justification for indigenous recognition, or non-recognition, for collectives like the Bedouin in Israel.[4] What will become clear is that the transit of law and the interplay between the international and the national not only produces inconsistencies, uncertainties and indeterminacy at the theoretical level but also generates tensions, hybridities, frictions and new subjectivities and new legal and political dynamics at the national and international level. Acknowledging the mutually informative nature of law and knowledge production, this study offers a unique insight into the ways in which international law is transformed and studied in the era of globalisation and global interconnections; a development that challenges key distinctions and categories upon which our concept of international law is premised.

This chapter can be divided roughly into three sections. Section II—The Concept of Indigenous Peoples in the International Realm—analyses how the concept of indigenous peoples is defined in international law. The study begins by tracing the origins of the concept and then goes on to explore its conceptualisation in scholarship and international law. Section III—The 'Vernacularisation of Human Rights' Model and the Transit of Law—offers a comprehensive conceptual framework, derived from the work of Engle Merry, to better understand how law transits between international and national realms. Section IV—The Concept of Indigenous Peoples in the National and Local Realm—endeavours to provide concrete insight into how the global becomes vernacularised domestically, which encompasses the national and the local level.[5] The case of the Bedouin citizens of Israel, and specifically the unrecognised village of Al-Araqib,[6] is illustrative in this respect.

[2] This is the first and only time I insert the term indigenous peoples in quotation marks. I do this in order to stress its questionable descriptive value and substantive content; however, for the remainder of the chapter I refrain from using quotation marks.

[3] The Negev is a desert and semi-desert area located in southern Israel, which is framed by borders with Egypt on the South and Jordan on the East. It extends over half of Israel's land area.

[4] See Kingsbury, '"Indigenous Peoples" in International Law: A Constructivist Approach to the Asian Controversy' (n 1) 444.

[5] Engle Merry (n1) 1.

[6] Unrecognised villages are not officially recognised even though some pre-exist the establishment of the State of Israel and others were set up during Israeli Military Rule (1948–1966), when the Bedouin tribes were relocated to an enclosed area called the *siyag* (Arabic for 'fence'). Today, they are formally classified as *pezurah* (Hebrew for 'dispersion'), or illegal clusters. These villages do not feature on maps and do not receive basic services such as water, health care, education and transportation. While it is difficult to obtain statistical data, it is believed that there are some 45 such villages with approximately 90,000 residents, all of whom are citizens of the State of Israel.

## II. THE CONCEPT OF INDIGENOUS PEOPLES IN THE INTERNATIONAL REALM

### A. Introduction

Scholars remain puzzled by the concept of indigenous peoples in international law. While recognising the conceptual challenges for theoretical analysis,[7] most commentators argue against 'a rigorous definition, one that in effect tries to close the intellectual borders where they were still porous'.[8] Even if unanimous consensus existed in theory, there remains the empirical question when determining a group's indigenousness,[9] in which a 'web of ethical, political and epistemological considerations' is at work.[10] Both practitioners and scholars agree that when a group is recognised as indigenous in international law, it is entitled to exercise a set of tailor-made collective rights, also referred to as special rights.[11] In the light of the concept's theoretical and practical ambiguities, which are arguably its most significant features, the purpose of this section is to unpack its contemporary meaning.

The section begins with a synopsis of the evolution of the term indigenous, followed by a sample of indigenous peoples' definitions formulated by scholars. This serves to set the stage for my examination of the concept of indigenous peoples in international law. It is helpful to outline the definitions developed by the International Labour Organization (ILO) and the World Bank, followed by a more extensive account of the definition by the United Nations (UN), which has taken the lead in its conceptualisation and legalisation at the international level.

[7] It is worth noting that indigenous peoples' analytical framework is one of several competing conceptual frameworks used to analyse indigenous peoples' claims. Besides the framework of indigenous peoples, Benedict Kingsbury lists four other conceptual frameworks applicable to indigenous peoples, which are: human rights and non-discrimination, minority rights, self-determination and historic sovereignty. See Benedict Kingsbury, 'Reconciling Five Competing Conceptual Structures of Indigenous Peoples' Claims in International and Comparative Law' in Philip Alston (ed), *Peoples' Rights* (Oxford University Press, 2008) 69.

[8] Ronald Niezen, *The Origins of Indigenism: Human Rights and the Politics of Identity* (University of California Press, 2003) 19. Opposing this position, Ian Brownlie argues that: 'The heavy reliance on the still relatively controversial category of "indigenous peoples" is difficult to understand and, frankly, it smacks of nominalism and a sort of snobbery.' Ian Brownlie, *Treaties and Indigenous Peoples: The Robb Lectures 1991* (Oxford University Press, 1992) 62.

[9] Anthony J Connolly, *Indigenous Rights* (Ashgate Publishing, 2009) xvi.

[10] Patrick Thornberry, *Indigenous Peoples and Human Rights* (Manchester University Press, 2002) 35.

[11] Similar to S James Anaya and Siegfried Wiessner, I use the term 'tailor-made collective rights' as an alternative to the term special rights. The special rights' position stands at odds with the universalist principle accorded to human rights, according to which rights are universal and serve all of humanity. I argue that indigenous rights, as a set of tailor-made collective rights, endeavour to protect them and to guarantee their basic survival and sustainability. Irrespective of their special character, Jeremy Webber describes indigenous rights as 'mediated rights'. In his discussion of the recognition of indigenous rights before the Australian courts, Webber remarks that there is a 'measure of translation and adjustment in the very act of recognition and this process may be unequal. Indigenous rights are mediated rights.' On 'tailor-made collective rights', see S James Anaya and Siegfried Wiessner, 'The UN Declaration on the Rights of Indigenous Peoples: Towards Re-Empowerment' (2007) Academic Commentary, available at www.jurist.org/forum/2007/10/un-declaration-on-rights-of-indigenous.php. On 'mediated rights', see Jeremy Webber, 'Beyond Regret: Mabo's Implications for Australian Constitutionalism' in Duncan Ivison, Paul Patton and Will Sanders (eds), *Political Theory and the Rights of Indigenous Peoples* (Cambridge University Press, 2000) 63.

## B. The Evolution of the Concept

The word indigenous derives etymologically from a Latin word meaning *native* or *born within*. It made its first appearance in the 1940s and 1950s as an English translation in official documents of the Spanish *indígena* and the French *indigène*.[12] In plain language, the contemporary meaning of the term depicts any given people, either an ethnic group or community, in a particular region or location over a period of time. Indigenous, however, has different meanings in different settings and can be evoked by different groups of differing shapes and sizes in a variety of social contexts.[13] It does not easily or non-pejoratively translate from English to different languages. There is an increasingly heavy emphasis placed on its proper and accurate allocation.[14] For these collectives, indigenous identification amounts to an expression of identity and is 'a badge worn with pride, revealing something significant and personal about its wearer's collective attachments'.[15] This pride differs from the historical labelling of indigenous peoples as 'the Other' as illustrated by the stereotypes of Western thought over the centuries.[16] The term indigenous, and other variations of the word such as 'noble', 'ignoble', 'savages' and 'barbarians'[17] can be viewed as a linguistic measure to 'mark the boundaries of a space and a time for the West to inhabit'.[18] Consequently, European colonisers and colonialists employed such terminology in order to keep the colonised in a specific space, separate from the dominating powers both physically and discursively.

It was only during the late twentieth century, around the time of the emergence of the indigenous movement, which took off in the 1970s, when the term indigenous peoples evolved into a distinct legal concept and category in international law.[19]

[12] Chris Tennant, 'Indigenous Peoples, International Institutions, and the International Legal Literature from 1945–1993' (1994) 16(1) *Human Rights Quarterly* 5. For the Spanish origins of the term, Tennant points to ILO documents from the 1940s and 1950s and for the French equivalent he refers to the debates on decolonisation that took place in the UN's Fourth Committee.

[13] James Clifford, *Returns: Becoming Indigenous in the Twenty-First Century* (Harvard University Press, 2013) 14.

[14] In Asia, for instance, the Alliance of Taiwan Aborigines (ATA) made a case before the UN Working Group on Indigenous Peoples (WGIP), challenging the UN translation of indigenous peoples as *tuzu renim*, which connotes 'primitive' and 'low cultural level'. ATA argued for the use of *yuanzu minzu* (indigenous peoples) and *yuanzu min* (indigenous people) as a more appropriate alternative. See Kingsbury. '"Indigenous Peoples" in International Law: A Constructivist Approach to the Asian Controversy' (n 1) 432.

[15] Niezen (n 8) 3.

[16] Here, I refer to Edward Said's account of Otherness in *Orientalism*. In the context of the Empire, Otherness is a term that underscores the perceived weaknesses of marginalised groups, while simultaneously stressing the alleged strength of those in positions of power. Edward Said, *Orientalism* (Penguin, 2003).

[17] See Anthony Pagden, 'Introduction' in Nigel Griffin (ed), *A Short Account of the Destruction of the Indies* (Penguin, 1992) xxix–xxx; Sharon Helen Venne, *Our Elders Understand Our Rights: Evolving International Law Regarding Indigenous Peoples* (Theytus Books, 1998); S Wright, *International Human Rights, Decolonisation and Globalisation* (Routledge, 2001) 46–60. See also S James Anaya, *Indigenous Peoples in International Law* (Oxford University Press, 2004).

[18] Tennant (n 12) 6.

[19] However, it should be noted that the subject of indigenous peoples as well as their involvement in international law has a longer history. The bilateral agreements between indigenous peoples and the European settlers—for example, the *Treaty* of *Waitangi* between Tāngata Whenua and the British Crown—formalised relations between them. Churches and civil society organisations were also

A major turning point for indigenous peoples is how the indigenous peoples and the concept 'featuring extreme localism has come to denote a global array' today.[20] Notwithstanding its terminological indeterminacy and inconsistency in law, this quintessential modern legal term has gained theoretical, legal and political clout, resulting in collective mobilisation, regional and international standard-setting, transnational networking and programmatic activity.[21]

Despite these theoretical and practical shifts, it continues to be an emerging area of legal development, with the potential for further transformation.[22] Attempts to grasp its international conceptualisation highlight '[t]he malleability of the concept of "indigenous" [which] is part of a muddy, but productive, and an ambivalent, but creative, terrain through which and with which indigenous delegates act to make radical claims to culture and territory at the UN'.[23] The legal concept, considered by many to be a social construction,[24] is complex in law and highly politicised because 'so much hinges on being formally identified as indigenous at international and domestic law' for it ultimately admits or denies access to a regime of indigenous rights.[25] Kingsbury succinctly captures the essence of the concept when he observes that if

> 'indigenous peoples' are deemed in international practice to have particular entitlements to land, territory and resources, based on historical connections, customary practices, and the interdependence of land and culture, the question whether a particular group is an indigenous people may take on great political and legal importance.[26]

actively involved with indigenous peoples, which set the stage for indigenous peoples' participation in international forums in the early twentieth century. As early as 1923, Cayuga Chief Deskaheh attempted to meet with the League of Nations as the representative of the Six Nations of the Iroquois. See also Anaya (n 17) 79. See also Manuhuia Barcham, '(De)Constructing the Politics of Identity' in Duncan Ivison, Paul Patton and Will Sanders (eds), *Political Theory and the Rights of Indigenous Peoples* (Cambridge University Press, 2000) 141.

[20] Clifford (n 13). Although the concept is often characterised for its historicity and cultural locality, it is simultaneously associated with global modernity. The latter has propelled the theorisation and legalisation of the concept, which is frequently framed in international, global and transnational terms. Shane Greene, *Customizing Indigeneity: Paths to a Visionary Politics in Peru* (Stanford University Press, 2009) 15.

[21] Kingsbury, '"Indigenous Peoples" in International Law: A Constructivist Approach to the Asian Controversy' (n 1) 414.

[22] Recognising its transformative potential for indigenous peoples, the UN declared the year 1993 as the International Year for the World's Indigenous Peoples. The decade from 1995 to 2004 was declared as the International Decade of the World's Indigenous Peoples under the theme 'Indigenous Peoples: Partnership in Action'. In acknowledgment of the continuing needs of indigenous peoples, the decade from 2005 to 2014 was declared the Second International Decade of the World's Indigenous Peoples. The second decade culminated with the first World Conference on Indigenous Peoples in September 2014, where perspectives and best practices were shared on how to achieve indigenous peoples' rights, specifically those laid down in the United Nations Declaration on the Rights of Indigenous Peoples (UNDRIP).

[23] Andrea Muehlebach, 'What Self in Self-Determination? Notes from the Frontiers of Transnational Indigenous Activism' (2003) 10(2) *Identities* 244.

[24] Anthony J Connolly contends that indigenous peoples represent a phenomenon of social construction, remarking: 'Given the often diverse nature of individual and collective beliefs and values within such communities, conceptual thought and practice is in fact often argumentatively dynamic.' He goes on to say that: 'Where important consequences follow for the peoples within conceptual communities in relation to the content of a concept, this dynamism may become inherently invest-ridden.' Connolly (n 9) xiii.

[25] Ibid.

[26] Kingsbury, '"Indigenous Peoples" in International Law: A Constructivist Approach to the Asian Controversy' (n 1) 444.

## C. Definitions by Scholars

The definitions of indigenous peoples formulated by individual scholars set the stage for the inquiry of the legal definitions formulated by inter-governmental organisations (IGOs). One of the most inclusive definitions of indigenous peoples is that of anthropologist John Bodley who defines indigenous people as 'a group of people who identify themselves with specific, small-scale cultural heritage'.[27] In contemporary anthropology, indigenous is considered a protean term and 'a work in progress, which therefore necessitates a broad definition of indigenous peoples'.[28] Political scientists, in their attempts to define indigenous peoples, also advance a broad definition,[29] and frequently base it on the notion of peoplehood.[30]

Similar to other academic fields, the main preoccupation of legal commentators is how to identify or define those properties, which render a (group of) people indigenous but they do so within a legal framework. These legal thinkers are interested in articulating the necessary and sufficient criteria that identify, or should identify, indigenous peoples as such in law.[31] For instance, Anaya, a legal scholar and former Special Rapporteur on the Rights of Indigenous Peoples, defines indigenous peoples as:

> The living descendants of pre-invasion inhabitants ... because their ancestral roots are imbedded in the lands in which they live, or would like to live, much more deeply than the roots of more powerful sectors of society living on the same lands or in close proximity. Furthermore, they are peoples to the extent they comprise distinct communities with a continuity of existence and identity that links them to communities, tribes or nations of their ancestral past.[32]

Thornberry points to the four overlapping strands, which he considers significant in determining indigenousness: firstly, the connection of a group 'with a *particular place* (usually lengthy) a locality, a region, a country, a State'; secondly, the group's '*prior inhabitation*—"we were here before you, so we are indigenous"'; thirdly, such collectives are seen as the '*original or first inhabitants*'; and fourthly, these groups usually amount to '*distinctive societies*'.[33]

Academic definitions for the most part are deficient in one way or another but they are, nonetheless, recognised as generalizable approaches, which allow for maximum inclusivity and flexibility. These academic approaches do not fully coincide with the more fixed legal approaches, formulated by IGOs, which set out to make the concept work in international law's practice. In contrast with academic definitions, these

[27] John H Bodley, *Victims of Progress* (Altamira Press, 2008) 4.

[28] Clifford (n 13) 14.

[29] For a standard definition, see Gerald R Alfred and Franke Wilmer, *'Indigenous Peoples, States and Conflict'* in David Carment and Patrick James (eds), *Wars in the Midst of Peace: The International Politics of Ethnic Conflict* (University of Pittsburgh Press, 1997) 27.

[30] For an overview of these definitions, see Jeff Corntassel, 'Who Is Indigenous? "Peoplehood" and Ethnonationalist Approaches to Rearticulating Indigenous Identity' (2003) 9(1) *Nationalism and Ethnic Politics* 92.

[31] Connolly (n 9) xiii.

[32] Anaya (n 17) 3.

[33] Thornberry (n 10) 37–39 (emphasis in the original).

working definitions have to balance practical fluidity and open-endedness against legal certainty and stability as will be shown below.

## D. Definitions by Intergovernmental Organisations

In the international community, IGOs, which are engaged directly or indirectly with indigenous peoples, have made several attempts to come up with a working definition of indigenous peoples. The main bodies involved in this enterprise are the ILO, the World Bank and the UN. The golden thread running through each of their definitions is that they are issue-oriented, apply a pragmatic approach, and favour context over abstraction. The ILO was the first international organisation to take up the question of indigenous peoples, when it started to address the working conditions of native workers living in European colonies in 1921. The first multilateral treaty on indigenous peoples was the Indigenous and Tribal Populations Convention, 1957 (No 107), whose original purpose was to assimilate and integrate indigenous people into mainstream society, resonating with the development discourse of the time, when it was adopted.[34] This was followed by the Indigenous and Tribal Populations Convention, 1989 (No 169), which explicitly broke away from its paternalistic approach and assimilative national policies towards indigenous groups.[35] Consistent with its standard-setting endeavours since the 1980s, the World Bank has been working to address poverty and social exclusion among indigenous peoples in client countries, where the organisation is actively engaged or finances projects, and has formulated a number of Operational Policies on Indigenous Peoples to this end.[36]

Compared to the ILO and the World Bank, the UN's working definition of indigenous peoples is the most controversial and politically-loaded because of what is at stake for the nation-state,[37] which is the working unit in UN law charged with making, implementing and enforcing international law domestically and extraterritorially. Against this backdrop, where states play the leading role in international

[34] ILO, *Indigenous and Tribal Populations Convention* C107, 26 June 1957.

[35] Ibid C169, 27 June 1989.

[36] Following its first policy on indigenous peoples in 1982, Operational Policy 4.20 was drafted in1991, which was revised in 2005 by Operational Policy 4.10. The 2005 policy retains the requirements that World Bank-financed projects are designed to avoid adverse impacts but also equally important, to provide culturally appropriate benefits. Moreover, the 2005 policy focuses on 'free, prior, and informed consultation'. Operational Policy 4.10, which was last amended in 2013, should be read with other relevant policies, which include: Environmental Assessment (OP 4.01), Natural Habitats (OP 4.04), Pest Management (OP 4.09), Physical Cultural Resources (OP/BP 4.11), Involuntary Resettlement (OP 4.12), Forests (OP 4.36), and Safety of Dams (OP 4.37). See Sia Spiliopoulou Åkermark, 'The World Bank and Indigenous Peoples' in Nazila Ghanea-Hercock and Alexandra Xanthaki (eds), *Minorities, Peoples, and Self-Determination Essays in Honour of Patrick Thornberry* (Martinus Nijhoff Publishers, 2005).

[37] An incident that reaffirmed the need for the UN to look into formulating a definition of indigenous peoples in international law was the participation of the Boers and the Rehoboth Basters in the UN WGIP in 1992. This marked a turning point which resulted in the UN compiling several studies that contributed to the debate, and culminated with the *UN Study in Treaties, Agreements and Other Constructive Arrangements Between States and Indigenous Populations* in 1999. Although no definition of indigenous peoples is contained in the document, Miguel Alfonso Martínez's report is significant because it points to 'the upsurge of the politics of recognition, which is not restricted to indigenous peoples but also includes other minority groups'. Thornberry (n 10) 33–34.

law, the UN was founded on the principle of universalism, with universal rights for all human beings.[38] However, subsequent decades witnessed how groups have come to feature prominently in UN law as confirmed by the UN treaty system.[39]

Yet it is often the case that groups are not expressly defined in the law of the UN treaty bodies. The omission of a formal definition of these groups has not been crucial to the UN's 'successes or failures in those domains nor to the promotion, protection or monitoring of the rights recognized for these entities'.[40] More problematic and a core concern for the UN, however, is how to categorise groups which share common characteristics, concerns and needs.[41] For example, since before the 1970s, UN officials have grappled with the minority/indigenous dichotomy due to the overlap between marginalised groups and their issues, and the difficulties in setting them apart from one another.[42] It was on the back of these reports, which set out to categorise and differentiate indigenous peoples from minority groups, that attempts were made to introduce a working definition of indigenous peoples.[43] It was actually the issue of discrimination and inequality experienced by indigenous peoples that marked a turning point in the treatment of indigenous communities by the UN, which subsequently led to the official UN definition of indigenous peoples.

After his initial attempt in 1972,[44] UN Special Rapporteur Martínez Cobo constructed a revised definition in his 1986 'Study on the Problem of Discrimination against Indigenous Populations' to the UN Sub-Commission on the Prevention of

[38] See, the Preamble of the Charter of the United Nations and Articles 1 and 2 of the Universal Declaration of Human Rights.

[39] For example, the Convention on Elimination of Discrimination Against Women (CEDAW), adopted in 1979, and the Convention on the Rights of Children (CRC), adopted in 1989, enshrined women's rights and children's rights in international treaties. Minorities were guaranteed tailored rights in 1992 Declaration on the Rights of Persons Belonging to National or Ethnic, Religious and Linguistic. Other groups covered in UN law include, inter alia, migrants, people with disabilities and LGBT persons.

[40] Department of Economic and Social Affairs, Division for Social Policy and Development Secretariat of the Permanent Forum on Indigenous Issues, 'The Concept of Indigenous Peoples', Workshop on Data Collection and Disaggregation for Indigenous Peoples of 19–21 January 2004, PFII/2004/WS.1/3.

[41] Ian Brownlie points to how the former UN Commission on Human Rights has commissioned various studies with different Special Rapporteurs, covering a vast range of groups and issues including Capotorti's report on the rights of persons belonging to ethnic, religious and linguistic minorities, Martínez Cobo's and Eide's report on indigenous populations and discrimination, Espiell's report on the implementation of UN Resolutions concerning the rights to self-determination of persons under colonial and alien control and Cristescu's report on the right to self-determination. See Ian Brownlie, 'The Rights of Peoples in Modern International Law' in James Crawford (ed), *The Rights of Peoples* (Clarendon Press, 1988) 15.

[42] See Erica-Irene A Daes and Asbjørn Eide, 'The Relationship and Distinction between the Rights of Persons Belonging to Minorities and those of Indigenous Peoples' Working Paper of 19 July 2000 in accordance with Sub-Commission Resolution 1999/23, E/CN.4/Sub.2/2000/10.

[43] The most notable UN officials, who have worked on peoples in international law including minorities and indigenous peoples, include Francesco Capotorti, Special Rapporteur of the United Nations Sub-Commission on Prevention of Discrimination and Protection of Minorities, José Martínez Cobo, Special Rapporteur of the Sub-Commission on Prevention of Discrimination and Protection of Minorities (1971), Erica-Irene Daes, Chairing the United Nations Working Group on Indigenous Populations (1984–2001), Rodolfo Stavenhagen, Special Rapporteur on the Rights of Indigenous Peoples (2001–2008), S James Anaya Special Rapporteur on the Rights of Indigenous Peoples (2008–2014) and Victoria Tauli-Corpuz, Special Rapporteur on the Rights of Indigenous Peoples (2014–present).

[44] José Martínez Cobo, 'Preliminary Report of the Study of the Problem of Discrimination against Indigenous Populations' 29 June 1972 (E/CN.4/Sub.2/L.566) para 34.

Discrimination and Protection of Minorities.[45] The latest version identified indigenous peoples from an international perspective. Hence it is commonly called the 'international definition' of indigenous peoples, and is the most cited definition by indigenous peoples, scholars and civil society organisations. Different from the previous definition, the international definition reads:

> Indigenous communities, peoples and nations are those which, having a *historical continuity with pre-invasion and pre-colonial societies* that developed on their territories, consider themselves *distinct* from other sectors of the societies now prevailing in those territories, or parts of them. They form at present *non-dominant sectors of society* and are determined to preserve, develop and transmit to *future generations* their *ancestral territories*, and their *ethnic identity*, as the basis of their continued existence as peoples, in accordance with their *own cultural patterns, social institutions and legal systems*.[46]

In Anaya's expert opinion, Martínez Cobo's definition 'is not so much about identifying which groups *should* be or are *entitled* to be considered indigenous, as it is about understanding which groups in fact share in the common characteristics of those groups that both call themselves indigenous and have this common agenda'.[47] In line with the IGOs' activity, the main international indigenous peoples' organisations, such as the International Work Group for Indigenous Affairs (IWGIA) and the World Council of Indigenous Peoples (WCIP), have drafted their own definitions of indigenous peoples, which bear a strong resemblance to Martínez Cobo's definition. However, it is worth noting that although a formal definition was argued against, indigenous rights NGOs have chosen to define the claims made by indigenous peoples under the following headings: physical survival, cultural survival and cultural identity, sovereignty, self-determination, self-government, land rights, control of land and its resources, compensation, non-discrimination, and affirmative action.[48]

## III. THE 'VERNACULARISATION OF HUMAN RIGHTS' MODEL AND THE TRANSIT OF LAW

As noted earlier, international law, irrespective of its sources and types, transits between international and national realms.[49] The previous section attempted to situate the concept of indigenous peoples within the international legal order, which will be fleshed out in the next section that focuses on the national and local level.

[45] José Martínez Cobo, 'The Study of the Problem of Discrimination against Indigenous Populations' (also known as the Martínez Cobo study) 1986 UN Doc E/CN.4/Sub.2/1986/7 and Add 1–4. The study was launched in 1972 and was completed in 1986, thus making it the most voluminous study of its kind with a total of 37 monographs.

[46] José Martínez Cobo, 'The Study of the Problem of Discrimination against Indigenous Populations' 1986 UN Doc E/CN.4/Sub.2/1986/7 and Add 1–4, para 379 (emphasis added).

[47] S James Anaya, *International Human Rights and Indigenous Peoples* (Aspen Publishers, 2009) 28 (emphasis added).

[48] Garth Nettheim, '"Peoples" and "Populations"—Indigenous Peoples and the Rights of Peoples' in James Crawford (ed), *The Rights of Peoples* (Clarendon Press, 1988) 116.

[49] Due to space limitations, this contribution will not discuss transnationalism and legal pluralism, two theoretical frameworks that are extremely relevant to unpack this legal phenomenon.

Together, these two sections explore and problematise our conceptual understanding of indigenous peoples, while also revealing the paradoxical practice of international law when it moves between different times and spaces. But before looking at the case study of the Bedouin, it is necessary to grasp the process, the manner by which international law transits from the international realm to the domestic realm and what actually happens in between these realms.

In short, this section aims to answer the simple question: how can we best capture the transit of international law? This section provides a model to help us understand this process, drawing primarily on Engle Merry's study on gender violence in the Asia-Pacific region and her model of the vernacularisation of human rights.[50] In short, this model shows the ways in which rights are appropriated, translated into the vernacular and subsequently mobilised, while simultaneously throwing light on the processes at play, the actors driving these processes and the role played by language, specifically rights language.

Owing to the absence of a formal definition in favour of working definitions, local interpretation is deemed mandatory as it accommodates collectives in different contexts, especially those groups who would not otherwise squarely fall under the framework of traditional indigenous peoples.[51] It is important to underscore that this amounts to a continuous process, in which the international abstract concept is made concrete through its contextualisation at the domestic level, and drives a constructivist approach put forward by scholars. Kingsbury, for instance, describes the construction process in the following terms: 'The abstract international concept of "indigenous peoples" has potential to be drawn from international society back into national society; the abstract is worked out and made particular in a specific context.'[52]

This leads to the simple question as to how the abstract legal concept, which is produced at the international level, becomes concrete at the national and local level? Elaborating on Kingsbury's call for a contextualised approach that enables its construction in different spatio-temporal settings, Engle Merry's framework, explaining how human rights are domesticated, is salient. The vernacularisation of human

[50] Vernacularisation can be traced to a nineteenth-century process, whereby Latin, the common shared language at the time, splintered into separate languages, creating a new sense of nationhood in Europe. Merry sees a parallel between this and contemporary human rights language; a universal language that is extracted and then adapted nationally and locally. Engle Merry (n 1) 219.

[51] By traditional indigenous peoples, I mean those collectives who inhabited an area that was subject to European settler colonialisation that took place at the time of the Renaissance, in the sixteenth century. Here, the settlers, who are characterised by their race (white), gender (male) and place of origin (Europe), came and never left. This covers the Aborigines in Australia, the Maori in New Zealand, the Native Americans in United States, and the First Nations in Canada. By contrast, cases that do not fall under the classical colonial model challenge the applicability of the definition of indigenous peoples. For example, Asia and Africa also experienced European settler colonisation. However, in instances of European settler colonisation, these countries were decolonised during the UN decolonisation process in the 1960s and 1970s to become independent states. The UN did not address other types of colonisation like internal colonisation. Any attempt to answer the question of who is indigenous to Africa and Asia is no easy task since the European colonial settlers left and all those remaining now claim to be indigenous.

[52] Kingsbury, '"Indigenous Peoples" in International Law: A Constructivist Approach to the Asian Controversy' (n 1) 450.

rights highlights the impact of an international production of human rights and the ways in which these rights are localised individually or communally.

To unpack Engle Merry's vernacularisation process, it is necessary to become familiar with three cultural flows that occur on the global and local levels; they are divided according to transnational consensus-building, transnational programme transplants, and the localisation of transnational knowledge.[53] In the first stage of transnational consensus-building, law is globally produced in the form of documents.[54] It is here that we have already witnessed a disjuncture between global law and local justice, noting in human rights making 'local context is ignored in order to establish global principles'.[55] In the second stage, we see transnational programmes, such as social service programmes and legal innovations, transplanted from one society to another.[56] Critical in this transplantation process are 'intermediaries who translate global ideas into local situations and re-translate local ideas into global frameworks' and act as the link between the grassroots and global activists.[57]

The third, and final, stage is where national and local actors localise transnational knowledge in order to bring rights home and for rights to enter the rights-consciousness at the local level.[58] In becoming rights-conscious and taking on rights, a key element is the notion of a shift in subjectivity, which depends on the individual but also, for Engle Merry, institutions that take rights seriously and implement human rights.

Interestingly, Engle Merry argues that rights consciousness is not necessarily permanent. In the case of indigenous peoples, this would mean they can collectively, and possibly individually, acquire a transient indigenous rights-consciousness. For the individual, there is much at stake in taking on rights and this can have a negative impact for relationships so it is not unusual 'that one would try on this identity, drop it, and try again'.[59] It is, therefore, possible for the concept of indigenous peoples to be tried and tested, dropped and tried again.

In this part of the vernacularising process of rights, actors play a key role and range from international actors, to national elites, grassroots groups and the individual.

[53] Engle Merry (n 1) 19–20.

[54] In this instance, Engle Merry details the process of creating human rights, the significance of reaching a consensus on contentious issues surrounding power imbalance, language barriers and so forth. What is interesting in this stage is the role and participation of NGOs, which are marked by ambivalence and tension with the states. It is also here that the issue of legitimacy becomes significant, and Engle Merry argues that international consensus-building is critical to the legitimacy of the human rights system as a whole.

[55] Engle Merry further asserts: 'To negotiate this divide [between global law and local justice] is a key human rights problem.' Engle Merry (n 1) 103.

[56] In the transplantation stage, the actual appropriation process and intermediaries are key. The success or failure depends on how the international rights framework is appropriated from the international to the local and on the intermediaries who are involved in blending international, national and local elements. Ibid 134.

[57] In this transplantation process, Engle Merry makes a distinction between appropriation and translation. Simply put, appropriation entails 'taking the program interventions and ideas developed by activists in one setting and replicating them in another' and translation entails 'adjusting the rhetoric and structure of these programs or intervention to local circumstances'. Ibid 135–37.

[58] Engle Merry argues: 'The rights framework does not displace other frameworks but adds a new dimension to the way individuals think about problems.' Ibid 180.

[59] Ibid 217.

Common to all these groups is the translator, who goes between all the various actors and communicates between them.[60] The lingua franca is rights language, which is either translated 'up' or translated 'down'.[61] In other words, rights language unifies all players and domains and it can be viewed as an open-ended text that groups can appropriate and redefine in context.[62] Despite the creation and formulation of rights language at the international level, the rhetoric is then articulated elsewhere, often far away places.

However, the global/local interplay in the vernacularisation of rights is not unproblematic, giving rise to scholarly attention. For instance, in her study of Nepalese Theravada Buddhists, Lauren Leve 'shed[s] light on characteristic dilemmas of the practice of human rights "between the global and the local," where positioned participants draw on transnational languages and forms of authority to conceptualize, advance, and support their own locally-determined ends'.[63] Developing these ideas of law's transit through various realms and the obstacles it encounters, Jane Cowan et al demonstrate the extent to which 'not only national but also international legal regimes, including the rights regime, dictate the contours and content of claims and even identities' and point to the 'intriguing ... dialectic between the discourses and practices—one might say, the culture—of human rights and those of the groups that appeal to them'.[64] Commenting on the ethical complexities, Cowan et al suggest that 'the ways in which rights discourse can be both enabling and constraining' represent a paradox—'paradox of rights'.[65] In the next section, the paradoxical possibilities and limits of the international definition and rights of indigenous peoples are illustrated in the case study of the Bedouin.

## IV. THE CONCEPT OF INDIGENOUS PEOPLES IN THE NATIONAL AND LOCAL REALM

Bridging the first two sections, explaining the theory and model relevant to law's transit, this section embeds the concept of indigenous peoples in the domestic realm that straddles the national and the local. The case of the Bedouin citizens of Israel offers a first-hand, practical account of how the concept of indigenous peoples transits from the international and anchors itself within a particular context.

[60] Ibid 204–12.

[61] Ibid 216. In her model, Engle Merry uncovers three dimensions in the translation of rights: framing, adapting to structural conditions, and redefining the target population. It is important to stress that Engle Merry acknowledge that 'even though programs are translated into new contexts and framed in culturally specific ways, they are never fully indigenized'. Ibid 137.

[62] Ibid 30.

[63] Lauren G Leve, 'Secularism Is a Human Right!: double-binds of Buddhism, Democracy, and Identity in Nepal' in Sally Engle Merry and Mark Goodale (eds), *The Practice of Human Rights: Tracking Law between the Global and the Local* (Cambridge University Press, 2007) 80.

[64] Jane K Cowan, Marie-Bénédicte Dembour and Richard A Wilson, 'Introduction' in Jane K Cowan, Marie-Bénédicte Dembour and Richard A Wilson (eds), *Culture and Rights: Anthropological Perspectives* (Cambridge University Press, 2001) 11.

[65] Ibid.

In short, by unpacking this concept, this section unravels the way in which the Bedouin in the Negev are *gradually*, and arguably *increasingly*, becoming indigenous peoples.

The Bedouin's shift to indigenousness articulated itself most explicitly in the 2000s, which culminated with a Bedouin group submitting a formal request for indigenous recognition at the UN in July 2005.[66] This action exemplifies the appropriation and translation of the concept in the local setting and its subsequent reproduction before an international forum. This turn to the international, specifically to the international law of indigenous peoples, is curious when we consider that historically the Bedouin were situated beyond the formal legal frameworks of the Ottoman Empire and the British Mandate and governed themselves according to their own customs and tradition.[67] The events of 1948, however, marked a turning point in the Bedouin way of life, when the Israeli State apparatus sought to bring the Bedouin collective under a Western-crafted legal order. To counteract these government practices and policies, some Bedouin citizens, principally the inhabitants of unrecognised villages, have recently attempted to re-invent and redefine themselves as indigenous peoples. In other words, the Bedouin are appropriating the concept of indigenous peoples and mobilising it at the domestic level, nationally and locally. Here, we witness a manifestation of the transit of the concept of indigenous peoples from the international realm to the national realm. We also see how it moves back again to the international, from time to time.

Due to this particular set of circumstances, questions arise as to why, when and how the term indigenous peoples entered the lexicon of the Bedouin.[68] A rough

[66] The Negev Coalition Forum for Civil Equality (NCF) presented a report to the twenty-third session of the UN Working Group on Indigenous Populations in July 2005. The report was titled 'Bedouins and the Rights of Indigenous People' and was prepared by Israeli academics and activists. Ms Ferial Abu Nadi, a Bedouin woman from the Negev, presented the document, noting that 'raising awareness about and putting the Bedouins (in Israel) on the international agenda signify a step forward in our struggle'. See Elana Boteach, 'The Bedouins in the Negev as an Indigenous Population—A report submitted to the UN Working Group on Indigenous Populations' The Negev Coexistence Forum Newsletter (Beer-Sheva, 2005) available at dukium.org/user_uploads/report-updated-3.pdf.

[67] In the early sixteenth century, historic Palestine was absorbed into the Ottoman Empire and remained under Turkish rule until the end of World War One. After British victory, Palestine was governed under the British Mandate from 1917 until 1948. Following the United Nations' plan to partition Palestine, the British troops withdrew from the region on 14 May 1948 and on the same day the State of Israel was established.

[68] It is difficult to pinpoint the exact date when the term indigenous was first used in reference to the Bedouin but Ghazi Falah, a Bedouin-Canadian geographer, began using the term in the 1980s. In his article from 1985, Falah describes the development in the Middle East generally, and Israel in particular, adding: 'Because of such activity and for many other reasons, the indigenous population of the Negev desert and other Bedouin groups in Israel have been frustrated in their attempt to improve their lives and welfare in a rapidly changing world.' See Ghazi Falah, 'How Israel Controls the Bedouin in Israel' (1985) 14(2) *Journal of Palestine Studies* 35. The application of an international definition of indigenous peoples to the Negev Bedouin, in its current format, can be traced to Ismael Abu-Saad, a local Bedouin scholar with tenure at the Educational Policy and Administration in the Department of Education at Ben Gurion University (BGU) in Be'er Sheva. The first time he employed the concept was in the early nineties when he wrote and presented a paper—'Higher Education among the Indigenous Bedouin Arabs of the Negev: The Last Frontier'—at an international conference hosted by Ben Gurion University and University of California, Los Angeles (UCLA). Since this time, he has actively and regularly written on the subject for both an international and local audience. Seth J Frantzman, Havatzelet Yahel and Ruth Kark,

translation of Bedouin means desert-dweller,[69] whereas the antonym *hadr* means 'sedentary', 'urban' and 'civilized'.[70] Consequently, and similar to indigenous peoples elsewhere, the Bedouin have been categorised in pejorative and simple terms. For example, Ratcliffe et al demonstrate that towards the end of the Ottoman Empire, European travellers and traders, such as John Lewis Burckhardt and Alois Musil, together with writers and missionaries who visited the region often viewed the Bedouin as bucolic, resonant with Rousseau's image of the 'noble savage' or biblical shepherds.[71] They add that these works were compiled as non-academic texts but today are considered as the precursor of formal academic studies on the Bedouin.[72] Later, in the early days of Israeli nation-state building, Middle East anthropologists and historians, who were often former military men, studied Bedouin customary laws and traditions as nomadic desert-dwellers.[73] These studies on the desert nomads for the most part minimised or ignored the political and ideological hegemonic forces at play.[74]

Since the 1960s, however, when the state's modernisation project sought to urbanise and sedentarise the Bedouin collective, Bedouin issues have become incrementally politicised and polarised. The latest turn in the academic discourse reflects and underscores the tension in Bedouin–Israel relations, emphasising the territorial and spatial features of the fractured relationship.[75] Building upon this land-focused scholarship,

'Contested Indigeneity: The Development of an Indigenous Discourse on the Bedouin of the Negev, Israel' (2012) 17(1) *Israel Studies* 87. The application of tailor-made collective rights, specifically indigenous land rights, to the Negev Bedouin manifested itself in a paper—'Land Settlement in the Negev in International Law Perspective'—authored by Alexandre Kedar, Law Professor at Haifa University, on behalf of Adalah, a Haifa-based NGO.

[69] The Merriam-Webster Dictionary defines Bedouin as follows: 'BED·OU·IN: noun, often capitalized \'BE-DƏ-WƏN, -DÜ-ƏN, 'BED-WƏN\, *Definition of BEDOUIN:* a nomadic Arab of the Arabian, Syrian, or North African deserts, *Origin of BEDOUIN*: Middle English Bedoyne, from Middle French bedoïn, from Arabic badawī (بدوي) desert dweller, from badw desert, desert dwellers, *First Known Use*: 15th century' The dictionary definition is interesting for several reasons. Firstly, the definition centres on the collective's ethnic background (Arab), movement (nomadic) and geographical location (the deserts of Arabia, Syria and North Africa). Secondly, badawī (بدوي), which translated into English means desert dweller, was imported from the East by the West, evoking an Orientalist representation of the Bedouin. Thirdly, when exactly the word first came into use remains unclear.

[70] Donald Powell Cole, 'Where Have the Bedouin Gone?' (2003) 76(2) *Anthropological Quarterly* 237.

[71] Richard Ratcliffe et al, 'Introduction' in Mansour Nasasra et al (eds), *The Naqab Bedouin and Colonialism: New Perspectives* (Routledge, 2014), 4.

[72] Ibid.

[73] Clinton Bailey, *Bedouin Law from Sinai and the Negev: Justice without Government* (Yale University Press, 2009). See also Emanuel Marx, *Bedouin of the Negev* (Frederick A Praeger Publishers, 1967) and Erwin Graf, *Das Rechtswesen der Heutigen Beduinen* (Verlag für Orientkunde, 1952).

[74] Critical legal scholarship on the Bedouin specifically has been comparatively scarce. This can be explained by the academic and popular preoccupation with the broader regional conflict, which detracts attention from narrower internal issues. Moreover, because the Bedouin constitute less than 1% of the approximately 20% Arab minority in Israel, scholars tend to work on the Arab minority as a single collective and treat the different Arab sub-groups (Muslim, Christian, Druze and the Bedouin) as a whole, which fails to take into account the fact that the Bedouin have distinct characteristics that differentiate their communal experience from that of the larger Arab minority.

[75] For example, scholars of legal geography expose the fractured relations between the pre-state inhabitants of the Negev desert and the State through an examination of how law is employed to simultaneously Judaize and de-Arabize the land. This discourse, which challenges the nation-state

the scope of the academic preoccupation has expanded to encompass critical studies that challenge and contest mainstream scholarship, which is viewed as Orientalist or colonial and as predominantly speaking from and to the hegemony.[76]

As noted previously, at the turn of the last century, the Bedouin attempted to locate themselves in a Western-crafted legality and resorted to redefining themselves, and their legal subjectivity and identity in particular. Crucial to this re-invention, or redefinition, is the concept of indigenous peoples in international law. During the mid 2000s especially, the Bedouin and local and nationwide NGOs recognised the political and legal leverage of this internationally-defined concept and the accompanying set of tailor-made collective rights.[77] While the Bedouin have achieved limited success in their struggle for indigenous recognition, primarily beyond Israel and within the UN forum,[78] this international recognition in no way reflects a national

paradigm, frequently gravitates towards theories of colonialism, specifically white-settler colonialism. Colonial studies scholars put forward three arguments: first, Zionism is a colonial movement; secondly, Israel is a neo-colonial state; and thirdly, Israeli society is oppressive. See Sammy Smooha, *Israel: Pluralism and Conflict* (University of California Press, 1978). It should be noted that legal geographer Oren Yiftachel explicitly applies the colonial paradigm to the Negev. See Oren Yiftachel, *Ethnocracy: Land and Identity Politics in Israel/Palestine* (University of Pennsylvania Press, 2006).

[76] In critical scholarship, not unrelated to land questions are identity questions—Bedouinness, Arabness, Palestinianisation, Islamisation—and studies on Bedouin culture, gender issues and development. Also, the study of Nakba and the Bedouin as part of the broader Palestinian peoples are increasingly under critical scrutiny. In contrast, mainstream academic discourse focuses on the land issues, specifically in relation to the Bedouin's irregular settlements in the Negev, and planning authorities. Oren Yiftachel, 'Naqab/Negev Bedouins and the (Internal) Colonial Paradigm' in Ahmad Amara, Oren Yiftachel and Ismael Abu-Saad (eds), *Indigenous (In)justice: Human Rights Law and Bedouin Arabs in the Naqab/Negev* (Harvard University Press, 2013) 290. It is important to note that the last few years have witnessed a growth in studies on and from the Bedouin that has given rise to a new, distinct sub-category of Palestinian Studies called Naqab Bedouin Studies. In 2013 and 2014, two edited volumes written by Bedouin, Israeli and international scholars were published. In the latest publication, it expressly defines this sub-category of Palestinian studies as 'Naqab Bedouin Studies'. See Ahmad Amara, Ismael Abu-Saad and Oren Yiftachel, *Indigenous (In)justice: Law and Human Rights for Bedouin Arabs in the Naqab* (Human Rights Program at Harvard Law School, 2013); Mansour Nasasra, Sophie Richter-Devroe, Sarab Abu-Rabia-Queder and Richard Ratcliffe, *The Naqab Bedouin and Colonialism* (Routledge, 2014).

[77] For example, in April 2004, Adalah: The Legal Center for Arab Minority Rights in Israel, an NGO located in northern Israel, submitted a report, entitled 'Land Rights and the Indigenous Palestinian Arab Citizens of Israel: Recent Cases in Law, Land and Planning' to UN Working Group on Indigenous Populations (UNWGIP) in order 'to establish a dialogue with the UNWGIP and to place the issue of land rights of Palestinian Arab citizens of Israel on the UNWGIP's agenda'. The report criticises the government's failure to recognise the Bedouin's 'native land rights' in its 2003 plan (known as the 'Sharon Plan') available at www.adalah.org/uploads/oldfiles/eng/intl04/unIndigpop.pdf.

[78] The UN treaty bodies in their recommendations have explicitly recognised the Bedouin as an indigenous group. For instance, in its Concluding Observations, the Committee on the Elimination of Racial Discrimination recommended that: 'The State party should withdraw the 2012 discriminatory proposed Law for the Regulation of the Bedouin Settlement in the Negev, which would legalize the on-going policy of home demolitions and forced displacement of the *indigenous* Bedouin communities.' Concluding Observations of the Committee on the Elimination of Racial Discrimination. Israel, CERD/C/ISR/CO/14-16 (9 March 2012) para 20 (emphasis added). Similarly, James Anaya, the previous UN Special Rapporteur on the Rights of Indigenous People, concluded that the Bedouin are entitled to international protection and entitlements as indigenous people. Acknowledging 'the State of Israel does not accept the classification of its Bedouin citizens as an indigenous people', the Special Rapporteur, however, considered the rights of Bedouin to fall under the purview of his mandate. *Report by the Special Rapporteur on the rights of indigenous peoples, James Anaya*, A/HRC/18/35/Add.1 (22 August 2011) para 21.

consensus on the question of the Bedouin's indigenous recognition and indigenous rights.[79] External definitions, specifically those emanating from the Israeli establishment, define the Bedouin as anything other than indigenous.[80]

As a result of the recent surge in the use and discourse surrounding the Bedouin's indigenous identity, scholars working in the field are embroiled in a contested debate as to whether the Bedouin are indigenous. In other words, they attempt to answer whether the Bedouin meet the legal criteria of indigenous peoples under international law. We see two distinct positions emerging.

One bloc argues the case of Bedouin indigenousness, while the other argues against such recognition. Somewhat remarkably, both sides employ the same international definition of indigenous peoples to back their cases. For instance, in their article 'Contested Indigeneity: The Development of an Indigenous Discourse on the Bedouin of the Negev, Israel' Frantzman et al provide a historical account of the discourse that depicts the Negev Bedouin as indigenous peoples which takes into account the processes and actions of those who have played a role in leading and crafting a narrative of an indigenous Bedouin identity.[81] The authors argue that the boom in international human rights efforts, notably in the UN, has helped create a 'consciousness movement' of indigenous people, which has not overlooked the Bedouin. The authors conclude that the Bedouin are not indigenous to the region according to international law, advancing three main reasons.

Firstly, they argue that the Bedouin settled in the Negev in the eighteenth century during the time of the Ottoman Empire, which negates the proposition that the Bedouin have inhabited the region since time immemorial.[82] Secondly, they contend that the Bedouin no longer engage in customary traditions and practices, which is a defining characteristic of indigenous peoples under international law. Here, they describe how the Bedouin do not collectively own the land like indigenous peoples elsewhere but their land ownership resembles property ownership in Western legal orders. Thirdly, the authors refer to other Bedouin groups in the Middle East and how they have not made a claim to indigenous peoples' law, making the Negev Bedouin's claim less plausible.[83]

Challenging and contesting this position, Nasasra examines the relationship between settler societies and indigenous people from an international law perspective.[84] Nasasra goes on to discuss the controversy over the indigenous identity of the Bedouin, who, in Nasasra's view clearly fulfil the criteria for indigenousness as enumerated by Special Rapporteur Martínez Cobo.[85] In support

[79] In parallel to the lack of recognition as indigenous peoples, Bedouin land rights are denied by the Israeli judiciary, and we see that on every occasion it has ruled against the Bedouin of unrecognised villages when Bedouin petitioners have submitted land claims against the State of Israel.

[80] Penny Maddrell, *Beduin of the Negev*, 1st edn (Public Interest Publication, 1990) 19.

[81] Seth J Frantzman, Havatzelet Yahel and Ruth Kark, 'Contested Indigeneity: The Development of an Indigenous Discourse on the Bedouin of the Negev, Israel' (2012) 17(1) *Israel Studies* 78.

[82] Ibid 95.

[83] Ibid 96–97.

[84] Mansour Nasasra, 'The Ongoing Judaisation of the Naqab and the Struggle for Recognising the Indigenous Rights of the Arab Bedouin People' (2012) 2(1) *Settler Colonial Studies* 81.

[85] Ibid 87.

of his claim to indigenousness, Nasasra lists the reasons, which include the fact that:

> [T]he Bedouins preserve affinity to their land: they have followed pastoralism as a way of life, used wells as a source of water, and maintained traditional agriculture. They have also maintained their cemeteries, their villages existed before 1948, they use their own language, laws, customs and beliefs that are based on those of their Islamic communities, they have the sense of belonging to tribes in relation to migration, and they preserve their traditional economy. Finally, the Bedouin today work at the political and juridical level for recognition of their land ownership according to traditional tribal laws.[86]

The lack of consensus amongst scholars highlights the concept's ambiguity and controversy when the Bedouin attempt to activate and mobilise this internationally-defined concept in national and local realms. In other words, the transit of indigenous peoples' concept from the international level to Israel on the national level, and the Negev on the local level present their own unique problems. The Bedouin's indigenousness is fixated on the legal definition, but behind the law there are multiple factors at work on the national and the local levels that manifest in Israeli society and the Bedouin community respectively. The transit of the concept of indigenous people to the Negev can be explained by the vernacularisation of human rights.

To explore and problematise the vernacularisation of the concept of indigenous peoples and the set of indigenous peoples' rights, this section concludes with a brief look at the concept at the local level in the Bedouin village of Al-Araqib. Al-Araqib is an unrecognised village, belonging to the Al-Uqbi, Al-Turi and Abu-Medeghem, Abu-Freih and Abu-Zayed tribes and is situated five miles (eight kilometres) north of Be'er Sheva.[87] In 1951, three years after the State of Israel was established, the villagers of Al-Araqib were removed from their ancestral lands by the Israeli military under the pretext that the lands were required for military training, and confined with 18 Bedouin tribes to the *siyag*, a fenced-off area in the northern Negev.[88] The Israeli military authorities indicated to the Bedouin village leaders that they would be allowed to return after six months.[89]

However, this promise was not kept and throughout the military regime, which lasted from 1948 to 1966, Al-Araqib villagers attempted unsuccessfully to return to their lands. In 1972, the Israeli authorities began to allow citizens to submit land registration applications under *Settlement of Land Rights Ordinance (Consolidated Text) 5729-1969*.[90] The residents of Al-Araqib submitted applications to claim back their land and made a concerted, though ultimately unsuccessful, attempt to return. Their claims to ownership of the lands have remained before the courts.[91]

[86] Ibid.
[87] Nadia Ben-Youssef, Suhad Bishara and Rina Rosenberg, *From Al-Araqib to Susiya* (Adalah, The Legal Center for Arab Minority Rights in Israel, 2013) 2.
[88] Ibid.
[89] Ibid.
[90] Ibid.
[91] Ibid.

Over the next two decades, little activity took place, save for an effort by the Israel Land Administration (ILA) to cultivate the land in 1991 and 1992 which prompted the villagers' intervention and resulted in the ILA issuing a public apology. In 1998, when the Jewish National Fund (JNF) showed an interest in Al-Araqib, villagers were afraid they would lose the land and they returned in order to defend their land from JNF afforestation.[92] Consequently, Sheikh Sayyah Al-Turi, his offspring and their 45 families, returned to their lands and began their struggle for official recognition of the village by the Israeli State.[93] In July 2010, the authorities began preparing the land for planting and, since then, the village has been demolished scores of times despite legal proceedings before the courts regarding the land's ownership.[94]

In the light of recent government activities, which include house demolitions, the villagers of Al-Araqib have organised themselves and responded to the JNF's afforestation plans. In July 2011, a year after the first demolition, and every year since, Bedouin residents of the village, along with activists from Israel and around the world, gather in solidarity for commemorative events, which run in parallel with their legal action demanding their right to remain on the land. Moreover, because of the ongoing demolition of the village, it acts as a visible rallying point for NGOs on the question of unrecognised Bedouin villages, and their specific rights issues.

In early 2012, the Be'er Sheva District Court dismissed the case of the Al-Ukbi tribe, which had attempted to register its lands in Al-Araqib; in its decision, the Court deemed the claimed land to be state property.[95] Significant for the purpose of this discussion, the question about whether the villagers amount to indigenous peoples was raised. The Court held:

> Another argument raised by the Plaintiffs concerns indigenousness and transitional justice. This issue which is of great importance and commanding the utmost respect, is a matter of policy which must be dealt with by the legislator and *at the present time the legislation in Israel does not recognize title rights based on indigenousness*. Besides which the El–Uqbi tribe arrived to [sic] the country when the Ottoman Authorities already ruled the country … as opposed to the minorities to whom the Plaintiffs refer, where foreign rule was established, after their arrival.[96]

[92] JNF's afforestation ambitions include 'Ambassador Forest' in the south and 'God-TV Forest' in the west. Ibid.

[93] Ibid.

[94] The home demolitions have been condemned by international NGOs, such as Amnesty International and Human Rights Watch (HRW) as well as Israeli NGOs such as Association for Civil Rights in Israel (ACRI), Coalition of Women for Peace, Gush Shalom, New Israel Fund (NIF), New Profile, Rabbis for Human Rights and Taayush.

[95] Ahmad Amara, Ismael Abu-Saad and Oren Yiftachel, 'Afterword' in Ahmad Amara, Ismael Abu-Saad and Oren Yiftachel (eds), *Indigenous (In)Justice: Human Rights Law and Bedouin Arabs in the Naqab/Negev* (Harvard University Press, 2013) 320.

[96] Be'er Sheva District Court Civil Case Nos 7161/06, 7275/06, 7276/06, 1114/07, 1115/07, 5278/08 *Sulieman Mahmud Salaam El-Uqbi v The State of Israel*, para 34 (emphasis added) (translation). According to the Expert Opinion of Professor Yiftachel, the El-Uqbi Tribe arrived in the Negev about 200 years ago. The case was appealed to the Supreme Court of Israel and in June 2014, it ordered mediation to reach a fair alternative. According to Yiftachel's analysis of the Supreme Court's ruling: 'The appeal also claimed that nationalizing Bedouin land in 2015 runs counter to Israel's 1992 liberal Basic Laws, and that the Bedouins constituted a typical *indigenous community* that should enjoy the protections provided by international law and norms. The court rejected all these claims, arguing that the tribe did not prove it

The case of al-Araqib reveals the significance of the concept of indigenous peoples and the role of actors—the translators in Engle Merry's vernacularisation model—in using and mobilising the concept and rights of indigenous peoples among the Al-Araqib villagers. Individuals and bodies, who activate and mobilise the concept, range from activists to international NGOs, as well as law centres and media representatives. NGOs and lawyers representing the villagers of Al-Araqib have incorporated indigenousness as part of their legal and political strategy in order to establish their permanency on the land and their right to basic services. However, in addition to seeking a legal remedy in the domestic court system, the Al-Araqib villagers have taken their land struggle beyond the national level to the international plane.[97] Here we see how these actors together with scholars, who write in English and not Hebrew or Arabic, endeavour to raise the international profile of the Bedouin, by centre-staging the Bedouin land issue, while taking Bedouin indigenousness as given.[98] To sum up, in seeking an international identity and rights protection based on indigenous peoples, the Al-Araqib villagers, in concert with others, are favouring international law, which can be seen as a brilliant or as a risky move.

## V. CONCLUSION

To conclude, this chapter has set out to map the manner in which the international concept of indigenous peoples transits between international and national realms. The concept's transit deviates off course, as captured and explained by Engle Merry's model on vernacularisation of human rights. In examining how the international concept becomes active and effective, through its appropriation and translation in the domestic setting, it also sheds light on how the concept has become the chosen legal identity and rights framework for groups, like the Bedouin in southern Israel. We see that this amounts to a very bold attempt by the Bedouin to re-think and redefine themselves in international law, which ultimately transforms their subjectivity and identity into a contested terrain. In short, by taking on the concept of indigenous peoples, the Bedouin attempt to maintain their 'Bedouin-ness' at and beyond the national realm.[99]

had a settlement before 1858; nor that it received any official permission to settle the land by the Ottoman authorities; and that it didn't prove cultivation or registration before 1921.' Oren Yiftachel, 'Supreme Court Decision on Al-Uqbi vs the State of Israel' May 2015 (emphasis in the original).

[97] For example, during the summer of 2012, the United Kingdom and South African ambassadors to Israel were given a tour of Al-Araqib by a coalition of local and nationwide NGOs. NCF provided an update on their website following the tours, which serves a dual purpose to raise awareness about the NCF and to raise awareness about the case of Al-Araqib. See, 'British Ambassador learns about NCF, visits Al Arakib' May 2012, available at www.dukium.org/eng/?p=1780 and 'Update from Negev Coexistence Forum' July 2013, available at www.dukium.org/eng/?p=1703.

[98] This literature lies somewhere between academic analysis and academic activism and targets the international audience. In *Indigenous (In)justice: Law and Human Rights for Bedouin Arabs in the Naqab*, for example, the village of Al-Araqib is expressly mentioned with regard to the Israeli demolition policy in the Negev. (n 76) 4.

[99] Bedouin-ness, I contend, sums up how the Bedouin seek to remain Bedouin but exactly what this is, is difficult to determine. This can be traced back to the fact that the Bedouin have been subject to dif-

Yet, this hints at another question as to why indigenousness and indigenous peoples' rights—as a legal identity and rights framework—was chosen and prioritised over other legal identities and rights frameworks. This is even more curious when we consider what is at stake for groups in taking on and utilising this legal identity and rights framework that is inherently incoherent, contradictory and unstable, and subject to change over time and place. Put another way, the concept of indigenous peoples amounts to an amalgamation of incoherent, contradictory and unstable ideas, practices and formulations. Nonetheless, this proves no deterrent to its continued appropriation, translation and reproduction, as demonstrated by the Bedouin and their indigenous turn in international, national and local realms.

ferent foreign regimes and have consequently undergone multiple identity transformations, while maintaining their distinct Bedouin traditions and customs. Donald P Cole, in his article 'Where have the Bedouin Gone?' (n 70) cites Sulayman Khalaf's depiction of Bedouin-ness as ethnic integrity. According to Sulayman Khalaf: '[N]ot one of simple and total transformation, but rather of an ongoing dialectic of continuity and change, an interplay between tradition and modernity. They are adjusting their material and political life to rapidly changing modern conditions and yet they continue to respect and adhere to a range of traditions that help them define and perpetuate their ethnic integrity, *their Bedouin-ness*.'Sulayman Khalaf, 'Settlement of Violence in Bedouin Society' (1990) 29(3) *Ethnology* 241 (emphasis added).

# 18

# *Fragmented Feminisms: Critical Feminist Thinking in the Post-millennium Era*

GINA HEATHCOTE*

## I. INTRODUCTION

CONTEMPORARY INTERNATIONAL LEGAL scholars have identified the fragmentation of the discipline as both a strength[1] and a danger[2] inherent within post-millennium developments. This contribution provides a feminist analysis of those debates; proposing feminist engagements with transnational legal processes as a path away from the potential stagnation within arguments on legal fragmentation. Karen Knop's work on transnational legal processes is used to consider how the uptake of ideas within a locale, region or nation might flow across legal structures in ways that significantly alter our perception of the development and deployment of international legal rules.[3]

Extending beyond Knop's focus on the translation of legal norms across structures I consider the deployment of plural subjectivities as the normative grounding of feminist approaches to international law. An emergent method of feminist inquiry, that draws on the bodies and subjects that populate feminist and gender theories, is then developed as a mechanism to bring together feminist writing on transnationalism and international legal approaches to plurality. In particular, the nomad,[4] the migrant[5] and the peripheral subject[6] are considered as forms of subjectivity that

* Dr Gina Heathcote, Senior Lecturer in Gender Studies and International Law, SOAS University of London. A longer version of this chapter is found in Gina Heathcote, *Feminist Dialogues on International Law* (Oxford University Press, 2016, forthcoming). Dr Heathcote wishes to thank Loveday Hudson for her generous help in presenting this paper in Vienna: multiple thanks Loveday! All errors remain my own.

[1] See generally, Martti Koskenniemi and Paivi Leino, 'Fragmentation of International Law? Postmodern Anxieties' (2002) 15 *Leiden Journal of International Law* 553.

[2] ILC, 'Summary Record of the 2468th Meeting' (23 July 1996) UN Doc A/CN.4/L.528, para 7.

[3] Karen Knop, 'Here and There: International Law in the Domestic Courts' (1999) 13 *New York Journal of International Law and Politics* 501.

[4] See generally, Rosi Braidotti, *Nomadic Subjects: Embodiment and Sexual Difference in Contemporary Feminist Theory*, 2nd edn (Columbia University Press, 2011).

[5] Avtar Brah, 'Diaspora, border and transnational identities' in *Cartographies of Diaspora: Contesting Identities (Gender, Racism, Ethnicity)* (Routledge, 1996).

[6] Ratna Kapur, 'The Tragedy of the Victimisation Rhetoric: Resurrecting the 'Native' in International/Postcolonial Feminist Legal Politics' in Ratna Kapur, *Erotic Justice: Law and the New Politics of Postcolonialism* (Glasshouse Press, 2005).

re-orientate contemporary accounts about the fragmentation of international law and re-assess the focus of feminist approaches to international law.

Knop's work on transnational legal processes demonstrates how legal innovations act across legal structures in ways that are not wholly hierarchal: top–down or bottom–up. Instead Knop engages with law as a non-vertical structure that relies on universal, or global, rules only to the extent that they are capable of being rendered with meaning in the local and/or national context. Extending Knop's focus on the translation of legal norms across jurisdictions, I present plural subjectivities as a feature of contemporary feminist theories that has resonance for approaches to legal pluralism and transnational legal processes within the international realm. In particular, I argue that the failure to recognise subjectivity as diverse and plural embeds a masculinist model of subjectivity that insufficiently facilitates meaningful local interpretations of international rules. In the context of fragmentation debates, this presents an important mechanism for further interrogating the ways in which critical engagements with fragmentation have reinforced, rather than disrupted, the status quo of international law and the global order.

## II. ON FRAGMENTATION AND INTERNATIONAL LAW

Scholarly understanding of the impact of legal fragmentation on international law has spawned both critical, mainstream international law scholarship (MILS)[7] and institutional activity. I draw on both critical and institutional accounts, leaving mainstream accounts out of the discussion. Relying on BS Chimni's account of MILS I assume these rarely reflect on the embedded inequalities and biases of any legal system. Consequently, MILS tends to assume that legal systems conform to a pre-exiting legal form within which specific rules are to be evinced. My research, in contrast, starts from the premise that existing legal forms embed specific legal histories and perspectives that benefit from exposure and transformation. Martti Koskenniemi's report to the International Law Commission (ILC) demonstrates the nexus between developments in critical legal scholarship and their currency within the mainstream of international law.[8] Fragmentation is regarded as a concurrent risk

[7] I use Chimni's terminology, see: BS Chimni, 'A Prolegomena to a Class Approach to International Law' (2010) 21 *European Journal of International Law* 57; BS Chimni, 'An Outline of a Marxist Course on Public International Law' (2004) 17 *Leiden Journal of International Law* 1, defining mainstream international law scholarship or MILS as 'an ensemble of methods, practices and understandings in relation to the identification, interpretation, and enforcement of international law' (at 2). Of the four features of MILS that Chimni identifies, the following is pertinent to the analysis in this chapter: 'the practitioners of MILS do not recognise that there are structural constraints in the international system that greatly limit the pursuit of common good through law' (ibid).

[8] ILC, 'Fragmentation of International Law: Difficulties arising from the Diversification and Expansion of International Law: Report of the Study Group of the International Law Commission—Finalized by Martti Koskenniemi' (13 April 2006) UN Doc A/CN.4/L.682 (Fragmentation of International Law); also see ILC, 'Report of the International Law Commission 58th Session' (1 May–9 June and 3 July–11 August 2006) UN Doc A/61/10, para 251.

to the international order and the site of the global order's potential consolidation. The ILC, in 2002, found:

> [F]ragmentation can be seen as a sign of the vitality of international law. It was also suggested that the proliferation of rules, regimes and institutions might strengthen international law. Attention was drawn to the fact that the increasing scope of international law means that areas that were previously unaddressed by international law are now being addressed. Similarly, there are advantages in increased diversity of voices and a polycentric system in international law.[9]

Yet in the same report the ILC regards its role as 'to assist international judges and practitioners in coping with the consequences of the diversification of international law',[10] and to provide 'what could be called a "toolbox" designed to assist in solving practical problems arising from incongruities and conflicts between existing legal norms and regimes'.[11] Both of these goals infer an assumed level of negativity and sense of challenges brought about by fragmentation alongside fragmentation as a site of renewal in terms of understanding, at a structural level, the inadequacies and the potentials of the system. Yet reports into the consequences of fragmentation insufficiently interrogate the structures of international law, asserting the persistence of fragmentation within international legal histories and, thus, fail to interrogate the persistent inequalities within those structures.

By 2006, when Koskenniemi had taken the lead in the ILC project on the fragmentation of international law, the project remained one that was driven by an attempt to balance understanding of the risk and potential of fragmentation. Importantly, analysis of Koskenniemi's report to the ILC finds no reference to 'women' or 'gender' within the study.[12] Yet the impact of fragmentation on gender perspectives within international law is of considerable importance, demonstrating how changes within the constitution of legal structures create specific outcomes. Women's rights and the Convention on the Elimination of Discrimination Against Women (CEDAW) process,[13] the women, peace and security framework within the Security Council,[14] developments within international criminal law with respect to gendered crimes,[15] as well as gender and development initiatives,[16] and anti-discrimination work,[17] all rely on some (assumed) shared goals, and yet function

[9] See Knop (n 3).

[10] Ibid para 2.1.

[11] Ibid para 21(e); also see 'Fragmentation of International Law' (n 8) para 14.

[12] This was established through a search for the words 'women' or 'gender' in the text of the Report; neither word was used.

[13] See generally, Marsha A Freeman, Christine Chinkin and Beate Rudolf (eds), *The UN Convention on the Elimination of all Forms of Discrimination Against Women: a Commentary* (Oxford University Press, 2012); Loveday Hudson, 'Women's Rights and Periphery: CEDAW's Optional Protocol' (2014) 25 *European Journal of International Law* 561.

[14] For a critical analysis and introduction, see Gina Heathcote and Diane Otto, *Rethinking Peacekeeping, Gender Equality and Collective Security* (Palgrave, 2014).

[15] For an introduction, see Alona Hagay-Frey, *Sex and Gender Crimes in the New International Law* (Brill, 2011).

[16] For a critique, see Ambreena Manji, '"The Beautyful Ones" of Law and Development' in Doris Buss and Ambreena Manji (eds), *International Law: Modern Feminist Approaches* (Hart Publishing, 2005).

[17] See Heathcote and Otto (n 14).

with considerable fragmentation, being located across the various institutional arms of the United Nations (UN).

The practical segmentation and division of work on women and gender across the institutions of the UN and throughout the various legal structures within international law, has had specific impact on the development of the feminist and gender transformation within international spaces.[18] Two key consequences are the continued focus of gender reform on issues centred on women's lives and therefore the increasing consolidation of the assumption that gender perspectives focus on women. First, even when men are considered as subjects within gender initiatives, for example, in work around male victims of conflict-related sexual violence,[19] a re-assertion of a gendered binary between men and women occurs rather than any serious attempt to reflect the sophisticated understanding of the diversity of gender politics or even an understanding of gender as varied within and across communities.

Second, the work on gender within the UN appears to have been 'ghetto-ised' into the umbrella body of UN Women, where gender mainstreaming is expected to be conducted by gender experts and institutions, so that individuals and laws that are not directly concerned with women remain untouched by the developments on gender, and women's rights, so effectively developed and promoted by UN Women. I come back to both of these points below, arguing that these are the expected consequences of fragmentation and that those feminist theories, which understand and deploy a diverse understanding of subjectivity, are starting points for addressing both the fragmentation of feminism and of international law generally.

At the same time, gender analysis of the rise of fragmentation can be linked to feminist reconstructive projects that are attentive to difference, that have resonance for moves toward legal pluralism. The continued framing of fragmentation as both a positive and a negative space is ultimately unhelpful, as it reasserts the status quo of international law, through the turn to functionalism, and leaves unquestioned the foundational components of international law that perpetuate inequalities. A broader feminist and gender framework can be used to better understand fragmentation and its consequences, and this is an approach that connects to the rejection of a specifically (and largely Western) masculine history of international law.

As such, the fragmentation of feminist approaches within international law is an important signifier of the poverty of mainstream approaches to fragmentation. As the study of 'women's issues' or 'gender issues' within international law immediately identifies an extremely partial account of international law (centred on international human rights law, collective security and international criminal law) and, while admittedly these spaces represent a series of useful developments within specific international legal spaces, they remain insufficient developments within gender perspectives or in terms of transforming the field of international law more generally.

[18] Although UN Women was established in 2010 to draw these strands together more effectively I would argue that fragmentation still occurs due to the very specific areas of attention that this work focuses on, the failure of gender mainstreaming initiatives and 'ghetto-isation' of work on gender.

[19] Chloe Lewis, 'Systematic Silencing: Addressing Sexual Violence against Men and Boys in Armed Conflict and Its Aftermath' in Gina Heathcote and Diane Otto (eds), *Rethinking Peacekeeping, Gender Equality and Collective Security* (Palgrave, 2014).

Despite the 1990s initiatives on gender mainstreaming, gender issues remain occasional and special interest topics rather than being knitted into the structures of international law. The next generation of feminist scholars should take this fragmentation as a serious indication of the politics behind the turn to gender in international spaces, which are often predicated on the legitimation of specific actors and institutions, rather than a commitment to the development of feminist law.

## III. FRAGMENTED FEMINISMS

Ultimately, I wish to document two splits in feminist approaches within international law that underscore the fragmentation identified in the previous section. When reflecting on paths forward, however, I return to larger debates and discussions on fragmentation to re-assert the relevance and necessity of feminist legal theories within the international realm as a series of interventions and reconstructive projects at the foundational level. The two splits I document in this section tally with the types of description Hilary Charlesworth, Christine Chinkin and Shelley Wright documented in 1991,[20] and again in 2005,[21] regarding the practical and substantive exclusions of women from the international sphere.

However, in contrast to these earlier accounts, rather than spaces of exclusion I argue for recognition of the post-millennium shift towards the partial inclusion of feminist approaches in a manner that ultimately fragments feminisms and reduces the impact of feminism on the structures and processes of international law. This, like the fragmentation debates, then risks the re-affirmation of the status quo and existing inequalities rather than a realisation of the transformative potential of feminist approaches to international law.

The first practical and most visible site of fragmentation exists in the organisation of 'gender issues' within international law. The real consequences of this are perhaps best understood by picking up and thumbing through any international law textbook in pursuit of an understanding of feminist approaches. Despite the multiple sites of feminist endeavours, gender perspectives and concrete legal developments, the topics of women, of gender, and of feminism are structurally invisible from the purview of the mainstream international lawyer. Gender is both present and absent in international law's self-representations. There are acknowledged sites where gender 'happens' and most, if not all, of these pertain to women's rights (and men's accountability for the violation of these rights in the most extreme cases) but these are not regarded as foundational to international law and both scholarly and policy focus seems only to pay attention from within the spaces that are labelled 'women', in particular the CEDAW Committee and UN Women. This constructs a practical fragmentation of feminist 'successes' and transformations within international

[20] Hilary Charlesworth, Christine Chinkin and Shelley Wright, 'Feminist Approaches to International Law' (1991) 85 *American Journal of International Law* 613, 631.

[21] Christine Chinkin, Shelley Wright and Hilary Charlesworth, 'Feminist Approaches to International Law: Reflections from Another Century' in Doris Buss and Ambreena Manji (eds), *International Law: Modern Feminist Approaches* (Hart Publishing, 2005).

law. Fragmentation then distances gender perspectives from the larger structures and foundations of international law, while a fragmentation of women, gender and feminist issues across the sub-disciplines of international law mirrors the rise of sub-disciplines explored in the ILC reports.

The second split occurs at a substantive level. This aspect of feminist approaches is less apparent from the international legal plane and concerns the diversity of these approaches, gender theory and even understandings of women's rights. Despite the practical divisions in the fragmented international legal frameworks on gender, there is an astounding consistency in the 'brand' of feminist politics that is taken up on the international plane. Reminiscent of Annelise Riles' analysis of the view from the international plane in colonial politics, where specific issues are transposed into international problems, a very specific form of feminist approach is continually asserted (or taken up) within international legal structures.[22] This fragments the diverse and changing sites of feminist and gender theory, constructing a largely liberal–radical model as the universal feminist approach and others, in particular postmodern, postcolonial and critical race feminisms as particularised fragments belonging in spaces outside of the international.

The complex movement of transnational feminist politics requires understanding of the non-vertical transplantation of ideas and their relevance, structurally, to both international law and feminist approaches. In this manner, Knop's transnational legal feminism is developed as a normative framework for attention to diverse forms of knowledge, subjectivity and being. The three specific ideas I draw into this discussion in this chapter are intersectionality, nomadic subjects and the migrant. The concrete conclusion, in line with Knop, is that each of these models has resonance both across and within specific communities and yet their translation relies on an understanding of the particular within any space or place.

## IV. FRAGMENTED SUBJECTS

> ... to talk of objects in the plural presupposes that they can be individuated[23]

Twining speaks of separating the empirical and normative accounts of legal pluralism. There is, he indicates, a need to account for the difference between studying, recognising and describing the varied legal spaces, structures and concepts and legal pluralism as a distinct commitment to an understanding of law as grounded in pluralism. The discussion Section III, on the fragmentation of feminist approaches follows a generally similar schema, although it is useful to think through the consequences and connections between the empirical and descriptive sites of pluralism with the normative.

[22] Annelise Riles, 'The View from the International Plane: Perspective and Scale in the Architecture of Colonial International Law' in Peter Fitzpatrick and Eve Darian-Smith (eds), *Laws of the Postcolonial* (University of Michigan Press, 1999) 127.

[23] William Twining, 'Normative and Legal Pluralism: a Global Perspective' (2010) 20 *Duke Journal of Comparative and International Law* 473, 478.

In this section I highlight the approaches of feminist theorists, in particular, Knop and the manner in which the foundational structures of international law are re-considered in her transnational legal feminism. The inherent legal pluralism within Knop's work then leads me toward additional feminist dialogues where foundational legal structures are re-imagined; in particular, Ratna Kapur's identification of peripheral subjects as a normative starting point,[24] Rosi Braidotti's conception of the nomadic subject,[25] and the study of migration via the framing of diaspora spaces in the work of Avtar Brah.[26]

Knop's perception of transnational legal processes, which I have labelled 'transnational legal feminism' for the purposes of this paper, considers the translation of legal rules, principles and norms between systems as an important theoretical and normative component of the international that has previously been misunderstood. For Knop, in focusing on the translation of laws in a transjudicial form, persuasive rules are understood as integral to the development of universal structures, such as human rights within specific legal contexts. Knop's approach permits and realises the development of a larger feminist commitment to representing diversity and understanding intersectional politics that emerge across temporal spaces and thus are attended to differently in various times and spaces. The juxtapositioning of the development of global—or transnational—patterns with an understanding of local renderings of those same rules reflects an understanding of the complexity of international law. It also provides a unique means to understand a range of false binaries within international law, including universalism and cultural relativism, monism and dualism, and rules and norms.

In constructing an understanding of international law, developed locally through translation into local rules, which in turn speak across and through legal forms to re-imagine the international, Knop embeds a commitment to legal pluralism in her project that I wish to extend into the recognition of the diverse subject as a necessary and transcendental figure within the international legal system. My reference to the diverse subject is an attempt to capture the varied subjectivities emergent within gender theories that, for legal scholarship, challenge the historical construction of a unitary masculine subject. In disrupting the expectation that legal norms filter down into the local/domestic space or that legal rules filter up into the larger international normative order, Knop equally facilitates recognition of the poverty of contemporary understandings of legal subjectivity, constructed on stories of masculine closure and unencumbered subjects. Instead, Knop shifts towards recognising the legal subject as always existing in relation to other legal subjects, be they states, non-state actors, international organisations, regional bodies or individuals.

Feminist legal theories then provide useful accounts of diverse subjectivity that feed into the analysis of the foundations of international law, re-asserting the capacity for a model of sources and authority within international law that is drawn from an expansive, changing understanding of subjectivity, and can thus be attentive to power relationships, inequalities and imperial histories. Unlike Twining's reflection

[24] Kapur (n 6).
[25] Braidotti (n 4).
[26] Brah (n 5).

that legal pluralism builds on the knowledge that pluralism assumes a level of individuation, Knop's transnational legal feminism takes as its starting point a recognition that legal systems, states and legal subjects, like individuals, function as separate and connected subjects: they are embedded in a network of legal forms facilitating cross-fertilisation and translation of ideas, in the same way as the legal structure, like individuals, asserts its separateness and individuality.

In the work of Kapur, via the articulation of the peripheral subject as a normative starting point for feminist theorising,[27] a robust critique of feminist approaches to international human rights law, and violence against women strategies within the international, is presented. Kapur's approach hinges on acknowledging the victim subject of liberal–radical feminist approaches to ask, and take seriously, how feminism constructs its subjects and thus its theories of knowing.[28] The peripheral subject, thus, is akin to transnational legal feminism, which acknowledges non-dominant legal forms as prevalent and relevant to our rendering of international/global laws. The peripheral subject acknowledges the perspective, agency and voice—as a normative force—outside of the masculine, Western unencumbered subject, imagined in liberal projects but also projected within feminist knowledge regarding agents and victims.

The nomadic subject enters Braidotti's work as a cross-boundary, stateless post-human whose subjectivity 'reflects the existential situation of the multicultural individual, a migrant who turned nomad'.[29] At the core of Braidotti's project is a commitment to 're-thinking the bodily roots of subjectivity' that acknowledges both the diversity of lived, bodily experiences and the epistemological projection of identity onto bodies in a manner that 'Others' specific subjects. Braidotti's account is then able to engage directly with the construction of subjectivity both through and within identity politics, across differentiations, to release understandings of subjectivity into the ranging, temporally shifting, and geographically mobile subjectivity of the nomad. Braidotti's work centres on the individual subject within philosophical work, so transferring and re-imagining this within the context of the international may seem counter-intuitive unless a return to understanding the sexed and gendered state is prefigured in our understanding of the state within international law.[30]

Despite early feminist work on international law directly addressing the sex and gender of the state, there has been a general decline in attention to this type of foundational concept within international law, from contemporary feminist and critical scholars alike. Braidotti's project is akin to Kapur's focus on subjectivity, although where Kapur draws on postcolonial subjects to frame a subject of resistance to the imperial legacy of international endeavours, Braidotti uses an account of postmodernism (as the contemporary temporal account rather than an ahistorical theory) and psychoanalytical accounts to explore the role of the affective and the role of desire in the formation of subjectivity.

[27] Kapur (n 6) 131.

[28] Ibid 107.

[29] Braidotti (n 4) 21.

[30] Hilary Charlesworth, 'The Sex of the State in International Law' in Ngaire Naffine and Rosemary Owens (eds), *Sexing the Subject of Law* (Law Book Co, 1997).

In terms of fragmentation debates, Braidotti's nomadic subject indicates a need to frame the fragmentation of international law as repressing the key affective and bodily accounts within the assumed spaces of international law. In particular, the state within fragmentation scholarship is insufficiently re-positioned in a series of discussions that fall back onto a series of expectations connected to legal formalism, or how the rules work and function despite fragmentation of the overarching structure. The transference from a stationary (as the state is assumed to be via its defined territory) to a nomadic subjectivity questions key assumptions that remain embedded within international law as a discipline, including within debates on fragmentation. In particular, the persistence of difference as a marker of inequality so that, in the words of Braidotti, 'the nomadism in question here refers to the kind of critical consciousness that resists settling into socially coded thoughts and behaviours',[31] such that the traversing of boundaries (between states, between ideas, and between fragmented forms of law) is grounded on understanding what it means to be human. Braidotti thus imagines a version of subjectivity that considerably transcends philosophical traditions that imagined the male body and experience of powerful men as the archetype of the human condition.

To Braidotti's and Kapur's projects, centred on subjectivity, Brah's work on diaspora furthers our understanding of the failure of categories of belonging within dominant philosophical–political accounts. The closure of identity politics and of mapping the world through the national state (or nationalism) destroys significant appreciation of the migrant's multi-located sense of belonging and the capacity for human empathy, memory and difference to be the site of our sense of belonging.

Like Braidotti and Kapur, Brah's account commences a project of acknowledging fractured subjectivity which has resonance within international legal accounts of fragmentation. However, rather than seeking a means to understand fragmentation within an (assumed) hermeneutically sealed world of legal relationships, rules and principles, Brah's work leads us to consider fragmentation as the space in which to know and understand the 'Other'. Then the international human rights lawyer, perhaps, might know and understand the theoretical and practical constraints of the international trade lawyer, that the humanitarian actor might hear and see the narratives of the environmental activist, that the development policy-maker might engage with the sanctions body, and in each case vice versa, to see maps of belonging and home, of language and law, as similar in their differences.

In contrast, fragmentation is a story of individualising and dividing international legal regimes in a manner that re-asserts the need for the state and the organisations of international law to function within the current foundational paradigms. Fragmentation scholarship pays little attention to how assumed stories of the origins of international law re-tell themselves as without particularisation or home. Kapur, Braidotti and Brah all present challenges to the feminist and the international lawyer alike—they demand a re-assessment of the types of engagements, both practical and substantive, that have evolved and emerged since the early 1990s. The expectation that legal arrangements might embrace contemporary gender theorists' formation

[31] Braidotti (n 4) 26.

and engagements with multiple, wandering subjectivities in the first two decades of feminist approaches to international law, is unrealistic.

The types of feminist developments within international law have instead mirrored the types of larger development within the discipline, including that of fragmentation. The consequence is a re-assertion and acceptance of the sexed and gendered foundations of international law. To shift beyond this point, a broader and complex feminist encounter within international law is required. This in turn, feeds back into larger debates on fragmentation to conceive of a post-fragmentation period in international law. Fragmentation is then perceived as a starting point for understanding a transnational legal framework where knowledge is able to traverse legal structures, in a nomadic fashion. This also encompasses a space for attention to (assumed) peripheral accounts of legal arrangements as normatively equivalent to the core. The nomadic and the peripheral then function to question any sense of belonging, or home, derived from a nationalist politics and deprived of the multi-consciousness of the migrant.

## V. DISRUPTIVE PLACES AND SPACES OF 'KNOWING'

In summary, this contribution has turned to the debates on fragmentation to further feminist engagements with the foundational structures—and developments—of international law and to map the development of feminist legal work within the international sphere. My initial impetus to undertake this study was driven by a sense of encountering two different spaces where legal pluralism and plurality were emergent themes and to ask what they might productively offer each other. The first site is work within critical legal scholarship which at once acknowledges and theorises legal pluralism, and connects this to the fragmentation debates within international law but does not read, see or tell, stories of gender and the connections between understandings of legal pluralism within feminist and gender theories.

As such feminist writing on plural subjectivities, or in the case of Knop, on transnational legal models, is the second set of scholarship I am interested in and I have tried to demonstrate the relevance of this to fragmentation discussions throughout this work. That is, feminist understandings of transnational legal approaches, the shifting between the spaces and planes of legal knowledge, and the need for an understanding of the complexity gained through attention to plurality, contribute to a counter-hegemonic theory of knowing the international where complexity, fluidity, choice and closure are demonstrated as at once outside the legal and eternally constructed by the legal.

Acknowledging this drives us to further see that there is, and must be, an ethical commitment within our projects. The unspoken ethical commitment of the fragmented approach to feminist legal advances within the international—where the non-Western woman is constructed and re-constructed as damaged, in need of protection, without voice and eternally cast as an actor defined through her assumed feminine body—is re-assigned a problematic gender ethic. The binary of m>f is re-told in the stories of international law as that of one's sexual and bodily vulnerability juxtaposed against the invisible normal subject that is male and intersects with other sites of power, including race, class, able-bodiedness and sexuality.

Feminist projects within international law must actively work to disrupt this sense of knowing, or assumption of gender politics, to use and develop plural understandings as a mechanism to intervene and disrupt precisely what we think international law *should* be. It is in stories of plurality that the knowledge to disrupt the intersectioning power relations, which persist in telling the particulars of international legal history as a universal, is made visible. In this chapter, I have used the debates on fragmentation to demonstrate how, from a feminist perspective, the fractal metaphor of international law is a repeating pattern that would benefit from the disruptive spaces of knowing that are spoken by the peripheral subject, the nomad, the migrant and bodies that defy the binaries of Western gender norms.

# PART VII

# INTERNATIONAL LAW AND SPORT

# 19

# 'For the Game, For the World'—And also for Human Rights? Analysing Human Rights Obligations of International Sports Associations

LARS SCHÖNWALD[1]

## I. INTRODUCTION

ORIGINALLY, HUMAN RIGHTS were designed to protect the citizen against the state.[2] Even today, states are the primary addressees of human rights obligations—at both the international and the domestic level.[3] However, at both levels, new actors, such as international organisations (IOs) and transnational corporations (TNCs), have emerged over time, which are as powerful as states (at least in a particular situation), and which can also infringe human rights.[4] For example, the liability of IOs for human rights violations was already confirmed, inter alia, by the European Court of Human Rights (ECtHR).[5] Similarly, the liability of TNCs for human rights violations has largely been debated before, inter alia, courts in the United States of America.[6] In fact, international sports associations can also infringe human rights, as the following five examples will demonstrate.

[1] The author is Doctoral Candidate at the Chair of Constitutional and Administrative Law, Public International Law, European and International Economic Law of Professor Dr Hans-Georg Dederer at the University of Passau.

[2] See Christian Tomuschat, *Human Rights—Between Idealism and Realism*, 2nd edn (Oxford University Press, 2008) 97.

[3] Cf Philip Alston and Ryan Goodman, *International Human Rights—The Successor to International Human Rights in Context* (Oxford University Press, 2013) 1461.

[4] See Jan Arno Hessbruegge, 'Human Rights Violations Arising from Conduct of Non-State Actors' 11 *Buffalo Human Rights Law Review* (2005) 21–75. Cf Human Rights Council, 'Report of the Special Representative of the Secretary-General on the issue of human rights and transnational corporations and other business enterprises, John Ruggie—Guiding Principles on Business and Human Rights: Implementing the United Nations "Protect, Respect and Remedy" Framework' UN Doc A/HRC/17/31 (21 March 2011). Cf also Tomuschat (n 2) 98–109.

[5] ECtHR, *Behrami and Behrami against France & Saramati against France, Germany and Norway*, A No 71412/01 and 78166/01, Decision of 2 May 2007.

[6] Supreme Court of the United States, *Kiobel, individually and on behalf of her late husband Kiobel, et al v Royal Dutch Petroleum Co et al*, No 10-1491, Decision of 17 April 2013, Syllabus available at www.supremecourt.gov/opinions/12pdf/10-1491_l6gn.pdf.

## A. Athletes' Rights: The Cases of Tommie Smith and John Carlos, Lance Armstrong, and Luis Suárez

When Tommie Smith won the gold medal, and John Carlos the bronze medal over 200 metres at the 1968 Olympic Games in Mexico City, they raised their fists at the podium to show solidarity with people fighting internationally for human rights and against apartheid in South Africa and racial segregation in the United States of America.[7] On the very same day, the two athletes were expelled from the Olympic Games by Avery Brundage, who was at that time the President of the International Olympic Committee (IOC).[8] Thus, the two athletes were sanctioned for the exercise of their freedom of expression. Still today, it is argued by international sports associations that there is no room for political messages at international sport events,[9] such as the Olympic Games[10] or Football World Cups.[11]

During his active career, Lance Armstrong won the most prestigious bicycle race on Earth, the Tour de France, seven times.[12] However, on 24 August 2012, the United States Anti-Doping Agency (USADA) decided to strip Armstrong of all competitive results achieved from 1 August 1998 onwards, and to issue a lifetime ban on Armstrong from any activity or competition for which the USADA has jurisdiction.[13] On 22 October 2012, the Union Cycliste Internationale (UCI) announced that it had accepted the USADA's recommended sanctions and carried them out.[14] Armstrong, who still denied the doping allegations but decided not to challenge the sanctions, said that the USADA had engaged in an 'unconstitutional witch-hunt' and was afraid of a 'one-sided and unfair' arbitration process.[15] In fact, the doping allegations against Armstrong—who later confessed to the use of

[7] See Tommie Smith with David Steele, *Silent Gesture: The Autobiography of Tommie Smith* (Temple University Press, 2007) 20–41; cf also Neil Amdur, 'Olympic Protester Maintains Passion', *The New York Times* (New York, 11 October 2011) 18.

[8] Cf Allen Barra, 'Fists Raised, but Not in Anger', *The New York Times* (New York, 23 August 2008), 19.

[9] Cf Teddy Cuttler, 'Moeen Ali banned from wearing pro-Palestinian wristbands: what happens when sport turns political?' *The Independent—Online*, 29 July 2014, available at www.independent.co.uk/sport/cricket/moeen-ali-banned-from-wearing-propalestinian-wristbands-what-happens-when-sport-turns-political-9635396.html.

[10] Ibid.

[11] Ibid. See also Nick Harris, 'Footballer falls foul of the rules as he shows his political colours', *The Independent* (London: 22 March 1997) 3.

[12] See Peter Kogoy, 'Wheel has turned, now even France embraces new Lance', *The Weekend Australian* (Sydney, 24 January 2009) 55.

[13] Robin Scott-Elliot, 'Armstrong in ruins as he is to be stripped of Tour titles; Doping chief claims legend is "admitting he is a drug cheat" by not fighting charges', *The Independent* (London, 25 August 2012), 16. See also United States Anti-Doping Agency, 'Reasoned Decision of the United States Anti-Doping Agency on Disqualification and Ineligibility: Report on Proceedings under the World Anti-Doping Code and the USADA Protocol—United States Anti-Doping Agency (Claimant) v Lance Armstrong (Respondent)' available at d3epuodzu3wuis.cloudfront.net/ReasonedDecision.pdf.

[14] See Richard Williams, 'Cycling: Armstrong loses titles as cycling chiefs lashes out at "scumbags": Hamilton and Landis are condemned', *The Guardian* (London, 23 October 2012), 48.

[15] Cf Juliet Macur, 'Armstrong Ends Fight Against Doping Charges', *The New York Times* (New York, 24 August 2012) 1.

performance enhancing drugs,[16] and accepted the imposition of the sanctions—raise questions about an athlete's right to work and related procedural rights, such as due process and fair trial.[17]

Luis Suárez became quite famous, even among non-football fans, during the FIFA Football World Cup 2014 in the Federative Republic of Brazil when he allegedly bit his opponent Giorgio Chiellini.[18] Two days after the incident, the Disciplinary Committee of the Fédération Internationale de Football Association (FIFA) banned Suárez from nine international matches—the longest ban in World Cup history.[19] In addition, he was banned from any football-related activity—including participating in team training and entering stadiums—for four months.[20] He was also fined.[21] Uruguay's football association, the Asociación Uruguaya de Fútbol (AUF), appealed the decision, but with no success.[22] Given that the ban was overwhelmingly criticised as being excessive,[23] it also raises questions about an athlete's right to work.

Taking only these three cases into consideration, it becomes apparent that international sports associations, as governing organisations for the respective sports, have significant power over athletes and therefore can infringe athletes' rights.

### B. Workers' Rights: The Cases of the Migrant Workers in Qatar, and of Labour Conditions in Bangladesh, India and Pakistan

The State of Qatar will host the FIFA Football World Cup 2022.[24] In order to do so, the country is undertaking significant infrastructure projects: stadiums, roads, bridges, highways, railways and ports need to be constructed.[25] It is also expected that hotels, restaurants, bars and so forth will be built.[26] These construction works

[16] See Mary Pilon, 'A Scandal Leaves Its Mark', *The New York Times* (New York, 16 February 2013) 1.

[17] Cf Verner Møller, 'Who Guards the Guardians?' (2014) 31(8) *The International Journal of the History of Sport* 934–50. See also Brian A Dziewa, 'Comment: USADA the Unconquerable: The One-Side Nature of the United States Anti-Doping Administration's Arbitration Process' (2014) 58 *St Louis University Law Journal* 875. Cf further Verner Møller and Paul Dimeo, 'Anti-doping: the end of sport' (2014) 6(2) *International Journal of Sport Policy and Politics* 259–72; Kayleigh R Mayer, '2012 Annual Survey: Recent Developments in Sports Law' (2013) 23(2) *Marquette Sports Law Review* 501–66.

[18] See Sam Borden, 'Uruguayan Star, Known for Biting, Leaves Mark on World Cup', *The New York Times* (New York, 25 June 2014) 1.

[19] Sam Borden, 'Suárez Suspended for 4 Months for Biting', *The New York Times* (New York, 27 June 2014) 12.

[20] Ibid.

[21] Ibid.

[22] Cf Martyn Ziegler, 'Sport: World Cup 2014: Suarez biting ban appeal rejected', *The Guardian* (London, 11 July 2014) 5.

[23] See Jack Pitt-Brooke, 'Suarez plunged into extraordinary legal battle after Fifa imposes four-months ban; Liverpool locks at grounds to join in appeal', *The Independent* (London, 27 June 2014) 1.

[24] See Jere Longman, 'Russia and Qatar Expand Soccer's Global Footprint', *The New York Times* (New York, 3 December 2010) 11.

[25] US-Qatar Business Council, 'Council News: Qatar Infrastructure Plans Toward 2022' available at www.usqbc.org/news-detail.php?newsid=155.

[26] Cf Satyendra Pathak, 'Completing infra projects on time challenge: Minister', *Qatar Tribune* (Doha, 3 June 2014) 3.

are mainly carried out by foreign workers, mostly from India, Pakistan, Bangladesh, Indonesia, Nepal and the Philippines.[27]

The migrant workers are monitored by the so-called *kafala system*,[28] meaning that every unskilled foreign worker needs an in-country sponsor (usually the employer) who is responsible for her or his visa and legal status.[29] Under the *kafala system*, the employer may withhold the passport of the migrant worker, making it impossible for the worker to change jobs or even leave the country.[30] Consequently, as several prominent human rights non-governmental organisations (NGOs) have pointed out, the migrant workers are vulnerable to systematic abuse[31] which amounts to modern-day slavery.[32] Also, with an increasing death toll among migrant workers, questions about labour standards and labour protection have arisen.[33]

The People's Republic of Bangladesh, the Republic of India and the Islamic Republic of Pakistan not only have great cricket teams[34] but also contribute significantly to world sports by manufacturing sport garments.[35] All major manufacturers of sports equipment operate production facilities in these countries.[36] The changes in the processing of raw materials for footballs from leather to synthetics in the 1970s and 1980s allowed for the production of footballs at home.[37] Consequently, middlemen began outsourcing the stitching of footballs to families working from home.[38] While this gave women, especially in Pakistan, the opportunity to work and earn

[27] See Human Rights Watch, *Building a Better World Cup: Protecting Migrant Workers in Qatar Ahead of FIFA 2022* (New York, Human Rights Watch, 2012) available at http://www.hrw.org/sites/default/files/reports/qatar0612webwcover_0.pdf 31–32.

[28] See for general information on the *kafala system*, Amrita Pande, '"The Paper that You Have in Your Hand is My Freedom": Migrant Domestic Work and the Sponsorship (Kafala) System in Lebanon' (2013) 47(2) *International Migration Review* 412–41.

[29] Human Rights Watch (n 27) 33–36.

[30] Ibid.

[31] Ibid. See also Amnesty International, *'My Sleep is My Break': Exploitation of Migrant Domestic Workers in Qatar*, (London, Amnesty International, 2014) available at www.amnesty.org.uk/webfm_send/358; International Trade Union Confederation, *The Case Against Qatar: Host of the FIFA 2022 World Cup* (Brussels, International Trade Union Confederation, 2014) available at www.ituc-csi.org/ituc-special-report-the-case 20–23. Besides NGOs, the UN and its specialised agencies are also addressing the situation in Qatar, see Human Rights Council, 'Report of the Special Rapporteur on the human rights of migrants, François Crépeau—Mission to Qatar' UN Doc A/HRC/26/35/Add.1 (23 April 2014) available at www.ohchr.org/Documents/Issues/SRMigrants/A-HRC-26-35-Add1_en.pdf; International Labour Organization, 'ILO: More decisive actions needed in Qatar' (Press release of 13 February 2014) available at www.ilo.org/brussels/press/press-releases/WCMS_235626/lang--en/index.htm.

[32] See International Trade Union Confederation (n 31) 25.

[33] Cf Human Rights Watch (n 27) 61–69.

[34] See International Cricket Council, 'ICC Ranking: Reliance ICC ODI Ranking' available at www.icc-cricket.com/team-rankings/odi.

[35] Cf Judy Mann, 'Working to Protect Children from Work', *The Washington Post* (Washington, DC, 8 December 1999) C14; International Labour Organization, *Bangladesh: Seeking Better Employment Conditions for Better Socioeconomic Outcomes* (Geneva, International Labour Organization, 2013) available at www.ilo.org/wcmsp5/groups/public/---dgreports/---dcomm/documents/publication/wcms_229105.pdf 19; Peter Lund-Thomsen and Khalid Nadvi, 'Global value chains, local collective action and corporate social responsibility: a review of empirical evidence' (2010) 19(1) *Business Strategy and the Environment* 1–13.

[36] Cf Sehr Hussain-Khaliq, 'Eliminating Child Labour from the Sialkot Soccer Ball Industry' (2014) 13 *Journal of Corporate Citizenship*) 101–107.

[37] Cf ibid.

[38] Ibid.

money, it also resulted in thousands of children aged seven to 14 leaving school and working at home, stitching footballs.[39]

In addition, the collapse of an eight-story building that housed five garment factories in Bangladesh on 24 April 2013 brought the labour conditions in so-called 'sweatshops' in Bangladesh to the attention of the international media.[40] It was reported that many workers have to work for 14 to 16 hours per day, seven days a week for less than the minimum wage and in an unsafe working environment with practically no labour rights.[41]

Although international sports associations do not directly infringe workers' rights, it is apparent that they contribute to these infringements as they require the construction of stadiums and other infrastructure, and as they chose, for example, a manufacturer of footballs who cares very little about workers' rights.

### C. Exclusivity-Clauses in Sponsoring Agreements and their Impact on Local Merchants and Producers

Whenever a country or city is chosen as the host for a major international sports event, it is very happy about it, in part because it is believed that the country or city will benefit economically from hosting the event.[42] Indeed, the new infrastructure can still be used long after the event is over and might contribute to economic development.[43] In addition, at least prior to and during the event, thousands of jobs are created.[44]

However, there is also an economic downside. Major international sports events are regularly sponsored by large corporations who, in return for sponsorship, want their products to be sold exclusively around the sports venues.[45] Consequently, local merchants are forced to close their shops if they do not exclusively sell the sponsors' products.[46] While local merchants at least have a choice, producers of goods are prevented from selling their products in or near the sports venues.[47]

[39] Ibid.

[40] See Julfikar Ali Manik and Jim Yardley, 'Building Collapse in Bangladesh Kills Scores of Garment Workers', *The New York Times* (New York, 25 April 2013) 1; Jason Burke, 'Engineers warn 60% of garment industry buildings in Bangladesh at risk of collapse: Survey conducted in wake of Rana Plaza disaster Factories set up with regulatory oversight', *The Guardian* (London, 4 June 2013) 17; Steven Greenhouse, 'Some Retailers Rethink Roles in Bangladesh', *The New York Times* (New York, 2 May 2013) 1.

[41] See Greenhouse (n 40) 1.

[42] Stephen Essex and Brian Chalkley, 'Olympic Games: catalyst of urban change' (1998) 17(3) *Leisure Studies* 187–206.

[43] Ibid.

[44] Ibid.

[45] Cf Simon Chadwick, 'The Nature of Commitment in Sport Sponsorship Relations' (2002) 4(3) *International Journal of Sports Marketing & Sponsorship* 257–74; Tony Meenaghan, 'Understanding sponsorship effects' (2001) 18(2) *Psychology & Marketing* 95–122; J Richard Shannon, 'Sports marketing: an examination of academic marketing publication' (1999) 13(6) *Journal of Services Marketing* 517–35.

[46] See National Public Radio (NPR) 'Want To Eat Brazilian Food At The World Cup? Please Step Outside' available at www.npr.org/blogs/thesalt/2014/07/05/328522903/want-to-eat-brazilian-food-at-the-world-cup-please-step-outside.

[47] Ibid.

The exclusivity clause is contained in the agreement between the sponsor and the host (normally the organising committee).[48] It triggers the question of how such a clause can have third-party effect, and even infringe the right to property, the right to work, or the general right to freedom of merchants and producers.

## D. The Impact of Massive Infrastructure Projects on the Rights of Affected People

As already mentioned,[49] the hosting of a major international sports event usually requires massive infrastructure projects to be carried out. This was the case particularly for the FIFA Football World Cups 2010 in the Republic of South Africa and 2014 in Brazil, but also for the Olympic Games in Beijing in 2008 and in Rio de Janeiro in 2016, where it has been reported that infrastructure projects led to forced displacements and evictions, lack of consultation of affected communities, and violent repressions of protests,[50] triggering questions about the rights of affected people with regard to housing, property, freedom of expression and the like. Again, it should be noted that the alleged human rights violations were not committed directly by FIFA or the IOC. However, international sports associations indirectly contributed to these human rights violations.

## E. Spectators' Rights

Finally, the rights of spectators might also be infringed. For instance, during the FIFA Football World Cup 2014 in Brazil, stewards confiscated banners with political messages.[51] In addition, spectators demonstrating with political messages on t-shirts or signs were not shown on television.[52] During the FIFA Football World Cup 2006 in Germany, Dutch supporters were criticised by the organising committee for wearing an orange garment which contained a reference to a sponsor's competitor.[53] During the Olympic Games 2014 in Sochi, protests and demonstrations were only allowed in designated areas.[54] The host countries of the next two FIFA Football World Cups—the Russian Federation (2018) and Qatar (2022)—have

[48] Joe Cobbs, 'Legal battles for sponsorship exclusivity: The cases of the World Cup and NASCAR' (2011) 14(3) *Sports Management Review* 287–96.

[49] See text at n 25.

[50] UN-HABITAT, *Enhancing Security of Tenure: Policy Directions—Enhancing Urban Safety and Security—Global Report on Human Settlements 2007*, Vol 2 (London and Sterling, VA: UN-HABITAT, 2008) vi–vii.

[51] Section 4.1(h) of the Stadium Code of Conduct for the 2014 FIFA World Cup Brazil, available, inter alia, at www.industry.siemens.com.br/home/br/pt/cc/phs/Documents/Stadium%20Code%20of%20Conduct%20for%20the%202014%20FIFA%20World%20Cup%20Brazil.pdf.

[52] Cf Luke Harding and Andrew Culf, 'Ambush marketing: The new World Cup rule: take off your trousers, they're offending our sponsor: Fifa bans shorts bearing logo of Budweiser's rival; Dutch supporters forced to watch game in pants', *The Guardian* (London, 19 June 2006) 3.

[53] Ibid.

[54] Cf Kathly Lally, 'Environmental protesters silent in Sochi', *The Washington Post* (Washington, DC, 15 February 2014) A09.

a poor reputation with regard to the rights of lesbian, gay, bisexual and transgender people (LGBT rights). Thus, the rights of spectators might also be (at least) indirectly infringed by international sports associations.

## II. INTERNATIONAL SPORTS ASSOCIATIONS AS ADDRESSEES OF HUMAN RIGHTS OBLIGATIONS

Having illustrated how international sports associations can infringe human rights, it has to be assessed whether and, if so, to what extent, international sports associations are addressees of human rights obligations.

### A. Determining the Legal Nature of International Sports Associations

In order to determine the legal nature of international sports associations, their legal status must first be determined. This requires an analysis of the statutes of the relevant international sports associations. It would go beyond the scope of this paper to consider every international sports association. Instead, this paper is limited to those associations which are recognised by the IOC[55]—which will also be analysed.

[55] These are, in alphabetical order, the Badminton World Federation (BWF), the *Confédération Mondiale des Activités Subaquatiques* (CMAS), the *Confédération Mondiale des Sports des Boules* (CMSB), the *Fédération Aéronautique Internationale* (FAI), the *Fédération Équestre Internationale* (FEI), the *Fédération Internationale de l'Automobile* (FIA), the *Fédération Internationale d'Escrime* (FIE), the *Fédération Internationale de Basketball* (FIBA), the *Fédération Internationale de Bobsleigh et de Tobogganing* (FIBT), the *Fédération Internationale de Football Association* (FIFA), the *Fédération Internationale de Gymnatique* (FIG), the *Fédération Internationale de Luge de Course* (FIL), the *Fédération Internationale de Motocyclisme* (FIM), the *Fédération Internationale de Natation* (FINA), the *Fédération Internationale de Pelota Vasca* (FIPV), the *Fédération Internationale de Quilleurs* (FIQ), the *Fédération Internationale de Roller Sports* (FIRS), the *Fédération Internationale de Ski* (FIS), the *Fédération Internationale des Échecs* (FIDE), the *Fédération Internationale des Luttes Associées* (FILA), the *Fédération Internationale des Sociétés d'Aviron* (FISA), the *Fédération Internationale du Hockey sur Gazon* (FIH), the *Fédération Internationale du Volleyball* (FIVB), the Federation of International Bandy (FIB), the Federation of International Polo (FIP), the International Association of Athletics Federations (IAAF), the International Biathlon Union (IBU), the International Boxing Association (AIBA), the International Canoe Federation (ICF), the International Cricket Council (ICC), the International Dance Sport Federation (IDSF), the International Federation of Netball Associations (IFNA), the International Federation of Sport Climbing (IFSC), the International Floorball Federation (IFF), the International Golf Federation (IGF), the International Handball Federation (IHF), the International Ice Hockey Federation (IIHF), the International Judo Federation (IJF), the International Korfball Federation (IKF), the International Live Saving Federation (ILSF), the International Orienteering Federation (IOF), the International Racquetball Federation (IRF), the International Rugby Board (IRB), the International Sailing Federation (ISAF), the International Shooting Sport Federation (ISSF), the International Skating Union (ISU), the International Sumo Federation (ISF), the International Surfing Association (ISA), the International Table Tennis Federation (ITTF), the International Water Ski Federation (IWSF), the International Weight Lifting Federation (IWF), the International Triathlon Union (ITU), the International Wushu Federation (IWUF), the Tug-of-War International Federation (TWIF), the *Union Cycliste Internationale* (UCI), the *Union Internationale de Pentathlon Moderne* (UIPM), the *Union Internationale des Associations d'Alpinisme* (UIAA), the *Union Internationale Motonautique* (UIM), the World Archery Federation (WAF), the World Baseball Softball Confederation (WBSC), the World Bridge Federation (WBF), the World Confederation of Billiard Sports (WCBS), the World Curling Federation (WCF), the World Karate Federation (WKF),

### *i. International Sports Associations as Associations under Domestic Civil Law*

Most international sports associations are associations under Swiss civil law.[56] Noteworthy exceptions are the FIQ, the IRF, the ISF, the ISA and the TWIF, which are

and the World Squash Federation (WSF), International Olympic Committee (IOC), 'International Sports Federations' available at <http://www.olympic.org/content/the-ioc/governance/international-federations/?tab=sportaccord>.

[56] Cf Article 15(1) of the 2013 Olympic Charter (IOC-Charter) www.olympic.org/Documents/olympic_charter_en.pdf, s (1)(1) of the 2013 Badminton World Federation Constitution (BWF-Constitution) www.bwfbadminton.org/file.aspx?id=555967&dl=1, ss 1.1.2. and 1.1.7. of the 2014 Statutes of the *Fédération Aéronautique Internationale* (FAI-Statutes) www.fai.org/downloads/fai/fai_statutes, Article 4.1 of the 2014 Statutes of the *Fédération d'Équestre Internationale* (FEI-Statutes) www.fei.org/sites/default/files/Statutes%2029%20April%202014%20-%20clean_NEW%20FORMAT_FLI_4May14.pdf, Article 1(1) of the 2013 Statutes of the *Fédération Internationale de l'Automobile* (FIA-Statutes) www.fia.com/sites/default/files/basicpage/file/Statuts%20FIA%20AGO%2006%2012%202013%20%28FR-EN%29-CLEAN_0.pdf, Preamble of the Statutes of the *Fédération Internationale d'Escrime* (FIE-Statutes) www.fie.ch/download/status/en/FIE%20Statutes%20ang.pdf, Article 2(2) of the 2014 General Statutes of the *Fédération International de Basketball* (FIBA-General Statutes) www.fiba.com/downloads/Regulations/2014/FIBAGeneralStatutes_ApprovedbyExtraordinaryCongress16March2014_English.pdf, s 2(1) of the 2010 Statutes of the *Fédération Internationale de Bobsleigh et de Tobogganing* (FIBT-Statutes) www.ibsf.org/images/documents/downloads/Statutes_2015-_E_final.pdf, s 1(1) of the 2013 Statutes of the *Fédération Internationale de Football Association* (FIFA-Statutes) www.fifa.com/mm/document/affederation/generic/02/14/97/88/fifastatuten2013_e_neutral.pdf, Article 1(2) of the 2013 Statutes of the *Fédération Internationale de Gymnastique* (FIG-Statutes) www.fig-gymnastics.com/publicdir/rules/files/main/STATUTES%202015%20%28english%29a.pdf, s 1(1) of the 2014 Statutes of the *Fédération Internationale de Luge de Course* (FIL-Statutes) www.fil-luge.org/fileadmin/user_upload/Documents/Statuten/Statutes2014_complete_Internet.pdf, s 4(1) of the 2014 Statutes of the *Fédération Internationale de Motocyclisme* (FIM-Statutes) www.fim-live.com/en/library/download/57328/no_cache/1/, s C 2 of the 2013 Constitution of the *Fédération Internationale de Natation* (FINA-Constitution) www.fina.org/sites/default/files/rules-print-pdf/7746.pdf, Article 7 of the 2012 Statutes of the *Fédération Internationale de Pelota Vasca* (FIPV-Statutes) www.fipv.net/media/docs/2013/02/21/estatutos-2012-es.pdf, Article I(1.2) of the 2007 Statutes of the *Fédération Internationale de Quilleurs* (FIQ-Statutes) www.fiq.org/fotos/FIQ%20STATUTES%287%29.pdf, ss 1(1) and 1(4) of the 2012 Statutes of the *Fédération Internationale de Ski* (FIS-Statutes) http://www.fis-ski.com/mm/Document/documentlibrary/Statutes/02/03/06/statutes-2012-complete_Neutral.pdf, s 1.1 of the 2012 Statutes of the *Fédération Internationale des Échecs* (FIDE-Statutes) www.fide.com/component/handboo k/?id=38&view=article, Article 1 of the 2013 Constitution of the *Fédération Internationale des Luttes Associées* (FILA-Constitution) www.fila-official.com/images/FILA/documents/ statuts/FILA_CONSTITUTION_2013.pdf, Article 1.1 of the 2013 Statutes of the *Fédération Internationale du Hockey sur Gazon* (FIH-Statutes) www.fih.ch/files/Sport/Coaching/2013-01-01%20Statutes%20passed%20by%20Congress%20on%2003%2011%2012.pdf, s 1.2.2 of the 2012 Constitution of the *Fédération Internationale du Volleyball* (FIVB-Constitution) www.fivb.org/EN/FIVB/Document/Legal/FIVB_Constitution_en_20120920.pdf, Article 1(1) of the 2013 Statutes of the Federation of International Bandy (FIB-Statutes) www.worldbandy.com/ckfinder/userfiles/files/Documents/FIB_Statutes_2012.doc, Article 1 of the 2012 Statutes of the Federation of International Polo (FIP-Statutes) www.fippolo.com/wp-content/uploads/2013/04/By-Laws-in-Spanish-Estatutos-2012-11-16-2.pdf, Article 1(2) of the 2013 Constitution of the International Association of Athletics Associations (IAFF-Constitution) www.iaaf.org/download/download?filename=109b892a-9520-4d2f-a182-57cf4f78d404.pdf&urlslug=IAAF%20Constitution, Preamble of the 2010 Constitution of the International Biathlon Union (IBU-Constitution) www4.biathlonworld.com/media/files/downloads/IBU_Rules_2012_cap1.pdf s 2.1 of the 2012 Statutes of the International Boxing Association (AIBA-Statutes) http://aiba.s3.amazonaws.com/2015/02/New-Version-of-the-2014-AIBA-Statutes.pdf, Article 1(3) of the 2013 Statutes of the International Canoe Federation (ICF-Statutes) http://www.canoeicf.com/sites/default/files/icf_statutes_2015_0.pdf, ss 1, 2 and 3 of the 1997 Memorandum of Association of the International Cricket Council (ICC-Memorandum) icc-live.s3.amazonaws.com/cms/media/about_docs/52fb1a7b80d96-ICC%20Mem%20and%20Arts%20%28approved%20by%20Conference%20June%202012%29%20-%20clean.pdf, Article 1(2) of the 2012 Statutes of the International Dance Sport Federation (IDSF-Statutes) www.worlddancesport.org/

associations under the civil law of the United States of America,[57] while the BWF, the IFNA, the IWSF and the WSF are associations and corporations respectively, under UK civil law;[58] the CMAS, the CMSB, the IAAF and the UIAA, which are associations under the civil law of the Principality of Monaco;[59] the FIA and the

Document/18455044380/WDSF_Statutes.pdf, Article 3 of the 2014 Statutes of the International Federation of Sport Climbing (IFSC-Statutes) www.ifsc-climbing.org/images/about-ifsc/IFSC_Statutes_2014.pdf, Article 1 of the 2012 Statutes of the International Floorball Federation (IFF-Statutes) www.floorball.org/Liitetiedostot/Statutes/IFF%20STATUTES%20Edition%202012.pdf, s 17.1 of the 2010 Constitution of the International Golf Federation (IGF-Constitution) igfederation.s3.amazonaws.com/wp-content/uploads/2012/11/Constitution_of_International_Golf_Federation_V2010.pdf, Article 1(1) of the 2014 Statutes of the International Handball Federation (IHF-Statutes) www.ihf.info/files/Uploads/NewsAttachments/0_01%20-%20Statutes_GB.pdf, Article I(1) of the 2012 Statutes of the International Ice Hockey Federation (IIHF-Statutes) www.iihf.com/fileadmin/user_upload/PDF/The_IIHF/2012-2014_IIHF_Statutes_and_Bylaws.pdf, Article 1.2 of the 2013 Statutes of the International Judo Federation (IJF-Statutes) www.intjudo.eu/editor_up/up/IJF%20Statutes%28%20Swiss%20Association%29%2023%2008%202013%20ENG%20-.pdf, Article 5 of the 2011 Statutes of the International Korfball Federation (IKF-Statutes) www.ikf.org/wp-content/uploads/2013/01/IKF-Statutes-2011final-rev.pdf, Article 1.3 of the 2012 Constitution of the International Live Saving Federation (ILSF-Constitution) www.ilsf.org/sites/ilsf.org/files/filefield/ILS%20Constitution%202012_0.pdf, s 1.2 of the 2010 By-Laws of the International Rafting Federation (IRF-By-Laws) www.internationalrafting.com/wp-content/uploads/2011/10/ByLawsVer1.2.pdf, s 2 of the 1996 Memorandum of Association of International Sailing Federation Limited (ISAF-Memorandum) www.sailing.org/tools/documents/CONSTITUTION-2014WEBSITE-%5B16614%5D.pdf, Article 1(6) of the 2014 Constitution and General Regulations of the International Skating Union (ISU-Constitution) static.isu.org/media/156160/constitution-and-general-regulations-version-july-15-2014.pdf, s 1.2.2 of the 2013 Constitution of the International Table Tennis Federation (ITTF-Constitution) www.ittf.com/ittf_handbook/2013/2013_EN_HBK_CHPT_1.pdf, s 1 of the 2013 Memorandum of Association of the International Waterski & Wakeboard Federation (IWSF-Memorandum) www.iwsf.com/org/memorandum/2009%20IWWF%20Memorandum%20of%20Association.pdf, s 1.1.1 of the 2013 Constitution of the International Weightlifting Federation (IWF-Constitution) www.iwf.net/wp-content/uploads/downloads/2015/02/IWF-Constitution_2015.pdf, Preamble of the 2013 Constitution of the International Triathlon Union (ITU-Constitution) www.triathlon.org/uploads/docs/ITU_Constitution-july112013v3.pdf, Article 1(1) of the 2013 Constitution of the International Wushu Federation (IWUF-Constitution) www.iwuf.org/upload/2014/1118/670358dfeea8a897c689436ca9fcf216c17258bd.pdf, Article 1(2) of the 2013 Constitution of the *Union Cycliste Internationale* (UCI-Constitution) www.uci.ch/mm/Document/News/Rulesandregulation/16/26/19/STA-20140926-E_English.pdf, Article 1 of the 2013 Statutes of the *Union Internationale de Pentathlon Moderne* (UIPM-Statutes) www.pentathlon.org/wp-content/uploads/UIPM-Constitution-Statutes-2014.pdf, Article 1 of the 2014 Statutes of the *Union Internationale de Motonautique* (UIM-Statutes) www.uimpowerboating.com/files/4613/9522/8367/2014_statutes_and_by_laws_for_publication_on_web.pdf, Article 1.1 of the 2014 Articles of Association of the World Baseball Softball Confederation (WBSC-Articles) isfsoftball.org/english/communication/WBSC_charter_eng_10May2014.pdf, Article 1 of the 2010 Constitution of the World Bridge Federation (WBF-Constitution) www.worldbridge.org/Data/Sites/1/media/documents/official-documents/WBFConstitution.pdf, Article 1.2 of the 2010 Constitution of the World Confederation of Billiard Sports (WCBS-Constitution) www.billiard-wcbs.org/WCBS_Constitution.pdf, s 1.2 of the 2013 Constitution of the World Curling Federation (WCF-Constitution) http://www.worldcurling.org/download/?dl==AFVxIkVWZ1RhxmRWR1aatWVFlVeW1mRTJlRah1UqZUV, Article 1.2 of the 2012 Statutes of the World Karate Federation (WKF-Statutes) www.wkf.net/pdf/wkf-statutes-english-nov2012.pdf, and s II of the 1996 Memorandum of Association of World Squash Federation Limited (WSF-Memorandum) http://www.worldsquash.org/ws/wp-content/uploads/2015/12/151116_Memorandum-Articles-of-Association.pdf.

[57] See for a general introduction, Marion R Fremont-Smith, *Governing Nonprofit Organizations—Federal and State Law and Regulation* (Harvard University Press, 2004).

[58] See for a general introduction, Robert S Lesher, 'The Not-Profit Corporation—A Neglected Stepchild Comes of Age' (1967) 22(4) *The Business Lawyer* 951–73.

[59] See for a general introduction, Karine Rodriguez, *Le droit des associations: Les règles générales* (Editions L'Harmattan, 2004).

UIAA, which are associations under the civil law of the French Republic;[60] the FIL and the IBU, which are associations under the civil law of the Republic of Austria;[61] the FIPV and the WKF, which are associations under the civil law of the Kingdom of Spain;[62] as well as the FIB, an association under the civil law of the Kingdom of Sweden;[63] the FIP, an association under the civil law of the Oriental Republic of Uruguay;[64] the ICF, an association under the civil law of the Kingdom of Denmark;[65] the ICC, an association under the civil law of the (British) Virgin Islands;[66] the IKF, an association under the civil law of the Netherlands;[67] the ILSF, an association under the civil law of the Kingdom of Belgium;[68] the IOF, an association under the civil law of the Republic of Finland;[69] the IRE, an association under the civil law of the Republic of Ireland;[70] the ISAF, a limited corporation under the civil law of the Isle of Man;[71] and the ISSF, an association under the civil law of the Federal Republic of Germany.[72]

### *ii. International Sports Associations as Subjects of International Law*

Despite their status as legal persons under domestic law, international sports associations act globally, are pretty much autonomous, and regulate their respective sports exclusively,[73] thus exercising some sort of sovereignty, which raises the question whether international sports associations are not only subjects of domestic law but also of international law. (a) International sports associations have some similarities with international organisations (IOs), but do not meet all required criteria, (b) As international sports associations do not meet all criteria to be treated in the same way as the International Committee of the Red Cross (ICRC), (c) NGOs, or (d) TNCs, it is suggested (e) that international sports associations should be considered as subjects *sui generis*.

[60] Ibid.

[61] See for a general introduction, Franziska Jaufer, *Recht im Sport* (Verlag Österreich, 2011).

[62] See for a general introduction, Santiago Catalá Rubio, *El derecho a la personalidad jurídica de las entidades religiosas* (Ediciones de la Universidad de Castilla-La Mancha, 2004).

[63] See for a general introduction, Rasmus Gustafsson and Maria Isaksson, *Ekonomistyrning i ideellaföreningar—En kvalitativstudiemedinriktningpåideellaidrottsföreningar* (Blekinge Tekniska Högskola, 2012) available at www.medieteknik.bth.se/fou/cuppsats.nsf/all/8b7bde7bc97a0692c1257a670035dba6/$file/BTH2012Gustafsson.pdf.

[64] See for a general introduction, Catalá Rubio (n 62).

[65] See for a general introduction, Jens Ewald and Lars Halgreen, *Sports Law in Denmark* (Kluwer Law International, 2011).

[66] See for a general introduction, Lesher (n 58).

[67] See for a general introduction, Aaron N Wise and Bruce S Meyer, *International Sports Law and Business*, Vol 2 (Kluwer Law International, 1997) 1349–51.

[68] See for a general introduction, Rodriguez (n 59).

[69] Cf Max Wesiack, *Europäisches Internationales Vereinsrecht* (Mohr Siebeck, 2011).

[70] See for a general introduction, Arthur J Jacobson, 'The Private Use of Public Authority: Sovereignty and Associations in the Common Law' (1980) 29 *Buffalo Law Review* 599–620.

[71] See for a general introduction, Lesher (n 58).

[72] See for a general introduction, Kurt Stöber and Dirk-Ulrich Otto, *Handbuch zum Vereinsrecht* 10th edn (Verlag Dr Otto Schmidt, 2012).

[73] See Jean-Loupe Chappelet, *L'autonomie du sport en Europe* (Council of Europe, 2010) 24.

1. Why International Sports Associations are not International Organisations

International sports associations are not IOs. An IO is defined as an 'organization established by a treaty or other instrument governed by international law and possessing its own international legal personality'.[74] In addition, the IO's 'existence is recognized by law in their member countries' and 'they are not treated as resident institutional units of the countries in which they are located'.[75] Furthermore, although international law does not require that the members of IOs are states,[76] the International Law Commission (ILC) points out that 'the presence of States among the members is essential for the organization' to be considered as an IO.[77] However, international law does not require that the whole state is a member of the respective IO. Instead, individual state organs or agencies can be members of the IO without any effect on the IO's legal status.[78] Unlike IOs, international sports associations are not established by a treaty or other instrument governed by international law. Instead, they are established by charters governed by domestic law.[79] Members of international sports associations are not states, but national sports associations, which are organised as private associations under domestic law and are thus not state organs or agencies.[80]

[74] Article 2(a) of the Draft Articles on the Responsibility of International Organizations (2011) YbILC 2011, Vol II, Part Two. See also Article 2(1)(i) of the Vienna Convention on the Law of Treaties between States and International Organizations or between International Organizations (1986, not yet in force) 25 ILM 543 (1986). See also Jan Klabbers, *An Introduction to International Institutional Law*, 2nd edn (Cambridge University Press, 2009) 7–12, who defines an IO as an entity created between states on the basis of a treaty and with an organ with a distinct will.

[75] Organisation for Economic Co-operation and Development (OECD), 'Glossary of Statistical Terms: International Organisations' available at stats.oecd.org/glossary/detail.asp?ID=1434.

[76] See Klabbers (n 74) 94–99.

[77] ILC, Draft Articles on the Responsibility of International Organizations, With Commentary (2011) YbILC 2011, Vol II, Part Two, 10.

[78] Ibid. An example of such an IO is the Arab States Broadcasting Union whose members are public broadcasting corporations from the Member States of the Arab League, Arab States Broadcasting Union, 'What's ASBU?' available at www.asbu.net/doc.php?docid=45&lang=en.

[79] Cf Article 15(1) IOC-Charter, s (1)(1) BWF-Constitution, ss 1.1.2. and 1.1.7. FAI-Statutes, Article 4.1 FEI-Statutes, Article 1(1) FIA-Statutes, Preamble FIE-Statutes, Article 2(2) FIBA-General Statutes, s 2(1) FIBT-Statutes, s 1(1) FIFA-Statutes, Article 1(2) FIG-Statutes, s 1(1) FIL-Statutes, s 4(1) FIM-Statutes, s C 2 FINA-Constitution, Article 7 FIPV-Statutes, Article I(1.2) FIQ-Statutes, ss 1(1) and 1(4) FIS-Statutes, s 1.1 FIDE-Statutes, Article 1 FILA-Constitution, Article 1.1 FIH-Statutes, s 1.2.2 FIVB-Constitution, Article 1(1) FIB-Statutes, Article 1 FIP-Statutes, Article 1(2) IAFF-Constitution, Preamble IBU-Constitution, s 2.1 AIBA-Statutes, Article 1(3) ICF-Statutes, ss 1, 2 and 3 ICC-Memorandum, Article 1(2) IDSF-Statutes, Article 3 IFSC-Statutes, Article 1 IFF-Statutes, s 17.1 IGF-Constitution, Article 1(1) IHF-Statutes, Article I(1) IIHF-Statutes, Article 1.2 IJF-Statutes, Article 5 IKF-Statutes, Article 1.3 ILSF-Constitution, s 1.2 IRF-By-Laws, s 2 ISAF-Memorandum, Article 1(6) ISU-Constitution, s 1.2.2 ITTF-Constitution, s 1 IWSF-Memorandum, s 1.1.1 IWF-Constitution, Preamble ITU-Constitution, Article 1(1) IWUF-Constitution, Article 1(2) UCI-Constitution, Article 1 UIPM-Statutes, Article 1 UIM-Statutes, Article 1.1 WBSC-Articles, Article 1 WBF-Constitution, Article 1.2 WCBS-Constitution, s 1.2 WCF-Constitution, Article 1.2 WKF-Statutes, and s II WSF-Memorandum.

[80] See Lucien W Valloni and Thilo Pachmann, *Sports Law in Switzerland* (Kluwer Law International, 2011) 67.

## 2. Comparing International Sports Associations with the International Committee of the Red Cross

International sports associations act globally and have a legal personality worldwide.[81] Similarly, the ICRC is also 'just' a private association established under Swiss domestic law, but it acts globally and has a legal personality worldwide.[82] In fact, the ICRC is considered to be a subject of international law.[83] Thus, an analogy between the ICRC and international sports associations is worth thinking about—but has to be rejected. Unlike international sports associations, the ICRC is not only mentioned in international treaties[84] but is also recognised as a subject of international law by states.[85] The ICRC's personality in international law is based on the fact that:

(1) the ICRC's and its personnel's privileges and immunities are, in practice, widely recognized by governments, by the UN, and by other international governmental organizations,
(2) the ICRC deals directly and in its own right with States, particularly States involved in an international armed conflict, with insurgent movements involved in an internal conflict, and with international governmental organizations, notably the UN and its various specialized agencies,
(3) it concludes agreements with States, particularly headquarters agreements, that clarify the position of the ICRC's delegation, of individual delegates, and of the ICRC's premises in a given country, and grant them quasi-diplomatic status,

[81] Cf Article 15(1) IOC-Charter, s (1)(1) BWF-Constitution, ss 1.1.2. and 1.1.7. FAI-Statutes, Article 4.1 FEI-Statutes, Article 1(1) FIA-Statutes, Preamble FIE-Statutes, Article 2(2) FIBA-General Statutes, s 2(1) FIBT-Statutes, s 1(1) FIFA-Statutes, Article 1(2) FIG-Statutes, s 1(1) FIL-Statutes, s 4(1) FIM-Statutes, s C 2 FINA-Constitution, Article 7 FIPV-Statutes, Article I(1.2) FIQ-Statutes, ss 1(1) and 1(4) FIS-Statutes, s 1.1 FIDE-Statutes, Article 1 FILA-Constitution, Article 1.1 FIH-Statutes, s 1.2.2 FIVB-Constitution, Article 1(1) FIB-Statutes, Article 1 FIP-Statutes, Article 1(2) IAFF-Constitution, Preamble IBU-Constitution, s 2.1 AIBA-Statutes, Article 1(3) ICF-Statutes, ss 1, 2 and 3 ICC-Memorandum, Article 1(2) IDSF-Statutes, Article 3 IFSC-Statutes, Article 1 IFF-Statutes, s 17.1 IGF-Constitution, Article 1(1) IHF-Statutes, Article I(1) IIHF-Statutes, Article 1.2 IJF-Statutes, Article 5 IKF-Statutes, Article 1.3 ILSF-Constitution, s 1.2 IRF-By-Laws, s 2 ISAF-Memorandum, Article 1(6) ISU-Constitution, s 1.2.2 ITTF-Constitution, s 1 IWSF-Memorandum, s 1.1.1 IWF-Constitution, Preamble ITU-Constitution, Article 1(1) IWUF-Constitution, Article 1(2) UCI-Constitution, Article 1 UIPM-Statutes, Article 1 UIM-Statutes, Article 1.1 WBSC-Articles, Article 1 WBF-Constitution, Article 1.2 WCBS-Constitution, s 1.2 WCF-Constitution, Article 1.2 WKF-Statutes, and s II WSF-Memorandum.

[82] Cf Antonio Cassese, *International Law*, 2nd edn (Oxford, Oxford University Press) 133–34.

[83] Silja Vöneky, 'Implementation and Enforcement of International Humanitarian Law' in Dieter Fleck (ed), *The Handbook of International Humanitarian Law*, 3rd edn (Oxford University Press, 2013) 647–700 at 691.

[84] See Article 9 of the 1949 Geneva Convention (I) for the Amelioration of the Condition of the Wounded and Sick in Armed Forces in the Field, 75 UNTS 31; Article 9 of the 1949 Geneva Convention (II) for the Amelioration of the Wounded and Sick in Armed Forces at Sea, 75 UNTS 85; Article 9 of the 1949 Geneva Convention (III) relative to the Treatment of Prisoners of War, 75 UNTS 135; and Article 10 of the 1949 Geneva Convention (IV) relative to the Protection of Civilian Persons in Time of War, 75 UNTS 287. See also Article 73 of the 2002 International Criminal Court Rules of Procedure and Evidence (ICC-Rules) available at www.icc-cpi.int/iccdocs/PIDS/legal-texts/RulesProcedure EvidenceEng.pdf.

[85] Cf International Criminal Tribunal for former Yugoslavia, *Prosecutor v Simić* (Decision of 27 July 1999) available at www.icty.org/x/cases/simic/tdec/en/90727EV59549.htm para 46.

(4) its relations with the host country Switzerland have been regulated by the Agreement between the ICRC and the Swiss Federal Council to Determine the Legal Status of the Committee in Switzerland of 19 March 1993,[86]
(5) the UN General Assembly (UNGA) has granted the ICRC observer status, and the ICRC's status at the UN is different from that of ordinary non-governmental organizations, as evidenced by the UNGA's voting a special resolution entitled 'Observer Status for the International Committee of the Red Cross, in Consideration of the Special Role and Mandate Conferred upon it by the Geneva Conventions of 12 August 1949'.[87]

In order to determine to what extent international sports associations can be compared with the ICRC, the following needs to be analysed: (1) whether international sports associations have the same or at least similar privileges and immunities; (2) whether they interact with other subjects of international law; (3) whether they conclude agreements with states; (4) whether they enter into an agreement with the respective host country; and (5) whether they are granted a special status by the United Nations or one of its specialised agencies.

### *The Privileges and Immunities of International Sports Associations*

The large majority of international sports associations analysed in this contribution are associations under Swiss civil law.[88] However, unlike 'ordinary' associations under Swiss civil law, international sports associations enjoy some privileges. For instance, they are largely exempt from tax duties[89] and from limitations with regard to the employment of foreigners.[90]

However, according to the Swiss *Gaststaatgesetz* (Host State Act),[91] only a few entities also enjoy further privileges, including immunities.[92] Among these entities are international organisations (Article 2(1)(a) *Gaststaatgesetz*), international institutions (Article 2(1)(b) *Gaststaatgesetz*), quasi-international organisations (Article 2(1)(c) *Gaststaatgesetz*), international conferences (Article 2(1)(h) *Gaststaatgesetz*), secretariats and other organs (Article 2(1)(i) *Gaststaatgesetz*), and other international organs (Article 2(1)(m) *Gaststaatgesetz*). The wording of Article 2(1)

[86] Under this agreement the Swiss Confederation guarantees the ICRC's 'independence and freedom of action' assures the inviolability of its premises, and grants immunity from legal process and execution, not only to the institution, but also to its staff in the exercise of their official functions, see 1993 Agreement between Switzerland and the International Committee on the Red Cross on the legal status of the Committee in Switzerland, 293 (1993 International Review of the Red Cross) 152–60, also available at www.icrc.org/eng/resources/documents/misc/57jnx7.htm.

[87] UNGA Res 45/6 (16 October 1990). The ICRC has also observer status with various UN agencies and with the major regional governmental organisations, cf Hans-Peter Gasser, 'International Committee of the Red Cross (ICRC)' in Rüdiger Wolfrum (ed), *Max Planck Encyclopedia of Public International Law* (Online Edition, Oxford University Press, 2008-) para 26.

[88] Text to n 56.

[89] Article 24(3) of the 2007 *Bundesgesetz über die von der Schweiz als Gaststaat gewährten Vorrechte, Immunitäten und Erleichterungen sowie finanzielle Beiträge* (*Gaststaatgesetz*, Host State Act) AS 2007 6637.

[90] Ibid.

[91] 2007 *Bundesgesetz über die von der Schweiz als Gaststaat gewährten Vorrechte, Immunitäten und Erleichterungen sowie finanzielle Beiträge* (*Gaststaatgesetz*, Host State Act) AS 2007 6637.

[92] Article 2(1) *Gaststaatgesetz*.

*Gaststaatgesetz* indicates that the list of entities which may be granted immunity under the *Gaststaatgesetz* is exhaustive.[93] Therefore, further analysis is necessary to determine whether international sports associations fulfil the criteria of these entities.

The definitions of international organisations pursuant to the *Gaststaatgesetz* and pursuant to international law are identical.[94] Consequently, as international sports associations are not IOs under international law,[95] they also do not meet the criteria of an international organisation pursuant to the *Gaststaatgesetz*.

International institutions (Article 2(1)(b) *Gaststaatgesetz*) are entities, which are similar to IOs, but do not meet all the criteria of an IO.[96] International institutions are not established by an international treaty, but nevertheless play an important role in the international field.[97] The lack of an international treaty is usually based on political reasons, but these reasons have vanished over time.[98] In addition, international institutions behave and act very similarly to IOs, and interact with states in many ways.[99] Examples of international institutions within the meaning of Article 2(1)(b) *Gaststaatgesetz* are the Organization for Security and Co-operation in Europe (OSCE) and the ICRC.[100] So far, the *Schweizerische Bundesrat* (Swiss Federal Council) has not granted any international sports association privileges under Article 2(1)(b) *Gaststaatgesetz*, which might indicate that these associations are not international institutions within the meaning of the act.

Quasi-international organisations (Article 2(1)(c) *Gaststaatgesetz*) are entities which are established pursuant to Swiss civil law and are quite similar to NGOs.[101] However, NGOs and quasi-international organisations can be distinguished based on their members, their financing, and their functions.[102] Members of quasi-international organisations are usually states or public entities, and these organisations are financed out of public funds.[103] In addition, quasi-international organisations usually carry out public functions, which would otherwise have to be carried out by the respective states.[104] An example of such a quasi-international organisation is the International Air Transport Association (IATA).[105]

Unlike quasi-international organisations, NGOs are composed of natural persons and private entities (such as associations), which are financed privately, and do not fulfil tasks of a general public interest.[106] While it can be questioned to what extent international sports associations fulfil tasks of general public interest, it has to be

[93] Cf Schweizerischer Bundesrat, 'Botschaft zum Bundesgesetz über die von der Schweiz als Gaststaat gewährten Vorrechte, Immunitäten und Erleichterungen sowie finanzielle Beiträge' (13 September 2006) AS 2006 8017 available at www.admin.ch/opc/de/federal-gazette/2006/8017.pdf 8030.

[94] Cf ibid 8031.

[95] Text to notes 74–80.

[96] Schweizerischer Bundesrat (n 93) 8031–32.

[97] Ibid.

[98] Ibid.

[99] Ibid.

[100] Ibid.

[101] Ibid.

[102] Ibid.

[103] Ibid.

[104] Ibid.

[105] See JWS Brancker, *IATA and What It Does* (Leyden: Sijthoff International Publishing, 1977).

[106] Schweizerischer Bundesrat (n 93) 8031.

noted that international sports associations are regularly composed of regional sports associations,[107] which are usually equal to associations in accordance with Swiss civil law.[108] They are regularly composed of national sports associations,[109] which are usually associations in accordance with the respective national civil law,[110] and are made up of natural persons and/or other private entities.[111] In addition, international sports associations are financed privately—through sponsorship and/or by generating profits through international tournaments.[112] Therefore, international sports associations are not quasi-international organisations.

International conferences (Article 2(1)(h) *Gaststaatgesetz*) refer only to those conferences which take place under the auspices of an IO, a group of states, or the Swiss Federation.[113] Although it can be observed that the number of participating NGOs and/or civil society participation as a whole is increasing and that occasionally NGOs are not only granted observer status, but full membership,[114] an international conference is still characterised by the participation of representatives of states.[115] Therefore, despite the fact that international sports associations regularly host conferences within the Swiss Federation[116] these conferences are not international conferences within the meaning of Article 2(1)(h) *Gaststaatgesetz*, as participants of these conferences are delegates of the respective member associations,[117] and not representatives of states.

Secretariats and other organs (Article 2(1)(i) *Gaststaatgesetz*) refer only to those secretariats and other organs that were established by international treaties.[118] This does not apply to the secretariats and other organs of international sports associations that were established by the respective statutes of the association, which is not an international treaty.[119]

Unlike the other entities listed in Article 2(1) *Gaststaatgesetz*, other international organs (Article 2(1)(m) *Gaststaatgesetz*) are not defined. Instead, the *Schweizerische Bundesrat* considers this alternative as an opening clause which allows for a dynamic adaptation of the *Gaststaatgesetz* in the event that a new entity is created that is not covered by the previous examples.[120] The *Schweizerische Bundesrat* emphasises,

[107] See n 80.
[108] Cf ibid.
[109] Ibid.
[110] Ibid.
[111] Ibid.
[112] See text to notes 422–555.
[113] Schweizerischer Bundesrat (n 93) 8036.
[114] An example of such a conference is the World Summit on the Information Society (WSIS) see World Summit on the Information Society, 'Basic Information: About WSIS' available at www.itu.int/wsis/basic/about.html.
[115] Schweizerischer Bundesrat (n 93) 8036–37.
[116] See International Olympic Committee, 'Calendar' available at www.olympic.org/content/the-ioc/governance/international-federations/?calendargroup=-1.
[117] See Amy Shipley, 'IOC Members Press USOC to Share the Wealth; Other National Committees Want Bigger Share of TV and Sponsorship Money', *The Washington Post* (Washington DC, 21 October 2008) E01 (relating to the United States Olympic Committee).
[118] Schweizerischer Bundesrat (n 93) 8037–38.
[119] See, for instance, Articles 21–60 FIFA-Statutes.
[120] Schweizerischer Bundesrat (n 93) 8036–37.

however, that this opening clause has to be applied restrictively.[121] Consequently, it declares that a new type of entity has to fulfil the tasks of general public interest.[122]

Although the organisation of major sporting events was considered to be a task of general public interest in ancient Rome ('*panem et circenses*'), and despite the fact that sports is an important field of public policy[123] and there are various advantages in hosting a major international sports event,[124] hosting such an event cannot be considered a task of general public interest that is transferred to the respective international sports association by the host country. Consequently, international sports associations do not fulfil tasks of general public interest.

Furthermore, the fact that the *Schweizerische Bundesrat* has not granted any international sports association immunity in accordance with the *Gaststaatgesetz*, and the fact that international sports associations are not listed in Article 2(1) *Gaststaatgesetz*, despite being active before the enactment of the *Gaststaatgesetz*, indicates that international sports associations were not considered to be eligible for immunity, and therefore do not fall under the opening clause of Article 2(1)(m) *Gaststaatgesetz*.

To sum up, international sports associations do not fall under Article 2(1) *Gaststaatgesetz* and are therefore not eligible for immunity under Swiss law. In addition, international sports associations do not enjoy immunity in any other jurisdiction. The indemnification clause usually contained in bidding and hosting agreements only refers to indemnifications for acts committed by the organising committee, not for acts directly committed by the international sports association and/or its own personnel.

### *Direct Interaction with States*

International sports associations do not interact with states—at least not on a regular basis. Even the agreement on the hosting of a major international sports event is not concluded between the international sports association and the host country, but between the international sports association and the organising team or organising committee, which is usually composed of members of the national sports association.[125] Politicians might be members of the advisory board of the organising team.[126]

It is up to the organising team to ensure that the government and the host cities support the international sports event.[127] The organising committee has to submit

[121] Cf ibid 8041.

[122] Ibid 8040–41.

[123] See Article 165 of the 1957/2007 Treaty on the Functioning of the European Union (TFEU) OJ (EU) C 326/47 (26 October 2012).

[124] Cf Essex and Chalkley (n 42) 187–206.

[125] See FIFA, 'Organising Committee for the FIFA World Cup' available at www.fifa.com/worldcup/organization/committees/index.html.

[126] Cf ibid.

[127] Cf FIFA, 'Bidding Agreement regarding the submission of bids for the right to host and stage the 2018 FIFA WORLD CUP or 2022 FIFA WORLD CUP', available at www.transparencyinsport.org/The_documents_that_FIFA_does_not_want_fans_to_read/PDF-documents/%2811%29FIFA-Bidding-agreement.pdf 26–28.

the declaration of support to the international sports association.[128] Thus, there is almost no direct interaction with states.

### *Conclusion of Agreements with States*

Besides concluding host agreements with the respective host country of the international sports association,[129] international sports associations do not make any agreements directly with states.

### *Agreement with the Host Country*

Some international sports associations have concluded host agreements with the host country.[130] These host agreements are, however, fundamentally different from the host agreement between the Swiss Federation and the ICRC.

### *Special Status Granted by the United Nations or One of its Special Agencies*

The IOC is the only international sports association that has been granted observer status by the UNGA.[131] The UNGA Resolution granting the ICRC observer status[132] is identical to the UNGA Resolution granting the IOC observer status.

### *Preliminary Conclusion*

Albeit having the same legal status as the IOC before the UNGA, the ICRC is a unique entity. It has been shown that the IOC is different from the ICRC. Furthermore, the other international sports associations do not even have observer status at the UNGA, thus they differ from the ICRC even more than the IOC. Consequently, international sports associations cannot be compared with the ICRC and therefore do not have the same legal status.

## 3. International Sports Associations as Non-governmental Organisations

As shown above,[133] international sports associations are composed of private entities (usually other associations pursuant to domestic civil law) and are financed privately. Further to this, with the possible exception of significant international

[128] Ibid.

[129] Cf ibid 2.

[130] 2000 Abkommen zwischen dem Schweizerischen Bundesrat und dem Internationalen Olympischen Komittee betreffend das Statut des Internationalen Olympischen Komitee in der Schweiz, AS 2001 845 available at www.admin.ch/opc/de/classified-compilation/20002659/index.html.

[131] United Nations General Assembly, 'Resolution adopted by the General Assembly on 19 October 2009: Observer status for the International Olympic Committee in the General Assembly' UN Doc A/RES/64/3 (22 October 2009).

[132] United Nations General Assembly, 'Observer status for the International Committee of the Red Cross, in consideration of the special role and mandate conferred upon it by the Geneva Conventions of 12 August 1949' UN Doc A/RES/45/6 (16 October 1990).

[133] Text at n 55.

sports events, such as the Olympic Games, the FIFA World Cup or a Formula One Grand Prix, international sports associations do not fulfil tasks of greater public interest—and even if the aforementioned events are considered to fulfil this role, it has to be noted that they are then fulfilled by the organising committee, and not the international sports association. Consequently, international sports associations meet all the criteria of an NGO.

Despite their expanding role, NGOs are not (yet) regarded as subjects of international law.[134] It is argued, however, that some NGOs which work within a legal framework of an organ or an IO should be awarded the status of partial legal subjects of international law.[135] Whether this argument should be upheld is irrelevant for international sports associations, as they are not working within a legal framework of an organ or an IO.

### 4. International Sports Associations as Transnational Corporations

Despite considering themselves as non-profit organisations,[136] at least some international sports associations, such as the IOC, FIFA and the FIA, generate massive profits.[137] Consequently, these international sports associations can be compared to other non-state actors acting globally and generating profits—TNCs. A TNC is defined as 'an entity that is legally separate from its members, and which enjoys its own personality and can hold rights and obligations in its own name'.[138] Moreover, it owns or controls production or service facilities in one or more countries other than the home country.[139]

As has been shown above,[140] international sports associations are associations pursuant (mostly) to Swiss civil law. Thus, they are entities which are legally separate from their members, and are the bearers of rights and obligations in their own

[134] See Steve Charnovitz, 'Nongovernmental Organizations and International Law' (2006) 100(2) *American Journal of International Law* 348–72; see also ILC, 'First report on responsibility of international organizations, by Mr Giorgio Gaja, Special Rapporteur' UN Doc A/CN.4/532 (26 March 2003) para 17.

[135] Stephan Hobe, 'Non-Governmental Organizations' in Wolfrum (n 87) para 44.

[136] Cf Article 15(1) IOC-Charter, s 1(1) BWF-Constitution, ss 1.1.2. and 1.1.7. FAI-Statutes, Article 4.1 FEI-Statutes, Article 1(1) FIA-Statutes, Preamble of the FIE-Statutes, Article 3(1) FIBA-General Statutes, s 1(1) FIBT-Statutes, s 1(1) FIFA-Statutes, Article 1(2) FIG-Statutes, s 1(2) FIL-Statutes, s 4(1) FIM-Statutes, s C 2 FINA-Constitution, Article 7 FIPV-Statutes, Article II FIQ-Statutes, s 1.1 FIDE-Statutes, Article 1 FILA-Constitution, Article 1.1 FIH-Statutes, s 1.2.1 FIVB-Statutes, Article 1.1 FIB-Statutes, Article 1 FIP-Statutes, Article 1(2) IAAF-Constitution, s 1.4 IBU-Constitution, s 2.1 AIBA-Statutes, Article 1(3) ICF-Statutes, ss 1, 2 and 3 ICC-Memorandum, Article 1(2) IDSF-Statutes, Article 3 IFSC-Statutes, Article 1 IFF-Statutes, Article 1(1) IHF-Statutes, Article 1.2 IJF-Statutes, Article 1.1 ILSF-Constitution, s 1.2 IRF-By-Laws, Article 1(6) ISU-Constitution, s 1.2.2 ITTF-Constitution, s 1 IWSF-Memorandum, s 1.1.1 IWF-Constitution, Preamble of the ITU-Constitution, Article 1(2) IWUF-Constitution, Article 1(2) UCI-Constitution, Article 1 UIPM-Statutes, Article 1 UIM-Statutes, Article 1.1 WBSC-Articles, Article 1 WBF-Constitution, Article 1.5 WCBS-Constitution, s 1.2 WCF-Constitution, Article 1.3 WKF-Statutes, and s II WSF-Memorandum.

[137] See TO Molefe, 'South Africa's World Cup Illusions', *The New York Times*, 25 June 2014 Op-Ed.

[138] Peter T Muchlinski, 'Corporations in International Law' in Wolfrum (n 87) para 1.

[139] Cf Malcom N Shaw, *International Law*, 6th edn (Cambridge University Press, 2008) 250.

[140] Text at note 57.

names.[141] As international sports associations govern the exercise of the respective sports globally, they are indeed very similar to TNCs.

## 5. International Sports Associations as Subjects of International Law *Sui Generis*

The list of subjects of international law is not exhaustive.[142] Therefore, international sports associations might be considered as subjects of international law *sui generis*.[143]

In its Advisory Opinion on Reparation for Injuries Suffered in the Service of the United Nations, the ICJ held that the necessary attribute of international personality is the power to enter, directly or indirectly, into a relationship (by treaty or otherwise) with other international persons.[144] As has been shown above, international sports associations enter indirectly—through the organising committees—into a relationship with the host country of an international sports event.[145]

Further, with regard to states as subjects of international law, it is argued that they derive their legal personality from the fact that they control territory in a stable and permanent way,[146] in other words they are sovereign over a specific territory. Of course, international sports associations do not exercise territorial sovereignty, but they do exercise some narrowly defined sovereignty. Each international sports association is the supreme authority for its respective sport.[147] Athletes have to agree to recognise the decisions of the respective international sports association.[148] Other entities, especially states, refrain from interfering in the affairs of international sports associations.[149] Consequently, international sports associations enjoy some sort of (international) autonomy. Therefore, I argue that international sports associations are 'limited' subjects of international law.

## 6. Preliminary Conclusions on the Legal Status of International Sports Associations

As has been shown, international sports associations are on the one hand associations under domestic civil law, thus subjects of domestic law, and on the other hand limited subjects of international law. On first view, this seems to be peculiar. On second view, it should be noted that domestic and international law are two separate legal orders. Consequently, all subjects of international law are at the same time subjects of domestic law.[150]

[141] Cf Article 60(1) of the 1907 *Schweizerisches Zivilgesetzbuch* (ZGB, Swiss Civil Code) AS 2014 210.

[142] Cf Shaw (n 139) 196–97.

[143] See generally for the notion of entities *sui generis*, James Crawford, *Brownlie's Principles of Public International Law*, 8th edn, (Oxford University Press, 2012) 124.

[144] ICJ, *Reparation for Injuries Suffered in the Service of the United Nations* (Advisory Opinion of 11 April 1949) ICJ Rep 1949, 174, 178–79.

[145] Text at n 130.

[146] Cassese (n 82) 71.

[147] See Valloni and Pachmann (n 80) 41.

[148] See Tony Buti, 'AOC Athletes' Agreement for Sydney 2000: The Implications for the Athletes' (1999) 22(3) *University of New South Wales Law Journal* 746–62.

[149] Valloni and Pachmann (n 80) 41.

[150] Cf Shaw (n 139) 195–96.

## B. International Sports Associations as Addressees of International Human Rights

Having determined the international legal personality of international sports associations, it has to be assessed to what extent international sports associations are addressees of international human rights. Besides the (non-binding) Universal Declaration of Human Rights (UDHR),[151] the most prominent international human rights instruments are the International Covenant on Civil and Political Rights (ICCPR)[152] and the International Covenant on Economic, Social and Cultural Rights (ICESCR).[153] In addition, regional instruments, such as the European Convention on Human Rights (ECHR),[154] the American Convention on Human Rights (AmCHR),[155] and the African Charter on Human and Peoples' Rights (AfCHPR),[156] play a significant role in the protection of human rights at the international level. Further, there are several instruments both at the international and the regional level providing for specific human rights, such as the Convention against Racial Discrimination[157] or the European Social Charter.[158]

### *i. International Sports Associations as Direct Addressees of International Human Rights*

Primarily, only Member States of these instruments are the addressees of the obligations.[159] However, the ECtHR held in the *Behrami and Saramati* case[160] that other actors can be addressees of the human rights obligations contained in the ECHR if these actors replace the state.[161] In the circumstances of the particular case, the United Nations (UN) was held responsible for human rights violations.[162] The ECtHR argued that the Member States of the UN had transferred parts of their sovereignty to the UN, making it impossible for the victims of the alleged human rights violations to seek remedies against the Member States. As a result, the human rights in question could only be enjoyed if the UN were also the addressee of the respective obligations.[163] More generally, whenever an actor enjoys some sovereign

[151] 1948 Universal Declaration of Human Rights (UDHR) UNGA Res 217A(III) (10 December 1948) UN Doc A/810 71 (1948).

[152] 1966 International Covenant on Civil and Political Rights (ICCPR) 999 UNTS 171.

[153] 1966 International Covenant on Economic, Social and Cultural Rights (ICESCR) 993 UNTS 3.

[154] 1950 European Convention for the Protection of Human Rights and Fundamental Freedoms (ECHR) 213 UNTS 221.

[155] 1969 American Convention on Human Rights (AmCHR) 1144 UNTS 123.

[156] 1981 African Charter on Human and Peoples' Rights (Banjul Charter, AfCHPR) 1520 UNTS 217.

[157] 1965 International Convention on the Elimination of All Forms of Racial Discrimination (Convention against Racial Discrimination, CERD) 660 UNTS 195.

[158] 1961 European Social Charter (ESC) 529 UNTS 89.

[159] See, for instance, Article 2(1) ICCPR, Article 2(1) ICESCR, Article 1 ECHR, Article 1(1) AmCHR, Article 1 AfCHPR, Article 2(1) CERD, Part II ESC.

[160] Essex and Chakley (n 5).

[161] ECtHR (n 4) paras 140–41.

[162] Ibid. This finding has been criticised, inter alia, by Aurel Sari, 'Jurisdiction and International Responsibility in Peace Support Operations: The Behrami and Samarati case' (2008) 8 *Human Rights Law Review* 151–70.

[163] Ibid. This was also held by the ICJ, *Injuries Suffered in the Service of the United Nations* (Advisory Opinion, 11 April 1949) ICJ Rep 1949, 174–220 at 185–86.

rights which might infringe human rights, the actor should also be the addressee of the respective human rights obligations.[164]

With regard to TNCs as subjects of human rights responsibilities, there is an extensive debate in international law.[165] The UN Special Representative on Human Rights and Transnational Corporations and other Business Enterprises, Professor John Ruggie, held that TNCs have a duty to respect human rights.[166] However, this is not the same duty as that which falls on states.[167] Instead, Ruggie pointed out that the TNCs' duty to respect human rights is rather a duty to act in a way that ensures compliance with human rights standards, and calls upon TNCs to act with due diligence, meaning that a TNC must become aware of, prevent and address adverse human rights impacts.[168] This requires TNCs to adopt a human rights policy, to carry out human rights impact assessments, to integrate human rights issues into their operations, and to track their performance in this regard.[169]

While it remains uncontested in international law that TNCs are subjects of human rights responsibilities,[170] it is still unclear whether they bear an obligation to address human rights responsibilities, and it is equally still unclear how far international law itself will set the normative content of possible corporate obligations.[171] It is argued, for instance, that the UDHR is addressed both to governments and to other organs of society—thus also to TNCs.[172] However, from a legal perspective, the UDHR is nothing more than a non-binding declaration.[173] Consequently, the TNCs' duty to respect human rights is based mainly on self-regulation and national supervision,[174] or on voluntary commitments.[175]

In this context it should be noted, however, that the voluntary commitments of TNCs with regard to their corporate social responsibility are not that 'toothless' anymore.[176] Instead, individual aspects of corporate social responsibility are being transformed into legislative acts.[177] For instance, in the context of the 'Strategy for

[164] See also Yaël Ronen, 'Human Rights Obligations of Territorial Non-State Actors' (2013) 46 *Cornell International Law Journal* 21–50.

[165] See Alston and Goodman (n 2) 1463–97; cf also Olivier De Schutter, *International Human Rights Law—Cases, Materials, Commentary* (Cambridge University Press, 2010) 365–460.

[166] United Nations Human Rights Council, 'Guiding Principles on Business and Human Rights: Implementing the United Nations "Protect, Respect and Remedy" Framework' UN Doc A/HRC/17/31 (21 March 2011), Principle 11.

[167] Cf Muchlinski (n 138) para 31.

[168] United Nations Human Rights Council (n 166) Principle 17.

[169] Ibid, Principle 15.

[170] Cf Alson and Goodman (n 3) 1465.

[171] Muchlinski (n 138) para 33.

[172] Ibid.

[173] Cf Tomuschat (n 2) 30.

[174] Muchlinski (n 138) para 33.

[175] Alson and Goodman (n 3) 1468–71.

[176] Cf Miriam A Cherry and Judd F Sneirson, 'Beyond Profit: Rethinking Corporate Social Responsibility and Greenwashing After the BP Oil Disaster' (2010–2011) 85(4) *Tulane Law Review* 983–1038.

[177] For instance, the Extractive Industries Transparency Initiative (EITI) requires that companies disclose their payments to governments, and governments disclose their receipt, Extractive Industries Transparency Initiative (EITI), "What is the EITI?" available at eiti.org/eiti. This initiative has been implemented in the Dodd-Frank Wall Street Reform and Consumer Protection Act and also incorporated into new EU directives, see Lars Schönwald, 'Overcoming the Resource Curse—Reducing Poverty by Making

Corporate Social Responsibility' of the European Union (EU), EU directives will be amended in order to oblige large corporations to report on non-financial issues such as environmental protection, social affairs, labour standards, and the like.[178] Similarly, Bangladesh signed an agreement with corporations, unions and NGOs under the auspices of the International Labor Organization obliging corporations to improve the working conditions of their suppliers.[179] Nevertheless, despite this positive development, it has to be noted that only a few TNCs are direct addressees of human rights obligations, meaning that international sports associations (which are to some extent also TNCs)[180] do not automatically have the same obligations as those few TNCs.

Taking the findings of the ECtHR in the *Behrami and Saramati* case into consideration, the question has to be asked: to what extent are states replaced by TNCs, and—further reduced to the scope of this chapter—to what extent are states replaced by international sports associations? As the hosting of major international sports events is considered to be a task of general public interest in special situations, the fulfilment of which is transferred to the organising committee under the auspices of the respective international sports association, and due to the association's autonomy,[181] states are partially replaced by international sports associations.

With regard to athletes, the examples given at the beginning of this paper[182] demonstrate that the respective international sports associations govern the individual sports. Athletes have to comply with the rules made by the international sports association in order to be allowed to participate in tournaments (for a professional athlete to do her or his job). If an athlete fails to comply with these rules, she or he will be sanctioned. There are opportunities for the athlete to challenge sanctions, but only within the legal regime of sports law.[183] The athlete is usually prevented from seeking judicial remedies from state courts.[184] Consequently, in relation to the

Mining More Transparent', Presentation given at the Workshop of the Interest Group on International Economic Law of the European Society of International Law (ESIL IGIEcL) in Vienna (Austria) on 3 September 2014 (not yet published).

[178] An example for such an amended directive is the Directive 2014/59/EU of the European Parliament and of the Council of 22 October 2014 amending Directive 2013/34/EU as regards disclosure of non-financial and diversity information by certain large undertakings and groups, OJ (EU) L 330 of 15 November 2014, 1–9 which entered into force on 6 December 2014. The mentioned obligations are contained in Article 1 of the directive and will become Article 19a of Directive 2013/34/EU (OJ (EU) L 182 of 29 June 2013, 19–76. See also European Commission, 'The EU Single Market: Transparency requirements for listed companies' ec.europa.eu/internal_market/securities/transparency/index_en.htm. See also Markus Kaltenborn and Johannes Norpoth, 'Globale Standards für soziale Unternehmensverantwortung—CSR-Leitlinien als neue Regelungsebene des Internationalen Wirtschaftsrechts' (2014) *Recht der Internationalen Wirtschaft* 402–10, 409.

[179] Cf International Labour Organization, 'ILO, EU, Bangladesh government adopt new compact on garment factory safety' (Press Release of 10 July 2013) available at www.ilo.org/global/about-the-ilo/activities/all/WCMS_217271/lang--en/index.htm. See also Kaltenborn and Norpoth (n 178) 409.

[180] Text at notes 136–141.

[181] Valloni and Pachmann (n 80) 41.

[182] Text at notes 7–23.

[183] See Richard H McLaren, 'The Court of Arbitration for Sport' in James AR Nafziger and Stephen F Ross (eds), *Handbook on International Sports Law* (Edward Elgar Publishing, 2011) 32–64.

[184] Ibid. However, decisions by the Court of Arbitration for Sport (CAS) can be challenged before the *Schweizer Bundesgericht* (Swiss Federal Court) cf Matthew J Mitten, 'Judicial Review of Olympic and

athletes and the exercise of their particular sports, the respective international sports association replaces the state completely. Therefore, based on the *Behrami and Saramati* decision, the international sports association is the addressee of human rights obligations such as the right to work with regard to athletes.

Similarly, international sports associations enact specific regulations governing spectators' behaviour inside (and to some extent around) the sports venue. In addition, they use stewards to enforce these rules.[185] In the event of gross misconduct, the international sports association might ban a spectator from attending future sports events—either for a defined period of time, or indefinitely, and either limited to a particular region, or globally.[186] However, unlike athletes, spectators generally have the opportunity to challenge these sanctions before 'ordinary' courts.[187] Thus, the state is not completely replaced by international sports associations with regard to spectators, but has a significant role, deterring international sports associations from acting arbitrarily, thus respecting the spectators' human rights.[188]

The exclusivity clause is contained primarily in the contract between the sponsor and the organising committee, and the organising committee and host country or city. In order to have legal effect, it has to be transformed into some sort of state regulation—usually a municipal regulation.[189] Thus, a sponsor's competitor is primarily infringed in her or his rights due to an act by the respective public entity and not the international sports association. However, the public entity has to adopt and enforce the regulation, as it would otherwise violate the agreement with the organising committee, and might even be de-selected as host.[190] Thus, the public entity is a tool of the organising committee, rather than an independent and willing subject.[191] Nevertheless, as sponsors contract with the organising committee and not the international sports association, there is no direct link between the violation of the rights of a sponsor's competitor and the international sports association.

Stadiums and other infrastructure projects needed in the context of international sports events are not constructed by the international sports association, and the workers have no legal relationship with the international sports association. Instead, the infrastructure projects are regularly carried out as public-private partnerships (PPPs).[192] Also, there are no direct contractual relationships between the workers producing sportswear and international sports associations. Instead, it is up to

International Sports Arbitration Awards: Trends and Observations' (2009) 10(1) *Pepperdine Dispute Resolution Law Journal* 51–67.

[185] Cf Harding and Culf (n 52) 3.

[186] Cf Robert CR Siekmann, 'Legal Aspects of Combating Transnational Football Hooliganism in Europe' in Robert CR Siekmann (ed), *Introduction to International and European Sports Law* (TMC Asser, 2012) 335–77.

[187] Cf ibid.

[188] Cf ibid.

[189] Cf Cobbs (n 48) 287–96.

[190] Cf ibid.

[191] Cf ibid.

[192] Anton Cartwright, 'Can mega events deliver sustainability? The case of the 2010 FIFA World Cup in South Africa' in Wolfgang Maennig and Andrew Zimbalist (eds), *International Handbook on the Economics of Mega Sporting Events* (Edward Elgar Publishing, 2012) 127–39.

private manufacturers to produce the articles and then either sell or receive sponsorship for them.[193] This means that the state is not replaced by international sports associations when it comes to workers' rights. Consequently, international sports associations cannot be held responsible for violations of human rights committed in the context of the construction of stadiums and other infrastructure projects.

### *ii. Third-Party Effect of International Human Rights*

In addition, there is a debate about the third-party effect of international human rights (*Drittwirkung*).[194] The notion of a third-party effect of human rights is quite well established with regard to domestic human rights.[195] At the international level, however, there is still some scepticism.[196] Despite this scepticism, it has to be noted that the third-party effect of human rights has been applied by the ECtHR[197] and the Inter-American Court of Human Rights (IAmCtHR).[198] In *Airey v Ireland*, for example, the ECtHR held that the third-party effect of human rights provided for in the ECHR is the only way to guarantee these rights effectively.[199] In *van Kück v Germany*, the ECtHR ruled that the rights guaranteed by the ECHR have a bearing on legal relationships between private individuals[200] and thus accepted a direct third-party effect of ECHR rights. Furthermore, the ECtHR held that it would be unacceptable for states to be allowed to privatise all public bodies, but at the same time not to answer for their human rights breaches, as it would undermine the whole system of the ECHR.[201] Thus, the ECtHR even recognised an indirect third-party effect of the rights contained in the ECHR.[202]

[193] See United Nations Global Compact, 'Human Rights and Business Dilemmas Forum: Combating child labour in football production' available at human-rights.unglobalcompact.org/case_studies/child-labour/child_labour/combating_child_labour_in_football_production.html#.U-EPQ2Nj_j5.

[194] See Béatrice Moutel, 'L'effet horizontal' de la Convention européenne des droits de l'homme en droit privé français: essai sur la diffusion de la CEDH dans les rapports entre personnes privées' (Université de Limoges, 2006), available at epublications.unilim.fr/theses/2006/moutel-beatrice/moutel-beatrice.pdf; Javier Mijangos y González, 'The Doctrine of the Drittwirkung der Grundrechte in the case law of the Inter-American Court of Human Rights' (2008) 9 *Revista para el Análisos del Derecho* 1–31.

[195] See with regard to France, Cour de Cassation (France) *Société Cogedipresse c Mme Grimaldi* (23 April 2003) 212 Gazette du Palais 2 (2003); Cour de Cassation (France) *Eva Joly et Sté Editions Les Arènes c Ordre des avocats de la Cour d'appel* (14 June 2005) Appeal No 03-17730 Bull civ I No 261; with regard to Germany, Bundesverfassungsgericht (Germany) *Lüth*, BVerfGE 7, 198, 205; Bundesverfassungsgericht (Germany) *Sozialplan*, BVerfGE 73, 261, 269; and for the United Kingdom, House of Lords *Campbell v MGN Ltd* (6 May 2004) [2004] UKHL 22; High Court of Justice for England and Wales *Max Mosley v News Group Newspaper Ltd* (9 April 2008) [2008] EWHC 687 [QB].

[196] See Rainer J Schweizer, 'Allgemeine Grundsätze' in Detlef Merten und Hans-Jürgen Papier (eds), *Handbuch der Grundrechte in Deutschland und Europa* (CF Müller Verlag, 2010) Vol VI/1, 77–124, 111.

[197] ECtHR, *Pla and Puncernau v Andorra*, App no 69498/01, Judgment of 15 December 2004, available at hudoc.echr.coe.int/sites/eng/pages/search.aspx?i=001-61900.

[198] IAmCtHR, *Comunidad de Paz de San José de Apartadó v Colombia* (Provisional Measures, 18 June 2002) IAmCtHR Ser E No 4.

[199] ECtHR, *Airey v Ireland*, App no 6289/73, Decision of 9 October 1979, para 24: 'The Convention is intended to guarantee not rights that are theoretical or illusory but rights that are practical and effective.'

[200] ECtHR, *van Kück v Germany*, App no 35968/97, Judgment of 12 September 2003, paras 145–46.

[201] ECtHR, *Costello-Roberts v United Kingdom*, App no 13134/87, Judgment of 25 March 1993 available at hudoc.echr.coe.int/sites/eng/pages/search.aspx?i=001-57804.

[202] Eirik Bjorge, 'Human Rights, Treaties, Third-Party Effect' in Wolfrum (n 87) para 9.

However, despite the fact that the third-party effect of human rights provided for in the ECHR is well established and the third-party effect of human rights contained in the AmCHR has been acknowledged by the IAmCtHR, it has to be noted that there is insufficient uniform state practice to grant the third-party effect of human rights the status of a norm of customary international law.[203]

### *iii. Preliminary Conclusion about International Sports Associations as Addressees of International Human Rights*

Consequently, under international law, states remain the primary addressee of human rights obligations. Only in situations where other actors exercise sovereign rights, thereby replacing or substituting the state, are these actors the addressees for the respective human rights obligation.[204] The notion of third-party effect of human rights applies only within the scope of the ECHR and the AmCHR.

As shown, in particular situations, international sports associations substitute for the state. Thus, they are the direct addressee of international human rights of athletes (right to work and procedural guarantees, such as due process and fair trial), competitors of sponsors (right to property, right to work) and spectators (freedom of expression, LGBT rights).

## C. International Sports Associations as Addressees of Domestic Human Rights

At the domestic level, human rights are generally contained either directly in the constitution of the respective state,[205] or in special legislation.[206] The primary addressee of the obligations contained in these human rights instruments is the state.[207] It is widely recognised, however, that human rights can also be infringed by others. As a result, there is a need for a third-party effect of domestic human rights.[208] Therefore, international sports associations, though not being direct addressees of domestic human rights, are indirectly bound by domestic human rights.

[203] See, for instance, Commission on Human Rights, Decision 2004/116 of 20 April 2004, contained in Commission on Human Rights, *Report on the sixtieth session (15 March—23 April 2004)* (United Nations, 2004) Part I, 345.

[204] See Lars Schönwald, 'International Human Rights and Non-State Actors', Presentation given at the Midyear Meeting and Research Forum of the American Society of International Law in Chicago (United States of America) from 6 to 8 November 2014 (not yet published).

[205] This applies, inter alia, to Australia, where human rights are contained in ss 41, 80, 116 and 117 of the 1901 Constitution of the Commonwealth of Australia, Germany, where human rights are contained in Articles 1 to 19 of the 1949 *Grundgesetz*, and the United States of America, where human rights are contained in the various Amendments to the 1787 Constitution of the United States of America.

[206] This applies, inter alia, to the United Kingdom, where human rights are contained in the 1689 Bill of Rights.

[207] Brid Moriarty and Eva Massa (eds), *Human Rights Law*, 4th edn, (Oxford University Press, 2012) 2.

[208] Greg Taylor, 'The Horizontal Effect of Human Rights Provisions, the German Model and Its Applicability to Common-Law Jurisdictions' (2002) 13(2) *King's Law Journal* 187–218.

## III. RESPONDING TO HUMAN RIGHTS VIOLATIONS BY INTERNATIONAL SPORTS ASSOCIATIONS

The fact that international sports associations can infringe human rights in various scenarios raises the question of how to respond to these human rights violations.

### A. Athletes

Since athletes have a direct relationship with their international sports authority, they can bring human rights claims directly. When issuing sanctions, the disciplinary committee has to take the athlete's rights and interests into consideration.[209] In other words, similarly to a negative administrative decision, the sanction has to be proportionate.[210] Specifically, it has to be considered whether professional athletes can compete only for a limited period of time. Consequently, if an athlete is banned from exercising her or his sport for months or even years, it might prevent her or him from enjoying her or his right to work.

As with administrative decisions, sanctions by international sports associations can be challenged.[211] Besides challenging the reason for a specific sanction,[212] the extent of the sanction can also be challenged.[213] Appellate bodies—and in the end the Court of Arbitration for Sports (CAS)[214]—have to decide, inter alia, whether a sanction is excessive, which requires balancing the offence committed by the athlete against the athlete's interests and rights.[215]

Decisions of the CAS can at least be challenged[216] before the Swiss Federal Court (*Schweizer Bundesgericht*), the Supreme Court of Switzerland.[217] The Swiss Federal Court, being an organ of Switzerland, is directly bound by human rights and therefore has to take them into account when rendering its decisions.

Therefore, the rights of athletes are well protected and can be enforced directly by the athlete.

### B. Workers

Workers who build and maintain the sports venues do not have a direct contractual relationship with international sports associations. A direct contractual relationship exists only between the worker and her or his employer. As the concept

[209] Cf, for instance, Article 39(4) of the 2011 FIFA Disciplinary Code, available at www.fifa.com/mm/Document/AFFederation/Administration/50/02/75/DisCoInhalte.pdf.

[210] Ibid.

[211] Cf, for instance, Article 79 of the 2011 FIFA Disciplinary Code.

[212] Ibid.

[213] Ibid.

[214] McLaren (n 183) 32–64.

[215] Ibid.

[216] Ibid.

[217] See Richard H McLaren, 'Sports Law Arbitration by CAS: is it the Same as International Arbitration?' (2001–2002) 29 *Pepperdine Law Review* 101–14.

of third-party effect of human rights originated in the field of labour law,[218] workers can bring claims against their employer for human rights violations—at least in theory. Depending on the degree of dependency of the worker on her or his employer and the legal system, it might be very difficult for workers to bring claims and thus to enforce their human rights.[219] Particularly in the context of the construction work for the FIFA Football World Cup 2022, it has been argued that the workers have almost no rights under the Qatari legal system, and no effective possibility to enforce their rights before Qatari courts.[220]

Taking into account that international sports associations are similar to TNCs[221] and considering that TNCs have the obligation, inter alia, to conduct human rights impact assessments prior to large projects,[222] international sports associations are equally obliged to conduct such an assessment.[223] Although such an assessment can never ensure that there will be no human rights violations it can raise awareness of a systematic endangerment of workers' rights. The latter may result in the international sports association calling for reforms in the respective country of its labour laws, or might even result in the non-consideration of an application.[224] Following the extensive criticism of working conditions in Qatar by well-known human rights NGOs, FIFA has already announced that it will conduct human rights impact assessments, prior to deciding who will host future FIFA Football World Cups.[225]

### C. Civil Society

Besides workers' rights, human rights impact assessments conducted by a sporting organisation should also assess the human rights situations of civil society in an applicant country prior to any decision on awarding international sports events. The 2014 FIFA Football World Cup in Brazil and the 2014 Olympic Games in Sochi both provide illustrative examples of the suppression of protests, which were only prima facie directed against the sporting event itself, but mainly criticised the government.[226] Neither the protests in Brazil, nor those in Russia, came as a surprise to political analysts.[227] Instead, they were highly predictable. Both countries are fast

[218] Cf John F Knox, 'Horizontal Human Rights Law' (2009) 102(1) *American Journal of International Law* 1–47.

[219] See International Trade Union Confederation, 'Qatar World Cup Workers' Standards: no legal enforcement, no worker rights' available at www.ituc-csi.org/qatar-world-cup-workers-standards.

[220] Ibid.

[221] Text to notes 136–141.

[222] United Nations Human Rights Council (n 166), Principle 17.

[223] Institute for Human Rights and Business, *Striving for Excellence: Mega-Sporting Events and Human Rights* (Institute for Human Rights and Business 2013) available at www.ihrb.org/pdf/2013-10-21_IHRB_Mega-Sporting-Events-Paper_Web.pdf, 32–33.

[224] Cf ibid.

[225] See Owen Gibson, 'Fifa could factor in human rights record when choosing World Cup hosts', *The Guardian—Online* (London, 8 June 2014) available at www.theguardian.com/football/2014/jun/08/fifa-factor-human-rights-record-choosing-world-cup-hosts.

[226] See Simon Romero, 'Protests Grow As Brazilian Blame Leaders', *The New York Times* (New York, 19 June 2013) 1.

[227] Cf ibid.

developing economies, belonging to the so-called BRICS.[228] Despite their significant economic development in recent years, not every citizen of those countries benefits from the process of development. The protesters criticising the fact that public funds were being used to host international sports events (which contributed only very little to the host country's economic development)[229], and not on projects which were beneficial for the whole population.[230] In addition, it is generally the poor who are evicted from their homes.

Often, there are in practice almost no opportunities for the poor to bring human rights claims. If there are legal procedures available at all, they are often costly, time-consuming, and offer little hope of success.[231] Hosting an international sports event might actually improve the human rights situation of the poor, if the international sports association applies a human rights impact assessment, as suggested above, and if it calls for reforms, and monitors progress.

## D. Merchants and Producers

Quite different is the situation with regard to competitors of sponsors. Despite the fact that their rights are infringed by the exclusivity clauses, it has to be noted that international sports events cannot be organised and carried out without external financing, to which sponsors contribute.[232] Of course, sponsors want something in return for their investment, which explains their interest in the exclusivity clause. Nevertheless, exclusivity clauses should be drafted carefully and it should be considered to what extent local producers and merchants are really a competitor for the sponsor and therefore have to be excluded from the sporting venues.

## E. Spectators

Finally, spectators have a direct relationship with international sports associations. When they purchase tickets for international sports events, they have to agree to the terms set by the international sports association and the organising committees.[233] Sanctions against spectators can be challenged in the ordinary courts in the respective country. The courts then have to take the spectators' rights into consideration when rendering their decisions.

[228] BRICS is the acronym for Brazil, Russia, India, China and South Africa, five fast-growing, yet not fully developed countries, see Institute of Development Studies, 'BRICS and Rising Powers' available at www.ids.ac.uk/idsresearch/brics-and-rising-powers.

[229] Harry H Miller, 'Post-event Outcomes and the Post-modern Turn: The Olympics and Urban Transformations' in Holger Preuss (ed), *The Impact and Evaluation of Major Sporting Events* (Routledge, 2009) 5–20.

[230] See Romero (n 226) 1.

[231] Cf Amnesty International, *Amnesty International Report 2013: The State of the World's Human Rights* (Amnesty International, 2013) 220–21 (relating to Russia).

[232] Chadwick (n 45) 257–74.

[233] Cf FIFA, '2014 FIFA World Cup Brazil General Terms and Conditions for the Use of Tickets' available at www.fifa.com/worldcup/organisation/ticketing/legal/terms-conditions/.

## IV. THE OBLIGATION OF INTERNATIONAL SPORTS ASSOCIATIONS TO ENFORCE RESPECT FOR HUMAN RIGHTS

It has been shown that international sports associations are addressees of international and domestic human rights, and that they therefore have to respect human rights. It has also been demonstrated, however, that international sports associations are often only the indirect cause of human rights violations. Therefore it is argued that international sports associations also have the obligation to enforce respect for human rights—against host countries of international sports events and against the sponsors of such events.

### A. The General Obligation to Enforce Respect for Human Rights

The obligation to enforce respect for human rights concerns not only the need for states to comply with human rights but also the need to ensure that all citizens can enjoy their rights.[234] This means that states have to ensure that human rights are also respected in private relations.[235] States therefore have the obligation to enact laws and regulations that govern private relations and give full effect to human rights.[236]

Thus, states must ensure that human rights are also respected in private relations. Consequently, if it is argued that international sports associations can to some extent replace states, it is coherent to argue that they also bear the obligation to enforce respect for human rights, especially in those situations in which the enjoyment of human rights is endangered.

### B. The Obligation of International Sports Associations to Enforce Respect for Human Rights against States

As mentioned previously, if TNCs have the obligation to carry out human rights impact assessments, this also applies to international sports associations, since they can be likened to TNCs. This means that international sports associations have to ask applicant countries to submit detailed information about the human rights situation and their labour laws in particular. International sports associations then have to assess whether minimum standards are at least observed. Countries should be called upon to improve the human rights situation, and reforms should be monitored carefully by independent experts. In order to do so, international sports associations can and should cooperate with prominent NGOs and/or specialised agencies of the UN.

If a state fails to comply with its human rights obligations, or if it turns out that the country made false statements about the human rights situation, international sports associations should consider re-awarding the tournament. Depending on the

[234] See s 11 August 2014 FIFA World Cup Brazil General Terms and Conditions for the Use of Tickets (n 233).

[235] Cf De Schutter (n 165) 365–460.

[236] Cf ibid.

precise situation, international sports associations can refer to the *clausula rebus sic stantibus* when re-awarding an international sports event.[237] This would also ensure that countries are more willing to improve their human rights situations.

### C. The Obligation of International Sports Associations to Enforce Respect for Human Rights against Sponsors

International sports associations are very dependent on sponsors. At the same time, large international sports associations in particular provide sponsors with the opportunity to address a large international audience. When it comes to equipping an international sports association, for example, with footballs, there is significant competition among manufacturers.[238] FIFA could use this competition to pressure manufacturers to improve working conditions.

## V. CONCLUSION

In conclusion, international sports associations are non-state actors which can infringe human rights in various cases. In addition, they are addressees of international and domestic human rights obligations. Consequently, international sports associations have to consider human rights when imposing sanctions against athletes and spectators as part of their duty to respect human rights. Furthermore, since international sports associations are sometimes the only basis for human rights violations committed by others, international sports associations may also have the duty to enforce respect for human rights.

Therefore, it is suggested that human rights should play a bigger role in the politics and decision-making of international sports associations. International sport associations should carry out human rights impact assessments prior to the award of international sports events, should pressure states for reforms which should be monitored, and should—as *ultima ratio*—also consider re-awarding an international sports event where there is evidence of serious human rights violations.

As a general conclusion, international sports associations as addressees of human rights is a topic which has only emerged recently, mainly in the context of awarding the FIFA Football World Cup 2022 to Qatar. It is quite promising that FIFA—which is often criticised for being too egocentric—is reacting to the debate and has considered requesting human rights impact assessments in the future. This provides some hope that other international sports associations will follow such a course.

[237] Cf Martyn Ziegler, 'Re-run of 2022 World Cup vote a possibility says Sepp Blatter', *The Independent—Online* (London, 19 May 2011) available at www.independent.co.uk/sport/football/news-and-comment/rerun-of-2022-world-cup-vote-a-possibility-says-sepp-blatter-2286380.html.

[238] Cf Barry Smart, 'Not playing around: global capitalism, modern sport and consumer culture' (2007) 7(2) *Global Networks* 113–34.

# 20

# *Emerging Fair Trial Guarantees*

JERNEJ LETNAR ČERNIČ*

## I. INTRODUCTION

ON 6 FEBRUARY 2012, the Court of Arbitration for Sport (CAS) delivered the eagerly awaited decision in the appeals arbitration procedure between the World Anti-Doping Agency (WADA), the International Cycling Union (UCI), the Spanish cyclist Alberto Contador and the Spanish Cycling Federation (RFEC).[1] As the UCI and the WADA disagreed with the decision made by the Spanish Cycling Federation in Contador's favour, they had appealed to the CAS.

The CAS upheld the appeal 'filed by WADA and … found Alberto Contador guilty of a doping offence'.[2] More specifically, the arbitration panel concluded that 'the Athlete's positive test for clenbuterol is more likely to have been caused by the ingestion of a contaminated food supplement than by a blood transfusion or the ingestion of contaminated meat';[3] that 'no evidence [had] been adduced proving that the Athlete acted with no fault or negligence or no significant fault or negligence';[4] that 'a two year period of ineligibility [should] be imposed upon the Athlete, running as of 25 January 2011';[5] and that 'the 2010 Tour de France result of Mr Contador [should] be disqualified as well as the results obtained in all competitions he participated in after 25 January 2011 when the ineligibility period [was] decided to have begun'.[6]

* Associate Professor of Human Rights Law, Graduate School of Government and European Studies, Kranj, Slovenia. An earlier version of this chapter was published in Jernej Letnar Černič, 'Fair trial guarantees before the court of arbitration for sport' (2012) 6(2) *Human Rights and International Legal Discourse* 259–83.

[1] CAS, CAS 2011/A/2384, *UCI v Alberto Contador Velasco & RFEC*, CAS 2011/A/2386 *WADA v Alberto Contador Velasco & RFEC*, Arbitral Award, 6 February 2012, available at wada-main-prod.s3.amazonaws.com/resources/files/cas-2011-a-2384-contador.pdf. RFEC initially decided in favour of Contador.

[2] CAS, 'Alberto Contador found guilty of an anti-doping rule by the Court of Arbitration for Sport: suspension of two years' media release, 6 February 2012, available at www.tas-cas.org/en/general-information/news-detail/article/alberto-contador-found-guilty-of-an-anti-doping-rule-violation-by-the-cas-suspension-of-two-years.html.

[3] CAS, CAS 2011/A/2384 *UCI v Alberto Contador Velasco & RFEC*, CAS 2011/A/2386 *WADA v Alberto Contador Velasco & RFEC*, Arbitral Award, 6 February 2012, available at wada-main-prod.s3.amazonaws.com/resources/files/cas-2011-a-2384-contador.pdf, para 512, a.

[4] Ibid.

[5] Ibid.

[6] Ibid.

The Court's decision in the above case did not come as a surprise. On the contrary, commentators had widely predicted the outcome of the Court's deliberations. Nonetheless, the decision still echoes in the international sports community and the determination has been widely criticised in the Spanish media,[7] while the public, including the highest representatives of the political parties,[8] still believe the story put forward by Mr Contador.[9] They have described the final CAS decision as unjust and unfair,[10] as has Contador himself.[11]

The right to a remedy for victims of human rights violations is a tenet of every functioning judicial system. The effectiveness of all other rights rests on access to an effective legal remedy. As such, the normative order places a burden, or obligation, on everyone not to breach their legal duties at the expense of third parties. The usual court systems are less suitable for resolving sports-related disputes owing to their long and complicated procedures and lack of specialised knowledge of sports law. In contrast, the sports arbitration procedure offers greater expediency and takes into account the wishes of the parties, while the arbitrators possess knowledge and experience in sports law.[12] As with commercial arbitration, the parties agree to abide by the sports arbitration procedure.

The Contador arbitral award illustrates the dilemma encountered by the CAS in reconciling two conflicting values in a contemporary sports competition. This concerns the issue of whether the prevention of doping may undermine the protection of athletes' fundamental human rights, and whether the protection of fundamental human rights may impede the suppression of doping. Jérôme de Montmollin and Dmitry Pentsov eloquently note that 'while the World Anti-Doping Program certainly has noble objectives, the fight against the evil of doping in modern sports must also be conducted by using noble means, ensuring respect for the human rights of the athletes'.[13] Traditionally, the protection of human rights has always concentrated on balancing the interests of the individual with those of society as a whole. More specifically, the Contador arbitral award concerns the exercise of delicately balancing the interests of the individual against those of sports society as a whole.

Such situations can be described as sports dilemmas. The arbitral award illustrates the general situation of fair trial guarantees in arbitral procedures before the CAS

[7] Lucas Ferrer Lucas, 'Posible, aunque improbable', *El Mundo*, 9 February 2012, available at www.elmundo.es/elmundodeporte/2012/02/09/masdeporte/1328798489.html.

[8] Cospedal, 'Es una injusticia y una arbitrariedad', *El Mundo*, 8 February 2012, available at www.elmundo.es/elmundodeporte/2012/02/08/ciclismo/1328704812.html.

[9] See, for example, *El Pais*, '¡Inocente, inocente!', 13 February 2012, available at ccaa.elpais.com/ccaa/2012/02/13/madrid/1329089263_556436.html; *El Pais*, 'Wert anuncia una nueva ley antidopaje para defender a España del caso Contador', 9 February 2012, available at deportes.elpais.com/deportes/2012/02/09/actualidad/1328775726_850215.html.

[10] 'Pinto homenajeará a su vecino Alberto Contador con la Glorieta del Ciclista', *El Mundo*, 15 February 2012, available at www.elmundo.es/elmundo/2012/02/15/madrid/1329324180.html.

[11] Pablo de la Calle, 'Contador: Perdí la confianza en la justicia deportiva', *El Mundo*, 7 April 2012, available at www.elmundo.es/elmundodeporte/2012/04/02/ciclismo/1333396783.html.

[12] Michael Straubel, 'Enhancing the Performance of the Doping Court: How the Court of Arbitration for Sport Can Do Its Job Better' (2005) 36 *Loyola University of Chicago Law Journal* 1205.

[13] Jérôme de Montmollin and Dmitry A Pentsov, 'Do Athletes Really Have the Right to a Fair Trial in "Non-Analytical Positive" Doping Cases?' (2011) 22(2) *American Review of International Arbitration* 239.

and raises a number of pertinent questions relating to minimum fair trial standards. Do fair trial guarantees apply and if not, should they apply to the sports arbitration proceedings before the CAS? If so, is the nature and scope of such fair trial guarantees broader or narrower than or the same as in regular judicial proceedings? What happens when the CAS violates one of the fundamental principles of a fair trial? What are the most appropriate ways to improve the guarantee of a fair trial before the CAS? Is the monitoring jurisdiction of the Swiss Federal Tribunal sufficient to guarantee procedural public policy guarantees, including fair trial guarantees?

The right to a fair trial is one of the backbones of the rule of law and a *conditio sine qua non* for the protection of human rights and fundamental freedoms. This contribution examines whether fair trial guarantees can also be exercised before the CAS. It attempts to identify whether the procedural rules and case law of the CAS should follow all four component parts of the right to a fair trial (the right to a fair hearing, the right to an independent and impartial tribunal established by law, the right to a public hearing and the public pronouncement of judgments, and the right to a fair trial within a reasonable time).

This chapter is devoted to exploring the concept of the right to a fair trial before the CAS. It will attempt to explore the nature, value and status of this concept through its fundamental principles developed in the jurisprudence of the European Court of Human Rights (ECtHR). The examination is divided into four parts. Section II discusses the CAS, in particular the different arbitration procedures it has available. Section III discusses and analyses the constituent parts of the right to a fair trial in the CAS's procedures and tries to establish whether a fair trial standard exists in the CAS's arbitration procedures subject to the monitoring jurisdiction of the Swiss Federal Tribunal, which examines whether the arbitration panel respected procedural public policy guarantees, including fair trial guarantees. Section IV assesses the right to a fair trial before the CAS, while Section V presents some proposals to improve the CAS's arbitration procedures from the viewpoint of fair trial guarantees. Based on the foregoing analysis, the conclusion in Section VI assesses the application of fair trial guarantees before the CAS. In general, the contribution seeks to argue that fair trial guarantees, as developed by the ECtHR, should also apply to proceedings before the CAS.

## II. THE COURT OF ARBITRATION FOR SPORT

The CAS is not part of the ordinary court systems. Rather, it was established by the International Olympic Committee (IOC) as its highest arbitration body for resolving sports-related disputes. It appears that it is not entirely clear whether the CAS is a court or merely an arbitration body. Richard McLaren describes it as 'a forum for the world's athletes and sports federations to resolve their disputes through a single independent and accomplished sports adjudication body'.[14]

[14] Richard H McLaren, 'Introducing the Court of Arbitration for Sport: The Ad Hoc Division at the Olympic Games' (2001) 12 *Marqette Sports Law Review* 515, available at scholarship.law.marquette.edu/sportslaw/vol12/iss1/20. See also M Reeb, 'The Role and Functions of the Court of Arbitration for Sport (CAS)' (2002) 2 *International Sports Law Journal* 21.

It was initially created by the IOC on 6 April 1983.[15] In 1994 it was placed under the International Council of Arbitration for Sport (ICAS), which was established to ensure the greater independence and impartiality of the CAS[16] and now regulates its administrative and financial matters.[17] Its normative position as an independent and autonomous body, exercising an arbitral function, is further regulated by the Statutes of the Bodies Working for the Settlement of Sports-Related Disputes (the Statutes).[18] Section 12 of the Statutes provides that 'the CAS sets in operation Panels which have the task of providing for the resolution by arbitration and/or mediation of disputes arising within the field of sport in conformity with the Procedural Rules'.[19] Parties must comply with the principle of *pacta sunt servanda* and can submit a dispute voluntarily to the Court.

Arbitration proceedings may arise from ordinary or appeals arbitration proceedings. Ordinary arbitration proceedings arise 'out of an arbitration clause inserted in a contract or regulations or of a later arbitration agreement'.[20] The CAS also rules over disputes relating to the Olympics. As a fundamental normative document of the Olympic movement, the Olympic Charter provides in Rule 59 that 'any dispute arising on the occasion of, or in connection with, the Olympic Games shall be submitted exclusively to the Court of Arbitration for Sport'.[21] Appeal arbitration proceedings deal with 'an appeal against a decision rendered by a federation, association or sports-related body where the statutes or regulations of such bodies, or a specific agreement provide for an appeal to CAS'.[22]

In the last few decades, the CAS has proved to be a very successful forum for resolving sports-related disputes. Its success was at first surprising.[23] In 2009 and 2010 alone it delivered 568 decisions, half of them stemming from football-related disputes.[24] All in all, the CAS has so far delivered 2,204 arbitral awards and 26 opinions up until 31 December 2013.[25] Nonetheless, its success rate may

[15] Tricia Kavanagh, 'The Doping Cases and the Need for the International Court of Arbitration for Sport' (1999) 22 *University of South Wales Law Journal* 721.

[16] The Statutes of the Bodies Working for the Settlement of Sports-Related Disputes provide at section S2: 'The task of the ICAS is to facilitate the settlement of sports-related disputes through arbitration or mediation and to safeguard the independence of the CAS and the rights of the parties.'

[17] See www.tas-cas.org/en/general-information/history-of-the-cas.html.

[18] Statutes of the Bodies Working for the Settlement of Sports-Related Disputes, 1 January 2016, available at www.tas-cas.org/fileadmin/user_upload/Code_2016_final__en_.pdf.

[19] Ibid Section 12.

[20] Ibid Procedural Rule 27.

[21] International Olympic Committee (IOC), Olympic Charter, Rule 61, 8 July 2011, available at www.olympic.org/Documents/olympic_charter_en.pdf.

[22] Statutes of the Bodies Working for the Settlement of Sports-Related Disputes, 1 March 2013, available at www.tas-cas.org/fileadmin/user_upload/Code20201320corrections20finales20_en_.pdf Rule 27.

[23] Mark Megan, 'The Court of Arbitration for Sport: Current Practice, Emerging Trends and Future Hurdles" (2009) 25(4) *Arbitration International* 591–602.

[24] Efraim Barak, 'CAS & Football: Principal rulings 2009–2011 and the new procedural regulations of the 2010 CAS Code' (on file with author), Real Federación Española de Fútbol, IV Congreso Internacional en Derecho de Futbol, Madrid, 1 October 2011, 2.

[25] The CAS's webpage, available at www.tas-cas.org/fileadmin/user_upload/CAS_Statistics_2013.pdf.

be described as debatable, although McLaren notes that 'the CAS is in the course of developing universal principles that will some day be widely recognized as the *lex sportiva*'.[26]

The CAS has the jurisdiction to deal with different aspects of sports-related disputes.[27] Procedural Rule 27 provides that 'such disputes may involve matters of principle relating to sport or matters of pecuniary or other interests brought into play in the practice or the development of sport and, generally speaking, any activity related or connected to sport'.[28] The CAS deals with a wide range of disputes, including doping cases,[29] disputes over eligibility,[30] contracts, registration and television rights. The next section turns to fair trial guarantees before the CAS.

## III. DOES THE RIGHT TO A FAIR TRIAL APPLY TO CAS PROCEEDINGS?

This section attempts to identify whether fair trial guarantees also apply to proceedings before the CAS. It examines the different component parts of the right to a fair trial before the CAS, as developed in the jurisprudence of the ECtHR.[31] The ECtHR is generally assumed to prescribe only minimum standards of human rights protection that are normally surpassed by national constitutional standards. The ECtHR's approach to fair trials has been chosen as a basic component of the right to a fair trial that is also enshrined as the lowest common denominator of European *ordre public* (public policy). In this way, it not only reflects the prevailing consensus about

[26] Richard H McLaren, 'The Court of Arbitration for Sport: An Independent Arena for the World's Sports Disputes' (2001) 35 *Valparaiso University Law Review* 381. Also see Darren Kane, 'Twenty Years on: An Evaluation of the Court of Arbitration for Sport' (2003) 4(2) *Melbourne Journal of International Law* 611.

[27] See, for example, Daniel H Yi, 'Turning Medals into Metal: Evaluating the Court of Arbitration for Sport as an International Tribunal' (2006) Paper 24, Student Scholarship Papers, available at digitalcommons.law.yale.edu/student_papers/24.

[28] Statutes of the Bodies Working for the Settlement of Sports-Related Disputes, 1 January 2012, Procedural Rule 27.

[29] See the World Anti-Doping Agency Code's World Anti-Doping Code 2009, available at www.wada-ama.org/Documents/World_Anti-Doping_Program/WADP-The-Code/WADA_Anti-Doping_CODE_2009_EN.pdf. The World Anti-Doping Code provides in section 13.2.1 for the compulsory jurisdiction of the CAS.

[30] See Matthew J Mitten and Timothy Davis, 'Athlete Eligibility Requirements and Legal Protection of Sports Participation Opportunities' (2009) 8 *Virginia Sports & Entertainment Law Journal* 71.

[31] European Convention for the Protection of Human Rights and Fundamental Freedoms, 213 UNTS 222, entered into force 3 September 1953. Article 6 (1) reads as follows: 'In the determination of his civil rights and obligations or of any criminal charge against him, everyone is entitled to a fair and public hearing within a reasonable time by an independent and impartial tribunal established by law. Judgment shall be pronounced publicly but the press and public may be excluded from all or part of the trial in the interests of morals, public order or national security in a democratic society, where the interests of juveniles or the protection of the private life of the parties so require, or to the extent strictly necessary in the opinion of the court in special circumstances where publicity would prejudice the interests of justice.'

At present, there are at least two cases pending before the ECtHR against arbitral decisions of the CAS: *Mutu v Switzerland* (Application no 40575, 12 February 2013) and *Pechstein v Switzerland* (Application no 67474/10, 12 February 2013).

fair trial guarantees in the ECtHR's case law but also fundamental principles of the constitutional orders of Council of Europe member states.

It is first necessary to examine whether arbitration proceedings or quasi-judicial proceedings fall within the definition of 'civil rights and obligations' in Article 6 of the European Convention on Human Rights (ECHR, or the Convention) on the right to a fair trial. What is important is the nature of the rights and obligations in question. Accordingly, in *Ringeisen v Austria* the ECtHR noted that 'the character of the legislation which governs how the matter is to be determined (civil, commercial, administrative law, etc.) and that of the authority which is invested with jurisdiction in the matter (ordinary court, administrative body, etc.) are therefore of little consequence'.[32] The ECtHR does not provide a fully fledged definition of civil rights and obligations, so the main question is whether Article 6(1) of the ECHR applies to arbitration proceedings, or whether it is enough that there is a possibility of appeal to a regular court, that is, the Swiss Federal Tribunal.[33]

This contribution argues that Article 6(1) of the ECHR applies to arbitration proceedings before the CAS subject to the monitoring jurisdiction of the Swiss Federal Tribunal, which examines whether the arbitration panel respected procedural public policy guarantees, including fair trial guarantees. In doing so, it argues that fair trial guarantees must be respected both before the CAS and also before the Swiss Federal Tribunal. Procedural public policy guarantees are found in Article 190(2) of Switzerland's Federal Code on Private International Law, which provides that the arbitral award can be challenged only

> if a sole arbitrator was designated irregularly or the arbitration tribunal was constituted irregularly; if the arbitration tribunal erroneously held that it had or did not have jurisdiction; if the arbitration tribunal ruled on matters beyond the claims submitted to it or if it failed to rule on one of the claims; if the equality of the parties or their right to be heard in an adversarial proceeding was not respected; and if the award is incompatible with Swiss public policy.[34]

Fair trial guarantees in the Swiss legal order also form part of the *ordre public*, which the CAS is obliged to observe. In other words, fundamental fair trial guarantees are included in the Swiss *ordre public*.[35] The Swiss Federal Tribunal has in several cases affirmed the importance of the fair trial guarantees in arbitration proceedings before the CAS. That fundamental fair trial guarantees also apply to the CAS was explicitly confirmed by the Swiss Federal Tribunal in *Marc Biolley [Representative of A Sport] v*

[32] ECtHR, *Ringeisen v Austria*, Application no 2614/65, para 94.

[33] See Alec Galič, 'Arbitration and the Right to Fair Trial: Constitutional Procedural Guarantees in Arbitration Proceedings' (2000) 7 *Croatian Arbitration Yearbook* 9.

[34] Swiss Federal Code on Private International Law, Switzerland's Federal Code on Private International Law, 18 December 1987, available at www.rwi.uzh.ch/lehreforschung/alphabetisch/haas/lehrveranstaltungen/fs2015/intro-sports-law/PILA.pdf.

[35] See generally, Juan Carlos Landrove, 'European Convention on Human Rights' Impact on Consensual Arbitration: an *état des lieux* of Strasbourg Case-law and of a Problematic Swiss Law Feature' in Samantha Besson, Michel Hottelier and Franz Weroro (eds), *Human Rights at the Centre* (Zürich, Schulthess Verlag, 2006) 73–101.

*Association Y & TAS*,[36] as regards the composition of a CAS panel, and *Canas v ATP*,[37] as regards the right to a fair hearing.

For instance, the Swiss Federal Tribunal noted in the *Lazutina* case the

> right to an independent ruling on the conclusions and facts submitted to the arbitration tribunal in compliance with the applicable procedural law; procedural public policy is violated when fundamental, commonly recognised principles are infringed, resulting in an intolerable contradiction with the sentiments of justice, to the effect that the decision appears incompatible with the values recognised in a State governed by the rule of law.[38]

The Swiss Federal Tribunal therefore considers that fair trial guarantees must also be employed before the CAS in its arbitration proceedings. Most fair trial guarantees certainly fall within the category of 'fundamental, commonly recognised principles' whose abuse may cause 'an intolerable contradiction with the sentiments of justice'. All in all, the Swiss Federal Tribunal considers that Article 6(1) guarantees also apply in arbitral proceedings.[39] It therefore monitors the extent to which fundamental fair trial guarantees belonging to public policy have been respected in proceedings before the CAS. However, the Swiss Federal Tribunal can only consider *ex post facto* whether the arbitration panel has respected procedural public policy guarantees, including fair trial guarantees, and provided that one of the parties has challenged the arbitral award on the basis of Article 190(2) of Switzerland's Federal Code on Private International Law.[40]

The ECtHR noted in *Osmo Suovaniemi v Finland* that a 'waiver may be permissible with regard to certain rights but not with regard to certain others. A distinction may have to be made even between different rights guaranteed by Article 6.'[41] The next sections therefore examine which fair trial guarantees before the CAS are protected by public policy and which can be waived in its arbitration proceedings.

## A. The Right to a Fair Hearing before the CAS

The right to a fair hearing must be complied with in arbitration proceedings before the CAS. The ECtHR noted that the 'right to a fair trial holds so prominent a place

[36] *Marc Biolley [Representative of A Sport] v Association Y & TAS*, 4A_506/ 2007 (2008) (Switz.), cited in Matthew J Mitten, 'Judicial Review of Olympic and International Sports Arbitration Awards: Trends and Observations' (2009) 10 *Pepperdine Dispute Resolution Law Journal* 57.

[37] *Canas v ATP*, Federal Tribunal 4P.172/2006 (Switzerland), judgment of 22 March 2007, 1st Civil Law Court, available at law.marquette.edu/assets/sports-law/pdf/2012-conf-canas-english.pdf.

[38] *A and B v International Olympic Committee (IOC) and International Ski Federation (FIS) (Lazutina)*, 4P. 267–70/ 2002 *(1st Civil Court 27 May 2003)* in Matthieu Reeb (ed), Digest of CAS Awards III 2001–2003 (2004) 691, cited in Mitten (n 36) 55.

[39] *X v Y*, 30 April, 1991, ATF 117 Ia 166 (1991) confirmed by unreported ATF *Hitachi v SMS*, 30 June 1994, 15 Bull. ASA 99 (1997) and *Egemetal v Fuchs*, 28 April, 2000, ATF 126 III 249 (2000), cited in Landrove (n 35) 96. However, the Swiss Federal Tribunal has so far refused to overturn CAS's arbitral awards on the merits, even though several sportsmen have attempted to challenge them on the basis of violation of Swiss public policy. See, for instance, *N, J, Y, W v FINA*, 5P.83/1999 (1999), cited in Mitten (n 36) 58.

[40] Swiss Federal Code on Private International Law, Article 190(2) (n 34).

[41] ECtHR, *Osmo Suovaniemi v Finland*, Application no 31737/96, 23 February 1999.

in a democratic society that there can be no justification for interpreting Article 6 (1) ... restrictively'.[42] This argument has been put forward by the Swiss Federal Tribunal on several occasions.[43] The Swiss Federal Tribunal obliges the CAS to follow this fundamental principle as it derives both from Swiss constitutional law and from the ECHR. As noted earlier, the right to a fair hearing belongs to the *ordre public* and must be respected in both compulsory and consensual arbitration proceedings. More specifically, Article 190(2)(d) of Switzerland's Federal Code on Private International Law provides for 'the equality of the parties or their right to be heard'.[44] The fairness of the arbitral proceedings therefore follows from two levels: the ECHR and the Swiss national legal order.

If the right to a fair hearing is not followed, the parties can challenge the arbitral award before the Swiss Federal Tribunal.[45] The right to a fair hearing refers to 'the right of access to court, a hearing in the presence of the accused, freedom from self-incrimination, equality of arms, the right to adversarial proceedings and a reasoned judgment'.[46] One of the most essential aspects of the right to a fair hearing is thus the right of effective access to a court. However, the right of access to a court is not so important an issue because the CAS is not a proper court but an arbitration tribunal. The right of effective access to the CAS therefore refers to access in fact and in law.[47]

The right of access to a court can be provided by right of appeal to the Swiss Federal Court from a CAS arbitral decision. Access to the CAS is open to any party that submits a request to the CAS.[48] Furthermore, 'unless it is apparent from the outset that there is manifestly no arbitration agreement referring to the CAS, the CAS Court Office shall take all appropriate actions to set the arbitration in motion'.[49] In most proceedings the arbitration is forced on the athletes. Montollin and Pentsov note that

> the athlete who wants to participate in such competition does not have a choice and must accept the arbitration clause, in particular by adhering to the by-laws of the sports federation containing the arbitration clause, all the more when the athlete is a professional. Otherwise, he would be confronted by the following dilemma: agree to arbitration or practice his sport as an amateur.[50]

[42] ECtHR, *Perez v France*, [GC], Application no 47287/99, ECHR 2004-I, 40 EHRR 909, para 64.

[43] See *Egemetal Demir Celik Sanayi ve Ticaret AS v Fuchs Systemtechnik GmbH* (2000) [Switzerland], ATF 126 III 249, 3c; *A v Union des Associations Européennes de Football (UEFA) et Tribunal Arbitral du Sport (TAS)* (2001) (Switz.), ATF 127 III 429, cited in De Montmollin and Pentsov (n 13) 212.

[44] See CAS 2006/A/117 *Aston Villa FC v B.93*, Copenhagen, 28 May 2007.

[45] Swiss Federal Code on Private International Law, Switzerland's Federal Code on Private International Law (n 34).

[46] Nuala Mole and Catharina Harby, *A Guide to the Implementation of Article 6 of the European Convention on Human Rights, Human rights Handbooks, No 3*, Council of Europe, (2006), available at rm.coe.int/CoERMPublicCommonSearchServices/DisplayDCTMContent?documentId=09000016800 7ff49, 30, 38.

[47] DJ Harris, M O'Boyle, EP Bates, and CM Buckley, *Law of the European Convention on Human Rights* (Oxford University Press, 2009) 236.

[48] Statutes, R 38.

[49] Ibid, R 39.

[50] Montmollin and Pentsov (n 13) 207.

It is debatable whether accepting the arbitration clause means automatically waiving the athlete's right[51] to bring the case before an ordinary national court.[52] For instance, an athlete cannot compete at the Olympic Games if she does not sign the Olympic entry form, which includes a mandatory arbitration clause.[53]

Equality of arms is another constituent part of the right to a fair hearing. The ECtHR noted in *Kress v France* that equality of arms 'requires each party to be given a reasonable opportunity of presenting his case to the court under conditions which do not place him/her at a substantial disadvantage *vis-à-vis* his/her opponent'.[54] The ECtHR describes the right to an adversarial trial as 'the opportunity for the parties to a civil or criminal trial to have knowledge of and comment on all evidence adduced or observations filed with a view to influencing the Court's decision'.[55]

The arbitral proceedings must also indirectly follow the equality of arms principle as all decisions may be subject to a potential challenge before the Swiss Federal Tribunal, which may examine CAS arbitral awards on the basis of Switzerland's Federal Code on Private International Law. Ultimately, the right to equality of arms can be waived by an agreement on arbitration, although the Swiss Federal Tribunal judicially monitors the arbitration proceedings from a procedural policy point of view. However, the Swiss Federal Tribunal is not a court of appeal. More specifically, the Swiss Federal Tribunal has noted that 'the Appellant confuses the Federal Tribunal with a court of appeal, which would oversee the CAS and freely review the accuracy of the international arbitral awards rendered by that private jurisdictional body'.[56]

Another important element of the fairness of proceedings is the standard and burden of proof. In the *Contador* case the CAS made a confident announcement about the banned substance and did not consider Contador's arguments to be plausible. The athlete carries the burden of proof in anti-doping procedures as they must prove

[51] See also *Case of Deliège v Ligue francophone de judo* (ECJ, C-51/96 in C-191/97) para 8.

[52] For example, Article 61(1) of the UEFA Statutes notes that 'the CAS shall have exclusive jurisdiction, to the exclusion of any ordinary court or any other court of arbitration, to deal with the following disputes in its capacity as an ordinary court of arbitration: a) disputes between UEFA and associations, leagues, clubs, players or officials; b) disputes of European dimension between associations, leagues, clubs, players or officials'. UEFA Statutes, Edition 2014, available at www.uefa.org/MultimediaFiles/Download/OfficialDocument/uefaorg/WhatUEFAis/02/09/93/25/2099325_DOWNLOAD.pdf. Further, Article 40 of the FIBA General Statutes (2014) see www.fiba.com/downloads/Regulations/2014/FIBA-GeneralStatutes_ApprovedbyExtraordinaryCongress16March2014_English.pdf. Also see *A v Union des Associations Européennes de Football (UEFA) et Tribunal Arbitral du Sport* (TAS) (2001) (Switzerland), ATF 127 III 429, 2a, cited in Montmollin and Pentsov (n 13) 208.

[53] Andrew Goldstone notes that 'an essential instrument in the IOC's campaign against doping is the mandatory arbitration clause contained in the Olympic entry form. In order to receive permission to compete in the Games, every athlete must sign this form. The language of the clause compels every Olympic participant to consent to mandatory, final and binding arbitration for any dispute that arises during the course of the Games.' See further Andrew Goldstone, Obstruction of Justice: The Arbitration Process for Anti-doping Violations during the Olympic Games, 7 *Cardozo Journal of Dispute Resolution* (2006) 386–87, fn 58.

[54] ECtHR, *Kress v France*, Grand Chamber, Application no 39594/98, para 72.

[55] ECtHR, *Vermulen v Belgium*, Application no 19075/91, para 33.

[56] Swiss Federal Tribunal, *Adrian Mutu v Chelsea Football Club Ltd*, 4A_458/2009, 10 June 2010, www.swissarbitrationdecisions.com/sites/default/files/10%20juin%202010%204A%20458%202009.pdf, 4.4.2.

that no prohibited substance entered their body in an unauthorised manner. The question is whether the institution of strict liability is appropriate for the exercise of anti-doping rules. The liability of athletes regarding the use of illicit substances must not override their right to a fair trial before an independent and impartial tribunal.

In the *Contador* case, as in previous cases, the arbitration tribunal met the standard of proof of likelihood (the balance of probabilities), and did not with certainty determine whether the presence of clenbuterol was due to the systematic use of banned dietary supplements. Applying this standard of proof in anti-doping procedures is likely to be controversial but it is often all that is possible since it is very difficult to demonstrate the use of illicit substances beyond a reasonable doubt.[57] Decisions in arbitration procedures before the CAS would be more convincing if the CAS were to decide beyond a reasonable doubt that in a particular case prohibited substances had been taken.[58]

On the other hand, such a standard of proof would render it largely impossible to combat the use of doping in sport. What should then be the more appropriate standard of proof? A more likely requirement would perhaps be that substantial grounds had been shown for believing that the person concerned had used prohibited substances. The applicable standard of proof would be whether there are substantial grounds for believing that the sportsman committed such offences. It is questionable whether 'proof beyond a reasonable doubt' would be more appropriate.

It may appear necessary to prove past events beyond reasonable doubt but such a high standard may not be appropriate in the context of the fight against doping in sport. It seems, however, that the application of any standard of proof, apart from beyond reasonable doubt, will be subject to a degree of speculation. Nonetheless, it seems that those two conflicting objectives should be reconciled by introducing a burden of proof which is not placed on the athlete. The CAS's decisions show that its case law in the fight against doping is developing, both in terms of the standards of evidence and in ensuring the fairness of the process. The *Contador* decision is an important development in the resolution of sports-related disputes. The decision also reveals some problems with the system, particularly the lack of equality of arms. The decision nonetheless suggests that the CAS could play a constructive role in efforts to improve its procedures so as to enhance the fairness of the procedure involved.

Andrew Goldstone notes, by referring to the comment made by high-ranking WADA and IOC officials on the *Tyler Hamilton* case, that a 'lack of due process protections during the arbitration process should expose the decisions of the panel to judicial review in national courts'.[59] Article 6(1) of the ECHR may provide for the possibility of applying for judicial review of arbitration decisions, but the question remains whether this would be to any national court. However, the fact that full fair trial guarantees before the CAS have yet to be developed does not imply that at the moment they are non-existent. On the contrary, it would be futile to argue that an arbitration procedure before the CAS will be wholly biased and unfair until it is

[57] See also *CAS 2010/A/2083 UCI v/Jan Ullrich & Swiss Olympic*; and *CAS 2009/A/1912 Claudia Pechstein v/International Skating Union.*

[58] See Straubel (n 12).

[59] Goldstone (n 53) 371.

accompanied by all constituent parts of the right to a fair trial as developed by the ECtHR. The next section considers the right to an independent and impartial tribunal established by law.

## B. The Right to an Independent and Impartial Tribunal Established by Law

This section examines whether the right to an independent and impartial tribunal established by law can also be exercised in proceedings before the CAS. Article 6 of the ECHR requires the tribunal to be independent and impartial. These requirements are interconnected and interdependent. The ECtHR noted that 'a court whose lack of independence and impartiality has been established cannot in any circumstances guarantee a fair trial'.[60] In this way, McClaren argues that is necessary to 'recognize the necessity for the arbitration panel to be independent, neutral, and impartial'.[61]

### *i. The Right to an Independent Tribunal*

The right to an independent tribunal requires that a tribunal is not dependent on an outside institution or person in its decision-making. The right to an independent tribunal refers to questions of how the tribunal members are appointed;[62] whether their position is permanent or ad hoc; if the former, how long their mandate lasts and whether it safeguards against external pressures;[63] and whether the tribunal displays an external appearance of independence.[64]

The CAS was established by the IOC but it was not until the case of *Gundel v Federation Equestre International* that its independence was first formally examined by the Swiss Federal Tribunal.[65] *Gundel* raised 'the organic and economic ties existing between the CAS and the IOC'.[66] The Swiss Federal Tribunal noted the inherent connection between the two institutions and held that 'it was desirable for greater independence of the CAS from the IOC'.[67] Consequently, the ICAS was established to govern the CAS.

In a later case, the Swiss Federal Tribunal noted that 'the CAS is more akin to a judicial authority independent of the parties'.[68] The ICAS selects arbitrators 'for a

[60] ECtHR, *Hulki Güneş v Turkey*, App No 28490/95, judgment of 19 June 2003, para 84.

[61] McLaren (n 26) 384.

[62] Mole and Harby (n 46) 30.

[63] Ibid.

[64] ECtHR, *Campbell and Fell v the United Kingdom*, 7 EHRR 165, para 78.

[65] *Gundel v Federation Equestre International* reprinted in Matthieu Reeb (ed), Digest of CAS Awards I 1986–1998 567 (Kluwer, 1998) cited in Yi (n 27) 11.

[66] Ibid 570, cited in Yi (n 27) 11.

[67] Ibid. The original in French reads as follows: 'il était souhaitable que l'on assurait une indépendence accrue du TAS à l'égard du CIO'. ATE 119 II 271 coinde 3B BGE 129 II 445, 451. See also, Matthew J Mitten, 'Judicial Review of Olympic and International Sport Arbitration Awards: Trends and Observations' Marquette University Law School Legal Studies Research Paper Series, Research Paper No 09-14, 5–6.

[68] *A and B v IOC and FIS* in Matthieu Reeb (ed), Digest of Case Awards *DIGEST OF CAS AWARDS III 2001–2003* (2004) 686, cited in Mitten (n 36) 56.

renewable period of four years'. The length of their mandates ensures their independence. However, the arbitrators do not hold a permanent position, only an ad hoc one. This rule opens the door to potential pressure on arbitrators. The list itself is reviewed every four years and 'there are at least one hundred and fifty arbitrators and at least fifty mediators'.[69]

At the moment there are over 354 arbitrators on the CAS's list.[70] The ICAS follows several principles in the selection process, in particular

> full legal training, recognized competence with regard to sports law and/or international arbitration, a good knowledge of sport in general and a good command of at least one CAS working language, whose names and qualifications are brought to the attention of the ICAS, including by the IOC, the international federations (IFs) and the National Olympic Committees (NOCs) and by the athletes' commissions of the IOC, IFs and NOCs.[71]

However, the phrase 'brought to the attention' reveals that the selection process is not as transparent as it would be in the case of an open call for candidates. Furthermore, it is unclear how the arbitrators are appointed in practice and whether the fact that they are appointed by the executive hinders their objectivity and independence. The selection process considers equal representation and 'fair representation of the continents and of the different juridical cultures'.[72]

By contrast, the arbitrators' independence seems to be ensured first by their obligation to declare their independence and second, by the possibility of their removal. More specifically, 'the CAS arbitrators and mediators sign a declaration undertaking to exercise their functions personally with total objectivity and independence'.[73] The external appearance of independence follows from the ability to remove the arbitrators. Section 19 of the Statutes provides that 'the ICAS may remove, temporarily or permanently, an arbitrator or a mediator from the list of CAS members if he violates any rule of this Code or if his action affects the reputation of ICAS/CAS'. Theoretically, such provisions ensure that the CAS fulfils the criteria of independence included in fair trial guarantees. However, the Swiss Federal Tribunal noted in the *Lazutina* decision that:

> An arbitrator's independence ... can only be evaluated on a case-by-case basis; there are no absolute grounds for a challenge. Doubts about the independence of an arbitrator must be based on the existence of objective facts which are likely, for a rational observer, to arouse suspicion concerning the arbitrator's independence. On the other hand, the purely subjective reactions of one party should not be taken into account.[74]

In order to underline the independence of arbitrators, the Statutes note that: 'CAS arbitrators and mediators may not act as counsel for a party before the CAS.'[75] Moreover, the Swiss Federal Tribunal, in the *Lazutina* decision, noted that 'members

[69] Statutes of the Bodies Working for the Settlement of Sports-Related Disputes, S13.
[70] See the webpage of the Court of Arbitration for Sport, available at http://www.tas-cas.org/en/arbitration/list-of-arbitrators-general-list.html.
[71] Statutes (n 69) S14.
[72] Ibid S16.
[73] Ibid S18.
[74] *Lazutina* (n 38) 691, cited in Mitten (n 36) 56.
[75] Statutes (n 69) S18.

of a tribunal are capable of rising above the eventualities linked to their appointment when they are required to render concrete decisions in the discharge of their duties'.[76]

Finally, the Swiss Federal Tribunal can examine CAS decisions from a procedural point of view. McLaren observes that 'the strongest proof that the CAS has achieved independence can be found within numerous decisions of the court. Indeed, the CAS has asserted its independence by overturning cases decided differently by the IOC and by criticizing the IOC where it has failed to act with decisiveness' (footnotes omitted).[77] Further, McClaren aptly notes that:

> An international arbitration system that is not independent and for which there is a political override, no matter how well intended, will ultimately bring both itself and its sports federation into disrepute. In the end, the international panel is no more independent in its actions than the national panels whose decisions they are reviewing.[78]

The right to an independent tribunal may be indirectly waived if the party to arbitration proceedings is inactive and is aware of potential doubts about the independence of the arbitrators. However, the Swiss Federal Tribunal must examine whether the arbitration panel which delivered the arbitral award followed the principle of independence.

From this analysis of the independence principle of the CAS, it becomes clear that a number of sources underline the CAS's commitment to ensuring independence.[79] The CAS has striven to ensure the independence of its arbitrators. Yet, in spite of these developments, the right to an independent arbitration panel through the CAS is still problematic as the appointment of qualified persons and their later selection in individual cases is not very transparent. Nevertheless, it appears there is growing support for the notion that the principle of independence should be evolved not only in theory but also in practice. Having gained an understanding of the right to an independent CAS, the next part of this section turns to the development of the principle of impartiality.

### *ii. The Right to an Impartial Tribunal*

Another important element of the right to a fair trial is the impartiality of those who resolve the disputes. In the case of the CAS, the arbitrators are persons entrusted with the decision-making. In *Piersack v Belgium*, the ECtHR held that:

> Whilst impartiality normally denotes absence of prejudice or bias, its existence or otherwise can, notably under Article 6(1) of the Convention, be tested in various ways. A distinction can be drawn in this context between a subjective approach, that is endeavouring to ascertain the personal conviction of a given judge in a given case, and an objective approach,

[76] *Lazutina* (n 38) 692, cited in Mitten (n 36) 56.

[77] McLaren (n 26) 383. See also Antoine Duval, The Court of Arbitration for Sport after Pechstein: Reform or Revolution?, 17 November 2015, Asser International Sports Law Blog, www.asser.nl/SportsLaw/Blog/post/the-court-of-arbitration-for-sport-after-pechstein-reform-or-revolution.

[78] Ibid 390.

[79] See also Straubel (n 12) 1233–47.

> that is determining whether he offered guarantees sufficient to exclude any legitimate doubt in this respect.[80]

The Statutes are clear on impartiality and require that 'every arbitrator shall be and remain independent of the parties and shall immediately disclose any circumstances likely to affect his independence with respect to any of the parties'.[81] Further, Rule 33 of the Statutes specifies that 'every arbitrator shall be and remain independent of the parties and shall immediately disclose any circumstances likely to affect his independence with respect to any of the parties'. This provision is further underlined by the provision for changing or removing an arbitrator.

If a legitimate doubt arises over the independence of an arbitrator, they may be challenged within seven days 'after the ground for the challenge has become known'.[82] Even the appearance of the possibility of bias towards one party will suffice to disqualify an arbitrator from further proceedings. If such a challenge proves justified, the ICAS or its Board decides on the removal of the arbitrator from the panel.[83] The Swiss Federal Tribunal also examines whether the arbitration panel acted impartially when judicially reviewing an arbitral award from a procedural policy point of view.

### *iii. A Tribunal Established by Law*

The right to a fair trial demands that the tribunal is established by law. The former European Commission of Human Rights noted in *Zand v Austria* that:

> It is the object and purpose of the clause in Article 6(1) requiring that the courts shall be 'established by law' that the judicial organisation in a democratic society must not depend on the discretion of the Executive, but that it should be regulated by law emanating from Parliament. However, this does not mean that delegated legislation is as such unacceptable in matters concerning the judicial organisation.[84]

It is still questionable whether the CAS is 'a tribunal established by law' in the strict meaning of the phrase because it was initially established by the IOC. Nonetheless, the CAS is a tribunal established by law; however its proceedings are arbitral, meaning that only the parties to a dispute can agree whether to bring it to an arbitral resolution.

The Swiss Federal Tribunal has so far prioritised the quick settlement of sports-related disputes before the CAS over an athlete's right to bring a case before the ordinary courts.[85] However, in the recent case of *UEFA v FC Sion*[86] concerning the illegal

80 ECtHR, *Piersack v Belgium*, Application no 8692/79 para 30.

81 Statutes (n 69) Rule 33.

82 Ibid Rule 32.

83 Ibid Rules 34 and 35.

84 ECtHR, *Zand v Austria*, Application no 7360/76. Further, the ECtHR noted in *Van de Hurk v the Netherlands* that 'the power to give a binding decision which may not be altered by a non-judicial authority to the detriment of an individual party is inherent in the very notion of a "tribunal", as is confirmed by the word "determination" ("qui décidera")', Application no 16034/90, para 45.

85 See, for example, *A, B v Comité International Olympique, Fédération Internationale de Ski (FIS) et Tribunal Arbitral du Sport* (TAS) (2003) [Switzerland] ATF 129 III 445.

86 See *UEFA Statement of FC Sion case*, available at www.uefa.org/about-uefa/executive-committee/news/newsid=1694975.html. See also Arbitration *CAS 2011/O/2574 Union des Associations Européennes*

registration of six players and the subsequent exclusion of FC Sion from UEFA, a Swiss regional court took another approach and issued a provisional measure and fined UEFA for illegally excluding the club from competition. Such a case re-opens the perennially controversial question concerning the legal nature of the internal rules of a sports association. Are such rules autonomous or are they dependent on a particular national legal order? Do domestic and international sports associations need to comply with the fundamental principles of national constitutional courts?

The ECtHR noted in *Osmo Suovaniemi v Finland*, one of the rare decisions on the waiver of rights, that 'the waiver of a right guaranteed by the Convention—insofar as it is permissible—must be established in an unequivocal manner' and that 'in the case of procedural rights a waiver, in order to be effective for Convention purposes, requires minimum guarantees commensurate to its importance'.[87] In this case, the ECtHR did not find a violation of an article as an unequivocal waiver had been given and therefore the bias of one of the arbitrators did not matter. It is also important that the waiver of a guarantee to a fair trial 'must not run counter to any important public interest'.[88]

It is necessary to examine whether a determination by the CAS is arbitral, judicial or a mixture of these.[89] The term judicial body refers to 'an independent and impartial body, competent to give, on the basis of the facts determined by due process, legally binding judgments'.[90] A quasi-judicial body is not a judicial body, yet it nonetheless carries out some judicial functions. Quasi-judicial bodies play a role in providing a right to an effective remedy. However, they are not always completely independent and their decisions are of a non-binding nature, often without sanctions. Even though some argue that only a court of law is competent to review complaints in relation to human rights violations, quasi-judicial mechanisms do have a role to play.[91] Brigit Toebes argues that 'the effectiveness of a decision does not always depend on its (non-)binding nature, so the impact of some decisions may be equal or similar to that of judicial bodies' decisions.'[92]

The issue of whether the CAS's awards are judicially binding or not cannot be answered with a simple yes or no. The response to this question is that it is more likely that both answers may be true in some respects. The CAS is primarily an arbitration tribunal which includes mostly arbitral and some minor judicial functions. The CAS is thus not a judicial body, although its arbitral awards show some 'important characteristics of a judicial decision'.[93] An issue of terminology also arises.

*de Football (UEFA) v FC Sion/Olympique des Alpes SA*, award of 31 January 2012 (operative part of 15 December 2011).

[87] ECtHR, *Osmo Suovaniemi v Finland* (n 41).

[88] ECtHR, *Hermy v Italy*, Application no 18114/02 para 73.

[89] See Brigit Toebes, *The Right to Health as a Human Right in International Law* (Hart Publishing, 1999) 168.

[90] GJH Van Hoof and K De Vey Mestdagh, 'Mechanisms of International Supervision' in P van Dijk (ed), *Supervisory Mechanism in International Economic Organizations* (Kluwer/TMC Asser Instituut, 1984) 15 quoted in Toebes (n 89) 168.

[91] EW Vierdag, 'The Legal Nature of the Rights Granted by the International Covenant on Economic, Social and Cultural Rights' *Netherlands Yearbook of International Law* Vol IX, (TMC Asser Press, 1987) 73, quoted in Toebes (n 89) 168.

[92] Toebes (n 89) 168.

[93] Ibid.

The CAS's arbitral awards are binding, however they do not have an *erga omnes* effect and only apply to parties in the arbitration procedure.[94] More specifically, the CAS has noted that 'in CAS jurisprudence there is no principle of binding precedent, or stare decisis'.[95] Ultimately, one can argue that despite the mainly arbitral function of the CAS, the right to an independent and impartial tribunal established by law must also be respected. However, the provision of guarantees can be supervised through the judicial review procedure of the Swiss Federal Court. Having acquired an understanding of the right to an independent and impartial tribunal established by law, the next part of this section turns to the right to a public hearing and the public pronouncement of judgments.

## C. The Right to a Public Hearing and the Public Pronouncement of Judgments

The guarantee of a fair trial requires hearings to take place in public. The right to a public hearing is an essential part of the right to a fair trial. However, a trial cannot be described as fair simply because it takes place in public—other constituent parts of the right to a fair trial must also be present. The ECtHR noted in *Martine v France* that:

> The public character of proceedings before the judicial bodies referred to in Article 6 § 1 protects litigants against the administration of justice in secret with no public scrutiny; it is also one of the means whereby confidence in the courts, superior and inferior, can be maintained. By rendering the administration of justice visible, publicity contributes to the achievement of the aim of Article 6 § 1, namely a fair trial, the guarantee of which is one of the fundamental principles of any democratic society.[96]

A public trial is therefore a *conditio sine qua non* for a fair trial. However, it is debatable whether this requirement must also be followed in arbitration proceedings such as those before the CAS. Michael Collins notes that 'strangers are to be excluded from the hearing of the arbitration'.[97] It was noted earlier that proceedings before the CAS have a quasi-judicial character. What is more, hearings before the CAS are not open to the public. The Rules note that 'proceedings under these Procedural Rules (of the CAS) are confidential. The parties, the arbitrators and the CAS undertake not to disclose to any third party any facts or other information relating to the dispute or the proceedings without the permission of the CAS.'[98] This rule derives from a traditional pillar of any arbitration—confidentiality.

[94] CAS 96/161, *ITU v Pacific Sports Corporation*, 4 August 1999, Digest of CAS Awards I, 560.

[95] Arbitration *CAS 2004/A/628, IAAF v USA Track and Field & Jerome Young*, award of 28 June 2004, 73 at 18, cited in Mitten and Davis (n 30) 71.

[96] *Martine v France*, Application no 58675/00, para 39.

[97] Michael Collins, 'Privacy and Confidentiality in Arbitration Proceedings' (1995) 30 *Texas International Law Journal* 121.

[98] Statutes (n 69) Rule 43.

Cindy Buys correctly notes that 'confidentiality is often cited as one of the main benefits of arbitration as opposed to litigation'.[99] One could also argue that in arbitration proceedings the publicity requirement may be waived. Nonetheless, Rule 43 of the Statutes[100] does not help to enhance the transparency and openness of proceedings. In fact, public proceedings would also ensure the greater legitimacy of the arbitral award and create a stronger appearance of independence. Currently, the confidentiality of CAS proceedings is at odds with the increasing interest in transparency on the part of sportsmen and their respective organisations.

Despite a commitment to confidentiality on the normative level, signs appear to be emerging of the CAS's greater openness to public hearings. For instance, the CAS website lists upcoming hearings and specifies the names of the parties.[101] This new development is a step in the right direction for ensuring the full fairness of procedures before the CAS since one could ask, what is the purpose of having compliance mechanisms if the procedure must remain confidential? This leads to a situation where arbitration procedures are potentially stripped of their *raison d'être*. By contrast, the former European Commission of Human Rights noted in *Nordström-Janzon and Nordström-Lehtinen v the Netherlands* that 'in some respects—in particular as regards publicity—it is clear that arbitral proceedings are often not even intended to be in conformity with Article 6, and the arbitration agreement entails a renunciation of the full application of that Article'.[102] However, the implementation of certain CAS decisions could be envisaged even if the proceeding were not open to the public. More importantly, it seems that the right to a public hearing and the public pronouncement of an arbitral award do not fall within the category of procedural public policy, which is judicially supervised by the Swiss Federal Court.

The fairness of judicial procedures is also ensured by the public pronouncement of decisions. However, Rule 43 provides that 'awards shall not be made public unless all parties agree or the Division President so decides'.[103] In practice, arbitral awards are not pronounced publicly. However, almost all of the more recent arbitral awards are publicly accessible in full on the CAS webpage.[104] This development illustrates the CAS's stronger commitment to public hearings and to ensuring the greater legitimacy of its decisions. Overall, the publication of proceedings has not yet gained a foothold as a fundamental principle in sports arbitration procedures. By contrast, the publication of arbitration proceedings is traditionally not required.

[99] Cindy G Buys, 'The Tensions between Confidentiality and Transparency in International Arbitration' (2003) 14 *American Review of International Arbitration* 121. See also Richard C Reuben, 'Confidentiality in Arbitration: Beyond the Myth' (2006) 54 *Kansas Law Review* 1255.

[100] Rule 43 of the CAS Statutes provides as follows: 'Proceedings under these Procedural Rules are confidential. The parties, the arbitrators and the CAS undertake not to disclose to any third party anyfacts or other information relating to the dispute or the proceedings without the permission of the CAS. Awards shall not be made public unless all parties agree or the Division President so decides.'

[101] See the website of the Court of Arbitration for Sport, available at www.tas-cas.org/en/general-information/news-detail/article/list-of-hearings-6.html.

[102] European Commission of Human Rights, *Nordström-Janzon and Nordström-Lehtinen v the Netherlands*, Application no 28101/95.

[103] Statutes (n 69) Rule 43.

[104] See the website of the Court of Arbitration for Sport, available at www.tas-cas.org/en/jurisprudence/recent-decisions.html.

However, with more concentration on the fundamental principle of transparency, the publication of the CAS's proceedings may gain traction and could gradually be included in all of its procedures and revision of its rules.

## D. The Right to a Fair Trial within a Reasonable Time

One advantage of arbitration proceedings is that, in theory, they should be finished within a reasonable time. Article 6 of the ECHR protects the right to a trial without undue delay. Allegations of a violation of the right to a trial without undue delay under Article 6(1) feature prominently among cases against several countries before the Strasbourg Court. The length of the proceedings is a very complex and systemic problem in many cases. The Venice Commission aptly noted that:

> The undue postponement of judicial decisions may result in a denial of justice for the parties to the proceedings (although it may happen that parties delay the proceedings on purpose). In more general terms and in the longer run, it risks to affect the confidence which the general public places in the capacity of the State to dispense justice, to decide disputes ... This may cause or even incite the recourse by individuals to alternative means of dispute settlement or dispensation of punishment. The deleterious effects on the rule of law of such a situation are evident.[105]

The length of proceedings before the CAS for an ordinary arbitration is between six months and one year, and for an appeals procedure it is three months.[106] The exact length of a case depends on the complexity of the case, the conduct of the parties, the conduct of the arbitration panel and the particularities of each case. For instance, the appeal procedures in the *Contador* case lasted three times longer than the time envisaged for such an appeal. Altogether, the *Contador* case took a year and half to resolve.

However, it is in the interest of the fight against doping that such procedures be speedy since it is thereby possible to protect the integrity of a sport and the athlete's rights. It is true that even here we can apply the criteria of normal court proceedings in terms of the duration of their assessment of the complexity of the case, the conduct of the parties to the proceedings and any other circumstances of the case.

Given the sensitivity of doping allegations, local sports associations and the CAS should strive to make decisions quickly without any undue delay. Undoubtedly, the CAS has a primary duty to protect human rights and freedoms first within its own proceedings. The CAS system does not suffer from a backlog of cases, which would undermine the importance of administering justice without delay and the right to

[105] European Commission for Democracy Through Law (Venice Commission), Report on Effectiveness of National Remedies in Respect of Excessive Length of Proceedings, CDL-AD(2006)036rev, Study number 316/2004, 3 April 2007.

[106] The CAS webpage, available at www.tas-cas.org/en/general-information/frequently-asked-questions.html. The CAS Statutes do not provide any time limits for arbitration at first instance in the so-called Ordinary Arbitration Division. By contrast, the appeals procedure provides for time limits. Rule 49 sets out the following time limits for an appeal: 'in the absence of a time limit set in the statutes or regulations of the federation, association or sports-related body concerned, or of a previous agreement, the time limit for appeal shall be twenty-one days from the receipt of the decision appealed against'. (Statutes, Rule 49).

an effective legal remedy. In short, the CAS must diligently pursue an interest in the proper functioning and use of justice; the inclusion of cost-effective management is another important element. Parties before the CAS do not have the option of filing an administrative action, pursuant to which someone alleging a violation of this right can bring a complaint before a court against lengthy proceedings in pending cases and request compensation for any damage caused.

## IV. ASSESSMENT

The arbitration procedures before the CAS reveal some problems with respect to fair trial guarantees, particularly the inability to challenge its arbitral awards apart from when there is a procedural public policy issue that calls for consideration by the Swiss Federal Tribunal, which nonetheless may be sufficient under Article 6(1) of the ECHR. However, the main question has been whether fair trial guarantees also apply in arbitration proceedings before the CAS. In other words, does it suffice that the Swiss Federal Tribunal has only *ex post facto* power to consider whether the arbitration panel respected procedural public policy guarantees, including fair trial guarantees, provided that one of the parties challenged the arbitral award on the basis of Article 190(2) of Switzerland's Federal Code on Private International Law?

The examination of the constituent parts of the fundamental right to a fair trial has shown that the right to a fair hearing and the right to an independent and impartial tribunal established by law must be respected at all times in arbitration procedures before the CAS as they form part of the *ordre public*, which is judicially supervised by the Swiss Federal Courts. As for the remaining constituent parts of the fundamental right to a fair trial, such as the right to a public hearing and the public pronouncement of judgments, and the right to a fair trial within a reasonable time, it is preferable that they should also be secured in the CAS's arbitration proceedings in order to assure their greater legitimacy and fairness.

Moreover, the waiver of any of the constituent components of the right to a fair trial is hardly voluntary and unequivocal. At best, such waivers are signed in order for an athlete to compete at the highest level in national and international competitions. Further, the absence of some elements of the right to a fair trial, such as the rights to an independent and impartial arbitration panel, to a public hearing and to the public pronouncement of judgments, do not contribute to the greater persuasiveness and legitimacy of the CAS's arbitral awards.

What is more, the *ex post facto* judicial review of respect for fundamental fair trial guarantees by the Swiss Federal Tribunal does not suffice to ensure the respect for fair trial guarantees before the CAS. Moreover, such *ex post facto* judicial review only takes place if the arbitral award is delivered and challenged before the Swiss Federal Tribunal. Accordingly, the most appropriate alternative would be for the CAS prospectively to ensure respect for fair trial guarantees in its proceedings.

CAS decisions highlight both the promise and pitfalls of the arbitration system. The arbitral awards suggest that the CAS could play a constructive role in efforts to improve state responsibility for human rights. Empowering the CAS to engage in binding judicial dispute resolution and to apply sanctions would, however, require a significant revision of its statutes, potentially undermining or strengthening the entire system in its current form. All in all, the nature and scope of fair trial guarantees before the CAS are narrower than in regular judicial proceedings, which is usual for arbitration proceedings.

When states interfere with the rights of individuals, effective complaint mechanisms have to be established to provide remedies for allegations of human rights violations. Similarly, when sports organisations interfere with the rights of athletes, effective complaint mechanisms have to be established to provide remedies for allegations of human rights law and sports law violations. The right to judicial review before the Swiss Federal Tribunal is the only option so far for challenging the CAS's arbitral awards; however, even this option is limited as it only provides for *ex post facto* judicial review and only for issues of procedural public policy.

The lack of fully effective access to a judicial organ in sports-related cases is still the major obstacle to the enjoyment of an individual's fundamental human rights. Given that there is only one relatively effective mechanism within the architecture of accountability, several more effective mechanisms would have to be developed. Many of the underlying weaknesses of the CAS's work can be directly tied to conundrums related to a weak respect for the right to fair trial guarantees in its arbitration proceedings, which cannot be corrected later by *ex post facto* judicial review of those proceedings by the Swiss Federal Tribunal.

To be clear, the argument here is not that the CAS should be dissolved. It plays a seminal role in resolving sports-related disputes. Instead, the argument is that the CAS could provide an incentive for sports organisations by setting up an advantageous and regulated judicial framework for resolving sport disputes. By all accounts, it is therefore not unreasonable to conclude that the CAS's arbitration procedure must at least be strengthened in order for the CAS system to comply effectively with fundamental fair trial guarantees.

## V. PROPOSALS FOR IMPROVEMENT

Transparent enforcement mechanisms and procedures are required to assess compliance with national and international sporting standards. Where a sports organisation fails to meet its obligations, adequate and effective remedies must be available to victims whose human rights have been violated. In future, the IOC could consider establishing an expert working group to examine whether existing sports dispute resolution mechanisms such as the CAS comply with fundamental human rights standards, including the right to a fair trial. Some commentators have already discussed the currently utopian possibility of a world court of human rights.[107] Such a

[107] For some proposals and discussion in this respect, see Martin Scheinin, 'Towards a World Court of Human Rights', Research report within the framework of the Swiss Initiative to commemorate the 60th anniversary of the Universal Declaration of Human Rights, 30 April 2009, available at www.eui.eu/Documents/DepartmentsCentres/Law/Professors/Scheinin/WorldCourtReport30April2009.pdf; Stefan Trechsel, 'A World Court for Human Rights?' (2004) 1 *Northwestern University Journal of International Human Rights*; Manfred Nowak, 'The Need for a World Court of Human Rights' (2007) 1(1) *Human Rights Law Review* 251.

complaints body might also consider individual communications from sports victims of human rights violations. The idea of such a court already envisages the possibility of hearing complaints directed against non-state actors as most international and national organisations are.[108]

Strengthening the CAS's existing arbitration system would help to overcome the shortcomings of the CAS when it comes to the protection of an athlete's human rights. Four proposals can be made for enhancing mechanisms under the CAS. First, it would appear possible to translate the arbitration mechanism under the CAS into a quasi-judicial organ which could also have the power of compulsory jurisdiction. To this end, an independent and impartial supervisory mechanism could be developed at the national level, possibly in the form of a sports ombudsman. Such an ombudsman would represent the public interest by investigating and addressing complaints made by any athlete. On the other hand, such a proposal might also seem overly bureaucratic when it would perhaps be better to change the internal workings of the CAS rather than adding an extra layer.

The second proposal is to introduce the ability to challenge the CAS's arbitral awards before the ECtHR. However, such a proposal would require substantial changes to the ECHR. A proposal along these lines has already been submitted.[109] However, in its jurisprudence the ECtHR has already observed that:

> [S]tates enjoy considerable discretion in regulating the question on which grounds an arbitral award should be quashed, since the quashing of an already rendered award will often mean that a long and costly arbitral procedure will become useless and that considerable work and expense must be invested in new proceedings.[110]

While such an amendment would ensure that the CAS complies with basic human rights standards, it would also mean that the ECtHR would be faced with the possibility of an even greater caseload. This step may thus seem questionable in light of the fact that several thousand cases are currently waiting to be examined by the ECtHR.

Third, the CAS has to strive towards an effective role in promoting fair trial guarantees in its arbitration procedures and ensuring transparency and accessibility. It could recognise that its main purpose is to serve parties in arbitration procedures and that such a service requires proper administration, including the acknowledgement of mistakes when they occur and the provision of appropriate remedies. In this context, the Swiss Federal Tribunal could examine all constituent parts of the right to fair trial, not only those which fall in the *ordre public*. Moreover, it appears necessary that some kind of preventive mechanism be established to monitor respect by the CAS for fair trial guarantees in its proceedings.

Fourth, irrespective of the structure adopted, for the instrument to work the CAS has to be informed, authoritative and command the confidence of all parties. A further revision of the wording of the CAS Statutes along these lines to ensure that they comply with fair trial guarantees would be the most appropriate solution.

108 See, for example, Article 6 of the Draft Statute of World Court of Human Rights (n 107).
109 De Montmollin and Pentsov (n 13) 239.
110 *Osmo Suovaniemi v Finland* (n 41).

Many criticise the Statutes for their vague wording and grand ambitions, which have proved difficult to implement effectively. A good way to remedy this drawback would be to initiate a comprehensive reform of the Statutes and to include fundamental rights principles so as to clarify the impact the new provisions would have, and how they would be interpreted and given effect. All in all, arbitration before the CAS is moving in the right direction as regards fair trial guarantees; what is needed is more detailed fine-tuning.

## VI. CONCLUSION

This contribution has attempted to examine fair trial guarantees before the CAS from the viewpoint of the principles and jurisprudence of the ECHR. The CAS holds jurisdiction over the resolution of sports-related disputes between all parties that have agreed to submit a matter for it to resolve. While it can be concluded that the arbitration procedures before the CAS generally abide by the majority of the constituent parts of the right to a fair trial, it is also evident that they could be better incorporated and implemented by ordinary and appeals arbitration procedures.[111] The underlying weakness of the CAS arbitration procedure is directly tied to the nature of its proceedings since an effective and coherent judicial system does not exist for resolving sports-related disputes.

The chief problems lie in the lack of procedural fairness, the non-publication of its proceedings, the issue of the burden and standard of proof and the absence of a right to an independent and impartial arbitration panel (the lack of transparency involved in appointing arbitrators to the CAS list). It seems that parties do not possess sufficient knowledge to respond adequately to the minimum standards of fair trial rights, as developed by the ECHR, in identifying the substantive obligations and responsibilities of relevant parties. Just as important is the question of how these obligations or violations can be identified in fair and equitable procedures. Judicial enforcement means the right to the effective protection of human rights and the right of access to an impartial judge or arbitration panel. It refers to questions of whether human rights have reached the individual. Parties to arbitration procedures before the CAS must have effective access to justice, with the ability to challenge the content of a CAS decision before a court of appeal.

However, the *ex post facto* judicial review of respect for fundamental fair trial guarantees by the Swiss Federal Tribunal does not suffice to ensure respect for fair trial guarantees before the CAS. Moreover, such *ex post facto* judicial review before the Swiss Federal Tribunal only takes place if the arbitral award is delivered and provided that it is challenged. Statistics on compliance with the CAS's determinations illustrate that the CAS's arbitral awards are rarely overturned.

Human rights, including in sports arbitration proceedings, are usually best protected within national legal orders. International sports arbitration enforcement can only be an emergency brake that complements judicial protection afforded

[111] CAS, CAS 2011/A/2384.

by national legal orders. An international arbitration sports regime should offer a clear set of minimum standards for the protection and promotion of fair trial rights guarantees. National sports associations should have to comply with these minimum standards and be a fortiori encouraged to go beyond them. In short, it may be necessary to explore the possibilities of constructing a stronger national sports judicial or arbitration rights regime, coupled with a stronger CAS to protect human rights better in sports arbitration or judicial procedures. Most of the normative framework for supporting the work of the CAS is already in place.

What appears to be missing is a clarification of the existing framework. However, until attempts are made to reform how the CAS operates, a vital part of athletes' access to justice will remain absent. The current state of the regulation of sports-related disputes before the CAS is a step in the right direction, although it does not fully advance the cause of the protection and promotion of procedural human rights in its arbitration procedures.

# 21

# *International Sports Law and the Fight against Doping: An Analysis from an International Human Rights Perspective*

CARMEN PÉREZ GONZÁLEZ*

## I. INTRODUCTION

THIS CONTRIBUTION FOCUSES on the relationship between public international law and sports activity. The existence of an international sports system operating as a self-regulating private legal order serves as the starting point for the analysis.[1] The central role played in this framework by international non-governmental organisations (NGOs), namely the International Olympic Committee (IOC), the World Anti-Doping Agency (WADA) and International Federations (IFs), is unquestionable. IFs are the bodies in charge of the organisation of sports activity at the international level and they act 'like global standard setters'.[2] The traditional structure which has organised sports activities could be defined as a multi-level top-down structure, which includes clubs, leagues and national and IFs on the one hand, and the IOC and the National Olympic Committees (NOCs), on the other.[3] This

* Lecturer in Public International Law and International Relations, University Carlos III of Madrid. Former member (2005–2014) of the Spanish Committee on Sports Discipline. Current member (since September 2015) of the European Commission High Level Group on Sport Diplomacy.

[1] As Professor Rigaux highlighted several years ago: '(l)'exploitation économique du sport et des divertissements a réussi à se soustraire à toute velléité de contrôle étatique. Il s'agit d'une vache sacrée qu'aucun gouvernement n'oserait réduire à la condition du bétail domestique': François Rigaux, 'Les situations juridiques individuelles dans un système de relativité générale' (1989) 213 *Collected Courses of the Hague Academy of International Law* 1, 379.

[2] Lorenzo Casini, 'Global Hybrid Public-Private Bodies: The World Anti-Doping Agency (WADA)' (2009) 6 *International Organization Law Review* 421, 426.

[3] As Casini describes it: 'The IOC recognizes only one IF for each sport, and only one [National Olympic Committee] NOC per country. The National Federations (NF's, charged with the regulation of each sport at the national level) are then associated to their respective IFs and NOC. This structure has been described as a "double pyramid", one relating to the relationship of IOC with the NOC's, the other relating to the relationship of the IFs to the NFs; however, the system seems better understood as a series of "multiple pyramids", meaning those that relate the IOC to the NOC's, on one hand, and to the many IFs of different sports ... and the respective NFs on the other. Further, these pyramids are linked to each other, both vertically and horizontally.' Ibid 424.

pyramidal structure has a hierarchical nature.[4] From a legal perspective, these international bodies are private associations, created in accordance with private domestic law and their members are national sporting associations that have been admitted into membership. They organise and coordinate their own international competitions and, in that sense, their activities have a transnational scope, and they can be considered international actors.[5] They have enjoyed a monopolistic position in this field for decades while, at the same time, maintaining that self-regulatory power was the only way of preserving good governance in sports.

In this context, and with self-regulation being a traditional basic element of sports organisations, national and supranational public authorities have met with serious difficulties when intervening in the sector. Those private organisations claim a so-called 'sport specificity' as a way to preserve regulatory autonomy and maintain in force private sporting rules, their own *Lex Sportiva*, even when they are in breach of essential principles of public law typically enshrined in international law.[6] Besides this, the emergence of a private mechanism for settling sports disputes through national and international sports arbitration bodies—the Court of Arbitration for Sport (CAS) being the supreme instance of this system[7]—seeks to avoid the intervention of national courts.[8]

[4] For more information about the sports governance system, see John Forster, 'Global Sports Organizations and their Governance' (2006) 6 *Corporate Governance* 72.

[5] It must be noted that the WADA has a different structure: both private sports bodies and public authorities, and also athletes (an Athlete Committee was established in 2005 to represent the views and rights of athletes worldwide) are part of its organs. See www.wada-ama.org/en/About-WADA/Governance/.

[6] A statement of the former vice-president of the International Amateur Athletics Federation (IIAF) gives us a clear idea about the strength of this claim: 'Courts create a lot of problems for our anti-doping work, but we say we don't care in the least what they say. We have our rules, and they are supreme', Ken Foster, 'Is There a Global Sports Law?' (2003) 2 *Entertainment Law* 1, 1.

[7] Adam Samuel and Richard Gearhart, 'Sporting Arbitration and the International Olympic Committee's Court of Arbitration for Sport' (1989) 6 *Journal of International Arbitration* 39; Bruno Simma, 'The Court of Arbitration for Sport' in Karl-Heinz Böckstiegel et al (eds), *Law of Nations, Law of International Organizations, World's Economic Law. Liber amicorum honouring Ignaz Seidl-Hohenveldern* (Heymanns, 1988); James AR Nafziger, 'Dispute Resolution in the Arena of International Sports Competition' (2002) 50 *American Journal of Comparative Law* 161.

[8] According to Article 68.2 of the Fédération Internationale de Football Association (International Federation of Association Football) FIFA Statutes:

The Associations shall insert a clause in their statutes of regulations, stipulating that it is prohibited to take disputes in the Association of disputes affecting Leagues, members of Leagues, Clubs, members of Clubs, Players, Officials and other Association Officials to ordinary courts of law, unless the FIFA regulations or binding legal provisions specifically provide for or stipulate recourse to ordinary courts of law. Instead of recourse to ordinary courts of law, provision shall be made for arbitration. Such disputes shall be taken to an independent and duly constituted arbitration tribunal recognized under the rules of the Association or Confederation or to CAS. The Associations shall also ensure that this stipulation is implemented in the Association, if necessary by imposing a binding obligation to its members. The Associations shall impose sanctions on any party that fails to respect this obligation and ensure that any appeal against such sanctions shall likewise be strictly submitted to arbitration and not to ordinary courts of law.

Similar clauses can be found incorporated in other IFs' Statutes. FIFA Statutes are available at www.fifa.com/mm/document/affederation/generic/02/14/97/88/fifastatuten2013_e_neutral.pdf. In addition, it has to be taken into account that according to WADA rules, cases arising from international events, or concerning international-level athletes, can only be appealed to the CAS.

For a long time, the sports system has been thought of as a self-contained regime where public law and state authorities did not have a clear role to play. However, in recent years, sports governing bodies have been challenged by strong demands from public authorities to increase their levels of legal scrutiny, democracy, transparency and respect for fundamental rights. This work defends the application of the fundamental principles of public law to sports activity. And due to the globalisation of sports activity, it maintains that the role to be played by public international law is one of the key elements of this process. This chapter explores this relationship.[9]

The fight against doping in sport will be used as a case study in this regard. Recent developments in the WADA framework have produced strong controversy, as they are considered contrary to certain athletes' human rights. This chapter argues that, as required by the 2005 UNESCO International Convention against Doping in Sports,[10] those anti-doping sports regulations and procedures should meet international human rights standards and, in this context, particular attention will be paid to the WADA Anti-Doping Program.[11] WADA has generated a World Anti-Doping *corpus iuris* composed of three elements: the Word Anti-Doping Code (the Code), the International Standards (IS) and the Model of Best Practices.[12] According to the Preamble of the Code, the purposes of both the Code and the Program are to protect the athlete's fundamental right to participate in doping-free sport and thus promote health, fairness and equality for athletes worldwide, and to ensure harmonised, coordinated and effective anti-doping programmes at the international and national level with regard to detection, deterrence and prevention of doping.[13]

As previously mentioned, when pursuing those goals, private sports organisations have approved specific sporting rules whose compatibility with international human rights law is controversial; in an increasing number of states those rules have been incorporated into domestic law. Since international human rights law imposes on states the obligation of securing certain fundamental rights to everyone within their jurisdiction, it was only a matter of time before athletes sought the protection of

[9] The problematic coexistence of these two legal orders has drawn the attention of academia. See, for instance, Massimo S Giannini, 'Prime osservazioni sugli ordinamenti giuridici sportive' (1949) 28 *Rivista di Diritto Sportivo* 19–29; Alegría Borrás, 'Existe-t-il un droit international du sport' in *Nouveaux itinéraires en droit. Hommage à François Rigaux* (Bruylant, 1993); Mohammed Bedjaoui, 'Droit et sport: une harmonie nécessaire pour un couple singulier' Concluding Report of the International Colloquium "Droit et Sport" organised by the IOC (CAS, 1994); Frank Latty, *La lex sportive. Recherche sur le droit transnational* (Martinus Nijhoff, 2007).

[10] UNESCO International Convention against Doping in Sport (adopted 19 October 2005, entered into force 1 February 2007) preamble, available at portal.unesco.org/en/ev.php-URL_ID=31037&URL_DO=DO_TOPIC&URL_SECTION=201.html (UNESCO Anti-Doping Convention).

[11] A deep global analysis of WADA anti-doping rules can be found at: Paul David, *A Guide to the World Anti-Doping Code: The Fight for the Spirit of Sport*, 2nd edn (Cambridge University Press, 2013).

[12] All of these are available at www.wada-ama.org/en/World-Anti-Doping-Program/Sports-and-Anti-Doping-Organizations/The-Code/Code-Review/Code-Version-4-0. Although these instruments had been modified during the third World Conference on Doping in Sport, hosted in Johannesburg in November 2013, the new versions only came into force in January 2015. For his reason, I will refer here to the versions of the Code and the IS currently in force.

[13] See the Preamble of the Code, available at wada-main-prod.s3.amazonaws.com/resources/files/wada_anti-doping_code_2009_en_0.pdf.

international human rights monitoring bodies. In my view, this intervention could turn out to be decisive in order to fix the limits of the international legal battle against doping in sports.

## II. PUBLIC INTERNATIONAL LAW AND SPORTS: A COMPLEX RELATIONSHIP

It has been said that: '(T)he governance of global sport, including the Olympics, involves considerable administration by private bodies and by hybrid public-private bodies.'[14] At the international level, the latter have created, based on their self-regulatory power,[15] a private set of sports rules and principles that can be labeled as 'private international sports law'.[16] Important questions arise in this regard: is there also a public international sports law?[17] If so, what is the relationship between these two sets of rules? Should private international sports law respect any limit imposed by public international sports law? Is there room for international human rights law in this field?

Elsewhere I have defended the premise that (public) international sports law has a key role to play regarding the promotion of democracy, transparency and good governance in sports and respect for fundamental rights.[18] Additionally, sport can

[14] Alec Van Vaerenbergh, 'Regulatory Features and Administrative Law Dimensions of the Olympic Movement's Anti-Doping Regime', IILJ Working Paper 2005/11 (Global Administrative Law Series) available at papers.ssrn.com/sol3/papers.cfm?abstract_id=871736. www.iilj.org/oldbak/papers/IILJ2005.11Vaerenbergh.html 1.

[15] At the European Union level, this self-regulatory power was formally recognised in the Nice Declaration of December 2008 on the specific characteristics of sport and its social functions in Europe. In the Declaration the European Council 'stresses its support for the independence of sports organizations and their right to organize themselves through appropriate associative structures'. This independence is not unconditional. Sports organisations must respect 'national and Community legislation' and act 'on the basis of a democratic and transparent method of operation'. What I maintain here is that these sports organisations are bound also by public international law, the Nice Declaration is available at www.consilium.europa.eu/uedocs/cms_data/docs/pressdata/en/ec/00400-r1.%20ann.en0.htm. Concerning the special legal status of sports activity within the EU, see Richard Parrish and Samuli Miettinen, *The Sporting Exception in European Union Law* (TMC Asser Press, 2008). The specific nature of sport is mentioned in the EU Treaties following the incorporation of an EU competence on sport in Article 165 of the Consolidated Version of the Treaty on the Functioning of the EU [2012] OJ C326/49. On the incorporation of this competence on sport, see the interesting analysis by Borja García and Stephen Weatherill, 'Engaging with the EU in order to Minimize its Impact: Sports and the Negotiations of the Treaty of Lisbon' (2012) *Journal of European Public Policy* 19, 238.

[16] Rigaux considered in 1989 that there were multiple transnational sports law systems: '(I)l n'existe pas "un" ordre juridique sportif transnational, chaque sport particulier étant régi par un système autonome. Sans doute relève-t-on une grande convergence entre les règles et les pratiques observées par chacun de ces systèmes particuliers, mais ils sont tous indépendants les uns des autres', Rigaux (n 1) 285. In the same sense, see Jean-Pierre Karaquillo, 'Droit international du sport' (2004) 309 *Collected Courses of the Hague Academy of International Law* 1, 22.

[17] According to Foster, a distinction between 'international' and 'global' sports law could be made. He defines 'international sports law' as 'the principles of international law applicable to sport' and global sports law as 'a transnational autonomous legal order created by private global sport institutions that govern international sports': Foster (n 6) 1–2.

[18] Carmen Pérez, 'International Sports Law' in Tony Carty (ed), *Oxford Bibliographies in International Law* (Oxford University Press, 2014). Regarding the concept and content of International Sports Law, see also, James AR Nafziger, 'International Sports Law: A reply of characteristics and trends' (1992)

accomplish some of the traditional functions of international law: promoting development and peace or fostering gender equality through sport can be considered good examples in this regard.[19] International sports law can be defined as the set of principles, rules and processes that guarantee those goals.

The potential tensions between public and private international sports law are not hypothetical. Certain recent developments in the fight against doping in sport have been challenged as not being compliant with human rights standards. In this sense anti-doping procedural rules regarding privacy rights and confidentiality are good examples. Also, some problems arise from the application of the strict liability principle in this framework and the compulsory jurisdiction of the CAS. Along with the interesting academic debate that is taking place,[20] the opportunity and eventual consequences of a possible intervention of the European Court of Human Rights (ECtHR) should be examined here.

## III. RECENT INTERNATIONAL DEVELOPMENTS IN THE FIGHT AGAINST DOPING IN SPORT

### A. General Approach

States, international organisations, sports governing bodies and athletes agree that doping is both unhealthy and contrary to fair play. It can be confirmed that there is an international consensus on the idea that doping in sports should be forbidden or, at least, limited. In general, this consensus is based on two different lines of reasoning.

On the one hand, the prohibition is linked to the protection of certain athletes' human rights, in particular, the right to health and the right to physical education.

86 *The American Journal of International Law* 489; Andreas Wax, 'Public International Sports Law: A "Forgotten Discipline"?' in RCR Siekmann and J Soek (eds), *Lex Sportiva: What is Sports Law?* (TMC Asser Press, 2012).

[19] Concerning the role of the Convention on the Elimination of all Forms of Discrimination against Women and its monitoring Committee in this regard, see Karen L Jones, 'Women's national leagues: does CEDAW go far enough?' (2013) 13 *International Sports Law Journal* 35–44.

[20] See, among others: Jan-Willen Soek, 'The Fundamental Rights of Athletes in Doping Trials' in John O'Leary (ed), *Drugs and Doping in Sport: Socio-Legal Perspectives* (Cavendish, 2001); Barrie Houlihan, 'Civil Rights, Doping Control and the World Anti-doping Code' (2004) 7 *Sport in Society* 420; Ryan Conolly, 'Balancing the Justices in Anti-Doping Law: The Need to Ensure Fair Athletic Competition Through Effective Anti-Doping Programs v the Protection of Rights of Accused Athletes' (2006) 5 *Virginia Sports and Entertainment Law Journal* 41; Robyn R Goldstein, 'An American in Paris: The Legal Framework of International Sport and the Implications of the World Anti-Doping Code on Accused Athletes' (2007) 7 *Virginia Sports and Entertainment Law Journal* 149; Dag Vidar Hanstad and Sigmund Loland, 'Elite athletes' duty to provide information on their whereabouts: Justifiable anti-doping work or an indefensible surveillance regime?' (2009) 9 *European Journal of Sport Science* 3; James Halt, 'Where is the Privacy in WADAS's "Whereabouts" Rule'? (2009) 20 *Marquette Sports Law Review* 267; Oskar Macgregor et al, 'Anti-doping, purported rights to privacy and WADA's whereabouts requirements: A legal analysis' (2013) 1(2) *Fair Play. Revista de Filosofía, Ética y Derecho del Deporte*, available at www.upf.edu/revistafairplay/anteriores/; Jan Lukomski, 'Arbitration clauses in sport governing bodies' statutes: consent or constraint? Analysis from the perspective of Article 6(1) of the European Convention on Human Rights' (2013) 13 *International Sports Law Journal* 60.

It is assumed, on the one hand, that both the use of a prohibited doping substance or a prohibited doping method could threaten an athlete's health. For the same reason and to the extent that doping in sport could be considered a matter of public health, the intervention of public authorities would be required. On the other hand, the prohibition constitutes a way to protect a 'collective interest': by providing an unfair or even an immoral advantage, doping in sports contravenes 'fair play' and contributes to weakening spectators' confidence in the honesty and integrity of sports competitions.

What I want to stress here is that this prohibition is contained not only in private sporting rules, but also in public international law instruments. The European Anti-Doping Convention was the first international treaty to impose such an obligation on States Parties.[21] According to the Explanatory Report of the Convention:

> Doping is contrary to the values of sport and the principles for which it stands: fair play, equal chances, loyal competition, healthy activity. Doping endangers the health of athletes, as they are using substances in ways that they were not designed for; sport is meant to be a life-enhancing activity not one that imperils life. In Resolution (76) 41 on the principles for a policy for sport for all—the European Sport for All Charter of 1975—the practice of doping was described as "abusive and debasing".[22]

Several years later, the UNESCO Anti-Doping Convention extended this obligation to the universal level.[23] The Preamble of the Convention expresses the concern of the UNESCO General Conference 'by the use of doping by athletes in sport and the consequences thereof for their health, the principle of fair play, the elimination of cheating and the future of sport'. The Preamble also declares that:

> [P]ublic authorities and the organizations responsible for sport have complementary responsibilities to prevent and combat doping in sport, notably to ensure the proper conduct, on the basis of the principle of fair play, of sports events and to protect the health of those that take part in them.

Article 19.1 imposes on States Parties the obligation of supporting, devising or implementing education and training programmes on anti-doping. These programmes should aim to provide updated and accurate information on both the harm of doping to the ethical values of sport, and the health consequences of doping.

As it has been noted: '(T)he rapid pace at which governments have adhered to this international instrument is without precedent.'[24] This is the most successful

[21] Adopted 16 November 1989, entered into force 1 March 1990, CETS No 135. According to Article 1: 'The Parties, with a view to the reduction and eventual elimination of doping in sport, undertake, within the limits of their respective constitutional provisions, to take the steps necessary to apply the provisions of this Convention.' Currently, 52 States are parties in the European Anti-Doping Convention, which is open to non-members of the Council of Europe. An Additional Protocol to this European Convention was adopted with the purpose of ensuring the mutual recognition of doping controls and to reinforcing the application of the Anti-Doping Convention (adopted 12 September 2002, entered into force 1 April 2004, CETS No 188).

[22] The Explanatory Report is available at www.conventions.coe.int/Treaty/Commun/QueVoulezVous.asp?NT=135&CM=8&DF=25/11/2014&CL=ENG.

[23] 180 States are parties to the UNESCO Anti-Doping Convention (n 10).

[24] Paul Marriot-Lloyd, 'Understanding the International Convention against Doping in Sports', available at unesdoc.unesco.org/images/0018/001884/188405e.pdf.

convention in the history of UNESCO in terms of speed of development and entry into force. In 2003, the United Nations General Assembly (UNGA) had adopted a resolution which considered that doping is one of the dangers faced by sportsmen and sportswomen, in particular young athletes, and invited governments to accelerate the elaboration of an international anti-doping convention in all sports activities.[25] It requested UNESCO, in cooperation with other relevant international and regional organisations, to coordinate the elaboration of such a convention. Only two years later, the UNESCO Anti-Doping Convention became a reality.

Besides these two international treaties, an important number of soft law instruments, such as Recommendations of the Committee of Ministers of the Council of Europe[26] and Communications from the European Commission,[27] have been adopted.[28]

Effective international cooperation among stakeholders appears indispensable to ensure maximum effectiveness in the fight against doping in sport. Any international cooperation framework created for this purpose has to take into account the diverse legal nature, both private and public, of its stakeholders.

## B. The World Anti-Doping Program: Some Critical Aspects

### *i. The Creation of WADA*

Harmonisation, coordination and effectiveness are key elements of the international anti-doping system. Due to the increasing number of doping scandals, the IOC convened a World Conference in Sport, held in Lausanne in February 1999. The Declaration on Doping in Sport, approved in the framework of the Conference, proposed the creation of an independent international anti-doping agency.[29] Following this indication, WADA was created in November 1999 to coordinate the fight against doping in sport at the international level.

[25] UNGA Res 58/5 (17 November 2003) UN Doc A/RES/53/5.

[26] See, for instance, the Recommendation No R (84) 19 on the 'European Anti-doping Charter for Sport', available at www.coe.int/t/cm/adoptedTexts_en.asp.

[27] See, for instance, the 'Communication from the Commission to the Council, the European parliament, the Economic and Social Committee and the Committee of the regions. Community support plan to combat doping in sport', COM (1999) 643 final, available at eur-lex.europa.eu/legal-content/EN/TXT/HTML/?uri=CELEX:51999DC0643&from=ES.

[28] Outside the European framework, the establishment of the Ibero-American Council on Sports in 1994 should be mentioned (Montevideo Treaty establishing the Ibero-American Council on Sports, adopted 4 August 1994, available at www.coniberodeporte.org/en/treaty. Among the aims of this International Organisation are the promotion of ethics and fair play in sports (Article 3(g)).

[29] The text of the Declaration is available at wcd.coe.int/ViewDoc.jsp?id=402791. According to paragraph 4 of the Declaration:

> An independent International Anti-doping Agency shall be established so as to be fully operational for the Games of the XXVII Olympiad in Sydney 2000. This institution will have as its mandate, notably, to coordinate the various programmes necessary to realize the objectives that shall be defined jointly by all the parties concerned. Among these programmes, consideration should be given in particular to expanding out-of-competition testing, coordinating research, promoting preventive and educational actions and harmonizing scientific and technical standards and procedures for analyses and equipment ....

From the legal point of view, WADA is a private foundation governed by its Constitutive Instrument, and by Articles 80 *et seq.* of the Swiss Civil Code.[30] From an organisational perspective, WADA constitutes a *sui generis* model, which has been considered 'emblematic of the emergence of the new forms of hybrid public-private governance mechanism in the global sphere'.[31] It is interesting to highlight that WADA's main governance organs include representatives from both the Olympic movement and governments.[32]

### *ii. WADA Anti-Doping Rules Regarding 'Whereabouts Requirements'*

As noted above, a universal normative framework has been approved under the auspices of WADA. The Code is considered to be the core document of WADA's anti-doping programme. Its main purpose is to harmonise anti-doping policies, rules and regulations within sport organisations and among public authorities around the world. Besides that, five IS (the List of Prohibited Substances and Methods, the IS for Testing, the IS for Laboratories, the IS for Therapeutic Use Exemption, and the IS for the Protection of Privacy and Personal Information) have been adopted with the purpose of harmonising and/or clarifying diverse aspects in the framework of the fight against doping.

The compatibility of some of these rules with international human rights standards is controversial. This is the case for WADA's 'whereabouts requirements'.[33] Article 2.4 of the Code considers an anti-doping rule violation to be the 'violation of applicable requirements regarding Athlete availability for Out-of-Competition Testing, including failure to file required "whereabouts information" and missed tests which are declared based on rules which comply with the International Standard for Testing'. It adds that 'any combination of three missed tests and/or filing failures within an eighteen-month period as determined by Anti-Doping Organizations with jurisdiction over the Athlete shall constitute an anti-doping rule violation'.[34] Article 10 of the Code regulates the sanctions for individual violations. According to subparagraph 3.3, for violations of Article 2.4 the period of ineligibility shall be a minimum one year, and a maximum two years, based on the athlete's degree of fault.

[30] WADA revised Statutes are available at wada-main-prod.s3.amazonaws.com/resources/files/WADA-Revised-Statutes-4-July-2014-EN.pdf.

[31] Casini (n 2) 424.

[32] WADA governance estructure is available at www.wada-ama.org/en/who-we-are/governance.

[33] 'Whereabouts are information provided by a limited number of top elite athletes about their location to the International Sport Federation (IF) or National Anti-Doping Organization (NADO) that included them in their respective registered testing pool as part of these top elite athletes' anti-doping responsibilities.' This definition is available at www.wada-ama.org/en/questions-answers/whereabouts#item-804.

[34] In the 2015 Code 'The window in which an Athlete may accumulate three whereabouts filings (Filing Failures Or Missed Tests) which trigger an anti-doping rule violation has been reduced from 18 months to 12 months': See the document about 'Significant changes between the 2009 Code and the 2015 Code' available at www.wada-ama.org/en/resources/the-code/significant-changes-between-the-2009-code-and-the-2015-code. According to this document the consensus behind this change was that 'twelve months is ample time for an Anti-Doping Organization to accumulate three whereabouts failures on an Athlete who is trying to avoid Testing and that shortening the window reduces the risk that Athletes who are simply careless in handling their paperwork will be found to have committed anti-doping rule violations'.

Specific whereabouts filing requirements are contained in Clause 11.3 of the IS for Testing.[35] This Clause sets out what whereabouts information must be provided by an athlete included in a Registered Testing Pool,[36] and when the information is required.[37] Where daily information is required, it must be provided for each day of the following quarter, even if the athlete is travelling, or competing, or on holiday, on any such day.

Besides this, Clause 11.4 of the IS for Testing regulates an athlete's obligations regarding availability for testing. Along with the information about residence and regular activities that must be regularly provided by athletes, they must also provide, for each day during the following quarter, one specific 60-minute time-slot between 6 am and 11 pm where he/she will be available for testing at a specific location.[38]

As established in the 'Guidelines for Implementing an Effective Athlete Whereabouts Program'[39] the basic principle in this regard is that it is the responsibility of the athlete to make him/herself available for testing. Thus, 'if the Athlete specifies a location for the 60-minute time-slot where it is not easy to find him/her, and/or he/she does not remain at that location for the full 60-minute time-slot, he/she risks a missed test'.[40]

## C. Do the Code and the International Standards Impose Obligations on States?

It goes without saying that private international and national bodies governing sports activity (that is, IFs, the Olympic and Paralympic Committees, Major Events Organizations and National Anti-Doping Organizations) are bound by the rules described above and that their decisions have a direct effect on individuals. Although it should be borne in mind that the participation of athletes in professional sport is voluntary, once he/she has decided to participate then he/she is forced to subscribe to the rules of the game. Breaches of these rules are punished with the athlete's exclusion from competitions.[41]

[35] I refer here to the version in force from January 2012. A revised version of IS for testing has come into force from January 2015. This new version is available at www.wada-ama.org/en/resources/world-anti-doping-program/2015-international-standard-for-testing-and-investigations-isti.

[36] Among the information required is the full address of the place where the Athlete will be residing (home, temporary lodgings, hotel, etc) and the name and address or each location where the Athlete will train, work or conduct any other regular activity, as well as the usual time frames for such regular activities.

[37] This information shall be provided on a date specified by the Responsible Anti-doping Organization (ADO), which will be prior to the first day of each quarter (ie 1 January, 1 April, 1 July and 1 October respectively) and for each day during the following quarter.

[38] Of course, circumstances can change so that the athlete may no longer be at that location at that particular time. In that case, he/she should update his/her 'Whereabouts Filing' to correctly identify a new time-slot and/or a new location.

[39] Available at www.wada-ama.org/en/resources/world-anti-doping-program/guidelines-implementing-an-effective-testing-program.

[40] Ibid, paragraph 3.3.

[41] 'Quant à la force de coercition des ordres juridiques sportifs, elle prend la forme de l'exclusion (analogue à l'excommunication du droit canonique), laquelle est souvent plus efficace que les actes matériels de contrainte physique appliqués par l'Etat sur son territoire, mais dont la force s'éteint au-delà de ses frontières', Rigaux (n 1) 66.

But the question I want to address here is the following: do states (or their public authorities) have the obligation to fulfill the requirements contained in the WADA Code and the IS? To answer this question, we have to take into account how both the UNESCO Anti-Doping Convention and the WADA Code conceive their mutual relationship.

On the one hand, we find a preliminary answer to this question in Article 4 of the UNESCO Anti-Doping Convention, regulating the relationship of the Convention to the Code. According to paragraph 1 of this Article:

> (I)n order to coordinate the implementation, at the national and international levels, of the fight against doping in sport, States Parties commit themselves to the principles of the Code as the basis for the measures provided for in Article 5 of this Convention.[42] Nothing in this Convention prevents States Parties from adopting additional measures complementary to the Code.

And according to paragraph 3 of Article 4, only Annex I (the prohibited list) and Annex II (IS for Granting Therapeutic Use Exemptions) to the Convention are an integral part of the Code. Article 4.2 establishes that most the current versions of Appendices 2 (IS for Laboratories) and 3 (IS for testing) are reproduced only for information purposes and are not an integral part of the UNESCO Convention. These two Appendices as such do not create any binding obligations under international law for States Parties.

On the other hand, Article 22 of the Code regulates the 'involvement of governments' in the implementation of the Anti-Doping Program. It establishes that 'each government's commitment to the Code will be evidenced by its signing the Copenhagen Declaration on Anti-Doping in Sport of March 3, 2003,[43] and by ratifying, accepting, approving or acceding to the UNESCO Convention'.[44]

The different paragraphs of Article 22 set forth the 'expectations' of the signatories. Among them: 'each government will take all actions and measures necessary to comply with the UNESCO Convention' (Article 22.1); 'each government will encourage all of its public services or agencies to share information with

[42] Which establishes that: 'In abiding by the obligations contained in this Convention, each State Party undertakes to adopt appropriate measures. Such measures may include legislation, regulation, policies or administrative practices.'

[43] Available at www.wada-ama.org/en/resources/world-anti-doping-program/copenhagen-declaration.

[44] As explained in the comment to Article 22:

> Most governments cannot be parties to, or be bound by, private non-governmental instruments such as the Code. For that reason, governments are not asked to be Signatories to the Code but rather to sign the Copenhagen Declaration and ratify, accept, approve or accede to the UNESCO Convention. Although the acceptance mechanisms may be different, the effort to combat doping through the coordinated and harmonized program reflected in the Code is very much a joint effort between the sport movement and governments.

The 2015 Code adds that Article 22 sets forth 'simply "expectations" since governments are only "obligated" to adhere to the requirements of the UNESCO Convention'.

Anti-Doping Organizations which would be useful in the fight against doping and where to do so would not otherwise be legally prohibited' (Article 22.2.); 'each government will respect arbitration as the preferred means of resolving doping-related disputes' (Article 22.3);[45] and 'all other governmental involvement with anti-doping will be brought into harmony with the Code' (Article 22.4).[46]

What are the consequences for the 'infringement' of these 'expectations'? Article 22.8 of the Code only refers to the consequences of a failure by a government to ratify, accept, approve or accede to the UNESCO Anti-Doping Convention or to comply with it. Such a failure may result in the ineligibility[47] to bid for events as provided in Articles 20.1.8,[48] 20.3.10[49] and 20.6.6.[50] Besides this, a government's failure to ratify, accept, approve or accede to the UNESCO Convention by 1 January 2010, or to comply with the UNESCO Convention thereafter may result in 'additional consequences', such as 'forfeiture of offices and positions within WADA; ineligibility or non-admission of any candidature to hold any International Event in a country; cancellation of International Events; symbolic consequences and other consequences pursuant to the Olympic Charter'.[51]

Although we can conclude from Articles 4 and 5 of the UNESCO Anti-Doping Convention and Articles 20.1.8, 20.3.10, 20.6.6 and 22 of the WADA Code that States Parties are only bound by the principles of the Code when adopting appropriate legislative, administrative, regulatory or policy measures for fulfilling the obligations contained in the Convention, and only NOCs and National Paralympic Committees, IFs and National Anti-Doping Organizations have to comply with the Code, a considerable number of states have incorporated these rules into domestic legislation. Eventual exclusion of their national teams or clubs from major sports events serves as a powerful incentive to do so. The problem is that, at some point, this legislation can be considered in breach of international human rights obligations assumed by those states. And it can be argued that, as a consequence of this assumption, they have the obligation to protect athletes within their own jurisdictions against breaches of fundamental rights committed through implementation of the WADA Anti-Doping Program.

[45] The 2015 version of the Code adds that arbitration will be subject to human and fundamental rights and applicable national law.

[46] This article has disappeared in the 2015 version of the Code.

[47] See n 41.

[48] This article includes among the roles and responsibilities of the International Olympic Committee '(t)o accept bids for the Olympic Games only from countries where the government has ratified, accepted, approved or acceded to the UNESCO Convention and the National Olympic Committee, National Paralympic Committee and National Anti-Doping Organization are in compliance with the Code'.

[49] According to this article, IFs should 'do everything possible to award World Championships only to countries where the government has ratified, accepted, approved or acceded to the UNESCO Convention and the National Olympic Committee, National Paralympic Committee and National Anti-Doping Organization are in compliance with the Code'.

[50] The Major Event Organizations shall 'do everything possible to award Events only to countries where the government has ratified, accepted, approved or acceded to the UNESCO Convention and the National Olympic Committee, National Paralympic Committee and National Anti-Doping Organization are in compliance with the Code'.

[51] See Article 22.6 of the Code.

## IV. DOES INTERNATIONAL HUMAN RIGHTS LAW IMPOSE LIMITS ON THE FIGHT AGAINST DOPING IN SPORTS?

Sanctions that disciplinary sporting bodies (including the CAS) may have decided upon, in accordance with WADA rules, may have a direct effect on an athlete's professional life. According to the Code, those sanctions should be adopted with full respect for procedural guarantees.[52] In my opinion, this does not exclude public intervention in this framework. Taking into account a state's obligation to guarantee fundamental rights to everyone within its jurisdiction, national legal systems should enable recourse to the courts, at least when one considers that the private system for sports does not give athletes sufficient protection.[53] It has been said, in this regard, that

> most national courts ... would not let the private nature of the actors stand in the way of an assessment of the rules and proceedings in the light of principles of administrative law (preliminary hearing, motivation on decisions, transparency and legal security ... and fundamental human rights (independence of tribunal, presumption of innocence...)[54]

In my opinion, review by the judiciary becomes essential in this field. And taking into account the fact that the anti-doping rules stemming from WADA have an international scope, the intervention of an international human rights body could clarify the extent to which international human rights obligations apply in the realm of sports activity.

In a different sense, the European Court of Justice (ECJ) has declared inapplicable certain sporting rules found contrary to EU law. The ECJ has repeatedly ruled that EU law applies to sports activity as far as it can be considered an economic activity. This means that sports activity falls within the scope of EU law only if, and precisely because, it takes place within the sphere of the economic and individual activities and freedoms with which that law is concerned. Exceptions would be justified only for legitimate aims compatible with EU law, for example, in the protection of public health or the promotion of educational values. In this sense, the ECJ has held that sporting rules are not subject to EU law only when they concern issues of purely

[52] See Article 8 of the Code (right to a fair hearing).

[53] According to Article 33 of the Spanish Basic Law 7/2006, 21 November, on health protection and against doping in sports, sanctions adopted by IF's disciplinary bodies were fully applicable in Spain and produced the effect of suspending the rights derived from sport license within Spanish territory. Article 22.2 of the same Basic Law incorporated a mechanism that allowed athletes challenging the compatibility of disciplinary measures, adopted by IFs or by the CAS, with fundamental principles of Spanish administrative law before the Spanish Committee on Sports Discipline. A decision of the latter could be challenged before ordinary administrative courts. Several IFs' decisions were declared incompatible and consequently inapplicable in Spain, according to the mechanism contained in Article 22.2 until the abrogation of Basic Law 7/2006. The new regulation, the Basic Law 3/2013, 20 June, on the protection of athletes' health and on the fight against doping in sport, does not contain this compatibility mechanism.

[54] Van Vaerenbergh (n 14) 17.

sporting interest. This is the case, for instance, of nationality-based criteria for the composition of national teams.[55]

The intervention of an international human rights body is not unconceivable, since whereabouts obligation rules, described above,[56] have been challenged before the ECtHR. In four cases that have been communicated to the parties, and must be still declared 'admissible', applicants have questioned the compatibility of national legislative measures, which have been adopted for incorporating into domestic legal order the rules contained in the WADA Code and related IS, with the European Convention for the Protection of Human Rights and Fundamental Freedoms (ECHR).[57]

In 2010 and 2012, France adopted domestic legislation aimed at protecting athletes' health and adapting the French Sporting Code to the WADA Anti-Doping Program.[58] Applicants in the first[59] and second[60] cases questioned the compatibility of the whereabouts requirements included in the French legislation with Article 8.1 of the ECHR (right to respect for private and family life) and Article 2 of Protocol 4 (freedom of movement).[61] In the other two cases, the applicants (a German national[62] and a Romanian national)[63] considered that arbitration

[55] For an analysis of the ECJ's decisions on the applicability of the right of free movement to third-country nationals in the context of professional sports activity and their impact in sports governance in Europe, see David W Penn, 'From Bosman to Simutenkov: The Application of Non-Discrimination Principles to Non-EU Nationals in European Sports' (2006) 30 *Suffolk Transnational Law Review* 203.

Regarding anti-doping rules, two cases before the ECJ are interesting. The first one is Case C-519/04 P *David Meca-Medina, Igor Majcen v Commission of the European Communities, Republic of Finland* [2006] OJ C. The Court set aside the judgment of the Court of First Instance of the European Communities of 30 September 2004 in Case T-313/02 *Meca-Medina and Majcen v Commission* and dismissed the action under No T-313/02 brought before the Court of First Instance for annulment of the Commission's decision of 1 August 2002 rejecting the complaint lodged by Mr Meca-Medina and Mr Majcen. The second one is Case C-269/12 P Guillermo *Cañas v European Commission World Anti-doping Agency, ATP Tour, Inc* [2013] OJ C. In this case, the ECJ decided on the appeal brought against the order of the General Court (Third Chamber) of 26 March 2012 in Case T-508/09 *Cañas v Commission*, by which the General Court dismissed the application for annulment of Commission Decision C(2009)7809 of 12 October 2009 in Case COMP/39471, rejecting for lack of Community interest a complaint concerning an infringement of Articles 81 EC and 82 EC allegedly committed by the WADA, the ATP Tour Inc and by the ICAS. Considering that the interest in bringing proceedings came to an end during the proceeding, the ECJ dismissed the appeal. Although both cases were dismissed by the Court, they prove that athletes are ready to search for protection outside the sporting arena.

[56] See Section III.B.ii.

[57] Adopted 4 November 1950, entered into force 3 September 1953, CETS No 005.

[58] Through the 'Ordonnance no 2010-379 relative à la santé des sportifs et à la mise en conformité du code du sport avec les principes du code mondial antidopage.' Also the Spanish Parliament has incorporated the same requirements into the Spanish legal order. A future decision of the ECtHR would then have effects in other States Parties to the European Convention on Human Rights.

[59] *National Federation of Sporting Syndicates (FNASS) and others v France* Application no 48151/11 (the case was communicated to the parties in June 2013).

[60] *Longo and Ciprelli v France* Application no 77769/13 (the case was communicated to the parties in June 2014).

[61] Adopted 16 September 1963, entered into force 2 May 1968, CETS No 046.

[62] *Pechstein v Switzerland* Application no 67474/10 (the case was communicated to the parties in February 2013).

[63] *Mutu v Switzerland* Application no 40575/10 (the case was communicated to the parties in February 2013).

proceeding before the CAS were in breach of Article 6 of the European Convention on Human Rights (right to a fair trial).

## V. CONCLUSION

An international consensus on the need to fight doping seems unquestionable.[64] This consensus can be extended to the traditional self-regulatory power maintained by sports governing bodies. To some extent, the relationship between public authorities and sports governing bodies has been ruled by a *non-intervention* principle. And public intervention in sports has been perceived by sports governing bodies as a violation of this principle.

While leaving open whether this self-regulatory power is strictly necessary, it has been affirmed in this contribution that specificity should not derogate from the application of fundamental principles of public law and good governance, including respect for fundamental rights. In particular, an eventual intervention of the ECtHR is considered desirable.

[64] Relevant arguments have been used in favour of doping in sports. One of the more well-known supporters of the legalisation of doping in sport is Professor Julian Savulescu from the Oxford University Uehiro Centre for Practical Ethics. A list of his publications and media appearances is available at www.practicalethics.ox.ac.uk/staff/staff/director/julian_savulescu. See also Jose Luis Pérez Triviño, *The Challenges of Modern Sport to Ethics. From Doping to Cyborgs* (Lexington, 2013).

# PART VIII

# INTERNATIONAL LAW AND THE ARTS AND HUMANITIES

# 22

# *Engaging International Law and Literature with Kafka, Deleuze and Guattari*

EKATERINA YAHYAOUI KRIVENKO*

## I. INTRODUCTION

THE FOLLOWING CONTRIBUTION will address the relationship between international law and literature using the work of Kafka[1] and its analysis by Deleuze and Guattari.[2] In doing so the contribution will also discuss the interplay of methodological approaches in both areas and will argue that international law informed by literary theory can uncover new potentials for a radical rethinking of many traditional notions of public international law.

The central notion from the point of view of literary studies will be the notion of minor literature.[3] As far as public international law is concerned, in order to have a more precise frame for discussion, I will concentrate on the constitutionalisation of international law.

The presentation will address three related points, namely the relationship between genres; the notions of law and justice; and the understanding of the political or possible lines of escape/revolutionary potential.

Firstly, the analysis of Deleuze and Guattari clearly demonstrates the artificiality of the theory of genres in literary studies.[4] Drawing a parallel between genres in

* Lecturer, Irish Centre for Human Rights, NUI Galway. Some ideas presented in this article are further developed in 'International Law, Literature and Interdisciplinarity' (2015) 9 *Law and Humanities* 103.

[1] Kafka's *The Castle* and *Before the Law* will be two main reference points. Franz Kafka, *The Castle* (trans. Anthea Bell, Oxford University Press, 2009), Frank Kafka, "Before the Law," in Nahum N Glatzer (ed), *Franz Kafka: The Complete Stories and Parables* 3-4 (New York: Quality Paperback Book Club, 1971)(Willa & Edwin Muir trans) However, other works by Kafka will also be used to the extent to which they provide better examples and illustrations.

[2] Gilles Deleuze and Félixe Guattari, *Kafka: pour une litérature mineure* (Les éditions de minuit, 1975) translated into English as *Kafka: Towards a Minor Literature* (University of Minnesota Press, 1986). All further references are to the English translation unless otherwise indicated.

[3] This notion is defined by Deleuze and Guattari through three characteristics: 'the deterritorialisation of language, the connection of the individual to a political immediacy, and the collective assemblage of enunciation'. Deleuze and Guattari, ibid 18.

[4] This has also been highlighted by others, eg Jacques Derrida and Avital Ronell, 'The Law of Genre' (1980) 7 *Critical Inquiry: On Narrative* 55.

literature and the division between different types of writings in public international law: jurisprudence, doctrine and official documents, I will investigate to what extent this division is justified and implemented in public international law, and what purposes it serves. What happens if we regard different types of writings in international law not as separate categories but as a single *oeuvre* as Deleuze and Guattari did when interpreting Kafka's letters, stories and novels?

Once this discussion has been concluded, I will take a renewed look at the expression of the constitutionalisation of international law, in different types of international writings. While doctrine comes first as the most obvious source, I will also draw on the case law of the International Court of Justice (ICJ). I will move between these different types of writings, imitating the movements of Deleuze and Guattari between the novels, stories and letters of Kafka.

Simultaneously with this analysis, these movements will be informed by Kafka's visions of law and justice as they emerge from Deleuze and Guattari's reading of his work. Will these new movements produce different visions and readings of international constitutionalism? Will they challenge the traditional approach to such a doctrinal issue as the constitutionalisation of international law? It will be left to other interpreters and readers to decide. However, the exercise will demonstrate the potential (or perhaps its absence) of applying methodologies of literary theory in the field of international law as a move towards a critical rethinking of international law.

Finally, based on this analysis, I will also develop some thoughts on the political and revolutionary nature of Kafka's work, and on the inherently political character of any minor literature[5] compared to the different politics of international law and international lawyers. Is international law revolutionary in this sense, and if so, how is it revolutionary and political? Can it be revolutionary at all? What would be the fate of a project centred on a radical rethinking of international law? We will thus return to the question of the relationship between international law and literature. The previous discussion will allow us to critically re-assess the interplay between them and their respective potentialities.

## II. MINOR LITERATURE AND GENRES

### A. What is a Minor Literature?

The notion of minor literature[6] is developed by Deleuze and Guattari as 'a means by which to enter into Kafka's work without being weighed down by the old categories of genres, types, modes, and style'.[7]

[5] See Deleuze and Guattari (n 2) 17, 26: 'There is nothing that is major or revolutionary except the minor.'

[6] The notion of minor literature originates in the works of Kafka himself. However, for the sake of brevity I will refer to this notion, almost exclusively as developed by Deleuze and Guattari, without discussing whether their interpretation is faithful to Kafka's ideas. For an example of such a discussion, see Lowell Edmunds, 'Kafka on Minor Literature' (2010) 33 *German Studies Review* 351; Stanley Corngold, 'Kafka and the Dialect of Minor Literature' (1994) 21 *College Literature* 89.

[7] Réda Bensmaïa, Foreword to Deleuze and Guattari (n 2) i, xiv.

Deleuze and Guattari's approach is based on a few fundamental principles that need to be emphasised from the outset. Firstly, they defy the search for a structure with formal binary oppositions.[8] Instead, they use their terminology of machinery, machines and assemblages to emphasise the interconnectedness of everything and the equal importance of every single element, movement and gesture. This also implies a lack of distinction between the inside and outside and an emphasis on process rather than on form.[9] Thus, they defy the search for some hidden and fundamental meaning, focusing instead on understanding functioning and the way a particular theme or image works within the author's *oeuvre*. In this sense, traditional literary interpretation has become useless.

The notion of minor literature appears in Deleuze and Guattari's discussion of Kafka's *oeuvre* in relation to expression. Expression needs, according to Deleuze and Guattari, to be considered by itself.[10] The importance of expression is related to Deleuze and Guattari's focus on functioning, processes and procedures. As they state: 'Seule l'expression nous donne le *procédé*.'[11] The problem of expression in Kafka is addressed, according to Deleuze and Guattari, not in the abstract but in relation to minor literature. Minor literature is defined as 'that which a minority constructs within a major language'.[12] According to Deleuze and Guattari, the following are the characteristics of minor literature: 'the language is affected by high coefficient of deterritorialisation'; 'everything in them is political'; and 'in it everything takes on a collective value'.[13]

Deterritorialisation is a term developed by Deleuze and Guattari in more detail elsewhere in their works published before and after their volume on Kafka.[14] In the present context it refers to a particular relationship between the author and the language he or she uses to write. At a very basic level it refers to writers writing in a language that is not their own: 'How many people today live in a language that is not their own? Or no longer, or not yet, even know their own and know poorly the major language that they are forced to serve?'[15] However, at a deeper level it concerns everyone and poses the question about the possibilities of a revolutionary use of any language: How to become a nomad in relation to one's own language?[16] How 'to be a sort of stranger within his own language'.[17] This particular use of language is distinct from any conventional use because it operates a disjuncture

[8] Deleuze and Guattari (n 2) 7.

[9] Ibid 7–8.

[10] The idea is clear in the original French version: 'Mais tant que l'expression, sa forme et sa déformation ne sont pas considérées pour elles-mêmes, on ne peut pas trouver de véritable issue, même au niveau des contenus.' Deleuze et Guattari, ibid 29.

[11] Ibid (emphasis in the original).

[12] Ibid 16.

[13] Ibid 16–17.

[14] See in particular, Gilles Deleuze and Félix Guattari, *Anti-Oedipus: Capitalism and Schizophrenia* (trans Robert Hurley et al, University of Minnesota Press, 1983) French original published in 1972, Gilles Deleuze and Félix Guattari, *A Thousand Plateaus: Capitalism and Schizophrenia* (trans Brian Massumi, University of Minnesota Press, 1987) French original published in 1980.

[15] Deleuze and Guattari (n 2) 19.

[16] Ibid.

[17] Ibid 26.

between content and expression. It 'oppose(s) a purely intensive usage of language to all symbolic or even significant or simply signifying usages of it'.[18]

For our purposes, it is important to realise that since any language fulfils a variety of functions, it creates 'multiple centers of power'[19] even though we might not want to admit or recognise this. Even the 'purely' linguistic approach to language is not a-political. Once we agree on this, it is easy to understand why Deleuze and Guattari argue that everything in minor literature is political. It's not only that each individual concern becomes immediately political[20] but also that minor literature's very use of the language challenges all traditional centres of power, conventions and the will to power and power itself: 'to oppose the oppressed quality of this language to its oppressive quality, to find points of nonculture or underdevelopment, linguistic Third World zones by which a language can escape'.[21] This gesture or dream of 'becoming minor' instead of so many attempts made by different styles, genres and literary movements 'to assume a major function in language, to offer themselves as a sort of state language, an official language'.[22] Deleuze and Guattari define this gesture, this movement of what they define as minor literature, as revolutionary. It is certainly revolutionary, it subverts the very foundations on which our conventional wisdom rests, it reminds us of Melville's Bartleby, of Benjamin's and Agamben's play with law[23] that in their attempt to situate themselves outside of power, to be a-political, they call for a radically new politics.

Since politics and power are so closely tied up with law, the notion of minor literature and the dream of becoming minor challenges, may destroy our vision of law, if not the very foundation of what it means to have a legal system. This, in turn, leads us to ask the question about the revolutionary potential of law. Can law be truly revolutionary? Or do we need to abandon law to become revolutionary? I will return to these questions. First, we need to consider precisely how Deleuze and Guattari depict and analyse the functioning of Kafka's *oeuvre* as a minor literature. What mechanisms do they believe allow Kafka to produce the minor or to become the minor?

## B. How it Works: Assemblages, Components, Blocs, Series and Connectors

To approach and understand the mechanisms that allow Kafka to operate as an author of minor literature, Deleuze and Guattari look at everything written by Kafka as a single *oeuvre*. Their first step is to extract the components of expression (or literary machine)[24] from Kafka's *oeuvre*. These components are letters, stories

[18] Ibid 19.
[19] Ibid 24.
[20] Ibid 17.
[21] Ibid 27.
[22] Ibid.
[23] Giogio Agamben, *State of Exception*, (trans Kevin Attell, The University of Chicago Press, Chicago and London, 2005), 64 and Walter Benjamin, Notizen zu einer Arbeit über die Kategorie der Gerechtigkeit, *Frankfurter Adorno Blätter* 4 (1992), 41.
[24] Deleuze and Guattari (n 2) 29.

and novels. In analysing each of these components the guiding idea is always to attempt to understand how each of the components functions and how they communicate with each other. Thus, they observe that letters were meant to disappear but constitute a 'motor part of the literary machine and put everything else in motion'.[25] As they explain: '[T]he letters are perhaps the motor force that, by the blood they collect, start the whole machine working. Nonetheless, for Kafka, it is a question of writing something other than letters—a question, then, of *creating*.'[26] Therefore the stories go further and constitute a particular mechanism that allows an absolute deterritorialisation of the individual.[27] Stories also erase subjectivity and the duality of a subject of enunciation and a subject of statement.[28] As stories have shortcomings, the need to create novels arises: '[T]he story will be perfect and finished but then will close in on itself. Or it will open but will open to something that could only be developed in a novel that would be itself interminable.'[29] Thus, the *oeuvre* of Kafka is described as an assemblage producing movements that are never complete, or finished, but through their communication with each other constitute a complete *oeuvre* whose success can be explained through the precedence of expression over content.

The assemblage in question is described as a *machinic assemblage*. Therefore, in order to understand it, and trace its movements and its development, we need to identify the building blocks that form the series through connectors, uniting these blocks and series. The goal is not to discover any final result or meaning produced by this assemblage but simply to understand how it functions. To me, this is one of the central ideas that emerge from Deleuze and Guattari's analysis for the purposes of rethinking international law that will be addressed below: 'It is absolutely useless to look for a theme in a writer if one hasn't asked exactly what its importance is in the work—that is, how it functions (and not what its "sense" is).'[30]

Of course, we need to understand what the building blocks are, what the connectors within the assemblage are, but these are just stepping stones towards the understanding of the functioning of the machinic assemblage.[31] When Deleuze and Guattari describe the way different blocks and series are connected in Kafka's *oeuvre* they identify two states or topographies that are sometimes used separately, but more often appear as a mixture in Kafka's works. The first state is described as a series of blocks that revolve around the centre and are separate from the centre and from each other (the 'astronomic model'). Blocks are distant and close. In the second state the blocks are also separated, but here they are placed on a continuous line. Each block/office has a door to an infinite hallway, but the doors are far away one from each other. On the opposite side to the door these blocks/offices merge; they

[25] Ibid.
[26] Ibid 35 (emphasis added).
[27] Ibid.
[28] Ibid 36.
[29] Ibid.
[30] Ibid 45.
[31] 'This functioning of the assemblage can be explained only if one takes it apart to examine both the elements that make it up and the nature of its linkages.' Deleuze and Guattari (n 2) 53.

have back doors that are contiguous. Blocks are far away and contiguous.[32] The first state dominates where Kafka has to deal with transcendental law and hierarchy. The second stage is associated with the new bureaucracy of capitalism and socialism or '[l]evels in a celestial hierarchy and contiguity of virtually underground offices'.[33]

The way Deleuze and Guattari depict the functioning of the machinic assemblage created by Kafka's *oeuvre* is particularly interesting. Running the danger of simplification, but keeping in mind the need for brevity, I would summarise the findings of Deleuze and Guattari which are essential for my further discussion as follows. The assemblage is first built through the creation of machinic indexes that will become parts of the assemblage and thus the assemblage in the process of being built seems to indicate some mysterious function. The best example of such machinic indexes is provided by Kafka's animal stories that can be read as complete finished works conveying some hidden meaning.

However, if we realise that these indexes are only parts or signs of an assemblage—and thinking of Kafka's writings as a single *oeuvre* helps us continue our reading at this stage—we can at some point understand how these parts fit together and what type of assemblage they compose. The assemblage at work becomes visible in novels.

And yet, Deleuze and Guattari distinguish assemblages from abstract machines that are also kinds of finished assemblages that don't function or no longer function.[34] The assemblages themselves can function in two ways: they can be in the process of being assembled, or they can work towards their own dismantling: 'Writing has a double function: to translate everything into assemblages and to dismantle the assemblages. The two are the same thing.'[35] Therefore, there is an intimate link between abstract machines and machinic assemblages. Abstract machines can help evaluate degree and mode of assemblages: to what extent assemblages are real in the sense of their capacity to dismantle themselves and not mere abstract machines. (Transcendental law and immanent field of justice can be given as examples of abstract machine and machinic assemblage respectively.)

This brief discussion of Deleuze and Guattari's approach to minor literature, and their way of looking at how this functions within the *oeuvre* of Kafka, has served to introduce the basic methodological tools that will be used to take a new look at public international law and its methodology. Before attempting a more substantive discussion of what could be the outcome of applying this methodology to public international law, I will first elaborate on the justifications for thinking that this is at all possible and that it could lead to any results that make sense.

Can we talk about an *oeuvre*, an assemblage or assemblages produced not by a single author but by many authors? Not by authors of literary *oeuvres* but by scholars (international lawyers in our case)? Since international lawyers produce written work, they also produce an *oeuvre*, although it is not a literary *oeuvre* in the traditional sense. It is more difficult to deal with a group of authors. I believe, however, that we can approach as a single *oeuvre*, not only the writings of a

[32] For a good visual illustration see ibid 74.
[33] Ibid 75.
[34] Ibid 47.
[35] Ibid.

particular international law scholar, but also writings constituting international law itself. International law abides by quite strict rules that determine its disciplinary boundaries, accepted styles, themes and so on. This produces a certain unity that can be analysed as a connected whole (like an assemblage or a machine as we shall see later).

## III. INTERNATIONAL LAW AND ...

### A. Envisaging International Law as a Minor Literature

The first characteristic of minor literature—deterritorialisation of language—resonates immediately with our experience of language in public international law. Through the fact that the dominant language of international law, namely English, is not the native language of the majority of international lawyers, a series of questions emerges. Does this fact make international law writings more susceptible to becoming minor literature? Does the diversity of origins of international scholars who have to operate to some degree in a position of dislocation, or deterritorialisation, have any influence on the minor character of international law? While it is important to keep this element in mind, international law as a discipline also operates in various degrees of re-territorialisation within its own disciplinary boundaries. The discipline allows only certain forms of language use.

Every international lawyer learns what the acceptable linguistic usages are within the discipline. As Martti Koskenniemi concludes in one of his articles: 'When Western speech becomes universal, its native speakers—the West—will be running the show.'[36] What could lead towards a new deterritorialisation of the speech and language of international law? What are the zones of international law for developing countries? Do international lawyers need to discover or create them? The discussion arising from these questions, and the questions themselves, illustrate how closely related, but at the same time distant, are the minor use of language and the use of language in international law. The same dynamic is visible as with other characteristics of minor literature.

As far as the political and collective nature of minor literature is concerned, international law seems to correspond with these characteristics. International law's connection to politics is an old tradition. However, international law and international lawyers as representatives of the discipline have always attempted to demonstrate that their discipline is severable and separate from politics. Despite these efforts, I think it is safe to state that international law stands in a very close relationship to everything political and in it even the most personal of affairs is potentially political, illustrated, for example, by the human rights complaints of individuals that are decided by treaty-monitoring bodies and courts.

[36] Martti Koskenniemi, 'Histories of International Law: Dealing With Eurocentrism' (2011) 19 *Rechtsgeschichte* 152, 160.

However, the important question is whether the political aspect of international law is political in the same sense in which minor literature is political: in a subversive, revolutionary way. As with the deterritorialisation of language, the similarity or proximity is only superficial and indicates distance. The same can be said of the collective value as the final characteristic of minor literature. By its very nature, international law appears to invoke and deal with everything that has collective value. However, a closer look reveals that the collectivity that international law takes into account is a select club.

Thus, the relationship between international law and minor literature is intriguing. They are both distant and close like the castle and the village in Kafka's work. For some reason, international law takes on the appearance of minor literature, or attempts to resemble minor literature or to be minor literature. My point is not to show this duality (to some extent to invoke any type of binary opposition is not saying anything new). What is more important is to provide an explanation for why and how this happens, that is how it functions.

## B. Genres and International Law

The division of different types of writings in international law into articles and monographs by scholars, judgments and other judicial and quasi-judicial decisions, official documents, including treaties, and so on can be compared to literary genres. As genres, these different types of writings are constructed in a particular way to respond to the expectations of the particular audience to which they are addressed, to make the message they want to transmit more susceptible of being accepted by the audience they want to reach.

Modern literary studies accept a certain degree of artificiality in this distinction between genres, while maintaining its utility. In public international law the distinction between different types of writings is closely linked to the theory of sources. Some types of writings are even expressly mentioned in Article 38 of the ICJ Statute: international conventions, judicial decisions and the 'teachings of the most highly qualified publicists'. On the other hand, the literature on the theory of sources recognises that there is a series of intimate links between different sources and thus different types of writings in international law. For example, judgments can rely on articles and books published by distinguished authors to interpret treaties and other official documents (for example, General Assembly resolutions). Despite these links, as in literary studies, the distinction as such is maintained and even jealously guarded by preserving styles and conventions linked to the production of each particular type of writing. The discipline of international law also attempts to preserve the boundary between what is considered 'serious' academic writing and other literary exercises in which international lawyers might be engaged. Although these other writings are recognised as a valuable part of overall written production, they certainly do not have the same impact as 'serious' academic writing. For example, the ICJ will never cite a poem written by a distinguished academic and will not engage in the writing of poetry.

Thus, the disciplinary boundaries, and the boundaries between different types of writing within the discipline, are still well preserved. However, Kafka also used his letters, stories and novels for different purposes and they fulfil different functions within his *oeuvre*. The important point from Deleuze and Guattari's perspective, is to take all writings as a single *oeuvre* and attempt to understand how these different components of the writing machine function and communicate with each other. More problematic is the complete exclusion of certain types of writing from consideration as a part of the discipline of international law and the imposition of very strict disciplinary conventions in writing.

## C. How it Functions

In order to illustrate how different types of international law writings function and communicate, I will use some examples in relation to the topic of the constitutionalisation of international law. This topic is selected because it encompasses several branches of international law. It will not be possible to draw a full picture but some of the most telling features will be highlighted.

The discussion around the constitutionalisation of international law is a notion developed by scholars in their theoretical work on some fundamental topics of public international law. It is a way of looking at the system of international law and interpreting it in a purposeful way. Scholars have articulated a variety of approaches to the constitutionalisation of international law but the structuring objective and the need to explain the purpose of international law remain present in all versions.

The need for purposeful fulfilment of international law resonates with the theme of transcendent law and guilt in interpretations of Kafka. The search for purpose and structure, and the energy and enthusiasm this topic attracts is comparable to the energy and enthusiasm with which some protagonists of Kafka's novels attempt to enter into contact with law (for example, K in *The Castle*: his desire to establish and maintain contact with the castle; or the man from the country in the parable 'Before the Law').

The parallel is reinforced by the fact that Deleuze and Guattari demonstrate how the idea of transcendental law is linked to hierarchy and hierarchical power relations. Kafka's protagonists always believe that if only they were able to reach out to a higher-ranking person, they would achieve their goal. Many versions of international constitutionalism are based on the very same belief: if only we had a clearly established hierarchy within the system of international law, problems would be solved. International lawyers working within this stream of international constitutionalism also attempt to demonstrate how this hierarchy emerges within the system of international law. The use of the notion of *jus cogens* is exemplary in this regard.

Like the law in Kafka's novels and stories, *jus cogens* remain inaccessible, always there for everyone, as for the man from the country in the parable 'Before the Law', but always delayed in their promise. All wronged parties attempt to call upon *jus cogens*, to bolster their testimony or to plead their invocation: Belgium in the name of the victims of international crimes in the *Arrest Warrant* case;[37] Bosnia and Herzegovina, in the name of the victims of genocide in the *Genocide Convention* case;[38] Italy and Greece in the name of victims of forced labour and war crimes in the *Jurisdictional Immunities* case.[39] But *jus cogens* has already gone or is not yet here; just like all the bureaucrats in The castle, and like Klamm, they are elusive.

You can get a glimpse of both bureaucrats and *jus cogens* through the keyhole but you can never actually speak to them. They might appear as an illumination when we do not know whether things are really getting darker around us or whether our eyes are merely deceiving us. But even this illumination appears only when it's too late and does not bring the expected. However, when you do not expect them, *jus cogens* are there although nobody needs them and they do not bring anything about: just as in the *Belgium v Senegal* case,[40] and the *Kosovo* Advisory Opinion.[41]

Other versions of constitutionalism mirror the disillusionment or rather a realisation that faces Kafka's protagonists, which is that justice is not hierarchy but contiguity, it is always 'in the office next door', and we are all functionaries of justice (for example, societal constitutionalism). But by framing their search and their discovery in constitutionalist terms the protagonists reveal their attachment to this justice, they reveal their desire for justice but even more their need for abstract machines of transcendental law.

Thus, there appears to be a very intimate relationship between absolute machines of transcendental law, linked to hierarchy, and machinic assemblages of immanence of justice and desire, linked to contiguity. As in Kafka's work, there are two movements: first the assemblage in the process of constituting itself and then the assemblage in the process of dismantling itself, each of which continues to reappear and to replace each other. The transcendental abstract machine of law does not exist separately or independently of the immanence of the machinic assemblage of justice. They are both necessary elements of the same assemblage: 'the transcendence of the law was an abstract machine, but the law exists only in the immanence of the machinic assemblage of justice'.[42]

The connectors between the abstract machine of law and the immanence of the assemblage of justice are international lawyers themselves. Justice is their desire which transforms itself into theories about international constitutionalism expressed

[37] Case Concerning the Arrest Warrant of 11 April 2000 (Democratic Republic of Congo v Belgium) Judgment of 14 February 2002, [2002] ICJ Rep 3, 23 para 56.

[38] Case Concerning Application of the Convention on the Prevention and Punishment of the Crime of Genocide (Bosnia and Herzegovina v Serbia and Montenegro) Judgment of 26 February 2007, [2007] ICJ Rep 43, 111 para 161.

[39] *Jurisdictional Immunities of the State (Germany v Italy*: Greece intervening) Judgment of 3 February 2012, [2012] ICJ Rep 99, paras 93 and 95 in particular.

[40] Questions Relating to the Obligation to Prosecute or Extradite (Belgium v Senegal) Judgment of 20 July 2012, [2012] ICJ Rep 422, 457, para 99.

[41] Accordance with International Law of the Unilateral Declaration of Independence in Respect of Kosovo, Advisory Opinion of 22 July 2010, [2010] ICJ Rep 403, 437, para 81.

[42] Deleuze and Guattari (n 2) 51.

in terms/blocks of traditional vocabulary, anchored in transcendence and hierarchy, with each of these blocks revolving around the invisible centre. Thus, the lawyers build an abstract machine of the hierarchy of desires for justice; the desire for justice drives them towards transcendental law and its hierarchy.

In doing so, there are times when they realise, like Kafka's protagonists, that justice is an immanent field; they realise its contiguity but because of the law's preference for content over expression, they continue to build hierarchical transcendental structures in the immanent field of justice. In addition, due to the disciplinary preference for finished abstract machines, it is difficult to continue working with assemblages that dismantle themselves without proposing something that is assembled or finished as an abstract machine. Besides, by definition an abstract machine is something that does not yet work or does not work anymore; therefore, it is easy to speculate about its significance without paying attention to its functions.

## IV. CONCLUSION

When I look at the way international law functions, I remember Kafka's castle. It has an appearance of a height and a centre around which everything moves, thus conveying an impression of a hierarchical system. However, the closer you come to it, the more you realise that the castle is actually a collection of cottages assembled into a little town and that the tower itself, which belongs to a dwelling, is not really a tower. You also realise that the most insignificant person can have as much influence as the most high-ranking bureaucrat. Thus, as in *The Castle*, the hierarchical structure is mixed up with the contiguity and fluidity of immanence. However, public international law has difficulty fully recognising the immanent field of justice, its machinic assemblage and its dismantling function. Law has learned to resist and counter these latter aspects of its functioning under the guise of abstract machines. Language, and its associated disciplinary boundaries, is one of the most important tools in this process.

The revolutionary character of minor literature emerges from the deterritorialisation of language and the particular use of language that this implies. This particular use of language extracts expressive, intensive use of language whereby the enunciation precedes content and statement. The language of international law rather operates in the opposite direction, re-territorialising any possible deterritorialisation that may have occurred, taking expression and enunciation for granted and focusing on statement and content. Only if this use of language by international law and international lawyers is disrupted can it fully develop its minor and truly revolutionary potential.

How is it possible that Kafka's works pre-figure the structure and functioning of international law and legal systems and that we find his works as relevant as ever today? Deleuze and Guattari demonstrate that Kafka's use of language throughout his *oeuvre* plays a fundamental role. For the time being, disciplinary boundaries and conventions do not allow international lawyers to fully embrace minor, and thus revolutionary, literature. The disciplinary boundaries and conventions create the impression that the blocks of international law compose an astronomic and hierarchical model, like the astronomic model described above. The intimate links with minor literature demonstrate that all these blocks that form a circle around the centre have, in fact, back doors that paradoxically are contiguous and emerge into an infinite immanent field of the revolutionary, that is, the very same field that works of minor literature occupy and dismantle. We simply do not yet have the courage to step out of these doors and into this field. We only glimpse the field through keyholes or tiny cracks in those back doors.

# 23

# *An Introduction to the Idea of International Law and the International Community in Contemporary Catholic Theology*

ALEŠ WEINGERL*

## I. INTRODUCTION

THIS CONTRIBUTION INTRODUCES the main elements of the idea of international law in contemporary Catholic theology, in particular in the Social Doctrine of the Catholic Church (hereinafter 'the Doctrine'). In presenting these elements, the contribution will reflect upon them from the perspective of the theory of international law. It will proceed from the implicit assumption that there are good reasons why an international lawyer today should study and refer to Catholic theology.

## II. FUNDAMENTAL ELEMENTS OF THE IDEA OF INTERNATIONAL LAW

It should be emphasised at the outset that the first context in which international law appears in the *Compendium of the Social Doctrine of the Church*[1] concerns the human person and human rights; more specifically, it appears in the section on the rights of peoples and nations.[2] The human person,[3] peoples and nations are thus the main coordinates for and cornerstones of the elaboration of the idea of international law in Catholic theology, which I propose to consider, by way of introduction, along the following fundamental elements.

* DPhil Candidate (International Law) (Oxford), LLM (i) (International Law) (Cambridge), Univ Dipl Iur *(cum laude)* (Ljubljana). Manuscript completed in 2015.

[1] The *Compendium* is a systematic presentation of the social teaching of the Church.

[2] *Compendium of the Social Doctrine of the Church* (Pontifical Council for Justice and Peace: Libreria Editrice Vaticana, Citta' del Vaticano 2004, reprint April 2005) para 157.

[3] The phrase 'human person' might appear to some as a pleonasm. However, it originates from the *Catechism of the Catholic Church* (Vatican, Libreria Editrice Vaticana, 1993) which sums up the belief of the Church and defines 'the dignity of the human person' as being 'rooted in his creation in the image and likeness of God', para 1700.

## A. The Principles of Human Rights Reflected in the Rights of Peoples and Nations

The first fundamental element is the close relationship between the concept of human rights and the rights of peoples and nations. This element derives from the Catholic philosophy of law, which considers the common good based on justice as 'the source of law, the reason(s) for law and the object of law'.[4] In this view, international law should be seen as a sort of extension of the Church's view of human rights. Human rights are conceived of as including the rights of peoples and nations. Thus, international law becomes primarily the law of human rights and their internationalisation. Catholic personalism[5] and anthropology appear to have transcended onto the level of peoples and nations on a global scale.[6]

Human rights are, of course, not an empty category, which anyone can fill in arbitrarily, and the present author believes that Catholic anthropology has something to say in this regard. In legal terms, they are defined as 'the criteria which the development of an international system of law must satisfy'.[7] The implementation of these criteria needs to be emphasised. The means are all well known and the Church is supportive of them: treaties, international organisations, support of governments and public opinion and so on.[8] Also known are their opponents, that is, the clash of national interests, cultures and ideologies, various forms of unjust domination, including slavery,[9] as well as the disregard of the rights of individuals and peoples.[10] The absence of solidarity, individualism, fragmentation and alienation within modern societies are also seen as important obstacles, which neglect the fact 'that society exists for men'.[11]

[4] Cf St John Paul II, 'Address to the International Court of Justice' (The Hague, 13 May 1985) ICJ Press Communiqué No 85/9, 4(8) available at www.icj-cij.org/presscom/files/5/9935.pdf?PHPSESSID=5c407 (also published in 78 *Acta Apostolicæ Sedis* (1986) 517–24).

[5] The term 'Catholic personalism' relates to a distinct philosophical school of thought particularly associated with St John Paul II. Its main principle is the idea that persons are not to be used, but to be respected and loved. Catholic personalism was also expressed in the Pastoral Constitution on the Church in the Modern World *Gaudium et spes* (1965). The Constitution affirms that 'man is the only creature on earth that God willed for its own sake and he cannot fully find himself except through a sincere gift of himself' (para 24). Pope Benedict XVI in *Caritas in Veritate* (2009) emphasised the *interpersonal* dimension of the human creature as a spiritual being: 'It is not by isolation that man establishes his worth, but by placing himself in relation with others and with God.' (para 53) Most importantly, this principle has also been extended to the level of *peoples*.

[6] Cf *Compendium of the Social Doctrine of the Church* (n 2) para 157.

[7] St John Paul II, 'Address to the International Court of Justice' (n 4) 3(7).

[8] Ibid.

[9] On globalisation of slavery and indifference, see: Pope Francis, 'No longer slaves, but brothers and sisters: message for the celebration of the World Day of Peace' (1 January 2015) available at w2.vatican.va/content/francesco/en/messages/peace/documents/papa-francesco_20141208_messaggio-xlviii-giornata-mondiale-pace-2015.html.

[10] St John Paul II, 'Address to the International Court of Justice' (n 4) 4(8).

[11] Ibid. Of course, this does not mean that it exists for men *only*. On the occasion of the Marian year in 1988, St John Paul II dedicated the Apostolic Letter *Mulieris Dignitatem* to the subject of the dignity and vocation of women, advocating 'Christian complementarism', ie the complementary roles of men and women. Moreover, in the context of the 1995 Beijing UN Conference on Women he wrote the *Letter to Women* concerning the rights and dignity of women, emphasising further the *feminine genius*.

### B. The Principle of Harmony between Particularity and Universality and Mediation Between Them

Closely related to the above element is the affirmation that 'what is true for the individual is also true for peoples'.[12] The *Compendium* is quite explicit in this respect: 'The rights of nations are nothing but "human rights" fostered at the specific level of community life.'[13] This element clearly reflects the unity of the idea of (international) law, in which the aggregate representations of the plurality of individuals in the form of national law find their balance and coherence within the representations of nations and peoples in the form of international law, and vice versa.[14] It is doubtful whether one should insist on a priori priority for international law or for national law given that each can be corrupted by the forces of international or national disorder respectively.

We can thus see that the idea of law in Catholic legal philosophy, focusing on human rights, performs a mediating function that balances 'particularity and universality'.[15] This mediating function is conceptualised as a requirement of the international order. The idea of law as such, and the idea of international law in particular, in the Doctrine are addressed to all nations, peoples and individual human beings.

### C. The Principles of Peace, Equal Respect and Solidarity

The primary obligation binding upon nations is 'to live in a posture of peace, respect and solidarity with other nations'.[16] Moreover, the Doctrine emphasises the 'principle of equal respect for States' and 'each people's right to self-determination.'[17] Equal respect for States is in turn derived from the respect for human rights, which also gives rise to the respect for the rights of peoples.

The right to independence in the Catholic idea of international law thus becomes a logical translation of the principles of peace, equal respect and solidarity.[18] Together with free cooperation between States and peoples, motivated by 'the higher common good of humanity', these principles are believed to provide a solid foundation for international peace as well as peace within nations.[19] The notion of respect is particularly significant because it sets higher standards of behaviour, which should

[12] St John Paul II , 'Letter on the Occassion of the Fiftieth Anniversary of the Outbreak of the Second World War', *L'Osservatore Romano* (English edition), 4 September 1989, 2.

[13] *Compendium of the Social Doctrine of the Church* (n 2) para 157.

[14] I leave the debate concerning the theory of representation on international and national level aside.

[15] *Compendium of the Social Doctrine of the Church* (n 2) para 157.

[16] Ibid.

[17] St John Paul II, 'Letter on the Occassion of the Fiftieth Anniversary of the Outbreak of the Second World War' (n 12) 2.

[18] St John Paul II , 'Address to the Diplomatic Corps', *L'Osservatore Romano* (English edition), 25 January 1988, 7.

[19] Cf *Compendium of the Social Doctrine of the Church* (n 2) para 157.

be contrasted with mere tolerance. The highest standard of behaviour would be that which would comply with the biblical law of love.

## D. The Right of Nations to Existence and the Principle of Spiritual Sovereignty

Two more aspects of the idea of international law deserve to be mentioned. The first is the affirmation of the 'fundamental right to existence' of a nation and the second is the concept of spiritual sovereignty. While the former is fairly self-explanatory and a reflection of the individual right to life, that is existence, the latter calls for more explanation.

Spiritual sovereignty is closely related but not limited to the international legal personality of the Holy See as the supreme authority of the Catholic Church. This personality stands as a reminder to States for all the unrepresented groups in the international community as well as an expression of spiritual sovereignty that should be contrasted with the sovereignty of States, which is based on the concept of territory and the effective exercise of personal jurisdiction over a State's population.

We read in the *Compendium* that 'sovereignty represents the subjectivity of a nation, in the political, economic, social and even cultural sense,'[20] and the *Compendium* goes on to emphasise this cultural dimension of sovereignty and proposes the concept of spiritual sovereignty[21] as an emanation of a people's culture and its identity. The principle of spiritual sovereignty thus includes the right of a nation to have and to express its language, culture, tradition, education and so on. It specifically excludes the abuse of basic human rights and 'the oppression of minorities'.[22] The right to religious freedom could also be included in this concept.[23] Spiritual sovereignty is a shield against the domination of various internationalised ideologies, for example, the dictatorship of relativism, and a medicine against the various forms of devastation that accompany them.

It is remarkable that the Doctrine constrained the potentially pathological charge of sovereignty by translating it into subjectivity, which of course in the sphere of international law becomes legal subjectivity, that is, legal personality, on the one hand and emphasised its spiritual dimension on the other. It seems that a potentially dangerous idea has been domesticated, while at the same time its transcendental and spiritual dimension has been brought into focus. The notion of spiritual sovereignty enables the preservation of national identity as a collective expression of transcendental individual human dignity, when faced with aggressive forms of domination.

[20] Ibid para 435.

[21] Ibid.

[22] Cf ibid para 157.

[23] See on the contemporary importance of concordats in promoting religious freedom: Maurizio Ragazzi, 'Concordats Today: From the Second Vatican Council to John Paul II' (2009) 12 *Journal of Markets & Morality* 113.

## III. CHALLENGES TO THE IDEA OF INTERNATIONAL LAW

Among the many challenges to the idea of international law, the notion of spiritual sovereignty points toward a particular challenge today. Spiritual sovereignty stands in stark contrast with 'heresies' like that of 'political theology' of the authoritarian kind. The concept of State should not be used in the same order of things in political theory as God in theology.[24] 'Secularised theological concepts', which inspired Carl Schmitt and some of his modern epigones, give the impression of empty pagan idols ('who have mouths, but cannot speak, eyes but cannot see').[25] When God is taken out of the picture, everything else, including the concepts themselves, loses its rationale, for what is purely human-made cannot endure for long. Therefore, it is both tragic and problematic to draw parallels between 'omnipotent God' and 'omnipotent lawgiver' or 'miracle in theology' and 'exception in jurisprudence'.[26] Life itself is akin to a miracle and, as such, not like an exception but rather like a general state of affairs, while the idea of an omnipotent lawgiver (on this side of the grave!) is alien to Catholic legal philosophy.[27] All lawgivers are constrained by law and should be its servants, not its masters. It is when lawgivers pretend to be omnipotent that humanity suffers.[28]

Atheist and even pagan deification of the State has in the past century given rise to the most tragic results in the domination of several totalitarian ideologies of dubious foundations, such as Communism, Nazism and Fascism. This is worth emphasising given the fact that Schmitt and his 'political theology' is being frequently evoked. I thus concur with those who think that international law would be better off without Schmitt's influence.[29] *Mutatis mutandis*, the pseudo-theological idolatry of the State (think for example, of ISIS/Daesh)[30] is an example of an extreme form of pathological fundamentalism and a most cruel abuse of religion for politically pathological passions and ends.[31]

Atheist and even pagan deification of the State and the pseudo-theological idolatry of the State have proved to be most brutal forms of idolatry and a work of a socio-pathological human mind. International legal theory will have to consider these

[24] *Contra:* Carl Schmitt, *Political Theology: Four Chapters on the Concept of Sovereignty* (George Schwab ed, Chicago, University of Chicago Press, 2005 (1922)) 36.

[25] Psalm 135:16.

[26] On the nexus between a purely legalistic idea of rights and individual *omnipotence* see: Armin von Bogdandy and Sergio Dellavalle, 'Reality and Transcendence: More Than a Religious Issue' in Marta Cartabia and Andrea Simoncini (eds), *Pope Benedict XVI's Legal Thought: A Dialogue on the Foundation of Law* (Cambridge, Cambridge University Press, 2015) 35–36.

[27] Jesus answered (Pontius Pilate): 'You would have no power over me if it had not been given to you from above. For this reason the one who handed me over to you has the greater sin.' (John 19:11).

[28] Cf St John Paul II , *Centesimus Annus (On the Hundreth Anniversary of Rerum Novarum)* (Vatican 1991) para 44. Cf *Catechism of the Catholic Church* (n 3) para 1904.

[29] Oliver Gerstenberg, 'What International Law Should (Not) Become. A Comment on Koskenniemi' (2005) 16 *European Journal of International Law* 125, 130.

[30] I leave the debate on whether the caliphate is truly a State aside. The term 'State' is here used in the international legal sense and not with a connotation of a modern State from political theory.

[31] When one reflects upon these sick signs of the present times, one should also meditate upon the episodes such as that of *la Terreur* (the Reign of Terror—1793–4) and its underlying motivation, which still haunts European conscience.

challenges and contemporary Catholic theology can help in arriving at a deeper understanding of these phenomena and propose ways out of the present crisis. To illustrate what is at stake, allow me to refer to Pope Benedict XVI, who at the *Collège des Bernardins* in Paris said the following:

> This tension between obligation and freedom ... presents itself anew as a challenge for our own generation as we face two poles: on the one hand, *subjective arbitrariness*, and on the other, *fundamentalist fanaticism*. It would be a disaster if today's European culture could only conceive *freedom as absence of obligation*, which would inevitably play into the hands of *fanaticism* and *arbitrariness*. Absence of obligation and arbitrariness do not signify freedom, but its destruction.[32]

## IV. FUNDAMENTAL ELEMENTS OF THE TRUE INTERNATIONAL COMMUNITY

International community cannot exist without values.[33] According to the Doctrine, there are three fundamental elements of the true international community. What is meant by the adjective 'true' is in fact the international community which has overcome or, rather, is effectively able to overcome all the various forms of man's and peoples' estrangement, alienation or division. A similar—but not altogether identical—aspiration can also be found in the Preamble of the UN Charter or the Universal Declaration of Human Rights. The fundamental elements, which reflect the values that the Doctrine proposes in order to build the true international community, are as follows.[34]

### A. The Centrality of the Human Person

The centrality of the human person[35] originates from the biblical account of creation and the place of the human person in the creationary undertaking of the Creator.[36] It is also the expression of the law of love, which so fundamentally pervades God's actions from the moment of creation onwards.

Moreover, the centrality of the human person is in fact a call to embark on the journey of finding the real truth about man and humanity, that is, something which is essentially the task of theology. This element finds its full expression in the

32 Pope Benedict XVI , 'Meeting with Representatives from the World of Culture' (Paris, Collège des Bernardins, 12 September 2008) available at www.vatican.va/holy_father/benedict_xvi/speeches/2008/september/documents/hf_ben-xvi_spe_20080912_parigi-cultura_en.html (emphasis added).

33 Values are, of course, not enough in and of themselves—virtues to implement these values are needed as well. I leave a debate on virtues in international law for some other occasion.

34 To understand these elements appropriately, it is necessary to bear in mind their biblical origins.

35 *Compendium of the Social Doctrine of the Church* (n 2) para 433.

36 We can fully understand this element in its international dimension, if we follow the human drama from the creation to the story of Noah, the tower of Babel, the death at Calvary, the Resurrection, and the Pentecostal mission of the Church. These important episodes offer a unique opportunity to contemplate the present state of the international community and international law.

Doctrine's consideration of human rights, which is permeated by Catholic anthropology and legal philosophy. The latter two recognise the human capacity to ask the most radical questions about man's existence and humanity's mission in the light of transcendental human dignity.[37]

## B. The Natural Inclination of Persons and Peoples to Establish Relationships among Themselves

'The natural inclination of persons and peoples to establish relationships among themselves' is a reminder that coexistence is a realistic possibility.[38] The view of the human person in the Doctrine is neither as pessimistic as Hobbes would have us believe, nor as excessively optimistic as utopian international idealists would have it. The Church is well aware of the fact that man is able to sin and that sin has an effect at a global and social level, not merely at a personal one.[39]

However, if persons and peoples act in accordance with natural law,[40] which is inscribed in individual hearts, the peaceful and prosperous coexistence of persons and peoples can become a reality. In 1985, St John Paul II had already recognised 'the new quality of interdependence between nations',[41] which illustrates the point at hand. The Church is convinced that the principal result of the coexistence between nations and peoples, that is, true peace, is possible, but notes that the main challenge resides in the will to achieve it.[42]

## C. Effective Universal Common Good

Hence, we must ask ourselves about the conditions for such fruitful coexistence. St John XXIII in *Pacem in terris*[43] offers values such as truth, justice, active solidarity and freedom. Blessed Paul VI mentions among the constitutive principles of the international community the principles of reason, equity, law and negotiation and condemns violence, war, discrimination, intimidation and deceit.[44] Here we meet the third fundamental element of the true international community, that is, 'the effective universal common good'.[45]

[37] See further for an interesting discussion on human dignity: Rafael Domingo, 'Human Dignity without God? Reflections on Some Relevant Speeches of Benedict XVI' in Marta Cartabia and Andrea Simoncini (eds), *Pope Benedict XVI's Legal Thought: A Dialogue on the Foundation of Law* (Cambridge, Cambridge University Press, 2015).

[38] *Compendium of the Social Doctrine of the Church* (n 2) para 433.

[39] See further the excellent study concering social sin: Maurizio Ragazzi, 'The Concept of Social Sin in Its Thomistic Roots' (2004) 7 *Journal of Markets & Morality* 363.

[40] On the modern exposition of natural law doctrine in law and philosophy see: John Finnis, *Natural Law and Natural Rights*, 2nd edn (Oxford, Clarendon Press, 2011).

[41] St John Paul II, 'Address to the International Court of Justice' (n 4) 2(6).

[42] Ibid.

[43] St John XXIII, *Pacem in terris (On Establishing Universal Peace in Truth, Justice, Charity, and Liberty)* (Vatican 1963).

[44] *Compendium of the Social Doctrine of the Church* (n 2) para 433.

[45] Ibid.

The *Catechism* teaches that 'this good calls for an organization of the community of nations able to provide for the different needs of men'[46] (for example, in the sphere of social life: food, hygiene, education and so on; and in certain occasional situations: alleviating the miseries of refugees and so on). The *Catechism* specifically insists that 'the order of things must be subordinate to the order of persons, and not the other way around' and that 'the common good is always oriented towards the progress of persons'.[47] The order in focus is the order 'founded on truth, built up in justice, and animated by love'.[48]

## V. CHALLENGES TO THE TRUE INTERNATIONAL COMMUNITY

The values mentioned above are universal values and it is *almost* impossible to disagree with them. Those who object, however, and claim that all value is subjective will have to come to concede that they essentially have a very negative, pessimistic, even Hobbesian vision of the human person and that the journey on which they have embarked will lead them to nihilism. Of course, every value can be seen as subjective for it must presuppose a human person, a human subject. However, this person is endowed with his or her conscience, which is a reflection of objective and universal natural law. The autonomy and the independence of the human person is a gift that was received by man in the Garden of Eden and his or her freedom is something that the Creator is not willing to sacrifice, even at the most precious price of the crucifixion of his only Son at Calvary. Such is the love of the Creator for his creation. And the end which Judas chose for himself shows how deep is the abyss into which a human person can fall, should the human person forget the loving mercy of his or her Creator. But this is not a necessity! It is the optional exercise of the human freedom.

The Doctrine is realistic and fully realises that 'the widespread aspiration to build an authentic international community' is not enough and that 'the unity of the human family [has] not yet becom[e] a reality'.[49] Moreover, it also identifies the sources of the present situation. These are the materialistic and nationalistic ideologies. The Church specifically condemns racism and racial discrimination as morally unacceptable.[50] Recently, Pope Francis has re-actualised the age-old problem of slavery.[51] The measure against which the Church considers these ideologies is the integral conception of the human person in all his or her spiritual and material, individual and community dimensions.[52] Problems which find bad solutions on a micro-level tend to reflect themselves on the macro-level and vice versa.

[46] *Catechism of the Catholic Church* (n 3) para 1911.
[47] Ibid para 1912.
[48] Ibid.
[49] *Compendium of the Social Doctrine of the Church* (n 2) para 433.
[50] Ibid.
[51] Pope Francis, 'No longer slaves, but brothers and sisters: message for the celebration of the World Day of Peace' (n 9).
[52] Cf *Compendium of the Social Doctrine of the Church* (n 2) para 433.

In light of the above, a question arises as to how far international law has acquiesced in the materialistic and nationalistic ideologies. And, how much has it retained its genuine force as an instrument of true progress towards the full realisation of the integral vision of the human person? How far has international law been compromised by the desires of what is called the realist school in the so-called science of international relations, or if you like, in the words of Philipp Allott, how far has international law given way to the passionate desires of the international 'Hofmafia'?[53] Moreover, how much space has it given to the reductionist vision of the human person and humanity? Pope Francis calls this phenomenon 'reductive rationality'.[54]

Moreover, is there enough strength in international legal scholarship to at least engage in a meaningful discussion with the Catholic vision of the true international community? Or, has the noise of those who ever since the French revolution and the Enlightenment have disproportionately relied on reason, reason alone and ultimately on *raison d'Etat* completely destroyed our ability to listen to that other voice? Do they not at least implicitly downplay that other equally important dimension of the human person, that is, the possibility of faith and of transcendence? It is believed that the transcendental dignity with which the human person is endowed is critically important if we want to escape past mistakes and tragedies and to resolve some of the present challenges.[55]

Allott, in his *Health of Nations*,[56] has elaborated a set of eight principles for *the new view of the human world and its law* and, on the face of it, his concept of international society bears several common traits with the true international community conceived by contemporary Catholic theology and the Doctrine. If nothing else, this is at least a proof that a meaningful dialogue between the present theory of international law and contemporary Catholic theology is possible. Allott has also recognised and emphasised the 'revolutionary mission' of the Church and has rightly called for 'a global *metanoia*'.[57] The convergence of certain of Allott's

[53] Cf Philip Allott, *The Health of Nations: Society and Law beyond the State* (Cambridge, Cambridge University Press, 2002) 396–97, para 13.33, 384, para 13.9.

[54] Pope Francis, 'Address to the Council of Europe' (Strasbourg, 25 November 2014), available at w2.vatican.va/content/francesco/en/speeches/2014/november/documents/papa-francesco_20141125_strasburgo-consiglio-europa.html.

[55] On the effects of ignoring transcendence for human liberty and dignity see: von Bogdandy and Dellavalle (n 26) 37–39. See also ibid for an interesting discussion of Gentili, Grotius, de Vitoria and Suárez in the context of Pope Benedict XVI's insistence that 'the Catholic God is a *logos* God and not an arbitrary God'. Von Bogdandy and Dellavalle, who share many of Pope Benedict XVI's views, however, propose a *secular* transcendence, which they regard as more than a religious issue. Cf ibid 42–45. It is difficult to grasp this idea of *secular* transcendence. How is it different from the cult of reason or from an ideology? Does it presuppose 'the limited, incomplete, or imperfect character of the revelation of Jesus Christ, which would be complementary to that found in other religions' (Congregation for the Doctrine of the Faith, *Declaration 'Dominus Iesus' (On the Unicity and Salvific Universality of Jesus Christ and the Church)* (Vatican 2000) para 6)? The present author is rather perplexed by this idea and has considerable reservations about it; however, it deserves a separate discussion outside the confines of the present contribution. See also n 67 and n 113.

[56] Allott, *The Health of Nations* (n 53) para 14.55.

[57] Philip Allott, 'International Society and the Idea of Justice' in Mary Ann Glendon, Juan José Llach and Marcelo Sánchez Sorondo (eds), *Charity and Justice in the Relations among Peoples and Nations (Acta 13: The Proceedings of the 13th Plenary Session of the Pontifical Academy of Social Sciences (27 April–1 May 2007))* (Vatican 2007) 48, para 32.

views and the Social Doctrine of the Church have also been noted by Krzysztof Skubiszewski.[58]

Furthermore, another question is: has international legal scholarship taken the lesson of the failure of the European Constitution? It seems that the architects of the Constitution for Europe, I think unintentionally, designed the Tower of Babel, which collapsed in my view, because Europe could not see itself in the mirror. It seems as if distorted reason and a reductionist rationalism prevented us from realising our Christian past and present.[59] I think we need to find a way to balance faith and reason, if Europe is to have a prosperous future, full of vigour, curiosity, idealism and enterprise. A meaningful dialogue between the secular and the religious lines of European thought is thus, in my view, much needed. Recently, Pope Francis made a similar appeal in Strasbourg, calling for the creation of 'a sort of new agora'.[60]

It seems that one of the main underlying problems of the present *Zeitgeist* concerns the relationship between faith and reason, which is, in essence, nothing but a quest for meaning, a quest for truth. St John Paul II noted this problem in his *Fides et Ratio* and realised that 'the search for ultimate truth seems often to be neglected'.[61] Consequently, what we have is a rise in agnosticism, relativism, scepticism, undifferentiated pluralism, proliferation of partial and provisional convictions and points of view aspiring to present themselves as the truth and a certain eclipse of philosophy's capacity to ask radical questions,[62] such as the ultimate meaning of human life and humanity's sense of being and sense of direction.

Hence, on one side we can see examples of the perversion of faith (for example, ISIS/Daesh) and on the other we can find examples of the perversion of reason (for example, the exclusion of the *invocatio Dei*, the denial of the Christian roots of Europe, the spread of Christ(ian)ophobia in Europe and the Buttiglione affair).[63] One hopes that Joseph Weiler, who realised in 2006 that 'if you are Christian you can be booted out',[64] is too pessimistic. One also wonders if this 'booting-out' is the correct application of the Enlightenment project and its enthronement of reason.

[58] Krzysztof Skubiszewski, 'Legal Regulation of the Use of Force by States' in Mary Ann Glendon, Juan José Llach and Marcelo Sánchez Sorondo (eds), *Charity and Justice in the Relations among Peoples and Nations (Acta 13: The Proceedings of the 13th Plenary Session of the Pontifical Academy of Social Sciences (27 April–1 May 2007))* (Vatican 2007) 321, para 35.

[59] See further on Christianity as an integral part of European culture, on Europe as an ethical community, Christophobia, tolerance, and withdrawal of religious phenomenon to private sphere: Joseph H Weiler, *Un'Europa cristiana. Un saggio esplorativo* (BUR Biblioteca Univ Rizzoli 2003). Our goal ought to be to aim higher than mere *tolerance*; *respect* is what one should aspire to in this context. See further on the explicitly public dimension of the freedom of religion: von Bogdandy and Dellavalle (n 26) 37.

[60] Pope Francis, 'Address to the Council of Europe' (n 54).

[61] St John Paul II , *Fides et Ratio (On the Relationship between Faith and Reason)* (Vatican 1998) para 5.

[62] Cf ibid.

[63] The Buttiglione affair refers to the controversy concerning the nomination of Rocco Buttiglione for the post of European Commissioner in 2004. His personal Catholic convictions caused his candidacy to collapse, notwithstanding – *nota bene* – that he gave assurances that they would not dictate his administration.

[64] Joseph H Weiler, 'Christophobia and Laicism' (Speech delivered on 27 April 2006 in Vienna) available at www.europe4christ.net/index.php?id=122.

The reason for this rather unhappy state of affairs was identified by Pope Benedict XVI. The Pope referred to St Augustine, who borrowed the phrase the 'zone of dissimilarity'—the *regio dissimilitudinis*—from Platonic philosophy, in order to designate his condition prior to conversion:

> (cf *Confessions*,VII, 10.16): man, who is created in God's likeness, falls in his godforsakenness into the 'zone of dissimilarity'—into a remoteness from God, in which he no longer reflects him, and so has become dissimilar not only to God, but to himself, to what being human truly is.[65]

## VI. A STRUCTURAL DEFECT IN THE THEORY OF INTERNATIONAL LAW?

Let us move forward and consider the relationship between these fundamental principles of the true international community according to the Christian vision. It will quickly become apparent that there might be a structural defect in the theory of international law. St John XXIII in *Pacem in terris* affirmed that 'the coexistence among nations is based on the *same values* that should guide relations among human beings: truth, justice, active solidarity and freedom'.[66]

It follows that insistence on a purely consensual and positivistic conception[67] of international law as well as exacerbating the divide between the international legal order and national legal orders stands in the way of the true international community. When national self-interest, which States pursue internationally, becomes the only measure of the international legal theory, are we not giving way to the 'heresy' that allows States to behave passionately, selfishly and materialistically? The same might be said, *mutatis mutandis*, of the various pressure groups that attempt to misuse international law in order to pursue their own selfish interests. If we

[65] Pope Benedict XVI, 'Meeting with Representatives from the World of Culture' (n 32).

[66] St John XXIII, *Pacem in terris* (n 44) para 80 (emphasis added).

[67] Pope Benedict, referring also to Hans Kelsen, reflected in the German Reichstag on positivism and the foundations of law in the following manner:

> A positivist conception of nature as purely functional, as the natural sciences consider it to be, is incapable of producing any bridge to ethics and law, but once again yields only functional answers. The same also applies to reason, according to the positivist understanding that is widely held to be the only genuinely scientific one. Anything that is not verifiable or falsifiable, according to this understanding, does not belong to the realm of reason strictly understood. Hence ethics and religion must be assigned to the subjective field, and they remain extraneous to the realm of reason in the strict sense of the word. Where positivist reason dominates the field to the exclusion of all else—and that is broadly the case in our public mind set—then the classical sources of knowledge for ethics and law are excluded.
>
> Where positivist reason considers itself the only sufficient culture and banishes all other cultural realities to the status of subcultures, it diminishes man, indeed it threatens his humanity.

(Pope Benedict XVI, 'The Listening Heart: Reflections on the Foundations of Law' (Berlin, Reichstag Building, 22 September 2011) available at w2.vatican.va/content/benedict-xvi/en/speeches/2011/september/documents/hf_ben-xvi_spe_20110922_reichstag-berlin.html. This view also seems to be shared by those who advocate a *secular* transcendence. See n 55 and n 113. See on the criticism of the majority principle by Pope Benedict XVI: von Bogdandy and Dellavalle (n 26) 36.

conceive of international law as nothing more than mutual consent between States, are we not enabling the order of things to run counter to the true international community? And, if one plays international law against national law or vice versa (without regard to the effective universal common good) is one not giving shelter to those who think in a somewhat Machiavellian manner that keeping faith in international commitments must ultimately be measured by self-interest and convenience?

International law is an expression of the interna(tiona)l personality of States and consent is important but it needs to be cautiously applied when it is supposed to give force to the passionate desires of nations and, indeed, some pressure groups that threaten the international legal order. I think international law is sufficiently equipped with tools to counter such desires. The principle of good faith (*bona fides*), most notably *æquitas* and common sense, should be applied whenever there is danger that inordinate passions might prevail.

Leaving the debate between dualism and monism aside, I think it would be a big step forward if one could stop playing one legal system against the other, international versus national and vice versa, and devote more attention to finding their common ground in the light of the effective universal common good. Reference to all of the three fundamental elements of the true international community can only be fruitful. There will be hard cases, but one must devote all efforts to finding solutions to legal problems, which correspond to the dictates of the 'effective universal common good', bearing in mind that 'the common good of a nation cannot be separated from the good of the entire human family'.[68]

What picture of international law can thus emerge? If all fundamental elements of the true international community are given their proper role in the theory of international law, international law can truly become the guarantor of an international order rather than an enabling device for international disorder and selfish passions.

## VII. THEORY OF INTERNATIONAL LAW IN THE LIGHT OF CONTEMPORARY CATHOLIC THEOLOGY

### A. Legal Personality of the International Community

The Doctrine dedicates a part of its attention to the concept of the State, its freedom and sovereignty, as well as the question of the possibility of an international order and the idea of international law which was presented above. It considers States (or nations) as sovereign entities operating *under* international law. In other words, sovereignty is not seen as an obstacle to the very idea of international law. This might appear to many international lawyers as rather surprising, but my understanding of the Doctrine confirms the view that the international community is given a legal personality of its own as it is defined as 'a juridical community founded on sovereignty of each member State'.[69] I understand that some lawyers would

[68] Cf *Compendium of the Social Doctrine of the Church* (n 2) para 434, referring to: St John XXIII, *Pacem in terris* (n 44) para 98.

[69] *Compendium of the Social Doctrine of the Church* (n 2) para 434.

interpret this definition contrary to what I propose; however, I think it would be illogical to deny legal personality to the international community given that it is, in fact, defined as a juridical community. In any case, this debate turns on the question of how one defines international legal personality. A juridical community without legal personality is, it is submitted, a non sequitur.

## B. States and International Law

The Doctrine thus considers the law of international community as a social rather than extra-social phenomenon. States are not absolutes in and of themselves. They are rather members of the international juridical community with a law of its own. Hence, international law cannot be simply the law that emanates from the activities of sovereign States alone, but must also take into account the effective universal common good of which the international community is a guardian. Thus, States are subjected to international law; they operate under its umbrella. This does not mean that States do not contribute to international law or that they are in any sense 'slaves' of the international legal order, but rather that the effective universal common good enshrined in international law may dictate a solution, which might appear to States as undesired or in some sense inappropriate. Such appearance is to be expected when States are estranged or alienated in one form or another. This principle, however, could also be applied *mutatis mutandis* to the international community itself when it becomes alienated, so that the effective universal common good can perform the healing function of *metanoia*. The effective universal common good is thus conceived as something objective, whereas States are seen as potentially—but not necessarily—subjective agents.

## C. Sovereignty and the Freedom of States

What role then is given to the concept of sovereignty in the Doctrine? States remain bound by the occasionally external norms of international law, as among themselves there exist no 'bonds of subordination that deny or limit its independence'.[70] Hence, sovereignty in the concept of the Doctrine simply evaporates into the principles of equality and independence. It is not given any extra-legal, let alone anti-social meaning. In particular, it does not cover any kind of international social pathology and cannot be a pretext for any misdeeds.

Moreover, the Doctrine spoken in the words of St John Paul II is explicit in confirming that the international community understood in this way 'does not in any way mean relativizing or destroying the different and distinctive characteristics of each people, but encourages their expression'.[71] There is thus a certain fine balance

[70] Ibid para 434.

[71] Cf ibid, referring to St John Paul II, 'Address to the Fiftieth General Assembly of the United Nations' (New York, 5 October 1995) available at w2.vatican.va/content/john-paul-ii/en/speeches/1995/october/documents/hf_jp-ii_spe_05101995_address-to-uno.html.

between the national and the international dimension. The Church is neither advocating a world State nor an alienated form of international law. It is simply being faithful to the principle of subsidiarity applied at the global level. On the one hand, genuine respect for sovereignty, seen as the expression of identity of peoples, avoids creating divisions that separate peoples or make them excessively self-centred. Such excesses can have destabilising effects globally.[72] On the other hand, a genuine opportunity for the social development of non-pathological faculties inherent in all peoples, men and women can be achieved when the internal and the international dimensions are harmoniously balanced.

This brings us to the question of the relationship between freedom of States and their sovereignty. According to the Doctrine, national sovereignty figures 'as an expression of the freedom that must govern relations between States'.[73] In other words, the freedom of States is conceived as a freedom in relation to the principle of (free) consent rather than as a pathological freedom that makes sovereignty run counter to the international legal order. St John Paul II noted 'the development of laws and mentalities ... based on the principle of absolute sovereignty of individual States'[74] and warned against the consequences of the absolutism of sovereignty. Similarly, we read in the *Compendium*:

> National sovereignty is not, however, absolute. Nations can freely renounce the exercise of some of their rights in view of a common goal, in the awareness that they form a 'family of nations'.[75]

Unfortunately, the language is perhaps reminiscent of the theory of auto-limitation but is actually radically different from it. The family of nations figures as a priori fact in the Doctrine, whereas in the scheme of the doctrine of auto-limitation, the family—if it is recognised at all—is only a fortunate by-product of the exclusively normative actions of States. The *Wimbledon* dilemma or paradox (concerning the existence of international law between sovereigns)[76] is solved in favour of international law and national sovereignty conceived as legal personality; in other words, for the Doctrine there is in fact no such dilemma or paradox.

## D. International Obligations and the Principles of Free Consent and Good Faith

In short, States cannot be forced to accept as legal obligations international commitments, which they see as opposing the effective universal common good. The effective universal common good on the other hand itself can induce States, through the medium of international law and the actions of the true international community, to realise the existence of international obligations that are not

[72] Cf *Compendium of the Social Doctrine of the Church* (n 2) para 434.
[73] Ibid para 435.
[74] St John Paul II, 'Address to the International Court of Justice' (n 4) 2(6).
[75] *Compendium of the Social Doctrine of the Church* (n 2) para 435.
[76] James Crawford, *Brownlie's Principles of Public International Law*, 8th edn (Oxford, Oxford University Press, 2012) 9.

dependent on their free consent. This is, of course, a theoretical postulate and the true challenge lies in its realisation in practice. In this context, diplomacy, including pontifical diplomacy, can play an important role.[77]

The principle of free consent is thus confirmed by implication, as is the principle of good faith without which no legal order can be sustained as the old Romans knew very well. In the *Compendium*, we read along the same lines that in the family of nations 'mutual trust, support and respect must prevail'.[78] Mutual trust, of course, calls for the principle of good faith as the medium that underlies the international legal order and informs its application.

## E. International Legislative Process and the Rights of Nations

The Doctrine laments the fact that:

> (T)here is still no international agreement that adequately addresses 'the rights of nations', the preparation of which could profitably deal with questions concerning justice and freedom in today's world.[79]

In other words, the only freedom that the Church is afraid of in this context is the freedom created by the absence of international legislation. St John Paul II, while noting limited progress, mentioned this problem and said that:

> (T)he contribution of the International Court of Justice to the development of new norms of international law will be impeded as long as the States do not agree on the fundamental principles and general rules of international law.[80]

Considering the stage in our international legislative process and contemplating the role exercised by the International Law Commission, a number of existential questions could be asked. For example, have we lost all faith in our international legislative project or is the project getting more and more difficult for other reasons? I am sure that the need for a world legal system is still alive today.[81]

## F. The Principle of Harmony, Universal Principles of *ius gentium* and the Rule *pacta sunt servanda*

The principle that 'the same moral law that governs the life of men must also regulate relations among States' has already been mentioned.[82] It will here be called the

[77] For the most recent example of the exercise of the pontifical diplomacy see: Holy See, 'Pope expresses joy for historic decision of United States and Cuba to establish diplomatic relations' (Vatican Information Service, 18 December 2014) available at www.news.va/en/news/pope-expresses-joy-for-historic-decision-of-united.

[78] *Compendium of the Social Doctrine of the Church* (n 2) para 435.

[79] Ibid, referring to St John Paul II, 'Address to the Fiftieth General Assembly of the United Nations' (n 71).

[80] St John Paul II, 'Address to the International Court of Justice' (n 4) 3(7).

[81] Cf ibid.

[82] *Compendium of the Social Doctrine of the Church* (n 2) para 436. See also Section II.B.

principle of harmony. Clearly, international and national law should never be set against each other if they are construed as expressing the effective universal common good. Both branches of law are merely reflections of the idea of law, which is a unitary and indivisible concept. This principle is closely related to the notion of the '*universal moral law*, written on the human heart'[83] that should apply equally within the State and the true international community.

Moreover, this principle is the basis for the respect and support that States and peoples owe to one another. This principle is a direct translation and internationalisation of the law of love that should exist on a personal level; it is inscribed in peoples' hearts. International law is as man-made law imperfect, but to the extent that it fulfils the criteria of justice and is motivated for the common good, it participates in the law's transcendental dimension.[84]

According to the Doctrine, international law based on the universal moral law 'is the necessary condition for the stability of international life'.[85] The Doctrine reaffirms validity of the universal principles that may be traced back to the period of *ius gentium*, that is, the period of 'juridical and theological reflection, firmly based on natural law'.[86] These principles, which are prior and superior to internal law, include

> the unity of the human race, the rejection of war as a means for resolving disputes, the obligation to cooperate for attaining the common good and the need to be faithful to agreements undertaken *(pacta sunt servanda)*.[87]

The *Compendium* particularly emphasises the principle *pacta sunt servanda* as a barrier against the temptation of the law of force. However, its importance goes beyond that. The principle finds its supreme expression as one of the sources of the legitimacy of international law; however, it originates in the *universal moral law*. As a principle with such provenance, the Doctrine cannot but realise that without it the entire edifice of international law could collapse.

## G. International Law, Negotiations and War

The Church strongly favours the application of international law in negotiations as a means of resolving international disputes. St John Paul II in *Centessimus Annus* advocates that it is 'indispensable to make use of common rules in a commitment to negotiate'.[88] Hence, for the Doctrine the notion of non-legal means of settling international disputes needs further qualification. In the same vein, it can be said that the idea that in negotiations 'the parties are free to negotiate on any terms they

[83] Ibid.

[84] St John Paul II, 'Address to the International Court of Justice' (n 4) 5(9). Cf on the importance of love (*agape*) in communication within legal epistemic community: von Bogdandy and Dellavalle (n 26) 35.

[85] *Compendium of the Social Doctrine of the Church* (n 2) para 437.

[86] On *ius gentium* before Hugo Grotius see James Brown Scott, *The Catholic Conception of International Law* (Washington, DC, Georgetown University Press, 1934).

[87] *Compendium of the Social Doctrine of the Church* (n 2) para 437.

[88] Ibid para 438, referring to St John Paul II, *Centesimus Annus* (n 28).

wish, and may exclude the application of rules of international law, which might bind them, except for those of *jus cogens*'[89] needs to be further developed. In the light of the conception of a State, the international community and the idea of international law according to the Doctrine, it is only natural to affirm that States remain bound by international law and are subjected to it when they engage in negotiations. Negotiations are not an international law-free area and the conditions of the effective universal common good should always be taken into account. But the Church is not naively utopian and the Pope also noted a specific inhibiting influence, saying

> even the peaceful settlement of disputes is often the province of a diplomacy determined more by self-interest than by the requirements of the common good of the international community[.][90]

The Doctrine devotes special attention to the question of war and the promotion of peace in Chapter Eleven of the *Compendium*. The extensive teaching of the Church on this topic adamantly opposes the idea that 'justice can be sought through recourse to war'[91] and thus remains faithful to Christian pacifism affirming the principle that peace is a fruit of justice and love. However, the Church realises that peace can be defeated but is equally realistic in realising that this need not be so and that peace is always an option, and it elaborates the requirements for legitimate defence based on the doctrine of *bellum justum*. The Church also emphasises the notion of defending peace and the duty to protect the innocent. It considers sanctions as measures against those who threaten peace, advocates disarmament and condemns terrorism. Special attention is also given to its own contribution to peace. Moreover, the Church fully affirms the UN Charter provisions on the prohibition of the threat and the use of force.[92] Recently, the Church spoke in favour of responsibility to protect.[93]

The question of whether international justice can ever be sought through recourse to war touches upon a most delicate debate on the relationship between religion and violence.[94] It should be emphasised that in line with Christian pacifism[95] religion cannot and should not be used to justify violence. On the other hand, the concept

[89] John G Collier and Vaughan Lowe, *The Settlement of Disputes in International Law: Institutions and Procedures* (Oxford, Oxford University Press, 2000) 24. As a matter of positive law, the idea is undoubtedly correct.

[90] St John Paul II, 'Address to the International Court of Justice' (n 4) 2(6).

[91] *Compendium of the Social Doctrine of the Church* (n 2) para 438, referring to St John Paul II, *Centesimus Annus* (n 28).

[92] *Compendium of the Social Doctrine of the Church* (n 2) para 438.

[93] Cardinal Pietro Parolin, 'Address at the 69th Session of the UNGA' (New York, 29 September 2014) available at www.vatican.va/roman_curia/secretariat_state/parolin/2014/documents/rc_seg-st_20140929_69th-un-general-assembly_en.html.

[94] Apart from this debate, there is also a most important debate on the relationship between coercion and faith. Pope Benedict XVI was explicit in stating that (Christian) faith can develop *only* in freedom. See a recent reflection on the consequences of this view: JHH Weiler, 'From Regensburg to Berlin: A Reflection on Pope Benedict XVI's Public Lectures' in Marta Cartabia and Andrea Simoncini (eds), *Pope Benedict XVI's Legal Thought: A Dialogue on the Foundation of Law* (Cambridge, Cambridge University Press, 2015).

[95] 'Then Jesus said to him, "Put your sword back into its sheath, for all who take the sword will perish by the sword".' (Matthew 26:52). Cf also Matthew 26:51, Luke 22:51, Ephesians 6:17, Hebrews 4:12 and Revelation 13:10.

of *bellum justum*, which was conceived by Catholic theologians, while it appears theoretically sound, has in practice too often, perhaps even (almost?) always, been misused due to passions and hatred which guide humans when deciding for and conducting war.

Moreover, one can observe today a certain pathological contentment that arises in some quarters when it comes to waging war and performing acts of violence, which should most definitely be rejected. Furthermore, the Doctrine recognises legitimate self-defence, which must be proportionate and rejects preventive strikes as well as so-called anticipatory self-defence. In this context, it should be emphasised that turning the other cheek is interpreted in Catholic theology as hyperbole and that Jesus Christ himself, who stood tied in front of Annas, when hit, asked for an explanation.[96] Recently, emphasis has been given to commitment to non-violence, just peace and pro-active peacemaking, including questioning the *bellum justum* doctrine.

Issues that are involved here are complex and deserve a separate and dedicated debate. It should be emphasised that one is dealing here with hopeless situations *in extremis*, that the dilemmas involved are not altogether easy, and that the human solutions at one's disposal as well as our understanding of the factual elements involved, are less than perfect. Sin is a grim reality of human existence and war may be its greatest eruption.

## H. The Primacy of Law in the International Community and the International Rule of Law

The main objective of the Doctrine in affirming the international rule of law and the primacy of law in the international community[97] is to prevent the dominance of 'the law of the more powerful'.[98] In this respect, the Church is animated by the same principles that apply to States internally. Just as private vendettas and reprisals are not acceptable internally, so it is the use of force motivated by revenge that is unacceptable internationally.

The Church places considerable reliance on the primacy of law in the international community, but is fully aware that international law has not yet reached the necessary maturity. The Doctrine proposes further strengthening of the principle of mutual confidence[99] and, above all, advocates what can be translated as effective universal compulsory jurisdiction, that is, 'a totally effective juridical authority in a peaceful world', which was mentioned by St John Paul II in his address to the International Court of Justice (ICJ).[100] He mentioned several concrete steps in

[96] 'If I have done something wrong, say so. But if not, why did you hit me?' (John 18:23).

[97] See the excellent article by Robert John Araujo SJ, 'John Paul II and the Rule of Law: Bringing Order to International Disorder' (2006) 45 *Journal of Catholic Legal Studies* 293. See also: Archbishop Bernardito Auza, 'Statement by the Permanent Observer of the Holy See at 69th Session of the UNGA concerning the Rule of Law' (New York, 13 October 2014) available at www.holyseemission.org/statements/statement.aspx?id=489.

[98] *Compendium of the Social Doctrine of the Church* (n 2) para 438.

[99] Ibid.

[100] Ibid para 439, referring to St John Paul II, 'Address to the International Court of Justice' (n 4) 3(7).

this direction: more intensive use of the ICJ and arbitration; wider acceptance of the ICJ's compulsory jurisdiction; proliferation of various international organisations at the regional level; and the development of international humanitarian and criminal law.[101]

Moreover, the Church advocates the reformulation of the dispute settlement instruments in order to strengthen their scope and binding force.[102] Other means of settling international disputes are welcomed, but they must be supported by the effective universal compulsory jurisdiction. In this sense, the primacy of law in the international community can truly lead to just peace according to the maxim *opus justitiæ pax* (peace is the work of justice). The Church considers that there can be no justice if the requirements of universal moral law are not met. On an institutional and a personal level, the Church is, of course, an advocate of judicial impartiality and objectivity.[103]

### I. Conscience of International Lawyers

It is remarkable that the only provision of an individual legal instrument which was mentioned by St John Paul II in his ICJ address was Article 20 of the ICJ Statute. This article is addressed directly to the newly appointed judges of the ICJ. They are to make a solemn declaration 'in open court' and promise to exercise their powers 'impartially and conscientiously'. Those who have undertaken such roles could perhaps witness the pressures they have had to face.

The conscience of international judges,[104] including those of international lawyers in general, is the primary addressee of the Doctrine. Conscience, moreover, should be re-discovered as the greatest treasure that all international lawyers have for the better development of international law, and contemporary Catholic theology could be a useful source of information in this regard. Independence and integrity against the politics of destructive power struggles and self-interest are the principal values, for which international judges and international lawyers must fight.[105]

## VIII. CONCLUSION

By way of a very rough introduction to the idea of international law and the international community in contemporary Catholic theology, I have asked some introductory guiding questions, which I think most of us have when it comes to the theory of international law. In answering these questions, it has been shown that

[101] Cf St John Paul II, 'Address to the International Court of Justice' (n 4) 3(7).

[102] *Compendium of the Social Doctrine of the Church* (n 2) para 439.

[103] St John Paul II, 'Address to the International Court of Justice' (n 4) 3(7).

[104] Pope Benedict XVI beautifully referred to Solomon's listening heart in his Reichstag reflection on the foundations of law. See: Pope Benedict XVI, 'The Listening Heart: Reflections on the Foundations of Law' (n 67). Cf 1 Kings 3:9.

[105] St John Paul II, 'Address to the International Court of Justice' (n 4) 4(8).

contemporary Catholic theology can provide reasonable (and compatible) answers that find their basis and reflection in the fundamental rules of the international community.

Finally, in line with the introduction to the Agora on *International Law and Theology*, convened at the 10th Anniversary Conference of the European Society of International Law on the *Boundaries of International Law and Bridges to Other Fields and Disciplines* in Vienna, where an earlier version of this chapter was presented, the importance of demands of conscience and morality in international affairs has been emphasised. It can be safely confirmed that not only has international law been long influenced by Catholic theology, but also that Christian theology,[106] a prominent part of which is contemporary Catholic theology, remains intertwined with international law.[107] Notwithstanding the effects of Enlightenment, secularism[108] and laicism, not to mention the pagan ideologies of Communism and Nazi-fascism, international law remains culturally Christian. Moreover, it also reflects to a certain degree Christian values. At the same time, the structure, grammar and language of international law, however imperfect, cannot be divorced from its cultural and traditional contexts.[109] While interconnections between international law and contemporary Catholic theology are ubiquitous, if only one is capable of and willing to see them, there could be much more interplay, in terms of interdisciplinary exchange, between current international legal scholarship and Christian theology in general[110] and

[106] On the influence of Protestantism, see: Pieter H Kooijmans, 'Protestantism and the Development of International Law' (1976) 152 *Recueil des cours de l'Académie de droit international* 79. On the interesting and important question of the various ways in which Christianity had an impact on law in general from its beginnings to the present day, see: John Witte Jr and Frank S Alexander (eds), *Christianity and Law: An Introduction* (Cambridge, Cambridge University Press, 2008). One thinks of the concepts such as justice, mercy, rule, equity and discipline, and also canon law, natural law and state law, as well as conscientious objection, civil disobedience, resistance, general contract law, and *pacta sunt servanda* etc.

[107] This raises the question of how one defines international law. Certainly, the Doctrine does not accept any reductionism, such as legal positivism, in this respect.

[108] On Pope Benedict XVI's recognition of the secular State and the problem of materially unjust positive law see: Martin Rhonheimer, 'The Secular State, Democracy, and Natural Law: Benedict XVI's Address to the Bundestag from the Perspective of Legal Ethics and Democracy Theory' in Marta Cartabia and Andrea Simoncini (eds), *Pope Benedict XVI's Legal Thought: A Dialogue on the Foundation of Law* (Cambridge, Cambridge University Press, 2015) 90–92.

[109] Cf Martti Koskenniemi, 'What should international lawyers learn from Karl Marx?' in Susan Marks (ed), *International Law on the Left: Re-examining Marxist Legacies* (Cambridge, Cambridge University Press, 2008) 33. Koskenniemi builds his 'progressive' argument concerning the 'international law's emancipatory promise' (ibid 51) on Marx's attack on religion; however, what is a source of concern for Koskenniemi and Marx is a source of hope for the present writer.

[110] Here are *some* notable examples:

An interesting and optimistic example of a call by a Protestant Thomist theologian for more attention to international law: Esther D Reed, *Theology for International Law* (London, Bloomsbury T&T Clark, 2013). See review by Philip Allott, 'Legislating in a God-made universe: Theology for International Law by Esther D Reed' The Tablet (14 November 2013) available at www.thetablet.co.uk/books/10/850/theology-for-international-law.

A political philosopher's affirmation of religious viewpoints on the idea of international order and justice: Jeremy Waldron, 'A Religious View of the Foundations of International Law' NYU School of Law, Public Law Research Paper No 11–29 (26 April 2011) available at ssrn.com/abstract=1823702.

contemporary Catholic theology in particular. The present chapter has briefly looked into the causes for this unhappy state of affairs but these cannot be discussed absent the more profound debate on the relationship between Christianity and culture.

As one struggles to understand international law in a broader context, one should not—however agnostic or atheist one might be—discard Christian and in particular contemporary Catholic theology as obsolete or irrelevant. Dialogue is an imperative, as religion will remain a fundamental and inherent dimension of human nature and human society in general; the more one attempts to marginalise it, the more it appears to be relevant.[111] The European fears concerning religion seem to originate from the essentially Nietzschean vision of a human person that wants to seek, but cannot believe,[112] and appear to persist even where one recognises the necessity of transcendence.[113] These fears can destructively paralyse our international project, which is without doubt in a crisis, because the denial of the inherent human capacity to believe carries with it also the nihilistic omen concerning the project itself, as Vera Gowland-Debbas seems to have realised in her Conference plenary lecture.

Rediscovering transcendental and spiritual values and virtues, which include justice but also love (*caritas*)[114] as the central point for saving our profession and project is a point where international lawyers could and should join forces with contemporary Catholic theology. It should be recalled that where there is *nothing* (in terms of faith, hope and love), ideology becomes *everything*. International law can be so much more than an ideology and it should certainly not descend to idolatry. Moreover, the present author, in line with Allott's optimistic vision (*metanoia*, that is, the change of mind, heart and life; also: repentance), believes that 'international law's emancipatory promise' could go far beyond and far deeper than simply the myth, suggested by Martti Koskenniemi.[115]

In summary, the present paper has introduced contemporary Catholic theology as a form of meta-legal reasoning. The Social Doctrine of the Church explains the normative quality of international law, which is so necessary at times marked by the fluctuating content of international law and the quest for its deeper meaning. Similarly, the Doctrine has something to say to the question, why should

For an appeal that law and religion need each other see: John Witte Jr , '"To Serve Right and to Fight Wrong": Why Religion, Human Rights and Human Dignity Need Each Other' in Marta Cartabia and Andrea Simoncini (eds), *Pope Benedict XVI's Legal Thought: A Dialogue on the Foundation of Law* (Cambridge, Cambridge University Press, 2015).

[111] See generally: Mark W Janis and Carolyn Evans, *Religion and International Law* (Leiden, Martinus Nijhoff, 2004).

[112] Cf Pope Francis, *Lumen fidei (On Faith)* (Vatican 2013) para 2. The Pope(s) refer(s) to Nietzsche's letter to his sister raising the problem of incompatibility of belief with seeking and of considering faith as the illusion of light.

[113] Cf von Bogdandy and Dellavalle (n 26) 44: 'if reason needs the light of faith, there is always the *danger* that it will be transformed into a maidservant, losing the freedom that defines it.' (emphasis added) But the role of faith is not to antagonise reason(!). Cf Marta Cartabia and Andrea Simoncini, 'A Journey with Benedict XVI through the Spirit of Constitutionalism' in Marta Cartabia and Andrea Simoncini (eds), *Pope Benedict XVI's Legal Thought: A Dialogue on the Foundation of Law* (Cambridge, Cambridge University Press, 2015) 26. See also n 55.

[114] Pope Benedict XVI, *Deus caritas est (On Christian Love)* (Vatican 2005).

[115] Koskenniemi (n 109) 51–52.

international law be followed? Moreover, as we struggle to see the whole picture marked by fragmentation and over-specialisation, both of which seem to threaten our holistic conception of international law, we need to consider not only what distinguishes international law from theology, but also how to link the good ideas of contemporary Catholic theology with contemporary international law scholarship. Hence, it is to be hoped that the times of Gentili's excommunication of (Catholic) theologians—*silete theologi in munere alieno*[116]—may be over.

[116] Translation: let theologians keep silence on matters outside their province. See: Alberico Gentili, *Alberico Gentili, De iure belli libri tres* (John Carew Rolfe and Coleman Phillipson trans, Oxford, Clarendon Press, 1933 (1585)) Liber I, Cap XII.

# 24

# *The Ideological Structure of the Early* Jus Gentium *and its Implications for the Current Debate about Normative Hierarchy and Public Policy in the International Community*

DIMITRIOS A KOURTIS*

## I. INTRODUCTION

ACCORDING TO THE Thomist approach, theology encompasses the study of that which is necessary by its own nature and does not receive validation from an external source, but instead necessitates each and every particle of its cosmos.[1] Assuming that we are not indulging in hubris, even though it is quite obvious that the Angelic Doctor was referring to the Divinity, this interpretation also appears pertinent to the all-inclusive discipline of international law. Despite the lack of unanimity concerning its *grundnorm(s)*,[2] international law exists by itself, validating all other branches of jurisprudence and every entity falling within its regulatory ambit. This analogy is, however, not even close to the existential bond forged between the theological doctrines and the law of nations during the flourishing years of its first era, and in particular the earliest years. For, within the foundations of international law rests a notion of sociability and an archetype of community as a natural impulse of all man-made institutions,[3] which is closer to the theological

* Attorney at Law; Scientific Associate for MP (Hellenic Parliament); LLM International Law (*cum laude*) Aristotle University of Thessaloniki, Greece; PhD candidate International Genocide Law, Aristotle University of Thessaloniki, Greece.

[1] Th Aquinas, *Summa Theologiæ* (Cambridge, Cambridge University Press, 2006) (henceforth *ST*) 1a.Q.1.

[2] See H Kelsen, *Pure Theory of Law* (Berkeley CA, University of California Press, 1967) 323–24.

[3] J Brown Scott, *The Catholic Conception of International; Francisco de Vitoria, Founder of the Modern Law of Nations* (Washington DC, Georgetown University Press, 1934) 481–82. After all, to paraphrase Schmitt's celebrated *dictum*, 'all significant concepts' of modern international legal theory are (at least to some extent) 'secularized theological concepts'; C Schmitt, *Political Theology: Four Chapters on the Concept of Sovereignty* (George Schwab trans, Chicago, University of Chicago Press, 2005) 36.

exegesis of *non est bonum esse hominem solum*[4] than to any scientific construction elucidating the formation of collective imagined communities.[5]

## A. From the *Civitas Christiana* to the *Civitas Gentium*

The first notion of spatial and social unity among nations was offered in the early phase of the mediaeval era through the conceptualisation of a *Civitas Christiana* or Christian Community. This Christian Community was dualistic in both its structure and its function, united and equally divided between kings and priests (*Reges et Sacerdotes*).[6] It enjoyed imperial and pontifical power and was regulated by the common law of the *Corpus Iuris* and consolidated by shared Christian moral principles and ethical imperatives.[7] Roman law was *written reason*[8] while canon law, as the only truly universal juridical concept, permeated the transnational Christian system, inter alia administering oaths, validating treaties and confirming the divine rights of kingship.[9]

This dualistic communitarian concept was to come to an end as soon as the imperial territorial order decayed and local kings claimed for themselves the *imperium* within the limits of their realms.[10] At the same time, the gradual evolution of the moral-juridical concepts of natural law and *jus gentium* or the law of nations, beginning in the twelfth century, moved the epicentre of the scholarly debate from godly verdicts to the ontology of human nature, thus re-establishing the human being as a naturally sociable and moral entity whose participation in the grand design stemmed from the utilisation of the *Recta Ratio* (Right Reason).[11] The Thomist concept of *synderesis* that allowed the human being to understand and co-discover basic moral imperatives through an instinctual and inherent mechanism[12] established—almost by Ciceronian epiphany[13]—natural law as the true common law of mankind.[14]

[4] *Nova Vulgata Bibliorum Sacrorum Editio* (ed 1979), Lib Genesis, Cap 2:18 (henceforth *NV*). The term *non est bonum esse hominem solumi* may be translated as 'it is not good for man to be alone'.

[5] B Anderson, *Imagined Communities: Reflections on the Origin and Spread of Nationalism* (revised and extended edn, London, Verso, 1991).

[6] According to the Melchizedekian archetype; see *NV* Genesis, Cap 14:18; Ibid, Lib Psalmorum (V), Psalmus 110:4. See W Ullmann, *The Growth of Papal Government in the Middle Ages* (London, Methuen, 1970).

[7] C Schmitt, *The Nomos of the Earth in the International Law of the Jus Publicum Europaeum* (GL Ulmen trans, New York, Telos Press, 2003) 60ff.

[8] R Phillimore, *Commentaries upon International Law*, 3rd edn, vol I (London, Butterworths, 1879) 34; J Westlake, *International Law*, 2nd edn, vol I (Cambridge, Cambridge University Press, 1910) 15; JL Brierly, *The Law of Nations: An Introduction to the International Law of Peace*, 6th edn (Oxford, Oxford University Press, 1963) 19.

[9] A Nussbaum, *A Concise History of the Law of Nations*, 1st edn (New York, Macmillan, 1947) 23ff.

[10] Ibid 46.

[11] Cf D Bauer, 'The Importance of Medieval Canon Law and the Scholastic Tradition for the Emergence of the Early Modern International Legal Order' in R Lesaffer (ed), *Peace Treaties and International Law in European History* (Cambridge, Cambridge University Press, 2004) 198ff.

[12] *ST* 1a.2æ.Q.91.

[13] MT Cicero, *De Republica* Lib III, s xxii (Augustinian annotation).

[14] Isidore of Spain, *Etymologiarum sive Originum Libri XX* (Oxonii, E Typographeo Clarendoniano, 1967) Lib V, s IV.

The aforementioned Thomist paradigm, understood through the lens of the Right Reason, inserted a primordial notion of hierarchy into the socio-juridical, since no human law (which was deemed to be *jus voluntarium* or voluntary law) could surpass or exceed the scrutiny of this *necessary law*. If found to be contradictory to the decrees of necessary law, positive law was not only to be disregarded but was also to be rendered null and void.[15] Thus Right Reason established itself as the measure of positive law's validity and the ultimate reference principle for the construction of legal categories.[16]

Later on, this principle proved ontologically fundamental for the discovery of the Americas because it brought to light a whole new perception of the globe, initiating a proper cosmogony[17] while confirming that the fate of the human world was not sealed, thus contradicting Augustine's prediction.[18] However, the new lands, inhabited by indigenous populations, appeared to be of disputed ownership, given that the Indians, as heathens, were deprived of juridical personality.[19] Since the newly discovered Indians possessed no status under human law, someone had to establish their position in accordance with the edicts of divine law. Consequently, Francisco de Vitoria, elected first-chair professor of theology at the University of Salamanca, and a member of the Oder of Preachers (Dominicans), embarked on an unprecedented intellectual *trivium*,[20] assessing their rights and powers vis-à-vis the law pertaining to the forum of mankind's conscience, a notion that was easily addressed by theologians, as savants of the conscience's dictates.[21]

## B. *Quod naturalis ratio* … and the Original Vision of Order

Resting in the forum of conscience, the quintessence of the issue in question called for the application of rules ascertained by the *Recta Ratio*. This pertinent set of norms was no other than *jus gentium*, a doctrinal category closely inter-connected with natural law and the Right Reason. According to the celebrated Vitorian definition, *quod naturalis ratio inter omnes gentes constituit, vocatur jus gentium*;[22] coining the term anew, not only did the great scholar reinterpret existing juridical and theological sources, but he actually construed a separate order, thus paving the way for the emancipation of the law applicable *inter gentes* or the law among nations, from both a civil and canonical jurisprudence.[23]

15 F de Vitoria, *De Indis et De Iure Belli* (Ernest Nys ed, Washington DC, Carnegie Institute of Washington, 1917) (henceforth *DIDB*) 152.

16 See H Kelsen, *General Theory of Law and State* (Anders Wedberg trans, Cambridge MA, Harvard University Press, 1949) 407–16.

17 J Brown Scott, *The Spanish Origins of International Law* (Oxford, Clarendon Press, 1934) 26ff.

18 Augustine of Hippo, *De Civitate Dei Contra Paganos*, Lib XXI.

19 de Vitoria, *DIDB* 120–21.

20 J Brown Scott, *Law, The State and the International Community*, vol I (New York, Columbia University Press, 1939) 554.

21 de Vitoria, *DIDB* 119–20.

22 Ibid 151 'what natural reason has established among all peoples is called the law of nations'.

23 Brown Scott, *The Spanish Origins of International Law* (n 17) 164.

The Vitorian law of nations was not a mere reiteration or abstraction of preexisting concepts but a normative order applicable to the intercourse of peoples and sovereigns, since both the Spanish metropolis and the Indian polities were sovereigns and owners under public and private law, each within their own jurisdictional boundaries.[24] Consequently, the New World's lands and populations could not have been acquired by occupation pertaining only to *res nullius* or no-man's land;[25] under these propositions, the supremacy of the Christian polities could not have been affirmed since each *commonwealth* or people knew no authority higher than itself.[26]

Instead, the territorial expansion of the mediaeval cosmos allowed a new idea to rise,[27] even to the detriment of Christianity's superiority.[28] Surpassing strict religious and cultural barriers, the Vitorian ideal type brought all polities, each perfect for its ultimate *telos* (purpose),[29] under a single normative order encompassed by fundamental values, all traceable back to the theological doctrinal narrative of the universe.[30]

These primary principles posed under scientific abstraction and departing from their articulate ornaments, comprise two fundamental notions, namely the communitarian value and the substratum of egalitarian independence.[31] The *prima principia* or primary principle, thus construed, gave rise to certain rights and elementary freedoms whose status appeared both ontologically and functionally superior when compared with the classical juridical concepts of municipal law, owing to their origin and their validating authority.

For example, for the Friar of Salamanca *jus gentium*, as an order, was not only a palimpsest of the Right Reason but was also communitarian law, established and sanctified under the will and conscience of all humankind, acting *qua* constituent authority. The origins of the system predetermined its end goal, which was the regulation of intercourse between humanity's collective formations, that is to say the plurality of independent States. Citing Ecclesiastes, the New Testament and the Digest as authorities of Natural Reason, the Friar-Preacher concluded that amongst nations there existed an inherent bond of sociability, as induced authoritatively by Augustine from the imprints of the divine lore concerning the imperative necessity of *loving thy neighbour as thyself*.[32]

[24] de Vitoria, *DIDB* 128.

[25] Later on the low (according to Western standards) level of the aboriginal polities' civilisation was considered to be a full and adequate title for their subjugation; see the *ratio decidendi* of *Johnson & Graham's Lessee v McIntosh*, 21 US 543 (SCt, 1823).

[26] See A Cassese, *International Law in a Divided World* (Oxford, Clarendon Press, 1986) 397, according to whom the Westphalian State is a collective community knowing no other superior than itself ('*communitates superiorem non recognoscentes*').

[27] P Vinogradoff, *Historical Types of International Law* (Lugduni Batavorum, Brill, 1923) 53ff.

[28] P Zapatero, 'Legal Imagination in Vitoria: The Power of Ideas' (2009) 11(2) *Journal of the History of International Law* 221, 221–22.

[29] See de Vitoria, *DIDB* 169.

[30] A Truyol y Serra 'Vitoria et la tradition scolastique' in YC Zarka (ed), *Aspects de la pensée médiévale dans la philosophie politique moderne* (Paris, Presses Universitaires de France, 1999) 69, 81–82.

[31] J Barthélemy, 'François de Vitoria' in A Pillet (ed), *Les fondateurs du droit international* (Paris, V Giard & E Brière, 1904) 1, 7–8.

[32] Cf CG Weeramantry, *Universalising International Law* (Leiden, Martinus Nijhoff, 2004) 9, 369.

Since all mankind was brought together under the said decree, clearly each and every human polity had to be considered the *proximus* to all the rest.[33] Established and forged by such natural inclinations, the grand polity of nations was existentially linked to its own constituted order. This was the *ordo ordinatus*, a normative system that was sufficiently derived from natural law and potent enough to produce legal effects but also generated rights and imposed obligations.[34] Even though the Right Reason had erected sufficiently clear commands and prohibitions among nations, for Vitoria several rules of *jus gentium* were created by the will and acquiescence of the plurality of co-existing States, in pursuit of their common purpose.

Similarly, Hugo Grotius also accepted the Friar's argument on the humanitarian and sociable nature of the *civitas gentium*, the grand polity of nations. For the great Dutchman, it was the ultimate manifestation of the *appetitus societatis* (the natural inclination towards sociability), which is intrinsic to human societies at large. The *appetitus* as a socio-legal notion derived from the Christian reiteration of the Stoic doctrines on humanity's moral and virtuous pre-disposition.[35] According to the Grotian narrative, this natural inclination towards the formation of societies (either national or supra-national) brought about the creation of a higher normative order in lieu of mere force or self-oriented conceptualisation of the international system.[36] Furthermore, it was of paramount importance that such an order was not diminished either in its completeness or in its enforceability vis-à-vis individual States.[37]

### C. *Totus Orbis, Jus Communicationis* and the Vitorian System for the Enforcement of International Obligations

As Vitoria envisaged, the normative order of the *civitas gentium* received not only the force of a pact, but also that of pure law—or so the Friar opined. Since the beginning of time, united polities (*totus orbis*) had the power to create laws, which were just and equitable for all persons.[38] Consequently, any State found in breach of these norms by deviating from the mandates of the collective will and conscience committed a 'mortal sin'.[39] As a result, when an actor of the international cosmos

[33] See Ch Tomuschat, 'International Law: Ensuring the Survival of Mankind on the Eve of a New Century; General Course on Public International Law' (1999) 281 *Recueil des Cours* 9, 73ff.

[34] See Ph Allott, *The Health of Nations: Society and Law Beyond State* (Cambridge, Cambridge University Press, 2002) 410, ss 14.36–14.37.

[35] H Grotius, *De Jure Belli ac Pacis Libri Tres* (FW Kelsey trans, Oxford, Clarendon Press, 1925) *Prolegomena*, 11ff.

[36] H Lauterpacht, 'The Grotian Tradition in International Law' (1946) 23 *British Year Book of International Law* 1, 24ff.

[37] Ch Wolff, *Jus Gentium Methodo Scientifica Pertractatum* (JH Drake trans, Oxford, Clarendon Press, 1934) *Prolegomena*, 12ff.

[38] A Truyol y Serra, 'Prémisses philosophiques et historiques du "totus orbis" de Vitoria' (1946–1947) 7 *Anuario de la Associación Francisco de Vitoria* 179; WG Grewe, *The Epochs of International Law* (M Byers ed, New York, Walter De Gruyter, 2000) 146ff.

[39] F de Vitoria, 'De Potestate Civili' in Brown Scott, *The Spanish Origins of International Law* (n 17) 219.

had violated the rules of the *totus orbis* or objected to their legal effects, the superior status of the former conferred a legitimate title on any injured party seeking restitution and redress all forms of coercive measures against the perpetrator.

This appeared especially true when the breached right was fundamental in that it incorporated a value stemming directly from the constituent principle of the system. Such was the case of the Indians, who supposedly breached an obligation under the law of nations by impeding the exercise of the most elementary of all freedoms, namely the tripartite right to travel, sojourn and trade with other nations (*jus communicationis*).[40] Conveniently enough the Spaniards were, among others, the holders of the breached right and thus the injured party of the aforementioned internationally wrongful act. The *jus communicationis* thus construed was immediately identified with the basis of the communitarian value itself. The authoritative articulation of this all-inclusive right left no room for speculation regarding its status and validity; *it was permissible from the beginning of the world for anyone to set forth and travel wheresoever he would.*[41] The oceans and rivers were created navigable, while the *terra firma* was explorable.[42] All States and their citizens were equally vested with the right to explore, travel and sojourn within the Creation.[43]

From this proposition, sanctioned by divine providence, the Great Savant induced a whole set of individual freedoms. The approachability of the New World, as a natural fact, established that interaction and trade were permissible between the sovereign members of the *totus obis*, while every human being was entitled to hospitable treatment,[44] provided that the population of the host State suffered no injury. This followed necessarily from the state of equality, naturally established among nations.[45] Unlike Augustine, who had foretold the end of the earthly polity *ad maiorem Dei gloriam* because States were to be considered the epitome of evil in the post-lapsarian society,[46] Vitoria considered independence and equality of States as the primary guarantee of fair and equitable treatment both between themselves and between their citizens, as synergistic actors in the perennial striving for progress.

Behind the liberal, almost mercantile, doctrines, we may discern that the Friar, being himself a member of the Order of Preachers, was not preoccupied with the creation of colonial peripheries or (even) the solidification of the Spanish Crown's

[40] Cf E Roucounas, 'The Idea of Justice in the Works of Early Scholars of International Law' in L Boisson de Chazournes (ed), *The International Legal System in Quest of Equity and Universality: Liber Amicorum Georges Abi-Saab* (The Hague, Martinus Nijhoff, 2001) 79, 84.

[41] On the importance of the Vitorian definition, see A Gómez Robledo, *Fundadores del derecho internacional* (México DF, Instituto de Investigaciones jurídicas/UNAM, 1989) 11 ff, especially 37–39.

[42] de Vitoria, *DIDB* 151.

[43] See also R Hernández, 'The Internationalization of Francisco de Vitoria and Domingo de Soto' (1991) 15(4) *Fordham International Law Journal* 1031, 1047ff.

[44] Cf I Kant, *Perpetual Peace: A Philosophical Essay* (Mary Campbell Smith trans, London, George Allen & Unwin, 1917) 117, 137ff.

[45] Brown Scott, *The Catholic Conception* (n 3) 20ff.

[46] The post-lapsarian degradation, namely the world after Original Sin (consuming the fruit from the tree of knowledge) and the Fall of Man (Adam and Eve's banishment from the Garden of Eden), is a constant element of the Augustinian doctrine; see PJ Weithman, 'Augustine and Aquinas on Original Sin and the Function of Political Authority' (1992) 30 *Journal of the History of Philosophy* 353; Bauer (n 11) 211.

juridical titles of conquest vis-à-vis the New World.[47] His major concern was the safeguarding of the *jus peregrinandi*, the right of worldwide travelling and trading of both products and ideas, which was of paramount importance for all preachers and missionaries.[48]

However, it was not commerce or material goods that intrigued the Friar but the trading of ideas, and the opportunity to ground once and for all, regardless of papal ambitions and sword doctrines, the right to preach (*jus prædicandi*),[49] that is, the right to communicate the divine word to the gentiles of the Western Hemisphere.[50] The construction of notions such as the freedoms of commerce and navigation were an intermediary step that linked the communitarian principle, itself emanating from a Thomist interpretation of the natural order,[51] to the great Thomist ideal of ecumenical peace through the evangelisation of the whole world.

Despite this doctrinal background, the conceptualisation of the Vitorian *civitas maxima* was by no means an ostensible articulation fostering solely a theologically-minted imperialism. The *prima sede* professor of Salamanca trusted highly in the order emanating from the law of nations.[52] And he could not do otherwise, since this order was prescribed by the most fundamental of all inherent human qualities, reason as opposed to will. For the mediaeval theologian, a rule imposed by the *Recta Ratio* was valid by and of itself, while a norm stemming from the will was sanctioned under the auspices of communitarian consensus.[53]

Consequently, any act diverging from the imposed limits was to be considered not only illicit *jure gentium*, but also mortally sinful. Similarly, rules established by common consensus, or revealed to the human conscience through rational imperative, were to bind all humans and every State regardless of their consent and/or objection.[54] Thus construed, the primeval notion of hierarchy disclosed a certain intellectual predisposal for some preferred values that must be served come hell or high water.[55]

To the Vitorian system, State equality and mutual respect of independence is deemed to be temporarilyinterrupted when breaches of fundamental norms occur. Inequity cannot pass unpunished, since *ex naturali ratione* where there is a wrong, Reason prescribes a remedy.[56] In Vitorian and Grotian times, the remedy rested in

[47] Cf A Anghie, *Imperialism, Sovereignty and the Making of International Law* (Cambridge, Cambridge University Press, 2004) 13ff.

[48] On its abuse by the Spaniards, see A Pagden, *Spanish Imperialism and the Political Imagination* (New Haven CT, Yale University Press, 1990) 20ff.

[49] Cf de Vitoria, *DIDB* 156.

[50] Barthélemy (n 31) 9.

[51] M Lachs, *The Teacher in International Law* (Dordrecht: Martinus Nijhoff, 1987) 43.

[52] P Zapatero (n 28) 232ff.

[53] Brown Scott, *The Spanish Origins of International Law* (n 17) 24.

[54] de Vitoria, *DIDB* 153.

[55] Cf JM de Aguilar, 'The Law of Nations and the Salamanca School of Theology' (1946) 9 *Thomist* 187, 216–17.

[56] Surprisingly enough, the Supreme Court of Cyprus has appealed to the inherent principles of natural justice—in a seemingly Vitorian and *jus naturalistic* manner—in order to set the limits of human rights' *Drittwirkung* (third-party effect);·see *Giallouros v Nikolaou* (= *Γιάλλουρος v Νικολάου*) [2001] 1 SCt Rep (= ΑΑΔ) 558 (in Greek).

recourse to the use of force and the waging of a just war; a war to protect the fundamental pillars of the system.[57] This was an act pertaining to the common good of the whole world that according to Augustine meant peace and security of the earthly city at large.[58]

As a result, what has been described as a 'force-suit' was the remedy the Founding Fathers granted vis-à-vis, inter alia, offences aggravating the moral status of mankind as a collective formation.[59] With the communitarian principle violated, the accessibility of the maritime routes at stake, and the tradability of goods and ideas repudiated given that Reason and persuasion could not serve justice, then armed force of a defensive nature could be employed, provided that, as Augustine had stipulated, necessity and proportionality were observed.[60]

Much like civil polities that possess the legitimate monopoly of the power to eliminate internal threats and punish civilians' illegal conduct, the *totus orbis* possessed the authority to exercise collective coercive action against the wrongdoer-State.[61] It could do so by employing force adequate and necessary for the restitution of the injury and the restoration of peace and tranquillity *inter gentes*.[62] Wars of this kind were deemed to be just, based on the assumption that the very foundations of the system were under severe threat. Furthermore, as the claim for restitution emanated from the failure to observe fundamental norms, every State possessed the competence to vindicate the rights of the community.[63] Meanwhile, the polity which exercised their authority was considered to be an agent of the *totus orbis*, performing a somewhat mixed function of the quasi-judicial and quasi-executive. Thus just war was conceptualised as a rudimentary mechanism of enforcement concerning breached obligations stemming from the law of nations. Needless to say, in spite of the original visions, enforceability was something of which international law was bereft from the very beginning.[64]

## D. In Defence of the International Organisation's Fundamental Pillars: Just War Revisited

Waging war under just title so as to defend the fundamental values of the *civitas maxima* may well be deemed as a theological pretext, justifying blatant expressions of temporal imperialism.[65] In fact, similar assertions can overshadow almost all of

[57] Cf Grotius (n 35) Bk II, Chap XX, 475 (citing Augustine).
[58] de Vitoria, *DIDB* 167.
[59] Brown Scott, *The Spanish Origins of International Law* (n 17) 240.
[60] de Vitoria, *DIDB* 154ff.
[61] See HG Justenhoven, 'Francisco de Vitoria: Just War as Defense of International Law' in WA Barbieri Jr (eds), *From Just War to Modern Peace Ethics* (Berlin/Boston MA, Walter De Gruyter, 2012) 121, 129ff.
[62] de Vitoria, *DIDB* 172.
[63] See Barthélemy (n 31) 11.
[64] Brown Scott, *The Catholic Conception* (n 3) 43–44.
[65] A Anghie, 'Francisco de Vitoria and the Colonial Origins of International Law' (1996) 5 *Social & Legal Studies* 321, 328ff.

the early doctrinal systems of the discipline's Founders. Vitoria appealed to Reason and humanity in order to justify Spanish colonialism; Suárez created the concept of modern customary international law by upholding European territorialism; and Grotius secularised biblical authorities and eventually established international law as a discipline that advocated Dutch mercantilism.[66] Thus, all three Founding Fathers may be held accountable for misinterpreting the Thomist doctrine on natural law.[67] These appear to be extremely important allegations, which one should not be willing to dismiss lightly, lest the scholar discover ulterior motives or methodological inconsequence in the *opera* of the Founders.

Yet this quest is almost as futile as arguing about the Grotian theology of international law: necessity subjugating ideas.[68] Grotian methodology, innovative, scholastic or liberal, pertained to the original vision, accepting an all-encompassing order as a guarantee for the peaceful striving of humans through Reason, itself a vehicle for the recognition of the fundamental order already prescribed by an inherent necessity.[69] Grotius, the perennially paternal figure of the discipline, considered the communitarian values as international law's *Grundnorm*, emanating from the theologically perceived rational nature of humanity and its institutions.[70]

Eventually, Vitoria—no less vehemently than Grotius—in departing from the classical religious doctrines and establishing the concept of normative imperative upon pure divinity, was able to utilise morality, theology and jurisprudence in order to address current issues of international life by adopting an new method. Most likely, this is the reason why the doctrinal contributions of the Founding Fathers prepared the way for the following generations of scholars who offered notions, propositions or ideas that were dearly held and widely used by what has been described as the 'invisible college of international lawyers'.[71]

Within the original vision's order, each State, bearing the responsibility of executing and ensuring execution of the obligations stemming from the fundamental communitarian principle, even to the detriment of equalitarian independence (non-intervention),[72] could seek the restoration of the injury caused by a delinquent peer, whose *sin* before the law of nations seems—to the present-day scholar—to be strangely connected to the notion of internationally wrongful acts. Once recognised as delicts under the law of nations, violation of fundamental norms could bring the wrongdoer within the jurisdictional competence of any other State. The actual polity that would use armed force to punish the wrongdoing body would

[66] J Thumfart, 'On Grotius's *Mare Liberum* nd Vitoria's *De Indis*: Following Agamben and Schmitt' (2009) 30(1) *Grotiana* 65.

[67] See the discussion in H Bull, 'Natural Law and International Relations' (1979) 5(2) *British Journal of International Studies* 171.

[68] See generally, L Henkin, *How Nations Behave: Law and Foreign Policy*, 2nd edn (New York, Columbia University Press, 1979).

[69] CA Stumpf, *The Grotian Theology of International Law: Hugo Grotius and the Moral Foundations of International Relations* (Berlin, Walter De Gruyter, 2006) 68.

[70] WP George, 'Grotius, Theology, and International Law: Overcoming Textbook Bias' (1999–2000) 14(2) *Journal of Law and Religion* 605, 612–15.

[71] See O Schachter, 'The Invisible College of International Lawyers' (1977) 72(2) *Northwestern University Law Review* 217.

[72] Barthélemy (n 31) 11–12.

not only wage a just war, but would also function as an enforcement agent of the *totus orbis*.[73] In this way, the theological tradition passed down to international jurisprudence not only the just war doctrine but, even more importantly, the idea that there is an order of values that must be defended for the earthly *civitas gentium* (or in twenty-first-century terminology, the international community) to function as a *katechon*, to borrow Carl Schmitt's vivid language, vis-à-vis the anarchy and segregation stemming from the parallel existence of a plurality of sovereign actors in the international arena.[74]

## II. THE MODERN DOCTRINE AND THE EVOLUTION OF VERTICAL NORMATIVITY

From divinely conceptualised necessities emanated a new 'creed' of international jurisprudential faith, pursuant to which certain values and the norms incorporating them—as pertinent to a higher ethical order, necessary for the preservation of the international community—stand omnipresent. They permeate the foundations of the system and compel every actor to respect them and guarantee their respect vis-à-vis the international community as a whole.

For Grotius, these principles constituted a higher immutable and eternal law.[75] Later on, other authoritative voices of classical international law declared that these values, encompassing and vertically penetrating the international system, prevented sovereigns from instituting 'voluntary law' (*jus voluntarium*) contrary to the moral imperatives of their order.[76] It has also been suggested that obligations arising from the *Vereinbarung* (agreement) of multiple States cannot be validly executed, if found opposable to the order of values inherent in the international system.[77] Thus, it came to pass that the very edifice of international law, grounded upon these precepts, generated the everlasting debate on hierarchies and orders. International lawyers understood this concept as well as the eternal struggle between *will* and *reason*, or—more aptly—between positivism and natural law theory.[78]

It is a truism that the scholarly debate has undergone several phases in theory without the realisation of equally important developments in the practice of international jurisprudence.[79] Although little less than a century has passed since the first

[73] Cf P Haggenmacher, 'La place de Francisco de Vitoria parmi les fondateurs du droit International' in A Truyol y Serra (ed), *Actualité de la pensée juridique de Francisco de Vitoria* (Brussells, Bruylant, 1988) 28, 44.

[74] Schmitt, *The Nomos of the Earth* (n 7) 59–60.

[75] Grotius (n 35) Bk I, Chap I, 38ff.

[76] E de Vattel, *The Law of Nations* (Northampton MA, TM Pomroy/S and E Butler, 1805) *Preliminaries* 52; Wolff (n 37) *Prolegomena* 10.

[77] See AW Heffter, *Das europäische Völkerrecht der Gegenwart auf den bisherigen Grundlagen* (Berlin, EH Schroeder, 1861) 155–56.

[78] M Koskenniemi, *From Apology to Utopia: The Structure of the International Legal Argument* (Cambridge, Cambridge University Press, 2006) 322–24.

[79] For a current exploration of the respective debate, see GI Hernández, 'A Reluctant Guardian: The International Court of Justice and the Concept of "International Community"' (2012) 83 *British Year Book of International Law* 13.

statement of hierarchical notions, at least as nominal values,[80] the scientific debate on hierarchy and the prospects of differentiated normativity still endure.[81] From as early as the 1930s, Professor Alfred Verdross believed that the existence of peremptory norms raised several objections amongst the devotees of voluntarism,[82] who know no other international law but voluntary law.[83] Although we may find no solid proof to the contrary,[84] it is justifiable to say that since the VCLT regime[85] authoritatively recognised the existence of peremptory norms, international scholarship is bound to accept the notion as a general legal category.[86]

It has been suggested by certain scholars that *jus cogens* is almost a reiteration of necessary law, as envisaged by the Founders of the discipline;[87] at the same time, it is deemed to be an open-ended concept,[88] while pursuant to the positive articulation of the notion (Article 53 of the VCLT) *jus cogens* can be modified. If someone tries to discern a solid doctrinal basis concerning the origin of the concept in question, including even the relative notion of obligations *erga omnes*,[89] some attention should be given to the original visions.

## A. Fundamental Juridical Concepts of the International Community

Although Pagden warns us that attempting to reinvent Vitoria as the ancestral figure of international organisation may generate several misconceptions,[90] we are bound to acknowledge that certain emanations of the concept hierarchy and restitution based on the importance of the underlying principles existed long before the

[80] *Oscar Chinn Case* (*UK v Belgium*) [1934] PCIJ Rep Series A/B No 63 149 (*Separate Opinion per Schücking J*). See also French-Mexican Claims Commission, *Pablo Nájera (France) v United Mexican States* (Arbitral Award No 30A of 19 October 1928) 5 RIAA 466, 472 (concerning the nature of the Covenant of the League of Nations, namely Article 18).

[81] See the classical contribution by P Weil, 'Towards Relative Normativity in International Law?' (1983) 77 *American Journal of International Law* 413.

[82] The turning point between positivism and voluntarism is traced back to the creation of the original voluntaristic myth; R Ago, 'Positive Law and International Law' (1957) 51 *American Journal of International Law* 691, 699.

[83] A Verdross, 'Forbidden Treaties in International Law: Comments on Professor Garner's Report on "The Law of Treaties"' (1937) 31 *American Journal of International Law* 571, 572.

[84] *Case of SS Lotus* (*France v Turkey*) [1927] PCIJ Rep Series A No 10 18.

[85] Vienna Convention on the Law of Treaties (adopted 23 May 1969, entered into force 27 January 1980) 1155 UNTS 331, Articles 53, 64 and 71.

[86] See in general, K Zemanek, 'The Metamorphosis of Jus Cogens: From an Institution of Treaty Law to the Bedrock of the International Legal Order?' in E Cannizzaro (ed), *The Law of Treaties beyond the Vienna Convention* (Oxford, Oxford University Press, 2011) 381ff.

[87] Cf A Gómez Robledo, 'Le ius cogens international: sa gènese, sa nature, ses fonction' (1981) 172 *Recueil des Cours* 9, 189ff; AA Cançado Trindade, 'International Law for Humankind: Towards a New Jus Gentium (I)' (2005) 316 *Recueil des Cours* 9, 335.

[88] Cançado Trindade (n 87) 360.

[89] *Barcelona Traction, Light and Power Company, Limited* (*Belgium v Spain*) (Second Phase) [1970] ICJ Rep 3, 32 [33]–[34]. Although different in notion [(1998) II *Yearbook of the International Law Commission* 76], it is certain that the two concepts interrelate ontologically; cf CJ Tams, *Enforcing Obligations Erga Omnes in International Law* (Cambridge, Cambridge University Press, 2005) 140–51.

[90] A Pagden, *The Uncertainties of Empire: Essays in Iberian and Ibero-American Intellectual History* (Aldershot, Ashgate Publishing, 1994) x.

Friar's era.[91] As already stated, the primary order of values recognised by the original visions was founded upon the concepts of community and equalitarian independence, with the former vindicating an all-encompassing primacy.[92] In defence of the values and respective norms, derived from fundamental communitarian principle, States could wage just wars, thus restoring the order of the *totus orbis*. This (secondary) order comprised—much like today—values such as peace, security, solidarity, sociability and the protection of the human life.[93]

In more recent times, the experiences of World War II—and specifically the atrocities committed during the war that shocked the conscience of civilised mankind—allowed for a revitalisation of ethical concepts in international legal scholarship and legal practice. Classical doctrines of natural law theory were rediscovered and updated, after a century of positivism, in an attempt to promote the evolution of the 'international community' into a morally encompassed construction. Thus the post-war international community was ultimately conceived as a formation based on fundamental communitarian values, which were understood as the unwritten constitution of the world at large.[94] Cogently, until now, the maxim *ubi societas ibi jus* (where there is a society, there is a law) retains its persuasive power.[95] However, without the inherent ideal of solidarity and sociability no community can be so identified.[96] Thus the ultimate evidence about survival of the original communitarian principle, as a concept of theology, natural philosophy and the founding vision, is none other than the construction of a new community of nations (*communitas gentium*), identified as the holder of rights and the guardian of obligations vis-à-vis individual States.[97]

The international community as whole has been acknowledged as the holder of rights and obligations *ab omnibus* and *erga omnes*.[98] This notion presupposes that some rules and the respective values underlying them are far too important to be left within the sphere of bilateral States' understandings and relations;[99] they

[91] With reference to the *Breisach Trial* (*Hagenbach Case*, 1474), see Georg Schwarzenberger, *International Law as Applied by International Courts and Tribunals*, vol II (London, Stevens & Sons, 1968) 462–66. Compare *USA v Ernst von Weizsäcker et alt* (*The Ministries Case*) XIII TWC 97 (US NMT, 11 April 1949).

[92] Cançado Trindade (n 87) 37–39.

[93] L Henkin, 'International Law: Politics, Values and Functions; General Course on Public International Law' (1989) 216 *Recueil des Cours* 9, 127ff.

[94] Ch Tomuschat, 'Obligations Arising for States Without or Against Their Will' (1993) 241 *Recueil des Cours* 195, 227.

[95] H Mosler, *The International Society as a Legal Community* (Alphen aan den Rijn, AW Sijthoff, 1980) 1–5.

[96] B Simma and AL Paulus, 'The "International Community": Facing the Challenge of Globalization' (1998) 9 *European Journal of International Law* 266, 276.

[97] E de Wet, 'The International Constitutional Order' (2006) 55 *International & Comparative Law Quarterly* 51, 54ff.

[98] Cf *Nuclear Tests Case* (*New Zealand v France*) [1974] ICJ Rep 253, 474 [51]. See also Tomuschat, 'International Law' (n 33) 75ff. For a general reappraisal, see M Ragazzi, *The Concept of International Obligations Erga Omnes* (Oxford, Clarendon Press, 2000) 44ff.

[99] B Simma, 'From Bilateralism to Community Interests in International Law' (1994) 250 *Recueil des Cours* 217, 233.

enshrine a collective interest, so fundamentally necessary for the maintenance of the community that all States may raise a claim for ensuring its observance.[100]

Based on what has been said about the Vitorian system of hierarchy, we may find that the concept of *erga omnes* is actually quite reminiscent of the former; fundamental communitarian values that are guaranteed through the 'extraordinary legitimization' of action by all State actors, who can stake a claim for the restoration of the breached obligation even if they are not the injured party. Of course, nowadays States are not permitted to execute such obligations by force, unlike in the times of Vitoria or Grotius. On the contrary, they may only seek peaceful means of redress. Ultimately the concept of obligations *erga omnes* is used for the recognition of those who can raise a claim for compliance and redress vis-à-vis breached fundamental norms and their *locus standi*.[101] Certainly, the latter parameter (*jus standi*) has long been stalled due to the primacy attached to the equalitarian principle underlying the consent-based system of international jurisdiction.[102] Even so, it should not come as a surprise that values such as peaceful intercourse[103] and the sanctity of human life remain at the epicentre of this secondary order of values, guaranteed through the schemes of *jus cogens* and *erga omnes*.[104]

Similarly, the communitarian principle is still able to revitalise itself by adjusting to the needs and developments within the international social sphere. It remains stable but its secondary order is still evolving, including new concepts necessary for the maintenance of the communitarian bond.[105] The communitarian value is involved as a stable pillar upon which a secondary order can be construed, acting in an almost constitutional manner.[106] The normative concept of this *ordre public* (international public order)[107] is quite old;[108] it was present in the Founders' vision as an articulation of rational imperatives drawing validating authority from the community

[100] *Barcelona Traction* (n 89) [34].

[101] CJ Tams, A Tzanakopoulos, 'Barcelona Traction at 40: The ICJ as an Agent of Legal Development' (2010) 23 *Leiden Journal of International Law* 781, 792.

[102] Cf *Case Concerning East Timor (Portugal v Australia)* [1995] ICJ Rep 90, 104–105.

[103] *Case Concerning Military and Paramilitary Activities in and against Nicaragua (Nicaragua v USA)* (Merits) [1986] ICJ Rep 14, 98 [186].

[104] *Reservations to the Convention on the Prevention and Punishment of the Crime of Genocide*, (Advisory Opinion) [1951] ICJ Rep 15, 23.

[105] Cf PM Dupuy, 'L'unité de l'ordre juridique international: cours général de droit international public' (2002) 297 *Recueil des Cours* 9, 31–42.

[106] See Ph Allott, 'The Concept of International Law' (1999) 10 *European Journal of International Law* 31, 37.

[107] SA Riesenfeld, 'Jus Dispositivum and Jus Cogens in International Law' (1966) 60(3) *American Journal of International Law* 511; Th Meron, 'On A Hierarchy of International Human Rights' (1986) 80(1) *American Journal of International Law* 1, 19; GA Christenson, 'The World Court and Jus Cogens' (1987) 81(1) *American Journal of International Law* 93, 96; J Tasioulas, 'In Defence of Relative Normativity: Communitarian Values and the Nicaragua Case' (1996) 16(1) *Oxford Journal of Legal Studies* 85; A Orakhelashvili, Peremptory Norms in International Law (Oxford, Oxford University Press, 2008) 8ff.

[108] See Gómez Robledo, 'Le ius cogens international' (n 87) 23ff. On the idea of a certain order within public international law during the classical positivist period, cf JC Bluntschli, *Das moderne Völkerrecht der civilisirten Staaten als Rechtsbuch dargestellt* (Nördlingen, CH Beck, 1886) 234ff; FF Martens, *Traité de droit international*, vol I (Alfred Léo trans, Paris, Librairie Marescq Ainé, 1883) 551.

itself.[109] Thus the communitarian principle can, finally, achieve a partial independence from the self-interests of individual States. Its interests can be protected through the conceptualisation of obligations *erga omnes*, and its order guaranteed under the concept of *jus cogens*, with the latter being conceptualised both as a mechanism and as a substantive normative phenomenon.[110]

## B. *Jus Cogens*: International Law's 'Higher' Norms and an Enforcement Mechanism

It is a truism that the function of *jus cogens* as an enforcement mechanism has attracted considerable controversy.[111] The mainstream voluntarist approach addresses the issue as hyper-customary law[112] while the polemic on the existence of the notion, although indirect, still persists. It is obvious that the mechanism, detached from the concept of a secondary set of values creating a core-concept of *ordre public*, appears quite nebulous. It has been asserted that international law, as a primitive system, lacks verticality, which is necessary for the creation of such an *ordre*.[113] However, the function of municipal public policy proves that the aforementioned argument cannot be accepted.

In the domestic system, the concept is employed to ensure that extra-legal communitarian considerations form an integral part of positive jurisprudence, guaranteeing that private actors cannot deviate from them when exercising their contractual freedom.[114] Consequently, the epicentre lies not in the degree of development but in the presence of the communitarian value that dictates the maintenance of such principles necessary for the preservation of the community as a whole.[115] Through the articulation of such a mechanism, the community asserts its vital interests in preserving the order against adverse juridical acts. The 'force-suit' of the Founding Fathers' vision, given the stage of systemic development, is replaced by a special instrument causing not annihilation of the wrongdoer, but invalidation of the wrongful act. Thus this institution acts as a safety mechanism protecting communitarian values, and herein lies the very teleology of peremptory law.[116]

[109] de Vattel (n 76) *Preliminaries* 56. For the current reconstruction, see Tomuschat, 'International Law (n 33) 85–88. A practical application in, *Prosecutor v Anto Furundžija* (Judgment) IT-95-17/1-T, ICTY T Ch (10 December 1998), paras 151–56.

[110] Cf R Kolb, *Théorie de ius cogens international: Essai de relecture du concept* (Paris, PUF, 2001), 172ff.

[111] See AL Paulus, 'Jus Cogens in a Time of Hegemony and Fragmentation: An Attempt at a Re-appraisal' (2005) 74 *Nordic Journal of International Law* 297.

[112] A de Hoogh, *Obligations Erga Omnes and International Crimes: A Theoretical Inquiry into the Implementation and Enforcement of the International Responsibility of States* (The Hague, Kluwer Law International, 1996).

[113] G Schwarzenberger, 'International Jus Cogens?' (1965) 43 *Texas Law Review* 455.

[114] Cf Orakhelashvili (n 107) 11–20.

[115] PM Dupuy (n 105) 270–71.

[116] M Byers, 'Conceptualising the Relationship between Jus Cogens and Erga Omnes Rules' (1997) 66(2) *Nordic Journal of International Law* 211, 219.

Furthermore, the almost unequivocal consensus regarding the *jus naturalistic* component of this particular law (that is, international peremptory law)[117] allows us to assert that the sub-concept in question brings into the twenty-first century the objective law envisaged by the Founding Fathers as a primary normative guarantee of the communitarian value. This higher law remains an open category that is perennially evolving, based on communitarian necessities. Unlike during the Founders' era, we do not find ourselves preoccupied with the *Corpus Iuris* or the Scriptures in trying to decode these norms, but we must refer to what has been described as an inherently Thomist reappraisal of the international community's rational edicts.[118] Thus, through State practice, multilateral treaties, concerted acts, and other emanations of international legislation (either soft or hard law documents) we are able to discover or reidentify the essential communitarian values by applying a deductive process.

Much as in the Founding Fathers' era, the need for an impartial adjudicator able to undertake this task is paramount. This third part (*tertia pars*) is sought through the ages, from Grotius to today.[119] We can all understand that the basic values stemming from the communitarian principle, namely peace, security, solidarity, sociability and finally the all-inclusive idea of justice, remain present through the ages and the different phases of international law's evolutionary process.[120] What we need is an authoritative pronouncement of their positive legal existence, adding to an already essential (though absent) mechanism of enforcement. This is the reason why, ultimately, the scholarly debate on hierarchy concludes with notions of justiciability and the functions of international adjudication.[121]

## C. A Kelsenian Exegesis of International Peremptory Law Adjudication: The '*Aiguilleur*' Theorem

In the international legal order, by the mere act of recognition of fundamental norms and values, the problem of the judicial guarantee vis-à-vis the aforementioned constituent elements of our juridical cosmos arises and demands a solution in harmony with the very nature of the system.[122] A possibly viable solution would be to entrust the tutelage of fundamental values to the international judiciary. All in all, the law-creating competence of international judicial fora appears as a salient point of the relevant legal discourse, from the consolidation of the very first permanent

[117] See Dupuy (n 105) 202; de Wet (n 97) 57.

[118] MH O'Connell, 'Jus Cogens: International Law's Higher Ethical Norms' in DE Childress III (ed), *The Role of Ethics in International Law* (Cambridge, Cambridge University Press, 2011) 78, 93–97.

[119] Cf Brown Scott, *The Catholic Conception* (n 3) 44.

[120] See the overall approach of Tomuschat, 'International law' (n 33) 91ff.

[121] On this point, see G Gaja, 'The Protection of General Interests in the International Community: General Course on Public International Law' (2011) 364 *Recueil des Cours* 9, 110ff.

[122] See, for instance, the discussion of the celebrated *Furundžija dictum* (ICTY T Ch, 1998) and its implications concerning the justiciability of claims arising from a breach of the *jus cogens* prohibition of torture in E de Wet, 'The Prohibition of Torture as an International Norm of Jus Cogens and Its Implications for National and Customary Law' (2004) 15(1) *European Journal of International Law* 97.

adjudicator to the outer limits of the international courts' and tribunals' excessive proliferation.[123]

However, fundamental values are defined by their communitarian nature and therein lies their necessary character. Consequently, by accepting that the constituent principles of the international order rest within the international community and its equally sovereign member States, the role of international justice is slightly altered.[124] To elaborate, the principle norm-creating powers are enshrined in the core of the international community as a collective entity and and the sovereign States as the primary subjects of the said community (i.e. international community). These are the only legislative actors of the international system able to produce both fundamental and ordinary norms.[125]

The role of the judiciary vis-à-vis this *quasi-constitutional* (fundamental) branch of international jurisprudence[126] cannot be rendered equally constitutive. On the contrary, it is both interpretative and declaratory.[127] Through the interpretation of the extant primary or raw juridical data, the judge can inductively identify positive emanations of quasi-constitutional principles and their secondary normative order (providing a positively consolidating interpretation).[128] For instance, this *stricto sensu* inductive approach or positively consolidating interpretation was exercised during the *Nicaragua* case before the International Court of Justice.[129] There, the International Court of Justice (ICJ) identified an intransgressible, fundamental norm (the general prohibition of the use or threat of force in international relations against the territorial integrity and/or the political independence of a sovereign State),[130] extending far beyond its conventional or customary status. It did so by means of an inductive process and the legal classification of raw juridical data.[131]

Even under this consolidating interpretative formula, judicial articulation is bound by the methods of generating peremptory law. Thus no international judicial organ can create or destroy what has been established as *jus cogens* without reference to the actual practice of the law-creating authority, namely the

[123] An exhaustive approach respecting the several hard cases of judicial legislation, see H Lauterpacht, *The Development of International Law by the International Court of Justice*, 2nd rev edn, (London, Stevens & Sons, 1958) 155ff. Compare also CJ Tams and James Sloan (eds), *The Development of International Law by the International Court of Justice* (Oxford, Oxford University Press, 2013).

[124] On the dilemmas posed by the proliferation of international judicial fora, see—in general—B Conforti, 'The Role of the Judge in International Law' (2007) 1(2) *European Journal of Legal Studies* 6.

[125] See the relevant *dictum* in *Legality of the Threat or Use of Nuclear Weapons* (Advisory Opinion) [1996] ICJ Rep 226, 237 [18].

[126] Cf Byers (n 116) 212, 219ff. See also Allott (n 34) 306; Robert Uerpmann, 'Internationales Verfassungsrecht' (2001) 56(11) *Juristenzeitung* 565, 569–71.

[127] Cf CA Ford, 'Adjudicating Jus Cogens' (1994) 13(1) *Wisconsin International Law Journal* 145, 168ff.

[128] See—with reference to the crystallisation of *jus cogens* normative emanations—G Schwarzenberger, *The Inductive Approach to International Law* (London, Stevens & Sons, 1965) 100ff.

[129] *Nicaragua* case (n 103) 100–101 [190].

[130] See Y Dinstein, *War, Aggression and Self-Defence*, 4th edn, (Cambridge, Cambridge University Press, 2005) 99–104.

[131] Certainly, the Court never refered directly to the quasi-constitutional character of the principle per se; however, the judicial articulation of the said norm was actually the first derogation from the classical doctrine on the modification of customary rules through a breach process. See PM Dupuy, *Droit international public*, 6th edn (Paris, Dalloz, 2002) 316ff.

international community and its sovereign members. For whoever accepts the communitarian principle as a source of normativity (actually as the *hierarchically* superior source)[132] is bound to accept the communitarian norm-creating process as the only possible procedural mechanism for the establishment of peremptory norms.

Furthermore, the judicial phase following the emergence of the rule is fundamentally different, since the norm, once duly articulated, becomes objective and escapes the absurdity of voluntary consolidation to the detriment of consent itself.[133] For, if peremptory law were consensual, even after its emergence there would be no cogent reason for pre-excluding the possibility of its alteration by the mere juridical fact of *consensus contrarius*. Nevertheless, one may not disregard the fact that peremptory law, as an objective concept, can and most probably will be altered.[134]

This modification process, however, will be equal to a quasi-constitutional amendment—to employ the domestic analogy—and will, consequently, demand legitimisation both subjectively (as a communitarian process) and objectively (as an alteration necessary for the preservation of the system).[135] Herein lies the very quintessence of the declaratory competence of international courts and tribunals, as the *'switchman'* of this process. Much like the Kelsen's constitutional law theory on the *juge aiguilleur* ('switchman' judge)[136] the court can only declare either that an alleged peremptory norm has or has not been duly articulated or that, given the consolidation of a similar norm, the alleged modification has or has not been effective.[137] The content of the norm, original or modified, cannot be judged per se.

[132] Whose normative outcome (*jus cogens*) is a body of 'supreme' or (international) 'constitutional' law; see A Cassese, *International Law*, 2nd edn, (Oxford, Oxford University Press, 2005) 202.

[133] See Tomuschat, 'Obligations Arising for States' (n 94) 306ff.

[134] To this end, see ILC, 'Draft Articles on the Law of Treaties with Commentaries' in the 'Report of the International Law Commission on the Second Part of its Seventeenth Session and on its Eighteenth Session' UN Doc A/6309/Rev.l in (1966) II *Yearbook of the International Law Commission* 177, 248; SA Riesenfeld (n 107) 514–15; M Virally, 'Réflexions sur le "jus cogens"' (1966) 12 *Annuaire Francais de Droit International* 5, 18–19 and n 13; Byers (n 116) 227.

[135] On the constitutional law analogy, see M Virally (n 134) 19 and n 13 and Byers (n 116) 227 and n 61. On the modification of *jus cogens* norms in general, see Ch Rozakis, *The Concept of Jus Cogens in the Law of Treaties* (Amsterdam, New York, Oxford, North-Holland Publishing, 1976) 85–94. According to B Fassbender, 'The Meaning of International Constitutional Law' in N Tsagourias (ed), *Transnational Constitutionalism: International and European Perspectives* (Cambridge, Cambridge University Press, 2007) 307, 318: 'The jus cogens perspective of international constitutional law is ... particularly value-orientated.'

[136] According to Kelsen, judicial engagement vis-à-vis constitutional law cannot be conceived in a norm-creating context. A judge facing litigation involving fundamental norms of a constitutional nature can only decide whether or not the fundamental norm exists; to express it differently, the judge can allocate the norm-creating competence. Consequently, the judiciary cannot decree on anything other than the existence of the competence to produce a fundamental norm and the existence or non-existence of the norm in question. Due to the constitutional judge's competence-allocating function, Kelsen utilised the term *judge-switchman* (*juge aiguilleur*). See H Kelsen, 'La garantie juridictionnelle de la constitution (La Justice constitutionnelle)' (1928) 45 *Revue du droit public et de la science politique* 197, See also Georges Vedel, 'Souveraineté et supraconstitutionnalité' [1993] *Revue Pouvoirs* No 67, 79; L Favoreu, *La Politique saisie par le droit: alternances, cohabitation et conseil constitutionnel* (Paris, Economica, 1989) 30ff.

[137] The ICJ—or any other international tribunal—may allocate the jurisdiction of generating or modifying a *jus cogens* norm, but it cannot do so under its own authority, because the titular bearer of the norm-creating authority is an entity different from the one administering justice in its name [on the problem of in whose name justice is served before international judicial fora, see A von Bogdandy and

To put it differently, the court has no legitimacy to rule on what is necessary for the perpetuation of the international communitarian system and cannot permissibly substitute the sovereign actors, as the only authors of this quasi-constitutional legislative process.

However, the judiciary can act as a Kelsenian peremptory law *switchman*, notifying all interested parties either that the consolidation of the norm is still in process or that a proposed amendment was not properly effectuated on the terms of subjective participation and/or compliance with the standard norm-creating procedure. It is true that, until now, international courts have demonstrated a great deal of self-restraint concerning their mission as quasi-constitutional judicial actors. Both the *East Timor* litigation[138] and the *Jurisdictional Immunities* case[139] illustrate the self-restrictive interpretation of the *aiguilleur* function. Nevertheless, the domestic analogy is not totally adequate to describe an international tribunal's dealing with the non-development or non-existence of a peremptory norm.

To elaborate, it is possible that such a ruling on the norm-creating procedure of a fundamental norm will develop indirect effects concerning the substance of the adjudicated rule. It would be completely justified for an international tribunal to declare that—given the present stage of international law's development—a certain norm (or a certain legal consequence of a norm), pertaining to the constituent principles of the international legal order, has not *yet* been crystallised. However, the international judge has no legitimacy or capacity to declare authoritatively that such a norm (or consequence) could not be accepted into the international legal order because of its content or its ontological antithesis to an already established non-peremptory norm. This is an indirect verdict on the substance of peremptory law and must not be accepted, even as an *obiter*, because it is not for a court of law but for the international community and its sovereign members to act as the final and ultimate judge of such a matter.

The substantialisation of the *jus cogens* debate,[140] subsequent to the ICJ's ruling on the *Jurisdictional Immunities* case may be identified as an indirect excess of this kind. The ICJ has ultimately decreed that *jus cogens* norms pertain to the substance while the institution of jurisdictional immunities is procedural in nature. Substance cannot affect procedure, and consequently a violation of *jus cogens* norms cannot develop any kind of procedural consequences, modifying the doctrine of jurisdictional immunities. Thus it left no room for States to either enhance or

I Venzke, 'In Whose Name? An Investigation of International Courts' Public Authority and Its Democratic Justification' (2012) 23(1) *European Journal of International Law* 7]; on the similar function of the *switchman theory* in municipal constitutional law, see D Baranger, 'The Language of Eternity: Judicial Review of the Amending Power in France (Or the Absence Thereof)' (2001) 44 *Israel Law Review* 389, 406–407.

[138] *Case Concerning East Timor* (*Portugal v Australia*) [1995] ICJ Rep 90, 102. See also *Armed Activities in the Territory of Congo (New Application: 2002)* (*DR of Congo v Rwanda)* (Jurisdiction and Admissibility) [2006] ICJ Rep 6, 32 [64].

[139] *Case Concerning Jurisdictional Immunities of the State* (*FR of Germany v Italy: Greece Intervening*) [2012] ICJ Rep 99, 140 [93].

[140] Cf S Talmon, 'Jus Cogens after Germany v Italy: Substantive and Procedural Rules Distinguished' (2012) 25 *Leiden Journal of International Law* 979.

impugn this particular procedural consequence of a *jus cogens* norm. Instead of *res judicata jus facit inter partes* (issue preclusion), it attached an indirect *inter omnes* effect, finally setting the terms of the modification debate on a dualistic confrontation between substance (*jus cogens* norms) and procedure (jurisdictional immunity).[141] Thus from a mere tension between the two concepts, pending a final settlement of the issue under the process envisaged by Article 53 of the VCLT, the Court effectuated a proper antinomy, which led to the controversial judgment of the Italian Constitutional Court which overturned—on grounds of unconstitutionality[142]—the domestic law ensuring compliance with the International Court's ruling in the *Jurisdictional Immunities* case.[143]

Consequently, under the *aiguilleur* scheme, a judicial intervention prior to the completion of the crystallisation or modification debate (regarding, of course, the secondary principles and their normative emanations) cannot be tolerated, for it is not an authoritative interpretation of the law as it stands, but an incoherent projection to a future point of juridical time, upon which the court concludes that the modification attempt will or will not become effective. Such a ruling effectively lacks legitimacy and cannot be grounded upon the law-declaring and law-enforcing function of the international judiciary.[144] The settlement of this kind of inter-state dispute calls for an extra-*aguilleur* interpretation of international peremptory law adjudication, which is reserved exclusively for States as primary actors in the international community. Certainly, the aforementioned disputes are legal and can be resolved pursuant to the law, but any settlement must necessarily be temporary in nature, given the pending phase of the process. Otherwise the very core of *jus cogens* as a practical emanation of the international order, that is, the order of the international community of equally sovereign States, will be substituted by a *sui generis* 'government' of the international judiciary.[145]

[141] This was an idea already adopted in the *Case Concerning the Arrest Warrant of 11 April 2000 (DR Congo v Belgium)* [2002] ICJ Rep 3, and further elaborated in the *Jurisdictional Immunities Case*. For a critique of this dichotomy between substance and process, see A Orakhelashvili, 'State Immunity and International Public Order Revisited' (2006) 49 *German Yearbook of International Law* 327; A Orakhelashvili, 'Peremptory Norms as an Aspect of Constitutionalisation of the International Legal System' in M Frishman, S Muller (eds), *The Dynamics of Constitutionalism in the Age of Globalization* (The Hague, Hague Academic Press/TMC Asser Press, 2010) 153; Ph Webb, 'Human Rights and the Immunities of State Officials' in E de Wet and J Vidmar (eds), *Hierarchy in International Law: The Place of Human Rights* (Oxford, Oxford University Press, 2012) 300, 308.

[142] C Const., Sentenza No 238/2014, GU 29 October 2014, No 45 (Italy, Const Ct, 2014). On the previous attitude of the Italian jurisprudence and the *Ferrini Case* (*Ferrini c. Repubblica Federale di Germania* 128 *ILR* 658), see M Iovane, 'The Ferrini Judgment of the Italian Supreme Court: Opening Up Domestic Courts to Claims of Reparation for Victims of Serious Violations of International Human Rights' (2004) 14 *Italian Yearbook of International Law* 165.

[143] Article 3 of Law of 14 January 2013, No 5, Gazzetta ufficiale, Ser Gener No 24, 29 gennaio 2013.

[144] See M Bothe, 'Remedies of Victims of War Crimes and Crimes against Humanities: Some Critical Remarks on the ICJ's Judgment on the Jurisdictional Immunity' in A Peters, E Lagrange and Ch Tomuschat (eds), *Immunities in the Age of Global Constitutionalism* (Leiden, Martinus Nijhoff, 2014) 99, 111–12; M Krajewski and Christopher Singer 'Should Judges be Front-Runners? The ICJ, State Immunity and the Protection of Fundamental Human Rights' (2012) 16 *Max Planck Yearbook of United Nations Law* 1, 30ff.

[145] Cf MA Kaplan and N Katzenbach, 'Law in the International Community' in RA Falk, SH Mendlovitz (eds), *The Strategy of World Order*, vol II (New York, World Law Fund, 1966) 19, 20.

## III. CONCLUSION

Even when facing the latter dilemma of a potential *sui generis* government, one cannot escape the necessity of an impartial third party who is able and willing to perform the *consolidating* (interpretative and declaratory) function, a condition *sine qua non* for the crystallisation and the enforcement of peremptory norms. Whether the existent international tribunals are the most appropriate *fora* for such a task remains to be seen.[146] Until then, it must be borne in mind that accepting the communitarian value's persistence is neither a commendation nor a repudiation of the consensualist tradition. It is a mere reiteration of the original and founding vision of the international legal order; communitarian bonds are forced out of natural necessity and these bonds give rise to certain secondary values, forming an order able to secure the maintenance of these bonds. These values, although receiving validation upon the existence of the community, are paramount for the system and universal for humanity itself. They were, more or less, present at almost every stage in the development of international law. Finally, we cannot disregard that international law is a legal system whose edifice is construed by independent States, and solidified through their consent; ultimately, it is a legal system founded upon the communitarian value and preserved by the fundamental pillars emanating from the latter.

[146] *In abstracto*, the function of the international judiciary as a promoting and empowering actor regarding the development of peremptory norms is undisputable, as it was in the initial phase of *jus cogens'* evolution. See in general, the discussion in Carnegie Endowment for International Peace, *The Concept of Jus Cogens in International Law* (Geneva, European Centre of the Carnegie Endowment for International Peace, 1967) 11–12.

# 25

# *The Inextricable Connection between Historical Consciousness and International Law: New Imperialism, the International Court of Justice and its Interpretation of the Inter-temporal Rule*

MIEKE VAN DER LINDEN*

## I. INTRODUCTION

EUROPEAN COLONIAL POWERS impaired the sovereignty of the native ruler, breached their obligations under the treaties that they had concluded with native polities, and violated customary international law. On the basis of customary international law, European States were bound to observe their obligations towards, and the rights of, African nations. More concretely, European States had a legal duty to observe the obligations they consented to in cession and protectorate treaties with African rulers. But they failed to do so. The excessive interpretation and employment of sovereign rights on the side of the European colonial powers after the conclusion of cession and protectorate treaties demonstrated disrespect for sovereignty and, subsequently, the property of the original population of Africa. The African rights of the *dominium* had to make way for European rights of *imperium*.[1]

With the conclusion that European colonisation of Africa at the end of the nineteenth century was illegal because cession and protectorate treaties had been violated, the first of the two questions posed at the World Conference Against Racism, Racial Discrimination, Xenophobia and Related Intolerance (WCAR Conference), which was held under the auspices of the United Nations in Durban from 31 August until 8 September 2001, the question whether colonisation was in accordance with

* The text of this chapter was completed while a post-doctoral researcher in legal history and international law at the Max Planck Institute of Comparative Public Law and International Law, Heidelberg.

[1] See M van der Linden, *The Acquisition of Africa (1870–1914): The Nature of Nineteenth-Century International Law* (Wolf Legal Publishers, 2014).

international law and valid at the time of colonisation, was answered. The second central issue discussed at the WCAR Conference, involved the establishment of responsibility for a historical wrongful act such as the colonisation of Africa. And, if the act was wrongful, were there remedies available within international law to redress this historical wrong? It would go beyond the scope of this contribution to answer both these questions on responsibility and remedies. Instead, this chapter addresses the origins of the problem of establishing responsibility and the available remedies for historical wrongs, which are comprised in the doctrine of inter-temporal law. It questions what the inter-temporal rule involves in the context of international law and how it is, and how it should be, applied with regard to the illegal nature of Africa's colonisation.

## II. THE INTER-TEMPORAL RULE

Time, in particular the lapse of time, confronts us with various problems and is sometimes even experienced as an obstacle in establishing the law in its historical context. Against this problematic lapse of time and the question whether we are able to assess past actions, according to the standards of the time, the question to be answered is under what conditions a claim of responsibility for international wrongful actions can be lodged. Between committing the internationally wrongful acts at the end of the nineteenth century and the claim for responsibility of (former) European colonial States lies a period of more than a hundred years that have hosted several generations of human society.

Parties who were affected by the internationally wrongful acts have passed away, which makes the treatment of a claim for responsibility and reparation almost impossible. They are succeeded by generations who live in their own contemporary societies and are usually little aware of the historic wrongs done to their ancestors.

Aside from lawyers, there are authors from the fields of political philosophy and history who argue that it is impossible and undesirable to re-evaluate the remote past: they claim that the past cannot be altered and that bygones should be bygones.[2] The lapse of time coincides with changing circumstances and the supersession of historical wrongs that consequently leads to the possibility of victims and their descendants having their claims rectified, fading over time. Moreover, under the assumption of *interest rei publicae ut finis litium sit*—it is in the public interest that legal procedures should have an end—which is better known as the principle of finality, the saying that old sores should be forgotten is commendable.[3] For now, however, the question is how legal scholars and practitioners should respond to the past and the responsibility for historical wrongs. Their innate reflex is, and should be, to rely on the doctrine of inter-temporal rule.

[2] See J Waldron, 'Superseding Historic Injustice' (1992) 103 *Ethics* 4–28. See also A De Baets, 'Historical Imprescriptibility' (2011) 59 *Storia della Storiografia* 142.

[3] De Baets (n 2) 142. See also MG Kohen, *Possession contestée et souveraineté territoriale* (Presses Universitaires de France, 1997) 183–200; and R Higgins, 'Time and the Law: International Perspectives on an Old Problem' (1997) 46 *International & Comparative Law Quarterly* 511.

The next two Sections outline the general features of the doctrine of inter-temporal law and provide an exposé of how the International Court of Justice (ICJ) understands and applies the doctrine.

## A. General Features of the Inter-temporal Rule

In situations of territorial conflicts—often having their roots in colonialism—the main issue is to ascertain the legal rights and obligations existing at a relevant period of time in the past. In this respect, the inter-temporal rule doctrine offers a way forward. Inter-temporal law formally[4] had its origin in the *Island of Palmas* case (1928),[5] in which arbitrator Max Huber had to decide on a rather common dispute. The United States, which was considered to be the legal successor to Spain with respect to title to the Philippines, based its claim to sovereignty over the Island of Palmas primarily on the basis of discovery of the island by Spain. The Netherlands, however, claimed that at the time of cession in 1898 they possessed title to the Island by way of effective occupation.

Alongside other fundamental conceptions, Huber articulated the inter-temporal rule as a response to the problem of changing conditions and circumstances that are relevant to international law and its principles after a certain time period when he stated that: '[A] juridical fact must be appreciated in the light of the law with it, and not of the law in force at the time when a dispute in regard to it arises or falls to be settled.'[6] Huber went on to say that:

> As regards the question which of different legal systems prevailing at successive periods is to be applied in a particular case (the so-called intertemporal law), a distinction must be made between the creation of rights and the existence of rights. The same principle which subjects the act creative of a right to the law in force at the time the right arises, demands that the existence of the right, in other words its continued manifestation, shall follow the conditions required by the evolution of law.[7]

With this, Huber pronounced the doctrine of inter-temporal law that has two components. The first component, better known as the non-retroactive application of rules, prescribes that acts should be understood and assessed in the light of contemporary law, that is, the law valid at the time of their creation.[8] The second component, however, holds that the evolution of the law has to be taken into account when assessing the continued existence of a right. As Judge Taslim Elias explained,

[4] Before the explicit formulation of the inter-temporal rule by Huber in 1928, the rule was already a recognised principle in international law. See H Lauterpacht, *The Function of Law in the International Community* (Clarendon Press, 1933) 284.

[5] *Island of Palmas (Netherlands v United States of America)* 1928, 2 RIAA 829.

[6] Ibid 831 and 845.

[7] Ibid.

[8] For a detailed reading on the non-retroactive application of international law, see JT Woodhouse, 'The Principle of Retroactivity in International Law' (1955) 41 *Transactions of the Grotius Society* 69–89. Woodhouse also shows that the acknowledgement of the existence of the principle of non-retroactivity already had a long history. Ibid 69.

'rights acquired in a valid manner according to the law contemporaneous with that creation may be lost if not maintained in accordance with the changes brought about by the development of international law'.[9] Or, in the words of Daniel-Erasmus Khan, 'acts must be assessed against the law of the time when performed but at the same time the claimant must keep up with the law in the course of the centuries in order to maintain their title'.[10]

Specifically, the second element of the inter-temporal rule could account for the criticism which was expressed by Phillip Jessup. He pointed out that, in the context of determining the precise title to territory: 'Every state would constantly be under the necessity of examining its title to each portion of its territory in order to determine whether a change in the law had necessitated, as it were, a reacquisition.'[11] As a result, Jessup concluded, chaos would reign.

In his argument, Huber had articulated the need to achieve equilibrium between the acquisition and the maintenance of a title to territory.[12] Paul Tavernier has rejected the idea of only mentioning one of the two rules as 'either the first rule which evokes the well-known adage *tempus regit actum* [the law in force at the time of the act], or the second rule which spells out the distinction between creating and maintaining a right. The choice to mention one without the other is evidently not neutral.'[13] Therefore, Tavernier claims that when mentioning the inter-temporal rule both parts deserve equal attention. The problem of the application and interpretation of rules in time is one of the most elusive in all legal systems and is not limited to the issue of the acquisition of territory. The non-retroactivity of norms of international law has been and still is a fundamental principle.[14] It is a matter of determining whether new

[9] TO Elias, 'The Doctrine of Intertemporal Law' (1980) 74 *American Journal of International Law* 286.

[10] D-E Khan, 'Max Huber as Arbitrator: The Palmas (Miangas) Case and Other Arbitrations' (2007) 18 *European Journal of International Law* 167.

[11] PC Jessup, 'The Palmas Island Arbitration' (1928) 22 *The American Journal of International Law* 740.

[12] Huber's findings were not uncontroversial, as has been mentioned already. However, Johnson puts this commentary in perspective by stating that 'many of these criticisms answer themselves provided it be understood that, whilst every title under international law must undergo a continuous process of "maintenance" or "manifestation," the degree of "maintenance" or "manifestation" required varies in accordance with the circumstances. In particular, it depends upon the absence or presence of competing claims.' DHN Johnson, 'Consolidation as a Root of Title' (1955) 13 *Cambridge Law Journal* 224.

[13] P Tavernier, 'Relevance of the Intertemporal Law' in J Crawford, A Pellet and S Olleson (eds), *The Law of International Responsibility. Oxford Commentaries on International Law* (Oxford University Press, 2010) 397.

[14] For an detailed reading on inter-temporal law and retroactivity, see O Bachelet, 'Face à l'alternative "rétroactivité ou immédiateté": la Cour européenne ne récidive pas' (2007) 18 *Revue trimestrielle des droits de l'homme* 233–45; D Bindschedler-Robert, 'De la rétroactivité en droit international public' in *Recueil d'études de droit international en hommage à Paul Guggenheim* (University of Genève Press, 1986) 184–200; A Cassese, 'Balancing the Prosecution of Crimes against Humanity and Non-Retroactivity of Criminal Law: *The Kolk and Kislyiy v Estoni* a Case before the ECHR' (2006) 4 *Journal of International Criminal Justice* 410–18; R Higgins, 'Some Observations on the Inter-Temporal Rule in International Law' in J Makaczyk (ed), *Theory of International Law at the Threshold of the 21st Century. Essays in Honour of Krysztof Skubiszewski* (Martinus Nijhoff, 1996) 173–81; Higgins, 'Time and the Law' (n 3); E McWhinney, 'The Time Dimension in International Law, Historical Relativism and Intertemporal Law' in J Makarczyk (ed), *Essays in International Law in Honour of Judge Manfred Lachs* (Martinus Nijhoff,

rules apply to facts, acts, or situations that took place or were established—or began to take place or to be established—before the entry into force of these new rules. Similarly, the application of rules to factual conditions raises the issue of whether these rules must be interpreted in the light of standards that existed at the time these circumstances took place or were established, or whether an 'evolving' interpretation is permissible. The issue that arises in the latter situation could be interpreted as a kind of retroactive application of law. In this respect, Edward McWhinney states that inter-temporal law presents

> both the contemporary conflict between the 'old' and the 'new' in legal doctrine—representing, on the one hand, the more traditional forces oriented to preservation of the political and economic status quo of yesterday, and also the newer political forces oriented to changing law in accord with changing society; and also the opportunities and challenge of judicial policy-making ... in behalf of a new and more nearly representative, in ethnic-cultural terms, World public order system, reflecting the new and more pluralistic World Community of today.[15]

However, the question remains whether a contemporary or an evolutionary interpretation prevails or should prevail. Although these components appear contradictory—the first component advocates a static and non-retroactive interpretation of international law, while the second reflects a dynamic and evolutionary perspective on international law—they are not. In 1975, the Institut de Droit International adopted a resolution on the phenomenon of inter-temporality in international law,[16] which underlined the interplay between the non-retroactive and evolutionary application of international law.[17] The non-retroactivity of rules is essential for the existence and application of international law,[18] but to be able to respond to the needs of current actors within international law an evolutionary interpretation of international law is unavoidable.

1984) 179–99; R Provost, 'Reciprocity in Human Rights and Humanitarian Law' (1994) 65 *The British Yearbook of International Law* 383–454 and P Tavernier, 'Recherches sur l'application dans le temps des actes et des règles en droit international public. Problèmes de droit intertemporel ou de droit transitoire' (1970) 21 *Revue internationale de droit comparé* 9–54.

[15] McWhinney (n 14) 180. Shaw also notes the paradox of the need for the stability and flexibility of international law in relation to inter-temporal law. See MN Shaw, *International Law* 6th edn (Cambridge University Press, 2008) 508.

[16] 'The Inter-Temporal Problem in Public International Law, Resolution adopted by the Institut de Droit International at its Wiesbaden Session' (1975) 56 *Annulaire de l'Institut de Droit International* 537.

[17] '[T]he legality or illegality of historical events must be judged according to the law in force at the time in question, but the continuing effects of these events can be judged by more recent standards.' D Shelton, 'Reparations for Indigenous Peoples: The Present Value of Past Wrongs' in F Lenzerini, *Reparations for Indigenous Peoples* (Oxford University Press, 2008) 63.

[18] The non-retroactive application of international law is a customary rule and codified in, for example, Article 4 of the Vienna Convention on the Law of Treaties (1969). See ibid. Not only does the law of treaties underwrite the non-retroactive application of law; the rule is also fundamental in the fields of international criminal law and human rights. See, for example, KS Gallant, *The Principle of Legality in International and Comparative Criminal Law* (Cambridge University Press, 2009) and G Lautenbach, *The Concept of the Rule of Law and the European Court of Human Rights* (Oxford University Press, 2013) 107–108.

These two components of legal security and development both complement and limit each other.[19] In this light, it can be said that they are interdependent and reciprocal.[20] Although rules should not be applied retrospectively, they have been created and have to function within ever-changing human societies. The evolutionary approach and the retro-active application of rules do not necessarily exclude each other.

The resolution of a responsibility or a reparations claim for historical wrongs require, therefore, the determination of the law applicable to (f)acts that commenced or were concluded in the past. But what does the inter-temporal rule, containing both the non-retrospective and the evolutionary component, mean for the particular question of the legality of the acquisition and partition of Africa? Or, what implications does the doctrine of inter-temporal law have for the central question of the responsibility claim arising out of the colonisation of Africa at the end of the nineteenth century? The applicability of the doctrine depends on the preliminary question whether or not the act of colonisation was legal.

On the basis of contemporary international law, it has to be established whether the conduct of European States could be considered as wrongful; and whether their acts were illegal according to the law valid at the moment of the commitment of these acts. If the illegality of these acts can be established, they do not have to be interpreted and assessed retroactively. In that case, the behaviour of European colonial powers was against the law in the international legal context during the colonial era. Moreover, the illegal nature of Africa's colonisation at the end of the nineteenth century was not annulled by the evolution of the law over the course of time. What happened back then is still not in accordance with international law.[21] In other words, on the basis of the inter-temporal rule and without any difficulty in its application, Africa's colonisation was an act which did not meet the standards of international law either then or now.

In the context of the colonisation of Africa during the Age of New Imperialism, the application of the inter-temporal rule does not cause direct problems. There are legal grounds on which the responsibility of former European colonial powers for the illegal acquisition and partition of African territory can be based. As we have seen, Europeans disrespected native landownership and sovereignty, breached treaty obligations and violated international law. On the basis of contemporary

[19] Elias (n 9) 291.

[20] See ibid 292.

[21] Nowadays, the unilateral extension of sovereign rights over territory by a State at the cost of the sovereignty of another State is a controversial issue and is rejected by most international legal actors. See J Crawford, *The Creation of States in International Law* (Oxford University Press, 2006); RY Jennings, *The Acquisition of Territory in International Law* (Manchester University Press, 1963) 37; Shaw (n 15) 197–216 and 492–95 and JG Starke, 'The Acquisition of Title to Territory by Newly Emerged States' (1965) 41 *British Yearbook of International Law* 413. In addition, the principle of non-intervention in the internal or external affairs of other States is fundamental for the existence of the international (legal) order—which had a determining role in the history of international law—and has a prominent place in Article 2(4) of the UN Charter. For a general elaboration on the principle, see Cassese (n 14) 53–54 and Shaw (n 15) 211–14. See also M Jamnejad and M Wood, 'The Principle of Non-Intervention' (2009) 22 *Leiden Journal of International Law* 345 and P Kunig, 'Prohibition of Intervention' in R Wolfrum (ed), *Max Planck Encyclopedia of Public International Law* (Oxford University Press, 2007).

nineteenth-century international law, the conduct of European States could already be considered as wrongful; their acts were illegal according to the law valid at the moment of the commitment of the wrongs. No backward legal evaluation of the factual conditions involved is, therefore, needed.

Problems regarding the application of the inter-temporal rule can, however, arise, especially in the case of emerging fields of international law. The rule has to be employed in cases of, for example, human rights violations. Our current arsenal of human rights instruments such as the Universal Declaration of Human Rights (1948) and the International Covenant on Civil and Political Rights (1966) cannot be employed to assess the colonial activities of the European States on the African continent and the subjection of African native peoples and lands to European power at the end of the nineteenth century. Further, neither the International Law Commission's Vienna Convention on the Law of Treaties (1969),[22] which partly reflects customary law[23] and forms the basis of discussions on the nature, content and procedures of treaties, nor the Articles on the Responsibility of States for International Wrongful Actions (2001) is applicable when considering the legality of treaties between Europeans and African natives and the possibility of the invocation of the responsibility of (former) European colonial States. Here, international judges play a vital role. Within the context of international adjudication and the understanding and application of the inter-temporal rule, the ICJ has enunciated decisions in cases in which it had to assess the validity of treaties, or to interpret their provisions.

## B. The International Court of Justice and the Inter-temporal Rule

The ICJ was confronted with the problem of inter-temporal law, notably in the *Kasikili/Sedudu Island* case (1999)[24] and the *Cameroons v Nigeria* case (2002).[25] Especially in the second case on the conflict between Cameroon and Nigeria, being the subject of further inquiry, the ICJ applied the inter-temporal rule and indirectly addressed the question whether the acquisition of a specific part of Nigeria by Britain was legal or not. As will be argued, the ICJ pronounced and motivated its

[22] See D Greig, 'The Time of Conclusion and the Time of Application of Treaties as Points of Reference in the Interpretative Process' in M Craven, M Fitzmaurice and M Vogiatzi (eds), *Time, History and International Law* (Martinus Nijhoff, 2007) 163.

[23] See *Legal Consequences for States of the Continued Presence of South Africa in Namibia (South West Africa) Notwithstanding Security Council Resolution 276 (1970)*, Advisory Opinion, 1971, ICJ Reports 16, 47 and *Fisheries Jurisdiction (United Kingdom v Iceland)* Judgment 1973, ICJ Reports 3, 18 and 55. See also Shaw (n 15) 902–55 and M Villiger, *Customary International Law and Treaties: A Manual on the Theory and Practice of the Interrelation of Sources* (Martinus Nijhoff, 1985).

[24] *Kasikili/Sedudu Island (Botswana v Namibia)* Judgment, 1999, ICJ Reports 1045. See JT Gathii, 'Geographical Hegelianism in Territorial Disputes Involving Non-European Land Relations: An Analysis of the Case Concerning Kasikili/Sedudu Island (Botswana/Namibia)' (2002) 15 *Leiden Journal of International Law* 581–622; Greig (n 22) 209–15; and P Tavernier, 'Observations sur le droit intertemporel dans l'affaire de l'Ile de Kasikili/Sedudu (Botswana/Namibie), Cour internationale de Justice, arrêt du 13 décembre 1999' (2000) 104 *Revue Générale de Droit International Public* 429.

[25] *Land and Maritime Boundary between Cameroon and Nigeria (Cameroon v Nigeria: Equatorial Guinea intervening)* Judgment, 2002, ICJ Reports 303.

judgment from a particular legal perspective, which did not reflect contemporary law, that is, the law valid at the time the (f)acts occurred, and practice. However, before drawing preliminary conclusions, the reasoning of the Court in the dispute between Cameroon and Nigeria, with a particular focus on the inter-temporal question, must be analysed.

A conflict between Nigeria and Cameroon emerged over the title to a particular piece of territory. The source of the conflict was a cession treaty concluded between Britain and a native ruler in 1884. In this case, one of the main questions with which the ICJ was confronted was the establishment of the location of the land boundary between Cameroon and Nigeria.[26] This determination eventually came down to the question for the Court to decide whether Britain had been entitled to pass title to a particular piece of territory on the basis of Articles XVIII–XX of the Anglo-German Agreement of March 1913.[27]

The issue called for an examination of the colonial history of this particular piece of territory, the Bakassi peninsula. Cameroon and Nigeria disagreed on the status and effect of the Anglo-German Agreement of 1913. On the one hand, Cameroon argued that this treaty determined the boundary between Britain and Germany in the involved area, which implied that the Bakassi peninsula fell under German authority and, after independence, it became Cameroonian territory on the basis of the *uti possidetis* principle. Nigeria, on the other hand, recognised that the 1913 treaty intended to place the involved area in German hands.

Nigeria argued, however, that the treaty could not effectuate this because at the time of the cession Britain had no sovereign rights over the peninsula, and was thus unable to transfer it. The reason for this, according to Nigeria, was that in the protection treaty, concluded between Britain and the Kings and Chiefs of Old Calabar in July 1884,[28] only limited rights were conferred on Britain but this treaty certainly did

[26] For an analysis of the whole case, see MD Evans and JG Merrills, '*Land and Maritime Boundary between Cameroon and Nigeri* a (*Cameroon v Nigeria: Equatorial Guinea Intervening*) Merits, Judgment of 10 October 2002' (2003) 52 *International and Comparative Law Quarterly*, 788–97. See also JN Anyu, 'The International Court of Justice and Border-Conflict Resolution in Africa: The Bakassi Peninsula Conflict' (2007) 18 *Mediterranean Quarterly* 40; NJ Bekong, 'International Dispute Settlement: Land and Maritime Boundary Between Cameroon and Nigeria: Origin of the Dispute and Provisional Measures' (1997) 9 *African Journal of International and Comparative Law* 287; DD Caron and PHF Bekker, 'Land and Maritime Boundary Between Cameroon and Nigeria' (2003) 97 *American Journal of International Law* 387; B Kwiatkowska, 'The Contribution of the 2002 Land and Maritime Boundary between Cameroon and Nigeria Judgment' (2005) 17 *Hague Yearbook of International Law* 95; EM Mbah, *Land/Boundary Conflict in Africa. The Case of Former British Colonial Bamenda, Present-Day North-West Province of the Republic of Cameroon, 1916–1996* (Mellen, 2008) 24–34; E Milano, *Unlawful Territorial Situations in International Law. Reconciling Effectiveness, Legality and Legitimacy* (Nijhoff, 2006) 75–77; MN Shaw 'Acquisition of Title in Nineteenth Century Africa' in P-M Dupuy, B Fassbender, MN Shaw, KP Sommermann (eds), *Common Values in International Law. Essays in Honour of Christian Tomuschat* (Engel, 2006) 1029, 1045–47 and NJ Udombana, 'The Ghost of Berlin still haunts Africa! The ICJ Judgment on the Land and Maritime Boundary Dispute between Cameroon and Nigeria' (2002) 10 *African Yearbook of International Law* 13.

[27] Agreement between Germany and Great Britain respecting the Regulation of the Frontier between Nigeria and the Cameroons and the Navigation of the Cross River, 11 March 1913, *Oxford Historical Treaties*, 218 CTS 23.

[28] Treaty establishing a protectorate between Great Britain and the rulers of New Calabar, 4 July 1884, HT, vol xvii, 131.

not involve transfer of sovereignty over the territory. Nigeria concluded by asserting that sovereign rights remained in the hands of the Kings and Chiefs of Old Calabar.

The Court held that the cession of the Bakassi peninsula to Germany in 1913 was effective notwithstanding the fact that it appeared to breach the terms of the earlier protectorate treaty between Britain and the 'Kings and Chiefs of Old Calabar'. First, the Court observed that the Treaty of 1884 did not specify the territory to which Britain was to extend protection, 'nor did it indicate the territories over which the kings and chiefs exercised powers'.[29] According to the Court, this was done intentionally by Britain. The ICJ concluded that the 'Treaty of protection' was, in the light of general European practice in Sub-Saharan Africa, not an agreement that recognised or maintained the sovereignty of the Kings and Chiefs of Old Calabar.[30] It stated that:

> [M]any factors point to the 1884 Treaty signed with the Kings and Chiefs of Old Calabar as not establishing an international protectorate. It was one of a multitude in a region where the local Rulers were not regarded as States. Indeed, apart from the parallel declarations of various lesser Chiefs agreeing to be bound by the 1884 Treaty, there is not even convincing evidence of a central federal power. There appears in Old Calabar rather to have been individual townships, headed by Chiefs, who regarded themselves as owing a general allegiance to more important Kings and Chiefs. Further, from the outset Britain regarded itself as administering the territories in the 1884 Treaty, and not just protecting them.[31]

The Court considered the status and effect of the protection treaty of 1884 and observed that there were two types of treaty of protection. The first created protected States from which sovereign rights in international law were not alienated. The second type of protection treaty, establishing the so-called colonial protectorate, however, was in essence a means of acquiring title to territory. Eventually, the ICJ concluded that there was no evidence that the protection treaty could be considered as falling into the first category.

In support of this assertion the Court referred to the *Island of Palmas* case (1928), in which Arbitrator Huber stated that a treaty of protection 'is not an agreement between equals; it is rather a form of internal organisation of a colonial territory, on the basis of the autonomy of the natives ... And thus suzerainty over the native States becomes the basis of territorial sovereignty as towards other members of the community of nations.'[32] Continuous meetings and debates between Britain and local rulers of the protectorate were considered characteristic of relationships falling under an international protectorate. Nigeria, however, failed to provide the evidence for the existence of these relationships. The Court, therefore, held that the 1884 treaty, transferring sovereignty over the Bakassi Island to Britain, established a colonial protectorate, which it considered to be a legal means to acquire title to territory.[33]

[29] Caron and Bekker (n 26) 390.

[30] M Craven, 'Introduction: International Law and its Histories' in M Craven, M Fitzmaurice and M Vogiatzi (eds), *Time, History and International Law* (Martinus Nijhoff, 2007) 19.

[31] *Land and Maritime Boundary between Cameroon and Nigeria (Cameroon v Nigeria, Equatorial Guinea intervening)* Judgment, 2002, ICJ Reports 103.

[32] *Island of Palmas* (n 5) 858–59.

[33] *Land and Maritime Boundary between Cameroon and Nigeria* (n 26) paras 203–209.

With this reasoning, the Court asserted Britain's acquisition of sovereignty over the Bakassi peninsula, on the basis of the treaty between Britain and the Kings and Chiefs of Old Calabar and the absence of sovereign powers on the side of the African treaty powers. The Court rejected Nigeria's arguments that the 1884 Treaty rendered the Anglo-German Agreement of 1913 defective,[34] and concluded that, according to contemporary law, Great Britain was able to establish an agreement with Germany on the determination of the boundary between Nigeria and Cameroon. It is noteworthy that Judge Koroma and Judge Ajibola, the latter of whom was appointed *ad hoc*, dissented by arguing that the Court had wrongly decided that the Bakassi peninsula fell under Cameroonian authority, and that the Court should have accepted Nigeria's arguments regarding the nature and content of the protection treaty of 1884.

In particular, Judge Koroma rejected the findings of the Court and accused the Court of 'recogniz[ing]] and consecrate[ing] political reality' instead of applying the law in ruling on the dispute before it.[35] He supported Nigeria's arguments by elaborating on the nature and implications of the 1884 Treaty of Protection and the principle of *pacta sunt servanda*.[36] In principle, he argued that the transfer of the Bakassi to Germany violated the internationally recognised legal principle of *pacta sunt servanda* and the rights of the people of Old Calabar. And, although Judges Rezek and Al-Khasawneh agreed on the arguments of the two dissenting Judges, they did not align with them, because they held that the Kings and Chiefs of old Calabar had consented to a transfer of sovereignty by their subsequent conduct and the absence of protest against the effectuation of the protection treaty in the period after the conclusion of the treaty.

Although the ICJ clearly tried to apply the inter-temporal rule correctly, the case between Nigeria and Cameroon, as Matthew Craven has noted, 'also exposes the limits of this kind of historical enquiry'.[37] The Court saw it as its task to interpret the treaty between Britain and the rulers of Old Calabar and to assess the status of the document by referring to the standards of treaty interpretation that were valid at the end of the nineteenth century, instead of referring to current rules. Concerning its approach, however, the ICJ made a step in its reasoning which can only be understood from a 'Euro-centric' perspective.[38] Craven analysed this line of argument as follows:

> Working from the apparent assumption that international law was largely Eurocentric in outlook, and actively facilitated the process of colonisation rather than resisted it, the Court seemed to conclude that relevant actors at the time would not have recognised the sovereignty and treaty-making capacity of the King and Chiefs, and hence that the treaty was not

[34] Ibid paras 193–99 and 201.

[35] Dissenting Opinion of Judge Koroma in *Land and Maritime Boundary Dispute between Cameroon and Nigeria* (*Cameroon v Nigeria, Equatorial Guinea intervening*) Judgment, 2002, ICJ Reports 303, 474, para 3.

[36] See ibid 480, para 15.

[37] Craven (n 30) 20.

[38] See P Singh, 'From "Narcissistic" Positive International Law to "Universal" Natural International Law: The Dialectics of "Absentee Colonialism"' (2008) 16 *African Journal of International and Comparative Law* 56.

> 'governed by international law' and did not affect the capacity of Britain to subsequently dispose of the territory.[39]

In other words, the Court considered the African treaty party as being non-sovereign and interpreted the treaty as being irrelevant in the context of, according to the Court, valid international law at the time of conclusion. That the African rulers, with whom Britain concluded a treaty, were not sovereign the Court presumed without any explanation. Eventually, the Court determined that the 1884 Treaty did not establish an international protectorate, in the true sense of the word, but a colonial protectorate, that is, a relation of protection between a sovereign and a non-sovereign political entity.

This finding, however, was and still is questionable.[40] As has been argued, despite the fact that protectorate treaties functioned first and foremost as a means of demonstrating a relationship of authority or control to other European powers, the conclusion of these treaties between European powers and African native rulers implied that the Europeans recognised, implicitly or explicitly, at least the internal sovereignty of the native ruler. This recognition also acknowledged the power of the same ruler to regulate existing and future property and subsequent rights within his territory. The Europeans concluded these treaties with the intention of also acquiring rights of internal sovereignty over the territory after the conclusion of the treaty of protection with the African rulers. Again, under the principle of *nemo dat quod non habet* (or, no one can give what he does not have), the Europeans assumed that the African rulers indeed possessed sovereign rights over territory, which they were able to transfer by treaty.

From this point of view, the Court takes an a-historic approach to interpreting the treaty and the status of the Kings and Chiefs of Old Calabar on the basis of the theoretical premise of cultural difference or a divided world. The Court took this one-sided or Euro-centric approach in its interpretation of the facts and its final judgment would probably have been different if the Court had conducted, for example, an analysis of the intentions of both treaty parties in the negotiations of the treaty. If the ICJ had included international law as it was applied in practice—and treaty practice proved that African rulers were considered sovereign—it would have concluded that the protectorate treaty only transferred rights of external sovereignty and that Britain did not legally acquire all-comprehensive sovereignty over the contested territory.[41]

Seen in this light, the Court would have judged that the later colonisation of the Bakassi peninsula by the British was illegal according to valid international legal standards at the time: as has been shown in the foregoing sections, the colonial protectorate was not a legal means to acquire territorial sovereignty, but a political

[39] Ibid.

[40] Craven refers to Koskienniemi who points out that nineteenth-century legal opinion was far from undivided on the question of the status of colonial treaties. Whilst there were those (such as Westlake and Rolin) who regarded such treaties as irrelevant to international law, there were also those (such as Bonfils and Fauchille) who assigned considerable significance to them. See Craven (n 30) 20.

[41] See J Gilbert, *Indigenous Peoples' Land Rights under International Law. From Victims to Actors* (Transnational, 2006) 53–54.

construct to justify the European colonisation of Africa afterwards. If the ICJ had pronounced on the illegality of the colonisation on the basis of all the available facts, acts and laws, it would have decided the case totally differently and no difficulties with regard to the inter-temporal rule would have arisen.

## III. INTERNATIONAL LAW IN ITS HISTORICAL CONTEXT

History and international law are inextricably and necessarily bound up with one another.[42] The lapse of time confronts legal theorists and practitioners with two interrelated problems, namely, providing evidence of causal relations and the legitimacy of counterfactual reasoning in determining how the present might have looked if that original illegal act had not taken place. Both causality and counterfactuals become increasingly indeterminate and complex over the course of time because of the changing circumstances under the influence of internal and external intervening factors. The increasing remoteness of historically wrongful acts runs parallel with an increasing complexity in establishing a claim for responsibility.

Historical awareness in the determination of the factual situation, therefore, is a preliminary requirement for lawyers. Especially in the field of international law, the necessity of a proper knowledge of historical developments is a constitutive condition in order to understand and deal with problems and conflicts. Before conflicts break out, they have already been lingering for years, decades, and sometimes even centuries. These disputes often have their origin in the remote past and develop over time, before they become legal conflicts, and are eventually brought before an international court or tribunal.[43] David Bederman has characterised this interrelatedness of international law and history as follows:

> International law as a discipline appears to be rooted in historical trends and realities to a far larger degree than other realms of law and jurisprudence, but the relationship between the domains of international law (as both an academic study and professional practice) and historiography remain cloudy and uncertain.[44]

The inter-temporal rule and its application in the context of international law make us aware of the fact that it is a delicate question to assess the past by current standards and knowledge, as the reasoning of the ICJ in the *Cameroons v Nigeria* case (2002) has proven. Here, reference should be made to Ronald Dworkin's thoughts. He would point to the vital importance of judicial interpretation being based on the historical and social characteristics of the contemporary legal order.[45] This remains true especially for lawyers operating at the international level. In this context, the three 'enduring truths', articulated by Bederman have to be taken into account by those who use historic materials in the pursuit of some legal objective, and, in

[42] See RCH Lesaffer, 'The Grotian Tradition Revisited: Change and Continuity in the History of International Law' (2002) 73 *British Yearbook of International Law* 103–39.

[43] See Kohen (n 3) 183–200.

[44] DJ Bederman, 'Foreign Office International Legal History' in M Craven, M Fitzmaurice and M Vogiatzi (eds), *Time, History and International Law* (Martinus Nijhoff, 2007) 43.

[45] R Dworkin, *Law's Empire* (Fontana, 1986) 245.

particular, the judges of the ICJ, who are time and again confronted with the fact that international law and conflicts have a long history. The first of these is that legal history and legal truth are not always the same thing, and they certainly cannot be ascertained by the same means and modalities. The second truth that international lawyers have to understand is that, no matter how hard one tries, the historic record is often sparse and incomplete, at least on the issues that matter to lawyers or judges. And that leads to a third enduring truth, and that is that even in cases where there is abundant historical material, the historic record can still be ambiguous or contradictory.[46]

Recognising the significance and seriousness of historical inquiry in international legal procedures is a fundamental issue, especially with regard to the questions whether the European acquisition and partition of African territory at the end of the nineteenth century was illegal and whether responsibility for these colonial acts can be established. Note, however, that lawyers should always be aware of the fallacy of 'presentism':[47] the anachronistic application of present-day norms and values to interpret and evaluate actions of the past should be avoided. Although anachronism should be avoided, interpretation and determination of facts in the past should not.[48] For now, the most important given to keep in mind is that the inter-temporal rule is not applicable in the particular case of violations of treaties and property rights by the European colonial powers at the end of the nineteenth century because these acts were, as has been argued above, illegal according to contemporary law.

## IV. CONCLUSION

To conclude, the historical consciousness of international lawyers, the judges of the ICJ included, is vital but delicate as the *Cameroon v Nigeria* case (2002) demonstrates, when it comes to establishing the illegality of past acts and redressing historical wrongs. As has been shown, the question whether colonisation, more specifically the acquisition and partition of Africa, was illegal could only be answered if it could be established whether the colonial acts were already contrary to the law at the time they occurred. Now it has been established that the acquisition and partition of Africa violated the legal standards at the time of colonisation, no difficulties arise with the application of the inter-temporal rule. International legal norms do not have to be applied retrospectively or in an evolutionary manner to evaluate the legal nature of colonialism.

This contribution has problematised the question of responsibility for the colonisation of Africa—as a wrongful act—by analysing and showing the consequences of the lapse of time and the application of the inter-temporal rule in international law.

[46] Bederman (n 44) 63.

[47] See T Govier and W Verwoerd, 'The Promise and Pitfalls of Apology' (2002) 33 *Journal of Social Philosophy* 7. See also De Baets (n 2) 145; P Burke, 'Triumphs and Poverties of Anachronism' (2006) 10 *Scientia Poetica* 291–92 and 298; DH Fischer, *Historians' Fallacies: Toward a Logic of Historical Thought* (Harper, 1970) 132–42 and H Ritter, 'Anachronism' in D Woolf (ed), *A Global Encyclopedia of Historical Writing* (Garland, 1998) 30–31.

[48] See De Baets (n 2) 146.

The interpretation and application of the inter-temporal rule—the non-retroactive application of law, but at the same time an evolutionary interpretation of law—is not obvious, though crucial, as the reasoning of the ICJ in the *Cameroons v Nigeria* case (2002) demonstrates. If the Court had employed an unbiased and historic interpretation of the inter-temporal rule, it would not have come to the conclusion that a colonial protectorate was a legal means for European States to acquire title to African territory.

Instead, the Court would have argued that the colonial protectorate was a political instrument to justify Africa's colonisation *a posteriori*, that Britain had breached its treaty promises and that the transfer of territorial sovereignty over Bakassi Island from the rulers of Old Calabar to Britain was not in accordance with nineteenth-century international law. The doctrine of inter-temporal law, therefore, underlines the relationship between international law and a proper understanding and awareness of the history of international law in general, and of legal disputes in particular.

PART IX

# INTERNATIONAL LAW AND THE AESTHETIC

# 26

# *Engaged Visual Art as a Tool for Normative Renewal in International Human Rights: The Case of Ariella Azoulay's* Potential History *(2012)*

EVA BREMS* AND HILDE VAN GELDER**

## I. INTRODUCTION

SINCE THE BEGINNING of the new millennium, a 'legal turn' has taken place within the visual arts. Artists, art theoreticians, art critics and curators have paid increasingly attention to human rights. Concerned about the numerous problems posed by the global crisis of the capitalist economy, they have sought a valid means to express social commitment. Since human rights law is a dominant language for talking about injustice, it has proven highly inspirational.

Artists have contributed to raising public awareness by exposing human rights violations in their works. A recent example of this engagement from the art world has been the acclaimed exhibition 'Newtopia: The State of Human Rights', held in Mechelen in 2012. The idea is not entirely new: ten years earlier, the world-leading visual art exhibition Documenta, which was held in Kassel in 2002, had already organised think tanks in order to exchange ideas about human rights issues.[1] Documenta 11 consolidated creative processes that had developed throughout the 1990s, in the wake of the influential legacy of critically-engaged visual art since the early 1970s. Academic research programmes engaged with this dynamic as, for example, with the interdisciplinary Human Rights Project at Bard College, founded in 1999.[2]

In such a productive climate, many visual artists now felt encouraged to move beyond merely representing human rights, in conformity with the artist's

* Eva Brems is a professor of Human Rights Law at Ghent University.

** Hilde Van Gelder is an associate professor of modern and contemporary art history at the University of Leuven, where she directs the Lieven Gevaert Research Centre for Photography, Art and Visual Culture.

[1] Okwui Enwezor et al, 'Democracy Unrealized', Documenta 11_Platform 1 (Hatje-Cantz, 2002).

[2] For more information on this project, seehrp.bard.edu/.

perception of current human rights standards. They thus entered into a critical dialogue with some of these standards' reigning norms and predominant mechanisms. Often they did so in collaboration with visual art theoreticians, art critics and curators—a group we further identify as 'art researchers'.[3] This paper focuses on one artist who may be situated in this school of thought. Throughout this case study, we examine the role of both engaged visual art making and visual art research in advancing the constant process of normative development that characterises international human rights law.

Until now, much of the engagement of human rights scholarship with the visual realm has been in relation to photography. More precisely, when discussing the human rights relevance of photography, scholars focus on photojournalism, with only scant attention paid to art photography.[4] They proceed from an instrumental approach, discussing the role and limits of photojournalistic pictures in exposing human rights violations and triggering reactions.[5] Additionally, critical approaches may be found, for example arguing that photographic representations of human rights violations may reproduce harmful stereotypes.[6] Only occasionally has it been claimed that photographic images may also contribute to shaping human rights discourse.[7]

Yet many believe that visual artists and visual art researchers may be among the actors who could advance the field of human rights. Former European Commission President José Manuel Barroso has recently said that 'artists are the unacknowledged legislators of this world'.[8] Our chapter examines the role engaged visual art can play today, as an instrument for activating a mobilising potential with regard to rethinking human solidarity in contemporary society. Underlying our collaboration lies the hypothesis that true interdisciplinary dialogue may help overcome scepticism about the lack of influence of engaged visual art.

This contribution is a first attempt at collaboration between an art researcher, Hilde Van Gelder, and a scholar of human rights law, Eva Brems, which we hope will develop into a fully fledged research project. In the first part of the chapter, Hilde Van Gelder shows how Ariella Azoulay's artistic and curatorial work leads to her theoretical positions on human rights, that is, how visual art talks to international

[3] Hilde Van Gelder, 'Art Research' in Janneke Wesseling (ed), *See it Again, Say it Again: The Artist as Researcher* (Valiz, 2011) 23–39.

[4] See, for example, Frank Möller, 'Rwanda Revisualized: Genocide, Photography, and the Era of the Witness' (2010) 35 *Alternatives: Global, Local, Political* 113–36.

[5] Sam Gregory, 'Transnational Storytelling: Human Rights, WITNESS, and Video Advocacy' (2006) 108(1) *American Anthropologist* 195–204; Liam Kennedy, 'Photography & Human Rights', available at www.photoconflict.com/casestudies/photography-human-rights/; Andrea Noble, 'Recognizing Historical Injustice through Photography: Mexico 1968' (2010) 27 *Theory Culture Society* 184–213; and Geoffrey Batchen et al (eds), *Picturing Atrocity: Photography in Crisis* (Reaktion Books, 2012).

[6] Roland Bleiker and Amy Kay, 'Representing HIV/AIDS in Africa: Pluralist Photography and Local Empowerment' (2007) 51 *International Studies Quarterly* 139–63.

[7] Daniel Joyce, 'Photography and the Image-Making of International Justice' (2010) *Law and Humanities* 229–49; Susie Linfield, *The Cruel Radiance: Photography and Political Violence* (University of Chicago Press, 2011).

[8] José Manuel Barroso, 'Inaugural Speech at the International Conference "A New Narrative for Europe"', Berlin, Akademie der Künste, 1 March 2014, full text available through a press release at europa.eu/rapid/press-release_SPEECH-14-168_en.htm.

human rights law in this case, and what it has to say. In the second part, Eva Brems explores whether and how international human rights law can rise to the challenge of, and address, the claims put forward by the artist and art researcher.

## II. VISUAL ART TALKS TO INTERNATIONAL LAW

In the spring of 2012, the political philosopher, photography theoretician, curator and artist Ariella Azoulay created an exhibition at both the STUK Contemporary Arts Centre in Leuven, Belgium, and the Center for Digital Art in Holon, Israel. Inside a black box, Azoulay's video *Civil Alliance* (2012), was on show. This 52:36 minutes long work portrays people of mixed Palestinian and Jewish background dressed in mid-twentieth-century clothing, gathering round a circular table that depicts a map of Mandatory Palestine. The group recite short stories in Arabic and Hebrew about civilian engagements and agreements achieved between January 1947 and May 1948. These narrated fragments testify to a joint civilian will to imagine a peaceful coexistence in the various villages that are marked, one by one, with dots on the map.

Azoulay provided a wider context for the viewer to understand *Civil Alliance* mostly through the simultaneous exhibition of black-and-white photographs encountered in formerly undisclosed Zionist archives, which she both installed on the projection room's exterior walls, and reproduced in a foldable booklet that was available free in the exhibition room.[9] When it was completely folded, the booklet's cover displayed only part of a photographic image, which shows a man in a costume firmly holding someone's hand. Upon opening the booklet, one finds that the second person is an Arab man. A further opening of the booklet shows a caption that reads: 'Ya'acov Epstein holding hands with Jabri Amin el Haj during a visit of Jewish settlers from Zichron Ya'acov to the Arab village of Subrin. Photographer: Zoltan Kluger, GPO 20.01.1940.' From the left-hand side of the picture, which reveals a third person's arm or back, one sees that the two men were not alone in the room.

Azoulay comments on this in the booklet, writing that the presence of other men provides a 'public meaning' to these two men's encounter 'that transcends their personal relations'. She adds to this that 'these openly public gestures of proximity turn them into a promise made in view of witnesses, one of whom is the photographer'. Thus, the picture unfolds before our eyes into a strong image of a 'civil alliance'.

In the exhibition, Azoulay combined such images with mural text fragments which she had written. Entitled *Potential History* (2012) the sequence began with a contemporary colour photograph of an encrusted wooden box that was looted from the former Palestinian village of Deir Yassin. The fragment of text tells us the following:

> The agreement between the inhabitants of Deir Yassin and Giv'at Shaul was violated not by local residents but rather by Jewish militiamen. This wooden box was looted from one of the houses in Deir Yassin and kept in the home of one of the Jewish assailants. For years

[9] Ariella Azoulay, 'Potential History' exhibition brochure (Leuven, STUK Arts Centre, 2012).

> its provenance was an open secret in the house where it was kept. It is now in my keeping. I regard it as a priceless deposit placed in my keeping until the story of this place be rewritten, until life as it was known here until the curse of partition took hold of it would be retold, and conditions would transpire for founding a shared museum—to tell how the national war machine ground to dust civil hopes for shared life. In this box borrowed time is stored.[10]

Now in Azoulay's possession, the box became a tool for her to claim the 'right not to be a perpetrator'.[11] On the same occasion, she pleaded for forgiveness and made a promise to make a case for the universal right of each and every one on this planet 'to imagine one's future'.

Our chapter focuses on Azoulay's first claim, that of establishing 'a right not to be a perpetrator'. Looting and destroying civilian property under circumstances of war is a violation of international law.[12] Basing herself on the metaphorical potential of this tiny box, Azoulay not only expresses her firm will but also claims her fundamental right to no longer participate in the continuation of such perpetrations. She pleads for a 'new declaration of human rights', which would protect not only victims of human rights violations, but also individuals who think that they may be susceptible of becoming (co-)perpetrators of human rights violations—even if only passively, that is, they are not actively committing the violation. On these individuals should be conferred a specific right to refuse to contribute to such perpetrations. Azoulay writes: a truly workable 'declaration of human rights ... should be based on the assumption that every time a right is violated, another right is also violated with it—the right not to be a perpetrator'.[13]

In recent years, Ariella Azoulay has thus constructed an influential theoretical, curatorial and artistic body of work in which she aims to push our spectatorial imagination as far as possible. She proposes no less than an understanding of engaged visual art as a most powerful tool to plant the seeds of new human rights.[14] At first sight, such intentions may sound completely utopian. For justifiable reasons, contemporary art theory is often situated as stopping short at the relatively inoperative level of visual imagination.

Our ambition is to explore under what conditions the visual arts can rise above the relatively inoperative level of 'a virtual community between spectators', as Sharon Sliwinski has so eloquently called it,[15] and to realise impact on the ground. Proposals for an engaged visual art that take up a particular position may be less wild than one would at first think. Human rights have, historically, always resulted from growing social consensus, and often in direct response to indignation about stories that had come to see the light of day.

[10] Ibid. This fragment also appears on screen at the end of Azoulay's video *Civil Alliance*, already mentioned.

[11] Ibid. Azoulay also elaborates in more depth on this claim in her 'Potential History. Thinking through Violence' (Spring 2013) 39 *Critical Inquiry* 548–74.

[12] See, for example, Geneva Convention IV of 1949.

[13] Ariella Azoulay, '"The Family of Man": A Visual Universal Declaration of Human Rights' in Thomas Keenan and Tirdad Zolghadr (eds), *The Human Snapshot* (Sternberg Press, 2013) 19, 42.

[14] A Azoulay, *Civil Imagination: A Political Ontology of Photography* (Verso, 2012).

[15] Sharon Sliwinski, *Human Rights in Camera* (University of Chicago Press, 2011) 5.

Samuel Moyn, in the catalogue to the exhibition *Newtopia: The State of Human Rights*, urged human rights law to reinvent itself by moving beyond its currently reigning standards.[16] If human rights law finds itself in an impasse today, he argues, this is because it relies too much on the judges in the courts and has insufficient contact with grassroots movements. As a result, it often lacks the reality checks made by such movements, which express human rights claims that do not necessarily reproduce the predominant status quo within the field of human rights, but instead represent human rights as they could or should be in the eyes of these activists.[17] It is our primary assumption that engaged visual art, and specifically the work of Azoulay, can be understood as such a productive 'grassroots movement'.

## III. HOW INTERNATIONAL LAW MAY ENGAGE WITH VISUAL ART (RESEARCH)

How can international law—and in particular international human rights law/international humanitarian law/international criminal law—respond to all this? If international lawyers want to take these claims seriously, what does this imply? As to *why* take it seriously, we submit that this type of artistic activism is one of many types of bottom-up expressions of or reflections about adequate responses to injustice. Bottom-up dynamics have often played a role in the formulation of new international standards or the adjustment of existing standards.

We refer to the role of women's organisations around the globe in achieving recognition of domestic violence as a human rights violation, and sexual violence as a war crime and crime against humanity. Other examples that have been explored in recent scholarship include the role of associations of families of disappeared persons in Latin America in the debates on the emerging right to the truth,[18] and the role of peasant movements in advancing a right to food sovereignty.[19]

Compared to such movements, artists are, of course, a different kind of actor, yet this difference does not make them less worthy of being taken seriously for two reasons. First, this is an actor who may suffer less from the myopia that may characterise the involvement in a highly personal struggle, as is the case for many grassroots movements; and second, this is an actor who arguably moves in a sphere that facilitates out-of-the-box thinking above and beyond politics.

### A. A Legal Role for the Universal Spectator

As discussed above, Ariella Azoulay talks about a 'universal spectator' as an implied absentee presence in the act of photography. Arguably, there is a similar central

[16] Samuel Moyn, 'The Future of Human Rights' in Katerina Gregos and Eelena Sorokina (eds), *Newtopia: The State of Human Rights* (Ludion, 2012) 46–56.

[17] Ibid 53.

[18] Patricia Naftali, *La construction du 'droit à la vérité' en droit international* (PhD thesis, Université Libre de Bruxelles, 2012–2013).

[19] Priscilla Claeys, 'The creation of new rights by the food sovereignty movement: the challenge of institutionalizing subversion' (2012) 46 *Sociology* 844–60.

figure that is implied in international human rights law: human rights law breaks into the sacrosanct principle of state sovereignty to turn horror and injustice into universal concerns. Human rights law and discourse thus invites the attention of the world. Wherever injustice is committed, the world is watching, and it may call perpetrators to account. In that sense, the universal spectator in international human rights law does more than look. Due to the strong normativity of human rights, the universal human rights spectator is always to some extent a universal prosecutor or judge. The human rights 'system' has institutionalised this universal spectatorship: the fact that injustice has been made a universal concern legitimises the role of international bodies that hold states and individuals accountable for human rights violations. This institutional turn, however, risks shutting out the role of individuals who are not directly involved in a human rights violation (either as a victim or as a perpetrator). The strong ethical power of human rights, that is felt—or supposed to be felt—by all human beings as spectators of human rights violations, is thus not matched by a legal role for human beings generally in addressing human rights violations.

Yet we may try to think of such a legal role for the universal spectator. It is submitted that this can be conceived in at least three ways, that is, as a duty, as a substantive right, and as a procedural right. It is not possible in this contribution to thoroughly discuss these different scenarios. Instead, we have focused on a more limited ambition, which is to 'translate' claims that were expressed in an artistic context, and to turn them into research questions in the field of international law. However, we intend to go further in the years to come, and to address these research questions with an interdisciplinary team of human rights lawyers and art researchers, in close contact with engaged visual artists.

In what follows, we shall briefly point out how the search for a legal role for the universal spectator may translate into questions of duties and of substantive rights, before going a bit more deeply into the matter of procedural rights, which in our opinion appears to offer the most promise.

## B. The Legal Duties of the Universal Spectator

Azoulay has conceived of the role of the spectator in the first place as a duty—an obligation to struggle against injuries inflicted on others and to avoid and resist political and economic situations that give rise to structural human rights violations.[20] Ethically speaking, this is a big claim that in many cases may result in a duty of mandatory heroism. It is true that systems of oppression and discrimination—from the holocaust and apartheid to the discrimination against women—cannot subsist without the silent collaboration—or at least the collaborative silence—of numerous people, many of whom may directly or indirectly benefit from such systems. For this reason, the idea of a legal duty to resist structural human rights violations cannot be

[20] Ariella Azoulay, *The Civil Contract of Photography* (Zone Books, 2008).

dismissed out of hand. Moreover, it resonates with the UN Declaration on the Rights and Responsibility of Individuals, Groups and Organs of Society to Promote and Protect Universally Recognized Human Rights and Fundamental Freedoms (hereinafter the UN Declaration on Human Rights Defenders).[21] This text declares a responsibility 'in safeguarding democracy, promoting human rights and fundamental freedoms and contributing to the promotion and advancement of democratic societies, institutions and processes', as well as a responsibility in contributing to the promotion of the right of everyone to a social and international order in which human rights can be fully realised.[22] Efforts to make these responsibilities concrete and operational, let alone legally binding, still need to be realised.

At the same time, one can think of a number of more specific duties that may potentially be more feasible as well as ways to legally facilitate living according to an *ethical* duty to resist human rights violations. In the first category of specific duties, one may explore, for instance, the feasibility of an international duty to assist victims or potential victims of human rights violations.[23] In our opinion, a legal obligation to protect a specific individual from a serious human rights violation that the person is suffering or that they might imminently be suffering, may—when one is in a position to do so, presumably with only limited risk to oneself—offer significantly better prospects than a legal obligation to resist a structural system of oppression.

Another limited duty one may conceive of is the duty to bring to light human rights violations of which one has knowledge—for example, in the exercise of one's profession, even where secrecy rules apply, so as to enable the competent authorities to hold perpetrators to account. If international law formulated such individual duties, it would oblige states to enact them in their legislation and to attach sanctions to them.

The second category of specific duties may offer an alternative, or a first step, to what is described above. Instead of obliging individuals to become whistle-blowers or to take other steps that may be perceived as risks to themselves, this scenario would leave it a matter of free choice whether or not to do so while focusing on containing or reducing the risks attached. This would imply, for instance, that states would need to have whistle-blowers' protection measures in place for those who bring to light human rights violations.[24] And states would be obliged to protect individuals who intervene in order to protect others against actual or potential human rights violations, against the risks such individuals run, and possibly also against any

[21] UN Declaration on Human Rights Defenders adopted by General Assembly of the United Nations on 9 December 1998, GA Res A/RES/53/144, available at www.ohchr.org/EN/ProfessionalInterest/Pages/RightAndResponsibility.aspx.

[22] Ibid, Article 18.

[23] We refer to the Belgian Criminal Law provision that makes it a criminal offence not to offer assistance to a person in serious danger (Article 422*bis* Criminal Code).

[24] Recommendation CM/Rec (2014)7 of the Committee of Ministers of the Council of Europe to Member States on the protection of whistle-blowers was adopted on 30 April 2014. It recommends that Council of Europe Member States have in place a normative, institutional and judicial framework to protect individuals who, in the context of their work-based relationship, report or disclose information on threats or harm to the public interest.

sanctions for offences that may be committed in so doing. The latter is not a new human rights obligation.[25]

## C. The Legal Rights of the Universal Spectator

When we think of individuals who are not directly concerned with a situation in which human rights are violated, and of the rights of such individuals pertaining to such violations, we can think of these rights either as substantive rights or as procedural rights.

### *i. An Individual Substantive Right Concerning the Human Rights of Others*

One may imagine a 'light' version of such a right, that consists essentially of the right to protest and advocate against violations of the human rights of others. This is a crucial right which, however, is not new, as it concerns freedom of expression, freedom of assembly and other rights of human rights defenders.[26]

A bolder version would be the right to live in a society where no structural or gross human rights violations occur. This comes closer to what Ariella Azoulay means by the right of the spectator not to become a perpetrator. It expresses the idea that human rights violations happening to others also damage our common humanity. Arguably, this is what is meant by Article 28 Universal Declaration of Human Rights (UDHR)[27] which reads: 'Everyone is entitled to a social and international order in which the rights and freedoms set forth in this Declaration can be fully realized.' In that sense, it is not a new idea. Yet while most rights expressed in the UDHR have been repeated and further developed in other international texts that are legally binding, this is not the case for this particular right. It is as yet not very clear what the practical effects of such a right would be, yet this is certainly worth exploring.

In addition to the autonomous meaning of this substantive right, it is submitted that it may also function as the substantive underpinning for the procedural right

[25] According to Article 12 of the UN Declaration on Human Rights Defenders (n 21).

> 1. Everyone has the right, individually and in association with others, to participate in peaceful activities against violations of human rights and fundamental freedoms.
>
> 2. The State shall take all necessary measures to ensure the protection by the competent authorities of everyone, individually and in association with others, against any violence, threats, retaliation, de facto or de jure adverse discrimination, pressure or any other arbitrary action as a consequence of his or her legitimate exercise of the rights referred to in the present Declaration.
>
> 3. In this connection, everyone is entitled, individually and in association with others, to be protected effectively under national law in reacting against or opposing, through peaceful means, activities and acts, including those by omission, attributable to States that result in violations of human rights and fundamental freedoms, as well as acts of violence perpetrated by groups or individuals that affect the enjoyment of human rights and fundamental freedoms.

[26] For example, Article 12(1) of the Human Rights Defenders' Declaration (n 21), as well as Articles 5, 6 and 7 of the same text and Articles 19, 21 and 22 ICCPR.

[27] Universal Declaration of Human Rights, adopted by the General Assembly of the United Nations on 10 December 1948, GA Res 217A (III).

discussed below. Azoulay builds on the 'right not to become a perpetrator' to make the very concrete claim that the recruitment of citizens taking part in human rights violations—*in casu* drafting citizens for service in the Israeli army in the occupied territories—should in itself be a human rights violation.[28] Currently, international law includes such a ban only for child soldiers;[29] it would seem an overly radical move to extend it to citizens generally, especially as every soldier was at one point a civilian, and every military operation in times of war may result in war crimes or other violations of international law.

Yet in this context as well, one may at the same time explore the matter further, and start thinking about lighter, more feasible approaches that realise part of the same ambition. In that sense, one may think of alternative ways of protecting citizens from becoming complicit in human rights violations and of conceptualising victimhood in perpetrators of human rights violations. This may include a reflection on the right to conscientious objection to military service and beyond, and the right to refuse to violate human rights[30] as well as appropriate accountability mechanisms for individuals who may be characterised as victim-perpetrators.

### *ii. An Individual Procedural Right Concerning the Human Rights of Others*

In our opinion, the most straightforward answer to the artistic appeal for the right of the spectator not to be a perpetrator is not the creation of a new substantive legal right but rather the extension of a procedural right, in other words access to a remedy that addresses these human rights violations. This would imply that where human rights violations are concerned, an *actio popularis* should automatically be possible.

To make clear what this means, we would like to present the case of Elisabeth Cohen. In June 2011, the Belgian parliament voted to adopt a law that is generally known as the 'burqa ban'.[31] The law prohibits going around in public with a face that is not recognisable.

Although it was clearly adopted to ban niqabs and burqas from the public sphere, it is formulated in general terms. Elisabeth Cohen is a Belgian woman living in Belgium. She is profoundly disturbed by this law, which she considers to be a type of religious persecution. She does not want a law that endorses this type of prosecution

[28] Azoulay, *Civil Imagination* (n 14) 246.

[29] Article 38, Convention on the Rights of the Child; Articles 3 and 4, Optional Protocol to the Convention on the Rights of the Child on the involvement of children in armed conflict (2002); Articles 8(2)(b)(xxvi) and Article 8(2)(e)(vii) Rome Statute of the International Criminal Court.

[30] Cf Article 10 UN Human Rights Defenders' Declaration (n 25) 'No one shall participate, by act or by failure to act where required, in violating human rights and fundamental freedoms and no one shall be subjected to punishment or adverse action of any kind for refusing to do so.'

[31] Act of 1 June 2011 'to institute a prohibition against wearing clothing that covers the face or a large part of it' was published in the *Belgian Official Journal* on 13 July and entered into force ten days later. The Act inserts Article 563*bis* into the Belgian Criminal Code. 'Subject to legal provisions to the contrary', the Article punishes persons 'who appear in places accessible to the public with their faces covered or concealed, in whole or in part, in such a manner that they are not recognisable' with a monetary fine of 150 euro and/or a prison sentence of one to seven days. Paragraph two of Article 563*bis* of the Criminal Code specifies that the prohibition contained in the first paragraph shall not apply when face covering is permitted or imposed by 'labour regulations or municipal ordinances owing to festivities'.

to apply in her country. Elisabeth Cohen herself does not cover her face, nor does she wish to do so. She is not a Muslim, instead she calls herself an atheist (although she has a Jewish background).

Elisabeth challenged the 'burqa ban' before the Belgian Constitutional Court, and when we met her she was also considering challenging it before the European Court of Human Rights (ECtHR). The Belgian Constitutional Court requires applicants to have an individual interest in the annulment of a legislative act and specifically does not allow an *actio popularis*. Hence in order for her to have an admissible claim, Elisabeth's attorney formulated her claim as one concerning her (privacy-related) right to cover her face in public, by 'oversized glasses, a shawl, a headscarf or an anti-bacterial face mask'. Only at the end of her argumentation did she add that Elisabeth also had 'an interest to live in a society that does not discriminate against religious minorities' and that in her opinion the face-covering ban signifies a cultural impoverishment and a uniformity that are not compatible with 'the fundamental rights of the society in which she lives and which are recognized by the European Convention on Human Rights'.[32]

Elisabeth's claim was found admissible on account of the potential application of the law to her as a person living in Belgium and being able to move freely in public, not on account of her real concern about the application of the law to others who significantly differ from her, but whose fundamental rights she feels she is entitled to see protected. As the Belgian Constitutional Court found no violation of fundamental rights, Elisabeth wanted to discuss the possibility of challenging the Belgian 'burqa ban' before the ECtHR. One thing she made very clear: she did not want the argument that would be made in her name in Strasbourg to be about the potential application of the ban to her. She wanted the legal claim to reflect her real concern, which is a concern about the rights of others, and about her right to live in a society that respects human rights. In this goal she could only be disappointed, as the ECtHR requires that the person, organisation or group of persons that applies to the Court must claim to be the victim of a human rights violation.[33]

If we look at international human rights law as a whole, standing rights to complain about violations that happen to other (unrelated) persons appear to be a matter on which there is very little or no consensus. The United Nations Treaty bodies accept that an individual complaint can be made on behalf of another, provided that this other person consents to the complaint being made. The same principle applies before the African Commission on Human and Peoples' Rights.[34] This solves Elisabeth's problem only in part, as first, it would narrow her concern to one about the application of the law in a specific case, whereas in reality it is a concern about the existence of the law as such and about all of its actual and potential applications,

[32] Belgian Constitutional Court, Judgment 145/2012 of 6 December 2012, para A.1.4.1, judgment available at www.const-court.be.

[33] European Convention on Human Rights, Article 34.

[34] African Commission on Human and Peoples' Rights, Guidelines for Submission of Communications, as interpreted in practice, see Filing a Communication before the African Commission on Human and Peoples' Rights; a Complainant's Manual, 2013, available at www.fidh.org/IMG/pdf/manual_to_the_african_commission_2013_en.pdf.

and second, it would require her to identify an individual victim and obtain her consent, which is not particularly easy in this case, because the number of face veil wearers in Belgium is very small (estimated at a maximum of 250 individuals out of a population of 11 million inhabitants), and the law has forced them indoors. The Inter-American system does allow individuals and organisations to act on behalf of a third person, particularly without the victims' consent or even knowledge.[35] Even though it remains necessary in this system to identify specific victims, it seems that this system would allow for an accommodation of Elisabeth's wish.

Hence it is submitted that one very feasible way of taking seriously the claim of the universal spectator of human rights violations who does not want to be complicit in such violations, is to recognise a universal right to legally challenge human rights violations. At a minimum, it seems that such a right would have to apply to all supranational judicial and quasi-judicial human rights complaint mechanisms. Yet it is obvious that it would be very meaningful to also extend it to domestic judicial fora. It seems that a victim consent requirement (and even a requirement for the identification of specific victims) is beside the point, as this is not about individuals or organisations defending the rights of others in the name of those others. Instead, it is about a separate interest/right of individuals to live in a society where human rights—not only their own rights, but also those of others—are respected, and of not being complicit in such violations. This includes those instances where the violations are committed in their name, in the case of a law voted by a democratically elected parliament, or because the violations are inherent in a societal structure from which the individuals benefit.

It is open to discussion as to how broad this universal individual standing right would be, and in particular whether some kind of link between the individual applicant and the state defendant would be required. If one refers purely to the idea of universal spectatorship, such a requirement may be undesirable. Yet if one refers to the 'right not to be a perpetrator', as the basis of the standing right, it may be justified to limit the standing right to individuals who have certain links to the issue or the state.

This is still rather embryonic, yet what we hope to convey is that the artist touches upon something that is not discussed very often in international human rights law, yet appears quite fundamental. International human rights law relies for its enforcement to a significant extent on peer pressure and peer review among states, for example, in the Committee of Ministers of the Council of Europe that supervises the implementation of ECtHR judgments, and in the Human Rights Council at the United Nations, as well as in bilateral and multilateral relations generally. It is common to express the success of human rights in triumphing over the doctrine of national sovereignty as the recognition that how a state treats people under its jurisdiction is not just its own business, but is also of legitimate concern to other states in the global community that is committed to universal human rights protection.

What the artist in this case has brought to the fore is that this state-based discourse cannot be the whole story of *human* rights. And that the point of universal

[35] American Convention on Human Rights, Article 44.

human rights is in the first place that the injustice suffered by one human being is of legitimate concern to another human being because it is an affront to shared values of humanity that have been entrenched in a universal human rights protection enterprise. With this procedural expression of the artist's claim, we feel that we have grasped the core of this notion—this is about a human rights mechanism relying on human beings acting for human beings. In addition to states watching each other's behaviour, human beings can be the ultimate permanent peer review mechanism for human rights.

## IV. CONCLUSION

In our opinion, a serious enterprise of translating artistic appeals to international law into the language of international law, in the form of new or amended standards or procedures, should proceed from a collaborative dialogue among international lawyers, artists and art scholars.

What this paper has done, is to show, using a specific artistic case as a starting point, that artistic claims may indeed point toward normative renewal in international law, and that such renewal may take many forms: within international human rights law, we have explored duties, substantive rights and procedural rights, all as potential legal conclusions from the same artistic claims. Similarly, we found that such claims may be translated in terms of radical normative reform, yet that this need not necessarily be the case: it may also concern the strengthening of existing standards, or support for developments that are underway. For us at least, this exploratory exercise has worked, in the sense that it has made us look at certain issues from a new angle, and has encouraged our creativity and our reflection on what is essential in this branch of international law.

# 27

# *Safeguarding Intangible Cultural Heritage: An Inter-disciplinary Approach to International Law*

JANET BLAKE*

## I. INTRODUCTION

SAFEGUARDING INTANGIBLE CULTURAL Heritage (ICH)[1] has, in reality, been an important priority and a requirement for a large majority of countries around the globe and their citizens long before the 2003 UNESCO Intangible Heritage Convention (the 2003 Convention) for its safeguarding was adopted.[2] Hence, despite its youth, as a subject matter of international regulation, the 'problem' of ICH was the lack of full international recognition of this pre-existing reality.[3] In addition, the pre-existing ICH protection paradigm was one that prioritised monumental cultural forms over local and indigenous ones and that, when it addressed

* Faculty of Law, Shahid Beheshti University, Tehran, Iran and Member of the Cultural Heritage Law Committee of the International Law Association.

[1] Now the accepted international law term of art for this range of cultural heritage is: 'the practices, representations, expressions, knowledge, skills—as well as the instruments, objects, artefacts and cultural spaces associated therewith—that communities, groups and, in some cases, individuals recognize as part of their cultural heritage', as defined by the UNESCO 'Convention for the Safeguarding of the Intangible Cultural Heritage' (adopted on 17 October 2003, entered into force 20 April 2006) 2368 UNTS 3 (2003 Convention) Article 2, para 1. It is manifested in five main, but non-exhaustive, domains: oral traditions and expressions, including language as a vehicle of the intangible cultural heritage; performing arts; social practices, rituals and festive events; knowledge and practices concerning nature and the universe; and traditional craftsmanship, see UNESCO 'Convention for the Safeguarding of Intangible Cultural Heritage' (adopted on 17 October 2003, entered into force 20 April 2006) 2368 UNTS 3, Article 2, para 2.

[2] In some countries, for example in Africa, ICH may constitute as much as 70–80% of their recognised heritage and can also serve as the main basis for health and other social services.

[3] The first international standard-setting in this area that took a broadly cultural approach (rather than a more narrow intellectual property approach) was the Recommendation on the Safeguarding of Traditional Culture and Folklore, see UNESCO, 25th Session of the General Conference, 15 November 1989, 'Recommendation on the Safeguarding of Traditional Culture and Folklore' (1989 Recommendation) available at portal.unesco.org/en/ev.php-URL_ID=13141&URL_DO=DO_TOPIC&URL_SECTION=201.html. Moreover, it was poorly implemented by Member States and regarded as not serving the needs of cultural communities well.

'traditional culture', did so from a heavily researcher-oriented viewpoint.[4] If we look now at the experience of countries that are Parties to the 2003 Convention, it is clear that this heritage in all its various forms is a rich social, economic and even political resource that can provide a variety of possible routes towards sustainable models of development.[5]

However, regulating this form of heritage brings with it new challenges or, at least, newly-appreciated ones, of which the question of how to address the gender dynamics of ICH and its safeguarding, is one that ties in with the broader issue of inter-disciplinary approaches in international law. With regard to the 2003 Convention, Hertz has asked the provocative question of whether 'true' ICH is not really a form of *matremoigne* (female inheritance), but one that has been placed within the essentially masculine framework in UNESCO.[6] This contribution explores this question by seeking to apply a more anthropological analysis to the gender issues thrown up by implementing it, although the author is an international lawyer by training and will no doubt do so through international law 'eyes'. Before addressing the specific question of gender and ICH, however, it is helpful to situate this Convention more broadly within international cultural heritage law and the wider context within which it was developed.

## II. THE 2003 CONVENTION—A PARADIGM SHIFT

Up until the 1970s, normative activity at UNESCO had been almost exclusively oriented towards material elements of what is often represented as a 'Eurocentric' conception of a monumental and prestigious culture. This was felt by many Member States from Africa and Latin America to ignore important parts of their heritage, much of which was the cultural practices of local and indigenous communities.[7]

In 1989, such non-material and often mundane cultural forms and expressions received a degree of international recognition and protection in the form of the 1989 Recommendation on the Safeguarding of Traditional Culture and Folklore (the 1989 Recommendation).[8] Although now criticised as too heavily researcher-driven and

[4] A criticism made against the 1989 Recommendation, in particular at the international conference 'A Global Assessment of the 1989 Recommendation on the Safeguarding of Traditional Culture and Folklore: Local Empowerment and International Co-operation', see UNESCO and Smithsonian Institution, 'Final Conference Report' (International Conference 'A Global Assessment of the 1989 Recommendation on the Safeguarding of Traditional Culture and Folklore: Local Empowerment and International Co-operation', Washington DC, 30 June—2 July 1999) available at www.folklife.si.edu/resources/Unesco/finalreport_eng.htm.

[5] The ways in which Parties are now setting development policies built around ICH is further explored in Janet Blake, 'Seven Years of Implementing UNESCO's Intangible Heritage Convention—Honeymoon Period or the "Seven-year Itch?"' (2014) 21 *International Journal of Cultural Property* 291.

[6] Ellen Hertz, 'Le matrimoine' in Marc-Olivier Gonseth, Jacques Hainard and Roland Kaehr (eds), *Le musée cannibale* (Musée d'ethnographie de Neuchâtel, 2002).

[7] In response, the World Heritage Committee (of the 1972 World Heritage Convention) launched its Global Strategy in the mid 1990s with the objective of achieving a greater 'geographic representation' of sites on the World Heritage list. See 'Evaluation of the Global Strategy for a Representative, Balanced and Credible World Heritage List (1994–2004)' adopted by the World Heritage Committee at its 28th session in China, 28 June—7 July 2004 [Doc WHC/04/28.COM13, 25 May 2004].

[8] See Recommendation on the Safeguarding of Traditional Culture and Folklore (UNESCO, 1989) cited at n 4.

using inappropriate terminology,[9] the 1989 Recommendation made it possible, later, for the 2003 Convention to be developed on the basis of the experience gained over the ten years from 1989 to 1999 and, importantly, to be conceived of as a broadly *cultural* Convention.[10] In tandem with this process, the *Operational Guidelines* to the 1972 World Heritage Convention underwent several revisions between 1992 and 2005, which increasingly allowed for non-material associated elements to be used as inscription criteria as well as for greater input from local communities in the design and implementation of management plans.[11]

I would suggest that a shift in the cultural heritage paradigm (according to UNESCO's standard-setting) has occurred and is occurring as a result of the adoption of the 2003 Convention. Here, I wish to describe briefly two main examples that demonstrate this and suggest that they are illustrative, in part, of the impact of regulating cultural heritage in an area in which anthropological and human rights values are so heavily implicated. First, the notion of the 'representativeness' of ICH that is to be given international recognition through inscription on the Representative List of Intangible Heritage of Humanity (the RL). The representative character of inscribed ICH elements is intended to celebrate the diversity of ICH worldwide and, as such, an element that fulfils the broad listing criteria,[12] is not regarded as being of special or outstanding significance (except, perhaps, to the cultural community) but rather as being one representative type of this heritage, the totality of which constitutes the global diversity of ICH. Hence, the significance of each element remains predominantly for the cultural community and the system of national and international cooperation designed to safeguard it is based on the imperative of the common interest of States in preserving the *diversity* of such ICH elements worldwide.

This notion, underlying not only the RL criteria but also the 2003 Convention as a whole, is a major departure from the idea of the subject of protection introduced by the 1972 World Heritage Convention (the 1972 Convention), predicated on the notion of a heritage of such 'outstanding' importance and 'unique' character that it transcends its local significance, rendering it a 'common heritage of mankind' for the protection of which international cooperation is required.[13] Over the 40 years of its operation, the 1972 Convention has slowly moved away from this notion

[9] The use of the term 'folklore', in particular, has later been heavily criticised as patronising and betraying a quasi-colonial view of this heritage. See Global Assessment of the 1989 Recommendation (n 4).

[10] Intellectual property rules are addressed in only one section out of six of the Recommendation on the Safeguarding of Traditional Culture and Folklore (UNESCO, 1989) namely Section E on 'Protection'.

[11] See Harriet Deacon and Olwen Beazley, 'Safeguarding Intangible Heritage Values under the World Heritage Convention: Auschwitz, Hiroshima and Robben Island' in Janet Blake (ed), *Safeguarding Intangible Cultural Heritage—Challenges and Approaches* (Institute of Art and Law, 2007).

[12] They include criteria such as historical continuity, a cultural community that identifies with it, community consent to inscription etc, Convention for Safeguarding of the Intangible Cultural Heritage, General Assembly of the States Parties to the Convention for Safeguarding of the Intangible Cultural Heritage 16–19 June 2008 and 22–24 June 2010 'Operational Directives for the Implementation of the Convention for the Safeguarding of the Intangible Cultural Heritage' (2008 as amended 2010) paras 1, 2.

[13] See Convention Concerning the Protection of the World Cultural and Natural Heritage, 29th Session of the World Heritage Committee 10–17 July 2005 'Keynote speech by Ms Christina Cameron and presentations by the World Heritage Centre and the Advisory Bodies UNESCO Doc WHC-05/29.COM/INF.9B (15 June 2005).

of outstanding and unique examples of monumental heritage towards the idea of examples that are 'representative' of the best cases available in a particular cultural area, region, theme or historical period.[14]

In order to resolve this apparent tension between the universal character and the (local) specificity of this heritage in the 1972 Convention, the World Heritage Committee has started to emphasise the 'representative' character of heritage sites as a 'particular dimension of universality'.[15] However, it remains true that the philosophy upon which the 1972 Convention was built and that of the 2003 Convention are fundamentally different and, to some degree, incompatible.

A second important shift in the heritage protection paradigm introduced in the 2003 Convention relates to the perception of the role of the State vis-à-vis other actors, who may be local communities, civil society groups and non-governmental organisations, local authorities and the private sector: these relationships have to be redefined in order to implement this Convention fully and to put new cultural policies in place over time.[16] Placing cultural communities closer to the centre of safeguarding and reducing the role of the State in identifying heritage is an important part of this process. The central safeguarding role given to communities in ICH safeguarding is a key aspect of the 2003 Convention[17] that sets it apart from other cultural heritage treaties and may even, later on, help to develop practice in the human rights field where participation is, of course, an important procedural norm.

Importantly, this notion of community participation is not limited to communities being passive interviewees for experts conducting ethnographic fieldwork in order to identify national ICH.[18] Rather, it assumes that communities will be involved in designing safeguarding strategies, conducting fieldwork themselves (in some cases) and managing safeguarding action plans in cooperation with state actors. Most Parties have taken this requirement on board, even if the degree of actual participation may differ widely.[19] In some cases, local people may propose ICH elements for

[14] Abdulqawi A Yusuf, 'Article 1—Definition of Cultural Heritage' in Francesco Francioni (ed), *The 1972 World Heritage Convention—A Commentary* (Oxford University Press, 2006).

[15] Allowing the World Heritage list to represent the diversity of all cultures around the world in their intellectual, aesthetic, religious and sociological expressions. According to Francesco Francioni in his 'Preamble' to Francesco Francioni (ed), *The 1972 World Heritage Convention—A Commentary* (Oxford University Press, 2006) at 20, the *Global Strategy* of the 1990s led to a dynamic interpretation of 'universality' and contains an evident anthropological dimension of cultural heritage, as opposed to a purely aesthetic and monumental art history approach.

[16] Antonio Arantes, 'Cultural Diversity and the Politics of Difference in Safeguarding Intangible Cultural Heritage' in Janet Blake (ed), *Safeguarding Intangible Cultural Heritage—Challenges and Approaches* (Institute of Art and Law, 2007).

[17] Convention for the Safeguarding of the Intangible Cultural Heritage (n 1) Articles 11(b) and 15. Article 15 reads: 'Within the framework of its safeguarding activities of the intangible cultural heritage, each State Party shall endeavour to ensure the widest possible participation of communities, groups and, where appropriate, individuals that create, maintain and transmit such heritage, and to involve them actively in its management.'

[18] This is very much the view taken in the 1989 Recommendation (n 4).

[19] An overview of the ways in which States Parties have done this can be found in the Summary of the Periodic Reports submitted to the Intangible Heritage Committee at its annual meetings. The relevant document for 2014 discussed at the 9th session of the Committee held in Paris 24–28 November 2014: Convention for the Safeguarding of the Intangible Cultural Heritage, 9th Session of the Intergovernmental

inscription, participate in completing inventory questionnaires, and may be consulted on safeguarding plans. In others, local interviewers (community members, representatives from local businesses, women's and children's associations, educational associations and so on) are trained to build up an inventory. NGOs also play a role as advisers to State organs in identifying ICH and for the operation of inventorying ICH and, in particular, providing expert advice on the methodology to be used.

## III. THE INTER-DISCIPLINARY CHARACTER OF REGULATING ICH

Of course, it is not peculiar to the international regulation of ICH that this process has been heavily influenced and deeply informed by other disciplines and that law-making in this area has followed from intellectual developments occurring in predominantly non-legal areas. This is true of many areas of international law (such as environment, trade, investment law and so on), but the way in which this influence has played out and continues to do so has implications for the Convention's implementation that may be subtly different and are worth examining further.

The term 'intangible cultural heritage' itself was used by anthropologists before it entered the legal lexicon and, thus it is no accident that a key UNESCO meeting in the history of developing the 2003 Convention was hosted by the Smithsonian Institution with a preponderance of non-legal scholars.[20] Once the decision was taken to elaborate a new Convention, the preliminary draft treaty text was prepared by a small group comprising non-lawyers and lawyers[21] and the input of anthropological (and related) experts was key. Equally, and I think unusually, the teams of governmental representatives during the inter-governmental stage of negotiation[22] commonly fielded cultural experts rather than legal ones. Non-legal experts have, of course, played a central role in international environmental policy-making and in the negotiation of some environmental treaties and instruments, such as the 1992 Rio Declaration.[23]

It is, however, the degree to which anthropologists, ethnographers and other cultural experts have continued to be deeply implicated in the process of

Committee for the Safeguarding of Intangible Cultural Heritage 24–28 November 2014 'Provisional Agenda: Examination of the reports of States Parties on the implementation of the Convention and on the current status of elements inscribed on the Representative List of the Intangible Cultural Heritage of Humanity, UNESCO Doc ITH/14/9.COM/5.a (22 November 2014).

[20] Global Assessment of the 1989 Recommendation (n 4). One of the recommendations to UNESCO of the Final Report of this conference, co-hosted with UNESCO, was to examine the question of elaborating a new standard-setting instrument for this aspect of heritage (still known as 'traditional culture and folklore').

[21] The history of this process is described in detail in Janet Blake, *Commentary on the 2003 UNESCO Convention on the Safeguarding of the Intangible Cultural Heritage* (Institute of Art and Law, 2006).

[22] Three sessions of the intergovernmental negotiations were held at UNESCO Headquarters in Paris between September 2002 and June 2003. These are briefly referred to in UNESCO 'Working Towards a Convention: Intangible Cultural Heritage' at 11–12, available at www.unesco.org/culture/ich/doc/src/01854-EN.pdf and described in detail in Janet Blake, *Commentary on the 2003 UNESCO Convention on the Safeguarding of the Intangible Cultural Heritage* (Institute of Art and Law, 2006) at 15–21.

[23] Philippe Sands, *Principles of International Environmental Law* (Cambridge University Press, 2003).

implementation (often acting as government officials in national cultural bodies) and setting national policies that may be significant here. In addition, they appear to be the main body of experts who commentate upon the treaty and its implementation, which is a key point and one that may have profound implications for its future development. If the situation continues as it is at present—where almost all the academic literature on this Convention, certainly in English, is written not by legal but by anthropological experts—while this can greatly enrich our understanding of the treaty and its implementation, it also carries dangers of serious misconceptions.

There has been a great deal of critical anthropology directed towards the treaty and this literature displays two predominant tendencies. First, there is a strong tendency to focus on the ICH elements listed on the RL in a highly critical manner but one that fails to recognise the legal techniques upon which this model relies and, importantly, ignores Part III of the Convention that contains the national safeguarding measures to be implemented by Parties (the heart of the Convention). Second, it betrays a failure to appreciate the basic realities of international law, including the principle of the sovereign equality of States, and a consequent lack of awareness of the limitations imposed by the international legal framework.

It is, of course, very healthy for the law (and lawyers) to be criticised from outside the discipline but some of this criticism is poorly targeted, fails to comprehend the legal requirements of the treaty and may lead to inappropriate policy approaches if it is not complemented by legal criticism. In addition, since the 2003 Convention enjoys the highly flexible structure of a main text, setting out broad purposes and principles (with few specific obligations), coupled with the work of the ICH Committee which develops the Operational Directives for implementation, the potential impact of such non-legal expertise is potentially very great and might, if insufficiently directed, result in unintended outcomes that may be harmful from a legal perspective.[24]

## IV. THE CASE OF GENDER AND SAFEGUARDING ICH

As a relatively youthful treaty, it is unsurprising that the 2003 Convention is still experiencing teething problems. For example, and probably inevitably, there has been a general over-enthusiasm about inscribing ICH elements on the RL which, in the case of some Parties, has been to the detriment of undertaking national measures for safeguarding ICH in general. Some Parties also appear to concentrate their safeguarding actions exclusively on internationally inscribed ICH. Although this could be positive in the long run by putting in place policies, institutional structures and legislative frameworks that can also contribute to safeguarding other ICH elements, it can also be read as a negative outcome of having such an international listing system in the first place. This is coupled with a serious misconception on the part

[24] For more on the issue of the role of experts from different fields (heritage studies and heritage law) in policy- and law-making in the cultural heritage field, see Lucas Lixinski, 'Between Orthodoxy and Heterodoxy: The Troubled Relationships between Heritage Studies and Heritage Law' (2015) 21 *International Journal of Heritage Studies* 203.

of many States Parties as to the conceptual basis of a 'representative' list and its essential difference from the notion of 'outstanding' on the World Heritage list (see discussion above at Section II).

Furthermore, the intellectual property (IP) aspects of safeguarding ICH have been a background issue since the inception of the Convention and are not yet fully resolved.[25] It is notable that several Parties (for example, Seychelles) have unilaterally included IP protection in their safeguarding approaches and have also, in a few cases, revised their IP legislation to take fuller account of the requirements of ICH under the Convention. Here, then, we see an emerging practice within States' domestic spheres that has the potential for informing the development of IP rules internationally. This is definitely an area that will need much further consideration and, in particular, how the work undertaken in WIPO since 2000 can (i) be harmonised with the operation of the Convention, and (ii) be directly informed by its experience.[26] Although the decision taken to develop a Convention that addresses ICH safeguarding on a broadly cultural basis, and not more narrowly as an IP issue alone (which was being strongly pushed at the time), was the correct one, this has left an important aspect of safeguarding without any certain approach and this needs to be resolved.

The main area of those challenges posed by the first eight years of implementing the Convention which this contribution seeks to address is one that may broadly be characterised as 'anthropological issues'. As mentioned above (at Section II), this treaty is one that cannot be easily divorced from questions relating to human beings as cultural actors since it concerns a form of heritage that is primarily located in human beings. This means that it immediately throws up a range of questions concerning social relationships and social power, including the gender dynamics at play both in the creation, enactment, expression and transmission of this heritage and also in its safeguarding. Of course, gender is not the only such question and both age and disability could also be appropriate subjects of a similar examination. Here, I have chosen to call these issues broadly 'anthropological' although they are very closely intertwined with human rights ones.

Indeed, the following case study on the gender dynamics of ICH and its safeguarding clearly shows the differences and the potential tensions between these two approaches and both aspects of the question are addressed here: the anthropological

[25] UNESCO and the World Intellectual Property Organization (WIPO) cooperated between 1970–1985 in order to develop a joint approach towards protecting traditional cultures and their expressions through intellectual property law (and related *sui generis* rules). By the mid 1980s there was a divergence whereby UNESCO began to explore a broader 'cultural' approach that went beyond the IP one. More recently, WIPO's work since 2000 on traditional cultural expressions and folklore can be seen as the continuation of this endeavour. For more on the history of this cooperation, see UNESCO-WIPO, World Forum on the Protection of Folklore 8–10 April 1997 '1967, 1982 and 1984: Attempts to Provide International Protection for Folklore by Intellectual Property Rights' UNESCO-WIPO/FOLK/PKT/97/19; and Janet Blake, *Developing a New Standard-setting Instrument for Safeguarding Intangible Cultural Heritage—Elements for Consideration* (UNESCO, 2001).

[26] A point noted in a recent internal evaluation by UNESCO of the 2003 Convention, 'Evaluation of UNESCO's Standard-setting Work of the Culture Sector: Part I—2003 Convention for the Safeguarding of the Intangible Cultural Heritage' (final report by Barbara Torggler and Ekaterina Sediakina-Rivière with Janet Blake as consultant) UNESCO Doc IOS/EVS/PI/129 REV.

issues are considered by looking at the *gender dynamics* of ICH and human rights questions are addressed with regard to *gender equality* in ICH and ICH safeguarding. Through this examination of the gender dynamics of ICH and of related issues of gender equality, I wish to illustrate the inevitable interactions between the operation of the 2003 Convention and questions more commonly understood to fall within the domain of the social sciences—its essentially inter-disciplinary character—and the implications that this has for its implementation.

## A. Gender Dynamics of ICH

Gender has largely been ignored in the heritage discourse[27] which is perhaps not surprising since the broader issue surrounding gender and heritage is related to the relative power of men and women in society. Moreover, in those cases where gender is directly addressed, it is usually reduced to 'women's issues' as if men have no gender. An important starting point in this discussion, then, is this recognition that gender should not be conceived as an isolated category but, rather, it should always be viewed within the context of other power relations in society. This fact has important implications not only for how we regard the gender dynamics of ICH and its safeguarding, but also, more broadly, how community participation in implementing the Convention is handled.[28] Above all, it clearly signals the fact that there is a great danger of viewing 'the cultural community' as if it is a monolithic structure and ignoring the diversity of experiences and aspirations of its members and, as a result, putting in place 'participatory' structures that favour certain community members' interests over others. To some degree this is inevitable, but having a better awareness of the diversity within communities—of which gender diversity is one aspect—can greatly help in designing participatory approaches that answer more appropriately to the needs of community members as a whole.

When dealing specifically with the question of gender, there are a number of assumptions that we commonly make which we need to be aware of and which we should attempt to avoid when developing a conceptual framework for addressing the gender dimensions of ICH. First and foremost, there is a common tendency in many societies (in particular, but not exclusively, Western ones) to conceive of gender as a dualistic male-female dichotomy. In reality, however, the differences that are often attributed to a woman's or a man's biological nature are frequently the result of their relative positions within the social structure and the expectations in terms of their behaviour placed on men and women by society.[29]

[27] Laurajane Smith, 'Gender, heritage and identity' in Brian Graham and Peter Howard (eds), *The Ashgate Research Companion to Heritage and Identity* (Ashgate Publishing, 2007) 159. She notes further at page 160 that 'Gender, alongside concepts of ethnicity and class, is perhaps one of the most unproblematized and naturalized aspects of identity within heritage discourses'.

[28] As noted in Section II, community participation in safeguarding is a fundamental requirement of the 2003 Convention and is required explicitly in Articles 11(b) and 15.

[29] Judith Lorber, *Paradoxes of Gender* (Yale University Press, 1995).

It has been argued that the current use of gender as a universal and timeless social category must be read in relation to the global dominance of European/American cultures and the ideology of biological determinism which underpins Western systems of knowledge.[30] Hence, there is no single, globally universal understanding of gender[31] as a result of which, for example, ICH documentation programmes in the Pacific region frequently misinterpret the nature of traditional gender roles and may ignore the gender complementarities that exist there.[32]

In addition to the danger of making false culture-bound assumptions, seeking to avoid these by applying the Convention in a 'gender-blind' fashion might itself actually reproduce or reinforce the discrimination and exclusion experienced by women and gender-based minorities.[33] It is important, therefore, to be aware of the risk of reinforcing, through approaches to ICH safeguarding, a mainstream gender order that assumes a dualistic form of gender based on biological sex alone.[34] Rather, it is necessary to apply a critical reflection to such concepts as gender instead of reinforcing them and to address existing stereotypes instead of reproducing them. The examples given below clearly indicate that gender is a much more complex phenomenon and that the variety of potential gender roles goes far beyond the male-female dichotomy. In order to address this diversity, we need to find a perspective that contextualises gender in the practices and activities of both men and women and the social power negotiations involved. It is possible to identify here certain questions that are key when considering gender and ICH and, in particular, to ask what impact recognising ICH and its practitioners, and implementing other safeguarding measures, will have on this.

The first question is how far the ICH created and practised by women and other subaltern gender groups in society is neglected and unidentified. As Nussbaum

[30] For example, Oyeronke Oyewumi has argued that the current use of gender as a universal and timeless social category must be read in relation to the global dominance of European/American cultures and the ideology of biological determinism which underpins Western systems of knowledge, see Oyeronke Oyewumi, *The Invention of Women: Making an African Sense of Western Gender Discourses* (University of Minnesota Press, 1997); and Oyeronke Oyewumi, 'Conceptualizing gender: the eurocentric foundations of feminist concepts and the challenge of African epistemologies' (Council for the Development of Social Science Research in Africa), available at www.codesria.org/IMG/pdf/OYEWUMI.pdf.

[31] Marilyn Strathern, *The Gender of Gift* (University of California Press, 1988) employed a feminist approach to argue that Papuan women are not being exploited, but rather that the definition of gender is different from the Western one.

[32] Lissant Bolton and Susanna Kelly, 'Women, Intangible Heritage and Development, a Feasibility Study—Pacific Region' (May 2001, Tehran) 33 state '[many ICH programmes] misunderstand the nature of traditional gender roles, and the way in which rights are locally understood and enacted ... Pacific gender models assume that men and women are very different but complementary, although in many societies men have greater apparent authority in decision-making.'

[33] Valentine M Moghadam and Manilee Bagheritari, '*Culture Conventions and the Human Rights of Women: Examining the Convention for Safeguarding Intangible Cultural Heritage and the Declaration on Cultural Diversity*' (2005)1 UNESCO Social and Human Sciences Papers in Women's Studies/Gender Research, available at www.unesco.org/new/fileadmin/MULTIMEDIA/HQ/SHS/pdf/Cultures_Conventions_HR_Women.pdf.

[34] Regina Frey and others, 'Gender Manifesto—A call for critical reflection on Gender-oriented capacity building and consultancy' (translated by Farah Alouidor and Rachel Andras, 2006) 2, available at www.gender.de/mainstreaming/GenderManifesto_engl.pdf notes that, through critical reflection on gender, 'the societal norm of heterosexual duality of sexes and its inherent causal connection of biological sex with gender and desire is thus called into question'.

and others have noted, women's productive work is often uncounted and made invisible,[35] and so is their contribution (and that of members of gender-based minorities) to the creating and safeguarding of ICH. This is, of course, an important issue for Parties when officially identifying and giving recognition to ICH and with regard to the international inscription of ICH elements under the 2003 Convention.

Second, it is important to consider the effect of the marginalisation of women and other gender-based groups from a public sphere generally dominated by men and their ICH. Ironically, this may often result in them becoming the privileged reproducers of certain ICH elements in their communities. This fact, then, leads us to ask whether giving it recognition and significance as a 'heritage' is positive for the communities, groups and individuals in question or whether it serves to reinforce their social marginalisation and subordination.

Tied to this issue is the following question: how do the interpretation, safeguarding and management of ICH legitimise gender stereotypes? For example, it may be necessary to re-examine the assumptions underlying the designation of certain ICH practices as predominantly 'female' ones (for example, handicrafts and textile weaving) and others as 'male' ones (for example, certain initiation rites). Taking such an approach will allow us to identify more easily the differences that exist between individuals in society (rather than between men and women) and help us to avoid taking a monolithic view of defining the essence of men and women, allowing us to take account of the processes of subordination and negotiation that are a part of social relations.[36]

## B. Gender as a Form of Diversity

The gender dynamics of ICH are many and various. As has been alluded to above, gender, in all its variety, is itself an important form of diversity that is manifested in many ICH practices, performances and enactments. Since the concept of gender diversity has its roots in culture, it should be a key idea applied when addressing the gender dynamics of ICH. Given that diversity is increasingly acknowledged as a value in international cultural policy,[37] it seems appropriate to ascribe a value to the diversity of gender roles and relations as expressed through ICH which are, essentially a cultural phenomenon. In order to be able to recognise the gender diversity manifested in ICH, however, the 'gender corset' of a bipolar and hierarchical understanding of gender needs to be loosened to make room for less deterministic understandings of gender.[38]

[35] Martha Nussbaum, *Women and Human Development: The Capabilities Approach* (Cambridge University Press, 2000); see also Joycelin Massiah (ed), *Women in Developing Economies: Making Visible the Invisible* (UNESCO Publications, 1994).

[36] Roberta S Sigel, *Ambition and Accommodation. How Women View Gender Relations* (University of Chicago Press, 1996).

[37] Although specifically celebrating cultural diversity, the 2001 Declaration on Cultural Diversity can be relevant here since the gender diversity expressed in ICH is itself, a cultural phenomenon.

[38] Regina Frey and others (n 34).

In the rite of the Châu van shamans' song from Viet Nam, for example, gender roles are reversed whereby female mediums assume traditionally 'male' roles and male dress, while male mediums take on traditionally 'female' gender roles, dress and behaviours.[39] In a similar way, the kabuki *onnagata* is a male actor who specialises in the art of performing female gender roles. For over 300 years, these performers developed rigorous performance techniques and stylised performance codes,[40] creating complex roles marked by gender ambiguity and transformativity that brought the binary/oppositional gender system of male and female into question.[41] By analysing kabuki, we can understand that the body is not a purely biological form but is, above all, a socio-cultural construct.[42]

The song and dance performances of the Acoli in Uganda represent another popular cultural form through which gender is performed and provide an example of a form of ICH in which men and women have clearly differentiated roles.[43] In Acoli, there is a binary dichotomy of gender identity which is seen as something that can be productively harnessed for the social organisation of society.[44] Through their performance women create for themselves a public space in which 'their' issues are forced onto the public agenda and they 'appropriate the existing binary gender notions and use them to their advantage'.[45]

This analysis appears to undermine much gender research which focuses on a critique of gender roles and generally regards all forms of gender differentiation as 'bad'. In contrast, in the Acoli song performance gender is embraced as 'good' and gender differentiation is used as a social resource.[46] This example reminds us, then, that gender differentiated roles in ICH enactment is not inherently negative.

[39] Barley Norton, *Songs for the Spirits—Music and Mediums in Modern Vietnam* (University of Illinois Press, 2009) 155–89. This rite has been nominated by Viet Nam for inclusion on the RL but reduced, for the purposes of nomination, to a performing art stripped of all of its deviant gender roles, religious content and 'superstitious' aspects. See fr.vietnamplus.vn/patrimoine-immateriel-nouveau-dossier-de-candidature-pour-lunesco/46512.vnp; and vovworld.vn/en-US/Sunday-Show/Chau-van-Vietnamese-ritual-singing/344354.vov.

[40] *Onnagata kata.*

[41] Katherine Mezur, *The Kabuki Onnagata: a Feminist Analysis of the Onnagata Fiction of Female-Likeness* (University of Hawaii at Manoa, 1998); see also Katherine Mezur, *Beautiful boys/ Outlaw bodies: Devising Kabuki female-likeness* (Palgrave, 2005); Minoru Fujita and Michael Shapiro (eds), *Transvestism and the onnagata traditions in Shakespeare and Kabuki* (Global Oriental, 2006).

[42] Galia Todorova Gabrovska, 'Gender and Body Construction in Edo Period *Kabuki*' (2009) 5 *Core Ethics* 71, 72.

[43] Benge Okot, 'Striking the Snake with its own Fangs: Uganda Acoli Song, Performance and Gender Dynamics' in VY Mudimbe (ed), *Contemporary African Cultural Productions* (Codesria, 2013).

[44] Ibid 109. Here it is noted that, traditionally, the African worldview took the human society as organic, in which all the members were considered relevant and effective for the survival of the society.

[45] Ibid 119–20. Through their own dance-songs, Acoli women have mobilised themselves into self-help groups to promote themselves and highlight issues affecting them as a gender category, namely 'women'.

[46] Ibid 110:

> Although it would seem the gender positioning tends to favour the males over the females, Acoli women generally have not attempted to change the performance of their gender to achieve 'equality' and 'democracy' as we would understand from the point of view of Western political ideology. Instead, it would seem, they have invested in gender as understood from the Acoli cultural perspective to achieve their aspirations within the patriarchal social system. Song performance plays a key role, not only as a catalyst but an integral part of this investment in gender.

Another ICH element that demonstrates a clear gender-based division of labour is the traditional manufacturing of children's wooden toys by villagers in Hrvatsko Zagorje (Croatia), using a technique that has been handed down within families for generations. The men gather soft willow, lime, beech and maple wood and then dry, hew, cut and carve it into toys using traditional tools; the women then decorate the toys with improvised floral or geometric patterns, painting 'from imagination', using environmentally-friendly paint. Similarly, in Taquile textile weaving in Peru, the pedal loom and needles are used only by men to make garments of Spanish colonial influence (trousers, hats) and the plain loom is used only by women to make more traditional garments (such as blankets). The Ceremonial Keşkek Tradition (Turkey) represents a more cooperative relationship; men and women work together to cook the ceremonial meal in huge cauldrons and then serve it to guests.

### C. Gender Equality and ICH

As has been suggested above, there is a distinction to be drawn between the fact of the gender dynamics of ICH and the diversity it contains, and the question of gender equality in the practice and safeguarding of ICH. While the former is primarily an anthropological issue, the latter implicates human rights directly. Moreover, it is clear that the fundamental predicates of the two approaches are different and, to some degree, potentially incompatible.[47] This presents a serious challenge if we want to preserve the gender diversity of ICH while respecting the human rights of individuals in the associated cultural communities and social groups.

In addition to treaty-based cultural rights,[48] the non-discrimination principle constitutes an important legal basis for defending the cultural practices and identities of minorities and other groups in society. Here, we understand discrimination to mean any distinction, exclusion, restriction or preference or other differential treatment that is directly or indirectly based on the prohibited grounds of discrimination (including sex) which has the intention or effect of nullifying or impairing the recognition, equal enjoyment or exercise of human rights.[49] Hence, the right to access and enjoyment of one's cultural heritage (based on the right to participate in cultural life)

[47] More broadly, William S Logan, 'Cultural diversity, cultural heritage and human rights: towards heritage management as human rights-based cultural practice' (2012) 18 *International Journal of Heritage Studies* 231 argues that human rights brought to the foreground when dealing with heritage as a cultural practice.

[48] International Covenant on Economic, Social and Cultural Rights (adopted 16 December 1966, entered into force 3 January 1976) 993 UNTS 3 (ICESCR) Article 15 on the right to participate in cultural life; International Covenant on Civil and Political Rights (adopted 16 December 1966, entered into force 23 March 1976) 999 UNTS 171 (ICCPR) Article 27 on the rights of ethnic, linguistic and cultural minorities, the human rights related to culture (freedom of expression, freedom of association etc) and the special rights of women, children, indigenous, disabled persons and migrants with regard to culture.

[49] See UN Economic and Social Council (ECOSOC), Committee on Economic, Social and Cultural Rights (CESCR), 43rd session 2–20 November 2009 'General Comment No 20 on "Non-discrimination in economic, social and cultural rights (art. 2, para 2, of the International Covenant on Economic, Social and Cultural Rights)"' Doc E/C.12/GC/20.

is one that all people and communities should enjoy equally with no discrimination on the basis, inter alia, of sex, age, race and so on.

In contrast to the anthropological view of gender presented above, the human rights principles of equality and non-discrimination are predicated upon the fact of biological sex, not on gender per se. Some feminist commentators have questioned the basis of the human rights notion of equality, regarding it as a male-dominated view that ignores issues of power and domination and fails to address the unequal and engendered structures of societies.[50] As we have seen above, 'female' gender roles derive from the position of women in the wider social structure and the expectations placed on them by society and not, immediately, from their biological sex itself.

With regard to human rights and gender equality, questions will continue to be raised about the validity of claims to preserve traditional cultural practices that include, and may even promote, non-egalitarian elements.[51] Such claims should be measured against the rights of women, children and others who are often marginalised and disempowered by the traditional cultural practices.[52] Hence, human rights-based limitations do exist on the right of everyone to take part in cultural life, in particular in the case of harmful practices attributed to customs and traditions that violate other human rights.[53]

However, these limitations must be proportionate and aimed towards taking the least restrictive measures in cases where a choice of measures exists.[54] Certain practices, such as forced marriage or foot-binding, can obviously never be condoned from a human rights perspective, but many others lie in a difficult grey area in which identifying the degree of harm to individuals can be extremely problematic and the thorny question is raised of who should make such determinations and how.

The Convention on the Elimination of Discrimination Against Women (CEDAW, 1979) addressed the issue of gender (and the role of women) with regard to cultural traditions in Article 5(a) on the elimination of 'prejudices and customary and all other practices which are based on the idea of the inferiority of either of the sexes

[50] See, for example, Hilary Charlesworth and Christine Chinkin, *The Boundaries of International Law: A Feminist Analysis* (Manchester University Press, 2000). Similar criticism is levelled by Laurajane Smith, *The Uses of Heritage* (Routledge, 2006) against what she terms the 'authorized heritage discourse' (AHD).

[51] It is important to distinguish here the term 'preservation' (keeping things exactly as they were) from 'safeguarding' (ensuring viability while recreating and/or adapting to change). The latter is the 2003 Convention's paradigm.

[52] It is clearly stated in the Convention on the Elimination of All Forms of Discrimination against Women (adopted 18 December 1979, entered into force 3 September 1981) 1249 UNTS 13, Article 5 that '[States Parties] shall take all appropriate measures to modify the social and cultural patterns of conduct of men and women, with a view to achieving the elimination of prejudices and customary and all other practices which are based on the idea of the inferiority or the superiority of either of the sexes or on stereotyped roles for men and women.'

[53] These might include infanticide (right to life), refusal to educate girls (right to education, equality of access), and certain public practices which may violate the individual's right to privacy.

[54] ECOSOC, Committee on Economic, Social and Cultural Rights (CESCR), 43rd session 2–20 November 2009 'General comment No 21 (2009) on The Right of everyone to take part in cultural life (art 15, para 1 (a), of the International Covenant on Economic, Social and Cultural Rights)' Doc E/C.12/GC/21, para 19.

or on stereotyped roles for men and women'. It is noteworthy that this article does not target the traditional cultural attitudes and practices themselves (or even any differentiated roles assigned to men and women) but rather any specific negative consequences that may result from them. These negative consequences may include regarding women as inferior to men and applying stereotyped roles to them (which dis-empower women or otherwise harm their interests). Hence the focus is, quite correctly, on those negative outcomes of certain cultural traditions (what would be the ICH elements in relation to the 2003 Convention) and this has an important consequence for the implementation of the Convention and the application of the 'human rights filter' it contains.[55]

However, bearing in mind the previous discussion of gender from an anthropological viewpoint, caution is required in applying this non-discrimination filter to avoid an over-strict or overly simplistic approach. It is important to understand the wider social context of the ICH element in question and the ways in which it may provide social benefits as well as losses. Work concerning gender and ICH should therefore be framed around avoiding negative social outcomes while celebrating potential positive outcomes for different members of society from enacting, practising and performing ICH.

Following this logic, ICH practices should not be discounted solely on the basis of the fact that they are, for example, sexually segregated. It is a reality in many societies worldwide that many social and cultural practices are segregated (on the basis of age, sex and other criteria) and this fact alone should not be taken as a sign that discrimination is taking place. It is only through applying a gender-based analysis (as set out above) that we will be able to recognise whether an element of ICH, that is, a social practice, ritual or oral tradition, is really discriminatory. As a corollary to this, it is not necessary for sexual segregation or other forms of sexual differentiation in practice and/or enactment to be involved for discriminatory aspects to be identified.[56]

## V. CONCLUSION

The interactions between gender and ICH performance (enactment, practice and so on) are complex and, to a degree, mutual. As a consequence, safeguarding approaches have the potential to impact on them in both positive and negative ways. From this, we see clearly how applying an anthropological analysis of gender and gender roles is vital for the appropriate implementation of the 2003 Convention: an inter-disciplinary approach is therefore a pre-requisite for ensuring the proper and

[55] The definition of ICH given in the Convention for the Safeguarding of Intangible Cultural Heritage (n 1) Article 2 para 1 limits the ICH that can be safeguarded under the Convention as follows: 'For the purposes of this Convention, consideration will be given solely to such intangible cultural heritage as is compatible with existing international human rights instruments, as well as with the requirements of mutual respect among communities, groups and individuals.'

[56] For example, violations of the following rights: the right to a private life (eg forced marriage); the right to education (cultural traditions that prevent girls from attending primary school); and the right to life (eg female infanticide or selective abortion).

successful operation of this Convention over the long term. The examples given in this article illustrate the variety of gender dynamics at play in ICH and, hence, the complexity of safeguarding these appropriately.

Therefore, in implementing the 2003 Convention, we need to consider a number of questions, which include the following: does official recognition of women (and gender minority) practitioners and transmitters of ICH contribute to their empowerment in contemporary societies? To what extent does ICH depend on gender-specific transmission? Can the concept of gender equality always be compatible with preserving traditional cultures?

When we consider the illustrative examples of gender diversity in ICH described in this article and the question of how to apply the theoretical and contextual considerations set out above to the implementation of the 2003 Intangible Heritage Convention, Kurin's observation that the Convention tends to reduce ICH to 'a list of largely expressive traditions, atomistically recognized and conceived' becomes relevant. He suggests that, as a result of this, the safeguarding actions it proposes tend to miss the larger, holistic aspect of culture of which its gender dynamics form a part.[57]

Heritage can be conceived as a point or *moment* of negotiation[58] that may occur during the performances of ICH or in relation to sites and objects of symbolic value. Although it is difficult to state definitively which comes first, gender identity or the performance of it,[59] the key point here is that heritage is a process in which identity (including gender identity) and social and cultural meaning are mediated, evaluated and worked out.[60]

Although human beings generally tend to assimilate/learn gender positioning by repeated acts right from childhood, gender identity is performative and it is possible to change the way we perform our gender.[61] One of the conclusions we can draw from this is that not only do we express our gender identities through ICH but they are also shaped to some degree by it and this process can be affected by safeguarding practices and interventions. This underlines the necessity both of applying a gender-sensitive approach to safeguarding and, as this article seeks to demonstrate, for an appropriate balance between legal and non-legal (anthropological) experts in this process in order to ensure a sufficiently nuanced but well-grounded approach towards gender.

[57] Richard Kurin, 'Safeguarding Intangible Cultural Heritage in the 2003 UNESCO Convention: a critical appraisal' (2004) 56 *Museum International* 66, 74–75, it is this holistic character—'the intricate and complex web of meaningful social actions undertaken by individuals, groups, and institutions', he argues, which is the very characteristic that makes culture intangible.

[58] Laurajane Smith, 'Empty Gestures? Heritage and the Politics of Recognition' in H Silverman and DF Ruggles (eds), *Cultural Heritage and Human Rights* (Springer, 2007).

[59] Okot (n 43).

[60] Smith (n 58).

[61] Judith Butler, *Gender Trouble: Feminism and the Subversion of Identity* (Routledge, 1990) 32; she also noted on page 25: 'There is no gender identity behind the expressions of gender; that identity is performatively constituted by the very expressions that are said to be its results.'

# 28

# Zero Dark Thirty: *International Law, Torture and Representation*

DANIEL JOYCE* AND GABRIELLE SIMM**

## I. INTRODUCTION

IN OUR MEDIATISED and visually-driven era, international law, its institutions and practitioners feel the pull of publicity, engage with techniques of communicative power, and increasingly negotiate the politics of representation. There is increasing attention given to the visual dimension of law and the normative power of the image.[1] In the fields of human rights and international criminal justice in particular, film has been used as evidence, and for advocacy and outreach. For recent examples one can think of the viral social media experiment *Kony 2012* or the earlier significance of film as evidence in the trials at the International Criminal Tribunal for the former Yugoslavia and later the International Criminal Court.

This chapter explores the relationship between film and international law against a historical and theoretical backdrop, foreshadowing the further development of international legal theory regarding the image and also engaging with relevant film criticism. We examine one recent feature film, *Zero Dark Thirty*, directed by Kathryn Bigelow and released in December 2012. The film focuses on a fictionalised account of the covert US operation to capture and kill Osama bin Laden. The contribution uses the film and its critical reception as a means to begin to consider related questions of genre, torture, gender, targeted killing and the dangers presented by their representation in a Hollywood film.

By focusing on the debates over the film, and its critical fallout, the intention is both to examine the power of pictures and the influence of the visual in the field of international law, but also to explore the accompanying risks. Having looked at the ambiguous visual record presented of the killing of bin Laden, we call into question the power of pictures and call for greater attention to be paid to the limits and ethics of representation in the practice and portrayal of international law.

* Lecturer, Faculty of Law, University of New South Wales.

** Chancellor's Post Doctoral Research Fellow, Faculty of Law, University of Technology Sydney.
A longer and extended version of this contribution has been published in the *London Review of International Law* (2015).

[1] See how these questions are entering mainstream journalism in 'Visibility Before All; Video and Human Rights', *The Economist*, 14 January 2012, 58–59.

## II. INTERNATIONAL LAW AND FILM

The power of images and the significance of film are most commonly understood and integrated within law at the evidentiary and documentary level.[2] Yet international law has also found itself to be the subject of larger and more commercial feature films, principally produced for audience entertainment and consumption, and less motivated by a functional or pedagogical purpose. At times this has been explicit but many older genres of popular film, such as those dealing with the criminal justice system, and with conquest and conflict, have an important international law 'resonance'.

From early film representations such as *Judgment at Nuremberg* (1961) to more recent human rights and international law-related films such as *Hotel Rwanda* (2004), *Blood Diamond* (2006) and *The Whistleblower* (2010), international law has found itself to be the focus of several important and popular feature films. This development has coincided with a broader post-cold war turn towards international law and its concepts in both media discourse and popular culture. International law's expansion, growing confidence and reach has also been a factor. Yet popular influence and political significance in times of war, transition and global connection have come with an attendant uncertainty, concern and caution. International lawyers both want and shun the spotlight; desire recognition and power, yet fear misrepresentation and spectacle.

Film is also culturally situated—the debate within international economic law about the treatment of cultural products is often a debate in shorthand about the pervasive cultural influence (and empire) of Hollywood and American film. Thus, film as a global economy is positioned within wider debates about community formation and even over the place of liberal internationalism and the hegemonic role of the United States. During the cold war, film and art were key products in the battle for cultural supremacy and public diplomacy. Film has often been held up as a mirror to society and as our own era has seen a growth in human rights discourse and the juridification of political debate about conflict and its resolution, it is perhaps no surprise that the discipline has found itself caught up with the world of cultural production and image-making. As Anne Orford has written, there is a danger that the representation of international law in media accounts, can itself feed off and profit from the imagery of suffering, whilst concealing deeper questions of responsibility.[3]

International law's treatment within film has been as varied as the many genres and narrative archetypes that populate the industry.[4] Films such as *Blood Diamond* and *The Whistleblower* have used international justice themes as a variation on familiar earlier genres such as docudrama, crime, conflict and even outlaw

[2] There is increasing, but still limited, scholarly interest in questions of visual representation, the image and law. See, for example, Costas Douzinas, *Law and the Image: the Authority of Art and the Aesthetics of Law* (University of Chicago Press, 1999); Richard K Sherwin, *Visualizing Law in the Age of the Digital Baroque: Arabesques and Entanglements* (Routledge, 2011).

[3] Anne Orford, *Reading Humanitarian Intervention: Human Rights and the Use of Force in International Law* (Cambridge University Press, 2003) 78.

[4] A useful resource on international law and film can be found at iiljfilms.blogspot.com.uk/.

narratives. Other films such as *The Interpreter* (2005) have used international law's glamour and even the UN's architecture as a backdrop for a traditional political thriller.

There have also been films with an explicit documentary aesthetic such as Errol Morris' work *The Fog of War* (2003) and *Standard Operating Procedure* (2008) exploring the cold war, Vietnam and Abu Ghraib through stark and revealing interviews with key participants. Another film, *The Act of Killing* (2012), uses documentary techniques to explore paramilitary violence and killings in 1960s Indonesia which have remained unaccounted for as crimes. This kind of aesthetic is almost film 'as justice', where participants illustrate the moral complexities in their various roles of witness, victim and perpetrator and urge mechanisms of international law and human rights to respond. *Hotel Rwanda* is another example of this type of film seeking to represent the Rwandan Genocide, though doing so in the context of UN failures to act and subsequent hesitant efforts at the International Criminal Tribunal for Rwanda (ICTR) to deliver justice.

Although *Hotel Rwanda* attempts to give quite an accurate picture of what occurred, it does so through a micro focus on a safe haven: an idealised space of bravery and hope, an oasis amidst desolation. In the face of the genocidal violence and killing outside the Hotel's walls the audience's attention is in the main fixed on the Hotel and we come to understand the tragedy through a small cast of characters, who we trust have faced evil, but who through courage and the human spirit cling to survival, and remain for the most part safe within the walls, abandoned by the West but still protected in some part by Western walls and local ingenuity.[5] Film is adapting to the broader changes in the digital media landscape and has migrated online both as commodified cultural product, and also as a YouTube clip and marketing tool. Here a recent example is the *Kony 2012* experiment in viral online film advocacy.[6]

Traditional epistolary and oral forms of civic engagement have been widened to include social and other forms of digital media advocacy, remaining heavily reliant on the development of an aesthetic and imagery associated with human rights and international criminal justice-related themes. These aesthetics have also fed back into the use of film as evidence at key trials such as the Lubanga trial at the International Criminal Court (ICC), with its echoes of the use of film at Nuremberg. The use of film at the Nuremberg trials was significant and yet has also been underplayed in subsequent accounts for the effect of the film also threatened spectacle and thereby potentially undermined the careful archival sensibility of much of the evidence.[7]

Of course, just because international law finds itself screened to global audiences both as entertainment and as advocacy, does not mean that the screening has been

[5] For a more developed reading of the film and an examination of the power of human rights-related films see: Lena Khor, 'Human Rights and Network Power' (2011) 33(1) *Human Rights Quarterly* 105.

[6] Daniel Joyce, 'Media Witnesses: Human Rights in an Age of Digital Media' (2013) 8 *Intercultural Human Rights Law Review* 231, 258–62.

[7] Telford Taylor, *The Anatomy of the Nuremberg Trials: A Personal Memoir* (Bloomsbury, 1993) 186–87.

successful or that this engagement with film comes without risk.[8] Kony remains on the run and the film is an example of a successful experiment in terms of its distribution, but a failure in terms of remedy.[9] *Blood Diamond* sits alongside other action adventures in online market places, largely divorced from ongoing debates regarding resources and conflict.[10] The complexity of the film, *Standard Operating Procedure*, with its reading of the perpetrators as potential victims and witnesses, has been largely lost in our indignation at the Abu Ghraib imagery and its entry into the realm of international law iconography.

Often international legal complexities have translated poorly onto the big screen. As with debates over international legality and the public demand for clarity from experts, the mediatisation of international legal subjects has resulted in a dilemma—how to acknowledge the politics, complexity and failures of the discipline, whilst also appealing to a form of normative certainty in its representation on screen as some form of moral internationalism or at least humanitarianism.

An example of the dangers of human rights heroism as film can be found in the documentary *E-Team* (2014) which follows the work of Human Rights Watch's emergency team as they themselves document, record and publicise violations of human rights and international law.[11] Does this kind of genre veer too close to advocacy at the expense of moral complexity or even visual power?

If international lawyers cannot always provide clear answers to complex questions, then for film-makers at least we are expected to provide adventure, strong narrative concerns and moral significance. How then to account for the technical and mundane elements within our discipline, for the fact that often international justice makes for poor viewing—just try the ICC or UN TV for starters.[12] How also to account for the competing demands of celebrity and justice? Celebrity can assist with publicity, but can it deepen processes of justice? Or is there a danger that it will trivialise and divert such efforts? This kind of concern is often personified in our view of Hollywood actors or musicians as UN ambassadors and moral agents. As Kristy Siegfried asks, how good are the UN's goodwill ambassadors?[13]

## III. *ZERO DARK THIRTY*

*Zero Dark Thirty* has also faced this difficulty. Will Kathryn Bigelow do for the aftermath of 9/11 what Leonardo DiCaprio did for blood diamonds and Nicole Kidman did for the UN interpreting service? Bigelow drew significant criticism for

[8] There is an emerging category of human rights film festival. See discussion of this phenomenon and an instrumentalist argument for human rights films, in Sonia Tascon, 'Considering Human Rights Films, Representation, and Ethics: Whose Face?' (2012) 34(3) *Human Rights Quarterly* 864.

[9] Sam Gregory, 'Kony 2012 Through a Prism of Video Advocacy Practices and Trends' (2012) 4 *Journal of Human Rights Practice* 463.

[10] For a counter argument see Khor (n 5).

[11] See further www.abc.net.au/lateline/content/2014/s4020784.htm.

[12] Proceedings stream 'live' from the ICC website. Cf UN TV at webtv.un.org/.

[13] See Kristy Siegfried, 'How good are Goodwill Ambassadors?' *IRIN*, 28 October 2013, available at www.irinnews.org/report/99012/how-good-are-goodwill-ambassadors.

her representation of torture and interrogation in the film and principally for failing to take an overtly political position regarding the abuse of human rights and violation of international law within the film. If her film is powerful in terms of her visual representation of significant events in recent political history, it is seemingly silent in terms of situating its subject matter explicitly within an international legal framework. What is especially interesting is the 'absence' of international law in this powerful film. The film also blurs the distinction between documentary and fiction. Bigelow faces the difficulty of taking on a subject of such contemporary significance and complexity when there has been arguably insufficient time to reflect on these 'events' and their full variety of meaning. As Keyan Tomaselli and Maureen Eke argue: '[M]ost films lack a sense of history as process. This is because films relate their messages in the perceptual present.'[14]

Yet the film opens explicitly contextualised by the events of 9/11 with the screen blank while recordings of victims play in the background. The audience is told that the film deals in real events and that its protagonists draw on stories and experiences that have been shared by historical figures. This aesthetic of 'authenticity' is blended throughout what is otherwise very much a Hollywood film. The film is punctuated by familiar and unfamiliar historical events and locations such as interrogations of terror suspects in 'black sites', the terror attacks in London, the shifting political sands of the US regarding torture and interrogation techniques following the election of President Obama, the targeting of the CIA in Pakistan and Afghanistan, and especially the hunt for and eventual assassination of bin Laden in Pakistan.

The central character, Maya, is a young CIA operative who has spent her entire professional adult life obsessed with capturing and killing bin Laden. She has lost colleagues and friends in this pursuit, and faced obstacles and criticism within the CIA for her work. She has also been tutored in the practice of torture and participates in gruelling interrogations of suspects with colleagues at black sites, all the while building an investigative trail leading to bin Laden. This hunt is thwarted by politics, the anti-torture lobby, the lazy careerism of her CIA superiors and simply by plain old human error and miscalculation.

Eventually her instincts regarding the significance and identity of a key messenger for bin Laden lead her, and the CIA and special forces team tasked to find him, to his bunker in Pakistan. It is an already familiar story, but now we are purportedly being given more detail than the media or official narratives have provided. Maya confronts office politics and bureaucracy, and is told to watch her back as political attitudes change to the interrogations, but her obsession with her target leads inexorably towards a high-risk covert mission to assassinate bin Laden—a mission which we know from the beginning to have been successful.

The film forms two halves. The first is immersed in the gritty, repulsive and unlawful world of interrogations where Maya is both participant and observer. The US is revealed as both victim and perpetrator, as powerful and weak. The second half largely revolves around Maya making the political case to her superiors for the

[14] Keyan G Tomaselli and Maureen Eke, 'Film and Human Rights: Whose Rights, Whose Interpretations, What Consequences?' (1997) 9 *Visual Anthropology* 353, 353.

resources to conduct the necessary investigative work; and then the audience follows the special operations team in seemingly real time as they undertake their darkened mission in stealthy helicopters into Pakistani territory.

But in a critical way the two halves are connected. The audience is led to believe that without the information gathered from the interrogations there would be no lead on the whereabouts of bin Laden. Do the unlawful means then justify the ends? Bin Laden is of course ultimately killed; his hard drives and files are retrieved, but what next? Is he in fact already history before he is killed? Maya identifies the body and flies home alone, finally able to cry. But the revenge motif is obscured. Is she grieving for her own loss and culpability? Does she represent America's loss or is she upset by the futility of it all? To her credit, Bigelow's film does not provide easy answers here and in some ways represents a screen upon which the audience can project its own anxieties and desires. The ending remains, after all, an anti-climax.

The reception of *Zero Dark Thirty* has been controversial and divided. At first, film critics applauded it as a powerful film presenting mainstream audiences with the difficult facts about the US 'War on Terror' and its use of torture in the hunt for Osama bin Laden. The film was nominated for five Academy Awards and named best picture of 2012 by the New York Film Critics Circle.[15] Yet when political journalists started to review the film, questions were raised about its claims to represent the truth and it was derided as 'a snuff film'[16] and as 'a failure on every level from the theatrical to the historical to the moral'.[17] Many journalists criticised the film as an apology for torture by inaccurately representing the fact that torture was critical in eliciting information that ultimately led the covert teams to bin Laden.[18] Such debates echoed those within our own scholarly community regarding torture and its legality.[19]

In addition to radical disagreement over whether the film supports or undermines the use of torture, critics cannot agree into which genre it falls. The issue of genre is important as genres raise expectations and critics may applaud a film adhering to or subverting generic tropes in unexpected ways. Finally, the gender of its heroine, Maya, has been an important factor in terms of how *Zero Dark Thirty* has been interpreted. She is presented alternatively as either a wonder woman figure succeeding improbably in a hyper-masculine, yet curiously bureaucratic, world, or as an asexual plot device whose significance for feminist progress is undercut by the familiar trope of the pleasure in looking at a beautiful monster.

[15] Steve Coll, '"Disturbing" & "Misleading"', *New York Review of Books*, 7 February 2013.

[16] Joann Wypijewski, 'Picture Show', *The Nation*, 18 February 2013.

[17] Bronwen Maddox, 'For lovers of truth, Zero Dark Thirty is sheer torture', *The Times*, 2 February 2013, 22.

[18] Slavoj Zizek, 'Zero Dark Thirty: Hollywood's Gift to American Power', *The Guardian*, 26 January 2013; Glenn Greenwald, 'Zero Dark Thirty: CIA Hagiography, Pernicious Propaganda', *The Guardian*, 15 December 2012; Jane Mayer, 'Zero Conscience in "Zero Dark Thirty"', 14 December 2012, *The New Yorker*; Naomi Wolf, 'A Letter to Kathryn Bigelow on Zero Dark Thirty's Apology for Torture', *The Guardian*, 5 January 2013; Coll (n 15).

[19] There is a significant critical literature here. See especially, Susan Marks, 'Apologising for Torture' (2004) 73 *Nordic Journal of International Law* 365; Fleur Johns, *Non-Legality in International Law: Unruly Law* (Cambridge University Press, 2013); Judith Butler, *Frames of War: When Is Life Grievable?* (Verso, 2009).

## IV. THE QUESTION OF GENRE

The predominant interpretations of *Zero Dark Thirty* are as either a police procedural (detective) story or as a war film. The focus on 'the endless technical invocations of military and intelligence life (satellite images, staged meetings in the CIA headquarters in Langley, Virginia, and other trappings of "tradecraft")'[20] and the ostensibly dispassionate detective work of tracking down bin Laden, leads some critics to see the film as 'the ultimate procedural',[21] and 'devoid of moral context'.[22] While Michael Atkinson refers to Bigelow as 'the Queen of the Asymmetrical war film',[23] Michael Boughn considers her to be fascinated with the genre of the war movie—'with the specific realities of war and their effects on those caught up in them'.[24] But as we know, the 'War on Terror' is characterised as exceptional, presented as a war without beginning or end and with an enemy largely imagined. Does this perhaps give rise to a certain degree of the film's interpretive ambiguity?

A compelling argument can also be made for seeing *Zero Dark Thirty* as a Western, which Vincent Malusa argues is the bedrock for Bigelow's cinema.[25] In the classic Western, cowboy hats are coded white for good guys and black for bad, with the natives forming part of the landscape or barbaric savages.[26] Glenn Greenwald sees *Zero Dark Thirty* as operating in similarly stereotypical ways:

> The CIA and the US government are the Good Guys, the innocent targets of terrorist violence, the courageous warriors seeking justice for the 9/11 victims. Muslims and Arabs are the bastardly villains, attacking and killing without motive (other than the one provided by Bloomberg) and without scruples. Almost all Hollywood action films end with the good guys vanquishing the big, bad villain—so that the audience can leave feeling good about the world and themselves—and this is exactly the script to which this film adheres.[27]

Central to the question of genre is the issue of whether the film should be considered as art or as journalism, human rights advocacy or even as history. This issue is directly related to the controversy over whether or not the film is an apology for, or represents a critique of, torture. Some have argued that while the film works as art, it is flawed journalism and history. Still others critique the idea that art 'excuses' the film's position on torture. Glenn Greenwald's excoriation of the film takes the

[20] Maddox (n 17).

[21] David Denby, '"Zero Dark Thirty" and "This is Forty"', *The New Yorker*, 24 December 2012.

[22] Mayer, 'Zero Conscience in "Zero Dark Thirty"'; *cf* Mahnola Dargis, 'By Any Means Necessary', *The New York Times*, 17 December 2012.

[23] Michael Atkinson, 'Duty Calls' (2013) 23 *Sight and Sound* 30, 33.

[24] Michael Boughn, 'The War on Art and Zero Dark Thirty' (2014) 91 *Cineaction*.

[25] Malusa argues, 'Le western est la base du cinema de Bigelow, et l'idee de deplacer le desert fondateur du grand Ouest dans les steppes ensablees du Moyen-Orient lui a permis de jeter un pont entre action pure, sensationalisme et regles de l'engagement.' (Gabrielle Simm's translation). Vincent Malusa, 'Contre-histoire' (2013) February *Cahiers du Cinema* 28.

[26] Ruth Buchanan and Rebecca Johnson, 'The "Unforgiven" Sources of International Law: Nation-building, Violence and Gender in the West(ern)' in Doris Buss and Ambreena Manji (eds), *International Law: Modern Feminist Perspectives* (Hart Publishing, 2005).

[27] Greenwald (n 18).

position that it should not be regarded as 'apolitical', but rather as amoral, clichéd and pretentious.[28] Genre matters for film as it does in providing a vocabulary for international law as language game, narrative and imagery.

## V. TORTURE, APOLOGY AND GENDER

Many support their interpretation of *Zero Dark Thirty* as questioning or apologising for torture by reference to the cinematic language of the film. The narrative structure of the film and its interpellation of the viewer through point of view shots are understood as producing certain responses in the audience. For example, critics of *Zero Dark Thirty* refer to the opening scene, a blank screen with actual audio recordings of the voices of some of those who died in the destruction of the Twin Towers. They argue that this opening is unjustifiably manipulative, especially in light of the fact that it is followed by a torture scene where Dan, a CIA operative, is interrogating Ammar for details of a lead on Osama bin Laden's whereabouts. This could be seen as implying a justification for the torture. By contrast, Michael Boughn argues that the 'attacks' on Bigelow are part of the 'war on art'. Boughn reads the same scene quite differently, reflecting that:

> [T]he camera angles down on Ammar and up at Dan. The shots down on Ammar embody a brutal power over a helpless, wounded victim. The shots up at Dan reinforce that sense of unbridled power and viciousness. The result is a deep emotional confusion, with the viewer's point-of-view destabilized. Since the scene comes hard on the heel of the 9/11 victim's voice, it ought to be a clear and unambiguous announcement of righteous anger and revenge. Dan's anger is palpable, but the viewer's ability to identify with it is troubled and subverted by the cinematography which forces her to sympathize with Ammar as well.[29]

Critics of Bigelow have also contended that the graphic and lengthy scenes of waterboarding and beating in the film, do not go far enough in representing the horrific intimacy and degradation of torture and thus 'grotesquely understate the reality of "enhanced interrogation", as any film director would if making a film for mass release: no genital torture, threat of electric shocks, [or] dispatch of prisoners to other, less constrained countries'.[30]

For international lawyers, it is both troubling and reassuring to see our discipline hidden from view; seemingly irrelevant, but also for once not presented as connected with these practices. The film has evoked moral outrage and extreme reactions. In likening Bigelow to Leni Riefenstahl, Naomi Wolf calls attention to the omission from the film of the more shocking record of torture from this period, taunting: 'By the way, you left out the scene where the CIA dude sodomizes the wrong guy: Khaled el-Masri, the German citizen unfortunate enough to have a similar name to a militant named Khaled al-Masri.'[31] According to Greenwald,

[28] Ibid.
[29] Boughn (n 25).
[30] Maddox (n 17).
[31] Wolf (n 18). See the *Case of El-Masri v The Former Yugoslav Republic of Macedonia* App no 39630 (ECHR, 13 December 2012).

'there is ample evidence to suspect that the film's CIA heroine is, at least in composite part, based on the same female CIA agent responsible for the kidnapping, drugging and torture of Khalid El-Masri in 2003'.[32] Another scene in the film is central to how readers understand its position on torture. In what could be construed as a rare reference to law, albeit law is not mentioned explicitly, three CIA analysts look at the screen when President Obama asserts that 'America doesn't torture'. Jane Mayer, whose work has focused on the approach to torture within the US administration, argues that, in the context of the film, this scene represents opposition to torture as legalistic and irrelevant:

> The lone anti-torture voice shown in the film is a split-second news clip of President Barack Obama, taken from a '60 Minutes' interview, in which he condemns torture. It flashes on a television screen that's in the background of a scene set in Pakistan; the movie's terrorist-hunters, who are holding a meeting, barely look up, letting Obama's pronouncement pass without comment. 'By this point in the film,' as the CNN national-security analyst Peter Bergen wrote recently, 'the audience has already seen that the C.I.A. has employed coercive interrogation techniques on an al Qaeda detainee that produced a key lead in the hunt for bin Laden. In the film, Obama's opposition to torture comes off as wrongheaded and prissy.'[33]

By contrast, Mahnola Dargis, reviewing the film for the *New York Times*, sees the scene as a blank screen onto which viewers will project their own interpretations:

> Ms Bigelow cuts to a close-up of … Maya. The analyst's face is blank. Maya's face reveals nothing and offers as much explanation as her silence. How viewers interpret this look will depend on them because here and throughout this difficult, urgent movie Ms Bigelow does not fill in the blanks for them.[34]

When asked about whether she had expected her film to provoke such controversy, Bigelow responded:

> It's perhaps a question of education in images and of capacity to read a film, to identify a point of view: what the film signifies occurs less in speech than in the mise en scène. If you aren't familiar with cinematographic language, interpretation loses its nuance and becomes very reductive and one-dimensional. In the press, the subject matter of the film has often been simplified, people only want to see black or white, good or evil. But reality is extremely complex. Torture has been a subject of debate in the United States since 2002, a subject which the film puts back on the agenda and which will continue to be debated for years, no doubt.[35]

Most of the critique of *Zero Dark Thirty* focuses on its troubling content and its failure to take an overt political or even moral position in relation to torture and the CIA's role in the 'War on Terror'. Critics argue that the film misrepresents the fact that torture was not crucial in obtaining the clues leading to the discovery and

[32] Greenwald (n 18).
[33] Mayer (n 18).
[34] Mahnola Daris, 'By Any Means Necessary', *The New York Times*, 17 December 2012.
[35] 'Dans le bunker: Entretien avec Kathryn Bigelow' (2013) February *Cahiers du Cinema* 24 (Gabrielle Simm's translation).

killing of Osama bin Laden.[36] Further, they argue that torture is not effective in eliciting reliable evidence.

Contrary to the character Dan's assertion in the film that: 'Everyone breaks in the end. It's biology', some victims of torture have died rather than reveal information, while others have provided misinformation to get the torture to stop. Some have based their critical reading of the film on its manipulative narrative structure, visual techniques and the absence of contrary perspectives and voices. This undercuts Bigelow's response, that her critics are not educated in cinematographic language and have consequently misunderstood the film's message.

As the first Hollywood female director to have won an Academy Award for directing, gender is read as important to Kathryn Bigelow's films. To what extent does the casting of Jessica Chastain in the role of Maya undermine the scopophiliac structure of narrative film as assuming a male viewer who identifies with a male hero whose gaze is directed within the film onto a female object?[37] Since news of Abu Ghraib broke, gender has been an important aspect of the 'debate' about torture, with 'gender coercion,' whereby American servicewomen 'perform acts designed to take advantage of their gender in relation to Muslim males,' by female American interrogators used to sexually humiliate male Muslim detainees in Iraq and Afghanistan.[38] What is Maya's role in torture in *Zero Dark Thirty* and how significant is her gender to this role?

David Denby celebrates Maya as a feminist heroine:

> That a woman is leading the charge is almost as surprising to the Americans as it is to the Muslim prisoners. After all the female avengers of the past fifteen years—Uma Thurman and Angelina Jolie kicking men in the ego and other places—American movies have at last produced a woman clothed, like Athena, in wilful strength and intellectual armour.[39]

However, for Susan Carruthers: 'The feminist gesture of casting a young woman as the central architect of bin Laden's downfall is undercut by the cinematographic reliance on Chastain's exquisite cheekbones, flawless skin, and lithe form to keep us fixated as Maya pursues her grail with Old Testament zeal.'[40]

While this film defies easy categorisation and invites multiple interpretations, most readers have interpreted Maya as little more than a plot device. The lack of information about her personal life means that she is interpreted as little more than a cartoon, but '[o]nce bin Laden is bagged, she becomes a girl again ... Naturally, she cries, for lost innocence?'[41]

[36] For example, Maddox (n 17); Coll (n 15); Mayer (n 18); Dexter Filkins, 'Bin Laden, The Movie', *The New Yorker*, 17 December 2012; Denby (n 21).

[37] Laura Mulvey, 'Visual Pleasure and Narrative Cinema' (1975) 16 *Screen* 6.

[38] Timothy Kaufman-Osborn, 'Gender Trouble at Abu Ghraib?' (2005) 1 *Politics and Gender* 597, 610.

[39] Denby (n 21).

[40] Susan L Carruthers, 'Zero Dark Thirty' (2013) Spring *Cineaste* 51.

[41] Wypijewski (n 16).

## VI. KILLING BIN LADEN

As examined above, a great majority of reviews of the film revolve around its depiction of torture, with reviewers often reflecting on their own position on the morality, legality and even the utility of torture. This is unsurprising, given that the first 45 minutes of the film are dominated by torture scenes which hang heavily over what follows. Yet very short shrift is given to the targeted killing of Osama bin Laden, other than that his killing is anticipated and desired.[42] International lawyers may have analysed the lawfulness of such targeted assassinations, yet this question has not received as much critical attention in the debates regarding the film.[43] As the ultimate target of the search, bin Laden is a plot device, necessary to generate the action rather than presented as a character. His agency and position are largely assumed, though there is uncertainty as to whether he remains a terror threat in real terms any more. In some ways this is an under-explored question for both international lawyers and critics of the film—is there presumed justice in the killing of bin Laden and should this be celebrated or condemned? Susan Carruthers argues powerfully that:

> Far more wholeheartedly than it endorses torture's efficacy, *Zero Dark Thirty* celebrates state-sanctioned, extrajudicial killing. 'Do your fucking jobs. Bring me people to kill,' thunders Maya's boss George ... 'Kill him for me,' she instructs the squad leader who is duly steeled by her conviction. That this uncritical embrace of assassination as a tool of statecraft should have passed entirely unremarked in the brouhaha surrounding *Zero Dark Thirty* tells us a good deal about the new normal in an era of secret kill-lists and escalating drone strikes.[44]

Further, Glenn Greenwald concludes: '[T]here is no event in the last decade that has inspired as much collective pride and pervasive consensus as the killing of Osama bin Laden.'[45] There is then guilty pleasure in the film's representation of the final killing of bin Laden, but there is little catharsis or room to reflect upon its legality.

## VII. CONCLUSION

This chapter has mapped out a variety of critical readings of the film *Zero Dark Thirty*, pointing to the broader international law-focused debates with which it can be connected, but also noting the absence of law in the film itself. In this example, the power of pictures can perhaps trigger a broader debate about the methods and manner of the mission to capture bin Laden—both a defining event within the 'War on Terror' and yet one which remains curiously hidden from view. We conclude by

[42] Carruthers (n 40).
[43] Some exceptions include Michael Atkinson, 'Duty Calls', February 2013 *Sight & Sound* 31, 32; and Logan Hill, 'Secrets of *Zero Dark Thirty*', *Rolling Stone*, 17 January 2013, 20. For a representative examination of targeted killing within international legal scholarship see APV Goodman and Dominic McGoldrick, 'Assassination and Targeted Killing—the Killing of Osama bin Laden' (2011) 60 *International and Comparative Law Quarterly* 778.
[44] Carruthers (n 40).
[45] Greenwald (n 18).

asking whether audiences now require images and pictures to analyse and assess such activity and its consequences in international law terms, and what might be lost in translation? Given the power of the image, but also its potential for manipulation and various interpretations, what are we to make either of the 'official visual narrative' provided by the CIA, or of this subsequent fictionalised attempt by Hollywood to provide the pictures and narrative behind the event? Should international lawyers equip themselves with a visual vocabulary and sophistication to match the technologies available and the demands which publicity increasingly makes of the discipline?

What is interesting about *Zero Dark Thirty* is that some viewers see it as ambiguous, raising questions about the efficacy and morality of torture, while others see it as a CIA propaganda film, built on crude stereotypes of American heroes and Muslim terrorists that leave no room for critical perspectives. So how do viewers reach such different conclusions from viewing the same film, reading the key scenes in radically divergent ways? Can such opposing conclusions be predicted from viewers' political beliefs? If film critics and political journalists are sharply split along disciplinary lines in their assessment of the film, how should international lawyers read *Zero Dark Thirty*? And how do non-lawyers understand the role of international law in this film?

What is unsettling about *Zero Dark Thirty* is that targeted killing and torture are presented as the subject of mass entertainment, without the director appearing to take a moral position or engaging in any form of debate surrounding the international legality of such actions. International law is largely surplus to requirements. This example then provides an opportunity to think more deeply about the potential and limits of our discipline's relationship with film. Does the power of pictures threaten to obscure the power of law? *Zero Dark Thirty* points to under-explored themes and techniques in international law, highlighting the need for the further development of a visual as well as a text-based international legal vocabulary as we grapple with filmic representations of international legal significance.

# 29

# À la Maison-Blanche: *le président des États-Unis se soucie-t-il du droit international lorsqu'il décide d'une intervention militaire?*

OLIVIER CORTEN*

## I. INTRODUCTION

À LA SAISON 5 de *À la maison-blanche* (*The West Wing*, en version originale), on apprend que l'Iran aurait effectué un essai nucléaire, ce qui lui permettrait à terme de disposer de l'arme atomique. Le président des Etats-Unis décide alors que, si ces faits sont avérés, des frappes unilatérales s'imposent contre cinq sites d'enrichissement d'uranium. Un membre de son équipe, Toby Ziegler, est chargé de rédiger un projet de déclaration, mais s'inquiète auprès de son chef de cabinet, Leo McGarry, de la nécessité d'obtenir l'aval de l'ONU. Celui-ci lui répond alors, manifestement excédé:

> The U.N. doesn't want this. They want to wring their hands and censure us after, but they expect us to take care of things like this. And after they've exhausted themselves calling us warmongers and imperialists they'll go home and quietly drink toasts to their relief.[1]

Si l'on s'en tient à cette scène, il semble que le droit international ne joue qu'un rôle très limité dans la décision de recourir à la force. Or, *À la maison blanche*,[2] dont les 7 saisons s'échelonnent entre 1999 et 2006 et qui sont encore régulièrement diffusées, est une série télévisée qui a connu—et connait encore—un succès considérable.[3] Si on la compare à d'autres séries contemporaines comme *24 heures chrono*[4] ou,

* Centre de droit international et de sociologie appliquée au droit international Université libre de Bruxelles.

[1] Toby Ziegler en *The West Wing*, Saison 5 (2003–2004) épisode 13.

[2] *The West Wing*, 7 saisons, 155 épisodes, 1999–2006.

[3] Peter C Collins et John O'Connor (eds), *The West Wing. The American Presidency as Television Drama*, (Syracuse University Press, 2003); Trevor Parry-Giles et Shawn Parry-Giles, *The Prime-Time Presidency. The West-Wing and US Nationalism* (University of Illinois Press, 2006).

[4] *24 heures chrono*, série créée par Joel Surnow et Robert Cochran; actuellement 9 saisons, 204 épisodes + 1 téléfilm (*Redemption*, 2008) 2001–2010/2014-?; v Jean-Baptiste Jeangène Vilmer, *24 heures chrono. Le choix du mal* (PUF, 2012).

plus récemment, *Homeland*,[5] *The West Wing* se caractérise par une place limitée donnée à l'action et une large prépondérance de scènes mettant en scène des débats politiques. Il s'agit sans doute de la série qui accorde la plus large place à la figure du président des Etats-Unis et de son équipe dirigeante dans la prise de décision, y compris en matière de politique étrangère.

Tout au long de la diffusion de cette série, les spectateurs ont régulièrement pu assister à des décisions de recourir ou de menacer de recourir à la force prises par le président des Etats-Unis, que ce soit contre des pays réels (Iran, Irak, Syrie, Corée du Nord, Chine) ou, parfois, imaginaires (le 'Qumar' et le 'Khundu'). Dans ce contexte, on peut se demander dans quelle mesure les représentations cinématographiques reflètent, et en même temps légitiment, la doctrine contemporaine des Etats-Unis relative au recours à la force, spécialement en ce qui concerne la portée et les limites que constituent les règles pertinentes du droit international.

La thèse qui sera privilégiée, sur la base du visionnage de l'intégralité des 155 épisodes de cette série, est que le droit international occupe un certain rôle dans la décision de recourir à la force. Une simple utilisation de la base de données permettant d'accéder au script de la série permet de le pressentir, puisque des entrées comme 'international law', 'Security Council', 'self-defense' ou encore 'Charter' renvoient tous à un nombre significatif d'épisodes.[6] Cette intuition se confirme au vu d'une série de scènes dont certaines seront exposées ci-dessous. Lors des saisons 3 et 4, le président Bartlet se demande même s'il ne risque pas d'être traduit devant une juridiction internationale: 'I'm going to need some cell-mates in Holland. So, what do we do now?'[7]

Si on compare *À la maison blanche* avec d'autres séries comme *24 heures chrono* ou *Homeland*, on constate d'emblée que les règles de droit international occupent une certaine place dans les débats, que ce soit à l'intérieur même de l'administration Bartlet ou dans les relations avec d'autres acteurs, qu'il s'agisse de journalistes ou de représentants d'Etats étrangers. La question se pose cependant de déterminer quelle est l'interprétation du droit international qui est proposée au téléspectateur. Comme on le sait, la série a été diffusée parallèlement à la proclamation de déclarations présidentielles définissant les conditions dans lesquelles les Etats-Unis étaient prêts à recourir à la force, que ce soit le président Clinton pour l'intervention humanitaire en 1999,[8] ou le président Bush pour la guerre contre le terrorisme, en 2002 puis en 2006.[9]

Notre thèse principale est que cette série populaire véhicule des représentations correspondant globalement aux doctrines présidentielles 'réelles'. On constatera en effet que *The West Wing* semble privilégier une représentation assez large non seulement de la légitime défense (II), mais aussi d'un droit d'intervention qui pourrait

[5] *Homeland*, série créée par Howard Gordon, actuellement 5 saisons, depuis 2011.

[6] www.westwingtranscripts.com.

[7] *The West Wing*, Saison 4 (2002–2003) épisode 2.

[8] Michael T Klare, 'The Clinton Doctrine' *The Nation*, 19 September 1999.

[9] *The National Security Strategy of the United States*, September 2002; *The National Security Strategy of the United States*, March 2006.

s'émanciper d'une autorisation du Conseil de Sécurité au nom d'une 'juste cause' (III). Dans un dernier temps, on montrera que la doctrine interventionniste véhiculée par cette série populaire peut plus largement être mise en relation avec les représentations qui se dégagent d'autres séries ou films mettant en scène la place du droit international dans la prise de décision du président des Etats-Unis (IV). Sur le plan méthodologique, on s'appuie sur une approche critique, visant non pas à évaluer la 'qualité' de la reproduction cinématographique sur un plan juridique, mais à dégager les représentations qu'elles véhiculent au sujet du droit international.[10]

## II. UNE REPRÉSENTATION ÉLARGIE DE LA LÉGITIME DÉFENSE

Pour résumer les traits caractéristiques des conceptions extensives de la légitime défense que l'on retrouve à la fois dans les doctrines Bush et Clinton et dans une certaine doctrine juridique,[11] on mentionnera:

— la possibilité de viser des Etats qui abritent ou tolèrent des groupes terroristes, sans qu'il soit nécessaire de démontrer que l'Etat concerné ait envoyé de tels groupes pour mener une action armée ou qu'il se soit impliqué dans une telle action;
— l'acceptation de la notion de guerre préventive, en application de laquelle la légitime défense peut être exercée avant qu'une agression armée n'ait pu être établie;
— l'accent sur le critère de nécessité davantage que sur celui du respect de la lettre des dispositions pertinentes de la Charte des Nations Unies.

Ces trois caractéristiques se retrouvent indéniablement dans divers épisodes qui jalonnent les saisons de *À la maison blanche*.

À la fin de la saison 3, on apprend que Abdul Shareef, le ministre de la défense d'un Etat du Golfe, le Qumar, est impliqué dans un acte terroriste.[12] La perspective de le juger aux Etats-Unis s'avère peu réaliste car, outre la question de l'immunité, les seuls éléments de preuve existants semblent avoir été obtenus sous la torture, et seraient donc probablement considérés comme irrecevables dans le cadre d'un procès. Le staff de la maison blanche envisage alors la piste d'une exécution extra-judiciaire, et le chef d'état-major estime que, en droit international contemporain, la différence entre état de paix et état de guerre s'est estompée, de sorte que l'on pourrait considérer Abdul Shareef comme une cible militaire légitime.[13] Le président

[10] Pour plus de précisions, v O Corten, 'Droit international et cinéma: quelle méthodologie ?' in O Corten et F Dubuisson, *Droit international et cinéma. Présentations et représentations du droit international dans les films et les séries télévisées* (Pedone, 2015), ainsi que, pour une application, 'Mais où est donc passée la Charte des Nations Unies? Représentations et sous-représentations des règles sur l'usage de la force dans les films d'action' in ibid.

[11] V par exemple Michael N Schmitt, *Counter-Terrorism and the Use of Force in International Law*, George C Marshall European Center for Security Studies, The Marshall Center Papers, No 5, 2002.

[12] Saison 3 (2001–2002) épisode 22.

[13] Trevor Parry-Giles et Shawn Parry-Giles, *The Prime-Time Presidency. The West-Wing and US Nationalism* (n 3) 141–45.

Bartlet hésite à franchir le Rubicon, mais son chef de cabinet, Léo, s'appuie explicitement sur la légitime défense. Le président donne alors l'ordre et l'exécution a lieu.[14] Mais l'affaire n'en reste pas là. Les services secrets tentent de maquiller la mort de Shareef en accident d'avion;[15] les autorités Qumar ne semblent pas convaincues et accusent bientôt Israël d'être impliqué dans l'incident.[16] Au vu de la tournure des événements, le président Bartlet commence à s'inquiéter d'une révélation de sa décision, et prend conseil auprès d'une spécialiste de droit international, Jordan Kendall. S'engage alors la conversation suivante, reproduite ici en version originale:

> BARTLET: Due respect, Ms. Kendall, ... Article 51 of the United Nations Charter says every nation has a right to wage war to defend itself.
>
> JORDAN: The article's incumbent on wars being declared.
>
> BARTLET: Wars don't work like that anymore.
>
> JORDAN: Laws work like that.
>
> BARTLET: 44 people are dead in Iowa, and most of them college kids. Shareef has murdered Americans in uniform. He's murdered Americans out of uniform. He was trying to blow up the Golden Gate Bridge, and I didn't have time to file an amicus brief.
>
> JORDAN: Anyway, at the moment I'm having trouble foreseeing the exact legal consequences on the international stage.
>
> BARTLET: Why?
>
> JORDAN: Because most in international law doesn't exist yet.[17]

Pendant ce temps, la tension monte, Israël bombardant des camps terroristes au Qumar, lequel affirme qu'il répliquer.[18] Le président Bartlet tente alors d'éviter l'escalade, et Leo McGarry convoque l'ambassadeur du Qumar, lequel se plaint que 'Israel launched and unwarranted, illegal, unilateral air attack against the people of Qumar'. Le chef de cabinet répond alors:

> The air strike was neither unwarranted nor was it against the people of Qumar. It was against two Bahji terrorist camps after the Israeli Foreign Minister was shot down by Bahji operatives of, by-the-way, Qumair citizenship. Educated, if we're going to use that word, in Qumari madrassahs and financed by fat members of the Qumari Royal Family, including the Sultan's brother, Abdul ibn Shareef.[19]

Se rendant compte que les Etats-Unis sont prêts à s'engager militairement aux côtés d'Israël, le Qumar renonce alors et la crise semble réglée. Mais, quelque temps plus tard, la responsabilité des Etats-Unis dans l'exécution d'Abdul Shareef éclatera au grand jour. Le président faisant fonction (Bartlet s'est retiré provisoirement en raison de l'enlèvement de sa fille) assumera alors clairement cette action lors d'une

[14] Saison 3 (2001–2002) épisode 23.
[15] Saison 4 (2002–2003) épisode 1.
[16] Saison 4 (2002–2003) épisode 2.
[17] Saison 4 (2002–2003) épisode 3.
[18] Saison 4 (2002–2003) épisode 5.
[19] Saison 4 (2002–2003) épisode 6.

conférence de presse. A un journaliste qui lui demande si cela ne remet pas en cause la protection des Etats, et à la suite d'une remarque selon laquelle 'acknowledging the assassination destroys a century's worth of progress toward international law', il rétorque simplement: 'terrorists aren't nations .... International law has no prohibition against any government, superpower or otherwise, targeting terrorist command and control centers. And Abdul Shareef was a walking command and control center.'[20]

Dans l'ensemble, la crise du Qumar met en scène l'opposition entre un droit international traditionnel hyper formaliste—la spécialiste du droit international va curieusement jusqu'à affirmer que l'applicabilité de l'article 51 de la Charte dépend d'une déclaration de guerre—, inadapté à l'évolution des relations internationales, et une légitime défense interprétée de manière raisonnable et appropriée à la situation. En résulte la légitimation des exécutions extrajudiciaires contre de présumés terroristes ainsi que des actions militaires menées contre des Etats qui les hébergeraient ou les toléreraient, sans qu'il soit besoin de démontrer l'existence d'une agression armée au sens du droit international traditionnel.

Cette conception élargie de la légitime défense se décline aussi sur le mode de la guerre préventive, comme on l'aura compris en découvrant l'extrait reproduit en ouverture de la présente contribution. Dans la saison 5 de la série, le président justifie en effet l'attaque ciblée de sites d'enrichissement d'uranium en Iran en raison des *risques* de l'acquisition de l'arme nucléaire par ce pays, et de sa *possible* utilisation pour perpétrer une agression.[21] En ce sens, la représentation qui émerge de la série fait écho à la doctrine Bush, qui justifie la légitime défense non seulement en cas de menace imminente—ce qui est déjà très contestable—mais aussi pour une menace lointaine ou diffuse.

Enfin, et plus fondamentalement, la série a tendance à présenter la légitime défense comme une institution devant être évaluée à l'aune d'un critère de nécessité, assez largement interprété, plutôt que sur la base de critères stricts ou rigides que l'on déduirait des textes juridiques applicables. La saison 1 s'ouvre pourtant assez rapidement sur une sorte de profil psychologique du président Bartlet, présenté comme un homme modéré, voire pacifiste:

> I'm not comfortable with violence. I know this country has enemies, but I don't feel violent toward any of them. I don't know whether that's a weakness or not, but I think I know how the Joint Chiefs would answer that question.[22]

Quelques minutes plus tard, le président apprend que son médecin personnel, à qui il confiait précisément les paroles que l'on vient de reproduire, était à bord d'un avion qui a été abattu par un avion de l'armée syrienne. Il réagit alors de manière impulsive, et s'exclame: 'I'm gonna blow them off the face of the earth with the fury of God's own thunder. Get the commanders.'[23] Lors de la réunion qui s'ensuit dans la 'situation room', Josiah Bartlet demande 'What is the virtue of a proportional

[20] Saison 5 (2003–2004) épisode 1.
[21] Saison 5 (2003–2004) épisode 13.
[22] Saison 1 (1999–2000) épisode 2.
[23] Saison 1 (1999–2000) épisode 2.

response?' Ses conseillers, quelque peu décontenancés, lui expliquent que c'est la procédure habituelle, qui réduit les pertes civiles et permet de garder les faveurs de l'opinion publique. Le président s'insurge alors, et propose une nouvelle doctrine, celle de la 'riposte disproportionnée': 'A disproportional response. Let the word ring forth from this time and this place, you kill an American, any American, we don't come back with a proportional response, we come back with total disaster!'[24] Quelques heures plus tard, le chef d'état-major lui propose un nouveau plan d'attaque massive contre la Syrie, avec des dégâts et des victimes considérables. Finalement, le président Bartlet renonce, et se résigne au scenario de la riposte proportionnée.

Dans un autre épisode, on apprend qu'un pilote est porté disparu, son avion ayant été abattu alors qu'il patrouillait dans la zone d'exclusion aérienne unilatéralement proclamée par les Etats-Unis dans les années 1990.[25] Le président doit prendre une décision, et on lui présente le profil du soldat, avec photo et relations familiales. Il décide alors de mener une action militaire de sauvetage, après s'être fait confirmer que le pilote n'avait pas ouvert le feu en premier, suggérant que c'est l'Irak qui est responsable de la première attaque. S'inquiétant des conséquences de l'opération militaire envisagée sur la vie du pilote, il déclare: 'Bill, if it ends up that Fitzwallace has to call this kid's parents, I swear to God I'm invading Baghdad.' Mais il ne devra pas en arriver là, le soldat étant effectivement secouru et le président pouvant lui-même délivrer la bonne nouvelle à ses parents.

Dans l'ensemble, les opérations militaires menées contre un Etat ennemi paraissent justifiées par la nécessité plus que par la démonstration de l'existence d'une agression armée préalable au sens de l'article 51 de la Charte. Ce sont les circonstances qui dictent à la fois la décision de déclencher l'attaque et les modalités de cette dernière. On retrouve donc trace de conceptions assez extensives du *jus contra bellum*, la légitime défense étant conçue soit comme un droit naturel dont l'appréciation relève principalement de l'appréciation subjective de chaque Etat concerné,[26] soit, dans une optique plus 'réaliste', comme n'étant tout simplement pas limitée par le droit.[27] Un schéma que l'on retrouve, *mutatis mutandis*, lorsque sera évoqué un droit d'intervention humanitaire dans d'autres épisodes de la série.

## III. UN DROIT D'INTERVENTION JUSTIFIÉ PAR UNE 'JUSTE CAUSE'

Si l'on veut synthétiser les principaux éléments de la doctrine favorable à un droit d'intervention de type humanitaire,[28] on peut souligner:

— une conception de l'ONU comme une organisation à la fois peu légitime et peu efficace;

[24] Saison 1 (1999–2000) épisode 3.
[25] Saison 1 (1999–2000) épisode 22.
[26] V par exemple Yoram Dinstein, *War, Aggression and Self-Defense*, 5th edn (Cambridge University Press, 2010).
[27] Trevor Parry-Giles et Shawn Parry-Giles, *The Prime-Time Presidency. The West-Wing and US Nationalism* (n 3) 125 et ss.
[28] V not Fernando Teson, *Humanitarian Intervention. An Inquiry into Law and Morality* (Transnational Publishers, 1997).

— l'insistance sur la justesse de la cause comme critère déterminant légitimant une opération militaire;
— la possibilité d'agir sur cette base à la fois pour sauver des vies humaines menacées et pour secourir ses propres ressortissants.

Une telle doctrine se développe principalement auprès de spécialistes de droit international et des relations internationales, et trouve plusieurs échos dans des déclarations ou documents des administrations Clinton (principalement au moment du déclenchement de la guerre du Kosovo en 1999) et Bush (y compris dans le cadre de la guerre en Irak).[29] Or, on retrouve ces différents éléments dans les représentations véhiculées par *The West Wing*.

La vision peu glorieuse de l'ONU a d'emblée été illustrée par les propos de Leo McGarry cités en introduction. On la retrouve encore à plusieurs reprises. Dans la saison 1, on apprend que les tensions se sont aggravées entre l'Inde et le Pakistan au sujet de la situation au Cachemire, avec un mouvement de troupes de 300.000 soldats indiens qui se dirigent vers la frontière.[30] Le président s'inquiète, mais annonce à ses propres collaborateurs que le Conseil de sécurité s'apprête à adopter une résolution appelant au cessez-le-feu. 'I feel better already' lui répond-on avec ironie. De fait, la crise sera réglée grâce à la médiation des Etats-Unis, sans que l'ONU—ni d'ailleurs le droit international—ne joue aucun rôle particulier. La même perception découle des épisodes consacrés au conflit israélo-palestinien. Alors que la tension est montée dans la bande de Gaza et qu'Israël a lancé plusieurs frappes militaires, le président Bartlet envisage lui aussi d'intervenir.[31] Il parvient cependant à réunir les parties à Camp David et à obtenir, après d'intenses et délicates négociations, un compromis supposé mettre fin au conflit.[32] Ici encore, ni l'ONU, ni le droit international ne semblent des cadres de référence pertinents, l'action étant dictée par une appréciation combinant réflexion éthique et prise en compte des impératifs de *Realpolitik*.

La prééminence de la 'juste cause' comme facteur déterminant est encore illustrée de manière particulièrement emblématique dans une sorte de mise en scène du génocide rwandais, transposé dans un Etat fictif, le Khundu. Dans le courant de la saison 4, on apprend qu'un conflit ethnique s'y développe, les 'Arkutus' massacrant de nombreux 'Induyés' à la machette. Dans un premier temps, le président se préoccupe surtout de la sécurité des ressortissants étatsuniens, mais sa conscience le travaille. CJ, l'attachée de presse du président, doit d'ailleurs subir les assauts répétés de certains journalistes, et s'en trouve particulièrement troublée:

> REPORTER STEVE: CJ, there's a 1948 UN Convention on Genocide, and the US is a signatory. Simply put, it says that if it's determined that genocide is taking place, the United States is compelled to intervene.
>
> CJ: The problem is that the Convention distinguishes between acts of genocide and genocide.

[29] V les sources citées ci-dessus.
[30] Saison 1 (1999–2000) épisode 11.
[31] Saison 5 (2003–2004) épisode 22.
[32] Saison 6 (2004–2005) épisodes 1 et 2.

REPORTER KATIE: It distinguishes between acts of genocide and genocide?

CJ: It does. Mark?

REPORTER MARK: How many acts of genocide constitute a genocide?

CJ: I don't know.[33]

Finalement, le président Bartlet convoque ses conseillers, initialement sceptiques, pour faire une annonce particulièrement solennelle:

> We're for freedom of speech everywhere. We're for freedom to worship everywhere. We're for freedom to learn ... for everybody. And because, in our time, you can build a bomb in your country and bring it to my country, what goes on in your country is very much my business. And so we are for freedom from tyranny everywhere, whether in the guise of political oppression, Toby, or economic slavery, Josh, or religious fanaticism, CJ. That most fundamental idea cannot be met with merely our support. It has to be met with our strength. Diplomatically, economically, materially. And if pharaoh still doesn't free the slaves, then he gets the plagues, or my cavalry, whichever gets there first. The USTR will go crazy and say that we're not considering global trade. Committee members will go crazy and say I haven't consulted enough. And the Arab world will just go indiscriminately crazy. *No country has ever had a doctrine of intervention when only humanitarian interests were at stake. That streak's going to end Sunday at noon.*[34]

La 'doctrine Bartlet' sera annoncée à la nation et, si elle suscitera un certain scepticisme, elle sera pleinement assumée:

> They're saying it's liberalism with a grenade launcher. But they're not saying it was badly written, so that's something. And they sure as hell know I was serious, so that's something else. Congratulations, folks. We've got ourselves a doctrine.[35]

L'ambassadeur du Khundu est aussitôt convoqué, et Bartlet lui annonce que son pays est envahi ('Strictly speaking, I conquered your country without the paperwork') avec le lancement d'une opération 'Safe Haven' destinée à mettre fin au génocide.[36]

Quelque temps plus tard, la 'juste cause' qui l'emporte sur la rigueur de la règle juridique sera mise en scène dans le cadre d'une opération de protection des ressortissants. Des soldats étatsuniens ont en effet dû s'éjecter, en raison d'incidents techniques, sur le territoire de la Corée du nord. Se pose alors le problème de leur récupération:

BARROW: We can't go get them. Sending a Special Forces covert retrieval team into North Korea will be seen as an act of war.

LEO: We're still at war with North Korea. We never signed an armistice ... .

BARROW: Mr President, if the North Koreans discover armed American soldiers on Korean soil ...

BARTLET: We go get'em.

[33] Saison 4 (2002–2003) épisode 15.
[34] Saison 4 (2002–2003) épisode 15; nous soulignons (emphasis added).
[35] Saison 4 (2002–2003) épisode 15.
[36] Saison 4 (2002–2003) épisode 16.

BARROW: Mr President, there are other…

LEO: We don't leave our people in harm's way, Mr Barrow. We bring'em home.[37]

Dans l'ensemble, tous ces exemples véhiculent une conception ambivalente d'un 'droit d'intervention'. D'un côté, les impératifs moraux l'emportent manifestement sur le respect des règles et des procédures, que ce soit pour mettre fin à un génocide ou protéger des ressortissants. Mais, d'un autre côté, les protagonistes de la série avancent certains arguments juridiques tendant à justifier l'action, comme le prétendu devoir d'intervention déduit de la Convention sur le génocide ou l'existence d'un état de guerre permanent avec la Corée du nord.

Ces interprétations sont particulièrement extensives, et on ne peut certainement pas affirmer qu'ils font l'unanimité auprès des spécialistes de droit international.[38] Mais l'essentiel semble être non pas de produire une analyse juridique rigoureuse et irréprochable, mais de parvenir à invoquer une argumentation venant à l'appui d'une décision dictée par de toutes autres considérations que le respect du droit international. De ce point de vue, le droit d'intervention pour une juste cause peut être mis en relation avec la conception élargie de la légitime défense telle qu'on l'a exposée plus haut, conception qui obéit manifestement à la même logique. Une logique que l'on retrouve d'ailleurs, au-delà de *The West Wing*, dans d'autres films et séries mettant en scène la décision de recourir à la force par le président des Etats-Unis.

## IV. UNE REPRÉSENTATION DE L'INTERVENTIONNISME EN PHASE AVEC LE CINÉMA ÉTATSUNIEN

En dépit de la variété des épisodes concernés, *À la maison blanche* véhicule ainsi une doctrine plutôt cohérente dans le sens d'une conception extensive du droit d'intervenir militairement. Le constat est d'autant plus remarquable qu'il ne vise que le droit international, le souci du respect des formes juridiques semblant s'appliquer bien davantage au droit interne, manifestement considéré comme plus légitime et plus contraignant.[39] Cette conception extensive caractérise d'ailleurs le cinéma américain existant, que ce soit lorsqu'il met en scène la légitime défense (*Delta Force* (1986), *Le pacificateur* (1997), *Zero Dark Thirty* (2013), …) ou qu'il traite du thème de l'intervention humanitaire (*Les rois du désert* (1999), *Les larmes du soleil* (2003), *John Rambo* (2008), …). Une place doit être réservée dans la filmographie existante au cas de *Air Force One* (1997), qui met en scène le président des Etats-Unis lui-même, James Marshall, incarné par Harrisson Ford. Le film s'ouvre sur une collaboration entre les armées des Etats-Unis et de la Russie, qui mènent une opération pour enlever le général Radek, qui gouverne d'une main de fer le

[37] Saison 5 (2003–2004) épisode 14.

[38] Olivier Corten, *Le droit contre la guerre* (Pedone, 2014).

[39] *À la maison blanche*, saisons 3 et 4, 2001–2002 et 2002–2003 (à propos des prérogatives présidentielles pour décider d'une action ciblée).

Kazakhstan. Le président Marshall est alors invité à Moscou, et visite des camps de réfugiés kazhakes, avant de prononcer un discours, visiblement ému:

> La vérité c'est que nous avons agi trop tard. Ce n'est que lorsque notre sécurité nationale s'est trouvée compromise que nous avons agi. Radek a fait massacrer 200 000 personnes. On a regardé ça à la télé. Nous avons laissé faire. Le carnage a duré plus d'un an. Nous nous sommes réfugiés derrière les sanctions économiques et la diplomatie. Comment avons-nous osé? Les morts se souviennent. La vraie paix, ce n'est pas seulement l'absence de conflit, mais le règne de la justice. Ce soir, je m'engage à changer la politique américaine. Jamais plus je ne laisserai l'intérêt politique nous détourner de notre devoir moral. Les atrocités et la terreur ne sont pas des arguments. A ceux qui les utilisent ... votre règne a pris fin. Nous ne négocierons jamais. Nous ne vous tolérerons plus. Nous ne tremblerons plus. C'est à vous de trembler.[40]

On n'aura pas manqué de relever le parallélisme avec le discours précité prononcé par le président Bartlet dans le cadre de la crise du Khundu. Plus fondamentalement, les limites de la Charte des Nations Unies, et plus spécialement la nécessité d'obtenir une résolution du Conseil de sécurité, ne sont pas plus présentes dans *Air Force One* que dans *The West Wing*.

Le même schéma ressort encore de séries particulièrement populaires, comme *24 heures chrono* ou *Homeland*. Tant l'ONU[41] que les règles de la Charte sont étrangement absentes, et ce alors même que plusieurs opérations militaires à l'étranger sont représentées, le plus souvent au nom de considérations de sécurité. La guerre contre les Etats tolérant des activités terroristes, dans le premier cas,[42] les exécutions ciblées, dans le second,[43] sont illustrées comme autant de possibilités légitimes de lutter contre le terrorisme. Dans *24 heures chrono*, on retrouve par ailleurs une réflexion sur le droit d'intervention humanitaire, spécialement dans le téléfilm *Redemption* (2008), sorti en prélude à la 7$^{ème}$ saison. Une crise y éclate dans un pays africain imaginaire, le Sangala, qui se révèle être le théâtre d'exactions commanditées par le président Juma contre la population civile, avec des campagnes de 'nettoyage ethnique' qui font la une des médias. Allison Taylor, qui vient d'être élue à la présidence, rend visite à son prédécesseur, le président Noah Daniels, qui exerce donc ses dernières heures de fonction. Il en résulte la scène suivante, au sujet de la situation urgente au Sangala:

> TAYLOR: On a des soldats dans la région. Une démonstration de force pourrait obliger Juma à plier.

[40] François Dubuisson, 'La doctrine américaine de l'intervention humanitaire dans *Air Force One*'; cdi.ulb.ac.be/la-doctrine-americaine-de-lintervention-humanitaire-dans-air-force-one-wolfgang-petersen-1997/.

[41] Avec une exception dans *Redemption* (2008), où l'ONU est incidemment discréditée; Jean-Baptiste Jeangène Vilmer (n 4) 150–51.

[42] V spécialement la saison 2 (2002–2003), pendant laquelle le président des Etats-Unis estime que, si un Etat du Moyen Orient est impliqué dans un attentat terroriste sur le sol étatsunien, une riposte militaire est nécessaire, la présidente développant le même raisonnement dans la saison 8 (2010), à l'égard du 'Kamistan', Etat imaginaire d'Asie mineure.

[43] V spécialement l'épisode 1 de la saison 3 (2013), dans lequel le directeur de la CIA dirige une opération lors de laquelle six présumés terroristes sont exécutés de manière coordonnée en quelques minutes, et ce dans six Etats différents.

PRÉSIDENT DANIELS: Et si ce n'est pas le cas, on se retrouve coincé dans un autre bourbier civil. Maintenant, c'est difficile à dire. En plus, il y a rien à Sangala qui vaille notre protection. Pas de ressources naturelles, pas d'attaches économiques, rien qui ne menace la sécurité de notre pays.

TAYLOR: La dernière fois que Juma a pris le pouvoir, il a initié une guerre tribale qui a tué des dizaines de milliers de civils. Notre implication aurait pu éviter un génocide.

PRÉSIDENT DANIELS: Et cette guerre va être aussi tragique. Mais, ce n'est pas notre guerre. Dès lors, j'ai demandé à l'Ambassadeur d'évacuer tous les ressortissants civils.

TAYLOR: C'est une erreur.

PRÉSIDENT DANIELS: Je refuse que des Américains soient pris dans les coups de feu quand Juma lancera l'offensive.

TAYLOR: Fermer l'Ambassade c'est dire au Monde que nous voulons vendre un allié démocratique à un criminel de guerre.

PRÉSIDENT DANIELS: J'apprécie votre idéalisme.

TAYLOR: Je ne peux en dire autant de votre cynisme.

PRÉSIDENT DANIELS: Reparlons-en ... après que vous vous soyez assise quelque temps dans ce fauteuil. En attendant, il y a des affaires dont nous devons encore discuter. Je propose que nous commencions.

Comme on le voit, le dilemme de l'intervention humanitaire est posé.[44] Mais, contrairement à ce qui a été mis en scène dans *A la maison blanche*, le droit international ou la Charte ne semble pas un cadre de référence digne d'être pris en considération, le débat semblant se résumer à une opposition de points de vue entre éthique et politique. *24 heures chrono* paraît donc traduire une conception plus réaliste tendant à ignorer largement l'existence d'un ordre juridique international. Il reste que, plus généralement, la doctrine interventionniste des Etats-Unis y est présentée, comme dans bien d'autres films et séries, sous un jour plutôt favorable.[45]

Ainsi, *A la maison blanche* semble s'inscrire dans une certaine tradition américaine dans laquelle les œuvres de fiction à destination du grand public relayent, et en même temps justifient, même si c'est généralement de manière involontaire voire inconsciente, les doctrines présidentielles qui sont conçues assez largement dans le domaine du recours à la force.[46] Cela ne signifie pas qu'*aucune* production

[44] Jean-Baptiste Jeangène Vilmer (n 4) 150.

[45] ibid, 152 (un parallèle étant opéré entre cette scène et la doctrine Clinton); v aussi Olivier Corten, 'La mise en scène des doctrines interventionnistes dans les films étatsuniens: *Ronnie goes to Hollywood*!' in *Actes du VIème festival 'ciné-droit'*, colloque de l'Université de Paris-Sud, avril 2014, à paraître.

[46] V not Anne-Marie Bidaud, *Hollywood et le rêve américain. Cinéma et idéologie aux Etats-Unis* (Armand Colin, 2012); Douglas Kellner, *Cinema Wars. Hollywood Films and Politics in the Bush-Cheney Era* (Wiley Blackwell, 2010); Jean-Michel Valantin, *Hollywood, le Pentagone et le monde. Les trois acteurs de la stratégie mondiale*, nouvelle édition, Paris, Autrement, 2010; Stephen Prince, *Firestorm. American Film in the Age of Terrorism* (Columbia University Press, 2009); Barthélémy Courmon et Erwan Benezet, *Washington-Hollywood. Comment l'Amérique fait son cinéma* (Armand Colin, 2007); François Dubuisson, 'Cinéma et idéologie: représentation et fonction du terrorisme dans le film d'action hollywoodien' in Olivier Corten et Barbara Delcourt (coord), *Les Guerres antiterroristes*, *Contradictions*, 2004, n°105, 53–79.

cinématographique ne puisse être interprétée comme une critique, comme peuvent l'illustrer, si l'on prend en compte la période couverte par notre étude, *Lions et agneaux* (2007) ou *W. L'improbable président* (2008), lesquels jettent de sérieux doutes sur la doctrine Bush et, plus spécifiquement, sur les principes—y compris juridiques—évoqués pour justifier les guerres en Afghanistan et en Irak. Cela ne signifie pas non plus que les producteurs de *The West Wing* puissent être réduits à de simples propagandistes visant à légitimer les administrations présidentielles en place. La représentation du droit international comme étant peu susceptible de limiter des opérations militaires perçues comme nécessaires ou justes aux Etats-Unis semble plutôt ressortir d'une représentation largement partagée par le public, représentation qui est à la fois relayée et renforcée dans cette série populaire. En ce sens, la force d'une telle représentation est certainement plus assurée et plus subtile que si elle apparaissait comme un pur produit de propagande, à l'instar de films comme *Les bérets verts* (1968) ou *Zero Dark Thirty* (2013). C'est là toute la spécificité du cinéma, à la fois produit et vecteur de l'idéologie dominante.[47]

## SUMMARY: *THE WEST WING*: DOES THE PRESIDENT OF THE UNITED STATES CARE ABOUT INTERNATIONAL LAW WHEN CONSIDERING A MILITARY ACTION?

> The U.N. doesn't want this. They want to wring their hands and censure us after, but they expect us to take care of things like this. And after they've exhausted themselves calling us warmongers and imperialists they'll go home and quietly drink toasts to their relief.

Those words, pronounced by Leo McGarry, President Bartlet's Chief of Staff, can make us think that international law is absent—or at least neglected—in the well-known *The West Wing* TV series (7 seasons, 1999–2006). However, a comprehensive viewing of its 155 episodes reveals a more subtle representation of international law, particularly as far as the UN Charter rules are concerned.

Generally, it can be said that *The West Wing* echoes, and at the same time supports, the traditional US doctrines about the use of force in international relations. Firstly, (preventive) self-defence is broadly conceived as an action that appears necessary in order to counter terrorist groups or States that support them: 'terrorists aren't nations ... International law has no prohibition against any government, superpower or otherwise, targeting terrorist command and control centers' says the President in Season 5. Secondly, a right to overpass the multilateral procedures

[47] Régis Dubois, *Hollywood, Cinéma et idéologie* (Sulliver, 2008); Shlomo Sand, *Le XXe siècle à l'écran* (Seuil, 2004).

enshrined in Chapters 7 and 8 of the UN Charter can be deduced from several scenes. In Season 4, for example, President Bartlet states that 'No country has ever had a doctrine of intervention when only humanitarian interests were at stake. That streak's going to end Sunday at noon.' At that moment, he proclaims a new US doctrine of humanitarian intervention without even mentioning the opportunity of requesting a Security Council's authorisation …

Finally, the representation of the UN Charter in *The West Wing* seems to correspond to the existing American film tradition, either in films like *Air Force One* (1997) and *Zero Dark Thirty* (2013), or in TV series like *24* (2001 –) or *Homeland* (2011 –): the powers of the president cannot be restrained by the existing rules; those rules must simply be interpreted as allowing any military action that could be necessary to protect the interests of the United States. Against this background, it is not surprising that US public opinion often shares this particular representation of international law when actual military interventions are triggered.

# EPILOGUE

# 30

# *'International Law and …' Variations on a Theme*

VERA GOWLLAND-DEBBAS*

## I. INTRODUCTION

THE THEME OF this 10th ESIL Anniversary Conference has been 'International Law and …' a loosely woven web of relationships between international law and a palate of other disciplines—from philosophy, economics and international relations to art, cultural heritage and music—but also covering in-house relationships between areas of international law once considered hermetically sealed off from one another—domestic/international, public/private.

What I'm proposing is not really a lecture but some ramblings on a variety of issues—reflections on the variations of these interactions of law with other disciplines and within its various functional fields. And while my title may evoke the Goldberg variations[1] and other similar musical pieces, I hasten to say that this isn't a sophisticated exposé about international law's interaction with music and its methods.

I will begin with some brief reflections on why this recent flurry of interest in extraneities to our discipline, looking beyond the confines of our narrow boundaries and the extent to which international law can draw on the insights of other disciplines and make increasing use of their methods. What is at stake in interdisciplinary practice? Are we risking very much in order to risk saying very little? Are we seeking strength and answers from other disciplines as a form of escapism from the problems we face in international law or is it a value-added exercise?

Next, I would like to focus on the question of 'International Law and …'—the discourse or lexicon which sprang up from international relations in the last decade, that is, post 9/11, and in counterpoint, as an example of the interaction between international law and the broader international system, the extent to which international law has resisted this penetration into the international legal system.

* Emeritus Professor of Public International Law Graduate Institute of International and Development Studies (IHEID), Geneva and former Member of the ESIL Executive Board, died 29 September 2015.

[1] For the tale of how the variations came to be composed, see Johann Nikolaus Forkel, *Johann Sebastian Bach: His Life, Art and Work* (Harcourt, Brace and Howe, 1920) 119.

## II. WHY THIS FLURRY OF INTEREST IN 'INTERNATIONAL LAW AND ...'

### A. Some Problems of our Discipline

We should start by taking stock of some of the current problems with our discipline, mainly though not entirely, originating in the globalisation process.

We are living through what at the start of the twenty-first century has been referred to as an 'erratic, dislocated world'. A 'runaway world ... of uncertain possible futures'[2] in which the globalisation process has been one of contradictions and confusions: homogenisation through 'glocalisation', that is, the universalisation of particular local systems, ideas and products (McDonald's or free elections, you take your pick)—alongside fragmentation of international society, hegemonic power alongside religious and cultural pluralism, rationalism alongside indeterminacy.[3] There is an even greater sense of dislocation in this second decade of the twenty-first century in which globalisation itself has been challenged by other competing ideas and ideologies, by economic and political crises and by a world marked by instability and chaos.

This feeling of dislocation has been reflected in the sentiments of many public international lawyers as this Tower of Babel has cast gloom over those seeking certainty and predictability in an anarchic world and faced with what appears to be the fragmentation or breakdown of the unity of the international legal system itself and its resulting so-called systemic crisis. For these external processes have, of course, had an impact on our discipline, including changes in our perception of international law and its functions.

The debate over 'fragmentation', a buzz word which in the last decade became an important part of the discourse of international law, challenged the vision of a coherent and uniform system of general international law in the face of the development of various subsets of norms. Fragmentation raised 'postmodern anxieties';[4] it has been referred to in terms of 'risks' and characterised as a pathological process. The term fragmentation presumes disintegration or decomposition of something which was once a unity (technically, it was also used in old computer language to denote the fragmentation of hard discs, of files broken up and stored in different locations thus slowing down system performance). This challenge to the unity of international law in the new millennium has been said to come from several sources.

The first source is an onslaught on the system of public international law from external legal sources. International law now has to contend with the phenomenon of legal pluralism which is challenging its monopoly of relations across borders, as various superimposed and interrelated juridical spheres have come to co-exist in

[2] Anthony Gidden, 'Runaway World: The Reith Lectures revisited' (1999–2000 Director's Lectures by Professor Lord Giddens, London) available at digital.library.lse.ac.uk/objects/lse:xet336par.

[3] In the words of Susan Marks, *The Riddle of All Constitutions: International Law, Democracy and the Critique of Ideology* (Oxford University Press, 2000) 76.

[4] Martti Koskenniemi and Päivi Leino, 'Fragmentation of International Law? Postmodern Anxieties' (2002) 15 *Leiden Journal of International Law* 553.

the same international space: transnational, suprastate, legal networks and orders; a revitalised *lex mercatoria* and an emerging *lex electronica* or a *lex sportiva*—all purportedly self-regulatory governance structures. 'Global law beyond the State', or post-State law as Teubner would have it.[5] Positivism, as someone once said, had made us lose God, nature and reason in law-making in favour of the State; were we now about to lose the State and its monopoly of law-making?

Second, the challenge to the unity of the system has also been said to come from within, resulting from the fragmentation and compartmentalisation of particular sectoral and functional fields of international law, set adrift as a result of a high degree of specialisation—trade, health, environment, and so on—reflecting the diversification of globalised society into areas which have become legalised or juridicised.[6]

There has been as a result, a breakdown in the unity of the content of the rules themselves as the concept of self-contained regimes emerged, or that relating to secondary rules from a growing diversity in the methods of law-making. The increasing technicity and complexity of the social environment, as well as cultural diversity, among other factors, have had an impact on the formal techniques of multilateral treaty-making, on the changing nature of State consent, or, again, on the practice required for the formation of customary international law, although the International Law Commission (ILC) continues to cling to the mantra of the two elements in the practice of States. This self-containment has also tended to produce a new breed of young international lawyers oblivious to all but their technical fields, be it criminal law or international economic law, unaware of the bridges between disciplines. We are also seeing a budding form of international legislation in the form of Security Council decisions on such issues as terrorism, arms control and protection of civilians eroding traditional State consent in treaty-making.

There have also been challenges to procedural or institutional unity, that is, the way the rules are interpreted and by whom, originating from the mushrooming of sectoral and specialised tribunals, quasi-judicial treaty bodies, or hybrid entities such as the Conferences of Parties (COPs) and Meetings of Parties (MOPs) of international environmental law, all bound by their own self-contained mandates and ethos. Regionalisation has been a growing trend, as witness the growing pervasiveness of EU regimes imposed even outside the region.

Finally, a well-discussed phenomenon is the contemporary heterogeneity of those who participate in the law-making process itself, the diversity of national, transnational and international authorities, global networks à la Anne-Marie Slaughter, non-governmental organisations (NGOs) (a variety of International NGOs (INGOs), Big International NGOs (BINGOs) and Government Organised NGOs (GONGOs)), leading us to query the very usefulness of the concept of international subjects. At the same time, there has been a breakdown in the monolithic character of States themselves with privatisation of State functions such as the running of prisons, immigration and the waging of war as cheaper and more

[5] Gunther Teubner, '"Global Bukowina": Legal Pluralism in the World Society' in Gunther Teubner (ed), *Global Law Without a State* (Aldershot, 1997) 11.

[6] Andreas Fischer-Lescano and Gunther Teubner, 'Regime-Collisions: The Vain Search for Legal Unity in the Fragmentation of Global Law' (2003–2004) 25 *Michigan Journal of International Law* 999.

cost-effective private military enterprises, responsible only to their shareholders, shoot their way through the streets of conflict zones. But there has also been a breakdown in the monolithic character of States externally, with States claiming differentiated obligations due to culture or power, or to a claimed division of the world into the good, the bad and the ugly. This leads even the least conservative of us who once decried that naughty 'S' word (to quote Louis Henkin) to pray for the comeback of the State, alone able to protect our public goods.

The buzz word of 'fragmentation' has been accompanied by the buzz words of 'deconstruction' and 'indeterminacy' of legal rules. Many from our new generation of young international lawyers have had their certainties in international law shaken and have turned away from the straight and narrow path just as the Pied Piper lured away the children of the town of Hamelin.

## B. 'International Law and ...' a Form of Escapism?

Have international lawyers, their faith in their traditional discipline shaken, latched on to others in the search for analogies and comparisons to justify their own? Is it our uncertainties, boredom or frivolity that has led to this fashion of 'international law and ...'? Or, as I've said, ultimately can we justify it as a value-added exercise?

It has been stated that:

> an increasingly common practice in the contemporary academy is precisely to look outside the narrowest disciplinary boundaries for potential insight in solving the puzzles presented by one's own disciplinary materials. To adopt Claude Levi-Strauss' famous notion, the essence of the post-modernist, ... post-structuralist interpreter is to be a bricoleur, who resourcefully and opportunistically borrows whatever tools might be available to solve particular problems at hand .... The bricoleur is not a self-conscious theorist. What justifies using any given tool is its usefulness. There is no theoretically a priori way of deciding what tools are either 'essential' or 'absolutely inappropriate.'[7]

Now let us begin by asking what we mean by the 'and' in the title of our conference—'International Law and ...'? For there are various ways in which the relations between international law and other disciplines may be articulated.

We can look at international law *in* another discipline, for example, the study of legal themes in literature, exploring how international law is interpreted or incorporated in classic or even popular literature—Ted Meron reflecting on the laws of war in Shakespeare, Susan Marks on the concept of punishment in Kafka or Olivier Corten on the US President's attitude to international law. It is good to see international law having a part to play in other disciplines. But to what extent may we export our methods?

In an *Opinio Juris* blog, Duncan Hollis has a standing offer for his services 'as a technical consultant for any Hollywood producer or New York Times best-selling

[7] Sanford Levinson and Jack M Balkin, 'Law, Music, and Other Performing Arts' (1991) 139 *University of Pennsylvania Law Review* 1597, 1604–605.

novelist looking for accuracy in popular portrayals of international law'.[8] Referring to a novel by Brad Thor, a thriller on military types fighting Al-Qaeda networks (which I have not read), he points out that it is replete with inaccurate references to international law, including claims that the 'Geneva and Hague Conventions' do not apply to terrorists when it comes to torture. He therefore queries why best-selling novelists cannot do as much consulting and research on international law as they do on covert tactics and operations. This makes me wonder why literature should concern itself with international law methodology—is it not allowed its inaccuracies as some form of poetic licence?

But of course to take the example of literature again, international law *in* literature is not the same thing as looking at international law *as* literature—as the Dormouse pointed out in *Alice in Wonderland* 'I breathe when I sleep' is not the same thing as 'I sleep when I breathe!' Law as literature is, of course, studying legal texts as a special form of literature, as a literary genre. It means importing literary theory, theories of language, deconstructionism and so on, seeking 'not merely to connect two related fields of inquiry (law and literature), but to change and transform the way we have understood law and literature by viewing both as forms of 'literary activity'.[9] In short, attempting to understand the nature of law through an understanding of the nature of language.

A construct of the relations between law, literature and music has also been made in this way. International law *in* music would be a stretch of the imagination—unless one takes into account the story of Beethoven's revocation in 1804 of his planned dedication to Napoleon Bonaparte of his Symphony No 3 (*Eroica*) after learning that Napoleon had declared himself Emperor because he too would 'tread under foot all the rights of man, indulge only his ambition … [to] become a tyrant'.[10] But there are examples of the use of international law *as* music, that is, use of music's methodology. Miguel Poiares Maduro, former European Court of Justice Advocate General, has applied contrapuntal principles to his study of the EU examining whether independent State actions in combination resulted not in a mere cacophony or dissonance but in counterpoint, establishing a harmonic relationship while retaining their individuality.[11] Edward Said, who was, in addition to his broad literary scholarship, also a music lover and piano player, developed contrapuntal analysis in interpreting different perspectives simultaneously of colonial texts, considering the perspectives

[8] Duncan Hollis, 'Wanted: Best-Selling Novelist Who Needs Advice on International Law' (*Opinio Juris*, 25 June 2012) available at opiniojuris.org/2012/06/25/wanted-best-selling-novelist-who-needs-advice-on-international-law/.

[9] Gary Minda, 'Law and Literature at Century's End' (1997) 9 *Cardozo Studies in Law and Literature* 245, 246–47.

[10] By Wikipedians (ed), *Ludwig van Beethoven. The Complete Guide* (PediaPress, 4 November 2015) 261.

[11] See transcript from the Symposium on 'Four Visions of Constitutional Pluralism' held at European University Institute on 11 January 2008, Matej Avbelj and Jan Komarek (eds), 'Four Visions of Constitutional Pluralism' (2008) EUI Working Papers, Law 2008/21 available at cadmus.eui.eu/bitstream/handle/1814/9372/LAW_2008_21.pdf?sequence=1; see also Miguel P Maduro, 'Contrapunctual (sic) Law: Europe's Constitutional Pluralism in Action' in N Walker (ed), *Sovereignty in Transition* (Hart Publishing, 2003).

of both the coloniser and the colonised as overlapping and intermeshed, point and counterpoint of patterns of power and domination accompanied by resistance and subversion, which in turn fed into Third World Approaches to International Law (TWAIL). Said saw history as 'a giant fugue of interweaving themes and voices, of subject and reply. A contrapuntal reading of culture entails the entire constellation of its "voices",'[12] all part of the same composition, but each distinct.[13]

Applying extraneous or extra-legal methodology to law is not new of course. Positivism was born out of a fascination with the scientific method. The relativism of modern physics or Darwin's aggressive survival of the fittest, has cut across the board of disciplines, including ours. More recently, the autopoietic paradigm drawn from biology, from the functioning of the cell, transposed to the legal system by, in particular, Niklas Luhmann and G Teubner[14] described law as having normative openness but operational closure. But to what extent should lawyers draw on methodology developed in other contexts? Is it methodological syncretism which Kelsen frowned upon claiming that one of the central aims of the Pure Theory was to avoid an 'uncritical mixture of methodologically different disciplines which obscured the essence of the science of law and obliterate[d] the limits imposed upon it by the nature of its subject-matter'[15] even though it has been maintained that he failed to do so?

One of the hopefully minor reasons for 'International Law and …', that is the turn to other disciplines, may quite simply be that we are bored with ours and are turning to others for comfort, reinforcement, credibility or mere frivolity.

A book entitled *Amusing Ourselves to Death*, written by Neil Postman in the mid-1980s but even more relevant today, set out to demonstrate how all fields of life—politics, journalism, education, religion or war—had become subject to the demands of entertainment, teaching us to expect life, including presentations of the horrors of war, to be entertaining.[16] We have only to look at the titles of some articles appearing in contemporary journals to realise the extent to which we feel compelled to entertain out of fear of boring our readers with more prosaic themes of international law. Social media has exacerbated this trend with its sound bites and tweets which demand a minimal attention span. Moreover, we live in a decontextualised world in which life is viewed as a series of unconnected, random events bearing no significance toward any larger picture.

12 Francis Baert, 'The United Nations Intellectual History Project and the Role of Ideas' in B Reinalda (ed), *The Ashgate Research Companion to Non-State Actors* (Ashgate, 2011) 47, 50.

13 For his views on contrapuntal reading, see Edward W Said, *Culture and Imperialism* (Alfred Knopf, 1993); George W Wilson, 'Edward Said on Contrapuntal Reading' (1994) 18 *Philosophy and Literature* 265.

14 First formulated in 'Biology' by H Maturana and F Varela, see Gunther Teubner, 'Introduction' in Gunther Teubner (ed), *Autopoietic Law: A New Approach to Law and Society* (Walter de Gruyter, 1988).

15 Deryck Beyleveld and Roger Brownsword, 'Methodological Syncretism in Kelsen's Pure Theory of Law' in SL Paulson and BL Paulson (eds), *Normativity and Norms. Critical Perspectives on Kelsenian Themes* (Oxford University Press, 1998) 145.

16 Neil Postman, *Amusing Ourselves to Death: Public Discourse in the Age of Show Business* (Penguin Group USA Inc, 1985).

This has led William Twining to state that from the perspective of some of the world's worst crisis areas, 'some of the more frolicsome aspects of critical legal studies, post modernism, law and literature, and other current fashions look rather like irresponsible rich playboys and girls fiddling while Rome burns'.[17] We have playfully deconstructed our discipline breaking down the borders separating law from other systems at the risk of bringing it down around our heads, thus undermining a normative and autonomous vision of law that may only serve to entrench the power of the dominant groups in society.[18]

But there is of course a more obvious traditional articulation between international law and other disciplines and that is the regulation of areas of international relations by international law. We are importing into international law the sectoral and functional diversifications of international globalised society which now constitute separate regimes whether in substantive, procedural, or institutional terms. This is not 'international law *and* ...'. This is international law *tout court*: health law, literature law (copyright and so on), economic law (as opposed, for example, to law and economics), environmental law, trade law and so on. This is a more assertive colonisation—the appropriation of other fugitive areas of society, or of other legal systems.

The increasing regulation of economic activity through public international law, has absorbed some of the substantive law emerging from the *lex mercatoria* in the form of soft law or standards, treaty law, or the law of international organisations such as the World Trade Organization (WTO), or again through harmonisation within the European Union, as for example, in the areas of competition law or the environment.

It has been stated that:

> [I]t is hard to conceive rationally of a contract *in vacuo*, as it were; a form of test-tube baby with no mother and no father. The force of the obligation in a contract comes from the force of the legal system that creates the obligation.[19]

As Teubner puts it:

How can authentic law 'spontaneously' emerge on a transnational scale without the authority of the state, without its sanctioning power, without its political control and without the legitimacy of democratic processes? Where is the global Grundnorm? Where is the global 'rule of recognition'?[20]

Nor can the *lex electronica* totally escape State-made regulation whether at the national or international levels though it has produced its own 'cyber-laws' to regulate substantive legal issues such as data protection and privacy rights. Nevertheless,

[17] W Twining, *Globalisation and Legal Theory* (Cambridge University Press, 2000) 60.

[18] As one American legal deconstructionist has said: 'Like all other kinds of rhetoric, we must use the practice of deconstruction responsibly, because the practice itself will not guarantee the purity of our motives or the goodness of our action.' Jack M Balkin, 'Transcendental Deconstruction, Transcendent Justice' (1994) 92 *Michigan Law Review* 1131.

[19] Keith Highet, 'The Enigma of the Lex Mercatoria' (1989) 63 *Tulane Law Review* 613, 613.

[20] Gunther Teubner, 'Global Bukowina. Zur Emergenz eines transnationalen Rechtspluralismus' (1996) *Rechtshistorisches Journal* 255, 267.

there is equally an attempt to reappropriate the *lex electronica* through State-made and international organisation regulation, with the Internet becoming increasingly anchored at least technologically, with geo-location software and linked to the sovereign right of States and their traditional jurisdiction, although the ability of States to black it out entirely has visibly failed. The rise of terms like Cyber war akin to the war on terror have also been encapsulated in international law, for example, the rules relating to the threat or use of force.

In short, it is not devoid of value to spend time in looking at 'international law in …', 'international law as …', and 'international law and …' for insights may be gained, so long as one does not neglect international law *tout court*. But there may be other ways to better understand law. It is necessary therefore to evaluate the articulation of law with other disciplines.

## III. INTERNATIONAL LAW AND THE NEW DISCOURSE

I want to turn to 'international law and …' the new discourse spewed, though not exclusively, by the post-cold war, post 9/11 world which we now take for granted, to examine how well it was received by international law and, as counterpoint, the extent of international law's resistance to such incorporation in the light of the articulation between international law and the broader system of international relations, or the passage of non-law into law.

Some of this vocabulary, as Orwell put it in one of his famous essays on politics, appears 'to make lies sound truthful and murder respectable, and to give an appearance of solidity to pure wind'.[21] Thanks to the exceptional and infinite inventiveness of some legal advisers, this modern political discourse embedded in the political changes which we have witnessed in the previous decade has received meaning, applicability and an iota of legitimisation in the form of legal concepts and categories, challenging the oldspeak of international law. But far from ushering in a brave new world, it reflected a shift in power relationships which aimed to undermine several areas of international law, to unravel the system so painfully set in place since 1945. Moreover, any struggle against it was perceived, again to quote Orwell, as 'a sentimental archaism, like preferring candles to electric light or hansom cabs to aeroplanes'.[22]

I am not using the term discourse in this context in any serious Foucauldian sense, but simply as euphemistic vocabulary, some of it worthy of Orwellian newspeak, which assumes only the semblance of novelty as in fact it only signifies the resurgence of an older pre-Charter law bringing with it a certain disillusionment with progress. But I would also like to point to a return to oldspeak—a resistance campaign against the attempts to unravel the *acquis* of the last seven decades or so.

[21] George Orwell, 'Politics and the English Language', available at www.orwell.ru/library/essays/politics/english/e_polit/.

[22] Ibid. He was speaking of resistance to the decline of the English language.

First, the weakening of the Charter system to constrain unilateral and collective uses of force as well as international humanitarian law (IHL) reflected in some contemporary military doctrines. As an example, it is telling that the planned initial military operation in Iraq in 2003, though ultimately abandoned, was dubbed 'Shock and Awe'. The object of such a concept was, according to a Pentagon-commissioned paper, 'to convince an adversary to accept our will in the Clausewitzian sense' resting 'in the ability to frighten, scare, intimidate and disarm' through the delivery of instant massive destruction.[23] This is not far from the Israeli Dahiya military doctrine, which the Goldstone report found had been applied in the 2008/9 Gaza war. The doctrine was named after a village in Beirut which had been razed during the 2006 onslaught on Lebanon. It is premised on a response which aims at 'the application of disproportionate force and the causing of great damage and destruction to civilian property and infrastructure [demanding long and expensive reconstruction processes] and suffering to civilian populations'.[24] It was stated by a number of Israeli Generals to be not a theoretical idea but an approved plan and this despite the evolution of the laws of war post-World War I and World War II.[25]

'Risk-transfer War' or 'Risk-Management' is another one of these innovative concepts traced by Martin Shaw in his book *The New Western Way of War* which refers to the containment of risks to the lives of Western soldiers in order to minimise political and electoral risk to governments, by transferring such risks to innocent civilians killed as part of collateral damage.[26]

[23] The concept of 'Shock and Awe' was first developed by the Pentagon's National Defense University (NDU) in 1996 as part of the 'Rapid Dominance' strategy. It claimed to produce the effect of a Hiroshima with conventional weapons 'directed at influencing society writ large, meaning its leadership and public, rather than targeting directly against military or strategic objectives ... striking directly at the public will of the adversary to resist' see Harlan Ullman and James Wade, *Shock and Awe: Achieving Rapid Dominance* (National Defense University Press, 1996) 23, 34. Parts of the following have drawn from Vera Gowlland-Debbas, 'Reflections on a Decade of International Law: Dark Ages or Renouveau?' in Denis Alland and others (eds), *Unity and Diversity of International Law: Essays in Honour of Professor Pierre-Marie Dupuy* (Martinus Nijhoff, 2014).

[24] The Dahiya doctrine was expressed by several Israeli Generals (Major General Gadi Eisenkot, the Israeli Northern Command, chief, Col (Ret), Gabriel Siboni and Major General (Ret) Giora Eiland), see UN Human Rights Council 'Report of the United Nations Fact-Finding Mission on the Gaza Conflict' (25 September 2009) UN Doc A/HRC/12/48, paras 1194–99.

[25] Writing in 1874, Henry Sutherland Edwards, *The Germans in France: Notes on the Method and Conduct of the Invasion. The Relations Between Invaders and Invaded (1874)* (Kessinger Publishing, LLC, 2010) 285–86, enumerated what he called 'the three great principles of invaders' law': 1. For every offence punish someone; the guilty, if possible, but someone. 2. Better a hundred innocent should suffer than one guilty man escape. 3. When in doubt shoot the prisoner.

[26] M Shaw, *The New Western Way of War: Risk Transfer: War and its Crisis in Iraq* (Polity Press, 2005). Michael Reisman wrote in connection with the June 1993 raid on Baghdad by the United States, that it represented 'one more claim to revise this part of the law of armed conflict by inserting a new corollary: the initiating state should use the most discriminating weapon *that exposes its forces to the lowest probability of casualty.* Note that in this claim, the relationship between attacker and collateral damage to civilians in the target state is perforce zero-sum. The greater margin of safety for the initiating forces translates into greater peripheral damage to civilians in the target', Michael Reisman, 'The Raid on Baghdad: Some Reflections on its Lawfulness and Implications' (1994) 5 *European Journal of International Law* 120, 130–31.

Proportionality has received yet another new meaning; for example in the case of house demolition as collective punishment, the Israeli court judgment in *Qawasmeh et al*, acknowledged that:

> [T]here is no dispute that the exercise of the authority under regulation 119 by way of seizure and demolition or sealing of residential homes severely violates the fundamental rights of the uninvolved inhabitants of said houses. Indeed, the demolition or sealing of a house in which lives a person who has not sinned is in contrary with the right to own property, the right to dignity and even the right to housing which is derived there-from ... cannot be reconciled with concepts of justice and basic moral principles ... [and is] contrary with the principle of the child's best interest, a principle which runs like a golden thread through a host of legal arrangements, local and international

while nonetheless upholding the relevant Israeli government regulation so long as it could be demonstrated that there was a 'weighty deterring purpose' which only the executive could evaluate. The Court at the same time held that it was 'impossible to conduct a scientific research which would prove how many terror attacks were prevented and how many human lives were saved as a result of taking the measure of house demolition'.[27]

In the context of the 'war on terror'—the most consequential buzzword post 9/11—one will recall the jargon or rhetoric of 'preventive self-defence' (going beyond an imminent threat and involving a vague 'security' threat with no requirement of concrete evidence, such as the notorious weapons of mass destruction), 'self-defence against non-State actors' (permitting the use of force against the territory of a sovereign State on which these nebulous forces operate), and 'deterritorialisation of war' (which allows for the expansion of the theatre of war literally to anywhere in the world). The term combatant has been broadened to include, for example, the police force or the administrative infrastructure.

The UN arena has also seen the invention of concepts such as 'implied' or 'continuous' Security Council authorisations to use 'all necessary means' (used for a cumulative interpretation of Security Council Resolutions 678 and 687 on Iraq, somehow said to have been revived by Resolution 1441, in order to justify the invasion and occupation of the country in 2003).

In turn, 'targeted killings/assassinations' have been put forward as minimising collateral damage.[28] While alien to international law, the term has been legitimised

[27] *Qawasmeh et al v Military Commander of the West Bank Area Judgment Verdict*, HCJ 5290/14 (11 August 2014) paras 21–24, available at www.hamoked.org/files/2014/1158616_eng.pdf; see also Shane Darcy, 'Collective Punishment Receives a Judicial Imprimatur' *EJIL Talk!*, 21 August 2014, available at www.ejiltalk.org/collective-punishment-receives-a-judicial-imprimatur/.

[28] See UN Human Rights Council 'Report of the Special Rapporteur Philip Alston, on extrajudicial, summary or arbitrary executions, Study on targeted killings' (28 May 2010) UN Doc A/HRC/14/24/Add.6; 'Targeted killing' as a term was popularised after 2000 by Israel's publicly proclaimed policy of targeting alleged terrorists in the Occupied Palestinian Territories, see *Public Committee against Torture in Israel v The Government of Israel*, HCJ 769/02 (14 December 2006), available at elyon1.court.gov.il/files_eng/02/690/007/a34/02007690.a34.pdf. Since 2009 targeted killings by the United States have escalated, primarily through an increase in unmanned drone strikes but also through US Special Operations kill/capture missions, the most notorious being the successful killing of Osama Bin Laden in May 2011, see Jonathan Masters, 'Targeted Killings' (Council on Foreign Relations, 23 May 2013) available at www.cfr.org/counterterrorism/targeted-killings/p9627.

within the framework of human rights law and international humanitarian law in which it has no place; for the former prohibits the arbitrary deprivation of life, permitting the use of lethal force only under very strict conditions (see, for example, Article 6 of the International Covenant on Civil and Political Rights) and the latter allows for the killing only of civilians taking a 'direct part in hostilities', but neither uses the vocabulary of 'targeted killings'. Besides, 'targeted' killing is a misnomer giving the impression of a clean surgical strike which belies the widespread civilian deaths surrounding the target.[29] While the term 'war on terror' has largely been unmasked in this new decade, we still lie within its shadows. In particular, targeted killings through the use of unmanned drones ('bug-splats' is part of the official drone-speak used in US Defense Department software for calculating and reducing collateral damage (dead civilians) resulting from airstrikes)[30] have raised numerous responsibility issues in international law.

And let us not forget R2P, the 'responsibility to protect' initially conceived as a euphemism for humanitarian intervention which the International Court of Justice (ICJ) in *Nicaragua* had considered incompatible with 'the protection of human rights—a strictly humanitarian objective'. Nor has this doctrine, at least if it connotes military intervention, any place within the collective security framework for the Security Council has no need of the concept to justify its competence under the Charter to determine that massive human rights abuses constitute a 'threat to the peace' and thus to authorise the use of 'all necessary measures'. Nor can one easily conceive the Council as having a 'duty' to intervene in the face of the Charter's in-built voting mechanisms although the unanswered question remains of an international organisation's (IO's) responsibility for its omissions in addition to its acts.[31]

[29] For example, in 2002 there was the killing in Gaza of Hamas leader Salah Shehadeh in which a one-ton bomb was dropped on a crowded Gaza apartment building in the middle of the night, killing eight children and seven adults and injuring well over 150 other people; one could also point to the unknown number of wedding parties and other groups of civilians killed through 'surgical strikes' in Afghanistan and Pakistan; see also Statement of the Special Rapporteur on Human Rights and Counterterrorism, Ben Emerson, following meetings in Pakistan, 14 March 2013 available at www.ohchr.org/EN/NewsEvents/Pages/DisplayNews.aspx?NewsID=13146&LangID=E#sthash.IepvKdAL.dpuf.

[30] This dehumanising language, the official term used by US authorities when humans are killed by drone missiles, is reminiscent of the reference to 'vermin' used by the Nazis or 'cockroach' which referred to the Tutsis during the Rwandan genocide, see Jennifer Robinson, '"Bugsplat": The ugly US drone war in Pakistan' *Al Jazeera* (US and Canada, Germany, Pakistan, United States, 29 November 2011) available at www.aljazeera.com/indepth/opinion/2011/11/201111278839153400.html, and Daniel Schwartz, 'Drone-Speaking lexicon: from "Bugsplat" to "Targeted killing"', *CBC News*, 8 February 2013, available at www.cbc.ca/news/world/drone-speak-lexicon-from-bugsplat-to-targeted-killing-1.1342966; for even John Yoo of the famous 2002 'Torture Memos' to state that 'those deaths from the sky violate personal liberty far more than the waterboarding of three al Qaeda leaders ever did' is telling of the controversy over the use of drones, see John Yoo, 'The Real Problem With Obama's Drone Memo' *Wall Street Journal*, New York, 7 February 2013, available at www.wsj.com/articles/SB10001424127887323951904578288380180346300.

[31] See ILC, 'Report of the International Law Commission on the Work of its 63rd Session' (26 April—3 June and 4 July—12 August 2011) UN Doc A/66/10, Articles on the Responsibility of International Organizations (DARIO) Art 12(3); Resolution 1973 on Libya, in which the Security Council authorised a 'no-fly zone' is not an example of R2P, as its preamble refers to the responsibility to protect as the duty of Libya itself and the parties to the armed conflict, not third parties, to protect the civilian population, see UNSC Res 1973 (2011) UN Doc S/RES/1973 (2011).

Finally, one should mention the terms used to baptise military operations—'operation just reward', 'operation cast lead', 'operation summer rain', 'operation Iraq freedom' and the latest, 'operation protective edge' or, a telling metaphor, 'mowing the lawn'—which belie the havoc left behind.[32]

This vocabulary has served to create a violent world, justifying ultimatums, fabricated evidence, and bombardment of towns and villages resulting in sizeable tolls of civilian deaths brushed aside as 'collateral damage', large-scale destruction of infrastructures, lethal remnants of war from Kosovo to Lebanon (depleted uranium or *soi-disant* 'self-destructive' cluster munitions) and shattered economies. Such terms and justifications have been partly responsible, for example, for leading to the chaos in Iraq and Libya among others and to the destruction in Gaza. They have also been open to expropriation in this new decade, leading President Assad of Syria to claim that his ruthless response was aimed at eradicating terrorism, President Putin of Russia to invoke the US memorial in the ICJ Kosovo case to justify the secession of Crimea, and Egypt and the United Arab Emirates to secretly launch airstrikes against Libya.

Second, we consider the unraveling of our human rights acquis since 1945 for the protection of the individual. The past decade has seen 'enhanced interrogation techniques' and 'ticking bomb scenarios',[33] 'unlawful combatants' placing these in the legal limbo of indefinite detention, 'extraordinary rendition' accompanied by 'diplomatic assurances' which have served to ease the conscience of well-meaning leaders of democratic States by transferring the task of torturing terror suspects to less sensitive governments of other States. As for the Security Council's policy of 'targeted sanctions', considered initially to improve on comprehensive sanctions with their humanitarian fallout on entire populations of States, this has resulted in numerous absurdities and due process challenges before regional and universal judicial and quasi-judicial bodies.

An older lexicon, but one just as worrying for human rights law, has served to undermine the 1951 Refugee Convention: 'Safe third country' concepts, subjecting individuals fleeing persecution to the risk of chain refoulement, 'manifestly unfounded applications', which signifies returning asylum-seekers without any screening of their request, 're-admission agreements' forcing countries to receive back their unwilling nationals, 'international airport zones', where individuals are left in the limbo of law-free zones, return in 'safety and dignity' shackled and hooded in airplanes, Australia's 'Pacific Solution' (transporting asylum seekers to detention centres on small island nations in the Pacific Ocean)—such euphemisms serving to prevent access to one's borders, have been the 'rule of law' response of 'rule of law' countries to the phenomenon of the *sans-papiers*, the *sans-états*, kept in quarantine outside our borders, reminiscent of nineteenth-century containment of the poor, a

[32] The importance of vocabulary is reflected in The Israel Project's 2009 Global Language Dictionary on the choice of words when addressing the media available at www.stopdebezetting.com/documents/pdf/090713Hasbara%20handboek_tip_report.pdf.

[33] See Philippe Sands, *Torture Team. Rumsfeld's Memo and the Betrayal of American Values* (Palgrave Macmillan, 2009); and Rafael Behr, 'So much for the rights of man' *The Guardian*, 4 May 2008, available at www.guardian.co.uk/books/2008/may/04/politics.

vocabulary serving to undermine the post-war 1951 Refugee Convention regime. The International Organization for Migration (IOM) reports that since 2000 over 22,000 migrants lost their lives in efforts to reach the European Union's southern border[34] while a large number of deaths have occurred during violent deportation processes. The privatisation of immigration detention centres has led to increasing cases of alleged assaults and beatings of asylum seekers in the UK which make painful reading.[35] The UK is by no means alone in this.

This new vocabulary has had an antisepticising effect, helping to shield international lawyers from the brutality of the social environment; for unlike social anthropologists, fieldwork is not a requirement for them.[36]

## IV. INTERNATIONAL LAW'S RESISTANCE MOVEMENT

How receptive has international law been to the onslaught from this new lexicon? We have been faced with a paradox. The greater the changes in our international environment, the greater the need to approach the international legal system as receptive to these changes; yet at the same time, the more open-ended, the more we are faced with the dilemma of ensuring international law's autonomy and with demarcating that 'thin red line' between law and non-law.[37]

But the changes engendered in international law have not been a faithful reproduction of the political and social changes which have taken place, although there have been different ways of envisaging the exchange between the international legal system and social change, that is, the transformation of non-law into law. It is a far more complex story as international law neither shares the 'rigidity of metal' nor 'the decomposition of smoke', and the relationship between, say, law and politics, can neither be disposed of altogether, nor analysed simply in terms of the impact of the one on the other. Law operates in the selection and transformation of political decisions into legally significant elements or acts with definitive and far-reaching legal consequences, which escape the ambit of political processes and in turn set new constraints on political action. The legal system provides its own means of

[34] International Organization for Migration, 'Fatal Journeys. Tracking Lives Lost during Migration' (2014) 20, the Mediterranean is the deadliest area, accounting for 75% of all deaths of migrants during 2014 available at www.iom.int/files/live/sites/iom/files/pbn/docs/Fatal-Journeys-Tracking-Lives-Lost-during-Migration-2014.pdf.

[35] See a report by Birnberg Peirce and Partners, Medical Justice and the National Coalition of Anti-Deportation Campaigns 'Outsourcing Abuse. The use and misuse of state-sanctioned force during the detention and removal of asylum seekers' (July 2008) available at http://medicaljustice.org.uk/new/about/mj-reports/139-mj-reports/411-qoutsourcing-abuseq-report-140708.

[36] A past illustration of this function of a specialised vocabulary is the concept of mega-deaths coined in 1953 by military strategist Herman Kahn of the RAND corporation as a unit for one million deaths in time of thermo-nuclear war, whose view was that alternate scenarios in which the USA suffers 10 instead of 100 mega-deaths should be weighed as 'tragic but distinguishable outcomes'. This was caricatured in Stanley Kubrick's film *Dr Strangelove or: How I learned to Stop Worrying and Love the Bomb*.

[37] To borrow from Bruno Simma who had apparently seen the film of the same name 'NATO, the UN and the Use of Force: Legal Aspects' (1999) 10 *European Journal of International Law* 1, 22.

validation, defining the threshold of normativity that must be crossed—whether we opt for rigid normative thresholds such as the formal sources of law, or soft law-making processes—provides for legal mechanisms for authoritative interpretation of its obligations by judicial and non-judicial organs exercising an element of judicial discretion, determines substance in addition to form, regulating not only the formal validity of the rule, but also its substantive validity based on empirical, teleological and axiological criteria (notions of effectiveness or legitimacy, finalities or essential values).

Thus political action is encapsulated within a legal framework, political organs bestow legal authority and normative quality on its decisions, including the attribution of legal significance to its practice (as both legal interpretation and legal development). The relations which law entertains with social reality have been likened to those between maps and spatial reality, a 'misreading' which is not chaotic but which 'occurs through determinate and determinable mechanisms'.

In constructing its own legal reality, international law also establishes its own language or meaning. This means that interdisciplinary theory-building which attempts to overcome the academic compartmentalisation of disciplines also has to cope with terminological barriers. One can think of the different connotations in law and politics of terms of art such as 'normative' or 'responsibility' or differences in vocabulary which partly cover the same object, such as 'regime theory' on the one hand, and 'treaty' or 'international organisation' on the other; or 'public good' so dear to economists and collective interests on the other.

International law has the paradoxical position of being both normatively open to 'the noise' or 'music' emanating from society and operationally closed, because society—and with it its teleology and value content—is reinterpreted or 'misread' in a legal context according to a specifically legal matrix. Hence it does not translate every happening into law; it is its own functioning that leads to its increasing diversification and complexity.[38]

In this process, international law has resisted to some extent the penetration into law of some of the manifestations of globalisation and the new lexicon.

## A. From Fragmentation to Unifying Processes

Rather than fragmentation, it is perhaps more accurate to speak of heterogeneity, a diversity of elements and constituent parts and therefore a certain enrichment of the system, which has a more positive connotation. Moreover, in contrast to

[38] See Gunther Teubner, 'The Two Faces of Janus: Rethinking Legal Pluralism' (1992) 13 *Cardozo Law Review* 1443, 1447; Michel van Kerchove and François Ost, *Le système juridique entre ordre et désordre* (Presses universitaires de France, 1988) 17; Boaventura De Sousa Santos, 'Law: A Map of Misreading: Toward a Postmodern Conception of Law' (1987) 14 *Journal of Law and Society* 279, 281–82; François Ost, 'Between Order and Disorder: The Game of Law' in Teubner, *Autopoietic Law* (n 4) 78. For its rather dehumanised approach to international law, however, see the critique of an autopoietic approach in Peter Goodrich, 'Anti-Teubner: Autopoesis Paradox, and the Theory of Law' (1999) 13 *Social Epistemology* 197.

fragmentation, we are seeing the construction of unifying, universalising processes which have resulted in the creation and expansion of a domain of general or public interest and the development of what can broadly be viewed, along the lines of some domestic legal systems, as an international public policy or *ordre public*. In parallel with market ideology, promoting the private interest, international law has thus created its own ideological and ethical components, representing the collective interest which has brought in its wake different assumptions and philosophical underpinnings. *Ordre public* is, of course, a very elusive concept even in domestic legal systems and both the notion and its content vary over time and place.[39] But its imprecision and vagueness should not invalidate the principle.[40] As in domestic law, international public policy arises from the need to protect overriding community values and interests of the international community as a whole, law having vital functions ranging from maintenance of international public order and the incorporation into law of a certain universal moral or ethical foundation to the very survival of our species.[41]

This breakdown of the monolithic nature of norms due to their hierarchisation in the framework of a value-oriented international law has paradoxically created an inverse movement of convergence rather than fragmentation, leading to linkages and permeability between different fields of international law and to a very visible process of reconciliation between hitherto hermetically sealed regimes. It is thus no longer possible to approach international law in a sectoral fashion, for it is evident, for example, that trade and investment are increasingly interlocked with non-trade areas, be they environment, health or human rights, that the continuing applicability of human rights in armed conflicts has been confirmed; that collective security and human rights are now intricately linked; and that environment and development can only be approached as two sides of the same coin[42] for global interests of the

[39] *Case concerning the Application of the Convention of 1902 governing the Guardianship of Infants (Netherlands v Sweden)* (Separate Opinion of Judge Percy Spender) 1958, 55 available at www.icj-cij.org/docket/files/33/2275.pdf; see also *Case concerning the Application of the Convention of 1902 governing the Guardianship of Infants (Netherlands v Sweden)* (Separate Opinion of Judge Moreno Quintana) 1958, 105ff available at www.icj-cij.org/docket/files/33/2271.pdf.

[40] *Kuwait Airways Corporation v Iraqi Airways Company and Others* [2002] UKHL 19, paras 16–18.

[41] The term international public policy was once used only in connection with *jus cogens* but today it obviously has a considerably wider use. The concept of international community in this context certainly does not correspond to a *Gemeinschaft* (with reference to Ferdinand Tonnies' *Gemeinschaft und Gesellschaft*, a society tending towards a higher degree of integration, with shared values and a feeling of solidarity), but it is nevertheless a working fiction by which a social grouping is attributed rights and obligations and a protection function, see Pierre-Marie Dupuy, 'L'unité de l'ordre juridique international. Cours général de droit international public' (2003) 297 *Recueil des Cours de l'Academie de Droit International de la Haye* 15, 247; see also Vera Gowlland-Debbas, 'An Emerging International Public Policy?' in Ulrich Fastenrath and others (eds), *From Bilateralism to Community Interest: Essays in Honour of Judge Bruno Simma* (Oxford University Press, 2011) 241–56.

[42] Thus judicial and quasi-judicial bodies have considered that the instruments they are mandated to protect should nevertheless not be read in 'clinical isolation' from the rest of international law, particularly in the light of contemporary concerns about the protection and conservation of fundamental norms, eg WTO, *United States: Standards for Reformulated and Conventional Gasoline–Report of the Appellate Body* (29 April 1996) WT/DS2/AB/R; See also Pierre-Marie Dupuy, 'Unification rather than Fragmentation of International Law? The Case of International Investment Law and Human Rights' in Pierre-Marie Dupuy, Francesco Francioni and Ernst-Ulrich Petersmann (eds), *Human Rights in International Investment Law and Arbitration* (Oxford University Press, 2009) ch 2.

international community have required an ever-greater need for overarching principles and holistic responses.

The ICJ has in its oblique manner reflected this hierarchisation by enriching the vocabulary—from *erga omnes* obligations and 'intransgressible' principles of international humanitarian law, to overriding considerations of humanity and *jus cogens* (though the latter only recently)—contributing to the shaping and clarification of the content and source of fundamental norms, from use of force to self-determination, grappling with the question of their sources (drawing on the underlying moral, ethical or constitutional foundations of the international community), and giving voice to the concept of collective interest embedded in multilateral treaties having a humanitarian purpose, such as the Genocide Convention. It has also pronounced on who could invoke the protection of fundamental norms, discoursed on both the rights and obligations of the international community; and insisted on the duty of all States to react to their violations.[43]

## B. The Resurrection of Article 2(4)

Any reference to Article 2(4) of the Charter today sounds like a playback to bygone times, an old-fashioned textual approach to an instrument which is intended to be, and has certainly been, dynamic and evolutionary. Yet one forgets the spirit behind the drafting of Article 2(4) and its intent—the desire not to revisit the 'scourge of war'. Since 1945, the trend has been the progressive limitation of resort to unilateral measures, not only through the outlawry of the traditional sovereign right to resort to military force—from war to military reprisals, from the League of Nations to the UN Charter—but also through efforts to constrain the exercise of unilateral non-military countermeasures by means of procedural and substantive limitations (for example, in the framework of the ILC's Articles on State Responsibility or of the WTO). This has gone hand-in-hand with the progressive institutionalisation of international society.

Faced with disputes arising from ongoing armed conflicts which States have surprisingly brought to it, the ICJ has tended to safeguard the Charter's oldspeak on the regulation of the use of force and has resisted efforts to unravel the post-Charter regime. In the same manner, it has refused to be deluded by the so-called 'progressive' nature of renewed State claims to widen the scope of Article 51 of the Charter.

The way in which the ICJ's judgments have contributed to strengthening and clarifying the normative basis of international peace maintenance is, of course, well known. It had opted in *Nicaragua* for a narrow construction of the meaning of armed attack, and hence of self-defence, by distinguishing between the most grave forms of the use of force constituting an armed attack within the meaning of

[43] See Vera Gowlland-Debbas, 'The Role of the International Court of Justice in the Formulation and Development of Fundamental Norms of International Law' in SS Caballero and RA Stoffels (eds), *Retos de la Jurisdiccion Internacional* (Thomson Reuters, 2012).

Article 5l, and other forms of lesser degrees of gravity, such as mere frontier incidents. It undertook a holding operation in both the *Wall* Opinion and the *DRC v Uganda* case, in which it addressed two situations involving enormous human suffering and continuing loss of life, by restrictively reading Article 51 as applying only in the case of an armed attack by one State against another State. It thus intimated that there was no right of self-defence against the acts of non-State actors (which does not imply there are no other means of recourse).

In *DRC v Uganda* it refused to widen State responsibility for the acts of non-State actors or be led down the path of 'preventive self-defence' for the safeguarding of 'essential security concerns'.[44] In addition, the Court stated in its *Wall* Opinion with reference to Israel's additional claim of necessity, that it was 'not convinced that the construction of the wall along the route chosen was the only means to safeguard the interests of Israel against the peril which it had invoked as justification for that construction'.[45] For all the Judges without exception recognised 'that a State which is the victim of terrorism may not defend itself against this scourge by resorting to measures international law prohibits'.[46]

In these cases, the Court was plainly acting as 'the guardian of Charter principles', as a bulwark against the development of international law in a particular direction by refusing to endorse the unilateral development of norms under the influence of a small group of powerful States.[47]

Even so, the Court was considered to have exercised 'inappropriate self-restraint' when supplied with the opportunity to play its role as principal judicial organ of the United Nations and was called on 'to take every opportunity to secure that the voice of the law of the Charter rise above the current cacophony'.[48]

[44] *Legal Consequences of the Construction of a Wall in the Occupied Palestinian Territory* (Advisory Opinion) 2004, para 139, available at www.icj-cij.org/docket/files/131/1671.pdf 13 March 2015; *Case Concerning Armed Activities on the Territory of the Congo (Democratic Republic of the Congo v Uganda)* (Judgment) 2005, paras 143–47, 301, available at www.icj-cij.org/docket/files/116/10455.pdf. In the latter case, the reference to irregulars is clearly to the sending of armed bands or irregular forces by a State and therefore to questions of attribution. In short, the Court rejected Uganda's argument that mere tolerance of irregulars or failure to take action 'creates a susceptibility to action in self-defence by neighbouring States', see *Case Concerning Armed Activities on the Territory of the Congo* (Separate Opinion of Judge Kooijmans) para 22 available at www.icj-cij.org/docket/files/116/10463.pdf.

[45] *Wall* Advisory Opinion (n 3) para 140.

[46] Ibid para 141; ibid, Declaration of Judge Buergenthal, para 2, available at www.icj-cij.org/docket/files/131/1687.pdf.

[47] On the two cases cited, see generally, Vera Gowlland-Debbas, 'The Conflict in the Democratic Republic of the Congo and the Role of Courts' in Thomas Giegerich and Alexander Proelß (eds), *Krisenherde der Welt im Blickwinkel des Völkerrechts* (Duncker & Humbolt, 2010) 167–200; Vera Gowlland-Debbas, 'The Responsibility of the Political Organs of the UN for Palestine in Light of the ICJ's Wall Opinion' in Marcelo G Kohen (ed), *Promoting Justice, Human Rights and Conflict Resolution through International Law. Liber Amicorum Lucius Caflisch* (Martinus Nijhoff, 2006) 1095–119.

[48] *Oil Platforms (Islamic Republic of Iran v United States of America)* (Separate Opinion of Judge Simma) 2003, para 6 available at www.icj-cij.org/docket/files/90/9735.pdf; *DRC v Uganda* (n 3) (Separate Opinion of Judge Simma) 2005, paras 2 and 8 available at www.icj-cij.org/docket/files/116/10467.pdf.

## C. The Reinforcement and Expansion of Human Rights Law

The 'war on terror' created legal black holes. In Guantanamo where detained aliens were subject to indefinite detention in a territory purportedly 'outside the jurisdiction' of the United States, with no possibility of access to a court to review the legality of their detentions, detainees were 'neither criminal suspects nor POWs, neither fish nor fowl, they inhabit a limbo of rightlessness'.[49] Israel denied human rights obligations extraterritorially in the Occupied Palestinian Territories and challenged the competence of the Human Rights Council to deal with IHL. The UK claimed the non-application of the European Convention on Human Rights in Iraq on the grounds that it had been superseded by Security Council Resolutions.

Yet judicial and quasi-judicial bodies have in recent years challenged such arguments, expanding human rights law to fill these black holes. Thus, human rights law has permeated such fields of international law as IHL, international criminal law and even collective security.

Even the ICJ could not remain impervious to an increasingly individually-oriented international law. Here, in contrast to its holding operation on the use of force, the ICJ, surprisingly for an inter-state court, has been at the vanguard of developments in the strengthening and indivisibility of human rights law, particularly necessary at a time of armed conflict. It has in recent years approached situations of armed conflict not only from the perspective of the rights and duties of States, but also from that of the rights of individuals, addressing in the *Wall* Opinion the continued applicability of human rights law to the extent of its non-derogability, which was to be interpreted either in the light of international humanitarian law as the *lex specialis*,[50] or more importantly, in complementary fashion.[51] It will be noted that the complementary nature of the relationship between human rights law and IHL was upheld in the *DRC v Uganda* case (and thus in a contentious case) not only in the Court's reasoning but in the very *dispositif* of the judgment.[52]

In the *Wall* Opinion, confirmed in the *DRC v Uganda* and *Georgia v Russia* cases, the Court also underlined the indivisibility of civil/political, economic/social/ cultural and children's rights, that is, the applicability of *all* human rights instruments, including regional ones in time of armed conflict, as well as confirmed their extraterritorial reach.[53]

[49] David Luban, 'The War on Terrorism and the End of Human Rights' (2002) 22 *Philosophy and Public Policy Quarterly* 9, 9–10.

[50] *Legality of the Threat or Use of Nuclear Weapons* (Advisory Opinion) 1996, para 25, available at www.icj-cij.org/docket/files/95/7495.pdf.

[51] *Wall* Advisory Opinion (n 3) para 106:

> As regards the relationship between international humanitarian law and human rights law, there are thus three possible situations: some rights may be exclusively matters of international humanitarian law; others may be exclusively matters of human rights law; yet others may be matters of both these branches of international law. In order to answer the question put to it, the Court will have to take into consideration both these branches of international law, namely human rights law and, as lex specialis, international humanitarian law.

[52] *DRC v Uganda* (n 3) paras 205ff, dispositive para 345(3).

[53] *Wall* Advisory Opinion (n 3) paras 107–13; *DRC v Uganda* (n 3) para 217; *Application of the International Convention on the Elimination of All Forms of Racial Discrimination (Georgia v Russian Federation)* (Provisional Measures) 2008, para 109 available at www.icj-cij.org/docket/files/140/14801.pdf.

Further consolidating the reach of human rights and IHL, the Court in the *Application of the Genocide Convention case*,[54] spelled out a duty to prevent, and underlined, in its *Wall* Opinion, the duty of third States under customary international law, as well as of the High Contracting Parties under common Article 1 of the Geneva Conventions, to react to breaches of fundamental norms of human rights and humanitarian law, including through non-recognition and non-assistance.[55]

The Court likewise innovated in calling for restitution and compensation for material damage to individual persons consequent to the construction of a wall in the Occupied Palestinian Territory,[56] though remedies are rare for individual victims of violations of IHL. It also considered in the *Georgia v Russia* case that the indication of provisional measures was required for the protection of individual rights, thus going beyond inter-State interests and rights, for the prejudice to the rights of individuals protected under the Committee on the Elimination of Racial Discrimination (CERD) was tantamount to the irreparable harm or prejudice that a request for provisional measures had to address.[57]

This is not to say, however, that the Court has been totally consistent in its defence of human rights as in the *Germany v Italy* case, rejecting a more progressive approach which would have taken into account contemporary developments in the tension between human rights and state immunities.[58]

The Court was ahead of the times in heralding the breakdown of the compartmentalisation of the laws of peace and war. The human rights bodies, whether universal or regional, have followed suit in that articulation between human rights law and IHL, alternating between using IHL as an interpretation of their respective human rights instrument or resorting to human rights exclusively in time of armed conflict in the absence of express derogations by the parties to the conflict.[59] Even the International Criminal Tribunal for the former Yugoslavia (ICTY) has pointed out that human rights law and IHL are mutually complementary and have similarities 'in terms of goals, values and terminology', going so far as to state that with regard to certain of its aspects, international humanitarian law can be said to have fused with human rights law, although one had to take into consideration the specificities of the latter body of law.[60]

The continuing applicability of human rights law in time of armed conflict has meant the availability of human rights treaty bodies which may be seized in respect of violations committed during armed conflicts, in the notable absence of IHL

[54] *Application of the Convention on the Prevention and Punishment of the Crime of* Genocide *(Bosnia and Herzegovina v Serbia and Montenegro)* (Judgment) 2007 available at www.icj-cij.org/docket/files/91/13685.pdf.

[55] Ibid dispositif, para 163 D.

[56] *Wall* Advisory Opinion (n 3) paras 151–53 and dispositif, para 163.

[57] Ibid para 142.

[58] *Jurisdictional Immunities of the State (Germany v Italy: Greece intervening)* (Judgment) 2012, available at www.icj-cij.org/docket/files/143/16883.pdf.

[59] See eg UN Human Rights Committee 'General Comment No 31' UN Doc CCPR/C/21/Rev.1/Add. 13; Vera Gowlland-Debbas and Gloria Gaggioli, 'The Relationship between International Human Rights and Humanitarian Law: An Overview' in Robert Kolb and Gloria Gaggioli (eds), *Research Handbook on Human Rights and Humanitarian Law* (Edward Elgar, 2013) 77–103.

[60] *Kunarac, Kovac and Vukovic* (Judgment) ICTY-2001- IT-96-23-T and IT-96-23/1-T (22 February 2001) paras 467, 471.

mechanisms. These bodies have in fact contributed to the evolution of IHL in a way which is more in keeping with contemporary mores. At times they have even, like the European Court of Human Rights (ECtHR), applied human rights law in armed conflict situations to the exclusion of IHL.[61] This has had a significant impact in that human rights law requires no threshold to come into operation; it is not based on the distinction between civilians and combatants, and the condition of proportionality is very differently assessed from that in IHL, permitting no more use of force 'than absolutely necessary' to achieve the permitted aim, while IHL balances military advantage with potential loss of civilian life.

Human rights bodies have forcefully addressed the arguments of those States wishing to divest themselves of their obligations under human rights instruments. The extraterritorial scope of the application of human rights obligations has become widely recognised, extending States' obligations to persons beyond their borders but subject to their effective control or authority, particularly in situations of occupation.[62] Extraordinary rendition has been condemned.[63] Targeted killings have been challenged;[64] as well as collateral damage from indiscriminate use of force, particularly in relation to hundreds of child casualties resulting from so-called 'clean surgical strikes'.[65] The ECtHR has condemned States for their treatment of refugees; the Parliamentary Assembly of the Council of Europe has also lashed out against the responsibility of European States in the case of the 'Migrants left to

[61] The ECtHR in its case law on the right to life in the context of terrorism or the intra-state conflict in Chechnya, has directly applied the provisions of Article 2 of the Convention on the right to life, rather than turn to humanitarian law as *lex specialis*, determining that where a State did not officially derogate from the ECHR, the military operations had to be 'judged against a normal legal background', see eg *Isayeva v Russia* App no 57950/00 (ECtHR, 24 February 2005) para 191.

[62] See the position of the Human Rights Council and the Human Rights Committee in the case of the Occupied Palestinian Territory, see UN Human Rights Council 'Consideration of Report Submitted by States Parties Under Article 40 of the Covenant. Concluding observations of the Human Rights Committee: Israel' UN Doc CCPR/C/79/Add.93, para 10 (1998) and 'Consideration of Report Submitted by States Parties Under Article 40 of the Covenant. Concluding observations of the Human Rights Committee: Second Periodic Report of Israel' (2003) UN Doc CCPR/CO/78/ISR, para 11; and the ECtHR in the case of Iraq, in *Al Skeini v United Kingdom* App no 55721/07 (ECtHR, 7 July 2011) paras 37–38.

[63] See eg *Case of El-Masri v The Former Yugoslav Republic of Macedonia* App no 39630/09 (ECtHR, 13 December 2012) para 221:'Having regard to the manner in which the applicant was transferred into the custody of the US authorities, the Court considers that he was subjected to 'extraordinary rendition', that is, 'an extra-judicial transfer of persons from one jurisdiction or State to another, for the purposes of detention and interrogation outside the normal legal system, where there was a real risk of torture or cruel, inhuman or degrading treatment', hence a violation of, inter alia, Article 3 of the Convention.

[64] In its 2003 Concluding Observations on Israel's report under the ICCPR, the Human Rights Committee clearly rejected targeted killings. It considered that 'All measures to arrest a person suspected of being in the course of committing acts of terror must be exhausted in order to avoid resorting to the use of deadly force,' see 2003 Concluding Observations on Israel (n61) para 15.

[65] In relation to the so-called 'clean surgical strikes', see Committee on the Rights of the Child, Optional Protocol on the involvement of children in armed conflict, 'Concluding observations on the second report of the United States of America' (28 January 2013) UN Doc CRC/C/OPAC/USA/CO/2) para 7: 'The Committee is ... alarmed at reports of the death of hundreds of children as a result of attacks and air strikes by the US military forces in Afghanistan over the reporting period due notably to reported lack of precautionary measures and indiscriminate use of force. The Committee expresses grave concern that in fact the number of casualties of children doubled from 2010 to 2011.' It urged the United States to 'Take concrete and firm precautionary measures and prevent indiscriminate use of force to ensure that no further killings and maiming of civilians, including children take place' see para 8 (a).

die' tragedy—72 to die and only nine left to tell the tale; despite distress calls and vessels passing by who ignored them, no one went to the aid of the boat.[66]

Human rights law—concerned with the protection of individuals—has paradoxically also gained centre stage in the context of the inter-State collective security system, requiring a fresh reading of the collective security provision laid down in Article 1(1) of the Charter in the light of such concepts as human security and of the recent linkages between collective security and principles of justice and international law (originally only associated with peaceful settlement of disputes). For not only has justice in the form of international criminal tribunals now been seen as instrumental to peace maintenance, but also references to international law and in particular to States' human rights obligations are now to be found in Council Resolutions.

Though rather wary at first of challenging the pre-eminence of Security Council Resolutions, courts have become emboldened in upholding human rights instruments over State implementation of Security Council Resolutions whether blacklisting suspected terrorists or authorising 'all necessary measures' against a State. Thus in *Abdelrazik*, a Canadian Court underlined the nonsensical result reached by Canada's interpretation of the 1267 travel ban and asset freeze, which prevented its own national from returning to Canada:

> According to their interpretation, the Resolution permits a citizen to enter Canada if and only if he happens to be standing at the Canadian border crossing, but it prevents that same citizen from reaching that border crossing as he cannot transit over land or through air to reach it.[67]

While in *Al-Jedda* the ECtHR, turning to the limitations placed by the purposes of the Charter on Security Council decisions, which included the promotion and encouragement of respect for human rights and fundamental duties, refused the automatic application of Article 103 of the Charter under which Member States obligations under the Charter and hence under Security Council decisions, prevailed over their international agreements, including human rights instruments to which they were parties. In rejecting the UK's argument that Security Council Resolution 1546 authorising it to use 'all necessary measures' in Iraq imposed on it an obligation to resort to indefinite detention without charge, the Court stated:

> Against this background, the Court considers that, in interpreting its resolutions, there must be a presumption that the Security Council does not intend to impose any obligation

[66] Council of Europe, Parliamentary Assembly 'Lives lost in the Mediterranean Sea: Who is responsible?' Report of the Committee on Migration, Refugees and Displaced Persons (05 April 2012) Doc 12895 http://assembly.coe.int/nw/xml/XRef/Xref-DocDetails-EN.asp?FileID=18095&lang=EN; Jack Shenker, 'Migrants left to die after catalogue of failures, says report into boat tragedy' *The Guardian*, 28 March 2012, available at www.guardian.co.uk/world/2012/mar/28/left-to-die-migrants-boat-inquiry. See also Case of *Hirsi Jamaa and Others v Italy* App no 27765/09 (ECtHR, 23 February 2012), Concurring Opinion of Judge Pinto de Albuquerque: 'Refugees attempting to escape Africa do not claim a right of admission to Europe. They demand only that Europe, the cradle of human rights idealism and the birthplace of the rule of law, cease closing its doors to people in despair who have fled from arbitrariness and brutality. That is a very modest plea, vindicated by the European Convention on Human Rights. "We should not close our ears to it."'

[67] *Abousfian Abdelrazik v The Minister of Foreign Affairs and the Attorney General of Canada*, 2009 FC 580 (4 June 2009) para 127.

> on Member States to breach fundamental principles of human rights. In the event of any ambiguity in the terms of a Security Council Resolution, the Court must therefore choose the interpretation which is most in harmony with the requirements of the Convention and which avoids any conflict of obligations. In the light of the United Nations' important role in promoting and encouraging respect for human rights, it is to be expected that clear and explicit language would be used were the Security Council to intend States to take particular measures which would conflict with their obligations under international human rights law.[68]

Rather than seeing a tension between human rights and peace maintenance, we have seen a shift in priority with human rights now forming a component part of the security fabric instead of, as originally intended, perceived as part of the longer-term creation of the conditions conducive to peace. In other words, the tension between human rights and other public order norms must be resolved in the light of the most 'reasonable way to apply them with minimal disturbance to the operation of the legal system'.[69]

A final word about the permeability of domestic and international law: there has been a universalisation of the language of law: the Geneva Conventions have been immortalised on CNN and Al-Jazeera. Public international law, once almost exclusively directed at States, is increasingly having a direct effect on private bodies and individuals, operating in every nook and cranny of our private lives: in that sense it is inescapable. In a world that has become increasingly interlocked, international obligations requiring universal adherence for their effectiveness make it increasingly untenable for States to retrench behind isolated domestic structures and international law is omnipresent in national systems. The integration of international human rights law into national constitutions has led also to a certain degree of harmonisation between legal systems.

In theory, the relationship between international law and municipal law has traditionally been approached from the perspective of the formal relations between two legal orders and the dual lens of monism and dualism. Yet increasingly, the relationship between the two orders is dependent not only on the systemic relations between them but on the degree of development of international law. As a result, contemporary international law has assumed the purpose not only of regulating interstate relations, but increasingly of harmonising domestic law, an interesting evolution in the manner in which international law is being imported into domestic legal systems, increasingly concerned with areas of shared common interest, such as the enforcement of human rights and humanitarian law. States, while resorting to disparate measures and means, have nevertheless succeeded in adapting their domestic legal systems to include a common minimum—though by no means monolithic—set of international norms.

To show the extent of the growing permeability between the two legal orders, not only in terms of substance or normative content, but also of legal subjects, it has

[68] *Al-Jedda v the United Kingdom*, App no 27021/08 (ECtHR, 7 July 2011) para 102.

[69] ILC, 'Fragmentation of International Law: Difficulties Arising from the Diversification and Expansion of International Law. Report of the Study Group of the International Law Commission' finalised by Martti Koskenniemi (13 April 2006) UN Doc A/CN,4/L.682, para 410.

been pointed out that the individual lives his life in both legal orders, for one must not ignore 'the all-prevailing reality of the universum of human experience' and even while both may claim to be autonomous, they are nevertheless 'harmonious in that in their totality the several rules aim at a basic human good'.[70] This development however does not take into account the burgeoning areas of chaos and relativist challenges that this new decade presages.

## V. WHO IS IN CONTROL OF INTERNATIONAL LAW-MAKING?

But what is the significance of the cumulative actions of judicial and quasi-judicial tribunals in challenging the new lexicon pushed by the practice of a small number of powerful States? What is the tally of these divergent trends? This raises the question of who ultimately is in control of international law formation, whose practice counts in the customary law process.

Recent challenges to the traditional formulation of the formation of customary international law have come principally from two divergent sources. The first consists in the claims of hegemonic States, among those 'who mark the soil more deeply with their footprints than others,' as De Visscher put it, although the ICJ had in the past noted that participation of the specially affected States must be accompanied by 'a very widespread and representative' participation of other States.[71] Such claims have been based not only on material power but on a professed moral superiority or exceptionalism which allow some States to act above the law, particularly in the fight against global terrorism.

At the same time, such hegemonic claims have been countered by contemporary developments in international society which have included the proliferation of actors on the global stage, the hierarchisation of norms, and the emergence of the concept of an international community.[72] At least in certain fields such as human rights, humanitarian law, international criminal law and environmental law, the notion of practice has been widened to include the notion of a broad consensus on the part of the international community as expressed, inter alia, by judicial decisions and resolutions of international organisations. Referring to the development of international criminal law, Simma and Paulus point to a detachment of international law from State practice in certain areas of international law.[73]

[70] DP O'Connell, *International Law*, Vol 1 (Stevens & Sons, 1965) 43.

[71] *Continental Shelf Case (FRG v Denmark, Netherlands)* ICJ Reports (1969) para 73.

[72] See Anja Seibert-Fohr, 'Unity and Diversity in the Formation and Relevance of Customary International Law' in Andreas Zimmermann and Rainer Hofmann (eds), *Unity and Diversity of International Law. Proceedings of an International Symposium of the Kiel Walther Schücking Institute of International Law, November 4–7, 2004* (Duncker & Humblot, 2006) and the response in Vera Gowlland-Debbas, 'Comment' in ibid.

[73] Bruno Simma and Andreas Paulus, 'Le rôle relatif des différentes sources du droit international pénal (dont les principes généraux de droit)' in H Ascensio, E Decaux and A Pellet (eds), *Droit international pénal* (Pedone, 2012) 60–61.

## VI. THE FINAL SCORE

A refusal to entrench the new discourse by a return to an older vocabulary is not necessarily conservative retrenchment but an attempt to safeguard certain *acquis* of international law which *are more in keeping* with contemporary values and interests. For the question of legitimacy is central. Whereas for Hobbes, Bentham, Ihering or Kelsen: 'a legal rule without coercion is a contradiction in terms, a fire which does not burn, a light that does not shine,'[74] surely the efficacy of the law depends also in the final analysis on the consensus prevailing within a society in relation to the legitimacy of the system and to shared understandings and commitments by the members of the legal system, all of which seem to be lacking today. Yet at the same time, we are faced with the fact that none of the efforts to import other disciplines, such as doctrines of liberal economics and legal recognition of the practice of powerful business enterprises by the rest of the world community, is value free and that momentous challenges from the area of religion are creating major fissures in international society.[75]

Judicial and quasi-judicial bodies, despite sometimes inconsistent and conflicting judgments, have generally resisted the incorporation of certain facts. This, of course, may create a gap between fact and law and make the discipline vulnerable to sceptical critique. But paradoxically, this gap may also contribute to the law's autonomy and its refusal to entrench certain developments may serve to erode the effectiveness of the factual situation itself. For legitimacy has today become a part of effectiveness—witness the invention of legal argument to bolster the legitimacy of political action and the intimidation and even physical threats to which opposing international lawyers have been subjected, thus showing the potency of lawfare. But international law also continually and paradoxically expands on the obligations of States, enmeshing them in an inextricable web of rules as well as soft processes, requiring them to penetrate even into the hitherto private sphere, despite their factual loss of power and hence increasing inability to perform certain obligations.

One should also underline the responsibility of international legal advisers in giving credence to a new lexicon without assessing the type of world they are thereby helping to usher in. Habermas has acknowledged the role of international lawyers as engaged constructors of social reality: 'At the level of norms and practices, I admire

[74] Rudolf von Ihering, *Law as a means to an end* (trans Isaac Husik, The Boston Book Company, 1913) 241; see Vera Gowlland-Debbas, 'The Security Council and Issues of Responsibility under International Law' (2011) 353 *Recueil des cours de l'Académie de droit international* 185, ch 1.

[75] One could add at this point one more 'international law and ...'—that of love. Some time ago, a farewell colloquium was organised for Brigitte Stern's retirement as adjunct faculty from our Institute. The theme was set to be: 'L'amour du droit international'. This proved to be one of the most challenging themes to which I have ever been invited to contribute. So I began by doing what most people do when they are at a loss for words—I googled 'love of international law' and ended up with multiple entries: 'Love and Law in Bollywood', 'Love and Law in Shakespeare's Macbeth', a song entitled 'Love is the Law', a poem by WH Auden entitled 'Law Like Love', and in recent literature, 'Law in the Courts of Love' by Peter Goodrich. While this understandably did not get me very far it may well be worth a reflection on how to articulate the two!

law as the most visible and the most rational form of what characterizes human culture in general—I mean the feature of constructing and intentionally shaping social reality.'[76] Again, 'realists' and 'deconstructionists' have been chastised for 'working against law when they—in exercising abstract rationality—break both the belief and the hope in the law without caring that belief and hope are a vital part of any law.'[77]

Finally, it is difficult to conclude on the extent to which the last decade's discourse is being overtaken. Let me therefore end with the words of TS Eliot in the fourth and final poem of his *Four Quartets*:

> 'For last year's words belong to last year's language. And next year's words await another voice.'[78]

[76] Armin von Bogdandy 'Discourse Theory and International Law: An Interview with Jürgen Habermas', *Verfassungsblog*, 12 May 2013, available at www.verfassungsblog.de/en/discourse-theory-and-international-law-an-interview-with-juergen-habermas.

[77] Carlo Focarelli, *International Law as Social Construct. The Struggle for Global Justice* (Oxford University Press, 2012) 56.

[78] TS Eliot's 'Little Gidding' in *Four Quartets* (Harcourt Brace, 1943).

www.ingramcontent.com/pod-product-compliance
Ingram Content Group UK Ltd.
Pitfield, Milton Keynes, MK11 3LW, UK
UKHW051448290926
15471UKWH00008B/1091

9 781509 908134